Encyclopedia of

Rap and Hip Hop Culture

ENCYCLOPEDIA OF

Rap and Hip Hop Culture

Yvonne Bynoe

GREENWOOD PRESS
Westport, Connecticut · London

Library of Congress Cataloging-in-Publication Data

Bynoe, Yvonne.
Encyclopedia of rap and hip hop culture / by Yvonne Bynoe.
p. cm.
Includes bibliographical references and index.
ISBN 0–313–33058–1 (alk. paper)
1. Rap (Music)—Encyclopedias. 2. Hip hop—Encyclopedias. I. Title.
ML102.R27B96 2006
782.421649'03—dc22 2005019215

British Library Cataloguing in Publication Data is available.

This book is included in the *African American Experience* database from Greenwood Electronic Media. For more information, visit: www.africanamericanexperience.com.

Library of Congress Catalog Card Number: 2005019215
ISBN: 0–313–33058–1

First published in 2006

Greenwood Press, 88 Post Road West, Westport, CT 06881
An imprint of Greenwood Publishing Group, Inc.
www.greenwood.com

Printed in the United States of America

The paper used in this book complies with the Permanent Paper Standard issued by the National Information Standards Organization (Z39.48–1984).

10 9 8 7 6 5 4 3 2 1

Contents

List of Entries

Preface

There have been numerous books written about Hip Hop that provide critiques, essays, or narrative histories. However, despite its thirty-plus-year history, much of the factual information related to rap and Hip Hop remains scattered among an array of disparate sources, including magazine articles, newspaper accounts, and Web sites. More problematic is that the quality of the information available on these topics remains widely uneven, with some material being blatantly incorrect. The *Encyclopedia of Rap and Hip Hop Culture* is the first comprehensive collection of factual information associated with the development and history of rap and Hip Hop. This text is a diligent effort to provide the most accurate information on these important subjects. The intent of this book is to provide scholars, students, and interested readers with one reference source.

Despite the mainstream emphasis on rap, Hip Hop is not just about music. Hip Hop is a cultural expression that encompasses music, narrative poetry, dance, and art as reflected by its original four elements: DJing, MCing, B-boying, and Aerosol art (also known as Graffiti Art). Each separate element is integral and equally important to the creation and advancement of Hip Hop. Scholars, and even Hip Hop cognoscenti, continue to debate whether or not Hip Hop qualifies as a legitimate culture in the anthropological sense. However, it is agreed that Hip Hop is a subcategory of African American culture that has been infused with characteristics from the African Diaspora, as well as from Europe and Asia. Moreover, although Hip Hop now commands a global audience and throughout the United States has spawned regional styles, slang, and references, it remains the lingua franca—the national unifier—for successive generations of young African Americans.

It would take several volumes to capture every person and event that contributed to the creation and advancement of rap and Hip Hop, however, this book represents a cross-section of people, events, and ideas that significantly shaped the genre. The entries, particularly those related to rap artists, represent contributors to rap and Hip Hop who gained prominence through critical acclaim and commercial sales. Overall, an effort was also made to include forgotten or often overlooked contributors who, while not household names, nevertheless impacted the development of Hip Hop regionally or nationally.

The dance and art elements of Hip Hop are the most difficult to evaluate because their purely creative nature does not lend them to empirical criteria or standards. Secondly, because of the fluidity of B-boy crews and graffiti writers coupled with these elements of Hip Hop receiving less media exposure than the others, there are many individuals and groups who have not been adequately documented within the history. In this text, frequently the B-boys and the graffiti artists are the best-known people, since their name recognition presumes that there is a general consensus about their influence on Hip Hop. However, readers should keep in mind that there may be lesser known or even unknown artists whose skills match or exceed those of the artists included.

In the main, rap artists were considered for inclusion based on the artist's (or group's) body of work and that collection's overall contribution to the genre. Generally, to warrant eligibility for inclusion, old-school artists (those artists who recorded before there were rap music albums), were required to have several single recordings, while contemporary rap artists needed to have at least two albums. In the deliberation process, there was no distinction made between independently released recordings and recordings released by major record companies.

In terms of the organization of this book, artists and personalities are listed and alphabetized by their real last names. For instance, singer Mary J. Blige is found under the letter "B." Artists or personalities best known by their stage names are listed and alphabetized by those first names. Using this format, The Notorious B.I.G. is listed as such under letter "N," and Biz Markie is listed under the letter "B."

Hip Hop is an interrelated genre, so readers will notice that entries can be cross-referenced. At the end of an entry, terms in boldface lettering send the reader to other related entries, for example, solo rap artist Lil' Kim is cross-referenced with Junior Mafia, the group she began her career with.

After the majority of music-related entries is a "Discography." The discography either details all known original recordings (rather than every iteration, remix, or re-issue) or, if that number of original recordings is large, the listed titles are a representation of the artist's full body of work. The "Selected Rap Discography" and the "Selected Bibliography" are resources provided to assist readers, at all levels, who wish to learn more about Hip Hop or a particular aspect of it. The Selected Rap Discography is a sampling of recordings that are generally acknowledged as Hip Hop classics by fans and critics. As a category, these Hip Hop classics are the foundation of the rap music canon. There are literally hundreds of books and thousands of articles associated with Hip Hop, therefore, the Selected Bibliography provides readers with some of the more credible Hip Hop–related books, articles, and Web sites as a starting point for further research and exploration. The order of the Selected Rap Discography and Selected Bibliography sections serves an organizational function and should not be construed as a rating system for the material.

This text also includes "Statements to Preserve and Appreciate Hip Hop Culture" that The Temple of Hip Hop, founded by KRS-ONE, presented at the United Nations in 2002. The significance of this document is that it attempts, in a thoughtful and broad manner, to codify the beliefs and understandings of Hip Hop for the purposes of preservation and transmission.

Hip Hop is a vastly complicated subject, and despite any author's best attempts, there is always room for different points of view. In that vein, I believe that providing my perspective may be helpful to readers. Rap music, although a commercially dominant force, is only one element of Hip Hop. In that connection, I do not use the terms rap and Hip Hop synonymously. In further exposing my language preferences, I do not readily use Hip Hop as an adjective to describe musical performers or the music connected to the genre. Additionally, in describing people who perform rap, I use the neutral term "rap artist," rather than the more judgment-laden term "MC," or "emcee." For many Hip Hop purists, the designation MC is only bestowed on those who meet subjective creative and performance standards.

Chronicling the history of a living genre requires regular revisions since new participants and creative ideas alter the landscape, although their importance may not be immediately apparent. As a practical matter, this collection of data was current as of 2005.

Y. Bynoe

Introduction

Hip Hop is not only music. It represents at least four different, interrelated art forms: MCing, or rap—the oral element; B-boying, break dancing, as it is commonly known—the dance element; DJing—the musical element; and graffiti, or aerosol art—the visual element. The acknowledged birthday of Hip Hop is November 11, 1973, the date that Afrika Bambaataa, one of the most important Hip Hop figures, established the Zulu Nation.[1] This former Black Spades gang member formed a communal organization that intended to eradicate street violence by using the arts as a means to squelch rivalries. Under the Zulu Nation, street gangs transformed into crews, whose members vanquished foes in battles using superior turntable skills, dance, or lyrical talents instead of weapons.

The prototypical B-boy, as Hip Hop followers were known, was a volatile mix of street knowledge, urban neglect, and American dreams. Without apologies or fears, Hip Hop was a vehicle that initially allowed its predominantly young and Black participants to artistically express the complexities of their lives. Framed within a new and unique aesthetic, the candor that Hip Hop adherents have expressed about their social and political beliefs (or lack thereof), sexuality, disdain for authority, and preoccupation with attaining wealth has continued to inform several mainstream American cultural idioms, including music, language, clothing, film, and advertising.

Like most cultural products, Hip Hop did not follow a linear progression. At its core level, Hip Hop was created in the early 1970s by African American, Caribbean American, and Puerto Rican youth in New York City. A more conceptual and historical context reveals that Hip Hop's ancestry is African, yet it is has always been heavily influenced by American popular culture. Rap, the spoken element of Hip Hop, stems from the African griots. The griots, storytellers and historians of their tribes, were indeed the first rap artists. These human links to the past often recited *praise poems*, detailing the greatness and histories of kings and queens, leaders and ordinary citizens. Over the centuries, the oral tradition of the griots would reemerge in the African Diaspora.

In the United States, slaves told Br'er Rabbit tales that covertly derided the slave master by skillfully using metaphors to describe how the slick rabbit [the slave] outwitted the mean, greedy old fox [the slave master]. Free Blacks created *toasts*, or narrative poems. Rather than just being mundanely recited, toasts were performed to be entertaining. Moreover, unlike literary poems, performers would tailor toasts to suit a particular audience's taste. The success of toasts like "Signifying Monkey," "Stagolee," and "Titanic" (which depict the trickster, the bad man, and the pimp hero, respectively) is that to common folks, the language was accessible, the characters were recognizable, and the meanings were clear.

The longevity of these Black folklore mainstays is evident in modern Hip Hop. Rap music utilizes updated versions of these characters as the basis for lyrics, as well as the foundation for many rap artists' public personas. Toasts could routinely be heard in male-only enclaves, such as local jails, street corners, pool halls, and at hangout spots frequented by poor and disenfranchised Black men. Like modern day raps, toasts, with central themes about violence, sex, and the futility of romance, were primarily the property of Black men. Women rarely performed toasts because, as with much of rap music, toasts often considered misogynistic and, therefore, women were probably disinclined to recite them.

Beginning in the 1940s, Black radio DJs demonstrating their verbal dexterity on the air were, in some respects, the precursors to modern rap stars. Using the latest bebop slang and the storytelling traditions of African Americans, DJs, such as Chicago's Al "the Midnight Gambler" Benson and Dr. Hepcat of Austin, Texas, promoted records and products using hip rhymes and melodic chatter. The preeminent DJ of the era was New York City's Douglas "Jocko" Henderson. Henderson's "Ace of Rockets" radio show not only influenced other American DJs, but also was instrumental in the development of Hip Hop via the Caribbean.

Reportedly, Clement "Coxsone" Dodd, a Jamaican producer visiting the United States, heard Jocko's on-air rhyming and upon returning to Jamaica helped sound system[2] DJ Count Machouki imitate Jocko's style. By the mid-1960s other Jamaican sound system DJs were toasting, or talking over, music. Jamaican immigrant DJ Kool Herc (Clive Campbell), considered the Father of Hip Hop, would bring the talking-over, or *dub* style,[3] of his native land, along with the sound system concept, to his Bronx, New York, audiences.

DJ Kool Herc recited simple toasts or raps to get the crowd moving while he mixed breakbeats between two turntables. Herc's spoken words over music would set the stage for the emergence of Hip Hop MCs such as Coke La Rock. Herc's innovative work with breakbeats would usher in B-boying. (A breakbeat is the portion of a song where the drums, bass, and rhythm guitar are distilled to their barest parts; the result is a vibrant percussionlike experience.) Successfully mixing breakbeats required intense concentration, so Kool Herc became the first DJ to use a dance crew, called *Break boys* or *B-boys*, to keep the party going as he manned the turntables. Pioneering Black youth, such as the duo called the "Nigga Twins," would blaze the B-boy trail; however, the art form would become strongly connected to New York City's Puerto Ricans. After the debut of Kool Herc's B-boys, Afrika Bambaataa's Zulu Kings dancers began exhibiting their own superior footwork. The early B-boy crews were primarily from the Bronx, with each neighborhood supporting its own local stars. The popularity of B-boying would help it to expand beyond the Bronx to Brooklyn, Manhattan, and Queens. In 1977, Jimmy D, JoJo, and JoJo's brother Eazy Mike would form The Rock Steady Crew, perhaps the most famous B-boy crew in the world. In 1979, The Rock Steady Crew added a Manhattan division, led by Richie "Crazy Legs" Colon, and its power moves would help the organization to gain international prominence.

B-boying appears to be related to *capoeira*, one of the ancient Manding–Kongo martial arts first practiced in Africa and later among Afro-Brazilians—where authorities outlawed the art form, fearing its potential to facilitate uprisings. Later, mainstream observers in the United States would likewise consider B-boying to be a renegade activity. B-boy moves are very similar to those of *capoeira,* with the exception of backspinning, which is an original B-boy move. In *capoeira*, the *roda* in which the movements take place is identical to the circle within which B-boys perform. In addition to the general movements of B-boying, the art form retained the *capoeira* idea of the challenge, which demands that participants compete against one another, and likewise retained the difficult headstand pose. The other important influence on the development of B-boying was the Asian martial arts. Asian martial arts became part of mainstream American popular culture with the 1972 premiere of the weekly television program "Kung Fu" and with the 1973 release of Bruce Lee's landmark movie, *Enter the Dragon*. B-boys incorporated Asian martial arts movements learned from television and movies into their performance routines.

The main instruments used in the practice of *capoeira* are drums, berimbau, shekere, agogo, and tambourine. Like its ancient counterpart, B-boying is dependent on percussion beats to propel the actors forward. In this connection, at the center of early Hip Hop stood that DJ who directed the party from behind his turntables. At the start there were no rap or Hip Hop records as such; instead, DJs combed record stores and their parents' record collections for distinctive and interesting recordings. Moreover, the reputation of a Hip Hop DJ was based on his ability to introduce new music to his audiences. The first Hip Hop DJs, by "digging in the crates" for "beats," experimented with an array of musical genres, including rhythm and blues, rock, Caribbean, Latino, and world music.

Not only were Hip Hop DJs audiophiles, they were also skilled technicians. Grand Wizzard Theodore (Livingston) is credited with inventing the needle drop and cutting, better known as "*scratching*" techniques.[4] Scratching altered the arrangements of songs by using duplicate copies of records and manually editing or repeating the break-beat portion by rubbing the record back and forth. Scratching would come to define the sound of early rap music. Coincidentally, Hip Hop legend Grandmaster Flash (Eric Sadler) mentored the younger Theodore and as the headliner of the Furious Five is primarily responsible for innovating scratching. Years later, turntablists like the collectives the Beat Junkies, and Invisibl Skratch would extend the range of Hip Hop DJing by using turntables as instruments and not just passive equipment for playing records.

It was scratching and other techniques, such as sampling, that allowed DJs to signify on the messages of recordings and create new works from prerecorded music. Sampling in fact was an updated version of older musical techniques found in the vocal interpolations of early African American popular ballads and jazz instrumental quotations. Moreover, cutting[5] and mixing were fundamental to early jazz performances, and even folktales. Sampling spawned debates about rap music's inherent originality, as well as its credibility as music, since it did not use instruments. The careers of older soul and funk artists, such as James Brown and George Clinton, were given second acts when rap artists began to sample their work. The practice, however, also resulted in numerous lawsuits instigated by artists who asserted that rap artists had sampled their work without their permission.

If DJs set the tone for the Hip Hop event, graffiti art[6] was the all-important backdrop. Not only did aerosol art decorate the venues where DJing, MCing, and B-boying took place, it also forced other New York City citizens to pay attention to the marginalized Black and Latino youth in their midst. Most graffiti makes the statement, "Yes, I am here, I do interact with society, and I do matter!" Creating graffiti thus, provides the author with a sense of establishing some sort of identity and, depending on the medium used, some sort of immortality.[7] Philadelphia, rather than New York City, is considered the place where Hip Hop graffiti began. Writers Cornbread and his partner Cool Earl wrote their names on numerous and varied sites in Philadelphia. The two became famous after Black news publications began reporting on their activities. Cornbread stopped writing in 1972, but during the middle 1970s the Broadway Style lettering of Philadelphia's Topcat 126 started to appear in New York City. Subsequently, New York City graffiti writers took advantage of their subway cars, something that Philadelphia lacked, and began to advance the art form.

In New York City graffiti painted on subway cars allowed writers' work to be seen by literally millions of people as trains traveled throughout the five boroughs. The New York City subway system also provided graffiti artists throughout the city with a way to communicate, a way to see each other's work.[8] Train painting became the primary canvas for New York City's *style wars*. The style wars a period when anyone who wanted to be recognized as the best artist of a subway line painted trains as often as possible. Rather than producing only the chaotic renderings of vandals, graffiti artists had acknowledged rules of engagement. To be designated a King or Queen, a writer could not just paint his or her name in a thousand different places. Rather, style and artistic talent were extremely important determining factors. The goal was to create subway car, or *burner* paintings as artistic statements that stood out based on originality, color, vibrancy, crisp outlines (meaning no drips), and overall aesthetic appeal.

Today, although DJing, B-boying, and graffiti continue to thrive in Hip Hop's underground scenes domestically and internationally, these elements have become less relevant to Hip Hop's mainstream fans. As Hip Hop left its local origins and its core urban audience, the MC or rap element became the easiest to commodify to a new consumer market. Not only did the MC supplant the DJ as the center of the Hip Hop universe, the success of an MC became far less dependent on demonstrating creativity and showmanship during live performances. As the appeal of rap music broadened, questions surrounding its authenticity arose. In the early 1980s, the initial Hip Hop chasm pitted long-term fans invested in selecting Hip Hop celebrities through neighborhood battles against new fans who chose MCs on the strength of studio recordings.

The commercial success in 1979 of the Sugar Hill Gang's song "Rapper's Delight," is pivotal to the transformation of Hip Hop from a local to an international entity. Not only did "Rapper's Delight" reach audiences outside of the New York metropolitan area and become the first rap record to make *Billboard*'s Top 40 list, it was also Hip Hop's first prefabricated group. Sylvia Robinson, owner of the New Jersey–based Sugar Hill Records, recruited Henry "Big Bank Hank" Jackson, Michael "Wonder Mike" Wright, and Guy "Master Gee" O'Brien to the Sugar Hill Gang, despite their lack of street credentials and live performance skills. Robinson, a former R & B singer, saw the Sugar Hill Gang as a way to capitalize on the growing popularity of rap music. Furthermore, Grandmaster Caz of the pioneering Cold Crush Brothers has long maintained that Sugar Hill Gang member Big Bank Hank, whom he knew, made unauthorized use of his rhymes on the groundbreaking "Rapper's Delight."[9] Ironically, for a musical genre whose mantra for so many years was "keeping it real," the mainstream ascent of Hip Hop may have been less than "real."

Not surprisingly, the Sugar Hill Gang did not have another major hit rap record. Sugar Hill Records, however, would record legendary Hip

Hop groups, such as the all-female Sequence, the Treacherous Three, and Grandmaster Flash and the Furious Five. Other Black-owned record companies, such as Paul Winley Records and Enjoy, would also enter the rap game. However, as business miscalculations forced the first rap labels from the industry, new ones emerged, such as Tommy Boy Records and Profile Records (run by young White entrepreneurs). Originally, rap music was an attractive business, because a twelve-inch rap record could be produced inexpensively and distributed directly to mom-and-pop record stores. A popular rap record, therefore, could net the independent record label a substantial profit. The enormous success of "Rapper's Delight" caused CBS records to want a piece of the rap music pie.

In 1979, Russell Simmons produced Kurtis Blow's single, "Christmas Rappin'" (Mercury/CBS). This would become the first rap record to be released by a major record label. The single also helped the fledgling Def Jam Productions, then primarily a management and promotions company, secure a reported $600,000 production deal with CBS records to sign, develop, and record talent. Aside from Kurtis Blow's hits, Def Jam would gain national prominence as the managers for Run DMC, who were initially signed to Profile Records. Run DMC was comprised of Russell Simmons's younger brother Joseph (Run), Darryl McDaniels (DMC), and Jason Mizell (Jam Master Jay). In 1984 Run DMC were the first rap artists to earn a gold album for *Run DMC*; in 1985 they were the first rap artists to go platinum with the album *King of Rock*. In 1986 Run DMC's *Raising Hell* was the first rap album to go multi-platinum. Run DMC with their gold chains and Adidas sneakers, is commonly considered the bridge from old-school artists such as Grandmaster Flash and the Furious Five and the Cold Crush Brothers to more current rap music artists.

In 1984 Def Jam Productions received a demo tape from a sixteen-year-old LL Cool J. At that point Russell Simmons and his partner Rick Rubin decided to form a record company, and each contributed $2,500 to the effort. The new Def Jam Recordings then signed LL Cool J, who remains with the label to this day. Def Jam Recordings dominated the rap music for nearly a decade by having management or recording agreements with many of the top rap artists, including LL Cool J, the Beastie Boys, Slick Rick, Public Enemy, Method Man, Foxy Brown, and Run DMC. Simmons believed that Hip Hop was marketable to a worldwide audience and looked for opportunities to expand Hip Hop beyond music. In 1985 Simmons produced the first rap movie when he acted and coproduced *Krush Groove*, a semi-autobiographical film. In 1988 after partner Rick Rubin left, Simmons established Rush Communications and became involved in everything from a clothing line (Phat Farm) to television comedy (*Def Jam Comedy*) to magazine production (*One World*).

Other young Black men—such as Luther "Luke" Campbell (Skyywalker Records), Jermaine Dupri (So So Def), Master P (No Limit), and Jay-Z (Roc-A-Fella Records)—would follow in Simmons's footsteps and establish lucrative rap record companies. Sean "P. Diddy" Combs has come the closest to building another Hip Hop empire. A former Uptown Records intern and protégé of Uptown's president Andre Harrell, Combs founded Bad Boy Entertainment in 1993. The company's first release was Craig Mack's contagious "Flava in Ya Ear," but it reached the next plateau with the 1994 release of The Notorious B.I.G.'s album *Ready to Die*. *Ready to Die* is widely recognized by fans and critics alike as one of the greatest rap records of all time. Combs's nonmusic business ventures have included several restaurants and a clothing line. Combs has also appeared in several films, and on Broadway in the 2004 revival of Lorraine Hansberry's play, "A Raisin in the Sun." Bad Boy Entertainment commanded the rap industry by using recognizable samples and Hip Hop flair. If Def Jam represented the grittiness of Hip Hop, then Bad Boy celebrates ghetto fabulousness.

Sean "P. Diddy" Combs has been unsurpassed in his skills at self-promotion. In true Hip Hop style, as head of Bad Boy Entertainment, he regularly appeared in his artists' music videos. Suge Knight, CEO of the California-based Death Row Records, publicly attacked Combs at the 1995 Source Awards for his video appearances, striking the first salvo in an East Coast–West Coast rap rivalry. Beginning with the 1992 soundtrack for the movie *Deep Cover*, Death Row Records, with producer Dr. Dre and rap artist Snoop Dogg, took the reins of the rap industry with hardcore rhymes laid over smooth, G-funk samples. Beefs between rap artists are commonplace in rap music, and are generally resolved "on wax" (that is, through their recordings). However, dispute between rap executives was new, and the fracas divided the loyalties of many rap fans and artists between Bad Boy Entertainment and Death Row Records.

The vitriol associated with the East Coast–West Coast conflict created an environment that, perhaps, contributed to the September 1996 murder in Las Vegas of Death Row artist Tupac Shakur. The twenty-five-year-old Shakur was a prolific writer whose raps exhibited an emotional honesty that garnered him a legion of devoted fans. The charismatic Shakur was also a poet and emerging movie star. In March 1997 Bad Boy Entertainment artist The Notorious B.I.G., aka Biggie Smalls, was gunned down in Los Angeles. Some speculate that he was killed in retaliation for Shakur's murder a year earlier. Biggie helped bring East Coast rap music back from the doldrums. He was a talented storyteller who possessed a keen sense of humor and an eye for detail. He rarely romanticized the violence of street life, instead displaying a clear-eyed realism that won him enormous credibility and respect. To date, no assailant in either of these slayings has been apprehended. The loss of these two stars devastated Hip Hop fans, underscoring the senseless violence that victimizes young African Americans. Many rap fans accused the media of fueling the East Coast–West Coast rivalry. In fact, the international scope of Hip Hop means that media outlets may indeed exploit controversies and disputes as a means to gain customers. On the other hand, rap artists and their record companies also rely heavily on the media to promote new projects. In that connection, the impact of the media, particularly music videos, cannot be underestimated in the commercialization of Hip Hop.

When "Yo! MTV Raps" debuted in 1988, Hip Hop had already existed in urban communities for over fifteen years. The weekly music video program, however, gave most of Middle America their first exposure to rap music and Hip Hop. White suburban teenagers subsequently helped to increase rap music's market share by becoming the largest consumers of rap music in the nation.[10] The advent of rap music videos, allowed a wider swath of young Americans to experience Hip Hop and created new Hip Hop consumers who were ready to purchase rap music, as well as anything else infused with Hip Hop style. Hip Hop's elements, particularly its language, music, and style, continued to develop organically among its traditional fan base, often underneath mainstream radar. However, for other fans more removed for Hip Hop's creative forces, they readily adopted the more homogenized and rap-centric version of Hip Hop that was broadcast to them on television.

Fashion was immediately impacted by rap music videos, with fans eager to buy the clothing worn by their favorite rap artists. This mainstreaming of Hip Hop fashion transformed it from ready-to-wear clothing, such as sheepskin coats, Kangol hats, Izod shirts, and Lee jeans that New York City B-boys and B-girls adopted and restyled to their tastes, into a new fashion category, "urban wear" designed by entities like Cross COLOURS, Karl Kani, Tommy Hilfiger, Phat Farm, and FUBU for Hip Hop consumers and sold in department and specialty stores. Today many rap artists are now also designers, hoping that their popularity as musical artists will translate into clothing sales. According to Jamel Spencer, president at Blue Flame advertising and chief marketing officer at Bad Boy Entertainment, "more than anything else, Hip Hop has been about marketing."[11] Hip Hop has indeed been used to sell urban music, film, television programs, and fashion, but also mainstream products such as video games, cars, and fast food. Hip Hop is no longer just a cultural expression; it is also a very powerful marketing term.

Hip Hop is amorphous. Every person has a different idea about what it is and who it represents. The 1999 release of Eminem's *The Slim Shady LP*, coupled with the media attention that this White rap artist received, reignited an intense philosophical debate as to whether Hip Hop is a native culture accessible primarily to African Americans still marginalized in our society or is rather a craft or trade open to anyone willing to engage in it. The debate remains current because, although White consumers buy rap music and Hip Hop products and primarily control the distribution and dissemination of Hip Hop, the public face of Hip Hop still is that of young African Americans. In the thirty-year history of Hip Hop, only the Beastie Boys and Eminem reached the higher echelons of the genre. Whether Hip Hop's mutability is its strength or its weakness is a matter of subjective judgment. Many academics and proponents hail Hip Hop as an empowering and important communication. Russell Simmons says, "The most important thing for race relations in America in the last, I don't know how many, years is Hip Hop."[12] According to Simmons, White rap artist Eminem and Black rap artist 50 Cent represent cross-racial commonalities, stating, "They're faced with the same struggle, and they recognize their common thread of poverty." Hip Hop's detractors, however, cite it as portraying young African Americans to a global audience stereotypically as pimps, thugs, and 'hos. Filmmaker Spike Lee states that much of today's rap reminds him of how Whites in blackface ridiculed Blacks in order to entertain Whites. "If you turn on Black Entertainment Television and watch some of these rappers, that stuff is borderline minstrel show. . . . It's horrible and they don't even realize it."[13] Lee adds, "The rap I grew up on originated in the South Bronx and was about having a good time: hip-hop, graffiti, break dancing. It was not about 'I got my 9mm, and I'll blow your [expletive] brains out.' When young African Americans live by the code 'Get rich or die trying,' it's a very sad state."

At its inception, Hip Hop was about young Black people coming together in their communities and expressing their ideas about the world and their life experiences. Today Hip Hop is a 1.6 billion dollar industry dependent on a worldwide network of consumers. The desired balance between art and commerce is a delicate calibration. The multifaceted nature of Hip Hop seems to suggest that, while its more visible corporate branch produces studio thugs and party music, its artistic and political branches nevertheless continue to provide an unfiltered voice for young Blacks and other marginalized groups. The dynamic character of Hip Hop means that it is poised for another transformation. What remains unclear is whether Hip Hop will stay its current course, veer off sharply in another direction, or even spawn something entirely new.

NOTES

1. See http://www.zulunation.com/hip_hop_history_2.htm. The organization is now known as The Universal Zulu Nation.

2. *Sound system* is a term to describe a mobile discotheque, which includes massive audio speakers and a DJ; In other accounts, Jocko's three-hour show was broadcast in Miami, Florida, on AM radio signals that could be heard on some nearby Caribbean islands.

3. *Dub poetry* is usually taken to refer to a particular brand of oral poetry performed to the accompaniment of reggae music.

4. There remains a debate as to whether scratching was developed by Grand Wizzard Theodore or Grandmaster Flash, since each man claims credit. Most, however, seem to agree that Grand Wizzard Theodore accidentally invented scratching while working on his turntables but that it was Grandmaster Flash who actually refined the technique so that it could be replicated.

5. The term *cutting* is probably derived from the Surinamese word *cutsingi*, which describes the interplay of folksongs and songs. Furthermore, the word 'cutting' is a fundamental term used among Haitian, Cuban, Caribbean, and African American musicians.

6. *Graffiti* is taken directly from the Italian word *graffiti* (singular: *graffito*), a term for drawings, paintings, or inscriptions made by passersby on walls and objects in public places.

7. Awareness of graffiti in the United States increased during World War II, when a cartoon with the phrase "Kilroy was here" began to appear on American ships and planes. Later, the phrase began to be seen throughout the world. Whether a political statement or a prank, this tag still spawns much debate about the identity and motives of the original writer. In the later 1960s an explosion of names on buildings and walls were seen in many cities, reflecting the social changes that the nation was undergoing. The peace sign was ubiquitous around college campuses. "Free Huey [Newton]" and "Off Tha Pig" exemplified the sentiments of Black Power activists. In many barrios, Puerto Rican flags were painted with the phrase "Viva Puerto Rico libre."

8. Graffiti appealed to a racially and economically diverse group of young New Yorkers, and it would be a fallacy to state that all graffiti writers were associated with the new Hip Hop phenomenon. Many writers preferred rock music or aligned themselves with punk culture. Moreover, writers often saw their work as their own personal statements, rather than as connected to any group or organization.

9. Davey D, "Grandmaster Caz Heats Up on Sugar Hill," http://www.daveyd.com/FullArticles/articleN432.asp [June 22, 2000].

10. MacLean, Natalie, "Bring on the Bling: Rappers Give Cristal and Hennessy Street Cred." *San Francisco Chronicle*, December 16, 2004. Cites that whites buy 70 percent of rap music; Kloer, Phil, "Rap's the Rage: The Numbers Prove It." *The Atlanta Journal-Constitution*, October 7, 2003. Cites that whites buy an estimated 80 percent of rap/Hip Hop music.

11. Ives, Nat, "Hip Hop Admen: Walk This Way, Shop This Way." *New York Times*, August 9, 2004, Business Section, pp. C1, C7.

12. Marriott, Michel, "The Color of Mayhem," *New York Times*, August 12, 2004, Circuits, pp. E1, E7.

13. Author Unknown, "Lee's Two Worlds," *The Week*, July 30, 2004, People section, p. 10.

A

A+ [Andre Levins]

A+ was one of the youngest rap artists of his era to be signed to a major label recording contract. The teenage rap artist won a national competition sponsored by **Def Jam Recordings** in 1995 and was discovered by manager Kedar Massenburg. A+ was just thirteen years old at the time his debut album, *The Latch-Key Child* (Kedar/Universal), was released in 1996. The album included contributions from major artists, including Q-Tip (**A Tribe Called Quest**), Prodigy (**Mobb Deep**), and AZ. Many rap music critics heard his debut single, "All I See," and compared his lyrical skills to those of **Method Man** of the **Wu-Tang Clan**. His sophomore album, *Hempstead High* (Kedar/Universal, 1999), was his last effort on a major record label. **DISCOGRAPHY:** *The Latch-Key Child* (Kedar/Universal, 1996); *Hempstead High* (Kedar/Universal, 1999).

A & R

A & R stands for *artist and repertoire*, a recording industry term for the division of a record label responsible for finding and developing talent.

ACEYALONE [Eddie Hayes]

A founding member of Los Angeles rap group **Freestyle Fellowship**, Aceyalone played an important role in the evolution of literate rap music on the West Coast during the 1990s, when so-called **gangsta rap** prevailed. In the aftermath of the breakup of Freestyle Fellowship, Aceyalone began a solo career. His work has not resulted in enormous mainstream success, but has allowed him to maintain his exalted place within the West Coast **underground** rap music scene. In 1995, he debuted as a solo artist with *All Balls Don't Bounce* (Capitol Records). The album was a critical success, but poor record sales caused it to be dropped from Capitol's catalog. Aceyalone continued recording on independent labels, following up with *A Book of Human Language* (Project Blowed, 1998). After a three-year absence from the Hip Hop scene, Aceyalone returned in 2001 with *Accepted Eclectic* (Ground Control). In 2003, *Love & Hate* (Red Urban Records) was released, featuring collaborations with El-P and Antipop Consortium. In 2004, Project Blowed secured the rights to *All Balls Don't Bounce* from Capitol and re-issued it with a bonus disc.

DISCOGRAPHY: *All Balls Don't Bounce* (Capitol Records, 1995; reissued by Project Blowed in 2004); *A Book of Human Language* (Project Blowed, 1999); *Accepted Eclectic* (Ground Control, 2001); *Love & Hate* (Red Urban Records, 2003).

ADIDAS SNEAKERS

The Adidas sneaker became an important fashion staple of early **B-boys**. The shell-toed Adidas sneaker, worn with loose shoe laces, was immortalized by rap group **Run DMC** on the single "My Adidas" from their third album *Raising Hell* (Profile, 1986). "My Adidas" was Run DMC's first Top 10 R & B single. In 1986, at a Run DMC concert, Adidas executives saw thousands of fans waving their unlaced shoes in the air, and, thereafter, the group reportedly was paid $1.5 million in 1986 to officially endorse the Adidas athletic shoe.

ADVERTISING AND HIP HOP

From the beginning, rap artists have routinely used the names of products in their rhymes. In the middle 1980s, mainstream advertisers realized the potential of young Black consumers and, as a way to sell to this new market, began to hire rap artists as product spokespersons.

In 1984, Swatch watches sponsored the Swatch Watch New York City Fresh Fest, the first national money-making rap tour. Participants included the **Fat Boys**, **Newcleus**, **Whodini**, **Kurtis Blow**, New York Dynamic Breakers, and **Run DMC**. The tour earned $3.5 million. The Fat Boys later signed a deal to appear in commercials and advertisements for Swatch. In 1986, Sprite cola hired Kurtis Blow, making him the first Hip Hop product spokesman in the United States. Future Sprite ads featured an array of rap artists, including **KRS-ONE**, **MC Shan**, **Grand Puba**, and **Kris Kross**.

Reportedly, in 1992 after a chance meeting at John F. Kennedy airport with Andy Hilfiger, Grand Puba was invited to a free shopping spree at the Tommy Hilfiger showroom. The idea was that, once Grand Puba was seen wearing Hilfiger clothing, the designs would gain popularity among Hip Hop fans. In 2003, **Jay-Z** struck a deal with Reebok and, with the release of the "S. Carter" athletic shoe, became the first rap artist to have a sneaker named after him.

The long list of rap artists who have endorsed products includes, in addition to those already cited, **MC Hammer** [**British Knights** (1990), Pepsi Cola (1991), Taco Bell (1991), Kentucky Fried Chicken (1992)]; **Ice Cube** [St. Ides malt liquor (1991)] KRS-ONE [Nike (1996), Sprite (1996)]; **Method Man** [Reebok (1996)]; **Busta Rhymes** [Mountain Dew (2000)]; **Lil' Kim** and **Mary J. Blige** [Viva Glam III/MAC cosmetics (2001)]; **Queen Latifah** [Cover Girl Cosmetics (2003), Lane Bryant (2000)]; **Ludacris** [Pepsi

Cola (2002) commercial pulled after protests], **Wyclef Jean** [Mountain Dew (2001)]; **Missy Elliott** [Vanilla Coke (2003), Gap (2003)]; **Eve** [Reebok (2003); one television ad with rap artist Fabolous, two solo print ads]; **LL Cool J** with **Run DMC** [Dr. Pepper (2003)]; and **Rakim** [Henessy 2003].

AEROSOL ART. *See* Graffiti

AFRIKA BAMBAATAA (aka Afrika Bambaataa Aasim) [Kevin Donovan]

Regarded, along with **DJ Kool Herc** and **Grandmaster Flash**, as an originator of Hip Hop, Bambaataa is respectfully known as the Godfather of Hip Hop. Bambaataa's music career began when he received his first set of turntables as a high school graduation gift from his mother. In 1976, he threw his first real party at the **Bronx River Community Center** and a year later Bambaataa would DJ against the reigning king, DJ Kool Herc, at the Webster Avenue Police Athletic League in the Bronx. Founder of the **Zulu Nation** (later Universal Zulu Nation), Afrika Bambaataa is largely responsible for the spread of rap music and Hip Hop culture through artist development and promotion of rap events, beginning with parties in the parks that featured rap artists, **B-boys**, **DJ**s, and **graffiti** art.

Afrika Bambaataa. *Courtesy of Photofest.*

As a teenager, the Bronx, New York, native joined the Bronx River Projects division of the Black Spades street gang and soon became a leader of the organization. Always a music buff, Bambaataa briefly played the trumpet and the piano at Adlai E. Stevenson High School. Bambaataa was also a serious record collector and he would later be known as the "Master of Records." His tastes were expansive and included Rock, R & B, African, Latin, calypso, and classical.

When the influence of street gangs, including the Black Spades, began to decline, Bambaataa founded a performing group. The group was originally called the Bronx River Organization, then simply The Organization. Kevin Donovan took the name Afrika Bambaataa (Bambaataa means "affectionate leader") after seeing the 1964 movie *Zulu*, which detailed the battles between British troops and the Azulu Tribe in 1879. Bambaataa then decided to form his own Zulu Nation and after about a two-year hiatus he reconstituted The Organization for that purpose. The Zulu Nation was first a five-member B-boy crew. These members were called the Shaka Zulu Kings (aka Zulu Kings); later there would also be Shaka Zulu Queens.

Over the years, Bambaataa's music spread through his DJing, and the Zulu Nation grew as other DJs as well as rap artists, B-boys, and graffiti writers followed Bambaataa's parties and were taken under his wing and made members of his Zulu Nation. Many audiocassette tapes, later known as **mixtapes**, were made of Bambaataa parties and the associated MC **battles.** These mixtapes were sometimes sold for $20 to $40 apiece. Setting the stage for **sampling**, during the long music segments when Bambaataa was DJing he would sometimes mix in recorded speeches from Malcolm X, Martin Luther King, Jr., and later Minister Louis Farrakhan.

Bambaataa formed the Soul Sonic Force, which originally consisted of approximately twenty Zulu Nation members but members formed groups within the group and Bambaataa would perform with these various entities. In the early 1980s, Bambaataa signed to Winley Records and released "Zulu Nation Throwdown Part 1" with the Cosmic Force and "Zulu Nation Throwdown Part 2" with the Soul Sonic Force, but Bambaataa was disappointed in the resulting recordings. He was further enraged when Winley released an unauthorized recording of one of the infamous Zulu Nation parties in "Death Mix, Parts I and II" (1983); this ended the business relationship.

In the early 1980s, Bambaataa met **Fab 5 Freddy**, a former graffiti artist and Hip Hop impresario, who introduced him to the largely White downtown New York City music scene. As a result, Bambaataa tried fusing familiar urban music sounds with the rock and alternative music that he was now being exposed to. Tom Silverman visited Bambaataa at one of his parties and did an article on him and the Zulu Nation for his own *Dance Music Report* magazine. In March 1981, Silverman, now president of Tommy Boy Records, released Afrika Bambaataa and The Jazzy Five's groundbreaking "Jazzy Sensation," produced by Arthur Baker and Shep Pettibone. In May 1982, Bambaataa and Soul Sonic Force released "Planet Rock" (Tommy Boy Records), sampling Kraftwerk's "Trans-Europe Express." By September 1982, "Planet Rock" had gone gold, and went on to sell over 620,000 copies in the United States. Bambaataa's next single, "Looking for a Perfect Beat" (Tommy Boy Records) was released about 1983, followed by "Renegades of Funk" (Tommy Boy Records); both singles were with Soul Sonic Force.

In 1982, Bambaataa was part of the first Hip Hop tour to Europe with Fab 5 Freddy, **Grand Mixer D.ST** & The Infinity Rappers, Rammellzee, **Rock Steady Crew**, the Double Dutch Girls, and graffiti artists Phase 2, Futura, and Dondi.

Due to his early use of drum machines and computer sounds, Bambaataa was instrumental in changing the way R & B and other forms of urban music were recorded. Beginning with the single "Planet Rock," Bambaataa's creation of electro music (or electro funk, as he called it) helped spark the development of other musical genres such as **freestyle**, electronica, house, and early techno. In 1984, with **James Brown**, Bambaataa recorded the landmark song "Unity" (Tommy Boy Records). The combination of Bambaataa and Brown was billed in music industry circles as "the Godfather of Soul meets the Godfather of Hip Hop." In 1985, Bambaataa and other music stars joined as "Artists Against Apartheid," recording *Sun City* (EMI-Manhattan) with Little Steven Van Zandt, **Run DMC**, **Kurtis Blow**, the **Fat Boys**, Lou Reed, and numerous others.

In 1990, Bambaataa was included in *Life* magazine's "Most Important Americans of the 20th Century" issue. Also in 1990, Bambaataa participated in a concert at Wembley Stadium in London for the African National Congress (A.N.C.) in honor of Nelson Mandela's release from prison. In connection with that event, the 1990 recording "Ndodemnyama (Free South Africa)" (Warlock Records) reportedly raised at least $30,000 for the A.N.C.

In 1994, Bambaataa began DJing on radio station Hot 97 (WQHT-FM, 97.1) in New York City, hosting the show ***Old School***. In 2002, Bambaataa produced *The True School Show*, featuring a diverse format of music airing on www.bringthenoise.com with that Web enterprise's cofounders **Chuck D** and Gary G-Wiz.

Over the years, Bambaataa has been featured in a number of **films**.

DISCOGRAPHY: *Singles* (over 45 total): "Jazzy Sensation" (Tommy Boy Records, 1982); Planet Rock (Tommy Boy Records, 1982); "Looking for a Perfect Beat (Tommy Boy Records, 1983). *Albums* (over 18 total): *Planet Rock: The Album* (Tommy Boy Records, 1986); *Beware (The Funk is Everywhere)* (Tommy Boy Records, 1986); *Lost Generation* (Hot Productions, 1996); *Dark Matter Moving At the Speed of Light* (Tommy Boy Records, 2004).

AFRIKA ISLAM

Best known for his production work with rap artist **Ice-T**, Afrika Islam is a talented DJ, able to spin four turntables at one time. He is recognized as one of the **Zulu Nation**'s original **B-boys** (the Zulu Kings) and host of the **WHBI** radio program, *Zulu Beats*, where he partnered with the Supreme Team to produce the the first Hip Hop mix show. Afrika Islam worked closely with **Afrika Bambaataa** and frequently warmed up the audience prior to Bambaataa's performance at Zulu parties in the 1970s, earning him the name "Son of Bambaataa."

In the early 1980s, Afrika Islam had a brief stint as the DJ for the **Rock Steady Crew**, after which he moved to Los Angeles and appeared in the films *Breakin' II* and *Pump up the Volume.* Islam also began doing production work for Ice-T, starting as a mixer on *Rhymes Pay* (Warner, 1987) and producing the albums *Power* (Warner, 1988), *Iceberg/Freedom of Speech/Just Watch What You Say* (Warner, 1989), *O.G.: Original Gangsta* (Warner, 1991), and *Body Count* (Warner, 1992). Through his work with Ice-T, Islam also began **remixing** for other artists, including Michael Jackson, New Order, and the Eurythmics.

In 1992, Afrika Islam exported his successful *Zulu Beats* show to Japan.

A.G. *See* Showbiz & A.G.

AKINYELE [Akinyele Adams]

A leading figure in New York's **underground** rap scene in the early 1990s, Akinyele got his start by appearing with **Nas** and **Large Professor** on **Main Source**'s single, "Live At The Bar-B-Que," from the *Breaking Atoms* album (Wild Pitch, 1991). By the time of his own debut album, *Vagina Diner* (Interscope Records, 1993), followed by *Bomb* (Interscope Records, 1994), Akinyele appeared to have a promising career, with classic tracks produced by Large Professor, Buckwild, and Dr. Butcher. Interscope Records, however, was not able to elevate him to star status.

After moving to Zoo Records, Akinyele found an underground radio hit with the sexually explicit title track from his 1996 EP, *Put It in Your Mouth*. In 1999, he followed up with the album, *Aktapuss: The Soundtrack* (Zoo Records). He also recorded "Juan Valdez" on Rawkus Records (though this was never formally released) and signed an album deal with Koch Records, releasing *AnaKonda* in 2001.

DISCOGRAPHY: *EP*: *Put It in Your Mouth* (Zoo Records, 1996). *Albums*: *Vagina Diner* (Interscope Records, 1993); *Bomb* (Interscope Records, 1994); *Aktapuss: The Soundtrack* (Zoo Records. 1999); *AnaKonda* (Koch International, 2001).

ALKAHOLIKS. *See* Tha Alkaholiks

ALMIGHTY RSO (aka Made Men)

With RSO standing for "Rock Solid Organization," the Almighty RSO is comprised of Ray Dogg [Raymond Scott], E-Devious [Marco Ennis], Rock [Rodney Pitts], Tony Rhome [Anthony Johnson], and DJ Deff Jeff

[Jeffrey Neal]. The Almighty RSO are probably best known for their controversial relationship with ***The Source*** magazine's president Dave Mays. In November 1994, without the knowledge of the editorial staff, Mays inserted a three-page story on the group in the publication; in response several of *The Source*'s editors resigned.

The Almighty RSO are rap music pioneers in the Boston area. They performed along with acts such as Roxbury Crush Crew, Fresh To Impress, Body Rock Crew, T.D.S. Mob, Disco P & The Fresh MC, Top Choice Clique, and Rusty The Toejammer. The Almighty RSO Crew was among the first to release rap songs in the Bean, among them "To Be Like Us" and "Call Us the All" in 1987 and "We're Notorious" in 1988. The group earned a Boston Music Award in 1987 for "Best Rap Group." Almighty RSO was later banned from performing in popular area venues, however, because of their pyrotechnic turntable show and in 1990 the fatal stabbing of Rock in a parking lot marred the group's burgeoning success.

The group signed with Tommy Boy Records and released the single "One da the Chamba" in 1992. Almighty RSO music appeared well into the 1990s, both on independent labels and on **Queen Latifah**'s Flavor Unit label. They later signed to RCA Records, which released their 1994 EP *Revenge Ov Da Badd Boyz*. In 1996, they released the full-length album, *Doomsday: Forever RSO* (Surrender/Rap-A-Lot/Noo Trybe Records). The album became a success on the strength of the hit single "You Could Be My Boo," which featured guest vocals by Faith Evans.

In 1999, the group later changed their name to Made Men. Ray Dogg would change his name to **Ray Benzino** and engage in a public **battle**, along with Dave Mays, against **Eminem**. In 2001, Benzino released his solo albums *The Benzino Project* (Universal, 2001) and *Redemption* (Elektra, 2003).

DISCOGRAPHY: *Singles*: "To Be Like Us" (1987); "Call Us the All" (1987); "We're Notorious" (1988); "One da the Chamba" (Tommy Boy Records, 1992). *EPs*: *Revenge Ov Da Badd Boyz* (RCA, 1994); *Doomsday: Forever RSO* (Surrender/Rap-A-Lot/Noo Trybe Records, 1996).

ANQUETTE

Recognized as the first female rap artist to represent Miami, Florida, Anquette would release several singles including, "Throw the P" (1986), a biting response to **2 Live Crew**'s song, "Throw the D," and "Ghetto Style" (1987) on **Luther "Luke" Campbell**'s Skyywalker Records. With her song "Janet Reno" (Skyywalker Records, 1988), she would immortalize former Attorney General Janet Reno, who as Florida's State Attorney prosecuted deadbeat fathers who did not pay child support. Anquette recorded only one album, *Respect* (Skyywalker Records, 1988).

ANT BANKS [Anthony Banks]

A prolific Bay Area producer who began working behind the scenes with rap artist **Too Short** as a member of his "Dangerous Crew," In 1992 Ant Banks was a producer for Too Short, Spice 1, and Pooh-Man. That same year, he appeared on two film soundtracks, *Juice* and *Menace II Society*. In 1992 Banks also signed a contract with Jive Records. He released his debut album, *Sittin' on Something Phat*, in 1993. The album featured live instrumentals, including the guitar playing of former Parliament Funkadelic member Michael Hampton.

Subsequent albums, *The Big Badass* (Jive Records, 1994) and *Do or Die* (Jive Records, 1995), showed Banks's skills on the microphone as well as on the mixing board. For his 1997 album *Big Thangs*, Banks recruited some of the West Coast's best rap artists to assist him, including **Ice Cube**, **Tupac Shakur**, Too Short, and **Ice-T**. In 1999, Banks released the CD single, "Drinks on Me" (Thump Special Products), with his T.W.D.Y. project. He followed up later in 1999 with the album, *Derty Werk* (Thump Special Prod) and experienced a big hit with the album track "Players Holiday—Mac Mall." In 2000, he followed with the second T.W.D.Y. album, *Lead the Way* (Thump Special Products).

DISCOGRAPHY: *Singles*: "Drinks on Me" (Thump Special Products, 1999). *Albums*: *Sittin' On Something Phat* (Jive Records, 1993); *The Big Badass* (Jive Records, 1994); *Do or Die* (Jive Records, 1995); *Derty Work* (Thump Special Products, 1999); *Lead The Way* (Thump Special Products, 2000).

ANTOINETTE [unknown]

A native of Queens, the self-proclaimed "Gangstress of Rap" Antoinette is best remembered for her on-wax **battles** with **MC Lyte**. She was introduced to rap music fans on producer Hurby "Luv Bug" Azor's 1987 compilation album, *Hurby's Machine (The House That Rap Built)* (Next Plateau), with the tracks "I Got An Attitude" and "Hit 'Em With This." After Antoinette allegedly dissed MC Milk (**Audio Two**), MC Lyte retaliated with the single "10% Dis" from her 1988 debut album, *Lyte as a Rock* (Atlantic). The two would continue to battle it out on wax, next on Antoinette's single "Lights Out, Party Over," followed by MC Lyte's single "Shut the Eff Up (Hoe)" from the 1989 album *Eyes on This* (Atlantic)—which effectively silenced Antoinette. In 1990, Antoinette recorded the album *Burnin' at 20 Below* (Next Plateau/Red) and in 1989 the album *Who's the Boss* (Next Plateau/Red).

DISCOGRAPHY: *Albums*: *Who's the Boss* (Next Plateau, 1989); *Burnin' at 20 Below* (Next Plateau, 1990).

ARABIAN PRINCE, THE [Mik Lezan]

Although this Compton, California, artist was a founding member of the rap group **N.W.A.**, The Arabian Prince has been largely deleted from N.W.A.'s official history. The Arabian Prince had been a producer and DJ since the early 1980s, however, and these talents helped him to sustain his career after leaving N.W.A.

The Arabian Prince began in the music business while still in middle school. His father worked at KACE-FM (103.9) in Los Angeles, and The Arabian Prince began his career recording **mixtapes** at the station after hours. He also DJed school dances and the occasional club date. In 1982–1983, Arabian Prince began recording his own tracks and coproduced the artists Bobby Jimmy & the Critters. He also did live appearances with **The Egyptian Lover**, **World Class Wreckin' Cru**, and the L.A. Dream Team.

His early singles "Innovator" (1985) and "Situation Hot" (1989) received critical acclaim on the Los Angeles club scene. One year after the release of the N.W.A.'s hit second album, *Straight Outta Compton*, in 1988, The Arabian Prince released his first solo full-length album, *Brother Arab, for Orpheus*. The single "She's Got a Big Posse" received some commercial recognition. Arabian Prince also produced the 1988 single "Supersonic," the only hit for Los Angeles-based female rap group **J.J. Fad**. In 1992, Arabian Prince released his second album, *Tha Underworld* (EMI-America). The 1995 album *Where's My Bytches* (Phantom) was his last, although he has pursued several musical projects, as well as ownership in a special-effects company and animation studio.

ARRESTED DEVELOPMENT

The group Arrested Development was comprised of Speech [Todd Thomas] and Headliner [Tim Barnwell] and at different times dancer Montsho Eshe [Temelca Gaither], singer Dionne Farris, drummer–singer–artist Rasa Don [Donald Jones], "spiritual adviser" Baba Oje, and singer–dancer–stylist–poet Aerle Taree [Taree Jones]. They popularized a humanist Afrocentric music, as did **De La Soul** and **P.M. Dawn**.

In 1992, in a rap music field dominated by so-called **gangsta rap**, the radio-friendly and spiritual sounds of Arrested Development were tagged as "alternative rap" by the media when they released their debut album, *3 Years, 5 Months and 2 Days in the Life Of . . .* (Chrysalis). The title reportedly represents the time that it took the group to get a record deal. Speech wrote all the songs and produced the group's debut album, which speaks of African American history and empowerment. The group's first hit, "Tennessee," discusses the reclaiming of Southern Black traditions from the racism that tainted their beauty. Their second

Arrested Development. *Courtesy of photofest.*

single, "People Everyday," was a skillfully updated version of the Sly and the Family Stone classic, "Everyday People."

Arrested Development released another CD in 1992, titled *Revolution.* The group dedicated the CD to any Black ancestors who were raped, hanged, or killed. The CD contained only five tracks; the first three have nearly identical versions of the song called "Revolution," which was used on the soundtrack for a 1992 Spike Lee film.

A native of Milwaukee, Wisconsin, Speech spent his summers in rural Tennessee with his grandmother. After moving to Atlanta, Georgia, to study music business and management at the Art Institute of Atlanta, he decided to start a musical group. He first met Headliner and then other members joined the group, including Speech's cousin Aerle Taree. The closeness of the group was legendary, to the point that the members referred to each other as a family.

Arrested Development received the 1993 Grammy Award for "Best New Artist" and for having the "Best Rap Performance by a Duo or Group" for its single "Tennessee." That year the group's sophomore effort was its popular *Unplugged* album (MTV). Also in 1993, Arrested Development performed in the Lollapalooza tour.

Arrested Development released their last album in 1994, *Zingalamaduni* (Chrysalis). Unfortunately, the group's antigangsta lyrics and image could not compete against the prevalent hardcore material, and the group officially disbanded in 1996. Speech would release three solo albums and singer Dionne Farris would release the acclaimed album, *Wild Seed—Wild Flower* (Sony, 1994).

DISCOGRAPHY: *3 Years, 5 Months and 2 Days in the Life Of . . .* (Chrysalis, 1992); *Revolution* (1992); *Unplugged* (MTV, 1993); *Zingalamaduni* (Chrysalis, 1994).

ARSONISTS, THE

A rap group from Brooklyn, New York, The Arsonists, comprised of Jise One, Swel Boogie, and Q-Unique, began with thirteen members in 1993, under the name Bushwick Bomb Squad. Over the years, the number would dwindle and by the end of 1999 there would be only three members remaining. After signing to the independent label, Fondle 'Em, they took the name The Arsonists. They released three innovative twelve-inch singles, "The Session" and "Geembo's Theme" with Fondle 'Em Records and "Venom" with Serchlite/Geffen, and a critically acclaimed 1999 debut album, *As The World Burns* (Matador), but then members Freestyle and D-Stroy left the group, leaving Q-Unique, Jise One, and Swel Boogie to carry the 2001 album, *Date of Birth* (Matador). Although mainstream success eluded The Arsonists, their creative and bold music, as well as their extraordinary stage shows, garnered them domestic **underground** star status and an international following.

DISCOGRAPHY: *Singles*: "The Session" (Fondle 'Em Records, 1996); "Venom" (Serchlite/Geffen, 1997); "Geembo's Theme" (Fondle 'Em Records, 1998). *Albums*: *As The World Burns* (Matador, 1999); *Date of Birth* (Matador, 2001).

A TRIBE CALLED QUEST. *See* Tribe Called Quest, A

AUDIO TWO

Audio Two, with members MC Milk [Kirk Robinson] and DJ Gizmo [Nathaniel Robinson], are best known for their 1988 single, "Top Billin'." The Brooklyn, New York, duo can definitely be called a one-hit wonder. MC Milk, MC Lyte's cousin, and DJ Gizmo had at best, average rap skills, however, they are responsible for a bona fide rap music classic. A decade later, **MC Lyte**, would cover the track on her album *Seven & Seven* (Elektra Asylum). "Top Billin'" easily stands as the best track on their 1988 debut album, *What More Can I Say* (First Priority/Atlantic)—thanks in no small measure to Daddy O's (**Stetsasonic**) tight and infectious production.

DISCOGRAPHY: *EP: I Get the Papers* (Atlantic/WEA, 1990). *Albums*: *What More Can I Say* (Atlantic, WEA, 1988); *I Don't Care: The Album* (First Priority, 1990); *The First Dead Indian* (First Priority, 1992).

AWESOME TWO

Special K and Teddy Ted, known as the Awesome Two, have the longest running rap music show in the world. The Awesome Two has been on the air for over twenty years. They began their radio program in 1983 on New Jersey's **WHBI-FM** 105.9 (now WNWK) and currently can be heard on the Sirius Satellite Radio program *Backspin Tuesdays*, which features Old School rap. The duo has been inducted into the Museum of Television and Radio for their achievements and longevity in the industry. By supplying a copy of the single "7 Minutes of Funk," Teddy Ted and Special K helped rap duo **EPMD** make their groundbreaking debut single, "It's My Thing," in 1987. The Awesome Two are also credited with being the first to play **Eric B & Rakim**'s debut single, "Eric B is President" (Zakia/4th & Broadway, 1987). The Awesome Two are also immortalized on Nice n' Smooth's 1989 single, "Ooh Child."

See also: KDAY-AM; Mr. Magic; DJ Kevvy Kev; and Kool DJ Red Alert

B

BACKSPIN

1. Turntable technique in which the **DJ** stops a record with his or her hand and rewinds it quickly. The result is a garbled sound that alerts the audience that the DJ is about to replay a portion of the record again.
2. A **B-boy** move that begins in a squatted position, tucking the arm and shoulder under the body, thereby touching the floor, then rolling onto the back and spinning.

BACKSTAGE. *See* Films

BAD BOY ENTERTAINMENT

The record company founded by **Sean "P. Diddy" Combs**, Bad Boy Entertainment is best known for following in the steps of Uptown Records by promoting glitz and street-influenced glamor within the Hip Hop aesthetic. When Combs was terminated from his position as Vice President at Uptown Records in July 1993, he formed Bad Boy Entertainment through a multimillion-dollar deal with Arista Records and released its first album, Craig Mack's *Project: Funk the World*. This album produced the hit single, "Flava in Ya Ear." **The Notorious B.I.G.**'s landmark album, *Ready to Die*, was released on September 1, 1994, and in the process helped to shape the direction of Bad Boy Entertainment.

During its first four years, the company sold $100 million in records, promoting artists including The Notorious B.I.G., **Lil' Kim** (on Undeas/Atlantic), Total, and 112. In June 2002, Bad Boy Entertainment ended its decade-long relationship with Arista Records. Combs, who been in a 50–50 partnership with Arista Records since 1996, took complete control of the label, including both the artist roster and the entire catalog. In February 2003 Combs signed a worldwide distribution deal with Universal Records for Bad Boy Entertainment. Under the terms of the agreement, Combs received a significant payment and also retained 100-percent ownership of the Bad Boy Entertainment label. Universal agreed to provide Bad Boy with promotions and marketing support and to distribute the Bad Boy catalog.

Bad Boy's current roster includes Sean "P. Diddy" Combs, Notorious B.I.G. (posthumous releases), Dream, Faith Evans, Carl Thomas, New

Edition, 8Ball & MJG, Loon, Mario Winans, Black Rob, Cheri Denis, G. Dep, Craig Mack, and Total.

BAHAMADIA [Antonia Reed]

A protégé of Guru (**Gang Starr**), Bahamadia is best known for her formidable rhyme skills and jazz-influenced music. The name Bahamadia is a combination of the Arabic words, *bahdai* (creator) and *hamdala* (thankful). A native of Philadelphia, Bahamadia grew up DJing house parties in the 1980s before stepping out in front of the turntables and grabbing the microphone in 1985.

In the early 1990s, she hooked up with producer–radio personality DJ Ran, who helmed her independent 1993 single "Funk Vibe," which caught the ear of Gang Starr's Guru. With the support of Guru and **DJ Premier**, Bahamadia landed a record contract with Chrysalis. In 1994, she released the single "Total Wreck" and in 1995 the single "Uknowhowwedu," winning critical praise for her jazz-inspired flavor, as well as **underground** notice. She also appeared on the second volume of Guru's acclaimed *Jazzmatazz Vol. 2 The New Reality* (Capitol Records, 1995) project. Her debut album, *Kollage* (EMI/Chrysalis), was released in 1996 and featured production by DJ Premier and fellow Philadelphia natives, **The Roots**. The critically acclaimed album was a blend of jazz-infused musical offerings.

A year later, Chrysalis folded and Bahamadia chose to wait out her contract before resuming her recording career. In the meantime, she solidified her underground reputation, making a string of musically adventurous guest appearances with artists such as The Roots, Sweetback, Roni Size, and Morcheeba. She also hosted a rap music radio show, *The B-Sides*, in Philadelphia on WPHI-FM (103.9) from 1997 to 1999. According to Bahamadia, the radio show was designed to "nurture grassroots-oriented" Hip Hop.

In 2000, she signed with the Los Angeles–based independent label Goodvibe and released the seven-track EP titled *BB Queen* (the BB is as in "beautiful black"), which received excellent reviews.

DISCOGRAPHY: *Single*: "Funk Vibe" (1993). *EP*: *BB Queen* (GoodVibe, 2000). *Album*: *Kollage* (EMI/Chrysalis, 1996).

BAKER, HOUSTON, JR.

An advocate for the inclusion of rap music in Black studies courses, Houston Baker, Jr., is a professor of English and African American literature at Duke University and past president of the Modern Language Association. Baker's polemical essay, *Black Studies, Rap, and the Academy* (University of Chicago, 1993), written in the aftermath of the 1992 Los Angeles riots, assesses the then-current state of Black Studies in academe and outlines its responsibilities to rap music, the newest form of Black expression. Baker robustly defends Black Studies programs and provides an extended commentary on the importance of rap.

BARNES, DEE

Best remembered as the television personality who was assaulted by **Dr. Dre (N.W.A.)**, Dee Barnes was the host of the pioneering rap music television show, *Pump It Up*. In 1991, Dr. Dre attacked Barnes after the program aired an unflattering segment on N.W.A. Barnes subsequently filed a lawsuit for $22 million. Dr. Dre pleaded no contest to the charges and the lawsuit was settled out of court. Barnes became a *cause célèbre* and fodder for discussions about **misogyny** in Hip Hop. In 1991, Barnes would host "Sisters in the Name of Rap," the first nationally televised concert featuring thirteen female MCs, including **Yo Yo**, Nefertiti, **Queen Latifah**, **MC Lyte**, and **Salt 'N Pepa**. On the track "Guilty Conscience." from **Eminem**'s 1999 album *Slim Shady* (Aftermath/Interscope Records), Dr. Dre refers to the assault with the line, "You gonna take advice from somebody who slapped Dee Barnes??!"

BATTLES; BATTLING

Hip Hop developed as a competitive art form, insofar as the public decided which rap artist, rap crew, or **B-boy** was the best in relation to his peers or challengers. In that atmosphere, attacks and insults are expected in battles for supremacy. Before there was recorded rap music, battles and battling were restricted to live performances and audiotapes with limited distribution. With the advent of rap records, personal **beefs** or disagreements were exposed to a national and later international audience, rather than just a particular local neighborhood or community. Classic Hip Hop battles involved **KRS-ONE** and **MC Shan**; **Roxanne Shante** and **The Real Roxanne**; **LL Cool J** and **Kool Moe Dee**; and **Tupac Shakur** and **The Notorious B.I.G.**

B-BOY (aka break boy); B-BOYING

B-boying represents the dance element of Hip Hop culture. **DJ Kool Herc** is credited with the term. The mainstream term is *break dancing*.

One of the most direct influences on B-boying may have been **James Brown**'s 1969 hit, "Get on the Good Foot." In film footage, James Brown does a dance called the Good Foot for the song. The Good Foot was a fast athletic dance and easily lent itself to dance battles between two opponents. Dancers who adapted the Good Foot style would dance in the "break" of a song, and so DJ Kool Herc called these dancers *breakers* or *B-boys*. This early B-boying was fast and furious; it was very physical, involving complicated leg work, and was all done on the floor.

Afrika Bambaataa recognized the art of B-boying and formed the first B-boy crew, the Zulu Kings, who went on to perform at various Hip Hop events and win countless battles. In 1977, with the emergence of the Manhattan chapter of the **Rock Steady Crew**, acrobatic elements were added to the floor work of the older styles. The new acrobatic moves included headspins, backspins, handglides (balanced on one hand, elbow tucked into the body while turning), and windmills (on the head and shoulders, spinning, with arms providing the momentum). Other terms associated with B-boying include "rockin'," breaking," "top rockin'," "burning," and "going off." Female dancers are known as B-girls.

BEANIE SIGEL [Dwight Grant]

Beanie Sigel is best known for his charismatic lyrical style and his ability to paint vivid pictures of street life. Rather than toiling in the underground for years, the Philadelphia rap artist had a rapidly rising career, beginning with an impromptu verse on **The Roots** track "Adrenaline," from their 1999 album *Things Fall Apart* (MCA) and with his appearance on one of **DJ Clue**'s **mixtapes**. Sigel would the make cameos on **Jay-Z**'s album, *Vol. 2: Hard Knock Life* (Roc-A-Fella/Def Jam Recordings), and subsequently sign his own solo deal with **Roc-A-Fella Records**. Sigel's distinctive delivery, tinged with a Southern drawl, and his smart but hard-hitting rhymes were displayed on his well-received 2000 debut album, *The Truth (*Roc-A-Fella/Def Jam Recordings), which reportedly sold 700,000 units. His sophomore album, *The Reason* (Roc-A-Fella/Def Jam Recordings) was released in 2001 and was generally considered to have surpassed the first in terms of flow and production.

Overshadowing his musical ability have been Siegel's legal troubles. In 1995, Sigel was convicted for drug trafficking, but was placed on probation and sentenced to house arrest rather than sentenced to prison. In July 2003, Sigel was arrested after a performance, allegedly for shooting an acquaintance in West Philadelphia. In April 2004, Sigel pleaded guilty to federal drugs and weapons charges, facing three years in prison.

DISCOGRAPHY: *The Truth* (Roc-A-Fella/Def Jam Recordings, 2000); *The Reason* (Roc-A-Fella/Def Jam Recordings, 2001).

BEASTIE BOYS

Comprised of Mike D [Mike Diamond], Ad Rock [Adam Horovitz], and MCA [Adam Yauch], the Beastie Boys became the first successful White rap artists. "Beastie" stands for "Boys Entering Anarchistic States Towards Internal Excellence." The former hardcore rock trio found international fame as the first crossover White rap. Unlike many of their Black counterparts, the members of this irreverent, New York–based rap trio all came from upper middle-class backgrounds.

Beastie Boys. *Courtesy of Photofest.*

The Beastie Boys debut album, *Licensed to Ill* (Def Jam Recordings, 1986), sold 1 million copies and at the end of November 1986 became the first rap album to top the U.S. pop charts. Original guitarist John Berry departed after the release of the EP *Polly Wog Stew* (Ratcage Records, 1982). The remaining members were Adam Yauch, Mike Diamond, drummer Kate Schellenbach, and new guitarist Adam Horovitz, who is the son of playwright Israel Horovitz and a former member of the band The Young And The Useless. In 1983, the reformulated Beastie Boys released the EP *Cookie Puss* (Ratcage Records). The single "Cookie Puss," a silly rap ditty based on a prank phone call made to Carvel Ice Cream, makers of the "Cookie Puss" novelty confection, became a surprise **underground** hit in New York clubs—particularly surprising, in that the Beastie Boys were a punk band. Schellenbach soon departed, reducing the crew to the core trio who were now going by names of MCA, Mike D, and King Ad Rock.

The group caught the attention of New York University student and aspiring record producer Rick Rubin, who signed the trio to his nascent rap music label, **Def Jam Recordings**. Def Jam officially signed the Beastie Boys in 1985, and that year they had a hit single from the soundtrack to the film ***Krush Groove*** with "She's on It," a rap music track that sampled the AC/DC single "Back in Black" and suggested the approach of the group's forthcoming debut album. The lead single from their debut album, the raucous "(You Gotta) Fight For Your Right (To Party!)," was a juvenile frat-boy type rant from the trio about parents confiscating their pornography or telling them to turn down the stereo. Remarkably the song became an anthem for pseudo-rebellious youth everywhere.

In 1984, when the Beastie Boys toured with Madonna on her "Like a Virgin Tour," the trio taunted the audience with profanity and was generally poorly received. In 1985, the trio gained their Hip Hop credentials on the Raising Hell tour, with **Run DMC** and **LL Cool J**. During 1988, there was a bitter lawsuit between the Beastie Boys and Def Jam and Rick Rubin. The Beastie Boys accused Def Jam of withholding royalties and Def Jam accused the Beastie Boys of withholding their follow-up album. Rick Rubin, who credited himself with the group's success, threatened to release outtakes as their second album. The Beastie Boys left Def Jam for Capitol Records, moved to Los Angeles, and began refining their sound.

In 1989, joining forces with an up-and-coming production duo called the Dust Brothers, the Beasties recorded their startlingly mature follow-up album, *Paul's Boutique* (Capitol Records). Abandoning heavy metal samples and childish rhymes in exchange for more complex arrangement of obscure samples and rhymes that referenced everything from cult fiction (e.g., Anthony Burgess's book, *A Clockwork Orange*) through to the Old Testament, *Paul's Boutique* confused both fans and critics and sold under 1 million copies. The album nonetheless spawned a minor hit in "Hey Ladies," which ranked number 36 on the Top 40.

In 1992, the Beastie Boys released the album *Check Your Head* (Capitol Records) which was recorded with a new keyboardist, Money Mark Nishita. The album revisited the group's punk days while adding touches of funk and old-school rap. Debuting in the Top 10, *Check Your Head* became a hit with college and alternative radio with the singles "So Whatcha Want" and "Pass the Mic." This album marked the transition of the Beastie Boys from the increasingly violence-filled world of rap music to the emerging alternative rock scene.

In 1993, Horovitz pleaded guilty to a charge of battery on a television cameraman during a memorial service for actor River Phoenix. He was put on two years of probation and was ordered to undertake 200 hours of community service and pay restitution costs.

In 1994, the Beastie Boys set up their own magazine and label, Grand Royal, whose first release was the EP *In Search Of Manny*, by Luscious Jackson (featuring Schellenbach, the original drummer of the Beastie Boys). Other signings included The Young And The Useless, DFL, DJ Hurricane (also of the Afros), Noise Addict, and Moistboyz, establishing the label as one of the most respected independents of the 1990s. In 1994, the Beastie Boys released the album *Ill Communication* (Capitol Records), which debuted at number 1 and went double platinum in two weeks. *Ill Communication* completed the group's shift to alternative rock music and garnered them top billing on the 1994 Lollapalooza tour. That same year, the trio released *Some Old Bullshit* (Grand Royal, Capitol Records), a compilation of their earliest punk recordings and Yauch founded the Milarepa Fund, a charity whose mission is to bring attention to and support the fight for Tibetan independence.

In 1995, the Beastie Boys released two EPs, the punkish *Aglio E Olio* (Grand Royal/Capitol Records), which contained eight songs blasted out in only eleven minutes, followed by *The In Sound From Way Out!* (Grand Royal/Capitol Records), comprised of B-sides and instrumental funk cuts from their previous two albums. Adam Yauch, a Buddhist convert and friends with the Dalai Lama, organized the two-day Tibetan Freedom Festival to benefit the Milarepa Fund. (The festival was repeated in 1997 and 1998.)

In 1998 the Beastie Boys released, *Hello Nasty* (Grand Royal/Capitol Records) their first full studio album in four years, a clever mix of old-school rap and more current music sounds. The album title was inspired by their agent's telephone greeting. After the funky feel of *Ill Communication*, the long-awaited *Hello Nasty* was a return to a cleaner, more rap-centered sound. The album debuted on U.S. music charts at number 1 in August 1998, staying at the top for three weeks. The following year they released a double CD greatest-hits package, *The Sounds of Science.*

After eight years of sustained growth, the Grand Royal label was forced to close down in September 2001. Mike Diamond cited "mounting debts, decreasing assets, and increasingly harsh industry conditions" among the reasons for the closure. In 2004, the Beastie Boys released the album, *To the Five Boroughs* (Capitol Records), an old-school style rap album that pays homage to the five boroughs of New York City.

DISCOGRAPHY: *EPs*: *Polly Wog Stew* (Ratcage Records, 1982); *Cookie Puss* (Ratcage Records, 1983); *Aglio E Olio* (Grand Royal/Capitol Records, 1995); *The In Sound From Way Out!* (Grand Royal/Capitol Records, 1995). *Albums*: *Licensed to Ill* (Def Jam Recordings, 1986); *Paul's Boutique* (Capitol Records, 1989); *Check Your Head* (Capitol Records, 1992); *Ill Communication* (Capitol Records, 1994); *Some Old Bullshit* (Grand Royal/Capitol Records, 1994); *Hello Nasty* (Grand Royal/Capitol Records 1998); *The Sounds of Science* (Grand Royal/Capitol Records, 1999); *To The Five Boroughs* (Capitol Records, 2004).

BEATBOXING; BEATBOXER; BEATBOX

In essence, beatboxing is making music with the mouth. Rhythm, beats, and melody are achieved with the mouth and throat alone, simulating anything from musical instruments to turntable **scratching** and creating a wide range of sound effects. Some of the most popular beatboxers have been **Doug E. Fresh**, **Biz Markie**, Buffy (of the **Fat Boys**), and most recently Rahzel (of **The Roots**).

BEATNUTS, THE

With members Psycho Les [Lester Fernandez], Junkyard JuJu [Jerry Tineo], and former member Fashion (aka Al Tariq) [Berntony Smalls], this Colombian–Dominican **underground** rap duo from Queens, New York, is best known for their self-produced party beats, on-wax bragging, and frequently X-rated rhymes.

They made their name in the late 1980s, when they began performing locally, eventually coming to the attention of the **Jungle Brothers**. The Jungle Brothers helped the duo to get production work and the duo racked up **remix** credits for Pete Nice, **Naughty By Nature**, **Da Lench Mob**, and **Cypress Hill**. They also did production for Chi-Ali, Da Youngsta's, and **Fat Joe**. Originally comprised of Psycho Les and Junkyard JuJu, lyricist Fashion was added when they began recording their own material.

In 1993, The Beatnuts released the EP *Intoxicated Demons* (Relativity Records), whose humorous raps won praise on the underground Hip Hop scene. The debut release had been delayed when Fashion was arrested on a drug-related charge and imprisoned for six months. Before joining the other two, he had recorded "Let The Horns Blo" with members of **De La Soul** and Chi-Ali in 1991.

The trio's eponymous 1994 debut album contained catchy rhymes and infectious beats. After *The Beatnut* album was released, Fashion left the group, converting to Islam and changing his name to Al Tariq. JuJu and Psycho Les continued to do production work, and in 1997 the duo released the album *Stone Crazy* (Relativity Records), which continued to display the duo's sardonic wit and great production. The following year The Beatnuts released the EP *The Spot (Remix EP)* (Relativity Records, 1998), and *A Musical Massacre* (Relativity Records) followed in 1999. The Beatnuts continued their winning style on *Take It Or Squeeze It* (Relativity Records, 2001), *Classic Nuts, Vol. 1* (Relativity Records, 2002), and *Milk Me* (Penalty (Ryko), 2004).

DISCOGRAPHY: *EPs*: *Intoxicated Demons* (Relativity Records); *The Spot (Remix EP)* (Relativity Records, 1998). *Albums*: *The Beatnut* (Relativity Records, 1994); *Stone Crazy* (Relativity Records, 1997); *Musical Massacre* (Relativity Records, 1999); *Take It Or Squeeze It* (Relativity Records, 2001); *Classic Nuts, Vol. 1* (Relativity Records, 2002); *Milk Me* (Penalty (Ryko), 2004).

BEAT STREET. *See* Films

BEEF

A beef is a disagreement or feud. Although the majority of beefs are between particular individuals, some beefs, especially within the music industry, respond to a message or statement that a person or another rap artist has aired in the media or on a record, but not directly to the respondent (e.g., **Stetsasonic** and James Mtume, "Talkin All That Jazz," Stetsasonic's response to musician James Mtume, who had disparaged rap music on a New York City radio program). Other beefs include that between Tim Dog and. **N.W.A.** (where "*F**k Compton*" is Tim Dog's response to N.W.A.'s "Straight Outta Compton") and between **KRS-ONE** and **MC Shan** (where "The Bridge is Over" is KRS-ONE's response to MC Shan's "The Bridge," the latter claiming that Hip Hop began in the **Queensbridge** Projects in Long Island City, New York).

BEEF: THE REAL WORLD OF MC BATTLES. *See* Films

BIG DADDY KANE [Antonio Hardy]
Big Daddy Kane is the original Smooth Operator of Hip Hop, outfitted in custom-tailored suits, a precisely cut **high top fade**, and effortless but lethal flow. Kane is an acronym for King Asiatic Nobody's Equal.

A member of **The Juice Crew All Stars**, The Brooklyn, New York, native began his rap career in 1984 after meeting **Biz Markie** in front of McCrory's department store in downtown Brooklyn. The two rap artists traded rhymes and quickly became friends. In high school Kane joined DJ Mister Cee and formed Magnum Force; the group dissolved but the duo stayed together and recorded his first solo single "Raw" (1987). Kane subsequently signed to **Cold Chillin'** Records and would go on to write many of Biz Markie's rhymes and also co-write **Roxanne Shante**'s single, "Have A Nice Day."

In 1988 Big Daddy Kane released his debut album, *Long Live the Kane* (Cold Chillin'), featuring the hit single "Ain't No Half Steppin'" and the **underground** classic "Raw." The album *It's a Big Daddy Thing* (Cold Chillin') followed in 1989, spawning the hits "Smooth Operator" and "I Get the Job Done." In 1990, Kane released another successful album, *Taste of Chocolate* (Cold Chillin'), on which he teamed up with crooner Barry White and with Rudy Ray Moore, better known as Dolemite.

Subsequent albums, *Prince of Darkness* (1991), *Looks Like a Job For . . .* (1993), and *Daddy's Home* (1994), did not capture the success of his earlier efforts. Kane moved from Cold Chillin' Records to Warner Bros. and then to MCA Records. Kane perpetuated his Black Casanova image by appearing nude in *Playgirl* magazine and in Madonna's 1992 photo book, *Sex* (New York: Warner Books), in which Kane, clad only in his underwear, was sandwiched between Madonna and model Naomi Campbell.

Kane appeared in the western movie *Posse* (1993), with **Tone Lōc**, and in *Gunmen* (1994), along with **Kid Frost**, **Eric B & Rakim**, and radio personalities **Dr. Dre** and Ed Lover. In 1998, Kane released *Veteranz Day* (Blackheart Records/The Label/Mercury).

DISCOGRAPHY: *Single*: "Raw" (1987). *Albums*: *Long Live Kane* (Cold Chillin', 1988); *It's A Big Daddy Thing* (Cold Chillin', 1989); *Taste of Chocolate* (Cold Chillin', 1990); *Prince of Darkness* (Cold Chillin', 1991); *Looks Like A Job for Big Daddy Kane* (Cold Chillin', 1993); *Daddy's Home* (MCA, 1994); *Veteranz Day* (Blackheart Records/The Label/ Mercury, 1998).

BIGGIE SMALLS. *See* Notorious B.I.G., The

BIG L [Lamont Coleman]

Big L gained fame for the 1998 **underground** hit "Ebonics (Criminal Slang)," released on his own label, Flamboyant Entertainment. Available only in twelve-inch format, "Ebonics" was hailed as one of the top five "independent records of the year." "Ebonics" accurately broke down the slang often used by members of New York's criminal underworld and did it to a radio-friendly beat. The Harlem rap artist was part of the group **Diggin' In The Crates Crew**, which also includes **Fat Joe**, O.C., **Diamond D**, **Lord Finesse**, and **Showbiz & A.G.**

Big L debuted on Lord Finesse's 1992 track, "Yes You May (Remix)." Big L was a member of the Children of the Corn, an Uptown crew whose alumni include **Mase** and **Cam'ron**. In 1993, based on the buzz from the promo-only single "Devil's Son," Big L received a record deal from Columbia Records. Big L's 1995 debut album, *Lifestyles Ov Da Poor and Dangerous* (Columbia/Sony), may be one of the most vulgar rap albums of all time. It features extremely violent threats on the tracks "All Black" and "Danger Zone." The track "Da Graveyard" featured an up-and-coming fellow Brooklynite, **Jay-Z**. After this first album, Columbia released Big L from his contract.

In February 1999 the twenty-two-year-old Big L was gunned down in front of his home on West 139th Street, in an area known as "The Danger Zone, and was pronounced dead at the scene. Big L's posthumous album, *The Big Picture* (Priority Records), was released in 2000. Where tracks were unfinished, top producers **DJ Premier** and **Pete Rock** stepped in to fill in the blanks. Along with several Big L tracks, the album features guest appearances from a long list of Hip Hop celebrities, including Fat Joe, **Kool G Rap**, Guru (**Gang Starr**), and Sadat X (**Brand Nubian**). On the track "Platinum" **Big Daddy Kane** shows that the years have not dulled his considerable skills. On the chilling "Deadly Contribution," the late **Tupac Shakur** appears to be speaking from the grave on behalf of another fallen rap artist. The album hit stores almost a year to the day after Big L's untimely death.

DISCOGRAPHY: *Singles*: "Ebonics (Criminal Slang)" (Flamboyant Entertainment, 1998); "We Got This" (Flamboyant Entertainment, 1999). *Albums*: *Lifestyles Ov Da Poor and Dangerous* (Columbia/Sony, 1995); *The Big Picture* (Rawkus Records, 2000; posthumous).

BIG PUNISHER (aka Big Pun) [Christopher Rios]

Big Pun was the first Latino solo rap artist to go platinum. The Puerto Rican rap artist from the Bronx, New York, released his debut album, *Capital Punishment* (Loud Records), in 1998. Big Pun, formerly known as Big Moon Dog, joined rap artists Triple Seis and Cuban Link to form the Full A Clips Crew. In 1995, the crew bumped into **Fat Joe** and Pun performed for Joe. Full A Clips Crew would eventually merge with Fat Joe and Argemenon to form the **Terror Squad**.

Big Punisher. *Courtesy of Photofest.*

Many first heard Big Pun when he appeared with Fat Joe and **Raekwon** on the track "Firewater," from the 1996 compilation album *Relativity Urban Assault* (Relativity Records). Big Pun would go on to ink a record deal with Loud Records and in 1998 released *Capital Punishment.* The album included performances from **Wyclef Jean**, **Busta Rhymes**, **Dead Prez**, Fat Joe & Terror Squad, Black Thought (**The Roots**), and Prodigy (**Mobb Deep**). From this album, the breakthrough single "I'm Not a Playa" exposed mainstream audiences to Big Pun's lyrical dexterity. The overweight artist died of heart failure on February 27, 2000.

Fat Joe served as the Executive Producer for Big Punisher's posthumous album, *Yeeeah Baby* (Loud/RCA), which was released in 2000.

DISCOGRAPHY: *Capital Punishment* (Loud, 1998); *Yeeeah Baby* (Loud/RCA, 2000; posthumous).

BIG TYMERS

The Big Tymers, a New Orleans-based rap duo, is comprised of Cash Money co-owner Brian Williams ("Baby") and local producer Byron Thomas ("Mannie Fresh"). The two met in 1992 and, together with Baby's brother, Ronald "Sugar Slim" Williams, formed Cash Money Records, one of the most successful rap music labels in the South. Baby and Sugar Slim ran the business side of the record company, while Mannie acted as in-house producer.

Big Tymers. *Courtesy of Photofest.*

The Big Tymers made their debut in 1997 with the BG **underground** classic, "It's All On U Vol. 2." The two went into the sound booth and started joking around on the microphone for an intro to the album. The result sounded so good that they decided to do a whole verse, and thus the Big Tymers were born. The two soon started collaborating in the studio and in 1998 they released their first album *How U Luv That* (Cash Money Records). The album sold over 100,000 copies with virtually no promotion. It was rereleased nationally later that year, when Cash Money signed a distribution deal with Universal Records. *I Got That Work* (Cash Money Records/Universal), the duo's second album was released in 2000. ("I Got That Work" is a street term for hustling.)

In 2002, the duo released their third album, *'Hood Rich*. Another rap ode to conspicuous consumption and sex, the album was notable a more radio-friendly tone and also for its omission of the Hot Boys (**Lil Wayne**, BG, Turk, and **Juvenile**), who had appeared on prior albums.

Mannie Fresh released his first solo album, *The Mind of Mannie Fresh* (Cash Money) in 2004.

BIG WILLIE

A late 1990s slang term, a Big Willie is a person who wields a great deal of power and financial resources. A possible origin is in the 1973 **blaxploitation** film, *Willie Dynamite*, a gritty drama about a high-living, flashy pimp who tries to outhustle a rival pimp and pays the price.

BIZ MARKIE [Marcel Theo Hall]

A rap artist born in Harlem, New York, and raised in Long Island, and known for his comic flair, Biz Markie began his rap career in the small clubs of New York.

He met producer **Marley Marl** in 1985, while rapping in the **Queensbridge** Projects. Marley Marl liked Biz Markie's sound and started producing demo tapes with him. As a member of **The Juice Crew All Stars**, Biz Markie began making a name for himself **beatboxing** for **Roxanne Shante**. Biz Markie was first heard on Roxanne Shante's single, "Get Retarded." He soon signed a recording contract with Prism Records, which became **Cold Chillin'**.

In 1988, Biz Markie released his debut album, *Goin' Off* (Cold Chillin' Records); it became an **underground** success, containing the hit singles "Vapors," "Nobody Beats the Biz," "Pickin' Boogers," and "Make the Music With Your Mouth." Biz Markie's follow-up, the 1989 *The Biz Never Sleeps* (Cold Chillin' Records), was even more successful. The album garnered crossover sales based on the singles and on videos for the tracks "Just a Friend" and "Spring Again."

Unfortunately for Biz Markie, his 1991 album *I Need a Haircut* (Cold Chillin' Records) gained national attention not for its sales, which were poor, but because he became the subject of a **sampling** lawsuit. Songwriter Gilbert O'Sullivan sued Biz Markie over the use of a sample of O'Sullivan's 1972 hit, "Alone Again (Naturally)," on Biz Markie's track "Alone Again." In one of the first lawsuits of its kind, Biz Markie was found guilty of copyright infringement. In federal court, Judge Kevin Thomas Duff awarded Sullivan punitive damages ruling that "sampling is theft under criminal law." The court ruling caused all rap artists to change how they used samples. Biz Markie's next release was aptly titled *All Samples Cleared* (Cold Chillin' Records, 1993).

After releasing "The Studder Step" in the mid-1990s and "Turn Tha Party Out" in 2001, Biz Markie and the once-mighty Tommy Boy Records released Biz Markie's first album in a decade, *Weekend Warrior* (Bizmont/Tommy Boy Records), in November 2003, without any major publicity campaign. Old School fans will appreciate Biz Markie's style and the tracks "Not a Freak," which features Erick Sermon (**EPMD**), and "Tear Sh*t Up," where **DJ Jazzy Jeff** (Fresh Prince and DJ Jazzy Jeff) takes over the wheels of steel. In 2004, Biz Markie released the EP *Friends* (Bizmont/Tommy Boy Records).

DISCOGRAPHY: *EPs*: *Friends Albums*: *Goin' Off* (Cold Chillin' Records, 1988); *The Biz Never Sleeps* (Cold Chillin' Records, 1989); *I Need a Haircut* (Cold Chillin', 1991); *All Samples Cleared* (Cold Chillin', 1993); *Weekend Warrior* (Bizmont/Tommy Boy Records, 2003).

BLACKALICIOUS

Comprised of The Gift of Gab [Tim Parker] and Chief Xcel [Xavier Moseley], Blackalicious is a northern California duo known for their spiritual and uplifting lyrics.

The two artists met through a mutual friend in 1987 at Kennedy High School in Sacramento, and in 1988 hooked up as GTI, an acronym for Gabby T [Parker] and Ice Ski [Mosley]. They changed their name to The Elements of Sound, then to Atomic Legion, and finally to Blackalicious in July 1991. Xcel was attending the University of California at Davis, where his friends were forming a crew called SoleSides, including DJ Shadow, Lyrics Born, and Lateef The Truth Speaker (the last two being known together as Latyrx). In January 1993, the first SoleSides record was released. The record was a double "A" side that included DJ Shadow's "Entropy" on one side and Lyrics Born's (then named Asia Born) "Send Them" on the other. The Gift of Gab had been featured on DJ Shadow's "Count and Estimate" and Chief Xcel was on "Back to Back Breaks," both segments of Shadow's "Entropy." The record received **underground** kudos.

In 1994, Blackalicious released their first EP, *Melodica* (Phantom), which received a great deal of support from college radio and mix shows with tracks such as "Rhymes For the Deaf" and "Swan Lake." In 1998, they signed to 3-2-1 Records, and in 1999 they released *A2G*, another EP. When 3-2-1 shut down, Blackalicious continued to record with DJ Shadow and the Latyrx crew, their label mates on SoleSides (now known as Quannum Productions). In 1999, under the Quannum label, the collective released the album *Quannum Spectrum*. The duo's debut album, *Nia* (Quannum Projects, 2000), continued to pursue Afrocentric themes (*nia* is a Swahili word for 'purpose') and included poet Nikki Giovanni reciting her poem "Ego Trip."

After selling over 100,000 copies of *A2G* and *Nia* on their own independent Quannum label in the United States, MCA/Universal won a recording industry bidding war and signed Blackalicious to a recording contract in late 2000. In 2002, the album *Blazing Arrow* (MCA/Universal) was released; it includes guest appearances by Zack de la Rocha (of Rage Against the Machine fame), ?uestlove (**The Roots**), and singer Gil Scott-Heron.

DISCOGRAPHY: *EPs*: *Melodica* (Phantom); *A2G* (3-2-1, 1999). *Albums*: *Nia* (Quannum Projects, 2000); *Blazing Arrow* (MCA/Universal, 2002).

BLACK EYED PEAS

Comprised of Will.I.Am [William Adams], Apl.de.Ap [Allen Pineda], Taboo [Jaime Gomez], and Fergie [Stacey Ferguson], the Los Angeles, California–based rap crew Black Eyed Peas is known for dabbling in different musical genres and for serving up radio-friendly tunes while maintaining the traditional Hip Hop base. Will.I.Am and Apl.de.Ap first met in 1989 as eighth graders and began performing around Los Angeles as Atban Klann.

After a stalled beginning with Ruthless Records, the duo recruited Taboo in 1995. The Black Eyed Peas were formed and signed a recording contract with Interscope Records. The trio's 1998 debut, *Behind The Front*, took a page from **The Roots**, with the three MCs fronting a live band, rather than relying on prerecorded samples. The Black Eyed Peas followed up in 2000 with *Bridging The Gap* (Interscope Records), an album that solidified the group as the spiritual and musical heirs of **A Tribe Called Quest** and **De La Soul**. From their third album, *Elephunk* (Interscope Records), the track "Where is the Love" features Justin Timberlake. The track, a response to the attacks of September 11, 2001, helped The Black Eyed Peas to gain mainstream attention.

The group became a quartet in 2003 when they added former backup singer Fergie to the line-up. The Black Eyed Peas performed in the pregame show for the 2005 National Football League Super Bowl Game. The group has received four Grammy Award nominations.

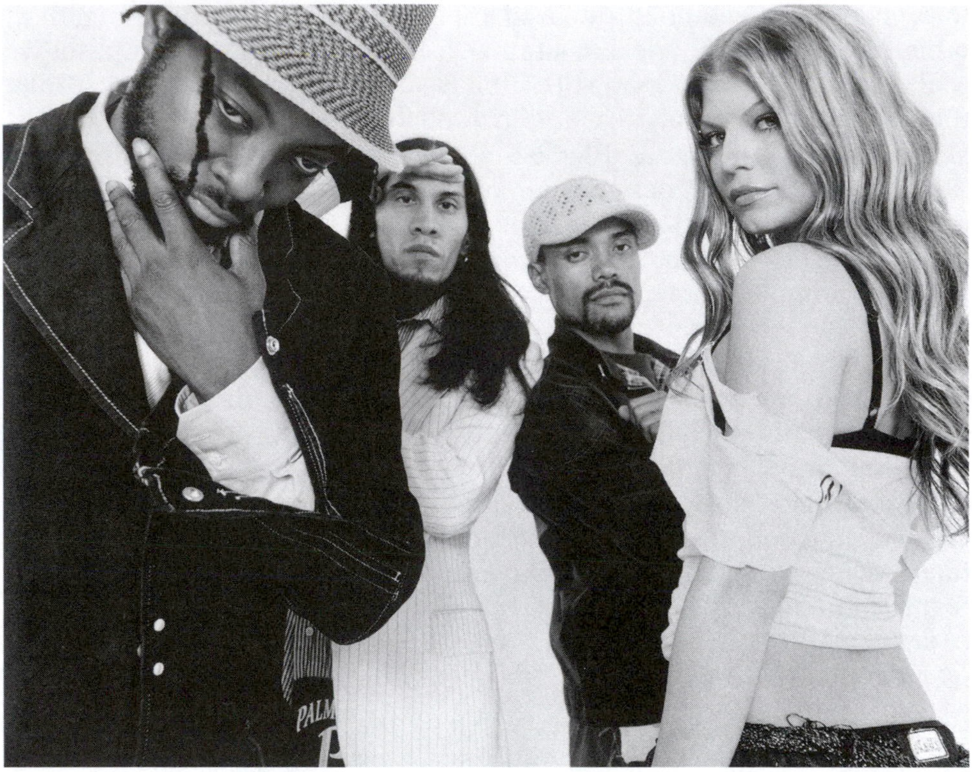

Black Eyed Peas. *Courtesy of Photofest.*

DISCOGRAPHY: *Behind The Front* (Interscope Records, 1998); *Bridging The Gap* (Interscope Records, 2000), *Elephunk* (Interscope Records, 2003).

BLACK LEATHER MEDALLIONS

Popularized in the late 1980s as the alternative to the heavy gold chains worn by rap artists and their fans. References to black leather medallions appear in **De La Soul**'s line: "Black medallions, no gold," from their song "Buddy" on the album *3 Feet High and Rising* (Tommy Boy Records, 1989). The medallions often depicted a map of Africa or the Lion of Judea, a symbol associated with Rastafarians, and had backgrounds in black, red, and green. These are the colors of the Black Nationalist flag, with black for the color of the people, green for the land of Africa, and red for the blood shed in liberation.

BLACK MOON

The Brooklyn, New York trio of Buckshot [Kenyatta Blake], 5FT [*unknown*], and DJ Evil Dee [Ewart Dewarde] joined forces in 1989. 5FT and Evil Dee met as students at Bushwick High School, when they formed a group called Unique Image. 5FT met Buckshot in his Brownsville neighborhood.

DJ Chuck Chillout helped the trio to secure a recording contract with the fledging Nervous Records. In 1992 the group released their first single, "Who Got the Props," which sold over 250,000 copies. Taking their time in the studio, Black Moon released their debut album, *Enta da Stage* (Wreck/Nervous) in 1993. Evil Dee and his brother Mr. Walt (aka Da Beat Minerz) produced the album, which earned the respect of rap music fans and critics alike. The trio's second hit single, "How Many MC's (Must Get Dissed)," was from this album. Black Moon released its third single, "I Got Cha Opin (remix)," featuring the now-famous Barry White "Ecstasy" loop. This **remix** garnered praise from both the Hip Hop **underground** and radio. The strength of the three singles helped propel album sales past 350,000 copies.

Buckshot was featured on the soundtrack for Spike Lee's 1994 film, *Crooklyn*, with the song "Crooklyn Dodgers," along with **Masta Ace** and **Special Ed**.

In 1995, the group broke up, however that year Nervous Records released 1995 the album *Diggin' In Dah Vaults*, which featured previously unheard tracks such as "Six Feet Deep," as well as tracks that were never previously available on CD, such as "Fuck It Up" and "Murder MC's." After years of internal and legal tensions, the group returned in 1999 with the album *War Zone* (Duck Down/Koch Entertainment). In 2004, Black Moon released the album, *Total Eclipse* (Duck Down/Koch Entertainment).

In March 2004, 5FT was charged with the alleged sale of an illegal substance, stemming from an incident in 2002, and was convicted.

BLACK NATIONALISM

A long-standing and complex set of beliefs, Black nationalism re-emerged during the Black Power era of the late 1960s and early 1970s, emphasizing the need for cultural, political, and economic autonomy for African Americans. The modern manifestation of the movement can be traced back to Marcus Garvey's Universal Negro Improvement Association of the 1920s, which sought to acquire economic power and to inculcate African Americans with a sense of community and group unity. As an alternative to being assimilated into a predominantly Eurocentric White America, Black nationalists sought to maintain and promote their separate identity as a people of African ancestry. Slogans such as "Black Power" and "Black is Beautiful," as well as natural hairstyles, Afrocentric clothing, renouncing of "slave names" (i.e., European-based names tracing back to those given by slavemasters to their slaves), and an interest in the languages and traditions of African nations were outward manifestations of Black nationalism.

BLACK SHEEP

Black Sheep, comprised of Dres [Andre Titus] and Mista Lawnge [William McLean] is best known for the 1991 rap hit, "The Choice Is Yours" (Mercury Records). Both rap artists were born in New York but raised in North Carolina (Dres the son of a military man), and both were rap fans. By the mid-1980s, Dres was an MC and Mista Lawnge was a DJ.

Mista Lawnge moved back to New York to pursue a recording contract. At an event, **Kool DJ Red Alert** introduced Mista Lawnge to Mike Gee of the **Jungle Brothers**. The Jungle Brothers were members of the **Native Tongues** movement, which included **A Tribe Called Quest**, **De La Soul**, and **Queen Latifah**. These new musical influences inspired Mista Lawnge to form Black Sheep and Dres joined him as MC.

In 1991 the duo released its first single, "Flavor of the Month" (Mercury/Polygram), which was considered one of the best songs that year. Black Sheep's self-produced debut album, *A Wolf In Sheep's Clothing* (Mercury) was released later that year. The album made the *Billboard* Top 30 in 1991, mainly on the strength of the successful single, "The Choice Is Yours." The single was a surprise hit with college radio stations, which at that time did not generally include rap music in their programming. The music video for "The Choice is Yours" was in heavy rotation on MTV and earned the duo an MTV music award. The humorous and imaginative *A Wolf In Sheep's Clothing* eventually sold nearly 1 million copies.

Unfortunately, in 1994, Black Sheep's star quickly fell with the release of their second album, *Non-Fiction*. The project was a disaster from the beginning. Possibly chasing the trends of the day, the duo attempted a somewhat tougher stance on this second album. Many fans and critics believed that *Non-Fiction* did not have the spark of *A Wolf In Sheep's Clothing*. Adding to the duo's woes, a dispute with the record company resulted in the label doing virtually nothing to promote the album. The lack of promotion did not help gain any airplay for the single, "Without a Doubt." After the failure of *Non-Fiction*, the duo split up.

In 1999, Dres released his solo album, *Sure Shot Redemption*. In 2000, Dres appeared in the film *Once in the Life*, which marked actor Laurence Fishburne's directorial debut. Black Sheep reunited to produce a track for the film's soundtrack.

DISCOGRAPHY: *A Wolf in Sheep's Clothing* (Mercury/Polygram, 1991); *Non-Fiction* (Mercury/Polygram, 1994).

BLACK STAR

Mos Def [Dante "Beze" Terrell Smith] and **Talib Kweli** [Talib Kweli Green] make up Black Star, an **underground**–aboveground duo epitomizing intelligent and Afrocentric rap music. The name Black Star comes from Marcus Garvey's Black Star Line, the first Black-owned passenger liner to go from the United States to the continent of Africa. The line's *S.S. Yarmouth* made its maiden voyage in November 1919.

The Brooklyn, New York–based duo released their album, *Black Star* (Rawkus), in September 1998. Evoking the best of Hip Hop's creativity, the album ignited the underground Hip Hop world. Drawing inspiration from the Black Power era, Black Star used intelligent lyrics and superior flow to celebrate Black art, political activism, and community strength. The album was not a commercial success, but nonetheless is considered to be one of the best, if not the best, rap album of 1998.

DISCOGRAPHY: *Black Star* (Rawkus, 1998).

BLAXPLOITATION

Blaxploitation describes a category of films, typically those produced between 1971 and 1979, that feature predominantly African American actors. According to the *Oxford English Dictionary*, the term *blaxploitation* was first used in the June 12, 1972, issue of *New York Magazine*, to characterize films marketed to Black audiences. Beginning with Melvin Van Peeble's 1971 controversial film *Sweetback's Badaass Song,* most were shot on budgets of less than $1 million, usually on budgets between $200,000 and $750,000. Approximately 200 to 250 of these films were made, featuring Black actors in lead roles and often having antiestablishment plots.

These films were often criticized for stereotypical characterizations and glorification of violence. The core of the genre consists of fast-paced movies packed with action, comedy, and sex. These films were called "exploitation" because, although African American filmmakers were substantially involved in making early movies in this genre, over time their participation in subsequent productions became minimal. Proponents of the genre, however, point out that these films gave Black actors lead roles, in a largely segregated system still used to casting Blacks casting primarily in subservient roles. Moreover, these films provided work for a score of Black actors and writers. Lastly, many of these films gave Blacks a voice in Hollywood, allowing themes associated with Black Power and "Black is Beautiful" to be the backdrop for many of these films.

Characters in blaxploitation were diverse, ranging from the hip private eye John Shaft in the original *Shaft* (1971), to the decadent hustler Youngblood Priest in *Superfly* (1972), to the flamboyant pimp Goldie in *The Mack* (1973), to the comedic Rudy Ray Moore in the "Dolemite" series. Many of the themes, characters, and soundtracks of these films have directly informed the creative products of Hip Hop culture, and also the personas of rap artists.

BLIGE, MARY J.

Universally known as the "Queen of Hip Hop Soul" because of her frequent collaborations with rap artists and Hip Hop producers, R & B singer Mary J. Blige credits her vocal style to old-school R & B and soul as well as to the rap music of her youth.

Mary J. Blige. *Courtesy of Photofest.*

Born in the Bronx, New York, and with a brief stint in Savannah, Georgia, as a young child, Blige grew up in Yonkers, New York. At the age of seven she began singing in her church's choir. In her teens, as her singing improved, she began to perform as a solo artist in church and at talent events. At seventeen, Blige recorded her first karaoke-style demo tape at a local shopping mall. Her stepfather gave out the demo tape and it eventually got into the hands of Uptown Records C.E.O. **Andre Harrell**. Harrell signed Blige to a recording contract, but it was **Sean "P. Diddy" Combs**, then an unknown producer at the label who would actually craft Blige's image and sound.

Her debut album, *What's the 411* (Uptown Records/MCA), was released in 1992. A strong single, "Real Love," pushed the album to number 1 and Blige into stardom. In 1993, she followed up her debut with *What's the 411 (Remix)* (Uptown Records/MCA), an album that had her going toe-to-toe lyrically with rap artists such as **The Notorious B.I.G.**, Craig Mack, and **Grand Puba**. Mary's third album, *My Life* (Uptown Records, 1994), which Combs executive-produced, spawned several hit singles: "All Night Long," "You Gotta Believe," "My Life," and "You Bring Me Joy." The album also gave listeners a glimpse into Blige's private life, particularly her turbulent and apparently painful relationship with K-Ci Hailey of the R & B group Jodeci. *My Life* also earned Blige a Grammy nomination for Best R & B album and a Grammy for Best Rap Performance by a Duo or Group for her duet with **Method Man** on his single "I'll Be There for You (You're All I Need to Get By)."

Coupled with lateness and cancellations, Blige's tough demeanor, honed in the Yonkers Schlobohm Gardens housing projects (residents call it Slow Bomb), gained her a reputation for being moody, demanding, and unprofessional. Furthermore, her raw and emotional lyrics combined with her tough, "around the way girl" public persona led to unwanted comparisons to the troubled singer Billie Holiday.

Blige took a break from recording and completed an artist development course taught by Angelo Ellerbee of DoubleXXposure, a Black-owned public relations firm. Ellerbee helped Blige, then a high school dropout, with everything from interview techniques and diction to personal finance. Ellerbee also encouraged her to begin to read books. Mary J. Blige returned to music on the *Waiting to Exhale* film soundtrack with the hit single, "Not Gon' Cry."

By her fourth album, *Share My World* (Universal, 1997), Blige had parted company with Combs and Uptown Entertainment, having left Uptown Entertainment in 1995 when Andre Harrell left the company for Motown Records. Her new deal with Uptown's parent company, Universal, granted her full authority over the album. Blige joined creative forces with producers, Jimmy Jam and Terry Lewis, and acted as her own executive producer. Critics were not enthused by the album's more traditional soul sound, but it nonetheless debuted at number 1 on the *Billboard* charts and proved another hit for Blige.

In 1998, she released a live album, *The Tour* (Universal), and the following year she released the heralded *Mary* (Universal, 1999). Fans and critics alike found a more mature singer, one who without sacrificing her own style channeled the empowering and beautiful soul music of prior eras. The most talked about track on the album was "Not Lookin'," which reteamed her with her former flame, K-Ci Hailey. The two had not dueted since the single, "I Don't Want To Do Anything" from her debut album. (It may be noted that the track was made without the two ever sharing the studio booth.)

Mary J. Blige entered the twenty-first century with *No More Drama* (Universal, 2001), featuring collaborations with powerhouse producers **Dr. Dre** and the **Neptunes**, and performances by **Eve** and **Missy Elliott**. On *No More Drama*, Mary expands the subject matter beyond relationship woes; musically, there is more diversity, with rocker Lenny Kravitz on acoustic guitar on "PMS" and the classical "Nadia's Theme" (popularized on the CBS soap opera, "The Young and The Restless") serving as the backdrop for the title track. The best track may be the Dr. Dre–produced "Family Affair," a classic party track and a major musical departure for Blige.

In 2002, Blige released *Dance for Me* (Universal), an album of dance music **remixes** of her hit songs. 2003's *Love and Life* (Universal) marked Bliges's reunion with P. Diddy. *Love and Life* included artists **Jay-Z**, P. Diddy, **50 Cent**, and Eve, as well as production by P. Diddy and Dr. Dre. Although the album went platinum, particularly on the strength of the singles, "Love @ 1st Sight" and "Not Today (featuring Eve)," critics and fans alike deemed it only a solid effort, not necessarily Blige's best album.

In January 2005, the song "Not Today," which also appears on the film soundtrack for *Barbershop 2*, was the subject of a lawsuit by pop artist Madonna. Madonna is suing Blige, Dr. Dre, and rap artist Eve, contending that Blige's song too closely resembles her classic 1983 hit, "Holiday." Although a music expert has concluded that the songs are not identical, the publishers of Madonna's song could receive at least $15 million if the case goes to trial and jurors determine that "Not Today" sounds notably similar to "Holiday."

Currently, Mary J. Blige is recognized as a philanthropist as well as a singer. She has filmed anti-drug public service announcements and worked with various education groups. For her efforts she received Rock The Vote's highest honor, the Patrick Lippert Award. She is a tireless fundraiser for people with AIDS and continues as the spokeswoman for MAC Cosmetics' Viva Glam IV (along with **Lil' Kim**), with all proceeds from the lipstick sales going to AIDS education and research.

DISCOGRAPHY: *What's the 411* (Uptown Records/MCA, 1992); *What's the 411 (Remix)* (Uptown Records/MCA, 1993); *My Life* (Uptown Records/MCA, 1994); *Share My World* (Universal, 1997); *The Tour* (Universal, 1998); *Mary* (Universal, 1999); *No More Drama* (Universal, 2001); *Dance With Me* (Universal, 2002); *Love and Life* (Universal, 2003).

BLING-BLING; BLING

A slang term for diamonds, bling-bling originally represented Hip Hop's love of conspicuous consumption as demonstrated by rap artist's penchant for extravagant diamond-crested jewelry. The term, like others before it (e.g., diss, **izzle**), has become a mainstream phrase.

BODY COUNT

The rap and heavy metal band Body Count, with rap artist **Ice-T**, in 1992 produced an album of the same name. This album contained the controversial track, "**Cop Killer**." The group had been playing a version of "Cop Killer" in concert for a year, including a performance at the 1991 Lollapalooza tour. The recorded version makes references to Rodney King, a Black motorist whose beating by Los Angeles police officers had been caught on videotape. The acquittal of the White officers set off the 1992 Los Angeles riots.

When the Los Angeles Police Department denounced the song as dangerous and inflammatory, Ice-T, who had himself played a cop in a 1991 movie, *New Jack City*, defended his right to use his art to protest police brutality. The public's ire was aimed directly at Ice-T, who became number two on the FBI National Threat list. "Cop Killer" also appeared in the

Body Count. *Courtesy of Photofest.*

Warner Bros. blockbuster movie *Batman Returns*, which consequently faced boycott calls. At a meeting for Time Warner stockholders, Charlton Heston (an actor and, at the time, National Rifle Association President) read aloud the lyrics to the track "KKK Bitch." Among other vocal opponents of Ice-T were Oliver North, a Marine Lieutenant Colonel who had been involved in the Iran Contra scandal, and then-President George H. W. Bush. The Dallas, Texas, police force called for a nationwide boycott of Time Warner, including its Disneyland properties. The promised boycott threatened to reduce Warner's stock value by the millions. The defining moment in the controversy came when Warner Bros. employees received death threats, whereupon the track "Cop Killer" was removed from the album.

Although Time Warner initially supported Ice-T and his right to free speech, the following year they dropped both the band Body Count and Ice-T from their roster.

See also: Censorship

BOMBER JACKETS

A waist-length leather jacket with fur hood, worn by men and women, the bomber jacket was popular among rap artists and Hip Hop fans in New York City in the 1980s.

BOMB SQUAD

Public Enemy's renowned production team, Bomb Squad members include **Chuck D**, Hank Shocklee [John Henry Boxley III], his brother Keith Shocklee [Keith M. Boxley], and Eric Sadler.

BONE THUGS-N-HARMONY

Bone Thugs-N-Harmony, a rap group from Cleveland, Ohio, is comprised of Krayzie Bone [Anthony Henderson], Bizzy Bone [Bryon McCane], Wish Bone [Charles Scruggs], Flesh-N-Bone [Stanley Howse], and Layzie Bone [Steve Howse]. Known for their fast and often undecipherable rhyming, they were instrumental in putting the Midwest of the rap map.

The group was formed in 1993; Layzie Bone and Wish Bone, who are cousins, first joined with Bizzy and Krayzie under the name Band-Aid Boyz. That same year, the group purchased one-way bus tickets to Los Angeles. Their destination was the offices of Ruthless Records, home to the legendary rap group **N.W.A.** According to legend, Bone auditioned over the phone, but **Eazy E** did not get back to them. When Bone heard that Eazy E was doing a show in their hometown, they scraped their money together and hustled back to Cleveland. They auditioned live for Eazy E backstage and he signed them on the spot, becoming their mentor.

Bone Thugs-N-Harmony. *Courtesy of Photofest.*

Eazy E was responsible for planning the group's 1994 groundbreaking debut EP, *Creepin On Ah Come Up* (Ruthless). The singles "1st of Tha Month" (which refers to when welfare checks are issued), "Thuggish Ruggish Bone," and "Foe Tha Love Of $" helped the EP to sell 4 million copies. The EP spent over seventy weeks on the *Billboard*'s Top 200 album chart, achieving both commercial and critical success. In 1995, the group released a full album *E. 1999 Eternal* (Ruthless), entering all of the music charts and at number 1 on the pop charts. The album sold 330,000 copies in its first week, eventually reaching over 5 million copies. The album's standout single was the spiritually charged "Tha Crossroads." The single went double-platinum, making history when it tied with the Beatles' thirty-two-year-old record (the 1964 "Can't Buy Me Love") for the fastest rising single on the pop charts. Moreover the track won the rap group a Grammy Award for Best Rap Performance for a Duo or Group.

In 1996, Flesh-N-Bone released *T.H.U.G.S.: Trues Humbly United Gatherin' Souls* (Def Jam Recordings), the first of what has become a string of Bone Thugs-N-Harmony solo albums. Flesh-N-Bone would also release the album *Fifth Dog Lets Loose* (Koch Records, 2000). In 1998, Bizzy Bone would release his first solo album, *Heaven'z Movie* (Ruthless). He would follow up with solo releases, *Gift* (American Music Corp, 2001) and *Alpha and Omega* (Bungaloo, 2004) In 1999 Krayzie Bone released his first solo album *Thug Mentality 1999*. Krazyie Bone's second solo album *Thug on da Line* (Sony, 2001) was released in 2000 as well as *The Collection Vol. Two* (Ruthless).

In 1998, Bone Thugs-N-Harmony released the album *Art of War* (Ruthless). That same year, the first of two Bone Thugs-N-Harmony compilation albums was released *The Collection, Vol. 1* (Ruthless, 1998). The Cleveland clan established their own Mo Thugs Records and released *Mo Thugs Family Scriptures* in 1996, to showcase other rap groups from their hometown. In 2000, the group released *BTNHResurrection* (Ruthless), considered a reunion album in the aftermath of the several solo projects since 1998's *Art of War*. The 2002 the group's album, *Thug World*, received mixed reviews, with some fans praising it as a brilliant effort but others panning it as their worst.

DISCOGRAPHY: *EPs*: *Creepin On Ah Come Up* (Ruthless). *Albums*: *E. 1999 Eternal* (Ruthless, 1995); *Art of War* (Ruthless, 1997); *BTNHResurrection* (Ruthless, 2000); *Thug World* (Ruthless, 2002).

BOOGIE DOWN PRODUCTIONS

Boogie Down Productions is comprised of **KRS-ONE** [Lawrence Parker] and Scott La Rock [Scott Sterling]. Although associated with the Bronx, KRS-ONE actually was born in Brooklyn, New York, and lived there before leaving home at age 14. KRS-ONE and Scott La Rock met at a homeless shelter in the Bronx, where Sterling was a counselor and Parker was a client. The two found common interest in music and began to collaborate, thus transforming into KRS-ONE and DJ Scott La Rock. Parker had written **graffiti** using the tag KRS-ONE (an acronym for Knowledge Reigns Supreme Over Nearly Everyone) and Sterling, a part-time DJ, used the name DJ Scott La Rock professionally.

In the summer of 1984, when Scott La Rock headlined the rap group called Scott La Rock and the Celebrity Three, they released the single, "Advance." The group was comprised of DJ Scott La Rock, MC Quality, Levi167, and KRS-ONE. Scott La Rock and the Celebrity Three broke up shortly following their debut, amid contract disputes with the group's record label.

While other rap artists were content to rhyme about partying and women, KRS-ONE rhymed about preventing nuclear war. In the winter of 1984, KRS-ONE wrote a song called "Stop The Violence," and he and Scott La Rock decided to reconstitute themselves as The Boogie Down Crew. In 1986, after receiving no money or rights to a record released by Sleeping Bag records, KRS-ONE and La Rock realized the importance of being the producers as well as the artists of their own music, so at this point they decided to change the name of their group from Boogie Down Crew to Boogie Down Productions.

Boogie Down Productions immediately became of the most important and influential rap music entities. In 1986, they independently released the single "Crack Attack." Boogie Down Production's groundbreaking 1987 debut album, *Criminal Minded* (B-Boy Records), a realistic account of life on the streets of urban America, was produced with the help of Ced Gee of a fellow Bronx crew, the **Ultramagnetic MCs**. *Criminal Minded* actively suggested that young Blacks were entitled to use "any means necessary" to overcome years of prejudice and discrimination. It sold over 500,000 copies.

As *Criminal Minded* was gaining steam on the **underground**, La Rock was fatally shot to death in the South Bronx as he tried to settle an argument involving Boogie Down Productions affiliate D'Nice and another man. KRS-ONE continued Boogie Down Productions with his brother, Kenny Parker, and D'Nice as DJs. In the aftermath of Scott La Rock's death, KRS-ONE's lyrics more vigorously encouraged Blacks to demand an end to violence and to educate themselves in order to survive and thrive.

In 1988, Boogie Down Productions left B-Boy Records for Jive Records and released their follow-up album, *By All Means Necessary* (Jive Records). The two album covers for *Criminal Minded* and *By All Means Necessary* (which reenacted a famous Malcolm X photo) sparked controversy for their depiction of guns. Unfortunately, some critics would credit KRS-ONE and Boogie Down Productions for beginning so-called **gangsta rap**—even though KRS-ONE led the ***Stop the Violence***

Movement, an all-star, antiviolence benefit song and music video. This was in 1988, after concertgoer Julio Fuentes was stabbed to death for his gold chain at a rap show at Long Island's Nassau Coliseum. Subsequently, Jive Records' Vice President of Artist Development, Ann Carli, and writer Nelson George assembled leading rap artists to do a benefit song titled, "Self Destruction." KRS-ONE, a Jive artist who had already penned the song, "Stop the Violence," was asked to lead the effort. The approximately $600,000 raised from the song was donated to the National Urban League.

In 1989 Boogie Down Productions released *Ghetto Music: The Blueprint Of Hip-Hop* (Jive Records), which contained the singles "You Must Learn" and "Jack of Spades." KRS-ONE began calling himself "the Teacher," promoting self-awareness and education in his rhymes. Around this time KRS-ONE began lecturing at universities and some of his writings appeared in the *New York Times*. Critics claimed that KRS-ONE had taken his role as "the Teacher" too far on the 1990 album *Edutainment* and dismissed it. Boogie Down Productions fans heard *Edutainment* differently, finding it an intellectual, insightful, and daring effort to debunk American hypocrisies. In 1992, KRS-ONE won over his critics with the powerful *Sex and Violence* (Jive Records), although the album was not a commercial success. In 1993, KRS-ONE abandoned the Boogie Down Productions concept and released his first solo album, *Return of the Boom Bap*.

DISCOGRAPHY: *Singles*: "Advance" (Sleeping Bag Records, 1984; released under Celebrity Three); "Crack Attack" (independent artist release, 1986). *Albums*: *Criminal Minded* (B-Boy, 1987); *By All Means Necessary* (Jive Records, 1988); *Ghetto Music: The Blueprint of Hip Hop* (Jive Records, 1989); *Edutainment* (Jive Records, 1990); *BDP Live Hardcore Worldwide* (Jive Records, 1991).

BOOM BOX

The boom box, an oversized portable radio that played audio tapes popularized in New York City during the late 1980s. Boom boxes gained wider mainstream recognition after one appeared in Spike Lee's film, *Do the Right Thing* (1989), via the film's character Radio Raheem, who carried one.

BOO-YAA TRIBE

The Boo-Yaa Tribe, comprised of Ganxsta Ridd [Paul Devoux], EKA [*unknown*], Rosco [*unknown*], Ganxsta OMB [*unknown*], the Godfather [Ted Devoux], and Don-L [*unknown*], is best known as Hip Hop's first Samoan rap group. T.R.I.B.E. stands for "Too Rough International Boo-Yaa Empire," and Boo-Yaa is slang for the sound of a shotgun being discharged.

Originally composed of six Samoan-descended brothers from Los Angeles, the Boo-Yaa T.R.I.B.E. offered a distinctly authentic brand of hardcore rap. Sons of a Baptist minister, the brothers grew up in a rough neighborhood of Carson and as members of the Mob Piru Bloods gang; every brother had done a stretch in prison for drugs or on weapons charges. When one brother, Robert "Youngman" Devoux, was shot dead, the remaining brothers decided that it was time to change their lifestyles and headed for Japan, staying with a Sumo wrestler cousin. The brothers formed a rap and dance troupe that they called the Blue City Crew.

Encouraged by their success in Japan, they returned to Los Angeles and in 1988 released a twelve-inch single called "Coming Hard to America." They rechristened themselves the Boo-Yaa T.R.I.B.E. and appeared in Michael Jackson's Walt Disney movie, *Captain EO* (1986) as street dancers, as well as on the television shows *Fame* and *The A-Team*. After a guest appearance on the Club Nouveau track "No Friend of Mine (1989)," the Boo-Ya T.R.I.B.E. signed with 4th & Broadway Records and in 1990 released their debut album, *New Funky Nation*. The album spawned a minor hit single with "Psyko Funk."

A second album, *Good Times Bad Times*, was recorded in 1992, but was never released. That year they performed on the Lollapalooza Tour and left 4th & Broadway Records to sign with Hollywood Records, which released their single, "Rumors of a Dead Man." In 1993, they collaborated with the heavy metal group Faith No More on the track "Another Body Murdered," from the *Judgment Night* film soundtrack. Signing with the smaller Bullet Proof label, the group released two more albums, *Doomsday* in 1994 and *Occupation Hazardous* in 1995. By this time, three members had adopted new aliases: Danny was Monsta O, Roscoe was Murder One, and Donald was Kobra Konvict (or just Kobra).

In 1996, the group released the EP, *Mentally Disturbed*. After forming their Samoan Mafia label, the collective unsuccessfully tried their hand at **rap-metal** on their 1997 album *Angry Samoans*. In 2000, they released the album *Mafia Lifestyle*. In 2003, **Eminem** raised the group's visibility by guest starring on the track "9-11" from their album *West Koasta Nostra* (Sarinjay).

DISCOGRAPHY: *Single*: "Coming Hard to America" (Villain Records, 1988). *EP*: *Mentally Disturbed* (First Kut, 1996). *Albums*: *New Funky Nation* (4th & Broadway, 1990); *Doomsday* (Bulletproof, 1994); *Occupation Hazardous* (Bulletproof, 1995); *Angry Samoans* (1997); *Mafia Lifestyle* (S.M. Records, 2000); *West Koasta Nostra* (Sarinjay, 2003).

BOSS [Lichelle Laws]

If Boss is remembered at all, it is as Hip Hop's first fake-hardcore female rap artist. Boss was the first female rap act to be signed to **Russell Simmons**'s Def Jam West label and later was discovered to have lied about her tough background, Boss and her sidekick Dee having feigned street credentials as a means to sell records. The product of solidly middle-class upbringing, Boss claimed that she and Dee had lived on the street, sold drugs, and spent time in jail. Boss and Dee hailed from Detroit, Michigan, but after a brief stint in New York, the pair headed west to Los Angeles before gaining the attention of **DJ Quik** and landing a record deal.

In 1993, boss released the album, *Born Gangstaz*. Boss's first and last record may be the most nihilistic rap album ever produced. According to Boss, life has no sacred purpose; there is no religion, no mercy, no love or romance. Even sex is reduced to kill or be raped. *Born Gangstaz* depicts life as violent and profane: a hail of bullets, then death. Although the lyrical message is bleak, producers Def Jef, Erick Sermon (**EPMD**), AMG, and MC Serch (**3rd Bass**) nonetheless create wonderfully layered, bass-heavy beats, often built on sultry guitar pieces.

After *The Wall Street Journal* revealed that her life on the streets was largely fabricated, Boss rapidly faded away.

DISCOGRAPHY: *Born Gangstaz* (Def Jam West, 1993).

BOX, THE

The Box was a Miami-based call-in video request line carried on cable systems that debuted in 1985. The Box offered music videos, twenty-four hours a day, seven days a week. The Box had a library of over 1,600 videos, including the newest pop, rock, and rap, as well as sexy R & B, Latin music, and country. Rather than waiting for programmers to select videos, viewers were able to request the videos they wanted by calling a 900 number and paying a $1.99 fee. The Box equalized the playing field for **underground** and regional rap groups. "Jacking The Box" became a term used within the music industry for record companies and artists who, through coordinated request efforts, created a false demand for particular records.

BOYZ N THE HOOD

Director John Singleton's 1991 debut film starring former **N.W.A.** rap artist, **Ice Cube**, *Boyz n the Hood* depicted the lives of several young men in working-class California. The movie presaged a slew of "hood" films portraying the friendships, rivalries, challenges, and tragedies that befall young Black men. John Singleton, at the age of twenty-three, was nominated for an Academy Award for Best Picture. The film also established Ice Cube as a credible actor.

BRAND NUBIAN

Natives of New Rochelle, New York, Brand Nubian, comprised of **Grand Puba** [Maxwell Dixon], Derrick X (aka Sadat X) [Derrick Murphy], Lord

Jamar [Lorenzo Dechelaus] and X's cousin, DJ Alamo [*unknown*], began performing together in the late 1980s. They created a smooth, funky Hip Hop sound backed by lyrics steeped in the teachings of the **Five Percent Nation**.

Their 1990 debut release, *One For All* (Elektra/Asylum), is considered a classic. It established these dynamic young artists as bona fide members of the East Coast rap community. In 1991, Grand Puba departed the group, with DJ Alamo. The remaining members recruited new member DJ Sincere and in 1993 released their sophmore album, *In God We Trust* (Elektra/Asylum). The album was buoyed by hits such as "Punks Jump Up To Get Beat Down," "Allah U Akbar," and "Love Me or Leave Me Alone."

Brand Nubian. *Courtesy of Photofest.*

Brand Nubian's third release in 1994, *Everything is Everything* (Elektra/Asylum), moved away from the Muslim doctrine to deal with social issues such as Black-on-Black crime and police corruption. In 1996, Sadat X released a solo album, *Wild Cowboys*, which spawned the hit "The Lump Lump." In 1998, Grand Puba returned to the group after recording solo albums *Reel to Reel* (Elektra, 1992) and *2000* (Elektra, 1995). Brand Nubian's fourth CD, *The Foundation* (Elektra), was released in 1998. Grand Puba released his third solo album, *Understand This* (Koch/In The Paint/Rising Son) in 2001.

DISCOGRAPHY: *All For One* (Elektra/Asylum, 1990); *In God We Trust* (Elektra/Asylum, 1993); *Everything is Everything* (Elektra/Asylum, 1994); *Foundation* (Elektra, 1998).

BREAKBEATS

The drum solo in funk, R & B, Soul, rock, jazz fusion, or other music is known as the breakbeat. Sometimes the breakbeat is accompanied by other percussion instruments such as congas, timbales, bongos, or by bass guitars and saxophones, usually in a 4/4 measure. Usually the breakbeat is found either in the beginning or in the middle of the song, typically with a gradual build up, often started with horns. Rap lyricists use breakbeats to rhyme over and **B-boys** use them to dance to.

BREAK DANCING. *See* B-boy

BRITISH KNIGHTS (aka BKs)

British Knights were a brand of sneakers popular in the 1980s. **MC Hammer** appeared in advertisements for BKs. BKs are also mentioned on **Missy Elliott**'s single, "Back in the Day," which talks about the time when "Hip Hop was fun." That track is from her 2003 album, *Under Construction* (Elektra).

BRITISH WALKERS

The British Walkers brand of dress shoes was popularized by young Black men in New York City in the late 1980s to mid-1990s, and immortalized on numerous songs such as **Masta Ace** and **Biz Markie**'s "Me and the Biz" (1990), **Organized Konfusion**'s "Who Stole My Last Piece of Chicken" (1991), and **Kool G Rap**'s "Money on My Brain" from the album *4,5,6* (1995).

BRONX RIVER COMMUNITY CENTER (aka Bronx River Houses Community Center)

The Bronx River Community Center serves the Bronx River Houses project, a public housing development. The Center is located at East 174th Street in the Morris Park section of the Bronx, New York. At this venue, pioneer **Afrika Bambaataa** held parties and rap **battles** that acted to advance the emerging arts of **DJing**, **B-boying**, **MCing**, and aerosol art (aka **graffiti**).

BROTHER D WITH COLLECTIVE EFFORT

Brother D [Daryl Aamaa Nubyahn] with his group Collective Effort recorded the twelve-inch "How We Gonna Make the Black Nation Rise?" (Clappers, 1980), the first rap record to openly discuss the status of African Americans. ("The Message," by **Grandmaster Flash and the Furious Five**, was not released until 1982.)

BROWN, JAMES

Soul singer James Brown has become the most sampled artist. **Afrika Bambaataa** collaborated with Brown on their 1985 song, "Unity Part 1 (the Third Coming)." The song "Give It Up or Turn It Loose" is considered by many to be the **B-boy** anthem.

BROWN SUGAR

A 2002 romantic comedy directed by Rick Famuyiwa that is also a tribute to Hip Hop. The storyline involves best friends since elementary school, who have been in love with rap music since they can remember. As adults their friendship remains, as does their relationship with Hip Hop. Dre (Taye Diggs) is making a successful living as a record executive, while Sidney (Saana Lathan) has just taken over as editor-in-chief at one of the nation's most popular Hip Hop magazines. Disillusioned with the mediocre rap music that his company continually puts out, Dre decides to start his own label. Sidney not only provides Dre with a needed business loan, but also with moral support. The platonic friends are then forced to confront their true feelings for each other. **Mos Def** and **Queen Latifah** provide hilarious supporting performances.

BUBBA SPARXXX [Warren Anderson Mathis]

A White rap artist from La Grange, Georgia, Bubba Sparxxx represents the New South, and he gained fame by giving props to his rural southern roots. Like many of his southern counterparts, Sparxxx's rap style is a combination of urban slang and country drawl.

Bubba Sparxxx entered the music world in 1996 and under the name Lil Devil formed the group One Card Shi with rap artist Jason Brown. When the pair parted ways, Mathis took the new name Bubba Sparxxx, Bubba being a childhood nickname and Sparxxx a catchy moniker.

In 1999, Sparxxx partnered with So So Def producer Shannon Houchins and released the album *Dark Days, Bright nights* on Noncents Recordings, a label that he co-owns. On the strength of this debut, Jimmy Iovine, President of Interscope Records signed Sparxxx. Iovine then struck a deal with producer **Timbaland**'s new Beat Club imprint to oversee the rerecording of *Dark Days, Bright Nights* for its major label debut. The retooled *Dark Days, Bright Nights* debuted at number 3 on the *Billboard* charts in 2001, with unique instrumentation that included a sitar sample on the hit "Ugly" and banjo on "Bubba Talk."

DISCOGRAPHY: *Dark Days, Bright Nights* (Noncents Recordings, 1999; re-issued by Interscope Records in 2001).

BURNER. *See* Graffiti

BUSTA RHYMES [Trevor Smith]

With his raspy voice, wild dreadlocks, and boisterous demeanor, Busta Rhymes, a member of the **Flipmode Squad**, is one of the most eccentric figures in Hip Hop.

The Brooklyn native came to rap music fame in the late 1980s as a member of the rap group Leaders of the New School. The group's 1990

Busta Rhymes. *Courtesy of Photofest.*

debut album, *Future Without A Past* (Elektra), earned Busta some notice, but Busta's lyrical skills and style were better highlighted when he appeared on **A Tribe Called Quest**'s 1991 classic track, "Scenario," and on Craig Mack's "Flava In Ya Ear" **remix**.

His solo debut album, *The Coming* (Elektra), was an instant hit in 1996. The single "Woo-Hah!! Got You All In Check" hit the Top 10 on U.S. record charts, the album went platinum plus, and Busta's unique videos made him a mainstay on MTV. In 1997, his sophomore album, *When Disaster Strikes* (Elektra), debuted at number 3 on U.S. music record charts and sold over 1.5 million copies. The single "Put Your Hands Where My Eyes Can See" and its innovative accompanying video solidified Busta's place among rap music's top artists. Capitalizing on his Hip Hop celebrity, Busta released his third album *E.L.E. (Extinction Level Events: The Final World Front* (Elektra) in 1998.

In the aftermath of the 2000 release of his fourth album, *Anarchy,* rumors began to circulate that Busta Rhymes was contemplating leaving Elektra for J Records, because he was displeased at their lack of promotion of the album. Busta had recorded for Elektra beginning in 1989 as a seventeen-year-old member of Leaders of the New School. After the demise of Leaders of the New School in 1993, Busta signed a production agreement with Elektra and formed Flipmode Entertainment, which has released albums by Busta, **Rah Digga**, and the Flipmode Squad.

Anarchy would be Busta's last album with Elektra and his first J Records album, *Genesis*, hit the streets in 2001. *Genesis* would contain the major **P. Diddy** collaboration, "Pass The Courvoisier." The song is credited with increasing sales for the upscale cognac. In 2002, Busta released his sixth album, *It Ain't Safe No More* (J Records); compared to his other efforts, this was a commercial failure. Busta thereafter terminated his relationship with J Records (as did fellow Flipmode Squad member Rah Digga) and in February 2004 joined **Dr. Dre**'s Aftermath Records. The two had collaborated on the single "Break Ya Neck" from the *Genesis* album. Busta's first Aftermath album, *Big Bang*, is slated for release in 2005.

Busta has appeared in such films as *Who's the Man* (1993), *Strapped* (1993), *Higher Learning* (1995), *Shaft* (2000), *Finding Forrester* (2000), and *Halloween 8* (2001).

DISCOGRAPHY: *The Coming* (Elektra); *When Disaster Strikes* (Elektra, 1997); *E.L.E. (Extinction Level Events: The Final World Front)* (Elektra, 1998); *Anarchy* (Elektra, 2000); *Genesis* (J Records, 2001); *It Ain't Safe No More* (J Records, 2002).

BUSY BEE [David Parker]

The legendary MC Busy Bee began his career in 1977 in New York City. Busy Bee's career took off when he MC'd a DJ **battle** between **Afrika**

Islam and Raheim against DJ Breakout with Baron and the Funky Four. Busy Bee so impressed the crowd that **Afrika Bambaataa** asked him to join his **Zulu Nation** and MC at their parties. Busy Bee established a reputation as one of New York's best MCs and eventually teamed up with Kool DJ AJ.

At the Disco Fever on December 30, 1981, Busy Bee took part in perhaps the most famous of battles in Hip Hop history, against **Kool Moe Dee**. In the 1982 film *Wild Style*, Busy Bee played himself; in a memorable scene, he spells out his name in money. Although most of Busy Bee's success was found playing at live parties, he also had some success on wax in the early 1980s on Sugarhill records, with hits such as "Making Cash Money" (1982) and "Busy Bee's Groove" (Sugar Hill Records, 1984).

In 1986, Busy Bee won the New Music Seminar's MC World Supremacy Belt. In the late 1980s he was as a member of the **Ice-T**'s Rhyme Syndicate and he subsequently dropped the hit singles "Express" (Uni, 1988) and "Suicide" (Strong City Records, 1987) and the albums *Runnin' Thangs* (Uni, 1988) and *Thank God for Busy Bee* (Pandisc Records, 1992). In 2002, **Busy Bee** released the twelve-inch single, "Keep it Moving," featuring DJ Kool (Blazin' Records).

DISCOGRAPHY: *Singles*: "Express" (Uni, 1988); "Suicide" (Strong City Records, 1987); "Rock the House" [*unknown*]. *Albums*: *Runnin' Thangs* (Uni, 1988); *Thank God for Busy Bee* (Pandisc Records, 1992).

BWP (aka Bytches With Problems)

The BWP trio Lyndah, Tanisha, and Michelle is often called the female **2 Live Crew** because of their rude and crude X-rated lyrics. According to the New York City natives, Bytches stood for "Beautiful Young Thing College Honeys en' Shit. BWP first appeared on the 1990 No Face album, *Wake Up Your Daughter*. The trio released its debut album, *The Bytches* (Def Jam/RAL/Columbia), in 1991 to a mix of outrage and indifference, which spawned a minor hit, "Two Minute Brother." BWP was subsequently signed by RAL-Chaos, and in 1993 released the album, *Life's a Bitch*. In 2000, they released the album, *Always on My Mind* (The Orchard). Critics of the BWP argued that the group promoted a stereotypical image of African American women. The trio faded from the rap music scene because, apart from their ability to match the crassness of their male counterparts, there seemed little else to the BWP. BWP never demonstrated more than mediocre creativity and rhyming ability, unfortunately coupled with lackluster production.

DISCOGRAPHY: *The Bytches* (Def Jam/RAL/Columbia, 1991); *Life's a Bitch* (RAL-Chaos, 1993); *Always on My Mind* (The Orchard, 2000).

C

CAMPBELL, LUTHER "LUKE" (aka Luke Skywalker; aka Uncle Luke)

Luther Campbell is best known for **2 Live Crew**'s obscenity trials in the early 1990s, trials that became a *cause célèbre* for First Amendment proponents. Campbell has worn many hats as one of Hip Hop's successful entrepreneurs, including concert promoter, founder of Skyywalker Records (later known as Luke Records), visionary behind the controversial rap group 2 Live Crew, author, and First Amendment advocate.

Raised in the rough Liberty City section of Miami, Luther Campbell began his music career DJing parties and making party tapes. Campbell would be recognized as being part of the first wave of the **Miami bass** music of the 1980s. In 1986, as the front man for 2 Live Crew he recorded the album *2 Live Crew Is What We Are* on his own Luke Skyywalker Record label. The single "Throw the D---" helped to garner the group a following in the Southeast. This album also prompted Luke to record "clean," or less explicit, versions of 2 Live Crew songs after a Florida record store clerk was charged with a felony for selling the album to a minor.

2 Live Crew would have some more success with the follow-up album, *Move Somethin'* (Luke Skyywalker, 1988). The first 2 Live Crew albums both reportedly sold over 500,000 copies. In 1989, 2 Live Crew released the multi-platinum-selling album *As Nasty as They Wanna Be* (Luke Skyywalker, 1989), a decidedly raunchy offering full of sexually explicit content and sophomoric humor that became the focus of a national campaign against allegedly obscene lyrics.

Spurred by the single "Me So Horny," Jack Thompson, a lawyer and an opponent of pornography, reviewed the lyrics and deemed album's content obscene; he sent copies to Florida's then governor, Bob Martinez, and to every sheriff in the state. The Broward County sheriff, Nick Navarro, then brought the album to a federal judge in Fort Lauderdale, who also declared it to be obscene. This ruling, that a music recording was obscene, was the first of its kind in U.S. history. In 1990, Charles Freeman, a Black man who owned a record store in Fort Lauderdale was arrested for selling *As Nasty As They Wanna Be.* Freeman's arrest, coupled with other record stores being fined for selling the album, led other storeowners to pull the album from their shelves. Shortly thereafter Campbell and 2 Live Crew member Chris Won were arrested in Broward County, Florida, for reciting obscene lyrics on stage during a performance at an adult-only show at Club Futura in Hollywood, Florida.

Now positioned as a crusader for the First Amendment, the twenty-nine-year-old Campbell raised the specter of racism as the reason why 2 Live Crew were being singled out when other, White artists (particularly the smutty White comedian Andrew Dice Clay) were not. At 2 Live Crew's obscenity trial, renowned scholar Henry Louis Gates, Jr., then a professor of English at Duke University, testified on behalf or 2 Live Crew, citing their risqué humor as part of a long-standing Western tradition. Musician Bruce Springsteen also supported Campbell and permitted the use of his song "Born in the U.S.A." on 2 Live Crew's 1990 album, *Banned in the U.S.A.* (Luke/Atlantic). The single "Banned in the U.S.A." championed the First Amendment and free speech and become the group's second Top 40 hit. Ironically, the album was still slapped with a "parental advisory" sticker.

After the release of *Banned in the USA*, 2 Live Crew members began to pursue solo projects. In that same year, 1990, Skyywalker Records would be renamed Luke Records after "Star Wars" films creator, George Lucas sued Campbell over the unauthorized use of the Skywalker name. Campbell also agreed to pay Lucas $300,000 to settle the copyright infringement lawsuit out of court.

In 1992, a federal appeals court overturned the lower court ruling that *As Nasty As They Wanna Be* was obscene, ending Campbell and 2 Live Crew's Cam two-and-a-half-year battle in Broward County over the album [*Luke Records v. Navarro*, 960 F.2d (1992)]. In 1994, Campbell MACROBUTTON HtmlResAnchor also won a Supreme Court decision with a ruling that his parody of the late Roy Orbison's song "Oh, Pretty Woman" did not violate the copyright held by Acuff-Rose [*Campbell v. Acuff-Rose Music*, 510 U.S. 569 (1994)].

In the years following these legal successes, Luke's career would have more valleys than peaks. He launched the short-lived career of R & B vocalists H-Town on Luke Records. In 1991, 2 Live Crew broke up after the release of their album, *Sports Weekend (As Nasty As They Wanna Be Part II)* and Luke embarked on a solo career, beginning with *I Got Sh*t on My Mind* (Luke, 1992). That same year, a state court ordered Campbell to pay $1.6 million to rap artist MC Shy D, who claimed that Campbell had cheated him out of record profits. In 1993 and 1994, Luke released two solo albums, *In the Nude* (Luke Records) and *Freak For Life* (Luke Records), with few rap fans noticing. In June 1995, Campbell filed for Chapter 11 bankruptcy. 2 Live Crew would become the property of Lil' Joe Records, founded by Luke's former business partner, Joe Weinberger. In 1997, Campbell made a financial comeback hosting "Luke's Peep Show," an erotic cable television program featuring rap artists and scantily clad women. In 1997, he released his fourth solo album, *Changin' the*

Game. In 2001, Luke returned to the studio and released the album *Luke Something Nasty* (Luke Records).

DISCOGRAPHY: *I Got Sh*t on My Mind* (Luke, 1992); *In the Nude* (Luke, 1993); *Freak for Life* (Luke, 1994); *Uncle Luke* (Luke, 1996); *Changin' the Game* (Luke, 1997); *Luke Something Nasty* (Luke Records, 2001).

CAM'RON [Cameron Giles]

Harlem-born rap artist Cam'ron may be remembered in Hip Hop annals more for his pink clothing in 2003 and his run-in with the National Basketball Association (NBA) than for his rhymes.

In 1998, Cam'ron released his gold-selling debut album, *Confessions of Fire* (Untertainment/Epic), and scored a hit with the single "Horse and Carriage" that featured fellow Harlem, New York, resident **Mase**. The two friends were members of the defunct rap group, Children of the Corn. Cam'ron second album, *Sports, Drugs & Entertainment* (Untertainment/Epic, 2000), created a firestorm when his then record label appropriated a version of the National Basketball Association's logo in a national advertising campaign to promote the artist's album. The print ad featured a silhouette of a man holding a gun while dribbling a basketball, a silhouette nearly identical to the NBA logo. On April 19, 1999, Untertainment placed a huge billboard on Malcolm X Boulevard in Harlem. Community activists, church leaders, and school officials, mistakenly concluded that the album was sponsored by the NBA, complained to the NBA and demanded action. The NBA quickly filed a lawsuit, contending that Untertainment had infringed upon their trademark and seeking damages and an immediate injunction against further use of their logo. The NBA secured a court order requiring the removal of the billboard and halting print ads in rap publications.

In 2002, after the closing of Untertainment and disputes with parent company Epic Records, Cam'ron released his third album, *Come Home With Me* (Roc-A-Fella Records). The album, which contained the hit single, "Oh Boy," featuring Juelz Santana, become Cam'ron's first platinum-selling album. That same year, Cam'ron also starred role in the **Roc-A-Fella**–produced movie, *Paid In Full*, which is loosely based on the lives of Harlem drug lords Rich Porter, AZ, and Alpo. On the heels of Cam'ron leaving Epic Records, the label released a compilation album, *Harlem's Greatest*, in 2002. In 2004, Cam'ron released the album *Purple Haze*; the title is taken from Jimi Hendrix's 1967 acid rock anthem of the same name. Unlike the classic album *Are You Experienced?* that spawned the original "Purple Haze," Cam'ron's album met with very mixed reviews: fans loved it, others not did not.

DISCOGRAPHY: *Confessions of Fire* (Untertainment/Epic, 1998); *Sports, Drugs & Entertainment* (Untertainment/Epic, 2000); *Come Home With Me* (Roc-A-Fella, 2002); *Purple Haze* (Roc-A-Fella, 2004).

CANIBUS [Germaine Williams]

Although initially heralded as the next big thing in 1998 after some memorable guest appearances, in the aftermath of his famous rap **battle** with **LL Cool J** Canibus proved to be little more than a fleeting talent. As a child Canibus, a native of Jamaica, West Indies, moved frequently; his mother's career required constant relocation. Canibus lived in Washington, DC; Atlanta, Georgia; London, England; and New Jersey. The constant upheaval forced Canibus to find solace within himself, which resulted in his penning lyrics.

Canibus began rhyming and in the mid-1990s joined a group called T.H.E.M. (The Heralds of Extreme Metaphors), which included his partner Webb. After the duo split, Canibus pursued a solo career and began appearing on mixtapes. By 1997, Canibus had appeared on a number of high-profile releases: "Uni-4-Orm," from the *Rhyme & Reason* film soundtrack; "Love, Peace & Nappiness," from the **Lost Boyz** *Love, Peace & Nappiness* (Universal, 1997) album; "Making a Name for Ourselves," from **Common**'s *One Day It'll All Make Sense* (Relativity Records, 1997); the nonalbum **remix** of **Wyclef Jean**'s (**Fugees**) "Gone Till November" from *Presents The Carnival: Featuring the Refugee Allstars* (Sony, 1997); and his most famous guest spot, on "4, 3, 2, 1," from LL Cool J's album, *Phenomenon* (Def Jam Recordings, 1997).

Of all of Canibus's guest spots, his appearance on "4, 3, 2, 1" was the most important. Aside from LL Cool J himself, the track put Canibus in the company of major rap music stars **Redman**, **DMX**, and **Method Man**. Shortly after Canibus's appearance on "4, 3, 2, 1," the up-and-coming rap artist bit the hand the fed him, lashing out at veteran LL Cool J on the Canibus track "Second Round K.O.," featuring heavyweight boxer Mike Tyson. LL Cool J, no stranger to rap **beefs**, replied with "The Ripper Strikes Back," from the *Survival of the Illest* soundtrack (1998), thus channeling even more attention toward Canibus.

Although the beef with LL Cool J attracted massive media attention for Canibus, it did little to spark interest in his 1998 debut album, *Can-i-bus* (Universal). The album, executive-produced by Wyclef Jean, was not well received by critics who were not impressed with Canibus's delivery and word of mouth from disappointed listeners led to sales of the album quickly dropping off. Canibus was further hurt by the fact that LL Cool J's "Ripper Strikes Back" was in comparison a large hit. After receding from the public eye, in 2000 Canibus returned with his follow-up album, *2000 B.C.* (Universal). The album went generally unnoticed.

After leaving Universal records, Canibus returned to the **underground** scene, recording albums on independent labels for his small but loyal fan base. In 2003, in a slam on LL Cool J, he came out with the album, *Rip the Jacker* (Babygrande), with beats by Stoupe, of Jedi Mind Trick fame.

DISCOGRAPHY: *Can-i-bus* (Universal, 1998); *2000 B.C.* (Universal, 2000); *Rip the Jacker* (Babygrande, 2003).

CAPOEIRA

Capoeira is a Brazilian art form that is alternatively a martial art, a dance, and a style of music. Developed in the sixteenth century by Africans enslaved in Brazil who were secretly training to fight, capoeira was outlawed at the end of the nineteenth century because authorities associated it with disorder and violence, as well as with possible slave uprisings.

The physical aspects of capoeira are performed within a *roda* or circle. Two figures swing their bodies in a dance of strategy and skill, punctuating their movements of circular kicks and timed exits with occasional headspins and back handsprings. A percussion orchestra, led by the berimbau (a single-stringed bow with a gourd resonator and a wailing tone) set the speed and style of the play.

Traditionally, women were not trained in the art of capoeira. Maestre Bimba (the first master to open a government-sanctioned academy in the city of Salvador, Bahia, when capoeira was legalized in 1937) did teach some women, although they did not perform or "play" in public. By the 1970s and the 1980s, middle-class Brazilians, wealthy university students, and people from various economic strata and ethnic groups in Brazil began to study the art form. Moreover, capoeira became Brazil's national sport. During this period, the *roda* transformed into a symbol of Africa's contribution to Brazilian society, stressing citizenship and equality.

The style and nature of capoeira indirectly informed the development of **B-boying** among Black and Puerto Rican youth in New York City. Ironically, both art forms have at times been banned because they were thought to disrupt society and to cause violence.

CAPONE-N-NOREAGA [Capone (Kiam Holley) and Noreaga (Victor Santiago)]

Capone-N-Noreaga (also known to their fans as CNN) are best known for their popularity among hardcore rap fans, particularly within the East Coast **underground** community. Both of members of this Queens, New York, rap duo endured difficult childhoods and numerous run-ins with the law. Capone grew up in the legendary **Queensbridge** Projects, and Noreaga was raised in the projects of LeFrak City. The two met in and became friends in 1992, at Collins Correctional Facility in New York, while serving kitchen duty together. When they left jail, they decided to join forces as rap artists, taking their names from gangster Al Capone and Panamanian president and drug smuggler Manuel Noriega.

In 1996, the duo signed to Penalty Records and released their first single, "Illegal Life." Their first major hit was their appearance on the single "L.A., L.A." (25 to Life Entertainment, 1996) with **Mobb Deep**, a response to **Tha Dogg Pound**'s diss record "**New York, New York**" (Priority Records, 1995).

With the release of their debut album, *War Report* (Penalty/Tommy Boy Records), Capone-N-Noreaga enjoyed massive street credibility. Before that album was completed, Capone had been sent back to prison for violating his parole on a weapons possession charge. Noreaga finished *The War Report* alone, and the album was released in 1997. The album garnered the duo enormous support among hardcore rap fans and sold 500,000 copies with little radio airplay. With Capone in jail, the duo's thugged out reputation appeared ever more legitimate.

On the strength of *War Reports,* which went gold, Noreaga remained loyal to Capone, but he also embarked on a solo career. Capone was given executive producer credits on Noreaga's solo albums, *N.O.R.E.* (Penalty, 1998) and *Melvin Flynt—Da Hustler* (Penalty, 1999). Capone left prison in 1999, and the duo released the album *The Reunion* in 2000. Dissatisfied with Tommy Boy's promotion of the project, Capone-N-Noreaga asked to be released from their recording contract; in 2001, the duo signed to **Def Jam Recordings**.

Capone continued to run afoul of the law, which may have hampered the ability of the duo to record an album. In 2002, Noreaga released his third solo album, *God's Favorite,* and Capone was reportedly working on his own solo debut at the same time. The duo's third album, *New Religion*, was due out in 2004, but it has been pushed back without a new release date.

DISCOGRAPHY: *Singles*: "Illegal Life" (Penalty, 1996). *Albums*: *War Report* (Penalty/Tommy Boy Records); *The Reunion* (Tommy Boy Records, 2000).

CASH MONEY MILLIONAIRES

The membership list of Cash Money Millionaires has included whatever rap artist is signed to Cash Money Records at the time. Initially, the group included Cash Money cofounder, Baby; producer, Mannie Fresh; and Hot Boys **Juvenile**, B.G., Turk, and **Lil Wayne**. In 2000, the group released the *Baller Blockin'* collection, which accompanied a straight-to-video film of the same name.

CAZAL GLASSES

Dark, heavy-framed, and worn without lenses, Cazal glasses were popular accessories for young men associated with Hip Hop in the 1980s.

The group Hot Boys. *Courtesy of Photofest.*

CB4: THE MOVIE. *See* Films

CELLA DWELLAS (aka Dwellas)

The Brooklyn, New York, duo of Ug [*unknown*] and Phantasm [*unknown*] are identified with the "horrorcore" subgenre of rap music popularized by groups such as the **Gravediggaz** in the 1990s.

The Cella Dwellas first received attention with their single "Land of the Lost," which originally appeared on the *Nudder Budders*, a CD sampler released by Loud Records in 1994. In early 1996, Flatbush natives Ug and Phantasm expanded on the horrorcore sound that influenced their debut single on their first album, *Realms N' Reality* (RCA), which combined hardcore New York–style rap music with the fantasy of a Saturday morning cartoon adventure. The tracks on the album seamlessly mixed funny rhymes and rugged beats with the role-playing found in **video games** such as "Dungeons and Dragons" with scenes that could have been taken from any number of horror films. *Realms N' Reality*, although it did not garner widespread attention, was considered an innovative and exciting album derived from the intellect of two warped minds.

Cella Dwellas faded from the rap scene for nearly four years but then returned in 2000, when the Dwellas released their sophomore album, *Last Shall Be First* (Relativity Records). Their second album met with mixed opinions: some thought it was stronger than the debut album, but others did not.

DISCOGRAPHY: *Realms N' Reality* (RCA, 1996); *Last Shall Be First* (Relativity Records, 2000).

CENSORSHIP

The notion that young people should be shielded from offensive lyrics is not new. One of the first instances of music censorship occurred in 1964, when The Kingmen's 1963 frat-boy song, "Louie, Louie," caught the attention of Indiana governor Matthew Welsh. Welsh believed that the song provided an anatomical reference, although the Federal Communications Commission (FCC) deemed the lyric in question indecipherable. Rap music has been at the center of many controversies and as such its lyrics and celebrities have been the subject of numerous censorship efforts. A sample of efforts is outlined here.

1989—**N.W.A.**, "Fuck Tha Police": The FBI sends out letters to police chiefs nationwide, singling out the song as an example of anti–law enforcement agitation.

1990—**2 Live Crew**, "Me So Horny": A Broward County, Florida, sheriff attempts to pull the record from stores and a judge rules the album obscene, but the U.S. Supreme Court, maintaining that the lyrics are protected under the First Amendment, overturns the decision [*Luke Records v. Navarro*, 960 F.2d (1992)].

1991—**Ice Cube**: Amid allegations that the album *Death Certificate* is anti-Semitic, the Simon Wiesenthal Center, a Jewish human rights group, lobbies major record stores to remove it from their shelves.

1992—**Body Count**: **Ice-T** pulls the single "**Cop Killer**" from the group's first album, of the same name, after protests and boycotts of Warner Bros.

1992—**Public Enemy**: MTV refuses to air Public Enemy's video for "Hazy Shade of Criminal" from the *Greatest Misses* (Def Jam Recordings, 1992), stating that it violates the network's criteria for violent content.

1992—Ice Cube: In the aftermath of the controversy surrounding the album *Death Certificate*, the state of Oregon makes it illegal to display Ice Cube's image in record stores. The ban also extended to Ice Cube's ads for St. Ide's Malt Liquor.

1993—Reverend Calvin Butts, pastor of New York's prestigious Abyssinian Baptist Church in Harlem, attempted to publicly and literally steamroll so-called offensive CDs and cassette tapes.

May 1994—**C. Dolores Tucker**, Chairwoman of the National Political Congress of Black Women and former Education Secretary, and conservative author William J. Bennett both addressed a Time Warner meeting and urged the company to eliminate all rap music with violent and/or sexually explicit lyrics.

June 1997—Insane Clown Posse: The purveyors of White Hip Hop have their album *The Great Milenko* pulled from store shelves and hours later are released from their record contact with Hollywood Records after the Southern Baptist church threatened a boycott of Disney, the parent company of Hollywood Records. Disney had been aware of the album's references to gang banging, drugs, and female anatomy for nearly a year prior to the protest.

2000—**Eminem**, "Kill You": After the release of "Kill You," the White rap artist becomes an example at the September Federal Trade Commission hearings on the entertainment industry marketing violence to children.

2002—Sarah Jones, "Your Revolution": Spoken-word artist Sarah Jones had her song "Your Revolution" pulled from airplay because the FCC considered some of the lyrics obscene. The FCC lodged a $7,000 fine against KBOO-FM, a radio station in Portland, Oregon, for playing the song. According to Jones, the song is a protest against the degradation of women in popular music. To bolster her position, Jones quotes some lyrics offensive to women from rap artists such as **LL Cool J** and **Biggie Smalls**.

CHUBB ROCK [Richard Simpson]

Weighing in at 250 pounds, Chubb Rock was often thought of as the Hip Hop Barry White (with whom he shared a duet on the song "And the Winner Is . . ."). Chubb Rock is best remembered as a nimble and affable lyricist.

Chubb Rock, a National Merit Scholar, was in a rap group while he was a teenager in New York; he first went on to Brown University, but then left to pursue music. Chubb Rock hit the scene in 1988 and released four albums in less than three years. His first album, *Chubb Rock Featuring Hitman Howie Tee* (Alldisc, 1988; Select, 1999), failed to garner mass appeal. His second album, *And the Winner Is ...* (Select, 1989), was released to greater commercial and critical acclaim, thanks to a **remixed** single version of "Caught Up" that was released prior to the album.

In the early 1990s, Chubb Rock scored hits with the singles "Treat 'Em Right" and "Just The Two Of Us," from the album *The One* (Select Records, 1991). In 1992, he released *I Gotta Get Mine Yo* (Select). Although Chubb Rock's smooth flow and ladies man appeal earned him some fans, the rap music environment during this period was dominated by hardcore music and his star soon descended. In 1997, five years after his last album, Chubb Rock released *Mind* (Select Records).

DISCOGRAPHY: *Chubb Rock Featuring Hitman Howie Tee* (Alldisc, 1988; Select, 1999) *And the Winner Is ...* (Select, 1989); *The One* (Select Records, 1991); *I Gotta Get Mine Yo* (Select, 1992) *Mind* (Select Records, 1997).

CHUCK D [Carlton Douglas Ridenhour]

The son of political activists and the founder of **Public Enemy**, Chuck D hails from Roosevelt, Long Island, New York. More than a rap artist, this elder statesman of Hip Hop has established himself as an intelligent thinker. Chuck D has became sought after as a speaker on the college lecture circuit and frequently provides commentary on television news programs.

When he was a graphics design student at Adelphi University, Chuck D made promotional flyers for Hip Hop events and also cohosted a mix show on the campus radio station with two future Public Enemy associates, Bill Stephney and Hank Shocklee. As a member of Spectrum City, a mobile DJ crew from Long Island, Chuck D (then known as Chucky D) had recorded "Lies," backed with "Check Out the Radio" (Vanguard Records), a single that made little splash. Under the name Chuck D, he appeared on Shocklee's demo single, "Public Enemy No. 1." The song caught the interest of **Def Jam Recordings** cofounder Rick Rubin but Chuck D, now a married man with a child, was not initially interested in making another record. At the behest of Rick Rubin, however, Bill Stephney convinced Chuck D to sign with Def Jam Recordings. Subsequently, Chuck D, using the concept of the demo, formed the group Public Enemy.

As the frontman for Public Enemy, Chuck D became known not only for his distinctive booming voice, but also for his political rhetoric. Public Enemy debuted in 1987 with the album *Yo! Bum Rush the Show* (Def Jam Recordings). The group followed up in 1988 with *It Takes a Nation of Millions to Hold Us Back* (Def Jam Recordings), *Fear of a Black Planet*

Chuck D. *Courtesy of Photofest.*

(Def Jam Recordings) in 1990, and then *Apocalypse '91 ... The Enemy Strikes Black* (Def Jam Recordings, 1994). By 1994, when *Muse Sick-N-Hour Mess Age* was released, the rap music climate had changed. Critics said that political rap was dead and that therefore the group had lost its power.

In 1995, Public Enemy went on hiatus and in 1996 Chuck D released his first solo album, *The Autobiography of Mistachuck*. The following year Chuck D published his autobiography, *Fight The Power: Rap, Race and Reality* (New York: Delacorte Press). In May 1997 Fox News announced that Chuck D would join them as a correspondent and commentator. In 1998, Public Enemy rejoined forces for the soundtrack to Spike Lee's 1998 film, *He Got Game*.

In March of 1998, Chuck D instituted a lawsuit in U.S. District Court in New York, charging the estate of Christopher Wallace; Big Poppa Music; C. Martin; Justin Combs Publishing; EMI April Music, Inc.; Gifted Pearl Music-EMI; **Bad Boy Entertainment**; and Arista Records, Inc., with two counts of copyright infringement and defamation based on the use of his voice on the single, "The Ten Crack Commandments." That single, which appeared on the 1997 **Notorious B.I.G.** two-CD release, *Life After Death* (Bad Boy Entertainment), features B.I.G. describing ten rules to follow when dealing crack, as Chuck D counts off the numbers. Chuck

D's vocal is sampled from Public Enemy's "Shut 'Em Down," which originally appeared on their 1991 *Apocalypse '91 ... The Enemy Strikes Black*. At issue was not the **sampling** of Chuck's voice, but its use in describing drug dealing. In November 1999, the Chuck D and the defendants in his defamation "Ten Crack Commandment" lawsuit reached a confidential, out-of-court settlement.

In 1999 Chuck D left Def Jam Recordings over the label's refusal to allow him to distribute Public Enemy music via free Internet downloads. After signing with the web-based Atomic Pop label, Chuck D became an outspoken proponent of MP3 technology. In that connection, in 1999 he made *There's a Poison Goin' On ...*, the first full-length album by a major artist to be made available over the Internet; the album was released on CD as well. In late 1999, Chuck D formed the now defunct streaming-radio Web site www.bringthenoise.com to provide music, news, and commentary on Hip Hop. In 2004, Chuck D signed on as a cohost of the radio show *Unfiltered*, broadcast on Air America, a politically liberal radio network.

CIPHER

A performance circle that signifies unity, the cipher is Hip Hop's sacred space, where MCs **freestyle**, passing the microphone or rhymes to one another.

C. L. SMOOTH [Corey Brent Penn]. *See* Pete Rock

COKE LA ROCK (aka A-1 Coke, aka Nasty Coke)

Coke La Rock, who worked with **DJ Kool Herc**, is thought to be the first Hip Hop MC or master of ceremonies. He is credited with such MC staple expressions as "To the beat y'all" and "Ya rock and ya don't stop."

COLD CHILLIN'

Founded by producer **Marley Marl**, the label would become associated with the **Juice Crew All Stars**, which included legendary rap artists **Big Daddy Kane**, **Biz Markie**, **Roxanne Shante**, **MC Shan**, and **Masta Ace**. Originally known as Prism, the first office for the record label was the living room of Marley Marl's sister's **Queensbridge** apartment.

COLD CRUSH BROTHERS

As the Cold Crush Brothers, **Grandmaster Caz** [Curtis Fisher], DJ Tony Tone [Angelo King], and DJ Charlie Chase [Carlos Mandes] made up one of the most popular and original of the early Hip Hop groups to come out of the Bronx at the end of the 1970s. This group has influenced a range of rap artists, as well as two generations of Hip Hop aficionados.

The 2001 song, "Izzo (H.O.V.A.)" from **Jay-Z**'s *The Blueprint* album (Def Jam Recordings) acknowledges the group. The original group lineup was DJ Tony Tone, Easy AD (Adrian Harris), DJ Charlie Chase, Whipper-Whip, Mr. T, and Dotarock. Whipper-Whip and Dotarock exited to The Fantastic Five and often met the Cold Crush Brothers on the lyrical battlefield. The Cold Crush lineup most recognized is DJ Charlie Chase and DJ Tony Tone, with four MCs: Grandmaster Caz, Almighty KG [Kenneth Pounder], JDL [Jerry Dee Lewis], and Easy "Girltaker" AD. The late Money Ray [Eric Hoskins] was added in the early 1980s. Formed in 1978 by DJ Tony Tone and DJ Charlie Chase, the Cold Crush Brothers had several MCs before reaching solidity with Grandmaster Caz. Before joining the group, Grandmaster Caz and JDL were once known as The Notorious Two. The Cold Crush Brothers' contribution to Hip Hop is somewhat obscured, from a mainstream perspective, because the group never recorded a full-length album. The group did release four singles: "Weekend" (Elite, 1982), produced by Ecstasy Garage owner Arthur Armstrong; "Punk Rock Rap" (Tuff City, 1983), featuring the "Oh, my God!" voice that would later be heard on **Slick Rick**'s hit single, "The Show"; "Heartbreakers" (Tuff City, 1984); and "Fresh, Wild, Fly, and Bold" (Tuff City, 1984).

The Cold Crush Brothers reputation grew in New York City during the early 1980s. Aside through their live performances, the group's music was circulated through bootleg audiotapes of their live shows at such clubs as the Ecstasy Garage, **T-Connection**, and **Harlem World**. The Cold Crush Brothers appeared in the classic Hip Hop film, *Wild Style*, for which the group recorded the theme song and battled rivals **Grand Wizzard Theodore** and the Fantastic Five. In 1982, the Cold Crush Brothers joined the first Wild Style tour of Japan and in the process they entered a deal with Tuff City, an independent New York–based record label. Tuff City released a series of the group's twelve-inch singles and then in 1994 a collection album, *Fresh, Wild, Fly and Bold (Old School Flava)*. The album *All the Way Live in '82* (Tuff City, 1995) would cull live performances from 1982 and 1983.

Afrika Bambaataa captures one of Cold Crush Brothers legendary **battles** with the Fantastic 5 on the album *Hip-Hop Funk Dance Classics, Vol. 1* (Planet Rock, 1991). The same recorded battle resurfaced in 1998 as *MC Battle From Harlem 1981* (Slammin', 1998), with **remixed** materials by DJ Charlie Chase. Like most other Old School artists, the Cold Crush Brothers did not survive the arrival of **Run DMC**. Subsequently, Grandmaster Caz launched a brief solo career in the late 1980s.

In 1995, the group returned with the twelve-inch single, "Ya Can't Do Me Nada" (Jazz Child). In 2000, The Cold Crush Brothers, experiencing a resurgence in popularity, performed at the grand opening of the new Experience Music Project in Seattle, Washington. In 2001, they also performed with **LL Cool J** during the Rock and Roll Hall of Fame and Museum's "Hip-Hop Nation: Roots, Rhyme and Rage" exhibit at the Brooklyn Museum of Art.

DISCOGRAPHY: *Singles*: "Weekend" (Elite, 1982); "Punk Rock Rap" (Tuff City, 1983); "Heartbreakers" (Tuff City, 1984); "Fresh, Wild, Fly, and Bold" (Tuff City, 1984). *Albums*: *Fresh, Wild, Fly, and Bold* (Old School Flava); *All the Way Live in '82* (Tuff City, 1995).

COLORS

This was the first Hollywood film to use rap music in the soundtrack for a nonmusical. Robert Duvall plays a veteran street cop assigned to a Los Angeles gang unit. He takes a headstrong young cop (Sean Penn) under his wing as a partner and shows him the ropes on Watts's mean streets. Penn soon realizes that his testosterone-fueled ways and hair-trigger temper will not get him very far when dealing with the gang-ridden neighborhoods of LA. *Colors* is a landmark movie in several respects. It helped bring director Dennis Hopper back into the spotlight after years of self-induced obscurity, and its success at the box office forced Los Angeles's gang problems into the public consciousness, prefiguring by several years the wave of "hood" movies (such as ***Boyz n the Hood***, *Menace II Society*, and *New Jack City*).

COMBS, SEAN "P. DIDDY" (aka "Puffy," aka "Puff Daddy," aka "Diddy") [Sean John Combs]

The rap impresario Sean "P. Diddy" Combs is one of the most important players in Hip Hop history. Dismissed by critics because of his lavish lifestyle and liberal use of samples, Combs is nonetheless one of the most commercially successful Hip Hop figures to date. Among his various ventures, Combs's empire includes **Bad Boy Entertainment**, Justin Combs Music Publishing, Daddy's House Studios, Justin's Restaurant (New York and Atlanta), and Sean John Clothing. Combs was nominated by the Council of Fashion Designers of America for the prestigious Perry Ellis Menswear Award in 2000 through 2004, with a win in 2004. In 2003, the five-year-old line reportedly sold $300 million worth of clothing in 2,000 locations.

Born in Harlem, New York, Combs moved as a child to Mount Vernon, New York, after the murder of his father. There he attended Mount Vernon Montessori School and Mount St. Michael Academy, a Catholic boys' high school. Combs attended **Howard University** in Washington, DC. When he began his pivotal internship at Uptown Records, his

Sean "P. Diddy" Combs. *Courtesy of Photofest.*

mentor was the company's president, **Andre Harrell**. Shuttling between Washington, DC, and New York City, Combs had advanced by age nineteen from intern to Director of **A & R** at Uptown Records. In his new position, Combs engineered the careers of Uptown Record artists Jodeci and **Mary J. Blige**. Not only did he oversee the production of their music, he also crafted their public images to mirror the ghetto-fabulous vibe seen in urban centers around the nation.

In 1993, Combs was dismissed from Uptown Records, but he reemerged later the same year with his own company, Bad Boy Entertainment. The company's first signings were Craig Mack and Biggie Smalls (aka **The Notorious B.I.G.**). The first Bad Boy hit was Craig Mack's "Flava in your Ear." Bad Boy would go on to sign, produce, and develop acts such as Faith Evans, the female trio Total, and the male vocal group 112.

In 1991, Combs had his first bitter taste of public tragedy. On December 28, at a charity celebrity basketball game he had organized at City College in New York with rap artist **Heavy D**, nine people were killed and twenty-nine others were injured as crowds pushed and shoved their way into the school gymnasium.

Bad Boy Entertainment would experience more adversity amid its growing success when a feud developed between Combs's company and Suge Knight's **Death Row Records**. The conflict became public during the 1995 Source Awards, when Knight mocked Combs onstage. The **East Coast–West Coast** rivalry was played out played on records by Death Row's **Tupac Shakur** and Bad Boy's The Notorious B.I.G. and by fans who took sides. In September 1996, Shakur was killed in a drive-by shooting in Las Vegas; six months later, The Notorious B.I.G. was murdered in Los Angeles.

In 1996, Combs was named ASCAP's "Songwriter of the Year." By 1997, Bad Boy Entertainment had sold nearly $100 million in recordings and had made a multimillion-dollar deal with Arista records. Combs was also able to extend his influence within rap music through the "Hitmen," his stable of platinum-selling Bad Boy Entertainment producers hired out to work with other artists.

In 1997, Puff Daddy and The Family released the album *No Way Out*, featuring the single, "Can't Nobody Hold Me Down," which held the number 1 spot on *Billboard*'s Hot R & B Singles chart for nearly two months. The album also included a Grammy Award-winning tribute to the slain The Notorious B.I.G., entitled "I'll Be Missing You." The track featured Biggie Smalls's ex-wife Faith Evans and the group 112, and used a sample of the Police's 1993 song, "Every Breath You Take." The album went on to win two Grammy awards, including Best Rap Album of the Year.

In 2000, Combs faced his biggest legal challenge when a stolen gun was found in his car and he was implicated in a New York City nightclub shooting. Combs was acquitted on all charges, but Bad Boy artist Shyne would be convicted. Shyne was sentenced to ten years in jail on charges of assault, gun possession, and reckless endangerment. In the aftermath of the trial, Combs, seeking to move away from the past, shed his nickname "Puffy" in exchange for "P. Diddy."

Combs moved to the big screen with small roles in the films *Made* (2001) and *Monster's Ball* (2001). In 2002, Combs starred in the television reality show, *Making the Band*. In 2004, Combs took on Broadway, starring in the role of Walter Lee Young in a revival of Lorraine Hansberry's play, *Raisin in the Sun*. (Sidney Poitier originated the role on Broadway in 1959 and played it again later in the film version.)

Aside from his entertainment activities, Combs is a philanthropist. His Daddy's House social program assists youths; he donated $1 million to **Howard University**; and in 2003 sponsored a New York marathon challenge that resulted in a $1 million donation to New York City Public schools. In 2004, Combs established the not-for-profit organization Citizens for Change, to encourage young people to vote. In 2004 Combs expanded his empire by opening the first Sean John retail store in Manhattan.

COMMITTEE ON ENERGY AND COMMERCE, U.S. HOUSE

On September 11, 1994, the U.S. House Subcomittee on Commerce, Competitiveness, and Consumer Protection held hearings on **gangsta rap**. Those who testified included author Nelson George, **C. Dolores Tucker**, Soul Train founder Don Cornelius, **Def Jam Recordings** President David Harleston, Representative Maxine Waters, and rap artist **Yo Yo**. Similar Congressional hearings have been held over the years, including the 2000 Drug Enforcement Agency investigation (involving Rap-A-Lot Records, its CEO James Prince, and Scarface) and the 2001 Media Marketing Accountability Act introduced by Senator Joseph Lieberman, which would have empowered the Federal Trade Commission to prohibit the marketing of "adult-rated media" to young people under seventeen years of age. Rap music lyrics were used to demonstrate the need for the legislation.

See also: Censorship

COMMON (aka Common Sense) [Rashid Lonnie Lynn]

A Southside Chicago, Illinois, native who relocated to Brooklyn, New York, Common is known for his superior lyrical talents, intellectual content, and unique hats.

Performing as Common Sense, he caught his first musical break when he was featured by ***The Source*** magazine in its October 1991 "Unsigned Hype" section. In 1992, he released his first single "Take It EZ," which also appeared on his debut album the same year, *Can I Borrow a Dollar?* (Relativity Records). Two subsequent singles, "Breaker 1/9" and "Soul by the Pound," solidified his reputation in the Hip Hop **underground**, although some critics complained that the records were colored by occasional **misogyny**. Common released his follow-up effort, *Resurrection* (Relativity Records), in 1994. The track "I Used to Love H.E.R." attracted substantial notice for its clever allegory about Hip Hop's decline from a nurturing force into a commercially exploitative one focused on sex and violence.

"I Used to Love H.E.R." spawned an **East Coast–West Coast** feud when former **N.W.A.** front man **Ice Cube** took offense to some of **Common**'s remarks about West Coast rap music and retaliated on the single "Westside

Common. *Courtesy of Photofest.*

Slaughterhouse," in collaboration with WC and **Mack 10**. Common Sense responded with the single "The Bitch in Yoo," which remains a classic diss track.

Common Sense was sued by a California ska band by the same name and was forced to change his stage name. Under the shortened moniker Common, he released the album *One Day It'll all Make Sense* (Relativity Records), which features **De La Soul**, Black Thought (**The Roots**), **Lauryn Hill**, **Canibus**, and singer Erykah Badu. The album was well received, and was consistent with the percolating "conscious" Hip Hop movement that was a counterweight to more money-, sex-, and violence-oriented rap fare.

Common's concerts continued to sell out, but when his records sales lagged he moved to major label MCA in 1999. For his third album, *Like Water for Chocolate*, released in early 2000, he teamed up with ?uestlove of The Roots, who executive-produced the project. The album also features an appearance by **MC Lyte** on the track, "A Film Called Pimp." With MCA's greater promotional muscle, a more spiritual tone, and radio-friendly singles such as "Sixth Sense" and the Grammy Award-nominated "The Light," Common attracted a wider audience and earned his first gold album. Unfortunately, the next album, 2002's *Electric Circus* (MCA), met with mixed reviews. The rock-infused album was deemed as creatively extending the range of rap music, by some fans, while more traditional fans found the effort an odd and jumbled collection.

DISCOGRAPHY: *Can I Borrow a Dollar?* (Combat Records, Relativity Records, 1992); *Resurrection* (Relativity Records, 1994); *One Day It'll all Make Sense* (Relativity Records, 1997); *Like Water for Chocolate* (MCA, 2000); *Electric Circus* (MCA, 2002).

COMPTON'S MOST WANTED. *See* MC Eiht

CONSCIOUS RAP

Traditionally, conscious rap music is described as music that incorporates themes of social justice and community upliftment. Conscious rap may also discuss the deleterious effects of materialism, criminality, drugs, and politics within the context of Black empowerment. Moreover, unlike the other types of rap music genres, which have been said to denigrate Black women and focus on sex, generally conscious rap portrays Black women in a positive light and supports functional interpersonal relationships. Nonetheless, conscious rap artists have not been above criticism. Artists have been brought to task for an array of concerns, including lyrics that are considered antigay or seem to advocate marijuana use. The personal lives of the artists have also come under question, particularly the issue of being unwed parents.

COOLIO [Artis Ivey Jr.]

Best known for his gravity-defying braids, Coolio combined Hip Hop party music with thoughtful insights on urban life. Before pursuing his music career, Coolio overcame an addiction to crack cocaine and spent time in jail for larceny after being convicted of attempting to cash a stolen money order. A resident of the notoriously dangerous South-Central and Compton neighborhoods of California, Coolio had associated with gangs, but the asthmatic child was a bookworm and not a gangbanger.

After graduating from high school Coolio attended Compton Community College, at which time he began performing raps in local contests. During one such event he was tagged with the name "Coolio Iglesias." Coolio became a regular on Los Angeles rap radio station **KDAY**, and he independently released the single "Whatcha Gonna Do," which is acknowledged to be one of earliest rap records out of Los Angeles. Unfortunately, Coolio's addiction to crack curtailed his budding music career. After completing drug rehab, he took a job as a firefighter in the forests of northern California.

Coolio returned to Los Angeles, and while trying to get back into music, he worked several odd jobs, including security at Los Angeles International Airport. He then released his second independent single, "You're Gonna Miss Me," which, like the first, was a failure. While making connections in the Los Angeles rap scene, Coolio eventually met WC and the Maad Circle. Subsequently, he appeared on their 1991 debut album *Ain't a Damn Thang Changed*. Thereafter and as a member of the collective called the 40 Thevz, he signed a deal with Tommy Boy Records. With the help of DJ Brian "Wino" Dobbs, Coolio recorded his 1994 debut album *It Takes a Thief* (WEA Int'l). Among a field of twenty-year-old rap artists, Coolio was nearly thirty when *It Takes A Thief* was released. The lead single "County Line" humorously detailed the humiliations of being on public assistance, but the standout track was "Fantastic Voyage," a rap version of the funk classic by Lakeside. The album was a smash, selling platinum on the strength of the single "Fantastic Voyage." Although a host of producers and songwriters worked on the album, it had the feel of a personal, yet accessible, collection of danceable rap that inextricably linked Coolio with good times.

His sophomore effort *Gangsta's Paradise* (Tommy Boy Records, 1995) provided a similar mix. The title track appears on the *Dangerous Minds* film soundtrack and became 1995's biggest single. The track is especially unforgettable because of its choral production, a result of Coolio teaming up with gospel-trained singer L.V. The backdrop for "Gangsta's Paradise" is Stevie Wonder's single "Pastime Paradise" from the album *Songs in the Key of Life*. Uncharacteristic of Coolio, "Gangsta's Paradise" is a powerful song that depicts the bleakness of the ghetto. In 1996, the track won him a Grammy Award for Best Solo Rap Performance.

Unfortunately, Coolio's career appears to have peaked with the triple platinum *Gangsta's Paradise*. In 1997, Coolio released the album *My Soul* (Tommy Boy Records), but changes in consumer tastes resulted in poor record sales. In the next few years Coolio would have several run-ins with authorities, including a 1999 gun conviction that netted him ten days in jail and forty hours of community service. Five years after the release of *My Soul,* Coolio released the album *El Cool Magnifico* on the independent label Riveria.

Coolio has recorded songs for several film soundtracks, including *Clueless* (1995), *Panther* (1995), *New Jersey Drive* (1995), *The Jerky Boys* (1995) *and Space Jam* (1996). He also penned the theme song for the

Keenan and Kel television program. In 1999 Coolio became the host of B.E.T.'s *Madd Sports* television program.

More recently Coolio won NBC's *Celebrity Fear Factor* reality show and earned $50,000 for his charity. He also won Fox's *Celebrity Boot Camp*'s top prize. Coolio has appeared on *The Weakest Link*, guest-starred on the WB's *Charmed,* HBO's *Arliss*, and was featured on MTV's reality special *Flipped.*

Coolio transitioned to films, securing small roles in *The Big Payback, In Pursuit, Leprechaun in the Hood, Judgment Day, Dear God*, and *Daredevil.*

DISCOGRAPHY: *Singles*: "Whatcha Gonna Do?" (independent release); "You're Gonna Miss Me" (independent release). *Albums*: *It Take's a Thief* (WEA Int'l, 1994); *Gangsta's Paradise* (Tommy Boy Records, 1995); *My Soul* (Tommy Boy Records, 1997); *El Cool Magnifico* (Riviera/D3, 2002).

"COP KILLER"

Body Count's controversial single "Cop Killer" was fronted by rap artist **Ice-T**. The single appears on the group's eponymous 1992 debut album released by Warner Bros. Records.

See also: Censorship

COUP, THE

The Coup, an Oakland-based rap duo with "Boots" Riley [Raymond Riley] and DJ Pam [Pam Warren] formed in the early 1990s, gained international recognition for the cover art on their fourth album, *Party Music* (75 Ark/Tommy Boy Records, 2001), a fictional depiction of the World Trade Center exploding.

The Coup released their debut album, *Kill Your Landlord* on Wild Pitch Records in 1993. The duo's confrontational political rap quickly earned them nationwide praise and respect from critics and fans alike. They next released *Genocide and Juice* (Wild Pitch, Capitol Records, 1994), another scathing political tome. After a four-year hiatus, the Coup returned in late 1998 with their third full-length album, the provocatively titled *Steal This Album* (Dogday, 1998).

The original cover art for the duo's fourth album, *Party Music* (75 Ark/Tommy Boy Records, 2001), unintentionally prefigured the World Trade Center calamity. According to Boots Riley the pictures were taken on May 15, 2001, and the final version was completed by the beginning of June. The cover art was supposed to be a metaphor for destroying capitalism. The Coup did not condone the September 11th attacks or terrorism, but when WEA [Warner/Elektra/Atlantic] objected to distributing the album as planned, the duo was adamant about keeping the cover.

DISCOGRAPHY: *Kill Your Landlord* (Wild Pitch, 1993); *Genocide and Juice* (Wild Pitch, Capitol Records, 1994); *Steal This Album* (Dogday, 1998); *Party Music* (75 Ark/Tommy Boy Records, 2001).

CRAZY LEGS [Richie Colón]

Invited to join **Rock steady Crew** in 1979 by founders JoJo and Jimmy D, Crazy Legs later became president and, arguably, its most famous member. Crazy Legs performed in many of the early Hip Hop tours, which established the culture. He has also appeared in such films as *Flashdance*, *Beat Street*, *Wild Style*, and *Style Wars*. He participated in the Peabody award-winning documentary, *Dance in America: Everybody Dance Now*, and in the "Great Performances 20th Anniversary Special." Crazy Legs also danced in a tribute to the Nicholas Brothers at the Kennedy Center. In 1991, he won the Bessie Award for choreography and in 1994 ***The Source***'s Hip Hop Pioneer Award. Crazy Legs is currently running his production company, Backspin Productions, and doing media consultation work.

CREW

Crew refers to a tight-knit group of friends and associates. A similar term is *posse*.

CRIMINALZ, THE

A rap supergroup formed with West Coast artists: Celly Cel, Spice 1, and **Jayo Felony**, The Criminalz released only one album, *Criminal Activity* (2001), on Celly Cel's Realside record label. Notably, although Jayo Felony performs throughout the album, only Celly Cel and Spice 1 appear on the album cover.

CROSS FADER

A cross fader is a machine that allows a **DJ** to segue from one record to the next seamlessly. The verb form is to cross fade.

See also: Mixer

CRUNK; CRUNKING

A type of high energy rap music that features bass-heavy beats and frenetic chanting, crunk originated in the Southern United States. **Lil Jon and The Eastside Boyz** helped to expand the popularity of this club-friendly music. Crunk is also a Southern slang term thought to derive from combination of the words "crazy" and "drunk." Others attribute the slang to an abbreviation for "cranked" or "cranked up." In any case, the word can be used as a noun, adjective, or verb. It can mean hype, phat, or excellent; or to have a good time; or to get drunk.

CYPRESS HILL

Comprised of Sen Dogg [Senen Reyes], B-Real [Louis Freese], and DJ Muggs [Lawrence Muggerud], the Cypress Hill trio from Los Angeles rose to fame not only because of their laid-back beats and tales of drugs and guns, but also because of their advocacy of marijuana. Tracks such as " I Wanna Get High, "Legalize It," and "Insane in the Brain" made them seem like the Hip Hop–era poster children for NORML (National Organization To Reform Marijuana Laws).

The original crew, DVX, was formed in 1988 by Sen Dog and his younger brother, Mellow Man Ace, and included former 7A3 members DJ Muggs and B-Real. When Mellow Man Ace left to start a solo career, the remaining trio renamed themselves Cypress Hill, after a street in South Central Los Angeles. (In 1994 Eric Bobo would join the group as percussionist.) Many have credited the group with producing Latin West Coast rap music; however, although MC Sen Dog hails from Cuba and MC B-Real is Mexica–Cuban, producer DJ Muggs is actually an Italian-American originally from New York City.

The trio's 1991 self-titled debut was initially only available in the UK as a import, but it created a buzz in the United States with the tracks "How I Could Just Kill a Man," "Hand on the Pump," and "Real Estate."

Cypress Hill. *Courtesy of Photofest.*

When released by Columbia, *Cypress Hill* would eventually go platinum. Unlike other groups with political messages or gangsta tales, Cypress Hill was a proponent of marijuana-induced escapism, a sentiment particularly appealing to alternative rock audiences. In 1993, the trio released their second album *Black Sunday* (Columbia), which debuted at number 1 on both R & B and Pop charts. The album contained the crossover hit, "Insane in the Brain," and also "Cock the Hammer" which appeared on the soundtrack for Arnold Schwarzenegger's film, *Last Action Hero*.

Cypress Hill's reputation for violent lyrics intensified when they appeared on the soundtrack for another movie, *Mad Dog and Glory*, accompanying a scene that involves a drug killing. The group responded that that they were not promoting violence, only interpreting what was happening. Cypress Hill also recorded tracks with the rock bands Pearl Jam ("Real Thing") and Sonic Youth ("I Love You Mary Jane") for the movie *Judgment Night*. With their third album, the moody, trip-hoppy *III: Temples of Boom* (Columbia, 1995), Cypress Hill lost college radio fans, but regained fans in the Hip Hop base.

In 1996, Sen Dog left the group to work with his punk–metal band SX-10 and was replaced by DJ Scandalous, who had already worked with the crew. *Unreleased and Revamped* (Columbia, 1996) followed, an EP of rare **remixes**, and then solo projects, with Muggs releasing "*Muggs Presents ... The Soul* Assassins *Chapter 1* and B-Real working with the Psycho Realm. Sen Dog rejoined Cypress Hill for their 1998 release *Cypress Hill IV*, which, although artistically sound, nonetheless failed to break into the U.S. Top 10. The double album *Skull & Bones* (Columbia, 2000) was divided equally between traditional rap music and more crossover-friendly music. Cypress Hill continued to migrate more into the realm of rap-rock on the albums *Stoned Raiders* (Columbia, 2001) and *Till Death Do Us Part* (Columbia, 2004).

DISCOGRAPHY: *EPs*: *Unreleased and Revamped* (Columbia, 1996). *Albums*: *Cypress Hill* (Columbia, 1991); *Black Sunday* (Columbia, 1993); *III: Temples of Boom* (Columbia, 1995); *Cypress Hill IV* (Columbia, 1998); *Skull & Bones* (Columbia, 2000); *Stoned Raiders* (Columbia, 2001); *Till Death Do Us Part* (Columbia, 2004).

D

DA BEATMINERZ

Da Beatminerz are DJ Evil Dee [Ewart Dewgarde], Mr. Walt [Walter Dewgarde], Rich Black [*unknown*], Baby Paul [*unknown*], and Chocolate Ty [*unknown*]. The production team, led by brothers DJ Evil Dee and Mr. Walt, became known for their boom bap sound, heavy on bass, kick drums, and snares. Though perhaps underrated, their contribution to rap music is undeniable.

Da Beatminerz sound can be described in one word—*grimy*. According to DJ Evil Dee, the best known of Da Beatminerz, "Songs that are too perfect lack warmth." He adds, "I like to keep music real." DJ Evil Dee had gained fame as a member of the rap group **Black Moon**; however, all the members honed their skills individually before joining forces in the late 1990s. Evil Dee's older brother, Mr. Walt, met Baby Paul at the record store, Music Factory in Jamaica, Queens, where he worked. During this period Evil Dee befriended Chocolate Ty, who has been part of the Shades of Brooklyn crew, and Rich Black who lived in his neighborhood and had been down with the Pitch Black.

Da Beatminerz would officially come together as producers for Black Moon's debut album, *Enter Da Stage* (Nervous Records, 1993). Two years later, their superior production skills would help the Smif-N-Wessun (later renamed Cocoa Brovaz) debut album, *Da Shining* (Wreck Records, 1995), receive critical praise. Da Beatminerz have done production for Boot Camp Clik (comprised of Buckshot of Black Moon, Cocoa Brovaz aka Smif-N-Wessun, Heltah Skeltah & OGC).

The production crew has worked with a host of artists including D'Angelo, **Dilated Peoples**, Joe, **Mos Def**, **Rah Digga**, **The Roots**, **Flipmode Squad**, **Nas**, **Talib Kweli**, and **Eminem**. After producing beats for a who's who of artists, Da Beatminerz released their debut album *Brace 4 Impak* (Rawkus, 2001). The album included collaborations with The Last Emperor, Flipmode Squad, Apani B. Fly, **Freddie Foxxx**, **Pete Rock**, Talib Kweli, **Naughty By Nature**, **Jayo Felony**, **Heather B**, Shades of Brooklyn, Lord Tariq, and others. The Beatminerz are also behind "Hot Sh*t," a twelve-inch single (D & D/Fat Beats, 2001) with appearances by **Big Daddy Kane**, Guru (**Gang Starr**), Sadat X (**Brand Nubian**), and Greg Nice. Mr. Walt produced the original version, while DJ Evil Dee did the **remix**. A second Da Beatminerz album, *Fully Loaded With Static* (Copter Records), originally slated for a 2004 release is rescheduled for first quarter 2005.

DISCOGRAPHY: *Singles*: "Hot Sh*t" (D & D/Fat Beats, 2001). *Album*: *Brace 4 Impak* (Rawkus, 2001).

DA BRAT [Shawntae Harris]

Da Brat, a native of Chicago, Illinois, became the first solo female rap artist to sell platinum with her 1994 album *Funkdafied* (So So Def). *Funkdafied* debuted at number 1 on the *Billboard* rap chart and also broke into the Top 20 of the Hot 200. The title single, which used a sample from the Isley Brothers classic "Between the Sheets," also went platinum and topped the rap single charts for eleven weeks.

Da Brat hit the rap music Hip scene in 1992 after winning a local rap competition sponsored by the cable television show, ***Yo! MTV Raps***. The contest prize was a meeting with the successful youth rap duo, **Kris Kross**. Kris Kross introduced Da Brat to their manager, **Jermaine Dupri**, who immediately signed her to his So So Def label.

Rather than exerting an overtly sexual persona, Da Brat at first was tomboyish and playful, with oversized pants and braids. Da Brat's hard-hitting rap style was cushioned by laid-back G-Funk rhythms. Her 1996

Da Brat. *Courtesy of Photofest.*

sophomore album, *Anuthatantrum*, attempted to put to rest critics, who had branded her simply another rap artist manufactured by Dupri. The album contained the hit single "Ghetto Love," featuring T-Boz, of the singing group TLC. In 2000, after taking time off to pursue an acting career, Da Brat made a strong comeback with the release *Unrestricted* (So So Def). The rap artist had an acting role in the Mariah Carey film flop, *Glitter*, prior to releasing her fourth album, *Limelite Luv and Niteclubz* (So So Def) in 2003.

DISCOGRAPHY: *Funkdafied* (So So Def, 1994); *Anuthatantrum* (So So Def, 1996); *Unrestricted* (So So Def, 2000); *Limelite Luv & Niteclubz* (So So Def, 2003).

DA LENCH MOB

Da Lench Mob, a West Coast rap trio comprised of Shorty [Jerome Muhammad], J-Dee [Dasean Cooper], and T Bone [Terry Gray], are protégés of former **N.W.A.** front man **Ice Cube**. The group is known for its confrontational messages that deal with social issues facing African Americans.

J-Dee accompanied Ice Cube to New York to record his 1990 album, *AmeriKKKa's Most Wanted* (Priority Records). J-Dee introduced his friend Shorty to Ice Cube, and Shorty toured with Ice Cube, initially as part of his security team during Ice Cube's solo concerts. As a teenager, Shorty had been a member of Los Angeles's notorious Marvin Gangster Crips and served time for robbery. In interviews, Shorty has claimed that Ice Cube not only used his and J-Dee's gang status to legitimize his own street credentials, he also culled aspects of their lives for use his albums.

Two years later, Ice Cube acted as executive producer on the group's gold-selling debut album, *Guerillas in tha Mist* (EastWest, 1992). Hard-hitting tracks such as "Freedom Got an A.K." and "Lost in Tha System" helped the trio to win over rap music fans. The album dealt with the horrors of racism and the ills of urban life, but angered some listeners, who objected to its advocacy of violence toward White people.

In February 1995, J-Dee was sentenced to twenty-nine years to life by a Los Angeles superior court for the 1993 murder of his girlfriend's male roommate. For their second album, *Planet of Da Apes* (EastWest, 1994), Da Lench Mob replaced J-Dee with Maulkie, an Oakland-based artist. Unfortunately, the poorly marketed *Planet of Da Apes* was not well-received by rap fans and the group disbanded soon after. In interviews, Shorty alleged that Ice Cube owed Da Lench Mob 1.5 million dollars and abandoned the group when they were in need.

Shorty independently released a solo album, *Short Stories* (Bow Tie Entertainment/Street Solid, 2002), which is most noted for the track "O'Shea's Great Adventure" that attacks former mentor, Ice Cube as a fake gangsta.

DISCOGRAPHY: *Guerillas in tha Mist* (East/West, 1992); *Planet of da Apes* (East/West, 1994).

DANA DANE [Dana McCleese]

Rap artist Dana Dane is known for light-hearted rhymes and a love of fashion. Dana Dane was raised in the Walt Whitman projects in Brooklyn and first displayed his talent as a member of the Kangol Crew, which Dana Dane and classmate **Slick Rick** formed at New York's High School of Music and Arts.

In 1985, after graduating from high school, Dana Dane signed to Profile Records and the following year he released his first single, "Nightmare." In 1987, he released his gold-selling debut album, *Dana Dane With Fame,* which features the tracks "Cinderfella Dana Dane" and "Delancy Street." Hurby "Luv Bug" Azor, best known for his production work with **Salt 'N Pepa**, produced the album. Dana Dane followed up with the albums *Dana Dane 4 Ever* (1990) and *Rollin' Wit Dane* (1995).

Dana Dane's tastes in clothing inspired him to open the IV Plai Boutique (later closed).

DISCOGRAPHY: *Singles*: "Nightmares" (Profile, 1986). *Albums*: *Dana Dane With Fame* (Profile, 1987); *Dana Dane 4 Ever* (Profile, 1990); *Rollin' Wit Dane* (Warner Bros. Records/Maverick, 1995).

DAPPER DAN

Before there was such a thing as "urban wear," there was Dapper Dan, the most famous name in Hip Hop fashion. In the 1980s this Harlem haberdasher custom-tailored clothing and accessories for the glitterati of New York City, among them rap artists, street hustlers, and a few downtown hipsters. Dapper Dan was famous for his leather products, such as the Gucci suits donned by **Eric B & Rakim** on the cover of their 1987 album, *Paid in Full.* Among sneaker aficionados, he won kudos for his Air Force Ones with the Louis Vuitton swoosh. Long before clothing designers lent their talents to SUV makers, Dapper Dan made Pierre Cardin interiors for the town cars of select clients. Recreating the styles of the 1980s for the **Roc-A-Fella**–produced film, *Paid In Full* (2002), Dapper Dan made two outfits for **Cam'ron**'s character Rico.

DAS EFX

Das EFX, the rap duo of Dray [Andre Weston] and Skoob [William Hines], are known for their Hip Hop scatting, producing rap songs made almost entirely of sounds.

Dray (from suburban Teaneck, New Jersey) and Skoob (from Brooklyn, New York) were juniors at Virginia State University when they entered a rap contest in Richmond on January 31, 1991. The judges for the contest were **EPMD**. The duo did not win the contest, but EPMD offered the duo an opportunity to perform professionally. Das EFX joined the Def Squad crew and signed with EastWest Records. The duo commuted between Virginia and New York as they worked on their debut album. They also mailed tapes to EPMD (on tour at the time), for their input.

In 1992, Dax EFX released the landmark album *Dead Serious*, which included the hit single, "They Want EFX." The single was both a Top 40 pop hit and a Top Ten R & B hit, and helped push sales of *Dead Serious* beyond platinum status. Not wanting to be pigeonholed as a novelty act, Das EFX changed their style on their second album, *Straight Up Sewaside* (EastWest, 1993), slowing down and de-emphasizing the sound effects. The sophomore effort, however, went only gold. Their third album, *Hold It Down* (EastWest, 1995) met with even less success. During this period, Dax EFX got caught in the crosshairs of the EPMD's acrimonious break-up, which led to a three-year hiatus. In 1998, the duo returned with the album *Generation Das EFX* (Elektra) but then faded again from the rap music scene until, in 2003, they resurfaced with the album *How We Do* (RT/Utr Music).

DISCOGRAPHY: *Dead Serious* (EastWest, 1992); *Straight Up Sewaside* (EastWest, 1993); *Hold It Down* (EastWest, 1995); *Generation Das EFX* (Elektra, 1998); *How We Do* (RT/Utr Music, 2003).

DAVY DMX [David Reeves]

David Reeves named himself Davy X after the Oberheim drum machine. A native of Queens, New York, he made his foray into Hip Hop by DJing locally. Davy DMX is credited with using Trouble Funk's single "Pump Me Up" to create the first sample loop.

In the 1980s as a guitarist he was a founding member of the band Orange Krush, which backed several tracks for **Run DMC**, Sweet G, and **DJ Lovebug Starski**. After the band broke up, he worked with **Kurtis Blow** as a DJ and guitarist, providing important contributions to the tracks "The Breaks" (1980) and "If I Ruled the World" (1985). His 1984 debut solo single, "One for the Treble" (Tuff City), became a Hip Hop classic. That single, coupled with the 1985 follow-up single "The DMX Will Rock" (Tuff City), helped to solidify him as a solo artist. In 1987, he released a full-length **Def Jam Recordings** album, *Davy's Ride*.

Apart from his production work, Davy DMX also appeared as a member of a comic group, The Afros, which was an offshoot of another group called Solo Sounds. In 1995, Old School Flava/Tuff City released a collection of four-track recordings called *FFFresh*, but without Davy DMX's knowledge.

DISCOGRAPHY: *Singles*: "One for the Treble" (Tuff City, 1984); "The DMX Will Rock" (Tuff City, 1985). *Albums*: *Davy's Ride* (Def Jam Recordings, 1987).

DEADLY VENOMS

The first female group connected to the **Wu-Tang Clan**, The Deadly Venoms are comprised of Champ MC (aka Shorty the Scorpion), Finesse (aka Chameleon), J-Boo (aka Viper), N-Tyce (aka Poison) [Amma Brown], and Lin Que (aka Isis) [Lin Que Ayoung]. The members of Deadly Venoms initially established careers as solo artists. Finesse is one-half of the late 1980s female duo, Finesse and Synquis, who released the album *Soul Sisters* (Uptown/MCA, 1988). J-Boo, N-Tyce, and Champ MC appeared on **Kurupt**'s 1998 double album, *Kuruption* (A&M Records). MC Champ also released several singles as a solo artist, including "Funhouse" (EastWest, 1994) and "Keep on the Real" (EastWest, 1994). N-Tyce came out in 1995 with the Father MC–produced single, "Sure Ya Right" (Wild Pitch). Lin Que, a former **X-Clan** member known for her lyrical skills, had brief success as a solo artist and released the album, *Rebel Soul* (1990), under the name Isis.

The Deadly Venoms were originally signed to A&M Records and had planned to release an album called *Antidote* in 1998. Although the album had been recorded, disputes with the label forced its cancellation. The Deadly Venoms subsequently signed to DreamWorks Records and in 2000 completed a new album, titled *Pretty Thugs*. They hit another streak of bad luck, however, advance copies of *Pretty Thugs* were leaked to the public, but the album was never commercially released.

DEAD PREZ

M-1 (aka Mutulu Olugbala) [Lavon Alfred] and Stic.man (aka Stic, aka Khnum Olubala) [Clayton Gavin] make up rap duo, Dead Prez, best known for their politicized rap with a defiant Black Power message.

The two men met in 1990 while at Florida A&M University. M1, a native of Jamaica, West Indies, grew up in Brooklyn, New York; Stic.man, in Florida. The scourge of drugs had personally touched both men, and as a result they became involved with Tallahassee's Black Survival Movement. Their activism eventually brought them to New York City and it was there that Lord Jamal (**Brand Nubian**) discovered them in 1995 at a Brooklyn block party. By 1996, Lord Jamal had helped Dead Prez to secure a recording contract with Loud Records.

Dead Prez has maintained that their music is a platform to address issues such as racism and economic injustice. Dead Prez debuted on Loud Record's '97 compilation *'97 Set Up* with the track "Food, Clothes, And Shelter," and gained more attention with the 1998, twelve-inch single, "Police State with Chairman Omali" (Loud Records/RCA). The track "Police State" discusses police brutality. In 2000, Dead Prez released their debut album, *Let's Get Free* (Loud Records/RCA), to widespread praise. The track "It's Bigger Than Hip-Hop," which critiqued the genre's crass materialism, and "Police State" helped to strengthen the demand for the album. Controversy arose, however, when Loud Records censored Dead Prez by slapping a parental advisory sticker on the CD cover. Loud Records thought that the image of South Africa youth, carrying rifles, during the celebration of an uprising against police in a township was problematic. The duo's political messages also caused them to be virtually banned from performing in clubs in New York City.

Dead Prez continued their activism through involvement in the National People's Democratic Uhuru Movement and by distributing the *Burning Spear* newspaper on New York's subway trains. In 2003, Columbia Records (who had acquired the artists when Loud Records folded) dropped Dead Prez, reportedly for low record sales: their debut sold 300,000 copies in the United States. Dead Prez released a two-volume **mixtape** project, *Turn Off the Radio: The Mixtape, Vol. 1* (Full Clip, 2002) and *Turn Off the Radio: The Mixtape, Vol. 2: Get Free or Die Tryin'* (Landspeed, 2003). The album title is perhaps a dig at **50 Cent**'s album title, *Get Rich or Die Tryin'*. The duo re-signed to Columbia Records and released *RBG: Revolutionary But Gangsta* in 2004.

DISCOGRAPHY: *Singles*: "Police State with Chairman Omali" (Loud Records/RCA, 1997). *Albums*: *Let's Get Free* (Loud Records, 2000); *Turn Off the Radio: The Mixtape, Vol. 1* (Full Clip, 2002); *Turn Off the Radio: The Mixtape, Vol. 2: Get Free or Die Tryin'* (Landspeed, 2003); *RBG: Revolutionary But Gangsta* (Columbia, 2004).

DEATH ROW RECORDS (aka Tha Row)

The quintessential **gangsta rap** label, Death Row Records blurred the line between art and reality, crime and business. Perceived as a record company run like a gang, or perhaps the other way around, Death Row seemed to confirm the public's worst fears about young Black men. The company nonetheless produced some of the most talented and controversial rap music artists of recent time. Ex-bodyguard Marion "Suge" Knight and former **N.W.A.** member **Dr. Dre** founded Death Row Records in 1993. The first major release for the label was the soundtrack for the 1992 film *Deep Cover*, which introduced Hip Hop audiences to Dr. Dre and to **Snoop Doggy Dogg**. The label's roster has included rap music luminaries such as Dr. Dre, Snoop Doggy Dogg, and **Tupac Shakur**. Beginning in 1995, Suge Knight initiated a bi-coastal feud with the East Coast's **Sean "P. Diddy" Combs**, head of **Bad Boy Entertainment** by ridiculing him at the Source Awards. In a direct reference to Combs, Knight told that audience that if they did not want record execs in their videos, they should sign with Death Row. The Death Row empire seemed invulnerable until the spring of 1996, when Dr. Dre grew frustrated with Knight's management style.

During this period Death Row was focused on Tupac Shakur's debut, the historic double album, *All Eyez on Me* (1996), and Snoop Doggy Dogg had just been acquitted of a murder charge related to a drive-by shooting. In an acrimonious split, Dr. Dre left the label in the summer of 1996 to form Aftermath, declaring gangsta rap dead. In September 1996 Tupac Shakur, who was in a car with Suge Knight, died of injuries from a drive-by shooting in Las Vegas.

In 1997, Dr. Dre's absence was being felt and Death Row sales fell. By the end of the year, Knight was imprisoned on racketeering charges and in 1998 Snoop Doggy Dogg had jumped ship for No Limit Records. During Knight's imprisonment, the record label struggled to stay afloat. In August 2001, Knight was released from prison; however, his continued run-ins with the law over alleged parole violations have not helped to reestablish Death Row as a viable record label.

DEE, WANDA

In the 1980s, when female rap artists were wearing little makeup sneakers, jeans, gold chains, and sweatsuits like the boys, the attractive Wanda Dee prefigured **Lil' Kim** by using a sexually charged, high glamour persona. The daughter of singer Freda Payne, Wanda was born in Harlem, New York, and raised in the Bronx.

Unlike today's cavalier attitude toward sexually provocative female rap artists, during one of her first performances in New York, Wanda Dee was booed off stage as audience members threw coins at her to imply that she was a prostitute. Moreover, other female rap artists were dismissive of her as promoting sex rather than lyrical skills with her revealing outfits. In the lyrics to her 1989 twelve-inch single "To The Bone," which, Wanda tells men to come "divide her and slide into her." On the record cover for the song, Wanda wears a tight leopard-skin body suit, standing before several skimpily dressed musclemen. She is often credited as being the first female Hip Hop DJ, and was the first female rap artist inducted into the **Zulu Nation**.

While still in her teens, Wanda Dee appeared in the film *Beat Street* (1984), which led to a European tour. Signed to Tuff City, she released the single "To the Bone," b/w "The Goddess." She wrote both of the songs. The DJ-turned-recording artist subsequently released *White Room* (Arista/BMG Records), a mélange of Hip Hop, techno, dance, tribal, rock, and pop. The album sold in excess of 15 million units worldwide, going platinum in seventy-seven countries. She went on to be the voice of a techno group, The KLF—after settling a lawsuit against them for **sampling** her hit "To the Bone." In 1990, she appeared in the pay-per-view broadcast, ***Rapmania***, produced by legendary promoter **Van Silk**.

Wanda Dee operates her own label, G.E.R.L. (Goddess Empire Record Label) with Eric Floyd, her husband, creative collaborator, and manager. (Floyd, also an actor, played "Jerome" on the hit television show *Fame*).

DEF

Def is a slang term for very good.

DEFARI [Duane Johnson]

A native of Southern Californi, Defari was a member of the **Likwit Crew** (**Tha Alkaholiks**, **King T**, **Xzibit**), as well as a history teacher at Inglewood High School. Defari commands the microphone with a smooth flow of intelligent lyrics and tight rhymes. He became regarded as a talented rap artist rather than merely a West Coast rap artist.

Defari began as a DJ in 1982, and then in 1987 he left the turntables for the mic. As a rap artist, he released his debut single, "Big Up," in 1995; produced by E-Swift, it was featured on *Next Chapter Compilation* (Immortal Records). In 1997, Defari joined with Evidence of the rap group **Dilated Peoples** and, on ABB Records, dropped the hit singles "Bionic" and "People's Choice." In May of 1998, Defari signed with Tommy Boy Records and became one of the first West Coast rap artists to transcend regional labels. In 1999, Defari released his debut album, *Focused Daily*, which he executive-produced. The result was one of 1999's most talked about albums of the year; an **underground** album with mass appeal. His deal with Tommy Boy Records ended shortly after his album *Focus Daily* was released. In 2003, Defari released his second album, *Odds & Evens*, on High Times Records, owned by the marijuana advocacy magazine of the same name.

DISCOGRAPHY: *Singles*: "Big Up" (Immortal Records, 1995); "Bionic" (ABB Records, 1997); "People's Choice" (ABB Records, 1997). *Albums*: *Focused Daily* (Tommy Boy Records, 1999); *Odds & Evens* (High Times Records, 2003).

DEF JAM RECORDINGS

Def Jam Recordings stands out as the record label most influential in the development of rap music. Through its charismatic leader, **Russell Simmons**, Def Jam Recordings for nearly two decades defined the look and sound of the genre. It was instrumental also in branding Hip Hop for worldwide consumption.

The origin of Def Jam Recordings' empire dates to when rap music promoter Russell Simmons met Rick Rubin, a New York University student. Simmons and Rubin shared a love of raw and street-wise rap music and became business partners. Def Jam Productions, the first incarnation of the Def Jam Recordings empire, managed rap artists and promoted rap music events. The first single to bear the Def Jam logo (and Rick Rubin's NYU dorm as the business address) was **T La Rock**'s "It's Yours"(1984). The song, though produced by Rick Rubin, was not a Def Jam product; at that juncture, Def Jam had no recording division. "It's Yours" was originally recorded and released by Arthur Baker's independent label, Streetwise Records.

Simmons managed rap artist **Kurtis Blow**, and (along with *Billboard* writer, Robert Ford, Jr.) co-wrote Blow's 1979 debut single, "Christmas Rappin'" (Mercury/CBS). Financier J. B. Moore put up the money to record the single. As a result of the success of ***Rapper's Delight*** (Sugar Hill Records, 1979), Def Jam secured a production deal with the Mercury division of CBS records. Through this deal, Blow became the first rap artist have his music distributed by a major record company. In 1982, Simmons's brother's rap group became clients of Rush Management and were given the name **Run DMC**. Run DMC, who initially recorded on Profile Records, would go on to become of the biggest groups in Hip Hop history. Alongside Kurtis Blow and Run DMC, other early clients of Rush Management included **Whodini**, **Dr. Jeckyll and Mr. Hyde**, Sparky D, and Jimmy Spicer.

In 1984, fifteen-year-old **LL Cool J** came to the attention of Rick Rubin and Russell Simmons through a demo tape he had mailed to the Def Jam office. Rather than shopping LL Cool J to other record companies, Rubin and Simmons decided to form a record company of their own. In 1984, the two partners put up $2,500 each and founded Def Jam Recordings. Def Jam then signed LL Cool J to a recording contract. The first official Def Jam Recordings release was LL Cool J's debut single "I Need a Beat" (Def Jam Recordings, 1984).

Over the next few years, Def Jam Recordings would become the preeminent record company in Hip Hop. In 1985, Def Jam signed a reported $1 million distribution deal with CBS records and entered the film industry with the *Krush Groove*. The film was loosely based on Russell Simmons's own career and starred Blair Underwood and Run DMC. In 1987, the dismal Def Jam film *Tougher Than Leather* came to the big screen. Other films would follow, including the 1997 romantic comedy *How to Be A Player*.

In addition to LL Cool J, the Def Jam roster would go on to include **Slick Rick**, **Public Enemy**, the **Beastie Boys**, **EPMD**, **3rd Bass**, **Onyx**, **Warren G**, **Foxy Brown**, **Redman**, **Method Man**, and **DMX**, among others. Rubin left Def Jam in 1988 to form the record company Def American, leaving Simmons the sole head of the company.

Lyor Cohen, a legendary figure known for his brashness, joined Def Jam's management division and would take over the daily operations of Def Jam Recordings. Cohen began his entertainment career running a nightclub in Los Angeles. In the early 1980s, he came to New York and obtained a job with Def Jam's management company, starting as road manager for Run DMC. Cohen became so important to the development of Def Jam Recordings that Simmons gave him equity in the company, which they sold to Universal for $130 million in 1999. When Universal Records merged Def Jam Recordings with Island Records, Cohen was put at the helm as Chairman. After twenty-one years at Def Jam Recordings, Cohen left for Warner Music Group in January 2004, making him responsible for acts far beyond rap.

In 1990, Russell Rush Associates was renamed Rush Communications. Rush Communications houses the various business entities tied to Def Jam and Simmons. In the winter of 1992, Def Comedy Jam debuted as a outgrowth of Rush's syndicated video show, *New Music Reports*.

Kevin Liles, who had joined Def Jam as an intern in 1992, became president in 1998. When LL Cool J threatened to leave, Liles was key to re-signing him. A cross-branding whiz, Liles also forged deals that tied Def Jam in with products ranging from clothing to **video games**. Liles brought a new professionalism to the label, which included establishing regular business hours at the label and implementing new standards by rejecting memos, reports, and other office documents with misspelled words. In July 2004, however, citing internal conflicts with new Island–Def Jam chairman Antonio "L.A." Reid, Liles left Def Jam Recordings. In December 2004, rap artist Shawn "**Jay-Z**" Carter, the cofounder of **Roc-A-Fella Records**, assumed the presidency of Def Jam Recordings.

DE LA SOUL

Posdnous [Kelvin Mercer], Trugoy the Dove [David Jude Joliceur], and Pasemaster Mace [Vincent Lamont Mason Jr.] make up the Long Island–bred trio De La Soul. They originally hail from Brooklyn (Pasemaster Mace, Trugoy) and the Bronx (Posdnous). The name De La Soul is Spanglish (a blend of Spanish and English) for "Of the Soul."

De La Soul have been rap innovators since their 1988 debut single "Plug Tunin'" (Tommy Boy Records). In 1989, the trio released their debut album, *3 Feet High and Rising* (Tommy Boy Records). Produced by **Prince Paul** of **Stetsasonic** fame, it contained the hit singles "Me Myself And I" and "The Magic Number." The album exemplified the new sound of Hip Hop, with its panorama of samples and styles, smart rhymes, and humor. De La Soul's music was less aggressive and more diverse than most of their contemporaries, using not only funk and soul sounds, but also pop, jazz, reggae, and psychedelic. De La Soul's treatment of rap music initially earned them kudos, but they found it difficult to survive as hardcore rap made its ascendancy.

As an expression of artists sharing a common musical vision, De La Soul, along with **Queen Latifah**, **Monie Love**, **A Tribe Called Quest**, and the **Jungle Brothers,** would form the **Native Tongues** posse. Tired of the "hippies of Hip Hop" label they had gained because their debut album promoted peace and love and declared the dawning of "the D.A.I.S.Y. age" (Da Inner Sound, Y'all)—the trio's second album, *De La Soul is Dead* (Tommy Boy Records, 1991), contained harder rhythms and fewer comedic touches.

The release of their second album was delayed for a year in the aftermath of a **sampling** lawsuit leveled against the group by the 1960s rock group the Turtles. The Turtles successfully sued De La Soul for sampling their song, "You Showed Me," on the *3 Feet High and Rising* track "Transmitting Live From Mars." As a result the trio painstakingly cleared the 100 samples used for their second album. The album received mixed reviews. Many critics simple did not favor the trio's new musical direction and panned the album.

Their third album, the 1993 *Buhloone Mindstate* (Tommy Boy Records), was a return to their original style and would be the last one produced by Prince Paul. The album generally received good press, but the popularity of De La Soul had ebbed and it fell quickly off the charts. The same held true for their 1996 album, *Stakes Is High* (Tommy Boy Records), which tried a tougher rap aesthetic but was no match for audiences now buying **gangsta rap**.

De La Soul embarked on an ambitious Art Official Intelligence (AOI) project, which not only helped reinvigorate the trio's reputation, but also proved to be highly innovative. The project's mission was to release three albums in as many years. The trilogy kicked off with the release *AOI: Mosaic Thump* (Tommy Boy Records, 2000), an album that debuted in the Top 10 and earned a Grammy nomination. The next installment, *AOI: Bionix* (Tommy Boy Records, 2001), actually trumps the first with flawless production, hypnotizing beats, and assertive lyrical styling.

In 2002, Warner Music Group, Tommy Boy's longtime partner, acquired the 21-year-old label's recorded music and music publishing, resulting in De La Soul going to Elektra. Elektra opted not to keep the group on their roster, and the trio wanted out of the Warner–Atlantic–Elektra corporate machine. De La Soul ended up at Sanctuary Urban Records Group, run by singer Beyoncé's father, attorney Matthew Knowles. De La Soul's 2004 *The Grind Date* is the first release on Sanctuary Urban, a division of a London-based record label, Sanctuary Records Group. De La Soul entered into a joint venture with Sanctuary that allows them to take on executive roles in the development and promotion of their albums. Critics and fans alike have hailed *Grind Date* as perhaps De La Soul's best album since *Stakes Is High*, giving it kudos for both its production and lyrical content.

The only downside to the current state of De La Soul is that the lack of a large promotion campaign, first at Tommy Boy with *AOI: Mosaic Thump* and *AOI: Bionix* and now at Sanctuary, with *Grind Date*, has resulted in many mainstream rap fans not even knowing that the trio has released these exceptional albums.

DISCOGRAPHY: *Single*: "Plug Tuning" (Tommy Boy Records, 1988). *Albums*: *3 Feet High & Rising* (Tommy Boy Records, 1989); *De La Soul is Dead* (Tommy Boy Records, 1991); *Buhloone Mindstate* (Tommy Boy Records, 1993); *Stakes is High* (Tommy Boy Records, 1996); *AOI: Mosaic Thump* (Tommy Boy Records, 2000); *AOI: Bionix* (Tommy Boy Records, 2001); *Grind Date* (Sanctuary Urban/Sanctuary Records Group, 2004).

DEL THA FUNKEE HOMOSAPIEN [Teren Delvon Jones]

Although Del Tha Funkee Homosapien, a member of the **Hieroglyphics**, is **Ice Cube**'s cousin, the Oakland, California, native distinguished himself by putting out non–hardcore rap music. Far from being gloomy, Del's rap music is buoyant and fun, and showcases his lyrical dexterity.

Ice Cube helped his seventeen-year-old cousin to get into the music industry. Del signed with Elektra records and released two albums for them, starting with *I Wish My Brother George Was Here* (1991), which was produced by Ice Cube and featured the West Coast signature G-funk sound. On his second album, *No Need For Alarm* (1993), Ice Cube was not on the boards and the music went in a jazzy direction. Unfortunately, *No Need for Alarm* was considered a commercial failure.

Del parted ways with Elektra and independently released the cassette-only album *Future Development* on the Hieroglyphics independent label Hiero Imperium in 1998. Del would go on to work on the Hieroglyphics album, *3rd Eye Vision* (Hiero Imperium, 1998). In 2000, he released his fourth solo album, *Both Sides of the Brain*, with collaborations with **Prince Paul** (**Stetsasonic**) and El-P (Company Flow), as well as production help from Hieroglyphic cohorts A+, Casual, and Domino.

DISCOGRAPHY: *I Wish My Brother George Was Here* (Elektra, 1991); *No Need For Alarm* (Elektra, 1993); *Future Development* (Hiero Imperium); *Both Sides of the Brain* (Hiero Imperium).

DIAMOND D

A member of the **Diggin' in the Crates** crew, Diamond D is both a rap artist and a producer. Although his verbal skills may not be exceptional, his beats are legendary. Diamond D has helped out with several of rap music's most acclaimed albums, including **A Tribe Called Quest**'s *The Low End Theory* (Jive Records, 1991) and the **Fugees** *The Score* (Ruffhouse/Columbia). He was instrumental also in the production of **Fat Joe**'s debut album, *Represent* (1993).

Diamond D recorded his first solo album in 1992, the **underground** classic *Stunts, Blunts & Hip-Hop* (Mercury). Released under the name Diamond & the Psychotic Neurotics, the album sold perhaps only about 300,000 units—but it contained the underground hit single, "Sally Got A One Track Mind," which gained the producer more respect and more work. He has done production for a who's who of rap artists, including **Xzibit**, **Mos Def**, **House of Pain**, **KRS-ONE**, **Pharoahe Monch**, **Freddie Foxxx** (aka Bumpy Knuckles), and **Pharcyde**.

Again as a rap artist, Diamond D released his second album *Hatred, Passion & Infidelity* (Polygram, 1997), which included performances by **Busta Rhymes**, Phife Dawg (A Tribe Called Quest), and **Pete Rock**.

DISCOGRAPHY: *Stunts, Blunts & Hip-Hop* (Mercury, 1992); *Hatred, Passion & Infidelity* (Polygram, 1997).

DIGABLE PLANETS

As the Digable Planets, Doodle Bug [Craig Irving], Butterfly [Ishmael Butler], and Ladybug [Mary Ann Vierra] are best known for their jazz-influenced sound and for the single "Rebirth of Slick (Cool Like Dat)." The members' names came from their admiration for the community structures of ants and insects.

Following in the steps of **De La Soul** and **P.M. Dawn**'s new styled rap, Digable Planets used lyrical wordplay and jazz samples to manifest the D.A.I.S.Y. (Da Inner Soul Y'all) mentality. The trio's integral use of jazz introduced Hip Hop audiences to artists such as Roy Ayers, Curtis Mayfield, Art Blakey, and Herbie Hancock. Departing from their predecessors, Digable Planets interjected a political slant into their productions. Their debut effort, *Reachin' (A New Refutation Of Time And Space)* (Pendulum, 1993) included the track "La Femme Fetal," an attack on the firebombing of abortion clinics. The hit single "Rebirth of Slick (Cool Like Dat)" rocketed the group to Hip Hop prominence, and the trio recreated the jazzy feel of their debut album by touring with live musicians.

The 1994 sophomore album, *Blowout Comb* (Pendulum), lacked a standout single and thus failed to reach the commercial success of their debut. The trio departed ways in 1996. Ishmael Butler reinvented himself as Cherrywine, releasing his debut album, *Bright Black*, in 2003.

DISCOGRAPHY: *Reachin' (A New Refutation Of Time And Space)* (Pendulum, 1993); *Blowout Comb* (Pendulum, 1994).

DIGGIN' IN THE CRATES

Diggin' in the crates refers to **DJ**s and producers looking for old, rare, and unique recordings to incorporate into their new musical creations. Originally, DJs stored and carried vinyl records in plastic milk crates.

DIGGIN' IN THE CRATES CREW (aka D.I.T.C.)

A collective of performers and producers comprised of **Fat Joe**, O.C., **Diamond D**, **Lord Finesse**, **Showbiz & A.G.** and the late **Big L** who worked together under the name Diggin' in the Crates Crew.

DIGITAL UNDERGROUND

An Oakland, California, group comprised of Shock G [Gregory E. Jacobs], Chopmaster [J. Jimi Dight], DJ Fuze [David Elliot], Money-B [Ron Brooks], and Schmoovy-Schmoov [Earl Cook], the Digital Underground is best known for its rap style built on bizarre humor and P-Funk samples. Their use of Parliament Funkadelic samples helped to resurrect the group for a new generation of rap music fans.

The group has featured numerous members, but Shock G has been a constant. The most recognized member of the group is Shock G's alter ego, Humpty Hump, a comical figure who sported large Groucho Marx-style glasses and a weird, stuttering voice. The character was immortalized on the group's single, "The Humpty Dance," from their 1990 debut album, *Sex Packets*.

Shock G with Chopmaster J. formed Digital Underground in 1987, and that year the duo released a single, "Underwater Rimes," which went to number 1 in the Netherlands. In 1989, the group signed with Tommy Boy Records, and that summer "Doowutchyalike" became an **underground** hit. During this period, Digital Underground was expanding its membership and featured DJ Fuze, Money-B, and Schmoovy-Schmoov. In 1990, they released the platinum-selling *Sex Packets* (Tommy Boy Records, 1990). In 1991, they released the gold-selling *This is an EP Release*, the first recording to feature rap artist **Tupac Shakur**, who had began his career as a roadie for the group. Their next EP, *Sons of the P*, went gold on the strength of the single, "Kiss You Back." The release of their third album, *The Body-Hat Syndrome,* in 1993 was a commercial failure; by now, hardcore rap was dominant. Ironically **Dr. Dre**'s production shared an affinity for George Clinton samples.

In 1996, Digital Underground made an anemic return with the album *Future Rhythm* (Radikal/Critique) and followed up in 1998 with *Who Got the Gravy?* (Interscope Records) and in 1999 with *Lost Files* (Little Butta).

DISCOGRAPHY: *Sex Packets* (Tommy Boy Records); *This is an EP Release* (Tommy Boy Records, 1991); *Sons of the P* (Tommy Boy Records, 1991); *The Body-Hat Syndrome* (Tommy Boy Records, 1993); *Future Rhythm* (Radikal/Critique, 1996); *Who Got the Gravy?* (Interscope Records, 1998); *Lost Files* (Little Butta, 1999).

DILATED PEOPLES

Like their fellow travelers **Jurassic 5**, **Freestyle Fellowship**, and **Hieroglyphics**, Dilated Peoples specializes in beats, rhymes, and production that is reminiscent of an old-school aesthetic.

The Los Angeles trio of DJ Babu [Chris Oroc] and MC-lyricists Evidence [Michael Peretta] and Rakaa-Iriscience [Rakaa Taylor] came together in 1992. The two MCs Evidence and Iriscience first met through **freestyle** sessions at the Hip Hop Shop. In 1993, the two signed a deal with Immortal–Epic, but that went south, leaving shelved a completed recording with cuts from a then-unknown DJ Homicide (Sugar Ray). In 1995, Evidence and Iriscience went the independent label route and released several popular twelve-inch releases on Oakland's ABB Records. The two eventually joined up with DJ Babu, a former member of "The Beat Junkies."

Dilated Peoples released several singles, including the 1997 "Third Degree" (featuring **Defari**) and the 1998 KutMasta Kurt–produced single, "Work The Angles." That single (which featured spots by artists such as **A.G.**, Defari, and **Xzibit**) landed on massive numbers of **mixtapes** worldwide. The 1999 follow-up, "Rework the Angles," included **remixes** of the original track. The long bubbling buzz on this **underground** group led Capitol Records to sign them, and in May 2000 they released the first full-length album, *The Platform*. The trio followed up in 2001 with the album *Expansion Team* (Capitol Records). The sophomore effort featured the talents of **DJ Premier**, ?uestlove (**The Roots**), JuJu (**The Beatnuts**), **Da Beatminerz**, and Alchemist. Their third album, *Neighborhood Watch* (Capitol Records, 2004) received production help from **Kanye West** and Alchemist.

In addition to his Dilated Peoples duties, DJ Babu has also released solo recordings, including 1997's *Wild Stylus*, 2002's *Duck Season*, and 2003's Duck Season 2.

DISCOGRAPHY: *The Platform* (Capitol Records, 2000); *Expansion Team* (Capitol Records, 2001); *Neighborhood Watch* (Capitol Records, 2004).

DISCO DADDY AND CAPTAIN RAP. *See* "Gigolo Rap"

DISCO FEVER

Possibly the most famous of the early venues for Hip Hop, Disco Fever in the Bronx, New York, is considered one of the three most important Uptown nightclubs in the development of old-school Hip Hop, alongside **Harlem World** (Manhattan) and **T-Connection** (Bronx). In 1975, veteran bar owner Albert "Allie" Abbatiello bought the original Disco Fever, located at Jerome Avenue and 167th street in the Bronx. Disco Fever was featured in the movie *Beat Street* (1984).

DISCO KING MARIO

The late Disco King Mario did not release any records or produce any records, but he is nonetheless a guiding force as one of Hip Hop's unsung pioneers. A Hip Hop DJ in the 1970s, his parties in the Bronxdale housing projects made him a household name. Disco King Mario and his crew Chuck Chuck City were mainstays in Hip Hop and were mentioned on many of the early **mixtapes**. Many Hip Hop fans familiar with the contributions of **DJ Kool Herc**, **Afrika Bambaataa**, and **Grandmaster Flash** are nonetheless unaware of Mario's influences on the genre, such as the fact that Disco King Mario helped Afrika Bambaataa get started by lending him DJ equipment. During this period, Disco King Mario was at the top of the elite DJs. To put his role into perspective, in earning his DJ stripes the novice Afrika Bambaataa faced Disco King Mario at his first official DJ battle at Junior High School 123 in the Bronx.

D.I.T.C. *See* Diggin' in the Crates

DJ; DJING (aka deejay)

An abbreviation for disc jockey, DJ refers to an announcer at a radio station and also to someone who plays recorded music at a nightclub or party. Within Hip Hop, the DJ is responsible for creating the instrumental portion of the music. Aside from merely playing records, early DJs developed techniques such as **scratching** and backspinning to manipulate and/or alter the sound of recorded music. Similarly early Hip Hop DJs learned to extend the **breakbeat** portions of the songs which was central to the development of **B-boying**. The basic DJ equipment is two turntables, speakers, a **mixer**, and numerous crates of records. Initially the DJ was the focal element of Hip Hop. DJs **Afrika Bambaataa**, **Grandmaster Flash**, and **DJ Kool Herc** are universally recognized as the pioneers of Hip Hop.

DJ CASH MONEY [Jerome Hewlett]

DJ Cash Money was the first inductee into the DJ Hall of Fame sponsored by **Technics**, the turntable manufacturers, in New York. In the 1980s, Cash Money began his career as a DJ in Philadelphia. He was the creator of transformer **scratch**, a turntable technique that allows DJs to mix records rhythmically; this style is still used by many Hip Hop DJs.

DJ CLUE [Ernesto Shaw]

A native of Queens, New York, DJ Clue revolutionized the **mixtape** industry through his ninety-minute compilations of star-studded **freestyles**, innovative blends, and never-heard-before exclusives. Street classics such as the mixtapes *Clue For President*, *Clueminatti*, and *Show Me The Money Part I* and *Part II* have gone round the world and back, serving as an infallible barometer for Hip Hop's hottest productions.

DJ Clue started out in 1989 fronting for a local rap group, MC Drama. After several sessions working on a friend's turntables, Clue realized that he would be better on the wheels of steel than on the mic and so became DJ Clue. After practicing on a pair of Linear-Tech DD 1700s with two copies of the Chic's "Good Times," Clue developed his own style.

In 1990, Clue released his first tape, *Clue #24*. According to Clue, he called it number twenty-four, so that people would assume that he was not new to the game and had twenty-three other mixtapes on the streets. The *Clue #24* tape was originally initially circulated on Jamaica Avenue, one of the main commercial strips in Queens. A DJ Clue tape is easy to recognize, because he tends to shout his name over the intros to tracks.

As Clue's reputation increased, his tapes distribution expanded to independent record stores throughout Brooklyn, Manhattan, and the Bronx. The appeal of Clue's mixtapes was that, unlike other tapes, his contain unreleased material and freestyles recorded live. Over the years, Clue has put out over 100 tapes, each receiving as much anticipation as a major label release and often selling just as well. Clue's first taste of big league success came in 1997, when he began hosting a syndicated show on New York City's Hot 97 (WQHT-FM, 9.1), along with **Funkmaster Flex**. Within a year, he was signed to **Roc-A-Fella Records** and in 1998 released his first major label release, *The Professional*. DJ Clue's fortunes continued to soar after he was the featured DJ on **Jay-Z**'s historically successful "Hard Knock Life" tour, which resulted in his second album, *DJ Clue Presents: Backstage Mixtape,* a commemoration of his role on the tour. In early 2001, DJ Clue released *The Professional Part 2*, which as usual was filled with exclusive material by some of the East Coast's top MCs.

DJ Clue and his manager, Rich Skane, founded their own record label, Desert Storm. Clue also established No Question Entertainment, his own production company, along with partner Ken Duro. Their production credits read like those of a veteran producer, including work with **Noreaga**, **Mase**, **Foxy Brown**, **Nas**, **LOX**, and the Player's Club Soundtrack.

DISCOGRAPHY: *The Professional* (Roc-A-Fella, 1998); *DJ Clue Presents: Backstage Mixtape* (Roc-A-Fella, 2000); *The Professional, Part 2* (Roc-A-Fella, 2001).

DJ DANGER MOUSE [Brian Burton]

The Los Angeles producer DJ Danger Mouse is credited with creating the first full-fledged **mash-up**, the taking of two separate songs and combining them into one. Using ACID Pro music-making software, DJ Danger Mouse created the *Grey Album* in 2004 by blending an a capella version of **Jay-Z**'s *Black Album* (Roc-A-Fella, 2003) with the music of the Beatle's *White Album*. Bootleg copies of the *Grey Album* were being distributed on the Internet, and **Jay-Z**'s lawyers issued the producer a cease-and-desist order. Jay-Z, along with Linkin Park, would go on to record the EP *Collison Course* (Warner Bros. Records, 2004), the first major label release of a high-profile mash-up.

DJ HOLLYWOOD [unknown]

DJ Hollywood is perhaps one of the most underrated and most often forgotten of the Hip Hop pioneers. As a disco DJ in the early to mid-1970s, he became one of the first people to rhyme over beats. He started a lot of the early rap music phrases, such as "Up my back and around my neck" and "Woo-Ha, got the girls in check." DJ Hollywood is widely credited with inventing the term "Hip Hop," although others say it was **DJ Lovebug Starski**.

DJ Hollywood was skillful at mixing **breakbeats**, but unlike his contemporaries, who used eclectic musical sources for the B-boy crowd, he focused on the disco hits played in the clubs. Hollywood gained a large following and went on to headline numerous parties, becoming one of Hip Hop's earliest celebrities. Around 1979, DJ Hollywood was so famous that his performances were showcased at Harlem's famous Apollo Theater in New York. Unfortunately, like other Hip Hop legends, Hollywood's earliest and most influential performances were not recorded—though they remain etched in the memories of those who attended his parties.

In 1980, DJ Hollywood released a single named "Shock Shock The House" (CBS Records). By the mid-1980s, he had largely faded from the Hip Hop scene, but attempted a comeback in 1986 with the singles "To Whom It May Concern"(Spring Records) and "Hollywood's Message" (Abdull-Akbar Records, Inc.). In 1987, he released the Teddy Riley–produced "Love in the Afternoon" (World to World, Inc.). In 1995, Hollywood again resurfaced, on **Doug E. Fresh**'s album *Play* (Gee Street), on the cut "The Original Old School" along with DJ Lovebug Starski, **Cold Crush Brothers**, and The **Furious Five**. In 1997, he performed on the single "Da Medicine" (Select) with Tha Veteranz, which included DJ Hollywood and Brucie B. More recently, he reunited with DJ Lovebug Starski on the album *Legends of Hip Hop* (Absolut Records, 2003) with Eddie Cheeba.

DISCOGRAPHY: "Shock Shock The House" (Epic/CBS Records); "To Whom It May Concern" (Spring Records, 1986); "Love in the Afternoon" (World to World, Inc.).

DJ JAZZY JEFF AND THE FRESH PRINCE

Two Philadelphia, Pennsylvania, natives, DJ Jazzy Jeff [Jeff Townes] and The Fresh Prince [Willard Smith] are best known for their playful rap

DJ Jazzy Jeff and The Fresh Prince. *Courtesy of Photofest.*

music, and for being the first rap artists to win a Grammy award. The duo was also unique for their time in that, by placing Jazzy Jeff's name first, they gave priority to the DJ rather than to the rap artist, which had become the norm.

Instead of aggressively representing the mean streets of America, these unabashedly middle-class rap artists provided good-humored stories about being teenagers. Not surprisingly, their "PG"-rated image proved a mixed blessing. Some other rap artists assailed them for selling out to White audiences and for ignoring the real problems of Black youth. On the other hand, the duo often toured more than their peers, because promoters believed that there would be less violence at their concerts.

They first performed as a duo in 1986, after separate careers in Philadelphia. That same year, the duo performed at the New Music Seminar, where Jeff placed first in the DJ competition. That win helped DJ Jazzy Jeff and The Fresh Prince secure a recording contract with Jive Records and as a result Fresh Prince turned down his acceptance to the Massachusetts Institute of Technology (M.I.T.). Their first single, the 1986

"Girls Ain't Nothing But Trouble," originally released on Word Up Records, used a sample of the theme from the 1960s comedy *I Dream of Jeannie*, and the humorous video made them an MTV favorite. In 1987, the duo released their first album, *Rock the House* (Word Up), which included their debut single. Based on the success of "Girls Ain't Nothing But Trouble," Jive Records bought the rights to release the duo's material and re-issued the album, which made a strong showing, going gold by selling some 600,000 units.

Stardom came the following year with the double album, *He's the DJ, I'm the Rapper* (Jive Records). With seventeen tracks, *He's the DJ, I'm the Rapper* is perhaps the first double rap album, and also one of the first rap albums to go double platinum. Both albums, but especially the second, found DJ Jazzy Jeff and the Fresh Prince offering rap music about the generation gap along with the routine and funny travails of being a teenager. The popular track "Parents Just Don't Understand" discussed the horror of shopping for school clothes with a mother with no fashion sense. The track made it to number 12 on the singles charts, selling gold, and in 1989 DJ Jazzy Jeff and The Fresh Prince were the first rap artists to win a Grammy award. The duo however boycotted the awards ceremony, because the presentation of their award would not be included in the televised coverage.

By 1989, the duo had far more competition from hardcore rap artists and as a result their release third album, *And in This Corner* (Jive Records) failed to match the success of the prior release. *And In This Corner* went gold off of the steam of the track "I Think I Could Beat Mike Tyson," a piece that pokes fun at a teenager's overactive ego.

The Fresh Prince's performances in the duo's music videos helped to land him the starring role the NBC sitcom, *The Fresh Prince of Bel-Air*, which debuted in 1990. The show was about a working class teenager from Philadelphia who moves to Bel Air, California, to live with his affluent relatives. DJ Jazzy Jeff was given a recurring role as the Fresh Prince's street-wise friend, Jazz; the show ran for six seasons.

In 1991, after taking time off to establish the sitcom, the duo, sparked by the greater public visibility, came back with their biggest hit single, "Summertime," from their album *Homebase* (Jive Records). The song provides an Old School vibe by using Kool and the Gang's 1974 single, "Summer Madness." Featuring outside production, the breezy party track waxed nostalgic about growing up in Philadelphia. The single resonated with all age groups and sold platinum; it became their first and only Top 5 pop hit, peaking at number 4. DJ Jazzy Jeff and the Fresh Prince would also pick up their second Grammy for the song.

In 1993, they released their fourth album, *Code Red*, which sold poorly in the United States. Ironically the single "Boom! Shake the Room" became their first number 1 hit in the United Kingdom. The Fresh Prince decided to focus full time on his acting career, but then returned to rap music as a solo recording artist known as **Will Smith**. DJ Jazzy Jeff meanwhile formed a production company called A Touch of Jazz, and worked as a producer and mixer for several rap artists, including Will Smith as well as R & B singer Jill Scott. In 2002, DJ Jazzy Jeff released his debut solo album, *The Magnificent* (BBE Records), a diverse album of **underground** rap music with house music, R & B, and spoken word.

DISCOGRAPHY: *Singles*: "Girls Ain't Nothing But Trouble" (Word Up, 1986). *Albums*: *Rock the House* (Word Up, 1987; re-issued by Jive Records in 1987); *He's the DJ, I'm the Rapper.* (Jive Records, 1988); *And in This Corner* (Jive Records, 1989); *Homebase* (Jive Records, 1991); *Code Red* (Jive Records, 1993).

DJ JAZZY JOYCE [unknown]

Bronx-born Jazzy Joyce is one of the pioneering female DJs, breaking into DJing in the 1980s. Jazzy Joyce began learning DJing at age eleven, from her cousin Chovie-Chove and DJ Whiz Kid. She later teamed up with The Sweet Trio and in 1986 they recorded the single "Non Stop" (Tommy Boy Records). DJ Jazzy Joyce then joined with MC Sweet Tee and recorded the classic hit, "It's My Beat" (Tommy Boy Records, 1986). DJ Jazzy Joyce continued to DJ, doing live shows, mixtapes, and radio work. Currently, DJ Jazzy Joyce works with DJ Coca Chanel and Angie Martinez on New York City's Hot 97 (WQHT-FM, 97.1) show "Ladies Night," one of the few all-female rap shows on the air.

DJ KAY SLAY [Kenneth Gleason]

The **mixtape** DJ Kay Slay is also known as the "Drama King," because he is the ringmaster of the rap rivalries that he captures on his mixtapes.

Originally from East Harlem, New York, Kay Slay began DJing in 1978 at the age of twelve. He expanded his career in Hip Hop as a **graffiti** writer, using the tag DEZ. Kay Slay appeared in the classic Hip Hop documentaries *Wild Style* and *Style Wars*. In the late 1980s, under pressure from then-Mayor Koch, the New York City Transit Police cracked down on subway graffiti and in the aftermath Kay Slay took up the turntables. As Kay Slay pursued a recording contract and financial stability, he made his way spinning records and releasing mixtapes.

Kay Slay hit the big time in 2001, when the **beef** between rap artists **Jay-Z** and **Nas** play erupted on his mixtapes. Subsequently, mainstream rap artists would send their insults to Kay Slay as part of their marketing and promotions campaigns. Moreover, new artists sent him their disses in the hope that he would include them on his mixtapes and jump-start their careers, the way he did for **50 Cent** in 1999 when he included his track "How To Rob" on a mixtape. Record company **A & R** staff looking for the next big thing would listen to Kay Slay (most recently on his

Thursday night show on New York City's Hot 97 (WQHT-FM). In 2004, Kay Slay joined **Shaquille O'Neal**'s DEJA34 record label, overseeing its A & R department.

DISCOGRAPHY: *Streetsweeper 1* (Sony, 2003); *Streetsweeper 2: The Pain From the Game* (Sony, 2004). The body of work includes thousands of independently released mixtapes.

DJ KEVVY KEV [Kevin Montague]

DJ Kevvy Kev's radio show, *The Drum*, is the second longest running rap music program in the world. Broadcasting from KZSU-FM in Stanford, California, the show airs on Sunday nights from 6 to 9 p.m. (The longest running show is the East Coast's ***Awesome Two*** radio program.)

"The Drum" operates on a completely open-door policy, which means that no person has been turned away, but *The Drum* does not play music that disrespects women or glamorizes the criminal life. In 1989, *The Drum* took a stand against **N.W.A.**'s gangsta-*vérité* masterpiece, *Straight Outta Compton*, refusing to play it. That decision offended the group, and in a memorable on-air moment *Drum* cohost Mookie D took **Eazy E**'s phone call live and offered Eazy explicit directions so that he could deal with him mano a mano; Eazy E declined the invite.

The radio show has been host to a veritable who's who in rap music. The son of an accountant and a stay-at-home mother, Kevvy Kev, is a native of Queens, New York. He attended the prestigious Bronx High School of Science. He began *The Drum* in 1984 as an undergraduate at Stanford University and as a member of the Members Only crew, which included Jonathan Brown, Richard "Rich D" Dwyer, Louis "Easy Lou" Carr, Todd "Todd T" Hosein, Mark "Rockmaster Markski" Hosein, and human **beatbox** Bruce "Casual B" Richardson. The crew exposed the Bay area to a New York-style mix-show format. They scratched and rhymed over records, took calls on the air, and invited guests in to **freestyle**. Most importantly, they were playing records that were big on the East Coast, but virtually unknown on the West Coast.

Kevvy Kev formed a tri-region college radio coalition with Will Strickland in Houston and legendary DJ Bobbito in New York. The three traded tapes and sent artists to each other for guest appearances. Kevvy Kev played Sway and Tech records before Power 92.7 FM's *The Wake-up Show* in Los Angeles ever existed and he had **DJ Q-Bert** as a regular for a while.

DJ KOOL HERC [Clive Campbell]

Known as the "Father of Hip Hop," DJ Kool Herc has maintained a somewhat lower profile than fellow pioneers **Afrika Bambaataa** and **Grandmaster Flash**.

DJ Kool Herc, who immigrated to the United States from Jamaica in 1967, was influenced by the sound systems of his native country. Sound systems are mobile DJ units, complete with turntables and massive speakers. "Toasting," or rapping, was also beginning to take hold in Jamaica during this time.

Herc was known for his DJ setup: twin turntables, a MacIntosh amplifer, and massive Shure speaker columns. In 1973, Herc played his first party, a birthday celebration for his sister in the recreation room located at 1520 Sedgewick Avenue in the Bronx, New York. Herc is credited with being the "Originator of **Breakbeats**," because he was the first DJ to extend the breakbeats by playing two identical records on twin turntables. The breakbeats provided music and inspiration for **B-boying**. Herc jealously guarded the names of records that he played from competitors by going as far as to soak the labels from records. Herc would also begin to "toast" by saying a few words over beats, thus introducing the concept of "rap" to partygoers on the emerging Hip Hop scene.

In 1977, Kool Herc would DJ against an upstart named Afrika Bambaataa at the Webster Avenue Police Athletic League in the Bronx. Despite his innovations in mixing and rapping, Herc nonetheless seemed to retreat from the forefront of Hip Hop around this time. Some of Herc's movement outside of the limelight was a result of him being stabbed one night outside of the Executive Playhouse as he intervened in a fight. Grandmaster Flash, however, is quoted as stating that Kool Herc had limited mixing skills, which would have prevented him from wanting to compete with younger DJs, like himself.

DJ LOVEBUG STARSKI (aka Luvbug Starski) [Kevin Smith]

Born in the Bronx, the legendary DJ Lovebug Starski began his career in 1971, as a record boy for local **DJ**s. After years on the scene, in 1978 Starski became the house DJ at the famed club **Disco Fever**, which was featured in the film *Beat Street*. Soon thereafter, he began DJing at the club **Harlem World**, home to many famous MC **battles** of the time. Some even credit Starski with coining the term "Hip Hop," although the more popular belief is that it was invented by **DJ Hollywood**.

Branching out to vinyl, Starski, recorded his first single, "Gangster Rock," in 1980 (Golden Flamingo Records). He followed up in 1981 with "Dancing Party People" (Golden Flamingo Records) and "Positive Life" (Tay-ster Records) with Harlem World Crew. In 1983, he released the single "You Gotta Believe" b/w "Live at The Fever Disco" (Fever Records), produced by Larry Smith and **Kurtis Blow**. In 1984, he followed up with "Do the Right Thing" b/w "Live at The Fever Part 2" (Fever Records). The 1986 single "Amityville (House On The Hill)" was also a hit.

Starski appeared on the soundtrack for the 1985 film, *Rappin'*, before recording his first CD, *House Rock*, on Epic Records the following year.

A five-year jail sentence curtailed Starski's activities in the late 1980s. In 1995, made a comeback when he appeared on **Doug E. Fresh**'s album, *Play* (Gee Street), on the cut "The Original Old School" with DJ Hollywood, **Cold Crush Brothers**, and **The Furious Five**. Two years later, he performed on the single "Da Medicine" (Select) with Tha Veteranz (DJ Hollywood and Brucie B). In 2002, Lovebug would also appear on the album *Legends of Hip Hop* (Absolut Records, 2002) with DJ Hollywood and Eddie Cheeba.

DISCOGRAPHY: *Singles*: "Gangster Rock" (Golden Flamingo Records, 1980); "Dancing Party People" (Golden Flamingo Records, 1981); "Positive Life" (Tay-ster Records, 1981); "You Gotta Believe" (Fever Records, 1983); "Do the Right Thing" (Fever Records, 1984); "Amityville (House On the Hill)" (Epic, 1986). *Album*: *House Rock* (Epic, 1986).

DJ MAGIC MIKE [Michael Hampton]

DJ Magic Mike is recognized for his contribution to bass music as an artist and as a label owner. A contemporary of **Luther "Luke" Campbell**, he is the first bass music artist to sell gold and platinum, as certified by Recording Institute Association of America (RIAA). *Vibe* magazine called Magic Mike the "Best Platinum Artist You Never Heard of." His work is distinguished from the more polished, pop-oriented productions by its gritty, raw musical texture.

The Hip Hop entrepreneur began his music career as a teenager, spinning records at a roller skating rink and selling **mixtapes**. By the age of fourteen, he was hosting a drive-time radio show in his native Orlando, Florida. After finishing high school, he focused his career on club work and in 1987 debuted on the single "Boot the Booty" (Vision Records). In 1988, he partnered with local promoter Tom Reich, owner of Cheetah Records. Under their new arrangement, Magic Mike released the single, "Drop the Bass" (Cheetah, 1989) with the Royal Posse, which became a regional hit. In 1989, he released his debut album, *DJ Mike and the Royal Posse* (Cheetah Records). Magic Mike would follow up his debut with the largely instrumental 1990 album, *Bass Is the Name of the Game* (Cheetah Records), which sold gold. In 1991, he released the single "Magic Mike Cutz the Record" (Cheetah Records) and also the album, *Ain't No Doubt About It* (Cheetah Records), which would garner Magic Mike more national attention. He would then release the albums *Bass: The Final Frontier* (Magic Records/Cheetah, 1993), *This Is How It Should Be Done* (Cheetah, 1993), and, with the Royal Posse, the album *Represent* (Magic Records/Cheetah, 1994). The two 1993 albums were released on the same day, with the *Final Frontier* album going gold.

Magic Mike continued to release albums throughout the 1990s, but none would reach the same levels of success as his earlier efforts. He has done commercial endorsements for Coca-Cola, Pioneer Electronics, and most recently Shure Electronics. During his career, Magic Mike has also worked with such artists as **Sir Mix-A-Lot**, **2 Live Crew**, and Poison Clan. More recently, he released *Magic's Kingdom* (Restless Records, 2000) and *Bootyz in Motion 2* (Down-Low, 2002).

DISCOGRAPHY: (Includes over seventy works.) *Singles*: "Boot the Booty" (Vision Records, 1987); "Drop the Bass" (Cheetah, 1989); Magic Mike Cutz the Record" (Cheetah Records, 1991). *Selected albums: DJ Mike and the Royal Posse* (Cheetah Records, 1989); *Bass Is the Name of the Game* (Cheetah Records, 1990); *Ain't No Doubt About It* (Cheetah Records, 1991); *Bass: The Final Frontier* (Magic Records/Cheetah, 1993); *This Is How It Should Be Done* (Cheetah, 1993); *Represent* (Magic Records/Cheetah, 1994) (with the Royal Posse).

DJ MARK THE 45. *See* Mark the 45 King

DJ POOH [Mark Jordan]

DJ Pooh began his musical career in the mid-1980s, when he produced **LL Cool J**'s album *Bigger and Deffer* (Def Jam Recordings, 1987). For the next decade, he continued to produce other rap artists, and he also made cameos in films and videos, where he usually accompanied **Ice Cube**.

In 1992, Pooh founded Da Bomb label and he became a highly sought-after producer following his work on **Tha Dogg Pound**'s album, *Dogg Food* (Priority Records, 1995), and on **Tupac Shakur**'s double-album, *All Eyez on Me* (Death Row Records, 1996). In 1995, DJ Pooh came out from behind the boards to costar in the Ice Cube film, *Friday*. In 1997, he executive-produced the compilation album, *Bad News Travels Fast* (Big Beat/Atlantic Records). In 2000, DJ Pooh starred in, wrote, and made his directorial debut with the comedy film *3 Strikes*. In 2001, he again put on his director's hat for the film *The Wash*, starring **Dr. Dre** and **Snoop Dogg**. DJ Pooh co-wrote *Friday After Next,* the sequel to *Friday*, which was released in 2002.

DJ PREMIER. *See* Gang Starr

DJ Q-BERT (aka DJ QBert) [Richard Quitevis]

DJ Q-Bert, recognized as the supreme **scratch** DJ, was a member of the now-defunct Invisibl Skratch Piklz (ISP), a collective of all Filipino-American turntablists. The Bay area native was influenced by an array of musical artists, including trumpeter Miles Davis, pianist Thelonius Monk and electric guitarists, Jimmy Hendrix and Les Paul, and he uses turntables as an instrument to reinterpret their compositions.

Q-Bert became a dominant figure in the DJ scene after winning the titles of the Disco Mixing Club (DMC) USA Champion (1991) and DMC World Champion (1992–1994). He was subsequently asked by the DMC founders to judge the 1995 DMC Championships. In June 1998, Q-Bert, along with fellow ISP member MixMaster Mike, received the DMC DJ Hall of Fame award for outstanding contributions to the competition and, more importantly, to the industry. As one of the most documented DJs in the world, he has been featured in numerous domestic and international publications, including *Urb*, *Details*, *XXL*, *Spin*, *Jazziz*, and the *Bay Area Magazine* (BAM).

Q-Bert also appeared in the documentaries *Hang the DJ* and ***Scratch***, and in *Modulations*, which focuses on the electronic music. In 1996 he contributed to Dr. Octagon's classic album *Octagonecologyst*. November 1998, Q-Bert released his solo debut album, *Wave Twisters Episode 7 Million: Sonic Wars Within the Protons* (G.B.H.). DJ Q-Bert was the only Hip Hop DJ to appear in Apple Computer's "Switch" commercials. In 2002, Q-Bert released his videos *Qbert's Complete Do-It-Yourself. Vol. 1— Skratching* and the follow-up *Qbert's Complete Do-It-Yourself. Vol. 2* (Thud Rumble, 2003).

DISCOGRAPHY: *Wave Twisters Episode 7 Million: Sonic Wars Within the Protons* (G.B.H., 1998).

DJ QUIK [David Blake]

Like fellow rap artists **N.W.A.**, **MC Eiht**, and Compton's Most Wanted, DJ Quik represents his hometown Compton, California. Unlike N.W.A., who focused on the harshness of street life of Compton, DJ Quik's music tends to celebrate the city's lighter side with songs about marijuana, alcohol, and of course women.

DJ Quik. *Courtesy of Photofest.*

DJ Quik began DJing at age of twelve, but it was the popularity of N.W.A. that led him to a career in rap. Quik began making tapes and one landed in the hands of Dave Moss, head of Profile Records Los Angeles office. DJ Quik signed with the label in 1991 and that year released his debut album, *Quik is the Name*. Having MCed, written, produced, and arranged this first album, Quik was often compared to Prince. The album spawned two hit singles, "Born and Raised in Compton" and "Tonite." The album went platinum and the two songs charted Top 20 on *Billboard*'s R & B chart, with "Tonite" being a crossover hit. Quik suddenly rose to the top of the West Coast rap scene. Although he would release successive albums, none reached the stature of the first.

In 1992 Quik released, his second album, *Way 2 Fonky* (Profile), which contained the single "Jus Lyke Compton." In 1995, for his third album, *Safe & Sound*, DJ Quik made Suge Knight his manager and the executive producer of the album. Quik refused to support *Safe & Sound* after battling with Profile Records about withheld royalties and other issues. The album contained disses to MC Eiht, and Quik and MC Eiht continued to trade barbs throughout the early and mid-1990s. In 1998, Profile Records sold its catalog to Arista Records along with the artists' contracts. That year on Arista Records, Quik released the album *Rhythm-Al-Ism*. While a commercial success, Quik fans did not like his new hardcore style. Two years later Arista Records dropped him after his album *Balance & Options* (2000), which peaked at number 18 on the *Billboard* 100, indicating lukewarm support.

Although Quik's MC career was on the wane, he continued to excel as a producer. Huge hit songs such as the 2001 "Buck Bounce" by Eightball & MJG and the 2002 "Addictive" by Truth Hurts featuring **Rakim** helped Quik to recapture some of his former star power. His comeback album, *Under Tha Influence* (Euphonic/Bungaloo, 2002), teams him up with **Dr. Dre**, **Talib Kweli**, and longtime collaborator AMG.

DISCOGRAPHY: *Quik is the Name* (Profile, 1991); *Way 2 Fonky* (Profile, 1992); *Safe & Sound* (Profile, 1995); *Rhythm-Al-Ism* (Arista, 1998); *Balance & Options* (Arista, 2000); *Under Tha Influence* (Euphonic/Bungaloo, 2002).

DJ RED ALERT. *See* Kool DJ Red Alert

DMC/TECHNICS U.S. DJ CHAMPIONSHIPS

Established in 1986, the DMC (Disco Mixing Club) is considered to be the premier DJ competition in the United States and around the world. The competition's format is that each contestant gets six minutes to work with two turntables, a **mixer**, and a mountain of vinyl records that they have preselected. The competitors are judged on technical skill such as beat juggling (moving back and for the between records on different turntables without losing the rhythm) and scratching (moving the needle back and forth on a record to produce a unique sound), on stage presence, and on originality.

DMX [Earl Simmons]

DMX is best known for his trademark bark and for reflective lyrics that focus primarily on the human struggle between good and evil rather than on the street tropes of money and "ho's." Born in Baltimore, Maryland, DMX was raised in Yonkers, New York. DMX's name is taken from the DMX digital sound machine. The moniker is apropos, since DMX initially developed his reputation as a local DJ.

DMX started out as the **beat box** in **freestyle** rap shows, but quickly received more recognition as a rap artist and so changed gears. In January 1991, DMX won ***The Source*** magazine's "Unsigned Hype" award. Subsequently Ruffhouse/Columbia Records released his promo single, "Born Loser," in 1992, but subsequently released him from his contract. Little was heard from DMX until the release of his 1994 independent single "Make a Move," but was convicted of a drug charge that same year. DMX stepped firmly back into the Hip Hop arena with an impressive performance on the **LL Cool J** 1997 track, "4, 3, 2, 1." His unique, gravelly voice then graced tracks by **Mase** ("24 Hours To Live"), The **LOX** ("Money, Power & Respect"), and a **remix** for **Ice Cube** ("We Be Clubbin'—Remix").

Upon signing to **Def Jam Recordings**, DMX released the powerhouse single "Get At Me Dog," in 1988 which was touted as a return to raw street rap. That same year he released his debut album, *It's Dark And Hell Is Hot* (Def Jam Recordings), which entered the U.S. *Billboard* album charts at number 1 and became a national sensation. His aggressive lyrical style had many calling him the successor to **Tupac Shakur**. Seven months later DMX followed up with *Flesh of My Flesh, Blood of My Blood* (Def Jam Recordings). The sophomore effort debuted at number 1 on U.S. charts and stayed there for three weeks during January 1999. This marked the first time in over twenty years that an artist had two

DMX. *Courtesy of Photofest.*

records debut at number 1 within the same year. DMX contributed to the Ruff Ryders' chart-topping album *Ryde Or Die Vol. 1* set, and in 2000 released ... *And Then There was X* (Def Jam Recordings), his third album in two years. Like its predecessors, this multi-platinum album debuted at number 1 on U.S. charts in December 1999.

DMX made his acting debut in the 1998 film *Belly*, with fellow rap artist **Nas**. In 2000, DMX was a scene-stealer in the gangland film *Romeo Must Die*, which starred martial artist Jet Li and the late singer Aaliyah. The following year, in the film *Exit Wounds*, DMX became a bankable star playing a street-wise crime kingpin who teams up with burnt-out cop Steven Seagal to battle police corruption.

In 2001, DMX's fourth album, *The Great Depression* (Def Jam Recordings), proved to be his most thought-provoking work, a reflection of his maturation as an artist. In 2003, DMX released his fifth album *Grand Champ* (Def Jam Recordings), which is claimed was last. The track "Thank You" features a performance by Patti LaBelle. With *Grand Champ*, DMX made history by becoming the first artist to debut at number 1 on the charts with his first five releases.

Also in 2003, DMX returned to films, in *Cradle 2 the Grave*, reteaming with Jet Li. In March 2004, DMX starred in the film *Never Die Alone*, based on the Donald Goines novel of the same name. In this graphic film, DMX stars in the role of King David, a stylish kingpin drug dealer, who returns to his hometown seeking redemption, only to meet a violent death.

Aside from music and film, DMX is also known for numerous run-ins with the law. In 1998, he was cleared of a rape charge after his voluntary submission of DNA samples. Other allegations followed, including gun and stabbing charges, although each one was subsequently dropped. His only convictions have been for fairly minor incidents. In 1999, DMX was charged with an obscenity violation in Trinidad following his concert performance, receiving a fine and a two-day jail sentence. In 2001, DMX served a fifteen-day sentence in New York State for driving without a license and failing to appear in court. In June 2004, DMX was charged with cocaine possession, robbery, and criminal impersonation after trying to steal a car then crashing his own vehicle through a car-park gate at New York's Kennedy International Airport, claiming he was a federal agent. For this, he faced up to seven year in prison. Authorities later brought DMX to Elmhurst Hospital in Queens, New York, after he allegedly became disruptive and appeared disoriented. In connection with his June 2004 charges, DMX pled guilty in December 2004 to driving under the influence and reckless endangerment, and his license was suspended for six months.

DISCOGRAPHY: *Single*: "Born Loser" (Ruffhouse/Columbia, 1992); "Make a Move" (1994). *Albums*: *It's Dark And Hell Is Hot* (Def Jam Recordings, 1998); *Flesh of My Flesh, Blood of My Blood* (Def Jam Recordings, 1998); ... *And Then There was X* (Def Jam Recordings,

2000); *The Great Depression* (Def Jam Recordings, 2001); *Grand Champ* (Def Jam Recordings, 2003).

DOGG POUND. *See* Tha Dogg Pound

DOOR KNOCKER EARRINGS

Oversized gold earrings worn by young women in the 1980s.

DOUG E. FRESH (aka Dougy Fresh) [Douglas E. Davis]

The self-proclaimed Original Human Beat Box, because of his skill in imitating the sound of a rhythm machine, Doug E. Fresh was born in St. Thomas, Virgin Islands, but raised in the Bronx and Harlem, New York. His first appearance came in 1983 on the single "Pass the Budda" (Spotlight), with **Spoonie Gee** and DJ Spivey. His introduction to most rap music fans however came a year later, performing behind the **Treacherous Three** in the film *Beat Street*.

In 1984, he released his solo efforts "Just Having Fun" (Enjoy Records) and "Original Human Beat Box" for Vintertainment. The artist gained attention on the classic 1985 single, "The Show," which was recorded with his Get Fresh Crew, including MC Ricky D (aka **Slick Rick**), along with Barry Bee and Chill Will. Doug E. Fresh matched the rhymes of MC

Doug E. Fresh, middle. *Courtesy of Photofest.*

Ricky D with human sound effects. Rather than being able to capitalize on the success of twelve-inch single "The Show" (with the B-Side "La Di Da Di") and take his place among Hip Hop's superstars, Doug E. Fresh ended up having to sue Reality Records for failing to pay him royalties on the hit song.

In 1986, the Doug E. Fresh sound chip was added to the Oberheim **Emulator**, to provide samples of his **human beat box** talents.

In 1987, he released his first solo album, *Oh, My God!*, which featured the moderate hit "All the Way to Heaven." His second album, the 1988 *The World's Greatest Entertainer*, broke into the *Billboard* charts on the strength of the hit single "Keep Risin' to the Top." Also in 1988, former sidekick Slick Rick would release his album, *The Great Adventures of Slick Rick*, which did comparatively better than Doug's.

In 1992, after a break, Doug E. Fresh released "Doin' What I Gotta Do," on **MC Hammer**'s Bust It label. In 1996, after he was reunited with Slick Rick and signed with Gee Street Records, he made a comeback with the release of the party record "I-Right (Alright)." In 1999, Doug E. Fresh again reunited with Slick Rick on the track "We Turn It Up," from Rick's album *The Art of Storytelling* (Def Jam Recordings).

Doug E. Fresh has lent either his performance or producing skills to a wide range of artists, including **Luke Campbell**, Prince, In Living Color, Kashif, Chico Debarge, Grover Washington, Jr., and most recently **Nas**, appearing on his album *Street Disciplines* (Columbia, 2004). In 2002, Doug E. Fresh stepped away from music to publish his first children's book, *Think Again* (Cartwheel), which tells the story of two kids who initially dislike each other because of their different races, but come to find out they have a great deal in common. The book is the first in the HipKidHop series of "Read and Rap-A-Long" children's stories written by rap stars. Intended for children between the ages of four and ten, the books include a two-track CD single. Doug E. Fresh also lectures at colleges. In June 2004, he participated in the historic first Hip Hop Political Convention in Newark, New Jersey, and modeled after the 1968 Gary Convention.

DISCOGRAPHY: *Singles*: "Just Having Fun" (Enjoy Records, 1984); "Original Human Beat Box" (Vintertainment, 1984); "I-Right (Alright)" (Gee Street, 1996). *Albums*: *Oh, My God!* (Reality, 1987); *The World's Greatest Entertainer* (Reality, 1988).

DOZENS

The term *dozens* refers to verbal insults traded between two participants. "Playing the dozens" has a long history in African American culture, as agile wordplay between both friends and adversaries. Onlookers may find the putdowns humorous, but essentially the winner is the person best at humiliating the other person. The ultimate barb is an insult to the other's mother and saying "Yo' Mama" alone is enough to provoke a fight. This activity has filtered into rap and Hip Hop and is manifested in **beefs** between artists and in actual **battles** taking place during live performances or via recorded music.

DR. DRE [Andre Young]

Dr. Dre, a producer and former member of **N.W.A.**, may be best known for production that is heavily influenced by the G-funk sound.

Dr. Dre began his career as a DJ at the Los Angeles nightclub Eve After Dark. Dr. Dre would go on to join the electro hop group **World Class Wreckin' Cru**. With Dr. Dre on the boards, the group hit the pop charts with the smooth jam "Turn Off the Lights" in 1998, which was the same year that N.W.A. released their second album. Dr. Dre met **Ice Cube**, and together they wrote songs for **Eazy E**'s record company, Ruthless Records. After HBO, a group signed to Ruthless, refused to record one of the songs written by Ice Cube and Dre, the three men formed their own group, N.W.A. (which stands for Niggaz With Attitude).

N.W.A. would gain a reputation for revolutionizing hardcore rap music. The group's first album was the independently released *N.W.A. and the Posse* (Ruthless Records, 1987). The following year, N.W.A. would release their breakthrough album, *Straight Outta Compton* (Ruthless Records). Ice Cube would leave the group in 1989 and forged a successful career as a solo rap artist. Like Ice Cube, Dr. Dre, citing management and financial issues, would leave N.W.A. in 1992. He co-founded **Death Row Records** with former bodyguard, Marion "Suge" Knight. Dr. Dre's first work for Death Row was the soundtrack for the film *Deep Cover* (1992), which also introduced **Snoop Doggy Dogg**.

Dr. Dre's first major success was his 1992 album, *The Chronic*. The multi-platinum album earned both critical acclaim and commercial

Dr. Dre. *Courtesy of Photofest.*

success. On the strength of singles such as "Nuthin' But a 'G' Thang" and "Dre Day," the album remained on the *Billboard* charts for eight months.

Backed by Dr. Dre's skillful production, Death Row Records became a leading rap music company. Aside from *The Chronic*, Dre's Death Row productions included Snoop Dogg's four-time-platinum debut album *Doggystyle* (Death Row Records, 1993) and his work with **Tupac Shakur** on the track "California Love" from his double album *All Eyez on Me* (Death Row Records, 1995/1996). During this period Dr. Dre also lend his talents to **Warren G** on his debut album *Regulate* and to the R&B group Blackstreet. On the track "Natural Born Killaz," from the *Murder Was the Case* album (Death Row Records), Dr. Dre reunited with Ice Cube, in addition to his overall production duties. He also produced the soundtrack for the film, *Above the Rim* (1994).

In 1996, Dre declared **gangsta rap** dead and departed Death Row Records. Aside from believing that the direction of rap music was changing, Dr. Dre also attributed his leaving Death Row to disagreement with Suge Knight's management style. Dre's split from Death Row was acrimonious and resulted in public threats and insults being hurled between the parties. In 2001, Dr. Dre obtained a restraining order against Knight. In the wake of Dre's leaving and Knight's imprisonment in 1996 for a parole violation in connection with a 1992 assault, Death Row went into decline. Dre then formed Aftermath Entertainment, a subsidiary of Interscope Records. Although his first release, the album *Dr. Dre Presents ... The Aftermath*, a compilation of artists, was not considered a success, the album contained the track "Been There Done That," which was a kiss-off to his former Death Row partner, Knight.

In 1999, Dre released the solo album *2001* (aka *Chronic 2001*) and its companion *2001 (Instrumentals Only)*. *2001* topped the Billboard R & B charts for three weeks. Dre's protégé Eminem is featured on the track "Forget About Dre." Dre also reteamed with Snoop Dogg on "The Next Episode." Although Aftermath was not blazing hot, Dre scored a major hit when he signed White rap artist **Eminem** to the label. Dre coproduced Eminem's 1999 debut album, *The Slim Shady LP*. Dre appeared on the track "Guilty Conscience." Dre also produced Eminem's hugely successful sophomore album, *The Marshall Mathers LP* (Aftermath/Interscope Records, 2000). In 2001 Dr. Dre appeared in the movies *The Wash* and *Training Day*, though he later stated that he does not intend to pursue a career in acting.

In July 2000, Detroit, Michigan, blocked Dre from showing explicit footage from his tour and Auburn Hills attempted to block it, but the video was shown after a federal judge overturned the city's order. Following Dre's Auburn Hills show, that city filed criminal charges against the rapper but the charges were eventually dropped. By October 2001, Dre had reached settlements with both cities over lawsuits that he had filed, asserting that their actions violated his First Amendment rights.

As part of the settlement, Dre received written apologies from the two cities and checks of $25,000 (from Detroit) and $28,346 (Auburn Hills).

Dr. Dre has had his brushes with the law. In 1991, Dr. Dre was charged with assaulting television host **Dee Barnes**, and the following year he hit a police officer at a New Orleans hotel and broke the jaw of a fellow record producer. In 1995, Dre spent five months in a Pasadena city jail for violating parole. He was back in court in 2001, but this time teaming up with Metallica's Lars Ulrich in their efforts to shut down Napster.

In 2003, Dr. Dre and Eminem produced **50 Cent**'s debut album, *Get Rich or Die Tryin'*, featuring the Dre-produced megahit "In Da Club." The release of *Detox*, which was to be Dre's final solo album, was planned for 2004 but the project seems to be cancelled.

DR. JECKYLL AND MR. HYDE

The Harlem, New York, rap duo of Dr. Jeckyll [**Andre Harrell**] and Mr. Hyde [Alonzo Brown] broke with the established Hip Hop style code by performing in suits and ties. Andre Harrell then put down the mic and become a record executive, first becoming a Vice President at Def Jam, then founding Uptown Records (later Uptown Entertainment), and then moving to Motown Records as president. After leaving Motown Records he consulted with **Bad Boy Entertainment**. Most recently Harrell cofounded Nu America, an agency and talent company.

In 1980, Dr. Jeckyll and Mr. Hyde first performed together as members of the Harlem World Crew. The two broke off from the group and formed Dr. Jeckyll and Mr. Hyde, later adding. DJ George Llado. In 1981, the duo became famous for their first single, "Genius Rap"(Profile Records), which incorporated a sample from the Tom Tom Club's "Genius of Love"; the single hit number. 31 on the Black singles chart. Between 1982 and 1984, Dr. Jeckyll and Mr. Hyde released the singles "The Challenge" and "Fast Life" b/w "AM, PM") (Profile Records, 1984), produced by **Kurtis Blow**, and "Gettin' Money" (Profile Records, 1983). In 1985, the duo released their only album, *Champagne of Rap*. They also released the singles "Yellow Panties" (Profile Records, 1985) and "Transformation" b/w "Scratch on Galaxy" (Profile Records, 1986).

In 1986, the duo split. Mr. Hyde briefly continued to record as a solo artist.

See also: Andre Harrell

DR. OCTAGON. See Kool Keith

D.ST (aka Grandmaster D.St, aka Grand Mixer D.XT, aka D.XT) [Derek Howells]

A member of Infinity 4 Emcees, D.St is best known for his contribution to jazz artist Herbie Hancock's song, "Rock It" (CBS, 1983). The name

D.St stood for Delancey Street in Manhattan, where he used to hang out. In 1989, feeling a need for change, he became known as D.XT.

D.XT began his career as a drummer. Around 1975, influenced by **DJ Kool Herc**, he began DJing. He gained reputation for both his DJ skills and showmanship at parties. D.XT would sometimes break out into a dance, or use body parts other than his hands to cut the records. **Afrika Bambaataa** took notice and invited D.XT to join him for parties. Later on, D.XT would become the DJ for the Roxy nightclub. In 1982, he was part of the **New York City Rap Tour**, the first Hip Hop tour to go to Europe, along with Afrika Bambaataa, Rammellzee, **Fab 5 Freddy**, **Rock Steady Crew**, the Double Dutch Girls, and **graffiti** artists Phase 2, Futura, and Dondi. He also appeared in the classic Hip Hop film *Wild Style* (1982). D.XT never recorded an album of his own, but he did release several singles. He continues to produce for current rap music groups, most notably **King T**. He is also prominently featured in the 2001 documentary *Scratch*, produced by the Hughes Brothers.

DISCOGRAPHY: "Grandmixer Cuts It Up" (Celluloid Records, 1982); "DST Cuts It Up" (Celluloid, 1982); "Crazy Cuts" (Celluloid, 1983); "Mega-Mix" with Herbie Hancock (CBS, 1984); "Megamix 2: Why Is It Fresh (Celluloid, 1984); "Mean Machine" with Jalaludin Mansur Nuriddin of the Last Poets (1984 Celluloid, 1984); "Home of Hip Hop" (Celluloid, 1985); "Rock the House" (1985).

DUNGEON FAMILY

An Atlanta-based musical collective modeled after Parliament Funkadelic. The Dungeon Family is a loose federation of musicians, MCs, and singers, comprised of the production team of Organized Noize (Rico Wade, Patrick "Sleepy" Brown, and Ray Murray), songwriters Marqueze Etheridge and Brandon Bennett, and their collective of MCs which includes **Outkast**, **Goodie Mob** members, Backbone, Cool Breeze, Witch Doctor, and Big Rube. In 2001, the Dungeon Family released their first album, *Even in Darkness* (Arista Records).

E

EAST COAST–WEST COAST RIVALRY

Rap artists sparring verbally in MC **battles** and on records is as old as the story of Hip Hop itself. The most notorious rap music feud occurred in the mid-1990s, and was so primarily because two of its principals, **Tupac Shakur** and **The Notorious B.I.G.**, were murdered. What remains unclear despite the fervent media speculation and reams of sloppy journalism about the matter is whether the deaths of these two talented rap artists were directly linked to the East Coast–West Coast rivalry or even to each other. Although the media simplistically made the dividing lines between the East Coast and the West Coast, the situation was more complex, because of the overlap between rap artists and rap fans' musical tastes. Furthermore, although rap fans expressed opinions about the rivalry and in some instances held strong alliances to one or the other coast, the disputes ultimately involved only two successful record companies and the artists associated with them.

Hip Hop's New York roots provided the East Coast, and particularly New York City, with the initial advantage in being the part of the country to establish the record companies, video shows, clothing stores, and magazines that were related to Hip Hop. In the late 1980s and early 1990s, East Coast artists routinely went to the West Coast to perform and West Coast artists such as **Ice-T**, **Ice Cube**, and Tupac Shakur, who started writing raps as MC New York, ventured to the East Coast to work with New York–based rap artists and producers. Some artists who became West Coast icons were ironically natives of the East Coast, including Ice-T, who was born in Newark, New Jersey; **Kurupt**, who hails from Philadelphia; and the Brooklyn, New York–born Tupac Shakur, who spent the early part of his life in New York and Baltimore, Maryland. What became apparent, however, was that much of the rap music industry was controlled by people whose tastes had been developed by the East Coast rap aesthetic (which was often called "Walkman music," because of its general emphasis on lyrics and tightly constructed beats).

Despite the commercial success of groups such as **N.W.A.**, **2 Live Crew**, and **The Geto Boys**, the East Coast's rap establishment did not automatically recognize other rap genres, particularly those emanating from the South and the West Coast, as legitimate forms of rap music. In 1992, **Dr. Dre**'s album *The Chronic*, which was released by **Death Row Records** became one of the biggest-selling album to date and with its laid back, jeep ready, G-Funk sound was appealing to rap fans across the country. With the release of *The Chronic*, the dominant creative force was, for the first time, the West Coast and not the East Coast. Death Row Records was established by former N.W.A. member Dr. Dre and former bodyguard and reputed Blood gang member, Marion "Suge" Knight.

During this period, West Coast artists such as **Snoop Dogg** and Tupac Shakur would experience huge commercial success, while East Coast rap artists, though still receiving the lion's share of the critical acclaim, were not faring as well as their West Coast peers in terms of overall sales.

In 1993, **Sean "Puffy" Combs**, as P. Diddy was then known, founded **Bad Boy Entertainment** after being fired from his vice president post at Uptown Records. At Uptown Records (Uptown Entertainment's original name), Combs, who gained fame for his work with **Mary J. Blige**, had become adept at not only producing music, but also in shaping the images of artists. With his first release, Craig Mack's infectious single, "Flava In Ya Ear," Combs revitalized East Coast rap by again making it marketable nationally. Bad Boy's subsequent release of the album *Ready To Die* by The Notorious B.I.G. proved that Bad Boy could not only produce hits that sold nationally, the label also—for better or worse—helped to redefine the Hip Hop with its aggressive promotion of conspicuous consumption and the lux life, in the public personas of its artists, their music videos, and their rap lyrics.

In 1994, Shakur was shot five times and robbed of approximately $40,000 worth of jewelry outside of the Quad recording studio in New York City, and in a *Vibe* magazine interview he accused former friend, The Notorious B.I.G., Combs, and **Andre Harrell** of setting him up. The three men vehemently denied the unsubstantiated charges. In 1995, Shakur would sign with Death Row Records, after Knight put up $1 million bail money for Shakur (incarcerated at the time on a sexual abuse charge). That same year, at the Source Awards, Knight took a public swipe at Combs—who had appeared in several Bad Boy music videos—by stating that anyone who did not want record executives in their videos should sign to Death Row Records. Many have speculated that Knight's public attack was connected to his personal concerns that Comb's rise in stature could diminish his own powerful position in the rap music industry.

In February 1996, Tupac Shakur, now on the Death Row label, released the first official double CD rap album, *All Eyez On Me*, which reached number 1 on the charts. In March 1996, Death Row and Bad Boy employees reportedly got into an altercation after the Soul Train Awards in Los Angeles. During this period Shakur had strongly suggested in the media that he had a romantic relationship with singer Faith Evans, then wife of The Notorious B.I.G. Going further, on the 1996 **underground** hit "Hit Em Up," which was the B-side to twelve-inch single version of "How Do You Want It" (Death Row Records), Shakur not only expressly stated that he had had a relationship with Evans, he verbally attacked a slew of East Coast artists, including B.I.G. associates **Lil' Kim**, and Lil Cease, as well as **Mobb Deep**, all using the melody line used in B.I.G.'s hit, "Get Money" (Bad Boy Entertainment).

On September 7, 1996, while driving in a car with Suge Knight after a Mike Tyson boxing match in Las Vegas, Tupac Shakur was shot several times and died of his injuries on September 13, 1996. On March 9, 1997, The Notorious B.I.G. was fatally shot outside Petersen Automotive Museum in Los Angeles, California, where he was attending an after-party for the Soul Train Awards. The assailants in both murders remain at large.

In the aftermath of these deaths, rumors about a continuing coastal rap war have also largely been laid to rest.

EASY MO BEE [Osten Harvey Jr.]

Grammy Award-winning producer Easy Mo Bee is known for producing sounds that combine the best of current day with the best of yesteryear. Easy Mo Bee grew up in the Lafayette Gardens Projects in the Bedford Stuyvesant section of Brooklyn, New York. By the age of twelve, the musical prodigy was playing drums in church and in the drum corps. Easy Mo Bee learned about music by listening to his father's record collection, which included greats such as Miles Davis, Count Basie, Aretha Franklin, Sam & Dave, BB King, and Billie Holiday.

Easy Mo Bee. *Courtesy of Photofest.*

Mo Bee began to see Hip Hop as it developed in the form of outdoor parties in his housing complex. While in high school, he bought his first DJ set with money he earned at an after-school job at a health food store. His purchase of two **Technics** turntables and a Gemini **mixer**. Spinning records would begin his lifelong relationship with music and his melding together different types of Black music. In 1985, Easy Mo Bee, with two other friends, started the group Rapping is Fundamental (RIF). The name was a play on a literacy program known as Reading Is Fundamental. The group doo-wopped and rapped, performing around their neighborhood and at local talent shows. Member AB went to Sara J. Hale High School in Brooklyn, New York, with rap artist **Big Daddy Kane**. AB had Mo Bee play his beats for Big Daddy Kane, and Mo Bee went on to produce the tracks "Another Victory" and "Calling Mr. Welfare" for Kane's 1989 album, *It's a Big Daddy Thing* (Cold Chillin').

In 1991, RIF, now signed to A&M Records, released the single "Rapping Is Fundamental," and Easy Mo Bee produced two **remixes** of the song. In 1991, he produced **GZA**'s first pre-**Wu-Tang** album, *Words From the Genius* (Cold Chillin'). That same year he would also produce the twelve-inch promotional single "Sexcapades" (Tommy Boy Records) for future Wu-Tang producer **RZA**, then known as Prince Raheem. In 1992, he won a Grammy award for his collaboration with jazz legend Miles Davis on Davis's album *Doo-Bop* (Warner Bros. Records).

Easy Mo Bee basically split production duties with **P. Diddy** on **The Notorious B.I.G.**'s groundbreaking debut album, *Ready to Die* (Bad Boy Entertainment, 1993), and did more production work on the 1997 album, *Life After Death*. Aside from The Notorious B.I.G., Easy Mo Bee has produced hits for a who's who of rap artists, including **LL Cool J** ("Pink Cookies in a Plastic Bag (Remix)"), **Heavy D** ("Black Coffee (Remix)"), Craig Mack ("Flava in Ya Ear"), **Lost Boyz** ("Lex, Coups, Bimaz, and Benz"), **Busta Rhymes** ("Everything Remains Raw"), and **Tupac Shakur** ("Temptations"), as well as film soundtracks from *The Show*, *Panther*, *Sunset Park*, and *New Jersey Drive*. Most recently, Mo Bee worked on Alicia Keys's second album, *Diary of Alicia Keys* (J Records, 2004).

DISCOGRAPHY: Contains over ninety items.

EAZY E [Eric Wright]

A native of Compton, California, Eazy E founded Ruthless Records (with Jerry Heller) in 1985 and would also be instrumental in ushering in the era of **gangsta rap**. In 1986, Eazy E with **Ice Cube**, **Dr. Dre**, MC Ren, and DJ Yella, formed the group Niggaz With Attitude (N.W.A.), one of the most controversial rap groups ever.

1987 saw the release of the eponymous debut album, *N.W.A. and the Posse*. Although the album was not a great success, the tracks "Dopeman" and "Boyz n the Hood" put Compton on the rap music map. The group's 1988 follow-up, *Straight Outta Compton* (Ruthless Records), quickly gained steam, based on the tracks "F**k the Police" and "Gangsta, Gangsta." The album has become a Hip Hop classic.

Eazy E released only one full-length album during his lifetime, the 1988 double-platinum *Eazy Duz It* (Ruthless Records), which was released shortly after N.W.A.'s sophomore album. Personality conflicts and financial disagreements would cause Ice Cube to leave N.W.A. in 1989, with Dr. Dre following Cube's lead and also leaving the group, in 1992. Eazy E and Dr. Dre fought bitterly over royalties and engaged in lyrical insults. In 1992, Eazy released the EP *5150 Home 4 Tha Sick* (Ruthless Records). In 1994, he released the single, "Real Muthaphukkin' G's," which was basically a rewrite of Dr. Dre's track "Dre Day," from *The Chronic* (Death Row Records). The same year Ruthless also released the EP, *It's On (Dr. Dre) 187um Killa.*

As a solo artist, Eazy E lacked the rap ability to regain the success of his N.W.A. days. After Eazy E publicly supported Theodore Briseno, one of the Los Angeles police officers who took part in the Rodney King beating, and then attended a Republican party fundraiser, Eazy E lost a great deal of credibility with rap music fans.

In 1994, Eazy E launched the careers of Cleveland, Ohio, rap group **Bone Thugs-N-Harmony** by signing them to Ruthless Records. In 1995, however, Eazy E succumbed to AIDS and was hospitalized for some time, finally dying of complications following a collapsed lung. The material he had been working on prior to his death was released posthumously in 1995 on the album *Str.8 Off Tha Streetz Of Muthaphukkin Compton.*

DISCOGRAPHY: *Single*: "Real Muthaphukkin' G's" (Ruthless, 1994). EPs: *5150 Home 4 Tha Sick* (Ruthless, 1992); *It's On (Dr. Dre) 187um Killa* (Ruthless, 1994). *Albums*: *Eazy Duz It* (Ruthless, 1998); *Str.8 Off Tha Streetz Of Muthaphukkin Compton* (Ruthless, 1995).

ED O.G. AND DA BULLDOGS (aka Edo G) [Edward Anderson]

Credited with putting Boston, Massachusetts, on the Hip Hop map, the young Ed made his break-dancing debut in 1983, as a sixth grader, in a talent contest held at the Martin Luther King Jr. Middle School in Dorchester, coming in second place. He subsequently moved from dancing to **beatboxing** and took the name Ed O. Rock. Ed Rock joined the Dorchester crew FTI (Fresh To Impress) and by 1986 the group had made a name for itself locally. The FTI's song "Suzie Q" was included on the 1986 compilation album *Boston Goes Def.*

With the emergence of Boston rap groups such as the **Almighty RSO** and the T.D.S. Mob, it appeared that Boston rap music would go national. Ed left FTI and launched a solo career as Ed O.G. In 1991, Ed O.G.

entered into a recording deal with Mercury Records and released the gold-selling album *Life of a Kid in the Ghetto,* which spawned the *Yo! MTV Rap* favorites "I Got Too Have It" and "Bug-a-Boo," as well as the moralizing classic "Be a Father to Your Child." Although titled as Ed O.G. & Da Bulldogs, *Life of a Kid in the Ghetto* is essentially a solo album.

Despite the album's success, it would be three years before Mercury Records would release Ed O.G.'s second album, *Roxbury 02119*. During this period, Mercury Records reportedly had a policy that an artist had to have a whole album done before a single would be released. Ed O.G. was on tour supporting his first album and, although he had singles ready for release, his album was not finished. In the interim, Ed O.G. would continue to tour in Europe and Japan. Mercury Records dropped Ed from the label and for several years he faded from the rap music scene.

Ed O.G. resurfaced in 1997 on the **underground** rap hit "Off Balance" by Laster, and for the next few years did cameos and twelve-inch singles. Renamed Edo G, he released the album *The Truth Hurts* in 2001 on Ground Control. The buzz on the **DJ Premier**–produced single "Sayin' Somethin'" was hot, but unfortunately sales of the album were not impressive. In 2004, he followed up with the album, *My Own Worst Enemy*, with production by Pete and the single "Wishing," featuring **Masta Ace**.

DISCOGRAPHY: *Life of a Kid in the Ghetto* (Mercury/Polygram, 1991); *Roxbury 02119* (Mercury/Polygram, 1994); *Truth Hurts* (Ground Control, 2001); *My Own Worst Enemy* (Fatbeats, 2004).

E-40 [Earl Stevens]

A California Bay Area rap artist best known for his unique rhyme delivery style, experimentation with overdubbed vocals, and creating slang terms such as "scrilla" (money) and "broccoli" (marijuana), E-40 has never fully gained mainstream success, remaining largely a regional sensation. Nonetheless, he has gained a large following spreads from the West Coast to the South.

Known by several nicknames, including "Charlie Hustle," "Forty Fonzarelli," and "40-Watter," E-40 aspired to follow the lead of **Too Short** and gained fame rapping about the "playa" lifestyle. Like Too Short before him, E-40 used **mixtapes** to create a street presence. E-40 began releasing singles in 1989 and started his own independent Sick Wid It Records in 1990, which helped to extend his music beyond his Vallejo, California, streets. His first release was the album *Federal* (Sick Wid It) in 1992. In 1993, with The Click, comprised of his brothers and sisters, he also released an album *Down and Dirty*. In 1994, E-40 received national attention with his EP *The Mail Man* and the single "Captain Save a Hoe."

E-40's talents reached Jive Records, and he subsequently signed a distribution deal with them for Sick Wid It's catalog. Under the deal in 1995, Jive Records rereleased older material as well as new music such as *In a Major Way* and the Click's *Game Related*. For his 1996 album, *Tha Hall of Game* E-40 again worked with longtime producer Mike Mosley but also collaborated with Bay Area heavyweight **Ant Banks**. The first single from the album, "Rapper's Ball," was an updated version of Too Short's 1987 single, "Playboy Short." This new version featured Too Short. Other standouts included "On The One," featuring **Digital Underground**'s Money-B and Da Funk Mob's G-Note, and "Things'll Never Change," which reinterpreted Bruce Hornsby's single "That's The Way It Is." This track included a contribution from E-40's then eight-year-old son, Lil' E. In 1998, *The Element Of Surprise* debuted at number 13 on the *Billboard* Top 200. In 1999, E-40 celebrated ten years on the rap scene with a semi-autobiographical album, *Charlie Hu$tle—The BluePrint Of A Self-Made Millionaire*. Subsequent albums included *Loyalty and Betrayal* (Jive Records, 2000); *The Ballatician: Grit and Grind* (Jive Records, 2002), and *Breakin News* (Jive Records, 2003).

DISCOGRAPHY: *Federal* (Sick Wid It 1992); *The Mail Man* (Sick Wid It 1994); *In A Major Way* (Sick Wid It/Jive Records, 1995); *The Hall Of Game* (Sick Wid It/Jive Records, 1996); *The Element Of Surprise* (Sick Wid It/Jive Records, 1998); *Charlie Hu$tle—The BluePrint Of A Self-Made Millionaire* (Sick Wid It/Jive Records, 1999); *Loyalty And Betrayal* (Sick Wid It/Jive Records, 2000); *The Ballatician: Grit & Grind* (Sick Wid It/Jive Records, 2002); *Breakin News* (Sick Wid It/Jive Records, 2003).

EGYPTIAN LOVER, THE (aka Jamie Jupiter) [Greg Broussand]

An innovative West Coast producer known for his electro Hop hits in the 1980s and his membership in **Uncle Jamm's Army**, The Egyptian Lover would release numerous singles during the mid-1980s that would influence rap music for years to come.

The Los Angeles native began recording in 1983 and released a twelve-inch single, "Egyptian Lover Theme" (Paradise Enterprise Records). Influenced by **Afrika Bambaataa**'s electro hit "Planet Rock" and **Man Parrish**'s "Hip-Hop Be Bop (Don't Stop)," in 1984 he released the West Coast anthem "Egypt, Egypt." The single "Egypt, Egypt" as well as the singles "What Is a DJ If He Can't Scratch," "And My Beat Goes Boom," and "Computer Love (Sweet Dreams)" were DJ mainstays throughout the 1980s and early 1990s. The majority of The Egyptian Lover's music was released on his own Egyptian Empire Records. *On the Nile* (Egyptian Empire, 1984), which can almost be categorized as a greatest hits compilation, was followed by *One Track Mind* (Egyptian Empire, 1986) and *Filthy* (Priority Records, 1988). In 1994, he returned with two albums *Back From the Tomb* (Egyptian Empire) and the following year released the album *Pyramix* (Egyptian Empire, 1995); *Get Into It* was released on Egyptian Empire in 1998.

DISCOGRAPHY: *Selected singles*: "Egyptian Lover Theme" (Paradise Enterprise Records). "Egypt, Egypt" (Egyptian Empire, 1984); "Girls" (Egyptian Empire, 1985); "Gotta Have Ya" (Egyptian Empire, 1994); "What Is a DJ If He Can't Scratch" (Egyptian Empire, 1984) "And My Beat Goes Boom" (Egyptian Empire, 1984); "Computer Love (Sweet Dreams)" (Egyptian Empire, 1984). *Albums*: *On the Nile* (Egyptian Empire, 1984); *One Track Mind* (Egyptian Empire, 1986); *Filthy* (Priority Records, 1988); *Back From the Tomb* (Egyptian Empire, 1994); *Pyramix* (Egyptian Empire); *Get Into It* (Egyptian Empire, 1998).

ELECTRO HOP (aka Electro)

A type of dance music combined with rap music that emerged in Southern California in the early 1980s. This subgenre of rap music (also known simply as electro) was popularized by rap artists such as **World Class Wreckin' Cru**, **The Egyptian Lover**, and **The Arabian Prince**. Electro hop was the prevailing form of West Coast rap during this period; however, many East Coast critics and rap music purists disliked electro hop and considered it a bastardized form of rap music. With the rise of hardcore rap artists such as **King T**, Toddy Lee, and **Ice-T**, electro ceased to be a dominant part of the rap scene.

EMCEE. *See* MC

EMINEM (Marshall Bruce Mathers III)

In 1999, Eminem, a protégé of **Dr. Dre**, entered the rap music scene and soon became one of its most controversial performers. Eminem's rhymes could be described as vile, **misogynistic**, homophobic, caustic—and sardonically witty. Eminem's music discussed many topics, including his dysfunctional family and his utter contempt for mainstream media and pop culture. His controversial lyrical content garnered him an inordinate amount of publicity, which pegged him alternately as a comic genius and foul-mouth sociopath. Moreover, being the first successful solo White rap artist provided him with a media platform not afforded to Black rap artists of equal or superior talent. Eminem nonetheless struck a cord with disaffected youth who could relate to his working class experience.

Born in St. Joseph, Missouri, near Kansas City, Eminem spent much of his impoverished childhood shuttling between his hometown and Detroit, Michigan. Attracted to rap music as a teenager, at age fourteen Eminem began performing in the basement of a high school friend. The two called themselves Manix and M & M, and the M & M soon became

Eminem. *Courtesy of Photofest.*

Eminem. As a White performer, Eminem's race was initially an issue when he decided to enter the performance side of the virtually all-Black world of rap music. He eventually won fans on the **underground** scene by battling other rap artists and freestyling.

Eminem stopped rapping briefly after his uncle's suicide, but upon his return, several other rap artists were vying to have him start groups. Eminem first joined the New Jacks, and then moved on to Soul Intent, which released Eminem's first recorded single in 1995. The birth of Eminem's child forced him to put his rap career on hold so that he could get a job and financially support his new family. Embittered by the turn of events, Eminem used his new experiences as fodder for his rhymes. After generally unfavorable reviews for his 1996 debut album, *Infinite* (WEB Entertainment), Eminem started downplaying the positive messages, creating Slim Shady, an alter ego that spoke his mind, uncensored. Slim Shady tapped into a reservoir of pent-up feelings about

Eminem's mother, whom he accused of mentally and physically abusing his younger brother, and about his girlfriend, who barred him from seeing his daughter. As Eminem used drugs, his material turned bleaker.

An unsuccessful suicide attempt convinced Eminem that music was the only way to escape his unhappy life. When he released the EP *Slim Shady* (WEB Entertainment) in 1998, a humorous, brutal, and thought-proving record, it made an impact on the underground because of his rapping style and because he was a White rap artist. For some, Eminem became Hip Hop's next "great White hope." In 1997, after Eminem took second place in the **freestyle** category at that year's Rap Olympics MC Battle in Los Angeles, Interscope chief Jimmy Iovine asked the rap artist for a demo tape. Iovine subsequently played the tape for **Dr. Dre**, who then contacted Eminem. Reportedly, Dr. Dre was initially taken aback that Eminem was White, yet within a hour of meeting they had already started recording "My Name Is."

Interscope Records signed Eminem and prepared to give him a massive push on Dre's advice. Dr. Dre agreed to produce Eminem's debut album and the single "Just Don't Give a F**k" was released to preview the new album. Eminem then appeared on Kid Rock's track, "Devil Without a Cause," helping to increase the buzz that was slowly building around him. In early 1999, *Slim Shady LP* (Shady/Aftermath/Interscope Records) reached the public, boosted by the lead single and video "My Name Is" and follow-up in "Guilty Conscience." Over the next year, the album went triple platinum. Controversy and debates surrounded the album's content, with critics assailing it for its graphic violence and fans proclaiming its edgy intelligence.

The Marshall Mathers LP (Shady/Aftermath/Interscope Records) appeared in the summer of 2000, selling approximately 2 million copies in its first week. Eminem's success helped keep him mired in controversies, including a bitter dispute with pop star Christina Aguilera over a lyric about a tryst between her and MTV's DJ Carson Daly. Eminem's mother also sued him for defamation of character, and Eminem attacked a Detroit club-goer after he allegedly witnessed the man kissing his wife. Fans loved the drama and continued to buy his records; however, mainstream media did not join the love fest, particularly as accusations of homophobia and sexism sprang from the inflammatory lyrics of the songs "Kill You" and "Kim." The track "Kim," in which Eminem depicted violently murdering his real-life wife, Kim Mathers, ended the marriage. Kim Mathers attempted suicide before they divorced. Nonetheless, the album was nominated for several awards. To quell critics, Eminem asked openly gay singer Elton John to perform with him at the annual Grammy Awards.

In 2001, he reteamed with several of his old Detroit friends and revived D-12, which had been formed years earlier. That same year,

Eminem released an album with the group on his Slim Shady label and toured with them that summer. After coming off tour, he made his acting debut as the star of the semi-autobiographical film, *8 Mile*. When he returned in 2002, Eminem made noise with the single "Without Me," which attacked artists Moby and **Limp Bizkit**. The album, *The Eminem Show* (Shady/Aftermath/Interscope Records), did not garner the controversy of his prior efforts. In a rather sober fashion, the second single, "Cleanin' Out My Closet," told of his unhappy childhood and detailed his intense hatred of his mother. Eminem was back in the spotlight, however, when he verbally attacked Moby for no apparent cause.

In November 2003, Eminem's race again became an issue when ***The Source*** magazine published lyrics from two old tracks (from 1993 and 1998) that use racial slurs and are derogatory to Black Women. In a statement, Eminem said, "The tape they played today was something I made out of anger, stupidity and frustration when I was a teenager. I'd just broken up with my girlfriend, who was African American, and I reacted like the angry, stupid kid I was. I hope people will take it for the foolishness that it was, not for what somebody is trying to make it into today." In June 2004, a federal court ruled that *The Source* had violated an injunction by publishing the aforementioned racist lyrics on its Web site. The court said that the publication of the lyrics had the ability to impair Eminem's "credibility" among rap music fans.

Eminem's fifth album, *Encore* (Shady/Aftermath/Interscope Records, 2004), considered overall a good one, nonetheless met with mixed reviews. Although Eminem employed the same formula of vitriol and wit mixed with Dre's production, the combination may have staled for some fans, who wanted Eminem to surprise them with something new.

See also: Censorship

DISCOGRAPHY: *EP*: *Slim Shady* (WEB Entertainment, 1998). *Albums*: *Infinite* (WEB Entertainment, 1996); *Slim Shady LP* (Shady/Aftermath/Interscope Records, 1999); *The Marshall Mathers LP* (Shady/Aftermath/Interscope Records, 2000); *The Eminem Show* (Shady/Aftermath/Interscope Records, 2002); *Encore* (Shady/Aftermath/Interscope Records, 2004).

EMULATOR

A product of California-based E-mu Systems, the emulator made its market debut in 1981 as the first machine dedicated to digital **sampling**.

ENJOY RECORDS

Enjoy Records, a Harlem, New York, label established in 1962 by Danny and Bobby Robinson, had been home to saxophone legend King Curtis.

In 1979, the label put out its first rap music single, "Rappin' and Rockin' in the House," by The **Funky Four + 1**. That same year, Enjoy would also release **Grandmaster Flash and the Furious Five**'s first twelve-inch, "Super Rappin." In 1980, **Spoonie Gee** recorded the twelve-inch "Love Rap" with **Treacherous Three**'s "New Rap Language" on the B-side. With Enjoy, the Treacherous Three would also record the singles "Body Rock" and "Put the Boogie in Your Body." In 1982, Enjoy sold its rap music roster to Sugar Hill Records.

EPMD

It is fair to say that few would have bet that EPMD, the duo of Erick Sermon (aka Funklord, E Double, the Green-Eyed Bandit, and MC Grand Royal) and Parrish Smith, would become stars, not with their sample-heavy productions and their monotone rap style—and yet they were among Hip Hop's best in the late 1980s and early 1990s.

Between 1988 and 1992, the duo gained fame mainly for concentrating on two themes: serving up weak MCs and recalling sexual exploits. The rhymes were tight if often undervalued because of the lack of variety in the delivery. EPMD were also skilled in finding good beats, and thus created numerous rap music classics, including "It's My Thing," "You Gots to Chill," "Get the Bozack," "Strictly Business," "Headbanger," You're A Customer," and "Rampage."

The two natives of suburban Long Island, New York, met in high school and both were determined to make a record together. They joined with DJ K. La Boss (later replaced by DJ Skratch). Smith began his career DJing for Rock Squad on a single released on Tommy Boy Records. In 1987, the two joined forces, naming themselves EPMD, short for "Erick and Parrish Making Dollars." They recorded "It's My Thing," in three hours. On this first release group's name was spelled Epee MD on the cover. The single sold an amazing 500,000 copies and was later licensed to Chrysalis Records. EPMD signed to Fresh/Sleeping Bag for their debut album *Strictly Business* (1988). The album, which cost approximately $15,000 to make, went gold on the strength of several singles, including "You Gots to Chill," "The Steve Martin," and "Jane." In only six weeks the album topped Billboard's Black LP charts. Their 1989 sophomore album, *Unfinished Business*, also went gold.

In 1990, the duo signed to **Def Jam Recordings** for a reported $700,000 advance. EPMD released the albums *Business As Usual* (Def Jam Recordings, 1991) and *Business Never Personal* (Def Jam Recordings, 1992). By 1992, EPMD had formed the **Hit Squad**, a group of artists including **Redman**, K-Solo, and **Das EFX**. In 1993, tension between Sermon and Smith caused EPMD to disband, however, each went on to record solo albums. In 1993, Sermon released his solo debut album, *No Pressure*, followed by the albums *Double or Nothing* (1995) and *Insomnia: The Erick Sermon Compilation Album* (1996). In 1994, Smith released his solo album, *Shade Business*.

The whole being stronger than the parts, the duo regrouped and in 1997 made a strong comeback with the album *Back in Business* (Def Jam Recordings). In 1999, *Out of Business* (Def Jam Recordings) was released. Erick Sermon, again as a solo artist, would score a magic hit with the title song from his 2001 album, *Music* (J Records). The song is a collaboration of sorts with the late R & B singer Marvin Gaye. In 2003 he released *React* (J Records). In 2004, Sermon released his fifth solo album, *Chilltown New York* (Motown/PGD).

DISCOGRAPHY: *Single*: "It's My Thing" (Fresh, 1988), as Epee MD. *Albums*: *Strictly Business* (Fresh/Sleeping Bag, 1988; re-issued by Priority Records in 1988); *Unfinished Business* (Fresh/Sleeping Bag, 1989); *Business As Usual* (Def Jam Recordings, 1991); *Business Never Personal* (RAL/Def Jam, 1992); *Back in Business* (Def Jam Recordings, 1997); *Out of Business* (Def Jam Recordings, 1999).

ERIC B & RAKIM

Eric B [Louis Eric Barrier] and Rakim (aka Rakim Allah) [William Griffin Jr] are ranked among the most influential and respected rap music artists of all time. This duo also represents the best of the second wave of New York City rap artists.

Eric Barrier, a native of Elmhurst, Queens, New York, started DJing in the early 1980s and by 1985 had displayed enough talent to land the coveted DJ slot on the WBLS-FM radio mobile unit. Eric B would meet Rakim; a native of Wyndanch, Long Island, New York, at one of these performances and the partnership was formed. At sixteen, William Griffin, Jr., the nephew of R & B singer Ruth Brown, converted to Islam, taking the name Rakim Allah.

In 1986, the new duo produced their first single, "Eric B Is President," b/w the B-side "My Melody," at Power Play recording studios in Manhattan for the independent Zakia label; 4th & Broadway Records, a division of Island Records, would later re-issue the singles. That same year, the single "Eric B. For President" would be released in the United Kingdom on London's Cooltempo Records. The duo recorded together for seven years, releasing four albums, which spawned numerous hit singles, including "I Know You Got Soul," "Follow the Leader," and "Let the Rhythm Hit 'Em."

Eric B & Rakim helped to shift the focus in rap music away from the DJ, who was the center of Hip Hop in its early days, to the MC. As a consummate lyricist, Rakim changed the art form; he is considered one of the best, perhaps the best MC ever. Rather than being a **battler**, **freestyler**, or hype man, Rakim took the time to write articulate poetical rhymes, delivered in a steely, smooth voice. Eric B's beat construction, which seamlessly cut together 808 drum kicks along with various samples, more than held its own against Rakim's verbal mastery. Never one to rely on gangster puffery, Rakim, a self-confessed "microphone fiend," used discussions of drugs and violence metaphorically, in sharp confirmations of his own intellectual brilliance.

Eric B & Rakim's first two albums, *Paid In Full* (4th & Broadway/Island, 1987) and *Follow The Leader* (Uni/1988), are considered classics and left an indelible mark on rap music with Rakim's trademark phrases: "Pump up the volume," "It ain't where you're from, it's where you're at," and "A pen and a paper, a stereo, a tape."

The 1987 single "I Know You Got Soul" (4th & Broadway), with its funky samples and jazzy textures encouraged a new generation of DJs and producer to "dig in the crates" for rare funk and soul music. The duo would release two more albums, *Let The Rhythm Hit 'Em* (MCA, 1990) and *Don't Sweat The Technique* (MCA, 1992). In 1992, a contract dispute would end the partnership and the two would never record again.

In 1993, Rakim's solo track "Heat It Up," appeared on the soundtrack of the film *Gunmen*. Two years later, Eric B released his self-titled solo debut on his own 95th Street label. In 1997, Rakim resurfaced with the album, *The 18th Letter* (Universal), with producers **Pete Rock** and **DJ Premier**; although critics felt that the effort did not break new ground, new and old fans were nonetheless happy for a return to cool and intelligent lyrics. In 1999, Rakim released the album *The Master* (Universal), a slept-on album that was, overall, given high marks by fans. However, even though the album had production help from **Mark The 45 King**, DJ Premier, and **Dr. Dre**, those who were critical of the album cited the beats, rather than Rakim's lyrics, as wanting. In 2000 Rakim signed with Dr. Dre and Aftermath Records. Rakim gained considerably more new school attention rapping the hook on the 2002 track "Addictive" (Interscope Records), by the artist Truth Hurts. In July 2003 Rakim, citing creative differences, left Aftermath, although it had been reported that his delayed album, *Oh My God*, would be released that summer.

In January, 2004 Eric B. and Rakim reteamed to file a lawsuit in New York against **Russell Simmons**, Lyor Cohen, Island Records, **Def Jam Recordings**, Universal Music Enterprises, and others for a yet-to-be-determined amount of money, alleging that they were never paid royalties from their classic 1987 album, *Paid in Full*. In 1998, 4th & Broadway/Island Records became part of the Island Def Jam Music Group, a subsidiary of the Universal Music Group. Eric B and Rakim contended that former managers Simmons and Cohen had misrepresented them and that Island/Universal has been illegally distributing the album. In

1998, a special "platinum edition" version of *Paid in Full* was issued by Island's 4th & Broadway imprint and in 2003 Island released a two-disc "deluxe edition" featuring bonus **remixes**. The lawsuit called for damages to be awarded based on accounting and sales of the album *Paid in Full* and the singles "Eric B. Is President" and "My Melody."

DISCOGRAPHY: *Singles*: "Eric B Is President" w/ "My Melody" (Zakia, 1986; re-issued by 4th & Broadway/Island); "Eric B. For President" (Cooltempo Records, UK, 1986). *Albums*: *Paid In Full* (4th & Broadway/ Island, 1987); *Follow The Leader* (Uni/1988); *Let The Rhythm Hit 'Em* (MCA, 1990); *Don't Sweat The Technique* (MCA, 1992).

EVE [Eve Jihan Jeffers]

Known as the first lady of Ruff Ryders, the rap artist Eve is also emerging as an actress and fashion designer. Calling herself Gangsta, the Philadelphia native began her career as a member of the female rap duo EDGP (pronounced "Egypt"), performing at local talent shows and club. When the duo dissolved, Eve pursued a solo career, changing her name to Eve of Destruction.

In the aftermath of her mother's remarriage, Eve moved to the Bronx, New York, and worked for a period as a dancer in a strip club. Determined to turn her life around, Eve again pursued a rap music career. Some of Eve's friends helped her get a meeting with producer, **Dr. Dre** in Los Angeles and turned it into an audition. Dr. Dre subsequently signed her to a one-year deal with his new label, Aftermath. Eve recorded several tracks, including "Eve of Destruction," which appeared on the 1998 soundtrack for the film *Bulworth*.

Due to transitions within Aftermath, Eve had not even begun to record an album before her contract with the label had expired. Fortunately for Eve, she met **DMX** when he was in Los Angeles promoting his debut album, *It's Dark and Hell Is Hot*. Eve was selected to join DMX's Ruff Ryders posse after participating in a **battle**-style audition. In 1999, she contributed to the Ruff Ryders compilation, *Ryde or Die, Vol. 1*. Eve's track on the compilation, "What Ya Want," was released as a single and reached the R & B Top Ten. In September 1999, Eve released her first full-length album, *Let There Be Eve . . . Ruff Ryders First Lady*. The album entered the charts at number 1, a first for a female rap artist, and went on to sell over 2 million copies. Eve also scored hits with the R & B Top Ten "Gotta Man" and the track "Love Is Blind," about domestic violence. Eve's sophomore album, *Scorpion*, was released in early 2001. The album received strong reviews, topping the R & B charts, while also debuting at number 4 on the pop charts. The second single, "Let Me Blow Ya Mind," a duet with No Doubt's Gwen Stefani, was a crossover hit and won a Grammy

Eve. *Courtesy of Photofest.*

in the newly created category of Best Rap/Sung Collaboration and helped boost *Scorpion* to platinum sales. Eve's third album *Eve-Olution* (Interscope Records) was released in August 2002, debuting in the Top Ten. The single "Gangsta Lovin'" featured guest vocals from Alicia Keys and the follow-up, "Satisfaction," was nominated for a Grammy.

Eve turned her talents toward acting and in summer 2002 made her film debut in *XXX* with Vin Diesel. Eve also appeared in the comedy films *Barbershop* (2002) and *Barbershop 2: Back In Business* (2004), written and directed by **Ice Cube**. In early 2003, Eve signed with the UPN network to produce and star in a multiracial sitcom about a fashion designer. In real life, Eve had entered the fashion industry with her Fetish clothing line.

DISCOGRAPHY: *Let There Be Eve . . . Ruff Ryders First Lady* (Interscope Records, 1999); *Scorpion* (Interscope Records, 2001); *Eve-Olution* (Interscope Records, 2002).

F

FAB 5 FREDDY [Fred Braithwaite]

Hip Hop's first renaissance man, Fab 5 Freddy became famous for using his connections in the media and on the streets to expose mainstream America and the world to Hip Hop. A native of Brooklyn, New York, the one-time **graffiti** artist took the "Fab 5" from the name of his former graffiti crew. In art circles, Fab 5 Freddy may be best known for his 1979 subway painting done with Lee Quinones in a tribute to Andy Warhol's Campbell's soup can paintings. The multitalented Hip Hop impresario also tried his hand at rapping and released the **underground** hit record "Change The Beat" (Celluloid, 1982).

Charlie Ahern enlisted Fab 5 Freddy to act and help create the landmark 1982 film, ***Wild Style***, which documents Hip Hop during its early years. Fab 5 Freddy also was part of the 1982 New York City rap tour sponsored by French radio station Europe1, which brought Hip Hop artists to Paris, France, and the groundbreaking Swatch Watch New York City **Fresh Fest** tour in 1984, the first rap tour of its kind. In August 1988, Fab 5 Freddy became the first host of ***Yo! MTV Raps***, and he has also produced music videos for rap artists such as **KRS-ONE**, **Snoop Dogg**, and **Queen Latifah**. He also had roles in the films *New Jack City* (1991) and *Juice* (1992).

FAT BOYS

Prince Markie Dee [Mark Morales], Kool Rock-Ski [Damon Wimbley], and the **Human Beat Box** [Darren "Buffy" Robinson] made up a trio known for their large size and their humorous rhymes. Originally known as the Disco 3, in 1983 the trio won a talent contest held by Charles Stettler, who would become their manager. The first prize included a recording contract with Sutra Records.

The Disco 3's first single, the 1983 "Reality," did not do well, so Stettler asked **Kurtis Blow** to help the group out for their second single, Blow is credited with the concept of comically exploiting their combined girth. Blow produced their 1984 single "Fat Boys," which introduces the human beat box. He would also produce their first two albums, *The Fat Boys* (Sutra, 1984) and *The Fat Boys Are Back* (Sutra, 1985). After playing in the 1985 film ***Krush Groove***, they came out with the album *Big and Beautiful* (Sutra, 1986). In 1987, The Fat Boys reached

Fat Boys. *Courtesy of Photofest.*

their career peak with their fourth album *Crushin'* (Tin Pan Apple/Polydor), a platinum-selling collection of entertaining party tunes that includes "All You can Eat" and "Wipeout," a collaboration with the Beach Boys. That same year the trio also starred in the film *Disorderlies*, with actor Ralph Bellamy.

As rap audiences changed, the Fat Boys style of humor lost its luster. Their next album, *Coming Back Hard Again* (Tin Pan Apple/Polydor, 1988), replicates the formula of *Crushin'*; it starts with a rap version of "The Twist" sung by Chubby Checker and includes a funny rendition of "Louie, Louie," in which the trio explains the songs.

The Fat Boys tried to expand artistically and build street credibility with the rap opera album *On and On* (Tin Pan Apple/Mercury, 1989); its failure spelled the end of the group. Their last album was *Mack Daddy* (Ichiban Records, 1991). In 1992, Prince Markie Dee, with the group The Soul Convention, recorded the R & B album *Free* (Columbia), following up in 1995 with the album *Love Daddy* (Motown). Prince Markie Dee subsequently developed a successful career an R & B songwriter and producer. In December 1995, Robinson died of a heart attack.

DISCOGRAPHY: *Singles*: "Reality" (Sutra, 1983); "Fat Boys" (Sutra, 1985). *Albums*: *Fat Boys* (Sutra, 1984); *Fat Boys are Back* (Sutra, 1985); *Big and Beautiful* (Sutra, 1986). *Crushin'* (Tin Pan Apple/Polydor, 1987); *Coming Back Hard Again* (Tin Pan Apple/Polydor, 1988); *On and On* (Tin Pan Apple/Mercury, 1989); *Mack Daddy* (Ichiban, 1991).

FAT JOE (aka Fat Joe Da Gangsta, aka Joey Crack) [Joe Cartagena]
A member of the **Terror Squad**, Fat Joe has said that he does not do Spanish rap, he's just a Spanish guy who raps. The Latino Bronx, New York, native was introduced to Hip Hop through his older brother, Angel, who brought home tapes of the rap music played at **Zulu Nation** events. The original sounds sparked Joe's interest in Hip Hop and as he got older he became involved not only with rap, but also with **graffiti** and **B-boying**. The streets would also influence Fat Joe, who hung with a crew and adopted the name Joey Crack to represent his stake in the local drug trade. Joe realized, however, that music, not hustling, was his means to success. He then parlayed his experience on the street and talent as a rap artist into a record deal with Relativity Records.

In 1993, recording under the name Fat Joe Da Gangsta, he released his debut album, *Represent*. Joe scored a surprise hit with the track "Flow Joe." In 1995, Fat Joe issued his sophomore album, *Jealous One's Envy*, which included a cameo appearance by **KRS-ONE**.

Fat Joe. *Courtesy of Photofest.*

Hoping to further expand his opportunities, Fat Joe left Relativity Records and signed a deal with Big Beat/Atlantic. In 1998, Fat Joe made his Atlantic records debut with the album *Don Cartagena*, which featured contributions by **P. Diddy**, **Nas**, **Big Pun**, **Jadakiss**, and **Raekwon**. During this period he had also established some nonmusic ventures: a clothing store called "Fat Joe's Halftime," a barber shop, and a fashion line called "FJ560." Joe employs neighborhood friends as a way to help them support themselves through legal means. His 2001 follow-up, *Jealous Ones Still Envy (J.O.S.E.)*, became a platinum-selling album. This album included the most-played single in Atlantic's history, "What's Luv," featuring R & B singer Ashanti. In 2002, Joe released his fifth album, *Loyalty*.

In 2004, the Terror Squad released the album *True Story*, which debuted on *Billboard* charts in the top five during its first week in stores. The first single, "Lean Back," topped the charts and spawned the dance "Rockaway." In January 2005, Face Dirty, a rap artist from Birmingham, Alabama, alleged that Fat Joe copied his song of the same name. Face Dirty has performed the song publicly on numerous occasion, had developed a dance, and also released a self-produced video of the song and the "lean back" dance. Face Dirty was contemplating a lawsuit if the matter is not resolved by the parties.

DISCOGRAPHY: *Respect* (Relativity Records, 1993); *Jealous One's Envy* (Relativity Records, 1995); *Don Cartagena* (Atlantic Records, 1998); *Jealous Ones Still Envy (J.O.S.E.)* (Atlantic Records, 2001); *Loyalty* (2002); *True Story* (2004).

FEARLESS 4

The Fearless 4 was The Great Peso [Mitchell Grant], the Devastating Tito [Wilfredo Dones], Mighty Mike C [Michael Kevin Clee], and DLB the Microphone Wizard [Daryl Barksdale] as DJs, with Master O.C. [Oscar Rodriguez, Jr.] and Krazy Eddie [Eddie Thompson]. When they signed with Elektra Records in 1983, the Fearless 4 became the first rap group to sign a contract with a major record company.

Tito and Master O.C. started the group when they were known as the Houserockers Crew, selling their tapes across Manhattan and the Bronx. The two recruited other members, first Mike Ski, then the Great Peso and Troy B, who arrived fresh from the Disco Four. Troy B was subsequently replaced by DLB, and Mike Ski got married and also departed. Mighty Mike C and Krazy Eddie (a second DJ who took his name from a New York City electronics store known for its loud pitchman and funny commercials) rounded out the group.

In 1982, the Fearless 4 had a hit with the single "Rockin' It" (Enjoy Records). The group followed up with the single "It's Magic" (Enjoy Records, 1982), based on a Cat Stevens song, and then they secured an

agreement with Elektra. At Elektra, they recorded the single "Just Rock" (1983) using a sample from Gary Numan's "Cars." The single flopped, even though it was **remixed** by legendary club DJ Larry Levan. In 1983, **Kurtis Blow** produced their nominal hit, "Problems Of The World Today" (Elektra, 1983). The group released two more twelve-inch singles: "Dedication" (Tuff City, 1983) and "After Tonight" (Mercury, 1987).
DISCOGRAPHY: "Rockin' It" (Enjoy, 1982); "It's Magic" (Enjoy, 1982); "Just Rock" (Elektra, 1983); "Problems of the World Today" (Elektra, 1983); Dedication (Tuff City"); "After Tonight" (Mercury, 1987).

FEAR OF A BLACK HAT. *See* Films

50 CENT (aka 50) [Curtis Jackson]

This rap artist had one of the most hyped debuts in Hip Hop history with the release of his 2003 debut album *Get Rich or Die Tryin'* (Slim Shady/Aftermath) By the time the album hit the streets on February 6, 2003, he had become the most talked about person in the music industry. Furthermore the record sold 872,000 units in the first five days, becoming the best-selling debut album since SoundScan started its tracking system in May 1991.

The Jamaica, New York, native not only talked the talk of hardcore rap, he had walked the walk. 50 Cent, like many rap artists before him had encountered the rough and grimy aspects of life on the streets. However, unlike many of his peers, 50 Cent lived the life that he rapped about experiencing first hand the drug trade, incarceration, and assaults on his life, which included stabbings and shootings. Like the mythical bad men of African American forelore, 50 Cent's appearance replete with bulging biceps, six-pack abdomen, tattoos, bulletproof vest and diamond-encrusted crucifix visually represented his hardcore demeanor.

50 Cent. *Courtesy of Photofest.*

Moreover, 50 Cent also attracted sizable media attention and fans with his penchant for public attacking wannabe rap music gangstas.

50 Cent's rap music career began in the mid-1990s, when after another run-in with the law he decided that, despite a lucrative street business, he should consider the legitimate hustle that is rap music. In 1996, he received a break when he met **Jam Master Jay**, who asked him to rhyme over beats recorded on a tape. Jam Master Jay liked what he heard and signed 50 to his JMJ Records label. Though nothing else materialized from the JMJ deal, 50 Cent met producers Trackmasters.

Trackmasters subsequently signed 50 to their label and they began work on his first album, *Power of the Dollar* for Columbia Records. Three singles from the proposed album were released: "Your Life's on the Line," "Thug Love" (featuring Destiny's Child), and "How to Rob." "How to Rob" became a hit because of its blatant lyrics that discussed how 50 would rob certain high-profile rap artists. Although **beefs** are commonplace with rap music, this type of impersonal frontal attack was relatively unheard of.

50's brashness may have almost cost him his life, because shortly after the release of "How to Rob," he was stabbed at the Hit Factory studio in Manhattan. Perhaps in an attempt to finish the job, in May 2000 just before the projected Columbia Records release of the *Power of the Dollar* album, 50 was shot nine times while sitting in the passenger seat in a car in Queens. After learning about these near fatal incidents, Columbia Records shelved his album and terminated his deal.

For the next few years, 50 went back to the **underground** and recorded **mixtapes** that would eventually earn him a solid reputation on the streets. Some of the tracks talked about his shooting, others clowned fellow rap artists, and some were raps over popular beats. One steady target of his mixtapes was rap artist **Ja Rule**, with whom 50 had an ongoing rivalry. The constant stream of 50's mixtapes garnered him street buzz and music industry attention. In 2002, *Guess Who's Back*, a collection culled from 50 Cent's mixtape appearances and his shelved debut album, was released on the independent Phantom label. The title pokes fun at the numerous rap artists whom 50 had dissed in the past.

When **Eminem** declared on a radio program that he thought 50 was a great rap artist, an industry bidding war ensued. In 2001, 50's talent and resiliency were rewarded when Eminem signed him to a reported seven-figure contract to Slim Shady Records, ushering in his rise to both rap and crossover stardom.

Work began on 50's debut album, *Get Rich or Die Tryin'* (Slim Shady/Aftermath). The track "Wanksta," which had been released on the underground, was rereleased in 2002 and became a huge success, reaching number 13 on *Billboard*'s Hot 100 charts. The lead single from the actual album, the **Dr. Dre**-produced "In da Club," reached number 1 on *Billboard*'s Hot 100 chart. The mammoth successes of the two singles demanded that the release date for the *Get Rich* album be moved up to combat bootlegging.

In early 2005, 50 Cent is scheduled to appear on an episode of the *The Simpsons* titled "Pransta Rap." According to press reports, the episode centers on Bart going to a 50 Cent concert without his parents' permission. The follow-up album, *The Massacre* (Slim Shady/Aftermath), is slated for release in early 2005.

DISCOGRAPHY: *EPs*: *Power of the Dollar* (Columbia Records, 2000; unreleased); *Guess Who's Back* (Phantom, 2002). *Albums*: *Get Rich or Die Tryin'* (Slim Shady/Aftermath, 2003); *The Massacre* (Slim Shady/Aftermath, 2005).

"FIGHT THE POWER"

A song by **Public Enemy** on the soundtrack for Spike Lee's 1989 movie, *Do The Right Thing*, "Fight The Power" (like the film) deals head on with the internal and external issues of race. The overtly political song represented young Blacks who saw their progress stalled by race and class conflicts. The importance of "Fight the Power" in the Hip Hop canon is that it did not simply reiterate the facts or cite problems—it was a forceful call to action, a demand for revolt. The song subsequently became an anthem for a generation of young people.

FILMS

The following is a selection from the increasing number of films and videos with Hip Hop–related themes. Hip Hop-related films are those movies that in some way document or critique the music or the culture.

Wild Style (1982): **Fab 5 Freddy** and writer–producer–director Charlie Ahearn captured Hip Hop at its beginnings. The stars of *Wild Style* form the pantheon of Hip Hop's pioneers: DJs **Grandmaster Flash**, **Grand Wizzard Theodore**, **Grand Mixer D.ST**; rappers **Grandmaster Caz** and the **Cold Crush Brothers**, The Chief Rocker **Busy Bee**, Double Trouble, Fantastic Freaks, and Rammellzee; and **B-boy** champions **Rock Steady Crew**. *Wild Style* stars the legendary subway artist Lee Quinones and the queen of the **graffiti** scene, Sandra "PINK" Fabara. Graffiti masters Dondi, Zephyr, and Daze also bombed for the movie.

Style Wars (1983): Directed by Tony Silver and Henry Chalfant, this historic PBS documentary tracks the rise and fall of subway graffiti in New York in the late 1970s and early 1980s.

Beat Street (1984): Directed by Stan Lathan, this musical drama details the roots of Hip Hop. Features **Afrika Bambaataa**, **Doug E. Fresh**, **DJ Jazzy Jeff**, **Kool Moe Dee**, and **Melle Mel**, among others.

See also: Disco Fever; US Girls

Krush Groove (1985): Directed by Michael Schultz, the film is roughly based on **Def Jam Recordings**. Features **Run DMC**, **Fat Boys**, and **Kurtis Blow**, among others.

Wild Style. *Courtesy of Photofest.*

Tougher Than Leather (1988): Directed by Rick Rubin, this Run DMC vehicle also features the **Beastie Boys**, Fat Boys, and **Slick Rick**.

Rapmania: Roots of Rap (1990). A live concert documentary featuring **Afrika Bambaataa**, **Big Daddy Kane**, **Biz Markie**, **Eric B & Rakim**, Grandmaster **Melle Mel**, **Ice-T**, Kool Moe Dee, Kurtis Blow, **LL Cool J**, Run DMC, Slick Rick, and **Tone Lōc**.

CB4: The Movie (1993): Directed by Tamra Davis, a comedy about aspiring **gangsta rap** artists, starring Chris Rock.

Fear of a Black Hat (1994): Directed by Rusty Cundieff, a comedy about **gangsta rap**.

The Show (1995): Directed by Brian Robbins, this documentary with performances and interviews features (among many others) **Dr. Dre**, **Russell Simmons**, **Biggie Smalls**, and Afrika Bambaataa.

Rhyme and Reason (1997): Directed by Peter Spirer, the documentary on Hip Hop culture features dozens of artist interviews (among them **Lauryn Hill** and **The Notorious B.I.G.**).

The Source: 1999 Hip Hop Music Awards, the first awards show.

Backstage (2000): Directed by Chris Fiore, this documentary follows the 1999 Hard Knock Life Tour with (among others) **DMX**, **Jay-Z**, **Method Man**, and **Redman**.

Jails, Hospitals & Hip-Hop (Kicked Down Productions, 2000): Directed by Mark Benjamin and **Danny Hoch**, the film is based on Mr. Hoch's stage monologue of the same name (which is also available in book form). The DVD was released in 2002.

Snipes (2001): A drama directed by Rich Murray.

Through the Years of Hip Hop. Vol. 1. Graffiti (2002). This DVD documentary on aerosol art features writers Seen, Vulcan, Lee Quinones, Dondi, and Phase 2, among others, and includes seven historical music videos. Three more volumes are projected for this series.

Freestyle: The Art of Rhyme (2002). Directed by Kevin Fitzergald. Shot over a period of almost ten years, explores the oral traditions of Hip Hop culture and the MC's mastery of the English language that allows the freestyler to subvert and reconstitute it as tool for empowerment or for sheer entertainment. Included, among many others, are **The Last Poets**, **Mos Def**, Black Thought (**The Roots**), **Freestyle Fellowship**, **Lord Finesse**, Supernatural MC, MC Juice of **Jurassic 5**, and **DJ Kool Herc**.

Whatz Beef: A Hip Hop Documentary On Beefs in 2002 (2002); and ***Beef: The Real World of MC Battles*** (2003): Directed by Peter Spirer, both documentaries focus on lyrical **battles**.

FIRM, THE

Nas's supergroup, The Firm, was originally comprised of himself, **Foxy Brown**, AZ, and Cormega. Nature replaced Cormega, reportedly after Cormega got into an acrimonious disagreement with Nas about financial matters. In retaliation for being booted from the group, Cormega came out with the **underground** single called "F**k Nas and Nature." Ironically, Cormega's label at the time was **Def Jam Recordings**, the same one as Foxy Brown.

The Firm's first appearance was with the song "Affirmative Action," on Nas's second album, *It was Written* (Columbia, 1996). In 1997, *The Firm: The Album* (Aftermath Records) was released, with the concept that it was the soundtrack to a film. Tracks such as "Phone Tap" and "Five Minutes To Flush," which used a sample from **Whodini**'s "Five Minutes of Funk," focus on gangster movie themes. The album is significant in that, in the aftermath of the **East Coast–West Coast** conflict, and the death of **The Notorious B.I.G.**, it is the first the West Coast–East

Coast collaboration, as represented by **Dr. Dre** and **Nas**. The raps are hardcore, but Dr. Dre's skillful production smooths them out.

Nature was the only member of The Firm who was already an established solo artist; however, his underground credentials kept the group connected to the street. Unfortunately, although The Firm looked like superstars on paper, the album did not live up to most critics' expectations. Even Dr. Dre gave himself a failing grade for his work on the album. Fan responses were more varied: some heralded *The Album*, others severely panned it and called it the first step in Nas's road to becoming a sellout. *The Album* eventually sold platinum.

FIRST HIP HOP CONFERENCE. *See* Howard University

FIVE PERCENT NATION (aka The Nation of Gods and Earths, aka Five Percenters)

The Five Percent Nation are a splinter group that broke away from the **Nation of Islam** (NOI) in 1964, under the leadership of Clarence 13X. The Nation of Gods and Earths has influenced Hip Hop insofar as numerous rap artists including **Brand Nubian**, **Poor Righteous Teachers**, **Big Daddy Kane**, **Rakim**, and **Wu-Tang Clan** have been involved, to varying extents, with the movement and thus the group's ideology has been transmitted through the artists' music. The name is derived from their central belief, which is that only five percent of the population knows and teaches the truth: these are the poor righteous teachers. Ten percent conspire to hide the truth: these are the devils, the slave makers of the poor. The remaining 85 percent have not yet received knowledge. Members of the Nation of Gods and Earths follow a moral code; rather than a formal religion followers describe the group as a culture or a way of life.

FLAVA FLAV (aka The Cold Lamper, aka The Joker, aka The Juice, aka Sparkplug) [William Drayton]

Best known as the colorful hype man of **Public Enemy**, Flava Flav is easily recognized by sight with his gold teeth, jumbo sunglasses, and the huge clock that hangs from his neck. The clock signifies metaphorically what time it is. By sound, fans know Flava Flav from his raucous "Yea Boy."

In the early 1980s, the Long Island, New York, native worked with **Chuck D** and his father at their U-Haul company. Chuck D, who was studying graphic arts at Adelphi University, was also a DJ on its radio station, WAMU-FM. After calling into the show, Flava Flav soon became a cohost. Flava Flav takes the lead on Public Enemy's catchy song, "911 Is A Joke" (*Fear of A Black Planet*), which castigates urban policy. Flava

Flav also does solo duty on the humorous "Can A Woman Make A Man Lose His Mind" (*Revolverlution*).

In 2004, Flava Flav appeared on cable channel VH1's reality program, *Surreal Life*.

FLIPMODE SQUAD

The Flipmode Squad is a collective comprised of **Busta Rhymes**, Rampage, Lord Have Mercy, Spliff Star, **Rah Digga**, and Baby Sham. Made up of Busta's Brooklyn friends and protégés, the crew first appeared on Rhymes's 1997 album, *When Disaster Strikes* (Elektra Records). Their official debut, *The Imperial*, was produced by Busta, **EPMD**'s DJ Scratch (who was also executive producer), Rockwilder, Swize, Tony Touch, and **Da Beatminerz**; it was released in October 1998 on Elektra Records.

FLY

A popular Hip Hop term, fly means stylish, hip, or impressive.

FLY GIRL

Fly girl is a slang term for an attractive, appealing, or fashionable young woman. An example appears in the title of Omar Tyree's 1993 novel, *Flyy Girl*. Also: fly betty; fly guy.

FONZWORTH BENTLEY (aka Farnsworth Bentley) [Derek Watkins]

Self-proclaimed leader of the Gentleman's Movement, Fonzworth Bentley is Hip Hop's first style maven. A native of Atlanta, Georgia, he has parlayed his sartorial acumen into a new position, the arbiter of sophisticated Hip Hop style.

Unlike unseen stylists who influence fashion by what they dress rap stars in, Fonzworth Bentley himself became a star for what he wore. Eschewing baggy jeans and jerseys for well-tailored suits and Turnbull & Asser shirts, Bentley began his career as **Sean "P. Diddy" Combs**'s personal assistant. In a photo opportunity designed to emphasize P. Diddy's wealth and power, Bentley was captured famously holding an umbrella over the rap mogul in St. Tropez. The immaculately dressed and uniquely styled Bentley then appeared in P. Diddy's video for the track "I Need A Girl Pt. 2," from the album *Bad Boy: We Invent the Remix* (Bad Boy Entertainment, 2002). In 2002, he attempted to transform a group of ungroomed rap artists who appeared in MTV's "The Making of the Band 2." Bentley appeared in three **Outkast** videos from their album *Speakerboxxx/The Love Below* (LaFace, 2003): "The Way You Move," "Hey Ya!," and "Roses." He also appeared in a commercial for Tommy Hilfiger jeans, has a line of upscale umbrellas in the works, and works as an "arbiter of taste" for Courvoisier Cognac, made famous in Hip Hop circles by the **Busta Rhymes** rap tune, "Pass the Courvoisier." Bentley is also awaiting the approval of his own reality show titled, "Borrow My Crew."

Although in the early 1980s the rap duo **Dr. Jeckyll and Mr. Hyde** performed in suits rather than jeans, Hip Hop style is still overwhelming premised on casual (albeit expensive) designer clothing. With the Hip Hop generation maturing—as manifested by P. Diddy's tailored suits and sophisticated clothing line, Andre 3000's being named Esquire magazine's "Best Dressed Man in The World," and Damon Dash's penchant for manicures—and given the myriad of occasions that call for Hip Hop professionals to be properly dressed, Bentley is intent on giving Hip Hop a makeover.

Bentley is suited to the position by having a background steeped in style and grace. The graduate of Morehouse College was born into a genteel Atlanta family, he studied violin, frequently read etiquette books, and has worked for Ralph Lauren retail shops in both New York and Atlanta. Rather than merely being a clotheshorse, Bentley's dandy character has a history rooted in African American culture. To be well-dressed free Black men was a subtle attempt to contradict the stereotypes often attributed to them. Golliwog dolls with wild hair and natty bowties was an attempt by racists to denigrate uppity Blacks. Similarly the fastidiously dressed minstrel character Zip Coon was another means to lampoon upstart Blacks. Therefore, rather than attempting to be unobtrusive and invisible, the well-dressed Black man challenges society's racial hierarchy through his impeccably tailored clothing and beautiful manners.

FORTÉ, JOHN

Rap artist and musician best known as a member of **the Fugees'** Refugee Camp. Forté, a native of the roughneck Brownsville section of Brooklyn, New York, was not the Hip Hop cliché. Forté won a full scholarship to Phillips Exeter Academy, a prestigious and predominantly White boarding school in New Hampshire, where he studied violin. After graduating in 1993, Forte briefly attended New York University, then left to pursue a career in the music business, working in Rawkus Records's A & R department.

A fan of the then little-known Fugees, he met **Lauryn Hill** and went on to write songs and do production work for their 1996 album, *The Score* (Ruffhouse/Columbia). His own 1999 debut album, *Poly-Sci* (Ruffhouse/Columbia), sold poorly, which resulted in his being released from his recording contract. Forté subsequently worked as a DJ and as a party promoter, attracting many celebrities to his functions.

In 2001, Forté was arrested at John F. Kennedy International airport in New York and charged with accepting a briefcase containing $1.4 million worth of liquid cocaine. Forté pleaded not guilty to the drug trafficking charges, claiming that he had no idea what was in the suitcase and was under the impression that he was merely picking up money for a friend. At trial, Forté was found guilty and sentenced to fourteen years in a Texas prison; he has been recently relocated to a facility in Fort Dix, New Jersey.

Forté completed his second album, *I, John* (Transparent Music, 2002), while on trial. A reflective memoir, it is not centered on rap but instead experiments with other genres, particularly soul, reggae, psychedelic rock, trip-hop, and jazz. Ironically, Forté did not have a reputation as a gangsta, but rather that of a smart guy who liked to have fun. Rather than gaining street credentials in the 'hood, Forte had gone to a private school, studied violin, spent summers on Martha's Vineyard, and counts Carly Simon among his closest friends and supporters. Simon even makes an appearance on *I, John* and continues to advocate for his innocence.

DISCOGRAPHY: *Poly-Sci* (Ruffhouse/Columbia, 1999); *I, John* (Transparent Music, 2002).

FOXY BROWN [Inga Marchand]

The Brooklyn, New York, native took her name from the title character of the 1974 **blaxploitation** film, *Foxy Brown*, starring Pam Grier. Before ever releasing even a single of her own, Foxy Brown had appeared on several platinum singles released between 1995 and

Foxy Brown. *Courtesy of Photofest.*

1996. In 1994, a teenage Brown **freestyled** on stage, having won a talent contest in Brooklyn. Producers Trackmasters took notice of Brown's talent; coincidentally, they were working on **LL Cool J**'s *Mr. Smith* (Def Jam Recordings, 1995) album, and they decided to let her rap over "I Shot Ya." The single was Brown's first recording credit, and was also a hit. Subsequently, she worked on other successful tracks, including Total's "No One Else"; **Jay-Z**'s "Ain't No N***" from his debut album, *Reasonable Doubt* (Roc-A-Fella/Priority Records, 1996); Toni Braxton's "You're Makin' Me High" (**remix**); and Case's "Touch Me, Tease Me." Despite Brown's other work, it is probably her pairing with Jay-Z that actually launched her career.

In early 1996, Brown's winning streak led to a bidding war among the major record companies, with **Def Jam Recordings** prevailing. Brown's 1996 album *Ill Na Na* sold over 1 million copies. Her 1999 follow-up *Chyna Doll* (Def Jam Recordings), which featured Jay-Z and **DMX**, made number 1 on the *Billboard* charts.

Brown's hardcore style, revealing outfits and overt sexuality has lead to comparisons with former friend and fellow Brooklyn MC, **Lil' Kim**. Brown joined rap artists **Nas**, AZ and Nature to form the supergroup, **The Firm.** She had a cameo role in the 1998 film *Woo* and appeared in print advertisements for clothing designer Calvin Klein. In 2001, she released the album, *Broken Silence* (Def Jam Recordings). In April 2003, Brown appeared on Wendy William's WBLS-FM radio show and made it clear that she wished to end her relationship with Def Jam Recordings, after her album *Ill Na Na Part 2: The Fever*, was shelved indefinitely. Brown left Def Jam Recordings after the completion of the project, but in January 2005 was re-signed to the label by the new Def Jam Recordings president, Shawn "Jay-Z" Carter.

DISCOGRAPHY: *Ill Na Na* (Def Jam Recordings, 1996); *Chyna Doll* (Def Jam Recordings, 1999); *Broken Silence* (Def Jam Recordings, 2001); *Ill Na Na Part 2: The Fever* (unreleased).

FREAK

Freak is a slang term for a sexually promiscuous woman.

FREDDIE FOXXX (aka Bumpy Knuckles) [James F. Campbell]

A Long Island, New York, native, Freddie Foxxx began rhyming in elementary school. In 1986, as "Freddie C," he made his first recorded appearance on the single "Co Handlin' Things," b/w "Come out Fresh" (Nia Records) as a member of the group Supreme Force. According to rap lore, Foxxx believed that he was destined to be a solo artist after standing alone on stage after winning his first **battle**. The fates must have agreed, because Foxxx missed a 1986 meeting with a DJ named

Eric B who was looking for an MC. (Rakim, another Long Island teenager, did make his meeting with Eric and the two became known as **Eric B & Rakim**.)

In 1989, Foxxx signed with MCA Records and released his debut album, *Freddie Foxxx Is Here*. After adding his brand of verbal jabs and punches to numerous albums and tracks, including **Kool G Rap & DJ Polo**'s "Money in the Bank" and the **Boogie Down Productions** "Ruff Ruff," Foxxx recorded his follow-up album, *Crazy Like a Foxxx* for Epic Records/Flavor Unit. Epic Records, however, decided to shelve the album and only a few promotional copies were made public. Foxxx went **underground** and resurfaced on singles by **Gang Starr** and **M.O.P.**

After his bad experiences with major record companies, Foxxx started his own label, Kjac, and received distribution from Landspeed for his second official solo record, *Industry Shakedown* (June 2000). *Industry Shakedown* is a verbal attack on the music industry, with production done by **DJ Premier**, **Diamond D**, and **Pete Rock**. Foxxx took on the new moniker, Bumpy Knuckles, after hearing someone discuss his fighting skills. In 2003, Foxxx–Knuckles released the album *The Konexion* (BBE/Rapster). Not only does the largely self-produced album solidify the veteran artist's reputation as an independent rap artist, it also spells out the evils of the music industry. Foxxx's hurls lyrical grenades at rap artists who do not know Hip Hop history, whether they are wannabe pop stars or studio gangstas. *The Konexion* is hardcore indeed, yet rather than rhyming about his own wealth and power, Foxxx seems to be seeking a connection with more important forces.

DISCOGRAPHY: *Freddy Foxxx is Here* (MCA, 1998); *Crazy Like A Foxxx* (Epic Records/Flavor Unit; unreleased); *Industry Shakedown* (Kjac/Landspeed, 2000); *The Konexion* (BBE/Rapster, 2003).

FREESTYLE

To freestyle is to create rhymes on the spot—spontaneously and contemporaneously—as opposed to memorizing and reciting previously written works.

FREESTYLE FELLOWSHIP

Comprised of freestyle rhyme specialists **Aceyalone**, Mikah 9, P.E.A.C.E., and Self Jupiter, the Freestyle Fellowship may be one of the more underrated rap groups.

The Los Angeles–based rap artists began in the 1990s and are alumni of the Good Life Café, the center of the **Los Angeles Underground Movement**. Their first album, *To Whom It May Concern* (Beats & Rhymes, 1991) had limited distribution since there were only 300 vinyl copies and 500 tapes produced; nonetheless, the positive buzz created a following. Often called "alternative" by the media, the group shunned the hardcore style favored by many West Coast artists. Instead, the group created free-flowing and imaginative verses indicative of their jazz and neohippie roots in Leimart Park, placing them on the periphery of the rap scene.

In 1995, the group released their second album, *Inner City Griots* (4th & Broadway/Polygram), considered a progressive masterpiece. Self Jupiter's incarceration, however, forced the group to take a hiatus. The band reunited briefly for one show in 1998 and then sporadically in 1999 to produce a few benefit concerts and participate in a "We Are the World"–style single called "Mumia 911," designed to raise awareness and funds for death row inmate Mumia Abu-Jamal. During this period members also took the opportunity to also record solo projects.

In 1999, Freestyle Fellowship's first album was rereleased on CD, and they released the new twelve-inch "Can You Find the Level of Difficulty in This?" (Celestial Records) as a new twelve-inch. In 2000, Freestyle Fellowship released their third album, *Version 2.0,* which is a collection of *To whom It May Concern* **remixes**. *Temptations* (Ground Control) followed in 2001 and *Shockadoom* in 2002.

DISCOGRAPHY: *Single*: "Can You Find the Level of Difficulty in This?" (Celestial Records, 1999). *Albums*: *To Whom It May Concern* (Beats and Rhymes, 1991); *Inner City Griots* (4th & Broadway/Polygram, 1995); *Version 2.0* (2000); *Temptations* (Ground Control, 2001); *Shockadoom* (2002).

FREESTYLE: THE ART OF RHYME. *See* Films

FRESH

Fresh is a slang term for cool or exciting.

FRESH FEST CONCERT

Titled the Swatch Watch New York City Fresh Fest, Hip Hop's first national tour debuted in 1984 on Labor Day Weekend in Greensboro, North Carolina, with twenty-seven dates booked through Christmas. Charles Stettler, who managed the **Fat Boys**, coproduced the New York City Fresh Fest. Stettler was instrumental in securing a reported $300,000 in sponsorship money from the Swatch Watch Company for the tour. The tour featured **Run DMC**, **Kurtis Blow**, **Whodini**, the **Fat Boys**, **Newcleus**, and New York's Dynamic Breakers. It grossed $3.5. million. The annual tour ended in 1988.

FUBU (Founders: Daymond John, J. Alexander Martin, Carl Brown Keith Perrin)
The apparel line FUBU was started in 1992 by four African American friends from Queens, New York. The clothing was initially endorsed by fellow Queens native **LL Cool J**. The "05" on FUBU jerseys is a company trademark. The company's name is an acronym for "For Us, By Us," expressing the founders' intent to create urban wear designed for African Americans, by African Americans. At the time of FUBU's inception, numerous clothing designers were targeting Black consumers, but few if any were totally Black-owned or Black-run businesses. The acronym FUBU, although meant as a positive statement of Black empowerment, was sometimes perceived as exclusionary and racist. The designers had assumed that Black youth would be their only customers; and, therefore, they were not using the company name to warn others not to purchase the clothing. Instead, the FUBU founders wanted young Blacks to see people like themselves as fashion designers and businessmen. In 1999, with a consumer base that extended beyond young Blacks, FUBU reported an annual sales volume of $200 million from its menswear business and $150 million from its licenses.

FUGEES
The Fugees, a group originally known as the Tranzlator Crew, formed in the late 1980s, in New Jersey, where **Lauryn Hill** and Prakazrel "Pras" Michel [Samuel Praskazrel Michel] attended high school. Michel's cousin Wyclef Jean joined the group and in 1993 the trio secured a record deal with Ruffhouse/Columbia records under the new name, the Fugees. The term *fugee* is a pejorative for Haitian immigrants, here taken on as a badge of honor; both Wyclef and Pras are of Haitian descent.

In 1993, the group released its debut album, *Blunted on Reality*. There are glimmers on the album, but most agree that it did not represent the true talents of the Fugees. The production was lackluster, and, rather than being innovative, the Fugees seem to emulate the gangsta-type rap style of the day. Rumor had it that Columbia Records was dissatisfied with the album and were strongly considering dropping the group. In response, on their own dime they **remixed** the track "Nappy Heads," which officially put the Fugees on the map. "Nappy Heads (re-mix)" demonstrates the smoother and more articulate sound that would turn up on their 1996 sophomore album, *The Score* (Ruffhouse/Columbia Records).

On *The Score*, The Fugees melded together R & B, reggae, and rap. *The Score* became the sleeper hit of 1996 and The Fugees won a Grammy for Best R & B Group for their remake of Roberta Flack's "Killing Me Softly" and another Grammy for Best Rap Album. The album would go on to sell approximately 5 million copies.

Although the group has not officially broken up, there have been public squabbles and the members have embarked on solo careers. In 1997,

Wyclef Jean released his first solo album, *Presents the Carnival: Featuring the Refugee Allstars* (Sony Records). The following year, Lauryn Hill released her smash solo debut album, *The Miseducation of Lauryn Hill* (Ruffhouse/Columbia Records). That same year, Pras would release his debut album, *Ghetto Superstar* (Ruffhouse/Columbia Records). Jean would go on to release more solo albums: *The Ecleftic: 2 Sides II a Book* (Sony, 2000); *Masquerade* (Sony, 2002), and *Preacher's Son* (J Records, 2003). In 2002, Hill released the live acoustic album *MTV Unplugged 2.0* (Sony Records), which contained snippets from her debut album and new material.

In late September 2004, the Fugees reunited as part of comic Dave Chapelle's "Block Party" event, held in the Fort Greene section of

Fugees. *Courtesy of Photofest.*

Brooklyn, New York. Other "Block Party" participants included singers Jill Scott, and Erykah Badu as well as rap artists **Big Daddy Kane**, **Kool G Rap**, and **Common**. Filmmaker Michel Gondry captured the event for a concert film and documentary (working title: *Block Party*). Chapelle was inspired by the 1973 documentary of the 1972 "Wattstax" concert held in the Watts section of Los Angeles, California, with humorous narration by comedian Richard Pryor.

DISCOGRAPHY: *Blunted on Reality* (Ruffhouse/Columbia, 1993); *The Score* (Ruffhouse/Columbia, 1996).

FUNKMASTER FLEX [Ashton Taylor]

The son of a Jamaican DJ, Funkmaster Flex was born in Brooklyn, New York. He purchased his first set of turntables at age sixteen, and was influenced by New York City DJs, such as **Kool DJ Red Alert**. In the late 1980s Flex began his radio career at New York City's KISS-FM as an assistant to Chuck Chillout. When Chillout transferred to WBLS-FM, Flex went with him and soon began playing at clubs and parties in New York City and his reputation began to grow. When programmers at New York City's Hot 97 (WQHT-FM) offered him a premier spot, Funkmaster Flex became one of the city's top Hip Hop DJs at the top-rated radio station in the nation's number one media market.

Throughout the 1990s, Flex was a chief tastemaker in the New York rap music scene. Through his high-profile position at Hot 97 (WKYS-FM), Flex had the ability to make or break artists. In the mid-1990s, in addition to his gig at Hot 97, Flex was also the weekly DJ at the Tunnel, at the time one of New York's top clubs. Lastly, Flex's radio show was also broadcast on Los Angeles's Power 106 FM (KPWR-FM), in America's second largest radio market.

In 1995, Flex joined the ranks of recording artists when he started commercially releasing **mixtapes**, beginning with *The Mix Tape, Volume 1: 60 Minutes of Funk* (RCA Records). In 1999, *The Mix Tape, Volume 2: 60 Minutes of Funk* (Relativity Records) and *The Mix Tape, Volume 3: 60 Minutes of Funk* (Relativity Records) were released. Additionally, in December 1999 he released the album *The Tunnel* (Def Jam Recordings). In 2000, he mixed a collection of that year's biggest rap songs, *Vibe Hits, Vol. 1* (Arista), and released *The Mix Tape, Volume 4: 60 Minutes of Funk* (Relativity Records).

At the end of the 1990s, his popularity only continued to rise, landing him a coveted position on MTV with his own daily show, *Direct Effect*. In 2003, Flex got another show, *Ride with Funkmaster Flex*, featuring celebrities and their cars, on Spike TV. Not since the days of **Afrika Bambaataa** and **DJ Kool Herc** has the DJ reigned, however, Funkmaster Flex's popularity has shifted the focus of Hip Hop back to the DJ.

FUNKY FOUR +1

Formed in 1979 with KK Rockwell [Kevin Smith], Keith Keith [Keith Caesar], Lil' Rodney Cee [Rodney Stone], and Jazzy Jeff [Jeffrey Myree], plus **Sha Rock** [Sharon Green-Jackson, this was one of the first rap groups to have a female MC. The group is best known for their classic single, "That's the Joint." Unlike today, Sha Rock was not looked at as a sex object, but simply as another member of the crew.

The crew was originally called the Brothers Disco. Original member Rahiem would leave and join **Grandmaster Flash and the Furious Five**; he was replaced by Lil' Rodney Cee. Although the group never released a full-length album, they are nevertheless important to Hip Hop. Their single "Rappin and Rockin the House," which uses a sample from Cheryl Lynn's "Got to Be Real," is over fifteen minutes long; it is probably the longest rap song ever. Notably, the drums on this track were programmed by Pumpkin, arguably rap's first great producers.

Other releases include "Do You Want To Rock," "King Heroin," "Square Biz," "Feel It," and "Superstars." In February 1981, the Funky Four +1 were the musical guests on *Saturday Night Live*, becoming the first rap group to make a national television appearance. By 1983, however, the group had split up. KK Rockwell and Rodney Cee formed the rap duo Double Trouble and Sha Rock joined two other female rappers to create **US Girls**. US Girls performed in the film *Beat Street*. Jazzy Jeff went on to record as a solo act with Jive Records.

DISCOGRAPHY: "Rappin and Rockin the House" (Enjoy, 1979); "That's the Joint" (Sugar Hill Records, 1980); "Do You Want To Rock" (Sugar Hill Records, 1982); "King Heroin," "Square Biz," "Feel It" (Sugar Hill Records, 1982); "Superstars."

FURIOUS FIVE. *See* Grandmaster Flash and the Furious Five

FU-SCHNICKENS

The trio of Moc Fu [J. Jones], Poc Fu [Lennox Maturine], and Chip Fu [Roderick Roachford] called themselves Fu-Schnickens. According to the group, the Fu stands for "For Unity" and the rest is a wholly original word meaning "coalition."

This group hailing from Brooklyn, New York, holds the distinction of being perhaps the oddest performers in Hip Hop history. Aside from their madcap antics, the group was masterful lyrically, weaving together tongue-twisting, ridiculous lyrics filled with an array of pop culture references including cartoons, television shows, and karate flicks. In addition to being influenced by dancehall reggae, Fu-Schnickens raps on occasion were words said backward, injected with humorous voice impressions, all at a high pitch. Their personas were equally colorful: sometimes they performed in kung fu outfits.

Their lyrical techniques and strange comic sense got Fu-Schnickens noticed in club in New York dates, and in 1991, the group performed at the first Hip Hop conference held at **Howard University** in Washington, DC, which led to a deal with Jive Records. Their first single, "Ring the Alarm" (Jive Records), was released in 1992. The dancehall-influenced track was popular and made the Top Ten on the rap singles chart. The trio's debut album, *F.U.: Don't Take It Personal* (Jive Records, 1992) followed; it includes the cult classic singles "La Schmoove" and "True Fu-Schnick."

In 1993, Fu-Schnickens received mainstream attention when they teamed up with NBA star **Shaquille O'Neal** on the single, "What's Up Doc?" (Jive Records). In 1994 the group released their second album, *Nervous Breakdown* (Jive Records), but their novelty had worn off. Although in Fu-Schnickens turned up on the soundtrack for the film *Die Hard With a Vengeance*, with the single "Got It Covered" (RCA Records), the trio seems to have faded from the rap music scene.

DISCOGRAPHY: *Singles*: "Ring the Alarm" (Jive Records, 1992); "What's Up Doc?" (Jive Records, 1993). *Albums*: *F.U.: Don't Take It Personal* (Jive Records, 1992); *Nervous Breakdown* (Jive Records, 1994).

G

GANGSTA RAP (aka Reality Rap)

Gangsta rap is a media-driven term to describe rap lyrics that portray street life and violence. Some prefer the term "Reality Rap" as a more accurate label for this type of the rap content.

In his book *Hip Hop America*, music critic Nelson George says that gangsta rap stems from a "suspicion of women, loyalty to crew, adoption of a stone face in confronting the world, hatred of authority" (New York: Penguin Books, 1999; p. 44). He attributes the adoption of these characteristics to the increased imprisonment of Black men in the 1990s as a result of tougher drug laws, failing public schools and the decline of jobs in urban centers. East Coast rap artists, rather than West Coast artists, would be credited with originating gangsta rap. The first acknowledged gangsta rap came from Philadelphia, Pennsylvania, rap artist **Schoolly D**, who independently released "PSK (Parkside Killers)—What Does it Mean?" (1985). Critics also cite the **Boogie Down Productions** album *Criminal Minded* (B-Boy Records, 1987) as an influence on the genre, because of the single "9 mm Goes Boom." Moreover, the album cover depicts **KRS-ONE** and Scott La Rock with guns, bullet belts, and grenades. **Just-Ice** would call himself the "original gangster of Hip Hop," and that image was solidified when he appeared on the television show *America's Most Wanted* as a murder suspect.

On the West Coast, **Ice-T** would popularize the genre with the single "6 'N in the Morning," from his debut album *Rhyme Pays* (Sire, 1987). **Slick Rick** would portray the gangster–pimp on tracks such as "Treat Her Like a Prostitute" and "Children's Story" from his debut album, *The Adventures of Slick Rick* (Def Jam Recordings, 1988) and, in a case of life imitating art, in 1991 Slick Rick would be convicted of attempted murder in the shooting of his cousin.

Kool G Rap & DJ Polo made their careers chronicling the gangster life, beginning with their debut album, *Road to The Riches* (Cold Chillin', 1989).

GANG STARR

DJ Premier [Chris Martin] and Guru [Keith Elam] are Gang Starr. These artists, like their music, are an original combination. Guru (the name stands for Gifted Unlimited Rhymes Universal) hails from Boston,

Gang Starr. *Courtesy of Photofest.*

Massachusetts, is the son of that city's first Black judge, and graduated from Morehouse College with a degree in business. Premier, from Brooklyn, New York, studied computer science at Prairie View University in Texas.

Premier was not originally a member. After moving to New York, Guru started Gang Starr with fellow rap artist Damo D-Ski and DJ Wanna Be Down. They signed to Wild Pitch Records, where they released the singles "The Lesson" and "Bust A Move," both produced by **Mark The 45 King**. While in Texas, Premier started the Inner City Posse (ICP) and was known as Waxmaster C when he sent the group demo to Wild Pitch. Guru, at Wild Pitch, listened to the tape, liked what he heard, and invited Waxmaster C to join Gang Starr. A few months later, after ICP dissolved and the other founding members left the scene, Waxmaster C changed his name to Premier.

Gang Starr are best known for their albums *Step in the Arena* (Chrysalis, 1991) and *Daily Operation* (Chrysalis, 1992). Even without attaining mass appeal or releasing a slew of albums, Gang Starr's contributions to rap music are nonetheless important. DJ Premier and Guru won the loyalty of fans and critics alike with their combination of socially conscious lyrics, no-nonsense stance, and jazz-influenced beats. Gang Starr's 1989 debut album, *No More Mr. Nice Guy*, was innovative in that the tracks were heavily steeped in a jazz aesthetic. Unfortunately, their first effort did not impress many listeners, aside from the tracks "Manifest" and "DJ Premier in Deep Concentration."

Two years later, Gang Starr released their sophomore album, *Step in the Arena*, which showed the maturity of the artists. The album is considered a Hip Hop masterpiece. Premier had refined his production and DJ skills, which allowed him to expand the way he used samples to give his beats their unique jazzy texture. As the MC of the duo, Guru, a former rebel, uses his trademark monotone voice to recite thought-provoking lyrics that greatly contrasted with the materialistic bent that dominated rap music during this period.

In 1992, the duo released *Daily Operation*, perhaps their greatest album. Although both *Step in the Arena* and *Daily Operation* would be highly praised by music critics and **underground** Hip Hop listeners, neither album spawned any mainstream hits. Gang Starr remains somewhat of an underground favorite. They are revered for songs such as "Just to Get a Rep," "Step in the Arena," "Take It Personal," and "Soliloquy of Chaos." Gang Starr refused to modify their style to the latest trends in order to chase "mass appeal," and they fiercely made that point with the track "Mass Appeal" on their 1994 album *Hard to Earn* (Capitol Records).

After a four-year hiatus Gang Starr returned with the album *Moment of Truth* (Noo Trybe/Virgin), which had the successful single "You Know My Steez," proving that the duo was still capable of making great music. In 1999, Gang Starr released *Full Clip: A Decade of Gang Starr* (Virgin Records), a two-disc greatest hits album that celebrated their tenth anniversary. Following the release of *Full Clip*, Premier and Guru took a break from Gang Starr but continued to be active in the music scene. Premier continued to produce for numerous artists and Guru continued to release solo album projects, which often had him collaborating with jazz and rap artists. In June 2003, Gang Starr released their seventh album, The *Ownerz* (Virgin Records).

The irony of Gang Starr may be while Premier produced winning tracks for mainstream rap artists, the duo themselves were uncompromising in the quality of their beat and their lyrical content. Stardom may have eluded them, but Gang Starr leave a legacy of excellent music.

DISCOGRAPHY: *No More Mr. Nice Guy* (Wild Pitch, 1989); *Step Into the Arena* (Chrysalis, 1991); *Daily Operation* (Chrysalis, 1992); *Hard to Earn* (Chrysalis, 1994); *Moment of Truth* (Noo Trybe/Virgin); *Ownerz* (Virgin, 2003).

GENIUS. *See* GZA

GETO BOYS, THE

For most of the 1990s, The Geto Boys—Bushwick Bill [Richard Shaw], Big Mike, **Scarface** [Brad Jordon], and Willie Dee [Willie Dennis]—would be embroiled in controversies about their ultraviolent and graphic lyrics. Without much airplay, the group nonetheless gained a loyal following.

In 1986, rap entrepreneur James "Lil' J" Smith formed the Ghetto Boys in Houston, Texas, and signed them to his Rap-A-Lot record company. The original lineup consisted of Prince Johnny C., the Slim Jukebox, and DJ Reddy Red. In 1988, the Ghetto Boys released the album *Making Trouble*. When in 1987 and 1988 Johnny C. and Slim Jukebox left, Smith added the diminutive dancer Bushwick Bill and two Rap-A-Lot solo acts: Ackshen (aka Scarface) and Willie "D" Dennis.

Former **Def Jam Recordings** partner Rick Rubin heard the group's independently released debut album, *Grip It! On That Other Level* and decided to **remix** and rerecord tracks from the album for release on his own record company, Def American. In 1990, at the point that the album was ready to be released, distributor Geffen Records refused to go forward because of the track "Mind of a Lunatic," which described necrophilia with a murder victim. By late 1990, Rubin had secured Giant Records as the album's distributor. That year, the newly minted **Geto Boys** released their eponymous *Geto Boys* album (Rap-A-Lot/Def American).

In 1991, with the release of their sophomore effort, *We Can't Be Stopped* (Rap-A-Lot), The Geto Boys continued to provide fodder for moralistic politicians intent on using them as examples of the decaying of American music. Prior to the release of the album, Bushwick Bill had lost an eye as a result of being shot by his girlfriend. The album cover showed Willie D and Scarface wheeling Bill into an emergency room, with a prominent image of his injured eye. The album's contents were considered by some to among the most extreme in the history of recorded music. Although radio did not readily support the album, by 1992 it had gone platinum, buoyed in part by the **underground** hit "Mind Playing Tricks on Me."

By 1993, all three members had recorded as solo artists. Willie D, citing artistic differences, was the only member to formally quit the group. Scarface and Bushwick Bill continued The Geto Boys with new member Big Mike, releasing *Uncut Dope: Geto Boys Best* (Noo Trybe/Virgin) in 1992 and *Till Death Do Us Part* (Rap-A-Lot) in 1993, after which the group split up. In 1996, the group reunited with Willie D. and released the album *The Resurrection* (Rap-A-Lot). They followed up with *Da Good, Da Bad & Da Ugly* (Rap-A-Lot) in 1998. Seven years after their last album, Bushwick Bill, Scarface, and Willie D came together for their latest album, *Foundation* (Rap-A-Lot), originally titled *War and Peace*.

DISCOGRAPHY: *Ghetto Boys: Making Trouble* (Rap-A-Lot, 1988); *Geto Boys: Grip It! On That Other Level* (Rap-A-Lot, 1988); *Geto Boys* (Rap-A-Lot/Def American, 1990); *We Can't Be Stopped* (Rap-A-Lot/Priority Records, 1991); *Uncut Dope: Geto Boys Best* (Rap-A-Lot, 1992); *Till Death Do Us Part* (Rap-A-Lot, 1993); *The Resurrection* (Noo Trybe/

Rap-A-Lot, 1996); *Da Good, Da Bad & Da Ugly* (Virgin, 1998).

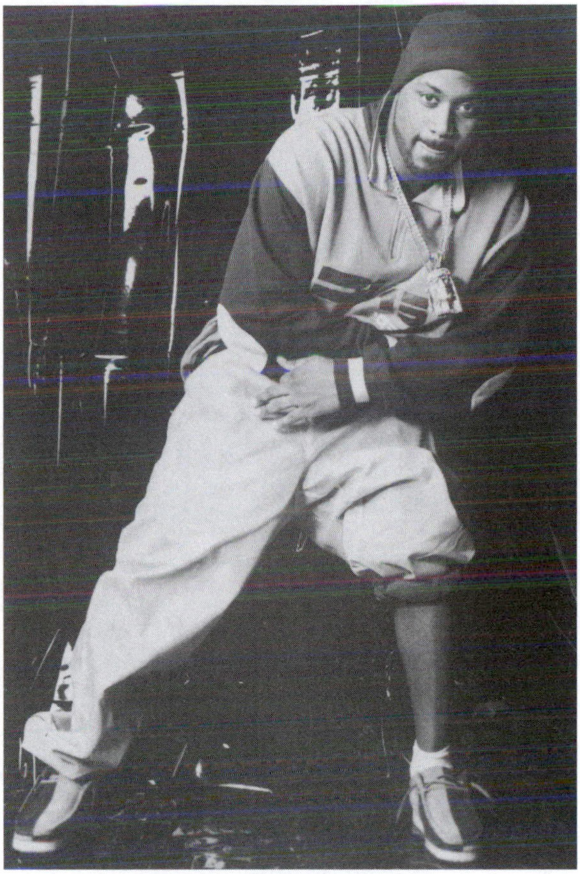

Ghostface Killah. *Courtesy of Photofest.*

GHOSTFACE KILLAH (aka Tony Starks) [Dennis Coles]

One of the original members of the 1990s rap group the **Wu-Tang Clan**, Ghostface Killah simultaneously launched a solo career, as did all other members of the Wu-Tang Clan. Although this native of Staten Island, New York, did not make an impact on the Wu-Tang Clan's 1993 debut album *Enter The Wu-Tang (36 Chambers)* (Loud/RCA), he received good reviews for his contribution to the album *Only Built 4 Cuban Linx* (Loud/RCA, 1995), by fellow Wu-Tang member **Raekwon**.

Ghostface is described as a superior lyricist who portrays his difficult childhood through both hardcore and occasionally gentle language. In early Wu-Tang Clan photos and videos, Ghostface wore a stocking cap to obscure his face, sparking rumors that he was wanted by the police and did not wish to be identified. In the Wu-Tang Clan's video for the song "Can It Be All So Simple," Ghostface removes the stocking cap. Subsequently Ghostface appeared on soundtracks for the films *Sunset Park* ("Motherless Child"), *Don't Be a Menace to South Central While You're Drinking Your Juice in the Hood* ("Winter Warz"), and *The Great White Hype* ("Who's the Champion").

Ghostface released his 1996 solo debut album, *Ironman* (RazorSharp/Epic), produced by **RZA**, to favorable reviews and was a great success in the Hip Hop **underground**. *Ironman* was also the first album to be released on Razor Sharp Records, RZA's record label. The follow-up album, *Supreme Clientele*, released in early 2000, was considered another hit. Unfortunately, his third album, the 2001 *Bulletproof Wallets*, got little attention, with some fans declaring that Tony Starks had "fell off." Taking time to regroup, at the end 2003 new Ghostface tracks, "Run" with **Jadakiss** and "Tush" with **Missy Elliott**, had started to appear on **mixtapes**. In April 2004, Ghostface dropped Killah from his

name and released the well-received, *The Pretty Toney Album*, his first album for **Def Jam Recordings**.
DISCOGRAPHY: *Ironman* (RazorSharp/Epic, 1996); *Supreme Clientele* (RazorSharp/Epic, 2000); *Bulletproof Wallets* (Razor Sharp/Epic, 2001); *The Pretty Toney Album* (Def Jam Recordings, 2004).

"GIGOLO RAP"

The first West Coast rap music song to be put on vinyl was "Gigolo Rap," by **Disco Daddy and Captain Rap** in 1981.

GO-GO AND RAP

Go-Go is a music indigenous to the Washington, DC, metropolitan area. The genre originated in the early 1970s by Chuck Brown and the Soul Searchers, who began by performing jazz. The benchmarks of Go-Go are "call and response" lyrics and percussion. Go-Go allows live bands to continue playing into the next song, or groove, without stopping. This was accomplished by letting the band's percussion section, particularly drums and congas, take center stage while an MC talks to the crowd.

The collaboration between rap music and go-go began when rap artist **Kurtis Blow** recorded his 1982 single "Party Time," with Essence Unlimited, known also as EU. **Grandmaster Flash and the Furious Five** recorded their own version of Trouble Funk's "Pump Me Up." Producer Herbie "Luvbug" Azor used go-go beats on the hit singles "My Mike Sound Nice" and "Shake Your Thang" by **Salt 'N Pepa** and on "Rollin' with Kid-n-Play" by **Kid 'N Play**. Producer Hitman Howie Tee also used go-go beats "Bang Zoom—Let's Go-Go" by the **Real Roxanne**. On the single "Rock the Bells," **LL Cool J** used a Trouble Funk loop in the bridge. **Heavy D** used a go-go breakdown in "Mr. Big Stuff," and **Doug E. Fresh** used a Chuck Brown backbeat in "All the Way to Heaven."

GOLD CHAINS

In the 1980s, before the emergence of diamond-encrusted or "iced out" platinum jewelry, large (called "fat" or "dookie") gold rope chains, often worn several at a time, were the *de rigueur* accessory for young men associated with Hip Hop. This style emulated that of former bodyguard Mr. T, a cast member of the television show *A Team*. Heavy Cuban link chains were also worn during this period, as were Mercedes Benz car emblems on a chain, worn alone or in conjunction with rope chains.

GOLD FRONTS

A dental accessory worn primarily by men, gold fronts are gold overlays worn on the front teeth, some of which include designs.

GOODIE MOB

Goodie Mob, a quartet from Atlanta, Georgia, became one of the most respected groups hailing from below the Mason-Dixon Line. When they arrived on the music scene in 1995, with members Cee-Lo [Thomas Burton], Khujo [Willie Knighton], T-Mo [Robert Barnett], and Big Gipp [Cameron Gipp], they were among the first to deliver issue-oriented lyrics from a Southern perspective. Goodie Mob's music represented a unique Black experience that was grounded in both the inclusive and urbane New South and the racist and parochial Old South.

While many rap artists from the Dirty South rose to prominence on the strength of irreverent lyrics or diatribes about street life, Goodie Mob

Goodie Mob. *Courtesy of Photofest.*

dealt with serious topics in a more thoughtful way. The Goodie Mob was passionately pro-South and pro-Black without sounding anti-White. Besides a message that spoke of optimism in spite of the odds, the group's soulful sound also distanced them from other Southern artists. The spiritual center of The Goodie Mob was Cee-Lo, the son of two deceased ministers. He is distinctive for his raspy voice and his chubby, 5-foot-tall frame.

The group's debut album, *Soul Food* (La Face/Arista, 1995) was one of the first Southern rap albums to be produced by a major record company. The album cover actually shows the group at a table praying. The album opens with "Free," a brief track steeped in the spirituals as a precursor to the message to come. Produced by Organized Noize, *Soul Food* evokes an Afrocentricity rooted in the gospels rather than in academe. Thematically, the quartet's sophomore effort, *Still Standing* (La Face/Arista 1998), continued to discuss subjects such as poverty, drug abuse, and Black power.

Creatively, they pushed the envelope by used live instruments, a rarity within Hip Hop. *Soul Food* and *Still Standing* broke new music ground within rap music with innovative rhyming and production, and gained The Goodie Mob a loyal following. Unfortunately, although the albums both sold approximately 500,000 units, those numbers fell far short of the platinum sales figures that have become the benchmark of a successful rap album. Perhaps under pressure to be more commercial and sell more records, the group's 1999 release, *World Party* (LaFace/Artista), was decidedly a more club-friendly album.

In 2002, citing professional and personal differences, Cee-Lo announced the end of Goodie Mob. That same year, he released his debut solo album, *Cee-Lo Green and His Perfect Imperfections* (Arista, 2002). In June 2004, the three remaining members of The Goodie Mob released the album *One Monkey Don't Stop the Show* (Koch), a sly reference to the much talked about departure of lead MC, Cee-Lo.

DISCOGRAPHY: *Soul Food* (La Face/Arista, 1995); *Still Standing* (La Face/Arista 1998); *World Party* (LaFace/Arista, 1999); *One Monkey Don't Stop the Show* (Koch, 2004).

"GOOD TIMES"

One of the earliest records to be sampled by rap music producers, Chic's single "Good Times" from their album *Risqué* (Atlantic, 1979) is also one of the most sampled songs in Hip Hop history. Sugar Hill Gang on "**Rapper's Delight**" (Sugar Hill Records, 1979) and **Grandmaster Flash** on "Adventures of Grandmaster Flash on the Wheels of Steel" (Sugar Hill Records, 1981) sampled or copied Bernard Edwards's bass line in full and in part. Initially, Bernard Edwards and Nile Rogers did not receive credit for composing the melody line for "Rapper's Delight," but were eventually acknowledged as co-writers. The song became a staple for a generation of emerging DJs and rap artists.

GORE, TIPPER

Tipper Gore is known for her activism as a founder of the Parents Music Resource Center (PMRC). In 1985, as the wife of then Senator Al Gore, Tipper joined a group of politicians' wives who objected to offensive lyrical content and held hearings on Capitol Hill advocating a rating system for recorded music.

See also: Censorship

GRAFFITI (aka Aerosol Art)

Graffiti—writing messages and drawing images in public spaces—is an ancient art. In more modern times, political activists used graffiti as a means to protest government policies and actions. Gang members have also used graffiti to mark their territory. Graffiti writing that uses spray paints is also known as aerosol art and became the visual component of Hip Hop.

The aerosol artwork associated with Hip Hop culture began in Philadelphia, Pennsylvania, during the mid to late 1960s and has its origins in *bombing*, or numerous writings of single names or messages. Philadelphia's Cornbread and Cool Earl are the first credited with a

Graffiti. *Courtesy of Photofest.*

conscious bombing effort. The two wrote their names throughout the city and garnered the attention of press, who made them celebrities by covering their activities. In New York, TAKI 183, a teenager from Greece named Demetrius, popularized tagging. Demetrius, who lived in the Washington Heights section of Manhattan, was first influenced when he saw "Julio 204" written on a street. Julio was a teenager who lived on 204th Street. Similarly, Demetrius took the nickname Taki and wrote it in front of the street where he lived, 183rd Street, creating the tag TAKI 183. Demetrius proceeded to write his tag in as many places as he could.

Philadelphia's Top Cat 126 is credited with moving away from tagging and developing the more complex "Broadway Style," which he would bring to New York City. The Broadway Style, along with the Softie or Bubble letters developed by Phase2, would form the foundation for aerosol art masterpieces. Writers such as LEE (Lee Quinones) began to paint intricate murals on the subway trains. After the Metropolitan Transit Authority began to *buff* or remove graffiti from the trains, LEE stopped painting his murals on the subway cars and went instead to creating his art on handball courts. LEE's handball court murals mixed cartoon characters with a moral awareness. One such mural appeal pleaded for an end to the arms race.

The original **writer's bench** in New York where graffiti writers gathered was located at 149th and Grand Concourse in the Bronx.

Some of the legendary graffiti artists include Cornbread (Philadelphia, Pennsylvania), Top Cat 126 (Philadelphia), Dondi (Donald J. White; Brooklyn, New York), Daze (Brooklyn), Futura2000 (New York City), Pink aka Lady Pink (Sandra Fabara, Queens, New York), LEE (Lee Quinones; New York City), Zephyr (New York City), and Phase2 (Bronx, New York). Super Kool 223 (Bronx) and WAP (Brooklyn) are both credited with first designing complex aerosol art, producing what would be known as masterpieces. NOC167 (Melvin Samuels Jr.) helped to develop "Wild Style." His famous car, called "Style Wars," is considered one of the best subway cars ever painted and was reproduced in 1991 for the "High and Low" exhibition at the Museum of Modern Art. Fabulous Five (Staten Island, New York) and The Death Squad (aka TDS; New York, all boroughs) were among the most significant and influential crews.

KEY TERMS: *Bombing*: Writing prolifically; *Burner*: A stylistically and technically well-done wild-style piece (burner also refers to subway cars); *Piece*: Term for a graffiti writer's artwork (short for masterpiece); *Style Wars*: A competition between graffiti writers to determine who has the superior talent; *Tag*: A graffiti writer's name or signature (as a verb, to write one's name or signature); *Throw-up*: A quickly drawn piece that may or may not have a thin layer of spray paint for fill-in; *Wild Style*: A complicated design of interlocking letters; *Writer*: An aerosol artist.

"GRAFFITI ROCK"

A single-episode television show that featured all of the elements of Hip Hop, "Graffiti Rock" aired on June 29, 1984, on New York's WPIX television station. Performers included **Run DMC**, **Kool Moe Dee**, and Special K of the **Treacherous Three**.

GRANDMASTER CAZ (aka Casanova Fly) [Curtis Fisher]

One of the unsung heroes of Hip Hop, Grandmaster Caz is known to many as the uncredited author of rhymes that Big Bank Hank used, without permission, to craft the Sugar Hill Gang's "Rapper' Delight (Sugar Hill Records, 1979).

Grandmaster Caz was the first to act simultaneously as both DJ and MC. The Bronx native saw **DJ Kool Herc** in 1974 and decided to also become a DJ. He purchased some equipment and named himself Casanova Fly. After learning how to DJ, he teamed up with JDL (Jerry Dee Lewis) and formed the rap duo Notorious Two; he became the first DJ to rap while working the turntables.

Casanova Fly became Grandmaster Caz and around 1978 or 1979 Caz and JDL joined the **Cold Crush Brothers**. The legacy of Grandmaster Caz and this group remains somewhat in the recesses of the Hip Hop annals, because the Cold Crush Brothers never recorded a full-length album. With emergence of **Run DMC**, many Old School rap groups, the Cold Crush Brothers among them, came to be considered passé and dissolved.

In the late 1980s after the end of the Cold Crush Brothers, Grandmaster Caz became a solo artist and on Tuff City recorded singles including "Mr. Bill," "Yvette," "Count Basie," "I'm Caz," "Casanova's Rap," and "Get Down Grandmaster." Unfortunately none of the singles were commercially successful, and he disappeared from the rap music scene. In the late 1990s, when exploring the roots of Hip Hop became more prevalent, Grandmaster Caz was recognized as one of its pioneers. In 1999, he made an appearance at a Hip Hop conference held at the Rock and Roll Hall of Fame. In 2000, he released the single "MC Delight," which addresses the "**Rapper's Delight**" controversy.

GRANDMASTER FLASH AND THE FURIOUS FIVE

Grandmaster Flash [Joseph Saddler] and the Furious Five crew, comprised of **Melle Mel** [Melvin Glover], Kidd Creole [Nathaniel Glover], Cowboy [Keith Wiggins], Rahiem [Guy Todd Williams], and Mr. Ness (aka Scorpio) [Eddie Morris] dominated Hip Hop in the early 1980s. With Grandmaster Flash on the turntables and MC Melle Mel's rhymes, the group produced several international hits, including the groundbreaking singles "The Message," "Freedom," and "White Lines (Don't Do it)."

Along with **Afrika Bambaataa** and **DJ Kool Herc**, Grandmaster Flash is considered one of the Holy Trinity of Hip Hop. In the mid-1970s, Grandmaster Flash learned the basic art of cutting between records from DJ Kool Herc, and then, along with Afrika Bambaataa, he became Herc's competition. Grandmaster Flash began his career performing at house parties and block parties, along with his partner "Mean Gene" Livingston, and they developed a following.

An innovative DJ, Grandmaster Flash had a key role in the development of **breakbeat** music. Unable to compete with DJ Kool Herc's massive sound system, he sought to use superior DJ skills to best him. An electronics major from Samuel Gompers Vocational High School, Grandmaster Flash perfected the art of mixing and "punch phasing." (Punch phasing is when a musical phrase or snippet from one record is quickly punched over the other record as it plays.) Grandmaster Flash was the first to master cutting the breakbeat on a record back and forth. He also installed a SPDT (single-pole double throw) switch on his **mixer**, which allowed him to hear what was playing on each turntable through a pair of headphones and cue records. (DJ Kool Herc, who cued records by sight, would not use headphones until much later.)

Grandmaster Flash was also the credited with using the electronic **beatbox**. He would put it between his turntables and used it to play beats in between records. His triumphant moment was playing before 3,000 people at Harlem's Audubon Ballroom on September 2, 1977. By 1978, Grandmaster Flash's popularity had surpassed that of DJ Kool Herc in popularity, but at the same time there was also a shift in Hip Hop, away from the DJ to the MC. During performances, Flash rapped and made shout-outs, but he realized that aside from his DJ skills he needed to join forces with some MCs. To stay relevant in the rap scene, he worked briefly in 1978–1979 with **Kurtis Blow**.

In 1980, Grandmaster Flash would receive mainstream recognition when punk rocker Debbie Harry rapped about him on Blondie's song "Rapture." During this period, Grandmaster Flash recruited his friends Cowboy, Melle Mel, and Mel's older brother Kidd Creole. The group called themselves the Three MCs and began writing their own rhymes. Next, The Three MCs added Rahiem Williams and Mr. Ness (Scorpio), and so became Grandmaster Flash and the Furious Five. The Under the name, "The Younger Generation" the group recorded the single "We Rap More Mellow" (Brass Records), and under the name Flash and The Five, they recorded a live version of "Flash To The Beat," released on Bozo Meko Records.

Grandmaster Flash and the Furious Five would go on to record *Super Rappin'* for **Enjoy Records** in 1976. In 1981, Grandmaster Flash displayed his superior cutting and scratching skills on the original twelve-inch single "The Adventures of Grandmaster Flash on the Wheels of Steel" (Sugar Hill Records). Rather than a song, Grandmaster Flash let loose a flurry of record sections, using parts of Blondie's "Rapture,"

Chic's "**Good Times**," and Queen's "Another One Bites the Dust," as well as parts of Furious Five releases.

Grandmaster Flash and the Furious Five are unquestionably known for the single "The Message," released in June of 1982. "The Message" was revolutionary, in that it was among the first rap records to discuss social themes (see Brother D with collective effort's 1981 song, "How We Gonna Make the Black Nation Rise"), paving the way for other artists like **Boogie Down Productions** and **Public Enemy**. The anti-drug song "White Lines (Don't Do It)" followed in 1983. By 1983, the ascendancy of **Run DMC** meant that Old School groups began to fade from the scene. Around this time, Grandmaster Flash sued Sugar Hill Records for $5 million in royalties. The lawsuit divided the group, with Melle Mel leading one faction and Flash the other. In 1984, Grandmaster Melle Mel and the Furious Five released the album *Work Party* (Sugar Hill Records) and the single "Beat Street" from the film soundtrack.

In 1987, the group reunited to record the album *On the Strength* (Elektra Records, 1988). It was not well received, and the group split up permanently. In 1989, the twenty-eight-year-old Cowboy died from the effects of drug abuse. The remaining members would continue to be involved in the music industry.

In 1990, Grandmaster Melle Mel and the Furious Five released their second album, *Piano* (Bon Ami Records). In 1997, Melle Mel and Scorpio released an album titled *Right Now* (Str8 Game Records). Melle Mel lent his vocal talents to the Sugar Hill Gang for their children's album *Jump on It* (1999), and in 2001, Melle Mel and Rondo released the album *On Lock*.

Grandmaster Flash released several solo albums: *The Adventures of Grandmaster Flash on the Wheels of Steel* (Sugar Hill Records, 1981); *They Said It Couldn't Be Done* (Elektra, 1985); *The Source* (Elektra, 1986); *Ba-Dop-Boom-Bang* (Elektra, 1987); *Grandmaster Flash Presents Salsoul Jam 2000: Dance Your Ass Off* (Salsoul Records, 1997); and *Flash Is Back* (Marlboro M, 1999). He became the musical director of HBO's *The Chris Rock Show*, and in 2002, Grandmaster Flash released *The Official Adventures of Grandmaster Flash* and *Essential Mix: Classic Collection*.

DISCOGRAPHY: *Singles*: Under the name The Younger Generation, "We Rap More Mellow" (Brass Records); under the name Flash and the Five, "Flash to the Beat" (Bozo Meko Records); "Super Rappin'" (Enjoy Records, 1976); "Freedom" (Sugar Hill Records, 1980); "It's Nasty (Genius of Love)" (Sugar Hill Records, 1982); "Scorpio" (Sugar Hill Records, 1982); "NY, NY" (Sugar Hill Records, 1983); "White Lines (Don't Do It)" (Sugar Hill Records, 1983).

GRAND PUBA [Maxwell Dixon]

Grand Puba is best known as the front man for **Brand Nubian**'s first album, *One for All* (Elektra Records, 1990), and their 1998 reunion album, *Foundation*. (Elektra Records).

The rap artist made his recording debut in 1988 with Masters of Ceremony, who released the album *Dynamite* (4th & Broadway). In 1992, after Grand Puba departed Brand Nubian, he released the album *Reel to Reel* (Elektra Records), which featured the standout singles "360 Degrees (What Goes Around)" and "Check It Out" (with **Mary J. Blige**). His sophomore album, *2000* (Elektra Records), was released in 1995 and his third album, *Understand This* (Koch Records). was released in 2001.

Beginning with his work with Brand Nubian, Grand Puba's rhymes have been influenced by his **Five Percent** beliefs. Grand Puba is also credited with popularizing the Tommy Hilfiger sportswear brand with Hip Hop fans. **DISCOGRAPHY:** *Reel to Reel* (Elektra Records, 1992); *2000* (Elektra Records, 1995); *Understand This* (Koch Records, 2001).

GRAND WIZZARD THEODORE (aka GrandWizzard Theodore) [Theodore Livingston]

A pioneering DJ who perfected the turntable technique known as needle dropping, and who is often credited as the inventor of **scratching**, Grand Wizzard Theodore was also the headliner for the rap group Grand Wizzard Theodore and the Fantastic Five, who **battled** archrival the **Cold Crush Brothers** in the seminal Hip Hop movie *Wild Style* (1983).

GRAVEDIGGAZ

The Gravediggaz are The Rzarector (aka **RZA**, from the Wu-Tang Clan) [Robert Diggs], The Gatekeeper (aka Fruitkwan, aka Frukwan, formerly of **Stetsasonic**) [Arnold Hamilton], and The Grym Reaper (aka Too Poetic) [Anthony Berkeley], with Dr. Strange (aka The Undertaker, aka producer **Prince Paul**) [Paul Huston] as producer.

The supergroup popularized a music called horrorcore, for its scary raps over hardcore beats. According to the Gravediggaz, their mission was to "resurrect the mentally dead," and they did so with mind-challenging lyrics. Their 1994 debut album, *6 Feet Deep* (titled *Niggamortis* for its European release), did fairly well, but their videos received very little airplay and MTV even banned the video for the track "Diary of a Madman," possibly because the song, with its discussion of death and killing, elicited enough gruesome images and the video itself was no less gruesome.

With each successive album, the membership dwindled. On their 1997 sophomore album, *The Pick, The Sickle And The Shovel*, Prince Paul was largely absent. This RZA-produced album introduces a new style, not as gloomy as the first album; the tracks depict life on the streets and reality in the ghettos. For the 2001 *Nightmares In A-Minor*, RZA was gone, leaving only Frukwan and Too Poetic. During the recording of this album, Too Poetic was battling metastatic colon cancer. When it was first diagnosed in 1999, he had been expected to live only a few more months. Too Poetic died on Sunday, July 15, 2001, leaving Frukwan as the sole Gravediggaz.

DISCOGRAPHY: *6 Feet Deep* (V2./BMG, 1997 re-issue); *The Pick, The Sickle and The Shovel* (V2./BMG, 1997); *Nightmare in A-Minor* (Empire Musicwerks, 2002).

GREAT DAY IN HIP HOP, A

The 1998 photograph inspired by the 1958 photograph titled, "A Great Day In Harlem," by Art Kane, depicts fifty-seven musicians representing three generations of jazz history who showed up that morning on the stoop of 17 East 126th Street, between Fifth and Madison Avenues in Harlem. The photo originally appeared in the January 1959 issue of *Esquire* magazine. In December 1998, the rap music publication, *XXL* magazine, decided to re-create that famous day forty years before, using the original location as the backdrop for rap music artists. Some 200 rap artists showed up for the photo shoot, spilling over three stoops.

GZA (aka Genius/GZA, aka Genius) [Gary Grice]

A Brooklyn, New York, native, GZA is the oldest member of the **Wu-Tang Clan**.

GZA officially began his career in 1991 with the release of his solo album titled, *Words From The Genius* (Cold Chillin' Records). The final album was not what GZA had in mind when he walked into the studio: a miserable failure, with sales of less than 31,000 units, even counting a rerelease in 1994. In the aftermath of his debut album flopping and fights with the label over marketing and payment issues, GZA was more prepared for his next foray into the music industry. GZA and his two cousins, **Ol' Dirty Bastard** and **RZA**, would form the rap group, All In Together Now. Three years later, others would join the trio and the group became the Wu-Tang Clan.

The Wu-Tang Clan released their debut album, *Enter the Wu-Tang (36 Chambers)* in 1993 on Loud Records. Known as a master craftsman, GZA fine-tunes his rhymes to dispense his street-bred wisdom. Critics often cite GZA's metaphoric and multiple-layered lyrics as genius—as his chosen moniker asserts. In 1995, the Genius released the gold-selling *Liquid Swords* (Geffen Records) and in 1999, *Beneath The Surface* (Geffen). Without RZA's production skills, some critics panned *Beneath the Surface*; however, many GZA fans hail it as among his best work. In 2002, he again satisfied his fans with his lyricism with the release of *Legend of the Liquid Swords* (Geffen/MCA).

DISCOGRAPHY: *Liquid Swords* (Geffen Records, 1995); *Beneath the Surface* (Geffen/MCA, 1999); *Legend of the Liquid Swords* (Geffen/MCA, 2002).

H

HARLEM WORLD

Harlem World is considered one of the three most important Uptown New York City venues in the cultivation of Old School Hip Hop. Along with **Disco Fever** (located near Yankee Stadium in the Bronx) and **T-Connection** (formerly at Gun Hill and White Plains Roads, also in the Bronx), Harlem World (located at 116th and Lenox Avenue in Manhattan) was an important venue for performances, **battles**, and parties in the early years of Hip Hop.

HARRELL, ANDRE

Andre Harrell is perhaps best known as the President of Uptown Entertainment and as mentor to **Sean "P. Diddy" Combs**.

Harrell however started his long career, as a rap artist, then he went on become a Vice President at **Def Jam Recordings** and after his departure from Uptown Entertainment, he went on to run the legendary Motown Records. The Bronx, New York, native began his career in music in 1977, at the age of fifteen, as one-half of the dapper rap duo **Dr. Jekyll and Mr. Hyde**. The twosome made their mark with such singles as "Genius Rap" (Profile, 1981) and "Fast Life" (Profile, 1984). Despite success as an artist, Harrell pursued his education and studied business administration at Lehman College (City University of New York). Harrell dropped out of school after the third year and began working full-time selling airtime on WINS radio in New York City, continuing to perform on the weekends. In 1983, Harrell joined **Russell Simmons** at Rush Communications as Vice President and General Manager. In 1986, when MCA Records offered Harrell his own record company, he entered into a joint venture with MCA and Uptown Records (later Uptown Entertainment) was formed.

Rather than replicating the street-wise persona of Def Jam Recordings, Uptown Records represented the "good life" that many young Blacks desired. The Uptown Records image was of performers draped in stylish clothing and surrounded by luxury, homes, furnishings, and cars. Harrell's protégé Sean "P. Diddy" Combs would go on to extend the "ghetto fabulous" sentiment of Uptown at **Bad Boy Entertainment**.

As president of Uptown, Harrell launched the careers of artists such as **Heavy D and The Boyz**, **Mary J. Blige**, Guy, and Jodeci. He also nurtured

Andre Harrell. *Courtesy of Photofest.*

the talents of producers such as Teddy Riley, Sean "P. Diddy" Combs, Eddie F. (former Vice President of **A & R** at LaFace Records), Poke (Trackmasters), and Heavy D. Harrell served as the producer and music supervisors for the film *Strictly Business* (1991). In 1992, MCA signed Harrell to a multimedia deal to recruit, sign, and develop talent for recording, motion picture, and television projects.

Harrell was responsible for creating the Fox network television show ***New York Undercover***, which deftly featured musical artists in episodes. Harrell served as co-executive producer of the hour-long police drama, which starred Malik Yoba and Michael DeLorenzo. In October 1995, Harrell was appointed President and CEO of Motown Records, succeeding Jheryl Bugsby. Two years later, however, Harrell had left Motown under mounting pressure after failing to have any major hits during his tenure. Next, Harrell worked at Bad Boy Entertainment as a consultant and later as president. Most recently, Harrell cofounded an ad agency and talent company, Nu America. Currently, Nu America's highest-profile client is Tommy Hilfiger. Nu America developed a new television campaign on MTV for Tommy Jeans.

HEATHER B [Heather B. Gardner]

The New Jersey–based rap artist Heather B is known primarily for her role on the first season of MTV's *The Real World*, filmed in New York City (1992). First, however, Heather B had established herself as a talented MC with appearances on **Boogie Down Productions's** *Edutainment* (Jive Records, 1990), on the track "Dee Jays" and *Sex & Violence* (Jive Records, 1992), and on the single "We In There?"

After appearing on *The Real World*, Heather B recorded a single for Elektra Records, "I Get Wrecked" (1992), and pressed her own copies of another single, "All Glocks Down," which Pendulum Records re-issued in 1995. In 1993, she released her debut album, *Heather B*, on Asylum Records, with a second album three years later: *Taking Mine* (EMI America, 1996).

Heather B. *Courtesy of Photofest.*

Although Heather B did not have the same commercial success as **Lil' Kim** or **Foxy Brown**, her debut album is no less hardcore or entertaining. Standout tracks include "If Headz Only Knew," the previously released "All Glocks Down," and "My Kinda Nigga." In 1998, she released the single "Do You" (MCA). In that same year she, along with **Lady of Rage** and Nikki D, formed the Underdogs, an all-female collective and support group for female MCs. In 2002, she released the album *External Affairs*. Unfortunately, while the quality of the album may have been good, its release on the little-known Sai Records International Records did little to raise the visibility of either the album or the artist.

DISCOGRAPHY: *Singles:* "I Get Wrecked" (Elektra, 1995); "All Glocks Down" (independent release; then Pendulum, 1995); "Do You" (MCA, 1998). *Albums: Heather B* (Asylum, 1993); *Taking Mine* (EMI America, 1996); *External Affairs* (Sai International Records, 2002).

HEAVY D AND THE BOYZ

Heavy D and The Boyz is comprised of Heavy D [Dwight Myers], DJ Eddie F, and dancers G-Wiz [Glen Parrish] and Trouble T-Roy [Troy Dixon]. Rap artist Heavy D was born in Jamaica, but his family migrated to the United States and settled in the Bronx, New York, the home of Hip Hop.

Heavy D began experimenting with rap music at age eight. In high school, Heavy D asked his friend DJ Eddie F to help him with writing lyrics. In 1986, Heavy D and The Boyz (by now including also G-Wiz and Trouble T-Roy) became the first act signed to Uptown Records. In 1987, their first album, *Livin' Large,* was released; this included the group's first successful single, "Overweight Lovers In the House." In 1989,

Heavy D and The Boyz. *Courtesy of Photofest.*

platinum-selling *Big Tyme* (Uptown Records) was released, and the single "We Got Our Own Thing" increased Heavy D and The Boyz's mainstream visibility. Unfortunately, the next year, Heavy D and The Boyz faced a tragedy when Trouble T-Roy died in a stage accident during a tour. Troy's death became the subject of Pete Rock and CL Smooth's elegiac hit "The Reminisce Over You (T. R. O. Y.)."

In 1991, Heavy D and The Boyz released the album *Peaceful Journey* (Uptown Records) as a tribute to Trouble T-Roy. The single, "Now That We Found Love," a remake of Third World's classic song, went gold. The song was one of the first rap hits with a distinct reggae beat. Heavy D would also team up with reggae artist Supercat on his 1991 single, "Dem No Worry We" (Columbia Records). In 1993, Heavy D and the Boyz released a gold album, *Blue Funk* (Uptown Records), and in 1994 Heavy D and The Boyz scored their last major hit with the single "Nuttin' But Love," from the group's final album of the same name.

In 1995, Heavy D succeeded **Andre Harrell** as president of Uptown Records. He had become vice president of A & R two years earlier. During this period, he signed, groomed, and released R & B group Soul for Real's debut album, *Candy Rain*. In 1997, Heavy D released his own debut solo album, *Waterbed Hev* (Universal Records) and left his post at Uptown Records to focus on acting. He wrote and performed the theme song for the Fox network television show *In Living Color*. As an actor, he appeared on the television shows *Roc*, *Living Single*, *Boston Public*, and *The Tracy Morgan Show*. He also appeared in films such as *Life* (starring Eddie Murphy and Martin Lawrence), *The Cider House Rules*, and *Big Trouble*. Heavy D also made his theatrical debut in the off-Broadway play *Riff Raff*, written and directed by Laurence Fishburne. In 1999 Heavy D released another solo album, *Heavy* (Universal Records).

DISCOGRAPHY: *Livin' Large* (Uptown Records, 1987); *Big Tyme* (Uptown Records, 1989); *Peaceful Journey* (Uptown Records, 1991); *Blue Funk* (Uptown Records, 1993); *Heavy D and the Boyz* (Uptown, 1994).

HENDERSON, DOUGLAS "JOCKO"

Often called the Grandfather of Rap, radio DJ Douglas "Jocko" Henderson gained popularity in the 1950s for rhyming in between records. The native of Philadelphia, Pennsylvania, become so popular that his fan club reportedly numbered over 50,000 people, and he would send tapes of his famous *Ace of Rockets* show to other radio stations around the country.

Artists in the Caribbean were influenced by Jocko's rhyming style and attempted to mimic him in what became known as *toasting*, or *dub talk-over*. There are two accounts of how Jocko reached Jamaica. One cites a radio station in Miami, Florida, having a signal strong enough to be picked up in Jamaica. Another account has a Jamaican music producer coming to the United States, where he heard Jocko and encourages the sound system DJ that he works with to replicate Jocko's style. By either means, sound system DJs such as U-Roy became known for rhyming. In turn, these DJs influenced a Jamaican immigrant named **DJ Kool Herc**, who is considered by many to be the Father of Hip Hop.

Douglas "Jocko" Henderson died in July 2000.

HERCULOIDS

Herculoids is the name of **Kool DJ Herc**'s sound system.

HIEROGLYPHICS

Hieroglyphics, an Oakland, California–based collective, are known as consummate **battle** lyricists. The group is comprised of artists **Del Tha Funkee Homosapien**, Souls of Mischief (A +, Opio, Tajai, Phesto), Casual, and Domino and the Prose (Pep Love and Jaybiz).

Most of the members had known each other since high school, if not before, and after Del obtained a record deal with the help of his cousin, **Ice Cube**, most of the Hieroglyphics crew received major label contracts of their own. Del, Souls of Mischief, and Casual established a loyal following, however the Hieroglyphics never produced a major star. The Hieroglyphics founded an independent label, Hieroglyphics Imperium, when its members' individual deals with major record companies fell apart. The Hieroglyphics debut recording was the 1998 album, *On Third Eye Vision* (Hiero Imperium), which they followed up in 2003 with *Full Circle* (Hiero Imperium).

DISCOGRAPHY: *On Third Eye Vision* (Hiero Imperium, 1998); *Full Circle* (Hiero Imperium, 2003).

HIGH TOP FADE

An extreme version of the fade, a 1980s haircut for Black men that was cut short of the sides and back and higher in the top. The rap artist Play, from the duo **Kid 'N Play**, had an extreme version of the haircut. The Gumby (named after the cartoon character) coming out of Philadelphia was a variation popularized by rap group 3X Dope in which the higher top was styled asymmetrically to lean toward one side.

HILL, LAURYN (aka L-Boogie)

This native of South Orange, New Jersey, is best known as a member of the **Fugees**. Hill began singing at an early age and at thirteen she competed in The Apollo Theater's legendary Amateur Night, singing the Smokey Robinson tune, "Who's Loving You." Hill did not win the contest, but nonetheless continued to perform. At the age of sixteen, Hill had a small but recurring role on the soap opera *As the World Turns*. She also appeared in the films *King of the Hill* (1993), *Sister Act 2: Back in the Habit* (1993), and *Restaurant* (1998).

In high school she would form the Tranzlator Crew, with friends Wyclef Jean and Prakazrel Michel. The trio, now called the Fugees, developed a following in the tri-state area and in 1993 they released their debut album, *Blunted On Reality* (Ruffhouse/Columbia). The much-hyped album failed to deliver and the Fugees almost broke up. That same year Hill enrolled at Columbia University. Their follow-up album, *The Score*, went multi-platinum, however, and the Fugees, particularly the telegenic Hill, achieved international success.

In 1998, Hill released her solo effort, *The MisEducation of Lauryn Hill* (Ruffhouse/Columbia Records). Hill wrote, arranged, or produced almost every track on the album. The album sails through many genres, including reggae, rap, and Old School soul, as evidenced the Motown-esque track "Doo Wop (That Thing)." Hill's solo album had the highest first-week sales of any album by a female artist at that point in time. In 1999, she received ten Grammy nominations for the album and took home five awards: Album of the Year, Best New Artist, Best Female R & B Vocal Performance, Best R & B Song, and Best R & B Album—the most ever received by a female artist. The album was also the first rap album in history to win a Grammy for Album of the Year.

Hill's creativity would be challenged by a lawsuit initiated by two musicians claiming they were denied full credit for their work on the album; the matter was eventually settled out of court. Although the Fugees never officially broke up, Hill's album led fans to believe that the trio was done. Rumors began to swirl about the Fugees internal conflicts, and many fans interpreted Hill's lyrics about stardom-seeking as a public criticism of Wyclef Jean.

Hill has continued shape her solo career, releasing *MTV Unplugged 2.0* (Columbia Records) in 2002, a double disc that showcases Hill's deeply personal performance. In addition to her own performing, Hill has written and produced hit songs for Aretha Franklin and CeCe Winans, and she has formed her own film production company. Hill is also the founder of The Refugee Camp Youth Project, which focuses on improving the quality of life of disadvantaged children.

DISCOGRAPHY: *The Miseducation of Lauryn Hill* (Ruffhouse/Columbia Records, 1998); *MTV Unplugged 2.0* (Columbia Records, 2002).

HIP HOP

Afrika Bambaataa credits **DJ Lovebug Starski** with first using the term *Hip Hop* to describe the new music and subculture. Around 1973 The **Zulu Nation** began widespread usage of the term Hip Hop as means to organize the new subculture.

HIPHOP APPRECIATION WEEK

Inspired by Carter G. Woodson's Negro History Week (now February's Black History Month), in 1998 **KRS-ONE** instituted Hiphop Appreciation Week, choosing the third week in May to honor Malcolm X, whose birthday is May 19. The week is recognized as a celebration and contemplation of Hip Hop's heritage. On May 14, 2001, Bronx Borough President Fernando Ferrer issued a proclamation recognizing Hiphop Appreciation Week.

See also: Appendix 2

HIP HOP HISTORY MONTH

The Universal **Zulu Nation** cites its own birthday as November 12, 1973, and the birth of Hip Hop as November 12, 1974. Since November 1974, strict followers of the subculture have celebrated Hip Hop History Month in November. On December 12, 2002, the New York State Senate officially proclaimed November as Hip Hop History Month.

See also: Appendix 2

HIP HOP CONFERENCE. *See* Howard University

HIP HOP LITERATURE (aka Gangsta Life Literature)

An increasingly popular style of writing that uses raw, often sexually explicit language to depict life in the ghettos of America has come to be known as Hip Hop literature, or sometimes as gangsta life literature. The genre stands in contrast to the nonfiction, fiction, and poetry written by authors of the Hip Hop generation such as Kevin Powell, Tony Medina, Willie Perdomo, Paul Beatty, Asha Bendele, Andrea Wren, and Jessica Care Moore, works that offer more varied portrayals and expressions of African American life.

These unvarnished tales of violent men and their women have provoked debate on the value of this brand of literature. The books have been criticized for glorifying thug life, criminality, and promiscuity and for thereby reinforcing negative stereotypes about African Americans. Moreover, with many of these self-published works, the writing is crude, grammatically incorrect, and filled with unintended misspellings.

Other critics have taken exception to applying the term Hip Hop to label these books, asserting that true Hip Hop fiction would have to concern some aspect of the cultural entity known as Hip Hop, or even its most commercial element, rap music. Otherwise, these critics say, Hip Hop is merely a stereotyped euphemism for Black and urban. As used by mainstream entertainment outlets, a Hip Hop label has the effect of marginalizing the multifaceted experience of young African Americans by heavily promoting the one-dimensional images of the drug dealer, drug addict, and baby's mama as the only authentic Black voices. Opponents of Hip Hop literature contend that if pulp fiction writers such as Donald Goines and **Iceberg Slim** were still alive today the books that they wrote would be marketed under the title Hip Hop fiction.

HIP HOP NATION EXHIBIT

In September 2000, the Brooklyn Museum of Art presented an exhibit, Hip Hop Nation. This was the first time Hip Hop artifacts were exhibited in a mainstream American cultural institution. The year before, the Rock and Roll Hall of Fame museum had organized an exhibit titled, "Hip-Hop Nation: Roots, Rhymes and Rage." It was a version of that exhibit, including a few pieces of **graffiti**, that was installed at the Brooklyn

Museum of Art. The museum's show was purported to be a comprehensive history of Hip Hop, showcasing sneakers, hats, clothing, and gold chains once worn by rap artists, as well as recordings, photographs, and other memorabilia. Critics cited too much focus on music, and a dearth of material relating to **B-boying** and graffiti arts. Furthermore, some visitors were also critical of its tepid treatment of the controversial rap lyrics and videos that have in part shaped Hip Hop.

HIP HOP THEATER FESTIVAL

Founded in 2000 by Clyde Valentin, **Danny Hoch**, and Kamilah Forbes in the summer of 2000, the New York City Hip-Hop Theater Festival was the first organized event showcasing the stories, characters, music, dance, and word of Hip Hop in one venue. The first festival brought together actors, playwrights, and **B-boys** and B-girls whose works represented the voices of the Hip Hop generation. Performances included Will Power's "The Gathering," Universe's "Slanguage," La Santa Luz Dance Company, and the two centerpieces: Sarah Jones's "Surface Transit" and Liza Colon Zayas's "Sistah Supreme." In 2002, the first Hip Hop Theater Festival in Washington, DC, was launched, supported by the D.C. Commission on the Arts. In 2003, the San Francisco Bay area held its first Hip Hop Theater Festival.

HIT SQUAD

The Hit Squad, an informal collective established in 1992 by rap duo **EPMD**, includes rap artists K-Solo, **Das EFX**, **Redman**, and Keith Murray.

HOCH, DANNY

Cofounder of the Hip Hop Theater Festival, Danny Hoch was one of the first artists to combine Hip Hop with theater. Hoch's work focuses on Hip Hop, race, class, and culture. Hoch's plays (*Pot Melting*, *Some People*, and *Jails, Hospitals & Hip-Hop*) have toured internationally. Hoch's writing and acting credits for television and film include *Bamboozled*, *Prison Song*, *SUBWAYStories*, *The Thin Red Line*, *Whiteboyz*, and *3 A.M.* Hoch is also a founding member of the Active Element Foundation (AEF), which builds relationships between grassroots youth activists, professionals, donors, and artists through grantmaking, technical assistance, and the development of Hip Hop-related arts projects.

Danny and his work have received numerous awards, including a National Endowment for the Arts Fellowship, Sundance Writers Fellowship, CalArts Alpert Award in Theater, Tennessee Williams Fellowship, two Obies, and a fellowship from the New School's Vera List Center for Art and Politics. His HBO special, "Some People," was nominated for a Cable Ace Award.

HOMEBOY

Homeboy is a slang term for a close friend or a person that one socializes with. *Also:* Homegirl.

HOODIES

Hoodies is a slang term for hooded sweatshirts.

HOUSE OF PAIN

House of Pain members include Everlast [Eric Schrody], DJ Lethal [Leor DiMant]; Danny Boy [Daniel O'Connor]. The raucous, Irish-American rap group is best known for the catchy 1992 crossover hit, "Jump Around." Everlast became interested in rap music while he was in high school and eventually became part of **Ice-T**'s Rhyme Syndicate. Everlast's relationship with Ice-T lead Warner Records to sign him and in 1990 he released his debut solo album *Forever Everlasting.* When his album proved to be a flop, Everlast formed House of Pain in 1990 with his high school friend Danny Boy and DJ Lethal, a Latvian immigrant. In 1992, the group released their eponymous debut on Tommy Boy Records, which included the track "Jump Around." Unfortunately, House of Pain's subsequent albums, *Same as It Ever Was* (1994), and *Truth Crushed to Earth Shall Rise Again* (1996), failed to come remotely close

House of Pain. *Courtesy of Photofest.*

to the level of success of their first single, thus relegating the group to the one-hit wonder category of rap history. Everlast resurfaced 1998 as a solo act, and gained critical acclaim for his album *Whitey Ford Sings the Blues*

DISCOGRAPHY: *House of Pain* (Tommy Boy Records, 1992); *Same as It Ever Was* (Tommy Boy Records, 1994); *Truth Crushed to Earth Shall Rise Again* (Tommy Boy Records, 1996).

HOWARD UNIVERSITY

Founded in Washington, DC, in 1867, Howard University is the premier historically Black academic institution in the United States. Howard University was the site of the nation's first Hip Hop conference. Held in 1991, the conference would be the model for subsequent college-based Hip Hop symposiums. Under the title, "Seizing the Cultural Initiative: Hip Hop at its Crossroads," the four-day conference was conceived and run by The Cultural Initiative, Inc., a student-based organization at Howard. The conference offered panel discussions (e.g., on artist ownership, gender oppression, creative control, the emerging Hip Hop fashion industry), new artist showcases, demonstration sessions, a fashion show, and after-parties. Panel participants included rap artists **Chuck D**, **Kool Moe Dee**, **MC Lyte**, and **Sister Souljah**.

HUMAN BEAT BOX. *See* Beatboxing; Doug E. Fresh; Fat Boys

HUSTLERS CONVENTION

The prototype for modern rap music and the first recording to directly connect the concept of the hustler to Hip Hop. The album *Hustlers Convention* (Douglas Records, 1973) was recorded by **Last Poets** member Jalal Nuriddin, under the name Lightnin' Rod.

Hustlers Convention presents the tale of a hustler named Sport and his friend Spoon, told in twelve prison-style toasts. The album was the first to feature raps over instrumentals from a host of jazz and funk musicians, including Kool and the Gang and Billy Preston. Moreover, *Hustlers Convention* vividly depicts the 1959 hustlers convention at Hamhocks Hall. In this particular story, Sport and Spoon win $172,000 from gambling, have some adventures, and end up facing the law. The close of the album focuses on Sport, who—having spent twelve years on death row—now renounces his life as a hustler. Some cultural critics of the day called *Hustlers Convention* a moralistic **blaxploitation** film on wax. *Hustlers Convention* was an **underground** sensation in the Bronx, influencing Hip Hop pioneers such as **DJ Kool Herc** and **Grandmaster Caz**.

HYPE MAN

An individual whose job is to highlight the MC during live performances by pumping up the audience and demanding that people listen to the MC's lyrics. Trailblazing hype men include Bobby Bird, who worked with R & B legend **James Brown**; Kid Creole of **Grandmaster Flash and the Furious Five**; DJ Code Money, who performed with **Schoolly D** and with **Flavor Flav** of **Public Enemy**; and **Sean "P. Diddy" Combs**, who highlighted the rhymes of **The Notorious B.I.G.**

I

ICE

A slang term for diamonds, *ice* is also used to describe a cool demeanor.

ICEBERG SLIM [Robert Beck]

The tough pimp persona and the street life that Iceberg Slim wrote about would come to resonate with several generations of young Black men. His writings would influence Hip Hop by emboldening rap artists to tell their own, sometimes raw and gritty stories, in their own language. Two rap artists, **Ice-T** and **Ice Cube**, pay tribute to Iceberg Slim through their own street names.

Iceberg Slim was born as Robert Lee Maupin in Chicago, Illinois, on August 4, 1918. He spent much of his childhood in Milwaukee, Wisconsin, and Rockford, Illinois, before returning to Chicago as a teenager. Abandoned by his father, Slim's mother supported the family, working as a domestic and operating a beauty shop. According to Iceberg Slim, his mother's pampering of him in childhood prepared him for the pimp lifestyle. Iceberg Slim briefly attended Tuskegee Institute in the mid-1930s, at the same time that Ralph Ellison was there, although they are not known to have met. At eighteen, Robert Maupin turned to street life, becoming a pimp and adopting the name Iceberg Slim. He would remain as such, located primarily in the Chicago area, until age 42. Iceberg Slim was incarcerated several times, including a stretch in Leavenworth. In 1960, when he spent a ten-month sentence in solitary confinement at Cook County, Iceberg Slim turned to writing about his life experiences.

In the 1960s, Maupin moved to California and, seeking to divorce himself from the past, changed his name to Robert Beck (Beck being his mother's married name at the time). In 1967, he published his first book, an autobiographical novel titled *Pimp: The Story of My Life*. Other books followed: *Trick Baby: The Story of a White Negro* [also published as *Trick Baby: The Biography of a Con Man*] (1967); *Mama Black Widow* (1969); *The Naked Soul of Iceberg Slim* (1971); *Long White Con* (1977); *Death Wish* (1977); *Airtight Willie & Me* (1979); and, a 1978 work published posthumously with an introduction by Ice-T, *Doom Fox* (1998).

Beck's books were published during the fervor of the Black Power movement and, ironically, Slim considered his success as a pimp as a rebellion against White oppression. The Black activists of the day did not share this perspective, and deemed his former profession as nothing more than the exploitation of Black people for personal gain. Iceberg Slim's books proved to be very successful and soon gained attention beyond Black communities in the United States. Over 6 million copies of his books have sold, the most popular being *Pimp: The Story of My Life*. His books have been translated into German, Spanish, and French. Despite his commercial success, and his status as a local hero to street kids, he remained an outsider in the square Black community.

In the early 1970s Universal Pictures purchased the film rights to *Pimp* following the success of the film *The Godfather*, but the project was considered too controversial and was shelved indefinitely. In 1973, however, his book *Trick Baby* was made into a film directed by Larry Yust. The cast included Kiel Martin as White Folks, Mel Stewart as Blue Howard, and Ted Lange as Melvin the Pimp.

In 1976, Beck released a spoken word album, *Reflections* (Warner Bros. Records), which found him reciting his lurid vignettes over suitably funky backing from the Red Holloway Quartet.

Also a writer and speaker, Beck was married with four children. He died on April 28, 1992, at the age of seventy-three.

ICE CUBE [O'Shea Jackson]

Ice Cube, a rap artist, actor, and director, began his career as a member of the infamous West Coast rap group, **N.W.A**. Ice Cube was the first member to depart from N.W.A. after conflicts with the group's manager. Ice Cube left the group in 1989 and quickly established himself as a controversial solo artist.

Raised in South Central Los Angeles by parents who worked at the University of California-Los Angeles (UCLA), Ice Cube did not become involved with rap music until his late teens. Ice Cube's adopted name pays tribute to pimp-turned-writer **Iceberg Slim**. In high school, he began writing rhymes, including "Boyz n the 'Hood." With his partner Sir Jinx, Ice Cube formed the rap duo CIA and began performing at parties hosted by **Dr. Dre**. Through Dr. Dre, Ice Cube eventually met **Eazy E**, who had founded Ruthless Records. Dre and Ice Cube went on to write for Ruthless, but when Ruthless artists HBO did not want to record the Ice Cube rap "Boyz n The Hood," Ice Cube, Eazy E, and Dre formed the original N.W.A.

In 1987, Ice Cube studied architectural drafting at the Phoenix Institute of Technology in Arizona. He returned to California in 1988, having obtained a one-year degree, just in time for the release of N.W.A.'s debut album, *Straight Outta Compton* (Ruthless Records, 1988). Within a year, *Straight Outta Compton's* hardcore lyrical content and its biting social commentary had made it a bona fide hit with the **underground** Hip Hop

Ice Cube. *Courtesy of Photofest.*

scene. These same characteristics also made the album the focus of massive criticism, as well as attention from the FBI.

Despite the wave of success that N.W.A. was riding, Ice Cube was not happy with their manager, Jerry Heller, and left the group in 1989. Ice Cube went to New York with his new posse, **Da Lench Mob**, and recorded his first solo album with **Public Enemy**'s production team, the **Bomb Squad**. Ice Cube's solo debut, *AmeriKKKa's Most Wanted* (Priority Records), was released in the spring of 1990. The album was an immediate success, going gold within two weeks of its release. Although many praised Ice Cube's lyrical skills and the album's production, touting it as a Hip Hop classic, others were highly critical of his often violent, homophobic, and **misogynist** lyrics.

Undeterred by his detractors, by the end of 1990 Ice Cube had released the EP *Kill at Will* (Priority Records). Ice Cube also produced the debut album of his female protégée, Yo-Yo, titled *Make Way for the Motherlode* (Atlantic Records, 1992). Continuing to cash in on his success, Ice Cube made his acting debut in John Singleton's film, ***Boyz n the Hood*** (1991). The film was acclaimed and Ice Cube was widely praised for his performance.

Rounding out 1991, Ice Cube released his second full-length album, *Death Certificate*. (Priority Records). Although *AmeriKKKa's Most Wanted* had been controversial, the furor around it was tepid compared to that which surrounded *Death Certificate*. In particular, the track "No Vaseline," a violent verbal assault on N.W.A. manager Jerry Heller, was called anti-Semitic, and the track "Black Korea" was perceived as a racist demand to destroy all Korean-owned grocery stores that do business in Black communities. The album provoked a public condemnation from *Billboard*, the leading music trade publication, the first such response in its history. Despite the maelstrom over *Death Certificate* the album went platinum.

In 1992, Ice Cube toured with the second Lollapalooza tour in a successful bid to galvanize his White fan base. That same year Ice Cube also converted to the **Nation of Islam** and that influence is felt on his third album, *The Predator* (Priority Records). When *The Predator* was released in December 1992, it became the first album to debut at number 1 on both the pop and R & B charts. The tracks "It Was a Good Day" and "Check Yo Self" helped to make *The Predator* Ice Cube's most popular album. Also in 1992, Ice Cube wrote and produced Da Lench Mob's debut album, *Guerillas in tha Mist* (Atlantic Records, 1992). Ice Cube also produced Kam's debut, *Neva Again* (Atlantic Records, 1993).

In 1993, Ice Cube released *Lethal Injection* (Priority Records) and, although it debuted at number 5 and went platinum, some fans were not pleased with its G-Funk sound. It would be some time before Ice Cube would record again; instead, he continued writing and producing for other artists. At the end of 1994, he released *Bootlegs & B-Sides* (Priority Records, 1994), a collection of **remixes** and rare material.

During this period Ice Cube also engaged in a short-lived feud with rap artist **Common** (then known as Common Sense). In 1994, Common's track "I Used to Love H.E.R." from his album, *Resurrection* (Relativity Records), attracted a lot of attention for its clever allegory about rap's descent into commercially exploitative sex-and-violence subject matter. Ice Cube, mistakenly deeming the song to be a diss to West Coast rap artists, publicly attacked Common on **Mack 10**'s single "Westside Slaughterhouse," from the album Mack 10 (Priority Records, 1995). Common fought back with the 1996 single "The Bitch In Yoo" (Relativity Records).

In 1995, Ice Cube reteamed with director John Singleton to appear in the film *Higher Learning*. Ice Cube also mended fences with Dr. Dre and performed a duet with him on the single "Natural Born Killaz," from the album *Murder Was The Case* (Death Row Records, 1994). During 1996, he also formed the rap group **Westside Connection** with Mack 10 and WC and released their debut album, *Bow Down* (Priority Records, 1996), at the end of the year. *Bow Down* went gold within its first month of release, and eventually double platinum. In the midst of the **East Coast–West Coast** conflict, Ice Cube seemingly forgot his old New York ties; *Bow Down* was a frontal attack on the East Coast.

In 1998, Ice Cube released the album *War & Peace, Vol. 1* (Priority Records). Although another Ice Cube album is not totally out of the question, for the past several years Ice Cube has spent more time on film sets than in recording studios. Ice Cube has acted in approximately twenty films, beginning with ***Boyz n the Hood***. Ice Cube wrote the screenplay for and starred in the 1996 hit comedy, *Friday*. Two years later, he would make his directorial debut with the film *Players' Club*. The Ice Cube production *Barbershop* (2002) would stir up a debate centered on free speech among African Americans when film characters openly criticized revered civil rights figures Rosa Parks and Martin Luther King, Jr. In a radical change from his original N.W.A. persona, Ice Cube most recently starred in the family-friendly film, *Are We There Yet*? (2004).

See also: Censorship

DISCOGRAPHY: *EP*: *Kill at Will* (Priority Records, 1990). *Albums*: *AmeriKKKa's Most Wanted* (Priority Records, 1990); *Death Certificate* (Priority Records, 1991); *Predator* (Priority Records, 1992); *Lethal Injection* (Priority Records, 1993); *Bootlegs & B-Sides* (Priority Records, 1994); *War & Peace, Vol. 1* (Priority Records, 1998).

ICE-T (or Ice T) [Tracy Morrow]

Many credit Ice-T as one of the founding fathers of **gangsta rap**.

Despite Ice-T's strong association with the West Coast, he was born in Newark, New Jersey. As a child, after his parents were killed in a car accident, he moved to California and was raised by an aunt. While a student at Crenshaw High School in South Central Los Angeles, he became heavily involved with rap music and adopted the name Ice-T, from **Iceberg Slim**, a pimp who later wrote novels. Ice-T memorized lines from Iceberg Slim's works, reciting them for friends and classmates.

In the early 1980s, after he had left high school, Ice-T recorded several marginal twelve-inch singles. As he attempted to forge his career, Ice-T also appeared in the low-budget Hip Hop films *Breakin'* (1984), *Breakin' II: Electric Boogaloo* (1984), and *Rappin'* (1985).

In 1987, Ice-T was signed to Sire Records and released his debut album, *Rhyme Pays*. Although *Rhyme Pays* was touted as Los Angeles rap, it was actually recorded in New York City and production was supervised by the **Zulu Nation**'s **Afrika Islam**. The mainly party-oriented album went gold. During that same year, Ice-T recorded the theme song for Dennis Hopper's film *Colors*, a depiction of life in urban Los Angeles. The theme song, also called "Colors," is more sophisticated and insightful than anything that Ice-T had previously recorded.

In 1988, Ice-T formed his own record label, Rhyme Syndicate, and released the album *Power* (Warner Bros. Records). *Power* was a strong album that garnered Ice-T positive reviews and his second gold album. His next release was *The Iceberg/Freedom of Speech ... Just Watch What You Say* (Warner, 1989), which ranks as a true force with Hip Hop. The album included thought-provoking lyrics and political commentary, particularly about censorship. In 1990, he rekindled his acting career by starring in the film, *New Jack City*, also recording "New Jack Hustler" for the film's soundtrack. "New Jack Hustler" became the focal point for Ice-T's 1991 album, *O.G.: Original Gangster* (Warner Bros. Records), which became his most successful album to date.

O.G.: Original Gangster also featured a track called "Body Count," which Ice-T recorded with his band of the same name, an all-Black heavy metal band. Ice-T and **Body Count** toured in the summer of 1991, including performances on the first Lollapalooza tour. Ice-T's participation in Lollapalooza increased his appeal with alternative music fans and with White suburban teens. That year he also appeared in the film *Ricochet* (1991), and the next year in the film *Trespass* (1992).

Ice-T's 1992 album *Body Count* (Warner Bros. Records) with the band Body Count would mark a pivotal point in his music career. The single "**Cop Killer**" was told from the killer's perspective. The rap artist came under fire from law enforcement, politicians, and Time Warner stockholders, and even from then-President George H. W. Bush. Publicly, Time Warner at first stood by Ice-T; however, they decided not to release his next album, *Home Invasion*, ostensibly because of the album cover. By year's end, Ice-T had left Warner Bros. Records.

Priority Records released *Home Invasion* in the spring of 1993, but the album received lukewarm reviews and sold only moderately. As Ice-T's music career progressed, his music style appealed less to urban Black teens and more to suburban White teens.

In 1994, he wrote the book *The Ice Opinion* (New York: St. Martin's Press), appeared in the film *Surviving the Game*, and released a second Body Count album, *Born Dead*, which received little attention from critics or record buyers. In 1995, Ice-T appeared in two science-fiction flicks, *Tank Girl* and *Johnny Mnemonic.* When Ice-T released *Ice T VI: Return of the Real* (Priority Records) in 1996 it was his first rap album since 1993. The album was met with mixed reviews and commercially was not a success. In 1999, Ice-T released *7th Deadly Sin* (Atomic Pop).

Throughout the 1990s Ice-T appeared in numerous straight-to-video B-movies, including *Stealth Fighter* (1999) and *Leprechaun in the Hood* (2000). On occasion Ice-T also appeared in theatrical releases, including *3000 Miles to Graceland* (2001) and *'R Xmas* (2001). After writing the introduction to Iceberg Slim's posthumous novel, *Doom Fox* (New York: Grove Press, 1998), Ice-T offered further insight into the pimp life in the documentary films *Pimps Up, Ho's Down* (1999) and *Pimpin' 101* (2002). He also costarred in the television shows *Players* (1997) and *Law and Order: Special Victims Unit* (2000–).

See also: Censorship

DISCOGRAPHY: *Rhyme Pays* (Sire Records, 1987); *Power* (Warner Bros. Records, 1988); *The Iceberg/Freedom of Speech ... Just Watch What You Say* (Warner Bros. Records, 1989); *O.G.: Original Gangsta* (Warner Bros. Records, 1991); *Body Count* (Warner Bros. Records, 1992); *Home Invasion* (Priority Records, 1993); *Ice T VI: Return of the Real* (Priority Records, 1996); *7th Deadly Sin* (Atomic Pop, 1999).

"IT'S YOURS"

"It's Yours" was the first record to bear the **Def Jam Recordings** logo. The 1984 song by **T La Rock** and Jazzy Jay and produced by Rick Rubin was initially released by Arthur Baker's independent label, Partytime/Streetwise, but the Def Jam logo was used on the record sleeve.

IZZLE

Izzle as a suffix or infix added to or inserted into any existing word was popularized by **Snoop Dogg**.

The origin of the infix (added to the middle of a word) is the 1985 **U.T.F.O.** song, "Roxanne, Roxanne," where the *izz* infix is used: "The *izzi* is the *grizzeat Kizzangizzo*." In 1991, Another Bad Creation in their song "Cooling at the Playground Ya' Know" sang, "Into the *Mizzark* chilling in the *pizzark* ... mother came home by *dizzark*." In the 1993 "Tha Shiznit" from Snoop Dogg's debut album, *Doggystyle,* Snoop raps, "Dr. *Drizzay*, so *Izzay* and *plizzay* with D-O-doubly *Gizzay*?" The first time that *izzle* is used as a suffix instead of an infix appears in Snoop Dogg's 2000 song, "Snoop Dogg (What's my Name, Part 2)," where he raps in the intro, "*Izzle Kizzle, fo' shizzle.*" Snoop Dogg's MTV show was titled, "Doggy Fizzle Televizzle."

Although Snoop has mainstreamed *izzle* as a suffix, its usage most likely has long-standing roots in Northern California, emanating from an earlier suffix, *eezy*. Bay area rap artists **E-40** and 3X Krazy used the *eezy* variant. In "Rappers Ball," from the album *Tha Hall of Game* (Jive Records, 1996), E-40 raps "We off the *heezy* fo' sheezy." On the same album, on the single "Record Haters," E-40 states, "3X Krazy laced me, taught me how to say fo' *sheezy.*" More recently, other rap artists have embraced *izzle* in their lyrics: **Jay-Z**'s 2001 "Izzo (H.O.V.A.)," "H-to the *izzo,* V to the *vizza*"; **Missy Elliott**'s "Gossip Folks" *Izzy kizzy* looky here"; and Chingy's 2003 "Holidae In" (cameo with **Ludacris**), "Fo' *Shizzle Dizzle,* I'm on track with Big Snoop *Dizzle.*"

The word is now used in mainstream advertisements and movies.

J

JACK THE RAPPER CONVENTION

The first commercial convention for Black music was founded in 1977 by radio veteran Jack "The Rapper" Gibson, known as the "Father of Black Radio." Jack Gibson, who died in 2000, began his radio career in the late 1940s. In 1949, the veteran radio disc jockey was hired as program director of WERD in Atlanta, Georgia, the first Black-owned and -operated radio station in the United States. He also appeared in radio's first all-Black soap opera, *Here Comes Tomorrow*.

The Jack The Rapper Convention was originally a sort of family affair, a meeting place for Black music and Black radio professionals who were generally marginalized at other music conferences. By the 1990s, the convention included rap music and would serve as the model for many Hip Hop conferences to follow. Regrettably, the addition of rap changed the tone of the Jack The Rapper convention, bringing to it violent confrontations and police interventions, which eventually ended the once-annual event.

JACOB THE JEWELER [Jacob Arabo]

Jacob the Jeweler, a New York City-based diamondeer, has been called the "King of **Bling-Bling**." He created oversized diamond-encrusted watches, chains, and bracelets for a host of rap artists, including **Sean "P. Diddy" Combs**, **The Notorious B.I.G.**, and **Mary J. Blige**, as well as pop stars such as Jessica Simpson, Christina Aguilera, and Elton John.

A Russian immigrant, Arabo began selling his gems in Manhattan's Diamond District in 1981. His first celebrity client reportedly was R & B singer Faith Evans, the former wife of The Notorious B.I.G. In the mid-1990s, Evans found his shop and reportedly fell in love with the jewels. Subsequently, she made a deposit on a ring and began to tell her celebrity friends about Jacob. In early 2004, Arabo signed a licensing deal with the National Basketball Association (NBA) for the rights to place the NBA logo and all twenty-nine teams on the face of his famous five-time-zone watches. In April 2004, it was announced that Jacob had teamed up with rap artist **Kanye West** to produce a line of "religious-themed" jewelry, which includes diamond-studded Jesus pendants. West's religiosity was evident on the track "Jesus Walks," which appeared on his debut album, *College Dropout* (Roc-A-Fella, 2004).

JADAKISS [Jason Phillips]

A native of Yonkers, New York, and a member of the rap group **The LOX**, Jadakiss is known for his gritty rhymes on street life. Along with fellow LOX members, Jadakiss became part of the Ruff Ryders crew in 1999.

Jadakiss released his debut solo album, *Kiss tha Game Goodbye*, in August 2001 on the Ruff Ryders/Interscope Records label. Three years later, his second album, *Kiss of Death* (Ruff Ryders/Interscope Records), was released.

On this album, the single "Why?" sparked controversy with the line, "Why did Bush knock down the towers?" As the first rap artist to directly link the Bush administration's actions to the 9/11 attacks, Jadakiss has received the most mainstream media attention of his career. Jadakiss has stated in interviews that, while he did not believe that President Bush was directly responsible for the 9/11 attacks, he believed that Bush should be held accountable for his administration's failure to do more to prevent such terrorist attacks. Jadakiss is quoted as saying, "They didn't follow up on a lot of things properly." He continues stating, "It's the president of the United States. The buck stops with him." Many radio station and video music shows have opted to play an edited version of the song that omits the reference to Bush.

DISCOGRAPHY: *Kiss tha Game Goodbye* (Ruff Ryders/Interscope Records, 2001); *Kiss of Death* (Ruff Ryders/Interscope Records. 2004).

JAILS, HOSPITALS & HIP-HOP. *See* Films

JAM MASTER JAY [Jason William Mizell]

Best known as the DJ for rap group **Run DMC**, Jam Master Jay was born in Brooklyn, New York.

As a boy of five, Jam Master Jay was playing drums and singing in the Universal Baptist Church's Young Adult Choir. When he was ten, the family moved to the Hollis section of Queens, New York. At thirteen, he began to DJ under the name Jazzy Jase. While at Jackson High School, JMJ played drums and bass in local bands, and met Darryl McDaniels and Joseph Simmons, the younger brother of **Russell Simmons**. In their late teens, the trio officially teamed up as a rap group and would become known as Run DMC. Soon thereafter, under the guidance of their manager, Russell Simmons, they signed a recording deal with Profile Records. The group's first single, "It's Like That/ Sucker M.C.'s," came out in 1983. Run DMC would go on to be the most influential rap group in Hip Hop history, setting a series of firsts for rap groups.

In 1988, Jam Master Jay lent his production skills to **The Real Roxanne** on the single, "The Real Roxanne," in her on-wax **battle** with **Roxanne Shante**. In the 1990s, Jay had his own label, JMJ Records, distributed by Def Jam Recordings, whose roster included artists such as **Onyx**, **50 Cent**, and **Jayo Felony**.

In November 2002, Jam Master Jay was killed in the lounge of his Queens, New York, recording studio with one shot to the head from a .40 caliber gun. As of January 2005, the murderer remains at large. The motive for the slaying has not been ascertained, although police have focused on the possibility of unpaid debts and Jay's association with controversial rap artist 50 Cent. Jam Master Jay had produced the single "Wankster," in which 50 Cent viciously mocked fake rap music gangstas, a track that led to gunshot attacks on 50 Cent.

JA RULE [Jeffrey Atkins]

Ja Rule became the premier artist on the Murder Inc. record label. He is also known as one of 50 Cent's main targets for verbal attacks.

Raised in the Hollis section of Queens, New York, the raspy voiced rap artist has been compared to fellow rap artist **DMX**. As an indication of his ambitions, he titled his 1999 debut album *Venni, Vetti, Vecci* (Murder Inc./Def Jam Recordings), a play on the Latin phrase reportedly uttered by Julius Caesar (*veni, vidi, vici*: "I came, I saw, I conquered").

Ja Rule was first heard on Mic Geronimo's 1995 "Time To Build," the B-side to Mic Geronimo's "Masta I.C." (TVT Records). Ja Rule is also remembered for his appearance on **Jay-Z**'s 1996 single, "Can I Get A . . . ," from *Reasonable Doubt* (Roc-A-Fella/Def Jam Recordings). In 1994, as a member of Cash Money Click, he signed a deal with independent label Blunt Recordings, distributed by TVT Records. Their first and only single was "Get The Fortune," b/w "For My Click" (Blunt/TVT, 1995). Thereafter, Ja Rule went solo and signed with Murder Inc.

The hardcore *Venni Vetti Vecci* debuted at number 3 on the *Billboard* pop chart. The breakout hit was the single "Holla Holla." The album quickly went platinum and gained Ja Rule a legion of fans. Ja Rule then appeared on the album *Irv Gotti Presents Murderers*, which included rap artists Jay-Z, **DMX**, **Busta Rhymes**, and Memphis Bleek. In 2000, Ja Rule followed up with the album *Rule 3:36* (Murder Inc./Def Jam Recordings). This album departed from the earlier tone, being less raw and more melodic. Rather than relying solely on rough and rugged lyrics, producer Irv Gotti paired Ja's thuggish style with three radio-friendly R & B singers: Christina Milian, Lil' Mo, and Vita. The collaboration produced three enormous hit singles: "Between Me and You," "I Cry," and "Put It on Me."

Taking his second album as a model, Ja Rule's third album, *Pain Is Love* (Murder Inc./Def Jam Recordings, 2001), teamed him up with

Ja Rule. *Courtesy of Photofest.*

Jennifer Lopez on the track "I'm Real (Murder Remix)" and with Ashanti on the track "Always on Time." Ja Rule also paired up with singer Case on "Livin' It Up," his version of Stevie Wonder's "Do I Do."

Like other rap artists before him, Ja Rule embarked on an acting career, making his debut in 2000 in the film *Turn It Up*. He followed the same year with *Da Hip Hop Witch*, a parody of *The Blair Witch Project*. In 2001, he appeared in the film *The Fast and the Furious* and in 2002 in the film *Half Past Dead*. Ja Rule, married and father of two, has referred to himself as the return of **Tupac Shakur**, but despite his success few others are willing to take that claim seriously.

DISCOGRAPHY: *Venni, Vetti, Vecci* (Murder Inc./Def Jam Recordings, 1999); *Rule 3:36* (Murder Inc./Def Jam Recordings, 2000); *Pain Is Love* (Murder Inc./Def Jam Recordings).

JAYO FELONY [aka Bullet Loco, aka Peer Pressure] [James Savage]

A San Diego–based rap artist perhaps best known for his **beef** with **Jay-Z**, Jayo Felony turned to music in the aftermath of a stay in prison (the result of teen years in a gang).

Jayo Felony recorded several **underground** tapes and he independently released the single "Pis* on Your Tombstone," selling it on consignment at local record stores. The strength of the single brought Jayo Felony to the attention of **Run DMC**'s **Jam Master Jay**. Jam Master Jay signed Felony to his JMJ label and in 1994 released the album, *Take a Ride* (JMJ/Def Jam Recordings). The album did not garner much enthusiasm on the street and quickly faded out. Four years later, Jayo Felony released his sophomore album, *Whatcha Gonna Do*? (Def Jam Recordings, 1998). In 1999, he released the album *Underground* (Eureka/Koch) and in 2001, *Crip Hop* (American Music Corp.).

Jayo Felony had a well-known beef with East Coast artist Jay-Z, alleging that Jay-Z prevented the song "Hotta Than Fish Grease," which dissed Jay-Z, from appearing on the compilation *Bullet Proof Love, Vol. 1*. (Henchmen Entertainment/Def Jam Recordings, 2001). Jayo Felony had earlier received "half a bar" in Jay-Z's song, "Takeover." Moreover, Jayo believed that many artists (including Jay-Z) who had no association with gangs were attempting to feign such ties for profit. After the fracas over "Hotta Than Fish Grease," Jayo Felony was let go by Def Jam.

On his album *Crip Hop*, Jayo attempts to take his revenge on Jay-Z with the track "Catch 'Em in the Morning." On the same album, Jayo Felony takes a shot at **Snoop Dogg** with the track "You's a Character."
DISCOGRAPHY: *Take a Ride* (JMJ/Def Jam Recordings, 1994); *Whatcha Gonna Do*? (Def Jam Recordings, 1998); *Underground* (Eureka/Koch, 1999); *Crip Hop* (American Music Corp., 2001).

JAY-Z [Shawn Corey Carter] [aka Jigga, Hova]

As an artist and cofounder of **Roc-A-Fella Records**, Jay-Z holds the dual distinction of being one of rap music's biggest selling artists and one of Hip Hop's most savvy businessmen.

A native of Brooklyn, New York, Jay-Z grew up in the Marcy Projects. Known as "Jazzy," the teenager made a name for himself as a member of the group **Original Flavor**. Although the group's second album, *Beyond Flavor* (Atlantic Records, 1994) failed to sell, the track "Can I Get Open" showcased Jay-Z's considerable talents. After the group disbanded, the solo Jay-Z would go on to perform with **Ol' Dirty Bastard** on **Big Daddy Kane**'s 1994 posse cut, "Show & Prove," from the album *Daddy's Home*.

Jay-Z. *Courtesy of Photofest.*

Having decided to form his own label rather than continuing to chase a recording contract, Jay-Z created Roc-A-Fella Records with friends Damon Dash and Kareem "Biggs" Burke. The label would release some singles, including "In My Lifetime." In 1996, after securing distribution with Priority Records, Jay-Z released the 1996 debut album *Reasonable Doubt,* already considered a Hip Hop classic. In 1997, he followed up with *My Lifetime, Vol. 1*, which reached number 3 on the *Billboard* album chart. *Vol. 2: Hard Knock Life* was released in 1998 and in 1999 he released his fourth album *Vol. 3: Life and Times of S. Carter* (Roc-A-Fella Records) his best-selling album to date. In 2000, *Dynasty Roc La Familia* was released.

Continuing to release an album a year, in 2001 Jay-Z delivered *The Blueprint*. Jay-Z had previewed the *Blueprint* track "Takeover" at the 2001 HOT97 Summer Jam Concert. "Takeover" disses New York–based rap artists Prodigy (**Mobb Deep**) and **Nas**, as well as California rap artist **Jayo Felony**. In a now famous lyrical sparring match, Nas responded to Jay-Z with the track "Ether," from his album *Stillmatic* (Columbia, 2001) and Jay-Z counterattacked with "Super Ugly." Jayo Felony also hit back with his diss track, "Catch 'Em in the Morning," from his album *Crip Hop* (American Music Corp.).

Jay-Z followed the successful *Blueprint* album by doing an *MTV Unplugged* (Roc-A-Fella, 2001) album, where he was backed by **The Roots**. In 2002, Jay-Z teamed with R & B star R. Kelly for the album *Best of Both Worlds* (Roc-A-Fella Records, 2002). In 2003, Jay-Z opened 40/40, an upscale sports bar located in Manhattan. In 2004, the album *Unfinished Business* (Def Jam Recordings) was a part two for the Jay-Z and R. Kelly match-up.

A 2002 tour to support the *Best of Both Worlds* album had been postponed because of R. Kelly's legal problems; when the tour eventually occurred in 2004, it ended disastrously. In November 2004, R. Kelly filed a lawsuit in New York State Supreme Court against Jay-Z, alleging that Jay-Z sabotaged his participation on the tour and the tour itself. R. Kelly seeks $15 million in lost income from cancelled dates and $60 million in punitive damages. Jay-Z takes a shot at R. Kelly on the "Drop It Like It's Hot" **remix**. In January 2005, Jay-Z countersued, stating in court papers that the tour promoter was forced to kick Kelly off the tour because of his erratic behavior.

In 2002, Jay-Z recorded a double album, *The Blueprint 2: The Gift & the Curse* (Roc-A-Fella Records). On this album, Jay-Z and his real-life girlfriend, Beyoncé Knowles, cover the **Tupac Shakur** single "'Bonnie & Clyde." Jay-Z also made an appearance on Beyoncé's catchy single, "Crazy In Love" (2002), and also appeared on the N.E.R.D. album *Unknown* (Star Trak/Arista, 2003) on the track "*Frontin'*."

In 2003, Jay-Z announced that his number 1 *The Black Album* (Roc-A-Fella Records) would be his last album, marking his retirement from recording. In June 2003, he would become the first rap artist to have an athletic shoe named after him, Reebok's "S. Carter" shoes in men's, women's, and children's styles. In August 2004, Jay-Z became a minority owner of the New Jersey Nets basketball team. In 2004, Jay-Z released the documentary *Fade To Black* about his retirement send-off concert at Madison Square Garden.

That same year Jay-Z paired up with hard-rock band Linkin Park for the album *Collision Course* (Roc-A-Fella/Warner Bros. Records, 2004). The two-disc CD/DVD, released in December, entered at number 1 on the *Billboard* album charts and includes **mash-up** tracks by both Jay-Z and Linkin Park.

Jay-Z became president of **Def Jam Recordings**, a label of Universal Music Group. As president of the company founded by **Russell Simmons**, Jay-Z would have authority over everything from album production to marketing for an artist roster that currently includes **LL Cool J** and **Ludacris**. He will also be allowed to sign a limited number of artists to his own Def Jam-distributed venture and, if he returns to the mic, his music would also be released through Universal.

DISCOGRAPHY: *Reasonable Doubt* (Roc-A-Fella, 1996); *My Lifetime, Vol. 1* (Roc-A-Fella, 1997); *Vol. 2: Hard Knock Life* (Roc-A-Fella, 1998); *Vol. 3: Life and Times of S. Carter* (Roc-A-Fella, 1999); *The Blueprint* (Roc-A-Fella, 2001); *MTV Unplugged* (Roc-A-Fella, 2001); *The Blueprint 2: The Gift & the Curse* (Roc-A-Fella, 2002); *The Black Album* (Roc-A-Fella, 2004); *Collision Course* (Roc-A-Fella/Warner Bros. Records, 2004).

JEAN, WYCLEF. *See* Fugees

JERMAINE DUPRI

The founder of So So Def Productions, Jermaine Dupri began his musical career before his teens. Dupri's father, record industry veteran Michael Maudlin, was then a manager in Atlanta, Georgia. In 1982, Maudlin had coordinated a Diana Ross performance and the young Dupri some how made his way on stage and danced along with Ross. After that, Dupri began performing around the country, appearing with Herbie Hancock and Cameo. In 1984, he opened the New York Fresh Fest, with **Run DMC**, **Whodini**, and **Grandmaster Flash**.

In 1987, Dupri moved from dancing to producing. The fourteen-year-old produced and secured a record contract for the Silk Tymes Leather trio. Their first and only album, 1989's *It Ain't Where Ya From ... It's Where Ya At* (Geffen Records), was a flop. Dupri then formed So So Def Productions in Atlanta, and within three years had found his first platinum act. Dupri saw the pint-size rap duo **Kris Kross** performing in an Atlanta mall, he subsequently signed them and prepared their debut album, *Totally Krossed Out*. The album, on the strength of the hit single "Jump," quickly sold 4 million copies and spawned a brief fad of wearing clothing backward. Kris Kross's success was short lived, but Dupri continued to work, producing tracks on TLC's first two albums, the multi-platinum *Oooooh—On the TLC Tip* (1992) and the ten-times-platinum Cra*zySexyCool* (1994); the combined albums sold over 15 million copies.

During 1993–1994, Dupri debuted the female R & B quartet Xscape with the album *Hummin' Comin' at 'Cha* (So So Def/Columbia) and female rap artist **Da Brat** with her album *Funkdafied* (So So Def/Columbia). Thanks to Dupri's production work, both debut albums went platinum.

By the end of 1994, Dupri was considered one the most respected producers in the business. Dupri's reputation was further enhanced with work on Mariah Carey's eight-times-platinum album *Daydream* (Arista, 1995). In 1997 Dupri would score another hit when he took over the production for teen singer Usher's sophomore album, *My Way* (LaFace/Arista); *My Way* sold over 2 million copies in its first three months of release.

Following the lead of **Sean "Diddy" Combs**, who had released a solo project in 1997, in 1998 Dupri released his single, "The Party Continues." In July 1998, Dupri released his debut solo album, *Life in 1472: The Original Soundtrack*, which featured collaborations with **Outkast**, **Snoop Dogg**, **Slick Rick**, **Nas**, and **Master P**, among others. 1998 also saw the debut of the male R & B group Jagged Edge, who debuted with the album *A Jagged Era*. In 2000, he would debut another multi-platinum album, with teenaged rap artist **Lil' Bow Wow**'s *Beware of Dog*.

In 2003, Dupri entered into an exclusive label/production deal with Arista Records. The deal brought Dupri's So So Def imprint to Arista and made Dupri a senior vice president in the company. Under the terms of the deal, So So Def, which was distributed by Columbia, would be distributed worldwide by Arista and Dupri would continue to act as a producer and solo artist, as well as produce exclusively for the BMG group. Moreover, the deal called for So So Def acts Bow Wow and Jagged Edge to remain with Columbia.

In January 2005 Dupri was tapped to run the newly created Virgin Records Urban Music. In his new capacity, he will be responsible for recruiting and developing new artists as well as steering the careers of established artists. Virgin already plays home to the likes of Lenny Kravitz, N.E.R.D., and Dupri's girlfriend, Janet Jackson.

DISCOGRAPHY: *Life in 1472: The Original Soundtrack* (So So Def, 1998).

JERU THE DAMAJA [Kendrick Jeru Davis]

In the 1990s, like **KRS-ONE** before him, Jeru the Damaja proclaimed himself the savior of Hip Hop and gained fame by decrying the decline of rap music. Jeru was highly critical of popular rap artists such as **Sean "P. Diddy" Combs** and the **Fugees**, which gained him few allies in the world of Hip Hop.

A Brooklyn, New York, native, Jeru began writing rhymes at age ten. In high school, he met Gang Starr's Guru and **DJ Premier** and landed a guest spot on their first album, *Daily Operation* (Chrysalis, 1992), on the track "I'm the Man." In 1993, Jeru toured with Gang Starr and released his own solo debut single, "Come Clean," on Gang Starr's Illkids label. Over a chilling marimba loop, Jeru chastised the studio gangstas who populate the music industry. "Come Clean" became an **underground** hit and led to his deal with Payday Records.

In 1994, Jeru his debut album, *The Sun Rises in the East* (Payday/ffrr), a lyrical assault on mindlessness within rap music. Produced by DJ Premier, the album was well-received, but Jeru received criticism for the track, "Da Bichez." In response, Jeru explained that most women did not fit into the category, but some did. Also in 1994, he made a guest appearance on the **Digable Planets** second album, *Blowout Comb* (Capitol Records). In 1996, he released a strong sophomore album, *Wrath of the Math*, which had production help from DJ Premier and Guru and contained the single "Ya Playin' Yaself."

In 2000, he released the independent album *Heroz4hire* (Knowsavage Records). Jeru's protégé Afu-Ra, debuted in 2000 with the album *Body of the Life Force*. Thereafter, Jeru faded from the limelight, although he did turn up on the superior track "Suntoucher," from Groove Armada's *Goodbye Country (Hello Nightclub)*. In 2003, Jeru made a comeback with the album, *Divine Design* (Ashenafi Records). Although many felt that Jeru's lyrics were still tight, without DJ Premier on the boards the production was considered lackluster.

DISCOGRAPHY: *The Sun Rises in the East* (Payday/ffrr, 1994); *Wrath of the Math* (Payday/ffrr, 1996); *Heroz4hire* (Knowsavage Records, 2000); *Divine Design* (Ashenafi Records, 2003).

JIMMY HAT

Jimmy hat is a slang term for condom.

J.J. FAD

J.J. Fad, comprised of M.C.J.B. [Juana Burns], Baby-D [Dania Birks], and Sassy C [Michelle Franklin], were the first female rap group to sell 1 million records. Unfortunately for this group, their only hit, the single "Supersonic," is considered by many to be emblematic of pop-oriented rap music.

In 1988, the three female rap artists from Compton, California, formed the group Just Jammin' Fresh and Def (J.J. Fad) and released their debut album, *Supersonic* (Ruthless Records), that same year. The placid title single was produced by **The Arabian Prince**, and producer **Dr. Dre** would also work on J.J. Fad's debut effort.

J.J. Fad instigated a **battle** with female artists on the **East Coast** when they released "Another Ho," an attack on female artists **Roxanne Shante**, **The Real Roxanne**, Sparky D, and **Salt 'N Pepa**. J.J. Fad also individually targeted Roxanne Shante on the single "Ya Going Down," which featured a cameo by **Ice Cube**.

Although they had loyal fans, particularly in South Central Los Angeles, J.J. Fad were never considered peers to the East Coast female rap artists that they dissed. Their follow-up, *Not Just a Fad* (Atlantic, 1991), did not do well and the group disbanded in 1992.

DISCOGRAPHY: *Supersonic* (Ruthless Records, 1988); *Not Just a Fad* (Atlantic, 1991).

JUICE CREW ALL STARS, THE

A collective of rap artists under producer **Marley Marl**'s **Cold Chillin'** records label established in the 1980s, The Juice Crew All Stars was comprised of rap artists **Big Daddy Kane**, **Biz Markie**, **Roxanne Shante**, **MC Shan**, and **Master Ace**.

See also: Queensbridge

JUNGLE BROTHERS

Mike Gee [Michael Small], DJ Sammy B [Sammy Burwell], and Baby Bam [Nathaniel Hall] teamed up in 1986 to form the trio known as the Jungle Brothers. Members of the **Native Tongues** Posse, the group predated fellow travelers **De La Soul**, **A Tribe Called Quest**, and **Digable Planets**, but somehow failed to gain substantial recognition from either rap music fan or mainstream audiences. One theory suggests that the Jungle Brothers were too musically diverse to develop a following. The group utilized Afrocentric ideology and house music, as well as **James Brown** and jazz samples; by contrast, most rap artists use only a single type of music to establish their signature sound and message.

In early 1988, the Jungle Brothers released the album *Straight Out the Jungle* on Idler Records, a label known for dance music, not rap. The standout single from the album was the innovative "I'll House You," a collaboration with house music producer Todd Terry. Although *Straight Out the Jungle* was not a commercial success, in 1989 Warner Bros. Records signed the Jungle Bros and they released their second album, *Done By the Forces of Nature.* Unfortunately for the Jungle Brothers, De La Soul released their groundbreaking debut *3 Feet High and Rising* (Tommy Boy Records) that same year and overshadowed their album. After the release of *Done By the Forces of Nature*, the Jungle Brothers, at the suggestion of Warner Bros. marketing department, took a four-year hiatus before releasing *J. Beez Wit the Remedy*. Although Warner Bros. aggressively pushed the album, the Jungle Brother had lost ground with fans during their absence and the album did not sell favorably. Again, Warner delayed the release of the fourth Jungle Brothers album, *Raw Deluxe*, until mid-1997. The album *V.I.P.* followed in early 2000, and *All That We Do* was released in 2002.

DISCOGRAPHY: *Straight Out the Jungle* (Idler Records, 1988); *Done By the Forces of Nature* (Warner Bros. Records, 1989) *J. Beez Wit the Remedy* (Warner Bros. Records, 1993); *Raw Deluxe* (1997); *V.I.P.* (2000); *All That We Do* (2002).

JUNIOR M.A.F.I.A. (Masters At Finding Intelligent Attitudes)

Hailing from the Bedford-Stuyvesant section of Brooklyn, New York, the 1990s collective known as the Junior M.A.F.I.A. was comprised of four separate acts: MC Clepto; the 6s (Little Caesar, Chico, and Nino Brown); the Snakes (cousins Larceny and Trife); and **Lil' Kim**.

In 1995, the crew gained immediate success with two hit singles, "Get Money" and "Player's Anthem," from their first and only album, *Conspiracy* (Undeas/Big Beat). Junior M.A.F.I.A.'s rhymed about a glamorous fast life of money, sex, and drugs. **The Notorious B.I.G.** was a friend of the collective's members and acted as their producer for the album. Lil' Kim, the only female in the group, was featured with The Notorious B.I.G. on the "Get Money" track, which helped set up her solo career. Lil' Kim would go on to record two platinum albums, *Hard Core* (Atlantic, 1996) and *The Notorious K.I.M.* (Atlantic, 2000). Her third album was the 2003 *La Bella Mafia* (Atlantic). In comparison, Lil' Cease's 1999 solo effort, *The Wonderful World of Cease A Leo* (Atlantic, 1999), flopped badly and the remaining members of Junior M.A.F.I.A. disappeared from the rap music scene.

DISCOGRAPHY: *Conspiracy* (Undeas/Big Beat, 1995).

JURASSIC 5

MCs Chali 2na [Charles Stuart], Zaakir (aka Soup) [Courtenay Henderson], Akil [Dante Givens], and Marc 7 [Marc Stuart] and DJs Cut Chemist [Lucas MacFadden] and Nu-Mark [Mark Potsic] make up the Jurassic 5. With strong vocal harmonizing and hyped funk-flavored beats, Jurassic 5 evokes memories of Old School Hip Hop: the nostalgia of park jams and block parties and playful boasting.

The Los Angeles–based group formed in 1993 as the merger of two separate rap groups, Rebels of Rhythm and Unity Committee. Cut Chemist and Chali 2na were also part of the Latin-hop collective Ozomatli, and Chemist himself recorded several mixtapes and also the wide-issue album *Live at the Future Primitive Soundsession* (Ubiquity, 1998) with Shortkut, from Invisibl Skratch Piklz. Jurassic 5's roots lie in the **Los Angeles Underground**, a Hip Hop movement that revolved around The Good Life Café open-mic venue in South Central Los Angeles's old jazz district, where dozens of MCs and DJs would gather regularly to perform. Rebels of Rhythm and Unity Committee originally came together to record the 1995 single, "Unified Rebelution" (TVT Records). The single was a hit with Hip Hop heads around the nation and sold extremely well in Europe. The critics praised the single as possibly the freshest in a decade. The one-time only single highlighted the chemistry that the artists have with each other and was the catalyst to the formation of Jurassic 5.

In 1997, they released an eponymous EP on their own independent label, selling tens of thousands of copies worldwide. After securing a recording contract with Interscope Records, they rereleased their EP and joined the ranks of **The Roots**, **De La Soul**, **Mos Def**, and **Talib Kweli** as artists providing another voice within the Hip Hop dialogue. Jurassic 5 is the rare rap group committed to performing live. In 2000, Jurassic 5 toured with Fiona Apple and on the Warped Festival, just in time for the release of their album *Quality Control* (Interscope Records) that summer. Jurassic 5 continued to perform do live shows during 2000–2001, and released the album *Power in Numbers* at the end of 2002. On the track "Day At The Races," classic lyricists Percee P and **Big Daddy Kane** appear as guest MCs. The song is based on a beat that Cut Chemist had created ten years before, paying homage to fast-talking Old School rap artists such as Big Daddy Kane and **Kool G Rap**.

DISCOGRAPHY: *EPs*: *Jurassic 5* (Rumble, 1997; re-issued by Interscope Records in 1999). *Albums*: *Quality Control* (Interscope Records, 2000); *Power in Numbers* (Interscope Records, 2002).

JUST-ICE [Joseph Williams, Jr.]

A former club bouncer, Just-Ice is recognized as the first New York rap artist to embrace hardcore rap. The Brooklyn, New York, native quickly gained attention for his lyrics, his looks, and his aggressive manner. With a mouthful of good teeth, a slew of tattoos, and a muscular build, Just-Ice stood out from the crowd.

He first hit the scene with his 1986 single, "Cold Getting' Dumb." His debut album *Back to the Old School* (Sleeping Bag Records, 1986) produced by **Mantronix**'s Kurtis Mantronik, with its hard rhymes and human **beatbox**, brought a new sound and style to rap music. In 1987, police in Washington, DC, held Just-Ice in connection with the murder of a drug dealer. Although he was never charged in the killing, Just-Ice's star rose because of it. In a classic power move, Just-Ice proclaimed a war on Washington, DC, **go-go** and dared to criticize the then-reigning kings of rap, **Run DMC**.

Although Just-Ice seemed destined for rap music stardom, the tide changed with the departure of Mantronik from Sleeping Bag Records. **KRS-ONE** took over the production duties for Just-Ice's second album *Kool and Deadly* (Sleeping Bag Records, 1987). Fans who had eagerly supported *Back to the Old School* were cool to the latest effort. In 1989, KRS-ONE put his producer's hat back on for Just-Ice's *The Desolate One*, but it failed to generate any excitement. In 1990, Just-Ice joined the Stop the Violence All Stars, who released the single, "Self Destruction." Throughout the early to middle 1990s, Just-Ice continued to release albums on small independent labels: *Masterpiece* (Fresh Records, 1990), produced by **Grandmaster Flash**; the reggae-influenced *Gun Talk* (Savage, 1993), with tracks produced by Mantronix; and *Kill The Rhythm (Like A Homicide)* (In-A-Minute, 1995), with KRS-ONE production. In the late 1990s, the renewed interest in Old School rap create a new demand for *Back to the Old School*, but Just-Ice did not attempt to exploit this opportunity.

DISCOGRAPHY: *Singles*: "Cold Getting' Dumb" (Fresh Records, 1986). *Albums*: *Back to the Old School* (Sleeping Bag, 1986); *Kool and Deadly* (Sleeping Bag, 1987); *The Desolate One* (Fresh Records, 1989); *Masterpiece* (Fresh Records, 1990); *Gun Talk* (Savage, 1993); *Kill The Rhythm (Like A Homicide)* (In-A-Minute 1995).

JUVENILE [Terius Gray]

The New Orleans-based rap artist Juvenile was raised in that city's infamous Magnolia Projects. He began his rap career as a youngster and at nineteen released the album *Being Myself* (Warlock Records, 1995). Instead of hustling, Juvenile took a series of odd jobs between music gigs. He eventually met Cash Money label owners, the brothers Ronald "Suga Slim" Williams and Bryan "Baby" Williams. After Juvenile signed with the label, he first came to national prominence with The Hot Boys' 1997 debut album, *Get it How U Live!* (Cash Money Records), followed by 1999's platinum album *Guerilla Warfare*. In 1996, Cash Money Records released Juvenile's solo album, *Solja Rags* (1996). The album became an **underground** sensation and set the stage for the release of his breakthrough sophomore album, *400 Degreez*, in 1998. The album went quadruple platinum and spawned the hit singles "Ha" and "Back That Azz Up."

In 1999, with Juvenile's popularity growing, Cash Money Records reissued *Solja Rags* nationally. Warlock Records, also trying to profit from Juvenile's rising star, released a **remixed** version of *Being Myself*. The year ended with the release of the platinum-selling *Tha G-Code*, two years later he followed up with *Project English*. Citing financial disagreements with Cash Money executives Ronald and Bryan Williams, Juvenile left the label in 2001; he had not been officially released from his contract. He rejoined the Cash Money Records fold in early 2003 and that year released *Juve the Great* (Cash Money Records/Universal), which spawned the summer hit "Slow Motion."

DISCOGRAPHY: *Being Myself* (Warlock, 1995); *Solja Rags* (Cash Money Records, 1996); *400 Degreez* (Cash Money Records, 1998); *Tha G-Code* (Cash Money Records, 1999); *Project English* (Cash Money Records, 2001); *Juve the Great* (Cash Money Records/Universal, 2003).

K

KANGOL

British-made Kangol hats became a popular fashion accessory for young men in the 1980s. The *Bedford/Ascot Ivy* cap (often worn backwards) and the *Ventair Snipe* were made famous by **LL Cool J**.

KARL KANI [Carl Williams]

Karl Kani was one of the originators of designer urban wear. Preceding clothing labels such as Enyce, **FUBU**, Phat Farm, Sean John, and Roc-a-Wear, Karl Kani (pronounced *Can-I*) gained a solid reputation for designing what he terms "street-savvy" sportswear, particularly attractive to young Black men like himself.

Born in the Flatbush section of Brooklyn, New York, Kani as a teenager began designing his own clothing to distinguish himself from his friends, who were wearing the popular designer jeans of that time. Kani had not studied tailoring or design, but he had a talent for coming up with unique and stylish ideas. He would then buy material and tell a tailor exactly what he wanted his garments to look like. Compliments on his clothing led to orders, and Kani eventually started a small clothing business.

In the late 1980s, Kani moved to Los Angeles, California where he opened a men's clothing store and started a mail-order business for his fashions. In 1990, Kani's fortunes changed dramatically when he teamed up with Cross Colours, the then-popular urban fashion label. Kani produced his designs under a Cross Colours subsidiary, Threadz 4 Life. The line was a financial success. By 1993, Karl Kani designs accounted for 65 percent of $97 million in Cross Colours sales. Unfortunately, success spelled disaster; the company could not keep up with increasing demands for both of its lines of clothes and Cross Colours had to close.

Kani took his profits from the Cross Colours venture (a reported $500,000) and used them to establish his own sportswear and licensing company, the Los Angeles–based Karl Kani Infinity. Karl Kani clothing is sold in department and specialty stores in the United States and abroad. Kani founded his own record label called Kani Life in 2001, adding Life as a new clothing logo in 2003.

KDAY-AM

In July 1983, Los Angeles radio station KDAY-AM 1580 began to play rap music. *The Mack Attack Mixmasters* show was created by KDAY Assistant Program Director/Music Director, Greg Mack, a native of Brooklyn, New York. The show was heard on Saturday nights from 8 to 11 P.M. and was where some of the best DJs in Los Angeles got to mix, including Tony G, Bobcat, Hen-Gee, Gemini, **Egyptian Lover**, and Julio G.

The first "Mix Masters" were **Dr. Dre** and DJ Yella, both of the **World Class Wreckin' Cru**. Dr. Dre and DJ Yella would go on to become members of **N.W.A.** Coincidentally, Mack is credited with turning N.W.A. from an unknown group to superstars. By the fall of 1983, KDAY had become the country's first rap-only radio station. Aside from being dedicated to promoting **underground** West Coast rap artists, KDAY was also the place for East Coast artists to break rap records in Los Angeles. The radio station also produced concerts and was the first to bring East Coast artists such as **Run DMC** and **Whodini** to Los Angeles. Moreover, KDAY was a boon to the local mom-and-pop record stores, which carried rap music at a time when large record chains did not.

In 1991, falling profits led KDAY's owner to sell the station and KDAY's all-rap format was replaced by business news. For rap artists from Los Angeles, KDAY had long symbolized their own uncensored voices and its demise represented their silencing.

KID FROST (aka Frost) [Arturo Molina, Jr.]

A pioneer in the field of Latino rap music, Kid Frost recorded some first records and helped bring exposure to other bilingual MCs. Although Kid Frost was raised primarily in East Los Angeles, he spent some time with his family on military bases in Guam and Germany.

Kid Frost. *Courtesy of Photofest.*

Kid Frost was already an accomplished break dancer when he joined **Uncle Jamm's Army** in 1982. His name, Kid Frost, was adopted as homage to **Ice-T**, whom he often **battled** at parties and in clubs in the early days of West Coast Hip Hop. During this period, Kid Frost released several twelve-inch singles, including "Rough Cut" (ElectroBeat Records) with **N.W.A.**'s DJ Yella and "Terminator" (ElectroBeat Records). Kid Frost stopped performing for a while, but returned in the late 1980s, when he teamed up with producer–DJ Tony G in 1990 and recorded the single "La Raza." This single from his debut album, *Hispanics Causing Panic* (Virgin Records, 1990), brought Kid Frost to the attention of a wider audience and became the anthem for Chicano rap music fans.

Hispanic Causing Panic was one of the first full-length Latino rap music albums, along with Mellow Man Ace's 1989 *Escape From Havana*. In the aftermath of "La Raza," Kid Frost pulled together a collective of bilingual rap artists called the Latin Alliance, which included ALT, Lyrical Engineer, and Markski. The group released its only album, *Latin Alliance* (Atlantic Records), in 1991. In 1992, Kid Frost released his second album, *East Side Story* (Virgin Records), with the singles "No Sunshine" and "Thin Line." Virgin records subsequently dropped Kid Frost from the label.

The mature artist omitted "Kid" from his name and became simply Frost. He signed with Ruthless Records shortly before its founder, **Eazy E**, died of AIDS in 1995. His 1995 album *Smile Now, Die Later* reinvented Frost as a hardcore MC rhyming over Latin-influenced G-funk beats. *Smile Now, Die Later* became Frost's first album to reach the Top 40 of the R & B charts. The single "East Side Rendezvous" was a minor success. In 1997, Frost followed up with *When HELL.A. Freezes Over*, but subsequently he left Ruthless Records. Frost reappeared on the independent label Celeb Entertainment, where he released two albums, *That Was Then, This Is Now, Volumes 1 and 2*, (1999 and 2000, respectively). In 2002, ten years after his debut album, Frost released *Still Up in This $#*+!* on the independent Hit-A-Lick Records. That same year Frost also produced, *Raza Radio*, a compilation album of Latino rap artists.

DISCOGRAPHY: *Singles*: "Rough Cut" (Electro Beat Records, 1984); "Terminator" (Electro Beat Records, 1985). *Albums*: *Hispanic Causing Panic* (Virgin Records, 1990); *East Side Story* (Virgin Records, 1992); *Smile Now, Die Later* (Ruthless Records, 1995); *When HELL.A. Freezes Over* (Ruthless Records, 1997); *This Was When, This Is Now*, Volumes 1 and 2 (Celeb Entertainment, 1999 and 2000, respectively); *Still Up in This $#*+!* (Hit-A-Lick Records, 2002).

KID 'N PLAY

Christopher Reid and Chris Martin are Kid 'N Play, a genial rap duo known for their fun, message-oriented music and their *House Party* movies. In 1988, Kid 'N Play released their debut album, *2 Hype* (Select Records). On the strength of the go-go–infused single "Rolling With Kid 'N Play," the album went platinum. The duo subsequently secured a media deal that involved films and a Saturday morning cartoon, a first for rap music performers.

Kid 'N Play first met while performing in rival high school rap acts; Kid was with the Turnout Brothers and Play with the Super Lovers. Their original name was the Fresh Force. In 1987, producer Hurby "Luv Bug" Azor, a former member of Super Lovers, became the duo's manager and helped them to sign a deal with Select Records. Although other rap artists were more successful, Kid 'N Play's clean-cut image (despite Kid's extreme **high top fade**) made them more appealing as film stars. In 1990, the Kid 'N Play movie *House Party* was released and was a moderate success. That same year, the duo released their second album, *Funhouse* (Select Records). The pop-flavored *Funhouse* did not fare well in a music environment dominated by hardcore rap. In 1991, Kid 'N Play appeared in *House Party II* and the teen film *Class Act*. In 1991, Kid 'N Play also released their final album, *Face the Nation* (Select Records). In 1993, another sequel to *House Party* was released.

DISCOGRAPHY: *2 Hype* (Select Records, 1988); *Funhouse* (Select Records, 1990); *Face the Nation* (Select Records, 1991).

KING T (aka King Tee) [Roger McBride]

One of the West Coast's pioneering rap artists, King Tee, later known as King T, released a number of commercially unsuccessful albums beginning in the late 1980s. In the early 1990s his record company, Capitol Records, dropped him. He then recorded an album for MCA. From a historical perspective, King T, a native of Los Angeles, stands alongside **DJ Pooh** and E-Swift as one of the premier West Coast producers of that era.

Although King Tee did not attain the same mainstream success of his peers, he nonetheless collaborated with some of the best of the West Coast's rap artists and producers, including **Too Short**, **Rappin' 4-Tay**, B-Legit, **Xzibit**, **Ice Cube**, **Ant Banks**, and **Ice-T**. He eventually became a member of the **Likwit Crew**, a loose affiliation that included **Tha Alkaholiks** and **Xzibit**. **Dr. Dre** attempted to use his newly minted Aftermath record label to reinvigorate King T's career. Unfortunately King T's performance on the compilation album *Dr. Dre Presents the Aftermath* (Aftermath/Interscope Records, 1996) and a poorly received solo album, *Thy Kingdom Come* (Greedy Green Ent., 1998), featuring some Dr. Dre production, did nothing to jump-start his career. King T maintained ties with Dr. Dre and made cameo appearances on his *2001* album (Aftermath Records, 1999) and on Xzibit's album, *Restless* (Sony, 2000). In 2004, he released the album *Ruthless Chronicles* (Bigga Ent.)

DISCOGRAPHY: *Act a Fool* (Capitol Records, 1988); *At Your Own Risk* (Capitol Records, 1990); *Tha Triflin' Album* (Capitol Records, 1993); IV Life (MCA, 1995); *Thy Kingdom Come* (Greedy Green Ent., 2002); *Ruthless Chronicles* (Bigga Ent.).

"KING TIM III"

"King Tim III," the first modern rap single, predating the release of "**Rapper's Delight**" (Sugar Hill Records, 1979), is a song by the funk group The Fatback Band, featuring rap artist King Tim (aka Personality Jock). It was released in 1979 on the Spring/Fantasy label as a B-side of the release "You're My Candy Sweet." It went initially unnoticed, but subsequently gained attention in the aftermath of the commercial success of "Rapper's Delight," released several months later.

KOOL DJ RED ALERT [Grant Smith]

A legendary Hip Hop radio personality and DJ, Kool DJ Red Alert was inducted into the Rock and Roll Hall of Fame in Cleveland, Ohio, with his own exhibit, the only DJ aside from the original pioneers so honored. Additionally, Red Alert was named one of the fifty most influential people in music by *Rolling Stone* magazine. He has also been named an honorary ambassador to the United Nations in recognition of his contributions in the field of music. Red Alert has appeared in over fifty music videos.

So named because of his red hair and "alert" response on the basketball court, Red Alert was reared in the Bronx by his maternal grandparents, who were from Antigua. During his last years at DeWitt Clinton High School, Red Alert went to the Saturday night parties thrown by **DJ Kool Herc** and his MC, **Coke La Rock,** at clubs throughout the west Bronx. After studying other DJs and getting his own equipment, Red Alert began to DJ parties himself, learning about various styles of music including dance, rock, reggae, and new wave. Red Alert met **Afrika Bambaataa** through his cousin, DJ Jazzy Jay. Red Alert became the DJ for Afrika Bambaataa and his **Zulu Nation**, joining the likes of **Afrika Islam**, the Soul Sonic Force, Grandmaster D.ST and the **Rock Steady Crew**.

In 1983, while DJing at the Roxy nightclub, Red Alert met Barry Mayo, then program director of New York's KISS-FM (WRKS-FM). Mayo hired Red Alert to inaugurate the *Dance Mix Party* program. Red Alert remained at KISS-FM for eleven years, becoming the top DJ at the station. In 1984, he released his first record, the twelve-inch *Hip Hop On Wax, Volume 2* (Vintertainment). Red DJed for female rap artist Sparky D and he also became a member of **Boogie Down Productions** and toured with them. In 1994, DJ Red Alert moved to New York City's Hot 97

(WQHT-FM), where he did two daily shows: the *"The Twelve O'clock Old School at Noon Mix* and the *"Five O'Clock Free Ride.*

Red Alert owns a production and management company, Red Alert Productions (RAP). The company developed a reputation for grooming and promoting new talent. Red Alert has been instrumental in launching the career of successful artists such as the **Jungle Brothers**, **A Tribe Called Quest**, **Black Sheep**, and **Queen Latifah**. In 2001, Red Alert returned to KISS-FM in New York City. Currently Red Alert hosts the *Old School Mix at Noon*, Monday through Friday, on New York City's Power 105.1 (WWPR-FM). On Sirius Satellite Radio, he presents the program *Classic Collections* on Fridays from 6 to 7 p.m.

DISCOGRAPHY: *Hip Hop On Wax, Vol. 2* (Vintertainment, 1984); *We Can Do This* (Next Plateau, 1988); *Kool DJ Red Alert: Let's Make It Happen* (Next Plateau, 1990); *Let's Make It Happen III* (Next Plateau/Red, 1990); *Kool DJ Red Alert—Propmaster Dancehall* (Sony, 1994); *Kool DJ Red Alert Presents* (Next Plateau, 1996); *Beats, Rhymes & Battles of Hip Hop 1* (Relativity Records, 2001).

KOOL G RAP & DJ POLO

Kool G Rap [Nathaniel Wilson] and DJ Polo [Thomas Pough] are widely recognized as one of the forebearers of hardcore rap music. A **Juice Crew All Stars** member, Kool G Rap—the name stands for "Kool Genius of Rap"—could easily be described as the Mario Puzo of Hip Hop. From classic songs such as "Talk Like Sex" to "It's A Demo" to "Streets Of New York," Kool G Rap and DJ Polo made classic rap music. Kool G Rap is best known as a formidable MC with a distinctive lisping delivery. Additionally, Kool G Rap's vivid narratives contained some of rap music's raunchiest rhymes.

Kool G Rap and partner DJ Polo were discovered by **Cold Chillin'** founder **Marley Marl**. In 1986, the Queens, New York–based duo released their first single, "I'm Fly," b/w "It's a Demo" (Cold Chillin'). Kool G Rap would, however, make his mark on the Juice Crew's group track "The Symphony," which included **Big Daddy Kane**, **Master Ace**, and Craig G. Marley Marl produced and co-wrote material for the duo's long anticipated debut album, *Road to the Riches* (Cold Chillin', 1989). Marley Marl would share production duties with **Eric B** and **Large Professor** (**Main Source**) for Kool G Rap & DJ Polo's sophomore effort, *Wanted: Dead or Alive* (Cold Chillin', 1990). This album featured guest performances by Big Daddy Kane and **Biz Markie**, and contained the duo's best-known song, "Streets of New York." The cover art for Kool G Rap & DJ Polo's third album, *Live and Let Die* (Cold Chillin', 1992), became the source of controversy. The album cover showed Kool G Rap & DJ Polo feeding meat to vicious dogs as two White men stood on chairs with nooses around their necks in the background. After the release of

Live and Let Die, Kool G Rap and DJ Polo parted ways.

Kool G Rap would go on and record as a solo artist. The album *4,5,6* (Sony, 1995), Kool G Rap's first without DJ Polo. One highlight from his solo debut is the track "Fast Life," which has Kool G Rap trading verses with **Nas**. In 1998, Kool G Rap would release *Roots of Evil* (Down Low Records) and in 2002, after a long delay, Kool G Rap's third solo album, *The Giancana Story* (Koch Records), was finally released. Rawkus Records signed Kool G Rap in the late 1990s and promoted it as being the Return of the King of the MCs. **DJ Premier** produced the track "First N*gga," which was a success in the underground scene, also receiving critical praise. Rawkus, however, continued to push back the release date of *The Giancana Story* and then the label closed its doors. The album was widely bootlegged during all the delays. Koch Records subsequently picked up Kool G Rap and in the deal got to release *The Giancana Story,* but without the DJ Premier cut and without the Hi-Tek produced track "Keep Going" featuring **Snoop Dogg** and Devin the Dude.

Kool G Rap. *Courtesy of Photofest.*

In 1997, DJ Polo recorded the single "Suzy Rose" with **Ice-T** as the B-side to the track "Freak of the Week" recorded with adult movie star Ron Jeremy.

DISCOGRAPHY: *Road to Riches* (Cold Chillin', 1989); *Wanted: Dead or Alive* (Cold Chillin', 1990); *Live and Let Die* (Cold Chillin', 1992). Kool G Rap solo: *4,5,6* (Sony, 1995); *Roots of Evil* (Down Low, 1998); *The Giancana Story* (Koch, 2002).

KOOL KEITH (aka Dr. Octagon, aka Dr. Dooom) [Keith Matthew Thornton]

A founding member of the legendary **Ultramagnetic MCs**, Kool Keith forged a solo career based on spaced-out, free-flowing rhymes and concepts.

Once a psychiatric patient at Bellevue Hospital, he released his debut single, "Earth People," under the name Dr. Octagon in late 1995 on the San Francisco, California-based Bulk Recordings. The single quickly became a hit on the underground rap music scene. His self-titled 1996 album was also an immediate success, featuring internationally renowned turntablist **DJ Q-Bert** with production by DJ Shadow and the Automator. The combination of superior turntable work, bizarre sounds, and impressionist lyrics found a wide audience, one that spanned hardcore rap music fans to rock music reviewers.

In 1997, the album *Sex Styles* was released on Keith's Funky Ass label. That same year, Keith signed a deal with Dreamworks and subsequently *Dr. Octagon,* retitled *Dr. Octagonecologyst*, was released, with a number of bonus cuts. In 1999, Dr. Octagon was killed off by Keith's alter ego Dr. Dooom on the album, *First Come, First Served* (Funky Ass). Keith then signed with Ruffhouse Records and released his second album, the 1999 *Black Elvis/Lost In Space,* under the Dr. Dooom name. In 2000 and 2001, Kool Keith released the albums *Matthew* (Threshold Recordings) and *Spankmaster* (Overcore), respectively. In May 2004, Keith released *Kool Keith Presents Thee Undatakerz*. That same year, Keith released *Diesel Truckers* with his old friend and producer, Kutmasta Kurt.

DISCOGRAPHY: *Singles*: "Earth People" (Bulk Recordings, 1995). *Albums*: *Dr. Octagon* (Bulk Recordings, 1996), re-issued as *Dr. Octagonecologyst* (Dreamworks, 1997); *Sex Styles* (Funky Ass, 1997); *First Come, First Served* (Funky Ass, 1999); *Black Elvis/Lost In Space* (Ruffhouse/MCA, 1999); *Matthew* (Threshold Recordings, 2000); *Spankmaster* (Overcore, 2001); *Kool Keith Presents Thee Undatakerz* (2004); *Diesel Truckers* (Method Recordings, 2004).

KOOL MOE DEE [Mohandes Dewese]

MC for the legendary **Treacherous Three**, one of the first Old School groups to record, Kool Moe Dee's tongue-twisting rhymes and speedy delivery were enough to vanquish most competitors. Kool Moe Dee was never one to back down from a fight. On December 30, 1981, the native of Harlem, New York, **battled Busy Bee** at the **Disco Fever**, which became one of the most famous match-ups in Hip Hop history. In another classic rivalry, Kool Moe Dee went to lyrical blows with **LL Cool J**.

In 1978, he began his musical career as a member of the rap group Treacherous Three. The group's friendship with rap artist **Spoonie Gee** led them to Gee's uncle's label, **Enjoy Records**. In 1980, the group released the single "New Rap Language" (Enjoy Records) and also the singles "Body Rock" (Enjoy Records) and "At the Party" (Enjoy Records). In 1981, the group signed to Sugar Hill Records and released the classic singles "Feel the Heartbeat" and "Whip It." In 1985, Kool Moe Dee effectively launched his solo career while still a member of Treacherous Three, when the single "Turn It Up" was released. According to Kool Moe Dee L.A. Sunshine had not come to the recording session for the single, and he erased Special K's quickly done rhymes because he considered them "sloppy." That same year he also lent his writing skills to the Sugar Hill Gang's single "The Down Beat." Kool Moe Dee would also record his own version of the song.

After graduating from the State University of New York at Old Westbury with a degree in Communications, Kool Moe Dee was ready for a solo career. By 1986 Kool Moe Dee had signed to Jive Records and released his first solo album, *I'm Kool Moe Dee*. On the hit track, "Go See the Doctor," a witty rap about venereal diseases, Kool Moe Dee teamed up with then-unknown producer Teddy Riley. In 1987, he released his second album, *How Ya Like Me Now* (Jive Records); on a track of the same name, he took on LL Cool J. Moe Dee was striking out at a new generation of rap artists for forgetting their predecessors. On the album cover, a red **Kangol** hat, LL Cool J's trademark, was being crushed by the wheel of a Jeep. and *How Ya Like Me Now* went platinum. In a war of words, LL Cool J fired back with the single. "Jack the Ripper." Kool Moe Dee shot back with "Let's Go." LL Cool J responded with "To The Break of Dawn." Finally, Kool Moe Dee landed the last punch with the single "Death Blow." It is up for debate as to who won this rap tournament.

In 1989, Kool Moe Dee participated in The Stop The Violence Movement single, "Self Destruction." That year he also released the gold-selling *Knowledge is King*, which led to his becoming the first rap artist to perform at the Grammy awards ceremonies. In 1989, Kool Moe Dee was also part of the Quincy Jones album, *Back on the Block*, released in November of that year. Kool Moe Dee appeared on the track of the same name, along with **Ice-T**, **Melle Mel**, and **Big Daddy Kane**, winning a Grammy award in 1991 for Best Rap Duo or Group. Kool Moe Dee released the EP *African Pride* (Jive Records) in 1990. His 1991 album *Funke, Funke Wisdom* (Jive Records) was not as commercially successful as his earlier efforts, and Jive Records dropped Kool Moe Dee after releasing his *Greatest Hits* album in 1993.

In 1993, with his talent still apparent, Kool Moe Dee recorded a Treacherous Three reunion album. In 1994, he signed to DJ Easy Lee's label for the 1994 album *Interlude* (1994). In 1997, Kool Moe Dee turned actor in the film *Gang Related*, which starred **Tupac Shakur**. In 1998, he performed in a science fiction clunker, *Storm Trooper*. The next year, Kool Moe Dee appeared on the track "Wild, Wild West" with **Will Smith** and Dru Hill, from the soundtrack for the 1999 film of the same name. Kool Moe Dee also turned up in the B-movies *Cypress Edge* (1999) and

Out Kold (2001), in the latter costarring with Ice-T. In 2002, Kool Moe Dee made a cameo appearance in the teen film, *The New Guy*.

In 2003, Kool Moe Dee released the book *There's a God On the Mic: The True 50 Greatest MCs* (New York: Thunder's Mouth Press), with a foreword by **Chuck D** and photographs by **Ernie Paniccioli**. Drawing on seventeen categories ranging from lyrical content, vocabulary, and free-styling capability to the length of an MC's career, the body of work, and the social impact of that work, the book compiles the definitive list of the greatest MCs of all time.

DISCOGRAPHY: *Single*: "Turn It Up" (Sugar Hill Records, 1985). *EP*: *African Pride* (Jive Records, 1990). *Albums*: *I'm Kool Moe Dee* (Jive Records, 1986); *How Ya Like Me Now* (Jive Records, 1987); *Knowledge is King* (Jive Records, 1989); *Funke, Funke Wisdom* (Jive Records, 1991); *Interlude* (1994). Grammy Award: 1991 for Best Rap Duo or Group [Quincy Jones's *Back on the Block* collaboration].

KRIS KROSS

Thirteen-year-old rap artists Daddy Mack [Chris Smith] and Mack Daddy [Chris Kelly] became famous in 1992 as Kris Kross.

Kris Kross. *Courtesy of Photofest.*

Producer **Jermaine Dupri** had discovered the duo at an Atlanta, Georgia, mall in 1991. Dupri mentored the young performers and, as a way to capitalize off the name, came up with the idea that the two wear all of their clothes backwards. The promotional gimmick worked, and Kris Kross's first single, "Jump," which sampled the Jackson Five's "I Want You Back," became the fastest-selling single in fifteen years. The single stayed at number 1 for eight weeks on the *Billboard* charts and helped sell over 4 million copies of their debut album, *Totally Krossed Out* (So So Def, 1992). The duo scored with the gold single "Warm It Up," and Kris Kross appeared on numerous teen-oriented television shows and toured Europe with pop star Michael Jackson. Unfortunately although the duo released two more albums, *Da Bomb* (So So Def, 1993) and *Young, Rich and Dangerous* (So So Def, 1996), Kris Kross never again attained the success of their debut album.

DISCOGRAPHY: *Totally Krossed Out* (So So Def, 1992); *Da Bomb* (So So Def, 1993); *Young Rich and Dangerous* (So So Def, 1996).

KRS-ONE (aka The Teacher) [Lawrence Krishna "Kris" Parker]

One of Hip Hop's most outspoken and enduring figures. KRS-ONE is a cofounder of **Boogie Down Productions**, a noted lecturer and author, and a founder of the **Temple of Hip Hop**. KRS is often credited with being one of the first rap artists to combine rap and reggae. KRS-ONE is also one of the first to rhyme off beat. Within an extensive body of work, the majority of KRS-ONE's notoriety comes from his ability to consistently reposition the character and content of the music by delivering thoughtful narratives with a direct and forceful style.

KRS-ONE. *Courtesy of Photofest.*

KRS-ONE was born Lawrence Brown (he took on the surname Parker when his mother remarried). Though associated with the Bronx, he was actually born in Brooklyn, New York. The rap artist reportedly left home at age fourteen and eventually ended up at a children's shelter in the Bronx. At age eighteen he landed at the Franklin Armory Men's shelter in the South Bronx, where residents called him Krishna because of his interest in the Hare Krishna spirituality of some of the antipoverty workers. Hare Krishna spirituality originated in ancient India and emphasizes mind elevation as the path to pleasure and tranquility.

Lawrence "Krishna" Parker spent his days playing basketball and reading books while watching Hip Hop develop around him. Soon he became an active participant, taking up graffiti and writing KRS-ONE, an acronym for Knowledge Reigns Supreme Over Nearly Everybody, a phrase that would soon become a philosophy. It is around this time that Krishna met Scott Sterling, a youth counselor and part-time DJ (aka DJ Scott La Rock). Realizing that they shared a common interest in music, the two began to work together.

Formally, KRS-ONE's music career began in the summer of 1984, when a rap group called Scott La Rock and the Celebrity Three released the single "Advance." Amid contract disputes with the record label, Scott La Rock and the Celebrity Three parted ways. In the winter of 1984, KRS-ONE and Scott La Rock started a new group, the Boogie Down Crew. After a bad experience working with Sleeping Bag Records, they changed the name to Boogie Down Productions (BDP). In 1986, Boogie Down Productions independently released a single called "Crack Attack." In 1987, Boogie Down Productions released the landmark album *Criminal Minded* (B-Boy Records). A few months after the album's debut, Scott La Rock was murdered in the Bronx, while trying to break up an argument dispute between rap artist D' Nice and an ex-girlfriend's boyfriend. Although many thought BDP would fold after Scott La Rock's death, BDP went on.

In 1988, BDP left B-Boy Records to sign with Jive Records and *By All Means Necessary* was released. BDP would go on to release three more albums: *Ghetto Music: The Blueprint of Hip Hop* (Jive Records, 1989); *Edutainment* (Jive Records, 1990); and *Live Hardcore Worldwide* (Jive Records, 1991). In 1992, KRS-ONE made headlines after he and his crew assaulted the rap duo **P.M. Dawn** at a live performance in a New York nightclub. KRS-ONE was angry over a comment made by Prince B about him in an interview that appeared in *Details* magazine. KRS-ONE later publicly apologized to P.M. Dawn for his actions.

In 1993, KRS-ONE released first solo album, *Return of the Boom Bap* (Jive Records). Other albums followed: *KRS ONE* (Jive Records, 1995), *Battle for Rap Supremacy* (Cold Chillin', 1996), a collaboration with his old rival **MC Shan**; and *I Got Next* (Jive Records, 1997). In 2001, KRS-ONE released *The Sneak Attack* (Koch International). The following year brought two albums: the gospel effort *Spiritually Minded* (Koch

International) and *The Mix Tape* (Koch International), the latter including the single "Ova Here," which was a response directed at rap artist **Nelly**.

In 2002, KRS-ONE and rap artist Nelly would engage in a public **beef** that hit a fevered pitch when the multi-platinum-selling Nelly publicly insulted the Teacher on Freeway's **remix** of "Rock The Mic." In response, KRS-ONE recorded the track, "The Real Hip Hop is Over Here," and called for a boycott of Nelly's album *Nellyville* (Universal, 2002).

Kristyles (Koch International) and *D.I.G.I.T.A.L.* (Cleopatra, 2003) were released in 2003. The album *Keep Right* (OTC/Grit) was released in 2004.

KRS-ONE has published two books. In 1995, he self-published *The Science of Rap*, which dissects the technical aspects of rapping. In 2003, KRS-ONE published his second book, *Ruminations*, an introspective exploration of a range of issues including popular culture, education, politics, and spirituality.

Often referred to as "The Teacher" or "The Philosopher," KRS-ONE has taken his melding of Afrocentric consciousness and street smarts around the globe as one of Hip Hop's elder statesmen. He has also lectured at some of this nation's most prestigious universities, including Harvard University, Yale University, Vassar College, Columbia University, New York University, and Stanford University.

Aside from being a performer, during his BDP years KRS-ONE also spearheaded movements such as Stop the Violence, which in 1988, which raised a reported $600,000 for the National Urban League and H.E.A.L. (Human Education Against Lies). In 1999, he created the Temple of Hip Hop, an organization dedicated to uplifting and promoting the stated principles of the culture. KRS-ONE and fellow BDP member Ms. Melodie were among the first rap artists to marry, but the union ended around 1990.

DISCOGRAPHY: *Boogie Down Productions: Criminal Minded* (B-Boy, 1987); *By All Means Necessary* (Jive Records, 1988); *Ghetto Music: The Blueprint of Hip Hop* (Jive Records, 1989); *Edutainment* (Jive Records, 1990); *BDP Live Hardcore Worldwide* (Jive Records, 1991). *Solo: Return of the Boom Bap* (Jive Records, 1993); *KRS-ONE* (Jive Records, 1995); *1996's Battle for Rap Supremacy* (Cold Chillin'); *I Got Next* (Jive Records, 1997); *The Sneak Attack* (Koch International, 2001); *Spiritual Minded* (Koch International, 2001); *The Mix Tape* (Koch International, 2002); *Kristyles* (Koch, 2003); *How Bad You Want It* (Koch, 2003); *D.I.G.I.T.A.L.* (Cleopatra, 2003); *Keep Right* (OTC/Grit, 2004).

KRUSH GROOVE. *See* Films

KURTIS BLOW (aka Kool DJ Kurt) [Curtis Walker]

Kurtis Blow was the first commercially successful solo rap artist, his first record, "Christmas Rappin'," being the first rap single distributed

Kurtis Blow. *Courtesy of Photofest.*

by a major record label (Mercury Records/CBS, 1979). His second single, "The Breaks" (Def Jam Recordings, 1980) became the first twelve-inch rap single to be certified gold, and only one of two ever to do so.

A native of Harlem, New York, Kurtis Blow participated in the emergence of Hip Hop in the early 1970s, first as a **B-boy** and then as a DJ. Under the name Kool DJ Kurt, Walker began performing in clubs and community events. After enrolling at City College of New York (CCNY) in 1976, Walker served as program director for the college radio station, and he teamed up with The Force, a group of party promoters that included fellow CCNY student **Russell Simmons**. The group sponsored parties in Harlem until 1977, when competition persuaded Russell Simmons to move the group to Queens.

Simmons renamed Kool DJ Kurt to Kurtis Blow and then promoted Kurtis Blow as "the #1 rapper in Queens"—although in fact Hip Hop had not taken off in Queens as it had in Manhattan and the Bronx, so the title was a marketing scheme, rather a legitimate superlative. Joseph Simmons, Russell's younger brother, would began to DJ for Kurtis Blow, calling himself "DJ Run, the Son of Kurtis Blow." Later he utilized the DJ and production skills of **Davy DMX**.

Between 1977 and 1978, Kurtis Blow's club performances in Harlem and the Bronx made him a celebrity in the emerging Hip Hop scene. As a result of his fame, *Billboard* magazine writer Robert Ford approached Simmons about making a record. Blow recorded the single, "Christmas Rappin'," which was co-written by Ford and financier J.B. Moore. Initially major labels were cool to the idea of releasing "Christmas Rappin'," on the theory that rap music was a passing fad. Opinions within the music industry changed, however, with the success of The Sugar Hill Gang's "**Rapper's Delight**." Simmons then signed a production deal with Mercury records, who released the single in 1979, thus making Kurtis Blow the first rap artist to have his work distributed by a major record label.

Blow's follow-up single, "The Breaks" (Mercury Records, 1980), was an immediate success and eventually went gold. Moreover, the single is considered a rap music classic. In 1980, Kurtis Blow released his eponymous debut album. One standout on the album is the single "Hard Times," perhaps the first stab by a rap artist at socially conscious lyrics. It would be **Run DMC**, however, that would popularize the song.

Blow had some difficulty surpassing the success of "The Breaks," although he released an album nearly annually in the 1980s. In 1981, Blow released *Deuce* (Mercury Records) and in 1982 the album *Tough* (Mercury Records), neither of which sold well. In 1983, Blow's *Party Time* (Mercury Records) EP paired him with the Washington, DC, **go-go** band E.U. and the title track was successful.

During this period, Blow began working as a producer and helped shape the sounds for a variety of rap artists, most notably the **Fat Boys**. After helping the Fat Boys secure a recording deal, Blow produced several of their records. In 1984, Blow released the album *Ego Trip* (Mercury), which sold moderately well on the strength of the tracks "AJ Scratch" (a tribute to DJs), "Basketball," and "8 Million Stories (a collaboration with Run DMC).

Blow appeared in the seminal Hip Hop film ***Krush Groove***, in which he performed the single "If I Ruled the World," his biggest hit since "The Breaks." In 1986, Blow and Dexter King, son of slain civil rights leader Martin Luther King, Jr., assembled The King's Holiday All Star Chorus (comprised of Run DMC, **Whodini**, Grandmaster **Melle Mel**, and The Fat Boys) to record the single "King's Holiday," in observance of the national holiday commemorating King's birthday. Unfortunately, musical tastes were changing, and that same year when Blow released his album *Kingdom Blow* (Mercury Records) it was not warmly received, though it did produce one final hit, "I'm Chillin'."

In 1988, Blow's comeback album, *Back by Popular Demand* (Mercury Records), was royally slammed by critics. Deciding that his recording career was over, Blow pursued other related endeavors. In the early 1990s, he spent several years hosting an Old School rap music show on the Los Angeles radio station Power 106 (KPWR-FM). In 1995, Blow appeared in Russell Simmons's rap music documentary, *The Show*. In 1996, using the same melody line **Nas** (with vocals from **Lauryn Hill**) would record his version of "I Ruled the World," for his album, *It was Written*. In 1997, as one of the elder statesmen of Hip Hop, Blow was hired by Rhino Records to produce, compile, and write liner notes for a three-volume series titled *Kurtis Blow Presents the History of Rap*. The same year, he was highlighted in the rap documentary *Rhyme and Reason*.

In 1998, the R & B group NEXT would sample "Christmas Rappin'" on their hit single, "Too Close." In 1999, Kurtis Blow appears on LEN's album, *You Can't Stop the Bum Rush*, on the track called "Cold Chillin'." In 2001, Blow founded the Alliance of Legends with **Grandmaster Flash**, an organization intent on officially documenting Hip Hop history. Releasing a Hip Hop history compilation album and a documentary film were among the new organization's objectives. Currently Blow hosts the Old School radio program *Backspin* on Sirius Satellite Radio every day from 6 to 12 P.M.

DISCOGRAPHY: *Singles*: "Christmas Rappin'" (Mercury, 1979); "The Breaks" (Mercury, 1980). *Albums*: *Kurtis Blow* (Mercury, 1980); *Deuce* (Mercury, 1981); *Tough* (1982); *Party Time* (Polygram, 1983); *Ego Trip* (Mercury, 1984); *Kingdom Blow* (Mercury, 1986); *Back by Popular Demand* (Mercury, 1988).

KURUPT (aka Kingpin, aka Kalhoon, aka Young Gotti) [Ricardo Brown]

A member of **Tha Dogg Pound**, Kurupt also gained fame as a member of the **Death Row Records** family, and yet struggled to establish himself as a successful solo artist. Born in Philadelphia, Pennsylvania, Kurupt moved to Hawthorne, California, as a teenager. He subsequently became friends with **Snoop Dogg** and was signed to Death Row Records.

Kurupt made his recording debut on **Dr. Dre**'s album *The Chronic* (Death Row Records, 1992), and thereafter performed on numerous Death Row releases. Kurupt became one-half of **Tha Dogg Pound**, a Snoop Dogg spin-off, when he teamed up with rap artist–producer Daz Dillinger. Kurupt, collaborating with Daz Dillinger and Snoop, enjoyed success with the debut of *Dogg Food* (Death Row Records, 1995), a Dogg Pound album that included the hit singles "Let's Play House" and "**New York, New York**," a diss to the Big Apple.

In 1998, Kurupt released a double-disc solo album, *Kuruption*, on Antra Records, a label that he cofounded. The album was only moderately successful. The follow-up album, *Tha Streetz Iz a Mutha* (Antra, 1999), though better produced, did not sell much better the first. Shortly before the release of that sophomore album, Kurupt made headlines when his bodyguard was fatally shot in front of the Los Angeles studio where he was recording.

Kurupt's third album, *Space Boogie: Smoke Oddessey* (Antra, 2001), had crossover aspirations, including guest performances by **Limp Bizkit**'s Fred Durst and Everlast (formerly of **House of Pain**). Unfortunately, the formula did not net Kurupt any more sales beyond his core fans. In 2001, Kurupt joined Daz Dillinger to record another Dogg Pound album, *Dillinger & Young Gotti*, which marked Kurupt's return to traditional rap music. (D.P.G. Recordz). This same year, Death Row released another Dogg Pound album, *2002* (Death Row Records, 2001), a collection of unreleased material from the mid-1990s. Unable to launch a viable solo career, in 2002 Kurupt returned to the moribund Death Row to assist Suge Knight in reviving the label.

DISCOGRAPHY: *Albums* with Tha Dogg Pound: *Dogg Food* (Death Row Records, 1995); *Dillinger & Young Gotti* (D.P.G. Records, 2001); *2002* (Death Row Records, 2001). *Albums*, solo: *Kuruption* (Antra, 1998); *Tha Streetz Iz a Mutha* (Antra, 1999); *Space Boogie: Smoke Oddessey* (Antra, 2001).

KWAMÉ [Kwamé Holland]

Rap artist Kwamé may be more known for his polka dot shirts than for his humorous, but intelligent rhymes. The Queens, New York, native was influenced musically by close family friends Stevie Wonder, Lionel Hampton, and Abdullah Ibraheem. As a child, Kwamé received a drum set from Lionel Hampton and a harmonica from Stevie Wonder. Kwamé went on to master several instruments, including piano, trumpet, and guitar.

In 1989, Kwamé released his debut album, *The Boy Genius* (Atlantic Records), and immediately began to develop a reputation with his good-natured style. Two of the album's singles, "The Man We All Know & Love" and "The Rhythm," helped to popularize the rap artist. Kwamé's penchant for bright polka dot shirts initiated a new fashion trend when his second album *A Day In The Life* was released in 1990. In that same year, Kwamé also produced the **remix** of "Lies" for the platinum-selling R & B girl group, En Vogue.

The following year, Kwamé was again working behind the scenes when he wrote the rhymes on Bell Biv Devoe's platinum-selling track, "Poison." In 1993, Kwamé released his third album, *Nastee* (Atlantic Records), and his fourth, *Incognito* (Wrap Records), in 1994, produced the infectious single "What's It Like (Like Butta Baby)." After taking several years off from recording Kwamé directed his talents to inspiring young children across the country to learn through music.

Kwamé added film work to his list of musical contribution, writing and performing songs for the films *Dancing in September* (HBO Films) and *Ghetto Dog* (Spartan Films) in 2001. Kwamé also produced the Nick Cannon track "Scared of You'" for the movie soundtrack for *Drum Line* (20th Century Fox Films).

Kwamé has produced for the likes of **Mary J. Blige**, **LL Cool J** and K Slay, and newcomer Lady May. Today, Kwamé continues to produce music in his Harlem, New York, studio.

DISCOGRAPHY: *The Boy Genius* (Atlantic, 1989); *A Day In The Life* (Atlantic, 1990); *Nastee* (Atlantic, 1993); *Incognito* (Wrap Records, 1994).

L

LADY B [Wendy Clark]

Lady B, a native of Philadelphia, Pennsylvania, stands among Hip Hop's pioneers. Her 1979 single, "To The Beat Y'all" (TEC Records), made Lady B one of the first female solo artists to release a rap single. Sugar Hill Records later picked up the single and released it on compilation albums. "To The Beat Y'all" would also make an appearance on the **Roots** track "Without a Doubt," from their album *When Things Fall Apart* (MCA 1999).

The seventeen-year-old Lady B began spinning rap records in 1979 on WHAT 1340 AM, and for several years she was the only DJ in Philadelphia playing rap music. Lady B went on to work at Philadelphia's WUSL Power 99 FM and then New York's WBLS FM before returning to Philadelphia in 1997 to host her *Street Beat* show on WPHI-FM, 103.9, the show currently airs on Sunday nights from 6 to 8 p.m.

In 1999, Lady B was chosen by the *Philadelphia City Paper*'s Readers' Choice as "Best Radio DJ." In addition to being a legendary DJ, Lady B served as the editor-in-chief of ***Word Up!***, an early rap music fanzine, and as National Promotions Manager at Sleeping Bag Records.

LADY OF RAGE, THE [Robin Yvette Allen]

Lady of Rage is recognized as the only female rap artist to record for **Death Row Records**. A native of Farmville, Virginia, she moved to New York and got a job at as a receptionist at Chung King recording studio. Lady of Rage then recorded vocals for the L.A. Posse's 1991 album, *They Come in All Colors* (Atlantic Records, 1991). Her skills and ferocity caught the attention of Death Row's **Dr. Dre**. Lady of Rage subsequently appeared on several tracks of the monumental album, *The Chronic* (Death Row Records, 1992).

In 1994, her debut single, "Afro Puffs," featuring Dr. Dre's production and vocals by **Snoop Dogg,** appeared on the *Above The Rim* film soundtrack. She would then appear on Snoop's 1996 album, *Tha Doggfather* (Death Row Records). Although Lady of Rage fans eagerly awaited her solo album, internal problems at Death Row Records meant that the release was repeatedly postponed. In June 1997, her album *Necessary Roughness* finally hit the streets. Unfortunately, Death Row Records was no longer the hit powerhouse and the album sold less than 200,000 copies. In 1998, along with **Heather B** and Nikki D, she formed the Underdogs, an all-female collective and support group for female MCs.

In 2000, The Lady of Rage hung up her mic to concentrate on her acting career. She had a recurring role on UPN's *Steve Harvey Show* and also appeared in the 2000 film "Thug Life," which also starred **Kurupt**. She returned to the mic on the track "Set it Off," from Snoop Dogg's album, *The Last Meal* (Priority Records, 2000) and again in 2002 in the track "Batman and Robin," from the Snoop album *Paid tha Cost to Be da Bo$$* (Priority Records, 2002).

DISCOGRAPHY: *Necessary Roughness* (Death Row Records, 1997).

LARGE PROFESSOR [William Paul Mitchell]

Large Professor is a prolific and skilled beat scientist who has done production for many of Hip Hop's heavy weights, including **Eric B & Rakim**, **Pete Rock and C. L. Smooth**, **Kool G Rap**, **Biz Markie**, **Big Daddy Kane**, **Gang Starr**, **A Tribe Called Quest**, the **Beastie Boys**, and **Nas**.

Large Professor officially entered Hip Hop in 1989, when he won a tryout held by **Main Source** members K-Cut and Sir Scratch. Main Source would release the classic album *Breaking Atoms* (Wild Pitch Records) in 1991. The track "Live from the Bar-B-Que" would introduce rap music fans to a fifteen-year-old Nas, and also **Akinyele**. Still a high school student, Large Professor became the group's MC and producer. Large Professor was the driving force behind Main Source's success; he would, however, part company with the group over creative differences.

At age seventeen, Large Professor went to school during the day and spent his evenings making beats, for Eric B & Rakim's album *Let the Rhythm Hit 'Em* (MCA Records, 1990). The skilled producer then got a call to work on **Kool G Rap**'s album, *Wanted Dead or Alive* (Cold Chillin'/Warner Bros. Records, 1990). Large Professor is credited with teaching **DJ Premier** the intricacies of a **Technics** SP1200 turntable, in effect passing on what he had learned from **Pete Rock**. Premier in turn introduced Large Professor to vintage vinyl, and brought Main Source to the attention of Wild Pitch Records. Large Professor also taught Prodigy of **Mobb Deep** his way around a recording studio.

In the 1990s, Large Professor signed a record deal with Geffen Records. He recorded two albums, but only the singles "Mad Scientist" (1996) and "I juswannachill" (1996) were released. In 2000, he released the EP *About That Time* (Matador Records) and followed up with the EPs *Rap Professionals* (Replay Records, 2000), *Blaze Rhymez* (Matador Records, 2001), and *Radio Active* (Matador Records, 2002).

In 2002, Large Professor released his first solo album, *1st Class* (Matador Records), comprised of sixteen tracks of first-class beats under the rhymes of old friends Nas, Q-Tip (of A Tribe Called Quest), Akinyele, and **Busta Rhymes**. The same year he released *The Large Professor Mix*

CD (Sandbox Automatic/HipHopSite.com), representing a complete retrospective of his dual career as rap artist and producer.

LAST POETS, THE

Considered the progenitors of modern rap music, The Last Poets performed politically charged spoken word pieces over drum and conga beats and instrumentations. In 1969, The Last Poets adopted their name from Little Willie Copaseely, a South African writer who believed himself to be among the last poets to exist before the start of warfare. The Last Poets' politically informed raps, tight rhythms, and focus on Black consciousness laid the groundwork for the emergence of rap music.

The Last Poets caught the attention of jazz producer Alan Douglas after performing on a local television program. In 1970, Douglas signed the group to his record label and supervised The Last Poets eponymous debut album. *The Last Poets* is a collection of songs that condemns both White oppression (e.g., "White Man's Got a God Complex") and Black stasis (e.g., "Niggas Are Scared of Revolution"). *The Last Poets* reached the Top 10 on U.S. album charts.

The second album, *This is Madness* (1971), featured more politically charged, radical poems, which got The Last Poets placed on President Nixon's counterintelligence lists. In 1973, Jalal Nuriddin, using the name Lightnin' Rod, would record a solo concept album, ***Hustlers Convention*** (Douglas Records, 1973), a cautionary tale about the sporting life. The album, popular with early Hip Hop DJs, is comprised of twelve prison-style toasts over jazz and became the prototype for rap music.
DISCOGRAPHY: *Selected albums*: *Last Poets* (Douglas, 1970); *This is Madness* (Douglas, 1971); *Chastisement* (Douglas, 1973); *At Last* (Douglas, 1974); *Oh My People* (Charley-UK, 1984); *Freedom Express* (Charley-UK, 1988).

LEADERS OF THE NEW SCHOOL

MC Charlie Brown, MC Dinco D, MC **Busta Rhymes** [Trevor Smith, Jr.], and Cut Monitor Milo formed the Leaders of the New School in 1989. They are best known for launching the career of rap wonder Busta Rhymes. The group from Uniondale, New York, was inspired by fellow Long Islander rap artists **Public Enemy** and **Eric B & Rakim**.

Shortly after The Leaders of the New School united, the group signed a recording deal with Elektra Records. Respected in the underground for their Afrocentric philosophy and hardcore rap style, they released their debut album, *Future Without A Past* (Elektra Records), in 1991. The group made some mainstream noise with the track "Teacher, Don't Teach Us Nonsense." Leaders of the New School would release only one more album, *T.I.M.E.* (Elektra, 1993), before breaking up the following year.

DISCOGRAPHY: *Future Without A Past* (Elektra Records, 1991); *T.I.M.E.* (Elektra Records, 1993).

LIKWIT CREW

The Likwit Crew is a loose affiliation comprised of Tha Liks (**Tha Alkaholiks**), **Xzibit**, and **King T**. Their debut compilation album, *Likwit Crew Presents* (JCOR), overseen by the collective's founding father King T, was to have been released in summer 2002, but it failed to materialize.

Lil' Bow Wow. *Courtesy of Photofest.*

LIL' BOW WOW [aka Bow Wow] [Shad Moss]

A protégé of **Snoop Dogg** and believed to be the youngest rap artist to be signed to a major record contract, Lil' Bow Wow first began to perform his raps when he was only six years old. The Columbus, Ohio, native performed as a warm-up act on the 1991 "Chronic Tour" and impressed rap artist, Snoop Dogg, who right away nicknamed the young artist Lil' Bow Wow and helped him to get signed to Death Row Records. The young rap artist made his recording a debut with a guest appearance on Snoop Doggy Dogg's 1993 multi-platinum album, *Doggystyle*.

Unfortunately, the Death Row deal did not produce an album for Lil' Bow Wow and thereafter he was signed to Epic Records and assigned to So So Def's **Jermaine Dupri**. Lil' Bow Wow's career moved rapidly and by the age of thirteen he had a long list of impressive industry credits. He worked on several film soundtracks, including *Wild Wild West* (1999), *Big Momma's House* (2000), and *Hardball* (2001). The single "Bounce with Me" from the *Big Momma's House* soundtrack gave Lil' Bow Wow wide exposure.

In 2000, Lil' Bow Wow recorded his debut album, *Beware of Dog* (So So Def/Columbia), under the mentorship of executive producer Jermaine Dupri. Lil' Bow Wow released his second album, *Doggy Bag* (So So Def/ Columbia) in 2001. The next year he made his debut as an actor in the film *All About The Benjamins*, with **Ice Cube**. He subsequently appeared in the films *Like Mike* (2002) and *The Johnson Family Vacation* (2004). In July 2003, upon turning sixteen, he abandoned the Lil' part of his name, debuting under the more mature moniker on the album, *Unleashed* (Columbia, 2003).

DISCOGRAPHY: *Beware of Dog* (So So Def/Columbia, 2000); *Doggy Bag* (So So Def/Columbia, 2001); *Unleashed* (Columbia, 2003).

LIL JON AND THE EASTSIDE BOYZ

Lil Jon [Jonathan Smith] is the self-proclaimed King of Crunk. Although **crunk** music has been around for more than a decade, Lil Jon has significantly helped to propel the subgenre. Wearing the hats of artist, collaborator, or producer, Lil Jon is behind many of crunk's biggest successes: his own "Get Low"; Petey Pablo's "Freek-A-Leek"; the Ying Yang Twins track, "Salt Shaker"; Ciara's "Goodies"; and Usher's "Yeah!" In 1993, So So Def President **Jermaine Dupri** invited Lil Jon, then a club DJ in Atlanta, Georgia, to work for the record company as executive vice president of **A & R**. Lil Jon also hosted an Atlanta radio show on V103 (WVEE-FM) and began producing and **remixing** tracks for such major artists as **Too Short**, Xscape, Total, and Usher.

In 1996, Lil Jon debuted his Eastside Boyz (Big Sam and Lil Bo) on *Get Crunk, Who U Wit: Da Album* (DM Records) and scored a club anthem,

"Who You Wit?" DM Records would rerelease the album in 2001. For the next five years, Lil Jon remained largely a regional success until he broke into the national market with the single "Bia', Bia'," featuring **Ludacris**, Too Short, and Chyna Whyte from the album *Put Yo Hood Up* (TVT Records, 2001). The double-platinum album *Kings of Crunk* (TVT Records, 2002) would follow; it includes the hit single "I Don't Give A. . . ." In November 2004, **Lil Jon and the Eastside Boyz** released their third album, *Crunk Juice* (TVT Records).

Comedian Dave Chappelle famously parodied Lil Jon's court jester antics on his show and during the 2003 MTV Awards, comedian Chris Rock joked that the dreadlocked, metal-mouthed Lil Jon resembled a "Black Cousin It." Lil Jon did not get angry at being lampooned: Chris Rock makes hilarious cameos on *Crunk Juice*, and Dave Chapelle's show has given Lil Jon exposure to a wider audience.

Following in the footsteps of **Nelly**'s "Pimp Juice," the trio have introduced into the marketplace their Crunk Juice tonic, a new energy drink mixed with top-shelf vodka.

DISCOGRAPHY: *Get Crunk Who u' Wit: Da Album* (DM Records, 1996, rereleased 2001); *Put Yo Hood Up* (TVT Records, 2001); *Kings of Crunk* (TVT Records, 2002); *Crunk Juice* (TVT Records, 2004).

LIL' KIM [Kimberly Jones]

The professional and personal specter of the late **Biggie Smalls** looms large over the diminutive Lil' Kim. A native of Brooklyn, New York, the self-proclaimed Queen Bitch began her career as a member of the rap group **Junior M.A.F.I.A.**, which was tightly aligned with **The Notorious B.I.G.** The only woman in Junior M.A.F.I.A., Lil' Kim had also received a great deal of the attention for her performances on the hit "Player's Anthem," the platinum-selling "Get Money" and for her generally aggressively sexual rhymes.

In 1996, Kim released her first solo album, *Hard Core* (Atlantic Records), executive-produced by Biggie Smalls with Lance "Un" Rivera. The controversial promotional poster for the album displayed a beautifully styled Kim, posed with her legs wide apart, displaying outlines of flesh beneath her leopard-skin panties. Later posters were artfully made less graphic, but the modifications did not quell the mounting debate about the role of female sexuality in Hip Hop culture. Kim became a hot commodity, and has made guest appearances on numerous rap tracks for leading artists, including **P. Diddy**, **Jay-Z**, **Jermaine Dupri**, **Missy Elliott**, **LOX**, **Mobb Deep**, Usher, Total, and Beyoncé.

With the assistance of plastic surgery, Kim transformed her image from a savvy "around the way" girl to a sexy moll. Kim has also become less of a rap artist and more of a celebrity. She is a member of the fashion elite, donning designer clothing and hobnobbing with fashionistas;

in 2000, she became a spokeswoman (along with singer **Mary J. Blige**) for VIVA Glam III lipstick by M.A.C. cosmetics. Kim, with her breast augmentation, rhinoplasty, blue contact lenses, and a penchant for long, blond wigs, continually stokes the fires related to mainstream and academic discussions about how Black women define themselves in a culture that extols Eurocentric standards for beauty.

Lil' Kim. *Courtesy of Photofest.*

Like many other rap artists, Kim has had her own brush with the law. In September 2004, her bodyguard, Suif Jackson, was sentenced to twelve years in prison for firing a gun outside of New York City's Hot 97 (WQHT-FM), in 2001. A grand jury indicted Kim on perjury and obstruction of justice charges and she is still awaiting trial as of early 2005. If convicted, she faces a maximum sentence of over thirty years. New York City police believe the dispute stemmed from an ongoing feud between Kim and **Foxy Brown**. As Kim and her entourage left, Capone (**Capone-N-Noreaga**) and his companions were entering. At the time, Capone-N-Noreaga's current album, *The Reunion* (Tommy Boy Records, 2000), contained the track "Bang Bang," on which Foxy Brown called Kim's album *Notorious K.I.M.* "weak" and "lame." Words were exchanged between the two groups before gunfire erupted.

Kim is often compared to Foxy Brown, another woman known for her sexually provocative raps. Early in their careers the former friends were both clients of Unlimited Management run by Lance "Un" Rivera and both had great success with their first solo albums. However, while Foxy Brown has struggled to remain relevant, Kim continues to stay in the spotlight.

In 2000, Kim released her sophomore album, *The Notorious K.I.M.* (Atlantic Records), which aside from some a little pop flavor, successfully builds on the sex and power themes that she debuted on *Hard Core*. In 2001, Kim teamed up with Pink, Mya, and Missy Elliott to redo the Labelle classic "Lady Marmalade" for the soundtrack for the film *Moulin Rouge*. In 2002, Kim appeared on the Christina Aguilera track, "Can't Hold Us Down," from her album *Stripped* (RCA Records).

In 2003, Kim released her third album, *La Bella Mafia* (Atlantic Records). Her rhymes remained strong, but despite having strong musical partners such as producer–artist Swiss Beats, Mr. Cheeks (**Lost Boyz**), and producer **Timbaland**, the overall effort failed to take off. As an example of Kim's staying power and crossover appeal, in November 2004 the English Department of Syracuse University offered the course "Hip-Hop Eshu: Queen B@#$H 101—The Life & Times of Lil' Kim." The course examined the cultural impact of Kim's sexuality in mainstream culture, and students analyzed the video as well as the lyrics.

DISCOGRAPHY: *Hard Core* (Atlantic Records, 1996); *The Notorious K.I.M.* (Atlantic Records, 2000); *La Bella Mafia* (Atlantic Records, 2003).

LIL' ROMEO [Percy Romeo Miller, Jr.]

The son of rap artist and No Limit Records CEO **Master P**, Lil' Romeo is part of the first father–son duo in rap music history. Lil' Romeo began appearing on his father's records at age four. At ten, he released solo his first CD *Lil' Romeo* (No Limit, 2004). The lead single, "My Baby," a song that shamelessly riffs off of the Jackson 5's "I Want You Back," rose to the top of the *Billboard* Hot 100 before the album even hit the streets.

Lil' Romeo has appeared in movies, including the 2003 film, *Honey,* and in a 2004 film with his father called *Uncle P.* He also has his own Nickelodeon show, *Romeo!* (also starring his father). On the show, Romeo wears his clothing line, P. Miller Shorties, and Master P wears his clothing line, P. Miller Signature Collection. Romeo's 2002 sophomore album, *Game Time* (No Limit) included a duet called "True Love" with Solange (sister of Beyoncé), which presages his entrance into puberty. In September 2004, he released his third album called *Romeoland* (Koch Records).

DISCOGRAPHY: *Lil' Romeo* (No Limit, 2001); *Game Time* (No Limit, 2002); *Romeoland* (Koch, 2004).

LIL WAYNE [Dwayne Carter]

Although Lil Wayne made his debut with the short-lived group The BG'z, which featured rapper B.G., this New Orleans rap artist gained prominence as the Cash Money's youngest Hot Boy. That supergroup of the 1990s was comprised of **Juvenile**, Turk, and B.G.

In 1999, Lil Wayne made his solo debut with the album *Tha Block is Hot.* The title single was a huge hit, selling platinum. In 2000, Lil Wayne released his second album, *Lights Out* (Cash Money Records), and his third, *500 Degreez* (Cash Money Records) in 2002. The title is a play on one of Cash Money's biggest albums, the four-times-platinum *400 Degreez* by label mate Juvenile. Cash Money and Hot Boy members, Juvenile, B.G., and Turk eventually parted company, leaving only Lil Wayne. With production by Mannie Fresh *500 Degreez* sold well, bolstered by the single "Way of Life." In 2004, Lil Wayne released his fourth album, *Tha Carter* (Cash Money Records).

DISCOGRAPHY: *Tha Block Is Hot* (Cash Money Records, 1999); *Lights Out* (Cash Money Records, 2000); *500 Degreez* (Cash Money Records, 2002); *Tha Carter* (Cash Money Records, 2004).

LIMP BIZKIT

Following in the footsteps of 1980s bands such as Anthrax, Red Hot Chili Peppers, and Rage Against The Machine, Limp Bizkit, a trio of [Fred Durst, DJ Lethal, Wes Borland], was one of the key bands in the **rap-metal** movement of the 1990s. One side of the hybrid was marked by raps and beats blended with conventional rock, the other by a merging of melodic death metal, traditional metal, and chomping beats. Most critics and fans alike acknowledge that, by 2002, the excitement about rap-metal had dissipated.

LL COOL J (aka Uncle L) [James Todd Smith]

LL Cool J, the first rap artist signed to **Def Jam Recordings** is the renaissance man of Hip Hop and remains with the label. LL Cool J is an acronym for Ladies Love Cool James.

LL Cool J. *Courtesy of Photofest.*

LL was born in the New York City suburb of Bay Shore, on Long Island, and was raised in the St. Albans section of Queens, New York. Back in the day, LL was known for his trademark **Kangol** hats, wearing one of his pant legs rolled up, and his lip licking, as well as for his six-pack abdomen and huge biceps. LL's long-standing appeal may be attributable to a rap style that is a balanced mix of street and sexiness.

In addition to recording rap music, LL had his own television series and appeared in over fifteen films. He is also known for his long-running feud with **Kool Moe Dee**. Kool Moe Dee, contending that LL disrespected pioneering rap artists like himself, used the single "How Ya Like Me Now" (the title track from his 1987 album) to take him on. LL Cool J fired back with the track "Jack the Ripper." Kool Moe Dee attacked back with "Let's Go." LL Cool J once again countered with "To The Break of Dawn."

LL's grandfather gave him his first turntables, when he was nine. By thirteen, LL was selling his demo tapes on the streets. New York University student Rick Rubin, the cofounder of the then-fledging Def Jam Recordings, received one of LL Cool J's tapes and signed a sixteen-year-old LL to a recording contract. Def Jam released its first official single, with LL Cool J's "I Need A Beat," in 1984. The record sold over 100,000 copies, establishing both the label and the rap artist.

LL dropped out of high school and recorded his debut album, *Radio* (Def Jam Recordings, 1985). The album was a surprise hit. Bolstered by the classic Hip Hop singles "I Can't Live Without My Radio" and "Rock the Bells," the album went platinum in 1986. In 1985, LL would perform part of the song in the film ***Krush Groove***. After the success of *Radio*, which marked Def Jam's first album release, LL began the now famous 1986–1987 "Raising Hell" tour, along with fellow legends **Run DMC** and the **Beastie Boys**. In 1986, LL also had a cameo appearance in the film Wildcats, and he made the theme song for that movie.

In 1987, a bare-chested, gold-chained LL emerged with his second album, *Bigger and Deffer* (Def Jam Recordings). The rap ballad "I Need Love" became a huge chart crossover hit and helped to solidify LL's star appeal. LL's ability to make rap music accessible to pop audiences has proven to be one of his greatest talents, as well as one of his weaknesses. On his third album, *Walking With A Panther* (Def Jam Recordings), LL experimented with new styles, but many music critics and fans panned his efforts, calling him a sellout. The album was perceived as more pop than rap, even though it spawned the platinum-selling single, "Goin' Back to Cali," which appeared on the film soundtrack for *Less Than Zero* (1988), and the gold single "I'm That Type of Guy." While touring to support the album, LL was booed at the legendary Apollo Theater in Harlem, New York.

LL teamed up with producer **Marley Marl** to answer his critics with his fourth album, the 1990 *Mama Said Knock You Out* (Def Jam

Recordings). The album became an enormous crossover success, primarily on the strength of the title single and other tracks, such as "Around The Way Girl" and "The Booming System." The track "Mama Said Knock You Out" would garner LL his first Grammy award, in the Best Rap Solo Performance category.

In 1991, LL Cool J made history by becoming the first rap artist to go acoustic on *MTV Unplugged*. That same year, LL made his acting debut in the film *Hard Way*, and followed up in 1992 in the film *Toys*, starring comedian Robin Williams. LL's fifth album, the 1993 *14 Shots To The Dome* (Def Jam Recordings), was released during the rise of so-called **gangsta rap**; it saw the emergence of a more hardcore LL. The album eventually became LL's fifth consecutive platinum album, with the hits "Back Seat," "I'm Coming," and "Pink Cookies In A Plastic Bag Getting Crushed By Buildings."

LL's broad appeal allowed him to be selected to perform at MTV's Inaugural Ball for President Clinton in 1993, and he became the first rap artist to be featured on MTV's *Rockumentary*. In 1995, LL landed his own NBC sitcom, *In the House* (1995–1999). That same year, the album *Mr. Smith* was released and proved the fans' unabated love by selling double platinum. The sexually charged track "Doin' It," as well as the track "Hey Lover," featuring the R & B group Boyz II Men, were standouts.

When LL remade LeShaun's 1988 underground hit "Doin' It" (Wild Thang Records) he ruffled the feathers of many female fans. LL had asked LeShaun to rhyme on the track, but then failed to include her in the music video for the remake. It was widely speculated that LeShaun's image was deemed not sexy enough for the music video, although LL said her pregnancy was the cause. "Hey Lover" brought LL his second Grammy award in 1996.

In 1996, LL released the album *All World* (Def Jam Recordings), a greatest hits album, and in 1997 he released his seventh album, *Phenomenon* (Def Jam Recordings). The title track climbed its way up the charts. The album would also spawn a **beef** between LL and rap artist **Canibus**. On the track. "4,3,2,1," Canibus originally rhymed about "borrowing" the mic tattooed on LL's arm and rocking it. According to Canibus, the line was meant to be a sign of respect; LL, however, took offense and told Canibus to rewrite his verse or be removed from the track. Canibus chose to rewrite his rhyme, but LL kept his verse dissing Canibus. Canibus then retaliated with a single, "2nd Round Knockout."

In 1997, LL published his autobiography, *I Make My Own Rules* (New York: St. Martin's Press/Ilion Books), which details his harrowing childhood and early career.

LL continued to act and appeared in films such as *Woo* (1998), *Caught Up* (1998), and *Halloween H20: 20 Years Later* (1998). As his acting talents improved, so did his film roles. He had significant parts in the films

Any Given Sunday, Deep Blue Sea, and *In Too Deep*, each role further proving his versatility.

To celebrate his fifteen years as a rap artist in 2000, LL released *G.O.A.T: The Greatest of All Time* (Def Jam Recordings), which sold double platinum. Continuing his rap career at Def Jam Recordings, the album *10* (Def Jam Recordings, 2002) made waves with the first single, "Luv U Better." With the help of producer **Timbaland**, LL released *DEFinition* album in 2004.

Aside from his work as an rap artist and actor, LL has become a family man, living with his wife of ten years and their four children in New York and Los Angeles. In 1992, LL founded Camp Cool J Foundation, a nonprofit organization that provides free year-round camping, educational, cultural, and recreational programs for underprivileged youth. In 1996, he was featured in a commercial for Major League Baseball. LL has also been the pitchman for The Gap, Coca-Cola and **FUBU** clothing.

DISCOGRAPHY: *Radio* (Def Jam Recordings, 1985); *Bigger and Deffer* (Def Jam Recordings, 1987); *Walking with a Panther* (Def Jam Recordings, 1989); *Mama Said Knock You Out* (Def Jam Recordings, 1990); *14 Shots to the Dome* (Def Jam Recordings, 1993); *Mr. Smith* (Def Jam Recordings, 1995); *All World* (1996); *Phenomenon* (Def Jam Recordings, 1997); *G.O.A.T: The Greatest of All Time* (Def Jam Recordings, 2000); *10* (Def Jam Recordings, 2002); *DEFinition* (Def Jam Recordings, 2004).

LOCKING

The West Coast–based dance called locking was developed by Don Campbell and popularized by Campellock Dancer, the late Fred "Rerun" Berry, on the 1970s television show *What's Happening?* and in other appearances by Lockers on the *Johnny Carson Show*, the *Dick Van Dyke Show*, the *Carol Burnett Show*, and *Saturday Night Live*.

Don Campbell, trying to imitate a local dance called the "funky chicken," added an effect of locking of the joints of his arms and body, thus creating his signature dance. He then established a dance group named The Lockers, which helped to develop locking as a dance. The lock is a specific type of movement, meshing combinations of steps and moves similar to a freeze or a sudden pause. Lock combinations can consist of a series of points done by extending the arms and pointing in different directions. The Lockers dancers combined complex step patterns with the legs and moves done in various sequences. The Lockers also jumped into half splits, knee drops, and butt drops, and used moves that took them down to the ground and back up to their feet again. The steps and moves created by these pioneers were called: the *lock, points, skeeters, scooby doos, stop n' go, which-away* and *the fancies*. Reminiscent of the legendary Nicholas Brothers, some

Lockers incorporated flips, tucks, dives, and other aerial moves into their routines.

See also: Popping

LORD FINESSE [Robert Hall]

Lord Finesse is a founding member of the **Diggin' in the Crates** (D.I.T.C.) crew and himself a legend of underground rap music.

A Bronx native, Lord Finesse got started with Hip Hop rhyming on the playgrounds, at age 14. In the mid-1980s his friend Mike Smooth, a DJ encouraged Finesse to rap, although Finesse wanted to DJ rather than MC. During this period, Finesse began to associate with DJs **Diamond D** and **Showbiz** and they, like Mike Smooth, thought that Finesse should rap. The two DJs schooled him on the turntables and he DJed as a way to make money. By the time he got to junior high school, Finesse had begun rhyming again. In high school, Finesse met **A.G.** in a **battle** in the yard of DeWitt Clinton High School in the Bronx. While in high school, Finesse also recorded his first demo called "Funky Dope Maneuver." The demo helped Finesse to get signed to Zakia Records in 1988. Problems at the label, however, resulted in the release of Finesse from his contract in the beginning of 1989.

Finesse's demo ended up at Wild Pitch Records, where it was heard by DJ Word and Guru (**Gang Starr**), who recommended it to the label's owner, Stu Fine. On May 5, 1989, Lord Finesse and DJ Mike Smooth were officially signed to Wild Pitch Records. In July, Finesse entered the 1989 MC Battle for Supremacy at the New Music Seminar. Although he didn't win the Seminar battle, Finesse created buzz in the industry when in the first round he defeated Mikey D, the New Music Seminar Champion from the previous year. After the New Music Seminar, Finesse and Smooth Mike joined forces with Diamond D, **Showbiz**, **DJ Premier**, and later **A.G.**, and started on their debut album, *Funky Technician* (Wild Pitch). The album, released on February 16, 1990, is considered by many to be among the best rap albums ever made. Unfortunately, although *Funky Technician* was hot on the streets, Finesse and Smooth Mike were not making much money from the album.

Subsequently, in 1990 Smooth Mike got a job and Finesse began making mixtapes. In the summer of 1990, on a routine stop to Rock and Will's on 125th Street, Finesse would discover the late **Big L**, who would join the D.I.T.C. crew. Finesse had made an impression on **Ice-T** during his performance at the New Music Seminar Battle for Supremacy in 1989. Ice-T would offer Finesse an opportunity to make money from his music, assuming that he could get released from Wild Pitch Records.

In July 1990, Wild Pitch released Finesse; in December 1990, Lord Finesse was signed to Rhyme Syndicate management and Giant/Warner Bros. Records. In August 1991, Finesse finished his sophomore album,

Return of the Funky Man (Giant/Warner Bros. Records), and on August 31 he departed for Europe with Ice-T, as part of the Rhyme Syndicate Original Gangster European Tour. *Return of the Funky Man* was released in January 1992. In May of 1992, Finesse, T-Ray, and a seventeen-year-old Big L entered Jazzy Jay's legendary recording studio and recorded the classic "Yes You May" **remix**. Finesse would go on to record two other albums, *The Awakening* (Tommy Boy Records, 1996) and *From The Crates to the Files: Lost Sessions* (Fat Beats, 2003).

Over the years, Finesse has appeared on and released numerous singles. His voice can also be heard on the hook to Fat Boy Slim's multi-platinum track, "Rockerfella Shank." As a platinum-selling producer, he has worked with artists such as artist as **The Notorious B.I.G.**, Big L, **Dr. Dre**, **Fat Joe**, and **Capone-N-Noreaga**.

DISCOGRAPHY: *Funky Technician* (Wild Pitch Records, 1990); *Return of the Funky Man* (Giant/Warner Bros. Records, 1991); *The Awakening* (Tommy Boy Records, 1996); *From the Crates to the Files: Lost Sessions* (Fat Beats Records, 2003).

LOS ANGELES UNDERGROUND MOVEMENT

The Los Angeles Underground Movement stressed lyrical skills and artistic style in rap. It was centered on The Good Life Café, located at 3631 Crenshaw Boulevard, in the heart of South Central Los Angeles's old jazz district. Bea Hall's Youth for Positive Alternatives hosted the weekly "Please Pas Tha Mic," an open-mic session, where dozens of MCs and DJs would gather to perform and where **A & R** representatives scouted for talent.

During its most active period between 1991 and 1994, the Los Angeles Underground was a mecca for musical innovation, spawning groups such as The **Pharcyde**, Urban Props, and **Freestyle Fellowship**. With its no cursing policy and with security furnished by the Fruit of Islam (an organization within the Nation of Islam), the importance of the Los Angeles Underground Movement was that it encouraged its artists to constantly balance progressive styles and good music, rather than simply relying on violent ghetto tales as the basis of their content.

See also: Lyricist Lounge

LOST BOYZ, THE

Made up of Freaky Tah [Raymond Rogers], Mr. Cheeks [Terrance Kelly], Pretty Lou [Eric Ruth], and Spigg Nice [Ronald Blackwell], The Lost Boyz, a quartet of brothers and cousins, was one of the first rap groups to join Uptown Records.

The group starting performing together as teenagers in their grandparents' basement and in their school cafeterias. The dreadlocked rap artists from South Ozone Park, New York, struggled for nearly a decade before tasting success. The name "Lost Boyz" is a response to the rejection that they experienced over the years. In 1994, the group released their first album *Diamond Dust* on the independent label Progressive International, with little fanfare. A year later, however, they released the hit single, "Lifestyles of the Rich and Shameless."

With the demise of Uptown Records, the now platinum-selling group signed with Universal Records. Their first album for a major recording company, *Legal Drug Money* (Universal), was officially released on June 6, 1996. The album included the hits " Jeeps, Lex Coups, Bimaz and Benz," "Music Makes Me High," and "Renee." The single "Renee" was based on a true story and was included on the soundtrack for the 1996 film, *Don't Be a Menace to South Central While You're Drinking Your Juice in the Hood.* Their second album, *Love, Peace & Nappiness* (Universal), followed in 1997 and went platinum. That same year, the Lost Boyz appeared in a commercial for Sprite soda.

Their third album, *LB IV Life* (Universal Records), was released in 1999 and would be the last Lost Boyz album. Freaky Tah was killed on March 28, 1999, after leaving Mr. Cheeks's birthday party in Queens, New York. In 2001, Mr. Cheeks released his solo CD, *John P. Kelly*, dedicated to his grandfather and to his cousin. The album included the club hit, "Lights, Camera, Action." On January 27, 2004, Sprigg Nice was sentenced to thirty-seven years in federal prison and ordered to pay $994,478 in joint restitution for committing, along with three accomplices, ten bank robberies throughout New Jersey.

DISCOGRAPHY: *Diamond Dust* (Progressive Int'l Records, 1994); *Legal Drug Money* (Universal, 1996; *Love Peace & Nappiness* (Universal, 1997); *LB IV Life* (Universal, 1999).

LOX, THE

Styles [David Styles], **Jadakiss** [Jason Phillips], and Sheek [Sean Jacobs] are known as The LOX.

As high school students, the Yonkers, New York, natives began their musical career as The **Bomb Squad**, performing and producing their own demos. The group gained a local reputation for their fierce lyrical style and through their underground mixtapes they continued to build their fan base. The group, now known as the Warlocks, teamed up with the Ruff Ryders crew. The trio would again change their name, now to The LOX, an acronym for "Living Off Experience."

Fellow Yonkers native **Mary J. Blige** would be instrumental in getting The LOX's demo to Bad Boy Entertainment CEO **Sean "P. Diddy" Combs**, who subsequently signed the group as writers. Between 1996 and 1997, the group wrote and performed on a number of Combs's productions, including his own "It's All About the Benjamins" and "I Got the Power," **Mase**'s

"24 Hrs. to Live," Mariah Carey's "Honey," **The Notorious B.I.G.**'s "Last Day," Mary J. Blige's "Can't Get You Off My Mind," and Zhané's "Saturday Night." The LOX penned several hits, including Biggie's "Victory," P. Diddy's "Seniorita," and Mase's "Can't Nobody Hold Me Down" (**remix**), as well as Faith's "You Used To Love Me." In 1997, The LOX received a career boost with their memorial track to the late Notorious B.I.G., "We'll Always Love Big Poppa," which reached sales in the millions. The single was the biggest hit of 1997, setting the stage for the January 1998 release of the LOX's debut album, *Money, Power & Respect* (Bad Boy Entertainment).

Money Power & Respect went platinum and reached as high as number 3 on the pop album charts. The LOX's debut album also helped to launch the career of producer Swizz Beatz. The title track featuring **Lil' Kim** helped to expand their audience and enhance their standing as hardcore rap artists.

In 1999, The LOX, unhappy with radio-friendly, ghetto fabulous image that **Bad Boy Entertainment** was using to market and promote them, the trio engaged in a public "Free the LOX" campaign (complete with picket signs, T-shirts, and protests) to be released from their recording contract. Successful, the trio signed a recording contract with Ruff Ryders' new label and in early 2000 they released their second album, *We Are the Streets* (Ruff Ryders/Interscope Records).

In 2001, Jadakiss released his solo album, *Kiss the Game Good Bye* (Interscope Records), and followed up with *Kiss of Death* (Interscope Records) in 2004. In 2002, Styles broke from The LOX with his debut solo album, *A Gangsta and a Gentleman* (Interscope Records), which included the Swiss Beatz–produced hit single, "Good Times."

DISCOGRAPHY: *Money Power & Respect* (Bad Boy Entertainment, 1998); *We Are the Streets* (Ruff Ryders/Interscope Records, 2000).

LUDACRIS [Christopher Brian Bridges]

The former Atlanta radio DJ holds the distinction of being the first rap act that Def Jam South President **Scarface** signed to the brand new label, Ludacris moves easily from **crunk** to **bling** to comedy to Old School flavor, making him difficult to pigeonhole and contributing to his crossover appeal.

Ludacris's love for rap music began as a youth. At twelve years old he joined a rap group called the Loudmouth Hooligans. That same year, he moved from Chicago, Illinois, to Atlanta, Georgia, and continued pursuing his music goal. At Banneker High School in College Park, Georgia, he started **battling** in the lunchroom, and later performed in talent shows and in clubs. He eventually got a job at Atlanta's then-new Hip Hop station Hot 97.5, producing the night show. Ludacris made his mark rapping on voice-over promos for the radio station. In the process, his voice became as recognizable as that of some DJs.

Ludacris. *Courtesy of Photofest.*

Ludacris realized that he wanted to create music, rather than just play it on the radio. In 1998, he appeared on the track "Phat Rabbit" from **Timbaland**'s *Tim's Bio: From the Motion Picture Life from Da Bassment* album (Blackground Records, 1998). In 2000, he recorded the album *Incognegro*, released independently on his own label, Disturbing tha Peace. On the strength of both the sexually provocative single "What's Your Fantasy" and Ludacris's reputation as a DJ, the album sold approximately 30,000 units regionally in the first three months.

Representing the Dirty South, Ludacris is skilled at creating street-wise party music. Ludacris's first album for Def Jam South, *Back For the First Time*, was released in 2000. His second album, *Word of Mouf* (Def Jam South, 2001), peaked at number 3 on the *Billboard* album chart in October. Ludacris's *Chicken-N-Beer* (Def Jam South, 2003) and *The Red Light District* (Def Jam South, 2004) were both hugely successful albums.

Ludacris made his film debut in *2 Fast 2 Furious* (2003) and also appeared in the film *The Wash* (2001). Ludacris is also a character in a **video game**, "Def Jam: Fight for New York."

In 2002, Ludacris became a pitchman for Pepsi Cola and quickly came under attack by Fox television commentator Bill O' Reilly. O' Reilly is quoted as saying that Ludacris "espouses violence, degraded sex and substance abuse." With pressure from Reilly's audience, Pepsi Cola pulled Ludacris's televisions commercials. Alleging a racial double standard, **Russell Simmons** and his organization, the Hip Hop Summit Action Network, threatened a boycott of PepsiCo products if Ludacris's commercials were not reinstated. Simmons contended that fellow Pepsi spokesmen, The Osbournes (family of rocker Ozzy Ozbourne), were not similarly dismissed, although their MTV reality program liberally involved profanity and drug use, and depicted a seriously dysfunctional family. A settlement (reached on February 11, 2003, on the eve of the boycott) has PepsiCo donating several million dollars for a multi-year period to the Ludacris Foundation. The Ludacris Foundation is a nonprofit organization in Atlanta that serves disadvantaged youth nationwide.

DISCOGRAPHY: *Albums: Incognegro* (Disturbing tha Peace Records, 2000); *Back for the First Time* (Def Jam South, 2001); *Chicken-N-Beer* (Def Jam South, 2003); *The Red Light District* (Def Jam South, 2004).

LUKE; LUKE SKYYWALKER. *See* Campbell, Luther "Luke"

LUNIZ, THE

As the Luniz, Yukmouth [Jerold Ellis, Jr.] and Numskull [Garrick Husbands] found themselves knocking Michael Jackson's album, *HIStory: Past Present and Future, Book 1* (Sony Records), off the top of the R & B charts in 1995, on the strength of their hit single, "I Got 5 on It," from their debut album, *Operation Stackola* (Virgin Records, 1995).

The rap duo from Oakland, California, first met in junior high; they were originally known as Luni Tunz. After six years in the rap game, they gained widespread attention on Dru Down's album, *Explicit Game* (Relativity Records, 1994). The Luniz's lyrics take a new and comedic approach to everyday issues as well as to sex and drugs.

In 1997, the Luniz released their second album, *Lunitik Muzik* (Virgin Records), which is considered one of the best album releases that year. The album contains the duo's eccentric humor, as well as guest appearance artists such as **Too Short**, **2 Live Crew**, and **Redman**. The album takes a serious turn on the track "Y Do Thugz Die," which discusses inner-city crime in the aftermath of the murders of **Tupac Shakur** and **The Notorious B.I.G.** In 1999, Yukmouth released a double solo album called *Thugged Out: The Albulation* (Virgin Records). In 2000, the Luniz released their third album, *Black and Silver* (Rap-A-Lot). In 2000, Clee & Drank-A-Lot (aka Numskull) released an album called *Good Laaawd That's a Lot of Drank* (Knockdiesel). In 2001, Yukmouth released another solo album, *Thug Lord: The New Testament* (Virgin Records) and followed up with two more solo albums, *United Ghettos of America* (Rap-A-Lot) in 2002 and *Godzilla* (Rap-A-Lot) in 2003.

DISCOGRAPHY: *Operation Stackola* (Virgin Records, 1995); *Lunitik Muzik* (Virgin Records, 1997); *Black and Silver* (Rap-A-Lot, 2000).

LYRICIST LOUNGE

The Lyricist Lounge, a New York City–based performance venue active during the 1990s, was dedicated to showcasing unsigned rap artists. Founders Anthony Marshall, Dan Castro, Rasheem Chapman, and Michael Thomas, operating under the name Kalodge Project, established the Lyricist Lounge in December 1991.

Members of the Kalodge Project got started by dancing in videos for artists such as **Special Ed** and also by being affiliated with music industry figures. Anthony and Dan were also performers with the group Figures of Speech. The idea of the Lyricist Lounge was not about competition, but instead was conceived as a place for artists from all of the boroughs to develop their skills (each session is videotaped), meet new people, and learn about the music business.

Beginning in a studio apartment on the Lower East side of Manhattan, the Lyricist Lounge eventually expanded to local clubs around New York City. The Lyricist Lounge eventually spawned a short-lived variety program of the same name on MTV (2000–2003).

See also: Los Angeles Underground Movement

M

MACK 10 [Dedrick Rolison]

An Inglewood, California, native and a founding member of rap trio **Westside Connection**, Mack 10 caught the attention of **Ice Cube** in the mid-1990s. Mack 10 was introduced to rap music fans through his appearance in Ice Cube's video for the 1995 single, "What Can I Do?" from the album, *Lethal Injection* (Priority Records).

That same year, Mack 10 released his eponymous debut album on Priority Records. Representing hardcore California rap, Mack 10's lyrics rarely strayed from street life and women. His first major success was the hit single, "Foe Life," which was co-written by Ice Cube and became an anthem for the West Coast. He followed his gold-selling debut album with the radio-only single, "Hoo-Bangin'," from the film soundtrack for *The Substitute*, which sold over 300,000 copies. Mack 10 then went into the studio with **Tha Dogg Pound** and in 1996 they released the smash single, "Nothin' But the Cavi Hit" (Priority Records), which appeared on the soundtrack for the rap music documentary *Rhyme and Reason* (1997).

In 1996, Mack 10 joined forces with mentor and label mate Ice Cube and rap artist WC to form the Westside Connection. The three had originally united for the track "Westside Slaughterhouse," from Mack 10's 1995 debut album. Westside Connection subsequently released the 1996 album *Bow Down* (Priority Records), a tribute to West Coast rap. The title track was a direct attack on East Coast rap artists, and other tracks on the album discussed the **East Coast–West Coast** rap conflict, which was at its height at that time.

During this period Mack 10 formed his own record label (Hoo Bangin' Records) and his own production company (Mack One-O), and had begun to establish a career as an actor through roles in the television series *The Jamie Foxx Show* (1996) and the film *Thicker Than Water* (1999). In 1997, Mack 10 released his sophomore album, *Based on a True Story* (Priority Records). The album, which includes the single "Backyard Boogie," is generally considered to be Mack 10's best work.

In 1998, Mack 10 returned with his third album, *Recipe* (Priority Records), which is remembered for the number of guest appearances, including **Master P**, **Mystikal**, **Jermaine Dupri**, and **Ol' Dirty Bastard**. Mack 10 appears alone on only one track on the album. Following the excess of *Recipe* in 1997, Mack 10's career went into decline, much like the West Coast gangsta rap scene that he represented. The public received

Mack 10's 1999 release, *Hoo Bangin': Mix Tape* (SUH 56), with little enthusiasm. The album primarily showcased new artists on Mack 10's Hoo Bangin' label, rather than his own material. In 1999, Mack 10 appeared in the film *Thicker Than Water*, with Ice Cube and **MC Eiht**. In 2000, Mack 10 released the album *The Paper Route* (Priority Records), but by this time his fans had gone elsewhere. Mack 10's public visibility was significantly increased in August 2000, when he married T-Boz of the R & B group TLC. In 2004, T-Boz filed for divorce from Mack 10, alleging adultery and threats against her life. The disappointment of *The Paper Route* led Mack 10 and Priority Records to part ways.

In 2001, Mack 10 in a surprise move signed with Cash Money Records, better known for representing the Dirty South. Mack 10's debut on Cash Money Records was *Bang or Ball*. Despite the **Dr. Dre**–produced track, "Hate in Yo Eyes," which interpolated the Bee Gees' "Stayin' Alive," the album got a lukewarm reception from the public. In summer 2002, Mack 10 regained some momentum with the release of *Mack 10 Presents Da Hood* (Riviera Records, 2002), which featured guest appearances by **Ice Cube**, **Cash Money Millionaires**, **Lil Jon**, and **Timbaland**. The track "L.A. Fo Ya" became an anthem for the city, and was customized by leading radio stations as well as by the Los Angeles Lakers and the Los Angeles Clippers basketball teams. Mack 10's most recent work includes 2003's *Ghetto, Gutter & Gangsta* (Ark 21) and roles in low-budget films *Dark Angel* (2000), *Random Acts of Violence* (2002), and *Cutthroat Alley* (2003).

DISCOGRAPHY: *Mack 10* (Priority Records, 1995); *Based on a True Story* (Priority Records, 1997); *Recipe* (Priority Records, 1998); *Hoo Bangin': Mix Tape* (SUH 56, 1999); *The Paper Chase* (Priority Records, 2000); *Bang or Ball* (Cash Money, 2001); *Mack 10 Presents Da Hood* (Riviera, 2002); *Ghetto, Gutter & Gangsta* (Ark 21, 2003).

MADE MEN. *See* Almighty RSO

MAD RAPPER [Deric "D-dot" Angelettie]

The Mad Rapper is a fictional, comedic character created to diss the rap artists who had criticized **Bad Boy Entertainment** and its leader, **Sean "P. Diddy" Combs**. Angelettie, then a member of Bad Boy Entertainment stable of producers known as "The Hitmen," first introduced the Mad Rapper on an interlude track from **Mase**'s album, *Harlem World* (Bad Boy Entertainment, 1997). He also appeared several tracks from *Bad Boy's Greatest Hits* (Bad Boy Entertainment, 1998), including the "Mad Rapper Intro." The Mad Rapper also makes an appearance on **Jermaine Dupri**'s 1998 track, "Get Your Sh*t Right," from the album *Jermaine Dupri Presents: Life in 1472* (So So Def Records).

Angelettie received his own record deal and in 1999 the Mad Rapper released his debut album, *Tell 'Em Why U Madd* (Sony Records). This album serves as a showcase for up-and-coming talent on Angelettie's own Crazy Cat label. Despite the humor and the beats, the album is mainly significant for including the **50 Cent** track, "How to Rob." Originally an underground hit, the track lyrically attacks numerous real-life rap artists. The Mad Rapper's identity, which had been concealed from the public, was exposed in a photograph in the December–January (1998–1999) issue of *Blaze*, a rap music publication. The photo, which ran without Angelettie's name, accompanied a music review of the Mad Rapper's single, "Gonna Beat Ya' All." Following the publication, in November 1998, *Blaze* editor Jesse Washington alleged in police reports that, as retaliation for running the photo, Angelettie and an accomplice physically attacked him in his office.

DISCOGRAPHY: *Tell 'Em Why U Madd* (Sony Records, 1999).

MAIN SOURCE

Comprised of **Large Professor** [Paul Mitchell], K-Cut [Kevin McKenzie], and Sir Scratch [Shawn McKenzie], Main Source is unique in its coupling of artists from Toronto, Canada, and New York City.

Toronto-born brothers K-Cut and Sir Scratch joined forces with the New Yorker, Large Professor, in 1989. Main Source is best known for its classic debut album *Breaking Atoms* (Wild Pitch Records, 1991). The album spawned the hit, "Looking at the Front Door." The legendary posse track, "Live at the Bar-B-Que" helped launch the careers of both **Akinyele** and **Nas**, who made his recording debut. Large Professor left the group after their first album, citing creative differences. K-Cut and Sir Scratch continued the group adding MC Mikey D.

Three years after the release of their debut album, Main Source released its sophomore album, *F*ck What You Think* (Wild Pitch, 1994). Perhaps unfairly compared to *Breaking Atoms,* the album was not without artistic merit, but nonetheless it failed to register with fans. The omission of Large Professor, as well as record company delays, contributed to the poor performance of *F*ck What You Think.* Subsequently, Main Source departed from Wild Pitch and MC Mikey D would then leave the group, claiming he did not get along with K-Cut and Scratch. Meanwhile, Large Professor, who had worked with **Eric B & Rakim** and **Kool G Rap** earlier in his career, continued to build a reputation as a talented producer, working with artists such as Nas and **A Tribe Called Quest**. In 2002, he released his solo debut album, *1st Class* (Matador Records).

DISCOGRAPHY: *Breaking Atoms* (Wild Pitch Records, 1991); *F*ck What You Think* (Wild Pitch Records, 1994).

MANTRONIX

DJ Kurtis Mantronik [Kurtis Kahleel] and MC Tee [Tooure Embden] combine their talents as Mantronix, considered one of the most innovative groups from rap music's early period.

Mantronik, a turntable master, used synthesizers and samplers to produce a rhythmatic mix, rather than merely using samples as hooks. Mantronik moved from rap music into electro, reggae, techno, and house. Although he never found a rap artist to match his superior production skills, Mantronik inspired dozens of Hip Hop and dance music DJs around the world during the next decade. He was born in Jamaica, West Indies, to a Jamaican mother and an Arabic father. His family moved first to Canada, and then, when he was a teenager, he moved to New York. Mantronik became interested in rap music after seeing a DJ scratching and bought himself two turntables to try it out himself.

In 1983, Mantronik met MC Tee while working at Downtown Records. The duo gave a demo tape to William Socolov, president of Sleeping Bag Records. Soon after hearing the tape, Socolov signed Mantronix and they released their debut single, "Fresh Is the Word." The track lit up New York's streets and clubs during 1985. That same year, Mantronix released his debut album, *Mantronix: The Album* (Sleeping Bag Records). The singles "Ladies" and "Basslines" became big street hits and even became among the first rap music to become popular in Great Britain. In 1986, Mantronix performed at the UK Fresh Festival held at London's Wembley Arena.

During this period Mantronik had also begun working on **A & R** at Sleeping Bag Records, where he signed **EPMD**, produced **KRS-ONE**'s first credit ("Success Is the Word" by 12:41), and helmed other intense tracks by Tricky Tee, **Just-Ice**, and **T la Rock**. Mantronix's second album, *Music Madness* (Sleeping Bag Records, 1986), continued to keep the duo popular in the clubs. The growing popularity of rap music allowed Mantronix the chance to leave independent Sleeping Bag Records and sign with a major record company, Capitol Records.

Mantronix's third album, *In Full Effect* (1988), was more a mixture of dance and R & B music rather than rap. After that release, MC Tee left to join the Air Force and Bryce Luvah (cousin of **LL Cool J**) replaced him and DJ Dee (Mantronik's own cousin). The album *This Should Move Ya* (1990) marks Mantronik's total move from Hip Hop into house music. Although he continued to use rap artists, he remained firmly in the dance music category and the group Mantronix faded from the music scene. In the mid-1990s, recording as Kurtis Mantronik he was providing **remixes** for EPMD and **Dr. Octagon**.

DISCOGRAPHY: *Single*: "Fresh is the Word" (Sleeping Bag Records, 1985). *Albums*: *Mantronix: The Album* (Sleeping Bag Records, 1985); *Music Madness* (Sleeping Bag Records, 1986); *In Full Effect* (Capitol Records, 1988); *This Should Move Ya* (Capitol Records, 1990).

MARK THE 45 KING [Mark James]

One of the most prolific producers in rap music history and considered a **breakbeat** legend, Mark The 45 King began his career in the late 1970s as the "record boy" for the legendary Bronx, New York–based group, the **Funky 4** (before the addition of Sha Rock as the "Plus One"). After leaving the Funky 4 crew, The 45 King spent the mid-1980s as a DJ on the New Jersey scene. His ability to make beats from obscure 45 rpm records gained him the nickname. In 1983, his production for MC Marky Fresh caught the attention of **Kool DJ Red Alert** of New York's KISS-FM radio (WRKS-FM).

The 45 King's career really began, however, in 1987 for his work for Wild Pitch Records artist Latee on his single "This Cut's Got Flavor." In 1987, The 45 King received widespread notoriety for his legendary breakbeat track, "The 900 Number." The strength of the independent single helped The 45 King obtain a production deal with Tuff City Records.

The 45 King used his deal to produce music for his crew, Flavor Unit. In 1988, Lakim Shabazz became the first Flavor Unit member to release an album. *Pure Righteousness* (Tuff City Records) was recognized creatively as a good first effort and spawned the minor hit "Black is Back." Tuff City's small budget and limited distributed were cited as reasons why the album was not more successful. The 45 King produced a demo record, "Princess of the Posse," for Flavor Unit member, **Queen Latifah**. He then gave the demo to **Fab 5 Freddy**, the host of ***Yo! MTV Raps***. The recording captured the attention of Tommy Boy Records and in 1988 Queen Latifah signed a recording contract. On her debut album, *All Hail The Queen* (Tommy Boy Records, 1989), The 45 King established himself as a first class beat-making, producing the hit tracks "Wrath of My Madness," "Ladies First," and "Inside Out." Later that year, The 45 King produced Flavor Unit member Chill Rob G's debut album, *Ride the Rhythm* (Wild Pitch Records, 1989). Although Chill Rob G received notice from the underground, the album failed to breakthrough to the mainstream.

By 1990, The 45 King's career was in decline. The 45 King produced Lakim Shabazz's sophomore album, *The Lost Tribe of Shabazz* (Tuff City Records, 1990), which was largely ignored. Tommy Boy Records dropped Queen Latifah, who went on to sign with R & B–focused Motown Records, which meant The 45 King's production services would no longer be requested. Unfortunately, The 45 King also developed a drug addiction that caused him not to lose not only a production contract with Warner Bros., but also the respect of the music industry.

Beginning in 1990 The 45 King salvaged his career by continuing to produce breakbeats, including *The Lost Breakbeat* series, *Breakmania*, and the *Breakapalooza* series. In 1996, his fortunes improved when Washington DC–based DJ Kool scored a big hit with the track, "Let Me

Clear My Throat," a call-and-response vocals over the "900 Number" beat. More important, DJ Kool acknowledged The 45 King as the song's originator, and The 45 King produced a **remix** version of the track for Kool.

In 1998, The 45 King partnered with **Jay-Z**, and produced the mega hit, "It's a Hard Knock Life (Ghetto Anthem)," which uses a looped chorus from the Broadway musical "Annie." In 2000, The 45 King produced the platinum track "Stan," for **Eminem**.

DISCOGRAPHY: Over sixty musical works. *Singles*: "900 Number" (Tuff City, 1987; originally independently released). *Albums*: *45 Kingdom* (Tuff City Records, 1990); *The Lost Breakbeat Vol. 1 & 2* (Tuff City Records, 1991); *Breakmania, Vol. 3* (Real Tuff Breaks, 1995); *Breakapalooza, Vol. 1* (Tuff City Records, 1997).

MARLEY MARL [Marlon Williams]

Founder of Cold Chillin' Records and producer behind the legendary **Juice Crew All Stars**, Marley Marl is recognized as one of rap music's first super-producers.

Marley Marl gathered a talented roster of rap artists under his **Cold Chillin'** Records. The Juice Crew All Stars included **Big Daddy Kane**, **Biz Markie**, **Roxanne Shante**, **Kool G Rap**, **Master Ace**, and his cousin **MC Shan**. The Juice Crew's on-wax **battle** with the Bronx's **Boogie Down Productions** ("The Bridge is Over"), about the origins of Hip Hop, remains one of the most compelling stories in rap music history.

Marley Marl, a resident of the **Queensbridge** Housing Projects in Long Island City, New York, would be instrumental in popularizing the use of samples, as heard on MC Shan's 1986 single, "The Bridge." Marley Marl also learned how to craft his own drum loops through **sampling**, which decreased rap music's dependence on drum machines and gave his production a more robust and modern sound. Aside from the classic "The Bridge," Marley Marl was also behind the posse track "The Symphony," with the original Juice Crew. Marley's productions spawned many other hits with Biz Markie, Big Daddy Kane, Kool G Rap, Craig G, and Roxanne Shante.

Marley Marl won a Grammy for his work with **LL Cool J** on his 1990 album, *Mama Said Knock You Out*, the first for **Def Jam Recordings**. In addition to working on the groundbreaking ***Mr. Magic's Rap Attack radio*** show, in 1989 Marl started his own radio show, called *In Control*. In 1994, Marley Marl teamed up with fellow producer **Pete Rock** when they took over as hosts on the *Future Flavas* radio program on New York City's Hot 97 (WQHT-FM). Marl continued producing into the late 1990s for such artists as **Capone-N-Noreaga**, **Rakim**, and **Fat Joe**.

DISCOGRAPHY: Over 135 works, including: *In Control, Vol. 1* (Cold Chillin'/Warner Bros. Records, 1988); *Queensbridge Session* (Ol Skool Flava, 1996); *Re-Entry* (BBE, 2001).

MARTIAL ARTS

Since the early 1970s, films such as Bruce Lee's *Enter the Dragon*, and television programs such as *Kung Fu*, have been popular among Black youth, and thus the martial arts became part of Hip Hop.

Rap artists have long peppered their lyrics with references to Shaolin, Kung Fu, and geishas. Within Hip Hop, **B-boys** may have had the strongest connection to the martial arts, primarily because both are competitive endeavors that have structured training and require consistent physical discipline. It is also widely recognized that B-boying has been informed indirectly by the Angolan martial arts, and the Brazilian martial arts of **capoeira**.

On a more direct level, B-boys imitated moves from karate and Kung fu films and television programs. Other aspects of Hip Hop culture that were culled from the martial arts include the concepts of clans or crews, elders, rites of passage, styles, and schools.

The connection between Hip Hop and the martial arts became more apparent with the emergence of the rap group the **Wu-Tang Clan** in 1993 and the films *Ghost Dog: The Way of the Samurai* (1999) and *Romeo Must Die* (2000). The rap group takes its name from the 1983 martial arts film, *Shaolin and The Wu-Tang*. The film is about a rivalry between the Shaolin clan and its offshoot, The Wu-Tangs. The rap group named its debut album, *Enter the Wu-Tang (36 Chambers)* (Loud Records, 1993). In martial arts lore, The Wu-Tang consists of 36 chambers, and in order to become a Shaolin warrior, one must pass each task with the 36 chambers. In *Ghost Dog: The Way of the Samurai*, Forest Whitaker plays Ghost Dog, a Samurai disciple and mafia hit man. The film was scored by **RZA**, who makes a brief appearance as the character the "Camouflage Samurai."

Romeo Must Die starring, Jet Li, rap artist **DMX**, and the late R & B singer Aaliyah, is a modern interpretation of Romeo and Juliet that combines martial arts with a Hip Hop aesthetic. An increasing number of martial arts film soundtracks include rap songs. Although rap music now has a worldwide appeal, its link to martial arts films may have to do with sudden rap's use of change of rhythm, as well as the intensity of both art forms. Rap artists use theirs to amplify a story line, while the martial artists, particularly in fight scenes, use their movements to further the plot.

MASE [Mason Durrell Betha]

Best known as the shiny-suited sidekick of **Sean "P. Diddy" Combs**, Mase was born in Jacksonville, Florida. At the age of six, he moved to Harlem, New York. In an attempt to protect him from the dangers of the streets, Mase's mother sent him to Florida as a teenager. Mase returned to New York and graduated from the Manhattan Center for Science and Mathematics. He was set to attend the State University of New York at Purchase on a basketball scholarship, however, rap won out over college.

Under the name Murder Mase he joined the rap group Children of the Corn, which included **Cam'ron**. The group separated after one member was killed in a car accident.

Mase's solo career took off in 1996 when he went to a music conference in Atlanta, Georgia. He attended the conference with the intention of meeting **Jermaine Dupri**, head of So So Def, but instead he ran into Sean "P. Diddy" Combs, who signed him to **Bad Boy Entertainment**. Mase first came to the public's attention on 112's 1997 smash hit single, *Only You (Remix)*, which also featured Bad Boy star **The Notorious B.I.G.** Mase then made guest appearances on the Bad Boy tracks "Can't Nobody Hold Me Down" and "Mo Money, Mo Problems."

In 1997, Mase released his debut album, *Harlem World* (Bad Boy Entertainment). Music critics gave Mase mixed reviews: some were impressed with his unique, laid back, and sometimes slurred flow, while others said he was terrible. The opinion of fans won out, however, with the album going quadruple platinum, helped by the single "Feels So Good," which also appeared on the film soundtrack for *Money Talks* and the album's follow-up single "What You Want."

Mase continued his guest appearances on singles such as the hit "Horse and Carriage," by friend and fellow Harlemite Cam'ron; Brandy's "Top of the World"; 112's "Love Me"; P. Diddy's "Lookin' At Me"; and "Take Me There," a collaboration with Blackstreet and Mya that appeared on the *Rugrats* film soundtrack. In 1999, Mase developed a group called Harlem World and released *The Movement* (Sony Records, 1999).

In April of 1999, shortly after his second album *Double Up* (Bad Boy Entertainment) was completed but before its release, Mase announced, without any apparent provocation, that he was retiring from the music industry in order to pursue his faith.

In comparison to his peers, Mase always maintained a fairly clean-cut image. His only brush with the law came in 1999 was charged in New York with disorderly conduct in connection with soliciting a prostitute; Mase vehemently denied the charge. However, in the aftermath of the deaths of The Notorious B.I.G. and **Tupac Shakur**, some speculated that Mase retired because he was fearful for his own life, given his high profile, rather than because of any religious revelation.

Although Mase granted interviews, he refused to do live shows to promote *Double Up*. It is unclear whether audiences had lost interest in Mase or whether the lack of promotion killed the album, but it reached only gold-selling status when it was released in the summer of 1999. In the meantime, Mase entered Clark Atlanta University, a historically Black academic institution in Atlanta, Georgia, and then founded the nondenominational group called S.A.N.E. (Saving a Nation Endangered). In the intervening years he worked with youth, become a sought after inspirational speaker on the religious circuit, and in 2001 published a memoir titled *Revelations: There's a Light After the Lime* (New York: Atria).

In 2002, he received an honorary doctorate of theology from New York's St. Paul's Bible Institute. Proving skeptical fans and industry observers wrong, during this period Mase did not perform or write any lyrics.

In 2004, Mase returned to the rap music scene and to Bad Boy Entertainment with his new album, *Welcome Back*." The album departs from his earlier efforts because it lacks explicit lyrics and the usual references to sex, drugs, or violence. The track "Keep It On" even advocates young women keep their clothes on and not give in to sex. The title track samples the theme from the 1970s television comedy, *Welcome Back Kotter*. The G-rated album is one that parents and kids can both enjoy and has potential within Christian rap audiences The second single, "Breathe, Stretch, Shake," is an entertaining club track.

Mase's return has not been controversy free. He caught some heat for his appearance on the **remix** for the **Terror Squad**'s single, "Lean Back." Although Mase does not use profanity or promote violence, the track included **Eminem**, who finished his verse by proclaiming "I got a pistol in my pants," and Remy Ma, who vowed to "leave your body in a vacant lot."

DISCOGRAPHY: *HarlemWorld* (Bad Boy Entertainment, 1997); *Double Up* (Bad Boy Entertainment, 1999); *Welcome Back* (Bad Boy Entertainment, 2004).

MASH-UP

The next phase beyond **sampling** records and **remixing** records, a mash-up allows two or more records to be fused into one new recording.

In May 2002 in Great Britain, Island Records released the single, "A Freak Like Me," an authorized mash-up of songs by new wave artist Gray Numan, the girl pop group Sugababes, and R & B singer Adina Howard. The single entered the Pop charts at number 1. Producer Richard X provided Island Records with newly mixed version of his popular, but illegal mash-up. In 2004, Producer **DJ Danger Mouse** combined the vocals from **Jay-Z**'s *Black Album* (Roc-A-Fella Records, 2004), with the music from the Beatles, *White Album* to create the Grey Album. The new recording gained international attention via the Internet. EMI Records would subsequently issue Danger Mouse a letter to cease and desist transmitting his mash-up. The first commercially released mash-up is "Frontin' on Debra," the hybrid of Beck's 1999 "Debra" and Pharell Williams's 2003 "Frontin'," which features Jay-Z. The mash-up created by New York-based DJ Reset was released by Interscope Records in October 2004 via iTunes, an Internet music company. In early December 2004, the *Collision Course* was released; this CD and DVD package featuring authorized Jay-Z/Linkin Park mash-ups had sold 792,000 units by December 19, 2004.

MASTER ACE (aka Masta Ace) [Duval Clear]

A luminary of the 1980s **underground** rap scene in New York, Master Ace is also the most unappreciated of the famous **Juice Crew All Stars**. Ace appeared on the 1988 classic posse cut, "The Symphony, Part1."

Ace, a native of the Brownsville section in Brooklyn, New York, broke into the music scene after winning a rap contest that netted him six hours in the studio with legendary producer **Marley Marl**. Ace's debut recording was the double A-sided single, "Simon Says" and "Keep Your Eyes On The Prize," which was included on Marley Marl's album, *In Control, Vol. 1* (Cold Chillin'/Warner Bros. Records, 1988), an album that also featured the track "The Symphony, Part 1."

In 1990, Ace released his debut album, *Take A Look Around* (Cold Chillin'/Warner Bros. Records). Although the album was not a big commercial success, it spawned the **underground** hit singles, "Music Man" and "Me and the Biz." In the popular music video for the single, Ace outclowns rap music's then reigning jokester **Biz Markie** by playing a ventriloquist who uses a Biz Markie puppet as part of his act. Biz Markie himself makes a guest appearance on the Marley Marl–produced album, Besides Marley Marl's beats, Master Ace, striking a balance between ghetto reportage and motivational speaking, talks about serious subjects without sounding morose. In that vein, the single, "Together" (actually a single from late 1989) includes the inspirational line, "we'll take a drink from the fountain of success, yo' let's all climb the mountain together."

After a three-year hiatus, Ace returned in 1993 with a new crew including vocalist Paula Perry, Lord Digga, and singer–writer Leschea. Now on the West Coast label Delicious Vinyl, the group released the album *SlaughtaHouse*. The album broke new musical ground because it combined East Coast lyricism with the synthesized West Coast sound. The popular single, "Born to Roll," a rap about cars and sound systems, helped to propel the album to national attention. In 2000, **De La Soul** used the "Born to Roll" beat on a **remix** of "All Good" that features singer Chaka Khan. *SlaughtaHouse* also produced the underground hits "Jeep Ass Niguhz" and "Style Wars."

In 1995, under the name, Masta Ace Incorporated, the group released their second album, *Sittin' On Chrome* (Delicious Vinyl Records). Building from *SlaughtaHouse,* Masta Ace continued to develop the sound that he called "Brooklyn bass music." In 1994, Ace joined **Special Ed** and Buckshot (Blackmoon) on a track for the soundtrack for Spike Lee's film *Crooklyn*.

Through the years, Ace has released singles that do not appear on his albums, including the rare 1996, twelve-inch single "Ya Hardcore" (the B-side of "Sittin' on Chrome"), which slams wet-behind-the-ears studio gangsters and rap artists. In 2000, Ace released "Hellbound" (Import-Generic), a duet with **Eminem**. The exclusive track was taken from the

American concept compilation album *Game Over* (Yosumi, 2000). The rare track is backed with two Ace tracks, "'Spread It Out" and "Rap 2k1."

In 2001, Ace released the album, *Disposal Arts* (Yosumi). The album is uneven, however, its best aspects are those tracks that have Ace analyzing himself, rap, and the world around him. One standout is "No Regrets," which allows Ace to look back at the highs and lows of his long career. In 2004, Ace released *Long Hot Summer* (Yosumi/M3), which he claims is his last album. *Long Hot Summer* is considered by both critics and fans alike to be a superb albeit slept-on album.

Never one for empty braggadocio and banal ghetto tales, Ace's international production team produces a jazzy vibe that complements Ace's reflective lyrics. Guest appearances by **The Beatnuts**, Big Noyd, **Edo G.**, Jean Grae, Punch & Words, and Rahzel (**The Roots**) help to complete the album's beautiful texture.

DISCOGRAPHY: *Selected twelve-inch singles*: "Ya' Hardcore" (Delicious Vinyl Records, 1996); "Cars"/"Keep Livin' (Do Ya Thang)" (INC Records, Distributor Tape Kingz, 1997); "Ghettolife"/"The Outcome" (Fat Beats Records, 2000); "Conflict," with Bald Head Slick (Landspeed Records, 2000). *EPs*: *Hellbound* (Import-Generic); *Disposal Arts* (Yosumi, 2001); *Long Hot Summer* (Yosumi/M3, 2004). *Albums*: *Take A Look Around* (Cold Chillin' Records, 1990); *Masta Ace Incorporated—SlaughtaHouse* (Delicious Vinyl Records, 1993); *Sittin' On Chrome* (Delicious Vinyl Records, 1995).

MASTER P [Percy Miller]

Founder of No Limit Records, Master P created a rap music empire by going against the grain. Based in New Orleans, Lousiana, his record label was outside the rap music power centers of New York and California. New Orleans is a city with a rich musical tradition, although the rap music scene at the time was underdeveloped. New Orleans was also a city with a violent underbelly that fueled the messages of No Limit's artists. Without much radio play, No Limit operated for some time under the mainstream radar. The independent label, not known for

Master P. *Courtesy of Photofest.*

having the best lyricists, nonetheless provided its audience with what they wanted, hardcore content wrapped in synthesizers and plenty of bass. Like any good business, No Limit consistently cranked out new albums, while keeping production and marketing costs down.

As a child of divorced parents, Master P moved between the homes of his mother who lived in Richmond, California, and his father, who lived in New Orleans. During his teens, rather than getting directly involved with street life, Master P was an avid basketball player and won a scholarship to the University of Houston. Master P left the school, however, and moved back to California and enrolled in Merritt Junior College in Oakland, where he studied business.

In the late 1980s, Master P's grandfather died and left him $10,000. Master P used his inheritance to establish his first business, a record store called No Limit in Richmond, California. As the owner of a record store, Master P realized that there was a rap audience whose tastes for raw content and street-level beats were not being met by the major labels. In 1990, Master P decided to turn No Limit into a record label and in 1991 he released his debut album, *Get Away Clean* (No Limit Records). The following year he released his second album, *Mama's Bad Boy* (No Limit Records) and then in 1994 he had an **underground** hit with his album, *The Ghetto's Tryin to Kill Me* (No Limit Records), which sold 100,000 units independently.

Master P soon moved No Limit back to New Orleans and began concentrating on building his label. By the mid-1990s, No Limit had its own production team, Beats by the Pound, comprised of Craig B., KLC, and Mo B. Dick, that worked on every one of the label's recordings. Supervised by Master P, Beats by the Pound produced nearly ten albums a year. The production team worked quickly, often using ideas from contemporary hits, and could record and release entire albums in as little as two weeks. The albums were then packaged inexpensively, and not necessarily tastefully, and sent to market.

In 1995, Master P released *99 Ways to Die* (No Limit Records), which sold 200,000 units without a major distributor. In 1996, he followed up with the album *Ice Cream Man* (No Limit Records). By the time the album *Ghetto D* (No Limit Records) was released in 1997, No Limit Records, without benefit of exposure on radio or music video shows, had become a mini-empire. With *Ghetto D*, Master P and No Limit Records experienced their first mainstream recognition with the extremely popular single, "Make 'Em Say Uhh!!" and with "I Miss My Homies."

The majors came calling on No Limit Records, the company having sold nearly a quarter of a million records as an independent label. In 1995, No Limit entered into a pressing and distribution deal with Priority Records. The first release under the new deal was **Tru**, a group formed by Master P with his younger brothers Silkk the Shocker and C-Murder.

Tru's debut album, *True*, sold over 400,000 copies and included the huge hit, "Bout It, Bout It."

Like **Russell Simmons** before him, Master P decided to make a movie about his success in the record industry. The 1997 film *I'm Bout It* is an autobiographical comedy-drama titled after Tru's breakthrough hit. Master P financed the production himself, and when he found no distributor, it went straight to video in the summer of that year. In the summer of 1998 he released his next film, *I Got the Hook Up,* which did appear in theaters, concurrent with the release of his album *MP Da Last Don* (No Limit Records).

In 1999, the former high school basketball star signed a contract with the National Basketball Association's Toronto Raptors, but was subsequently cut from the team. The Charlotte Hornets had waived Master P the prior year, after he sustained an injury. Through his No Limit Sports Management, formed in 1998, he negotiated the National Football League contract of Heisman Trophy winner Ricky Williams (a contract that many called disastrous because of its incentive-driven terms). In 2000, athletes, including Williams, begin to exit the sports agency, some citing Master P's lack on focus as he pursued his own hoop dreams.

In 1999, Master P released the album *Only God Can Judge Me* (No Limit Records) and in 2000 released *Ghetto Postage* (No Limit Records). Feeling that No Limit Records needed room to expand, Master P left Priority Records. He signed a distribution deal with Universal Records in 2001—a move intended to get more exposure and profit for No Limit. He also changed the name of the record label from No Limit Records to New No Limit Records. The 2001 album *Game Face* was the first New No Limit Records release. Headed in a more radio-friendly direction, *Game Face* liberally uses music from big hits, such as Funkaelic's "One Nation Under a Groove," **Kurtis Blow**'s "The Breaks," and the Bee Gees' "More than a Woman." The old No Limit peeks through on the album's big single "Ooohhwee," a club track meant to appeal to ladies and thugs alike.

In December 2003, New No Limit Records quietly filed for bankruptcy. Master P left Universal Records and entered into a partnership agreement with Koch Records, subsequently releasing the double album *Good Side: Bad Side* (New No Limit Records). The album went gold within the first week of its release. In late August 2004, The New No Limit and Koch formally renewed their partnership agreement, which calls for Koch to provide The New No Limit with promotion, marketing, and distribution services for all New No Limit initiatives and releases.

In 2002, Master P was ordered by a Pomona, California, judge to pay 79-year-old Geneva Burger $105,000 in punitive damages in connection to her 1999 lawsuit that asserted her voice was put on a No Limit Records track discussing marijuana without her knowledge or consent. The track appeared on Magic's 1998 album, *Sky's the Limit* (No Limit

Records). A jury had previously found Master P not personally liable, but the 2002 ruling held his record company at fault. **Snoop Dogg**, who appeared on the track, settled out of court with Burger for $75,000, and Priority Records, the album's distributor, reportedly gave Burger $300,000 before the trial.

Two years later, Master P would be back in court pleading guilty to tax fraud charges in federal court in Baton Rouge, Louisiana. He had failed to file a corporate tax return reporting first-year earnings for Bout It, Inc, the company he founded in 1996 to oversee No Limit Records. The tax crime carries a sentence of up to five years probation, a fine of $200,000 or twice the financial gain or loss (whichever is greater), and court costs. In 2003, Master P was ranked on *Fortune* magazine's "40 Richest Under 40" list, with an estimated $361 million in holdings.

With his son **Lil' Romeo**, Master P made rap music history as the first father-and-son artists. Romeo released his self-titled debut album in 2001 at age 10. Master P currently appears with Lil' Romeo on his Nickelodeon show, *Romeo!*

See also: Tru

DISCOGRAPHY: *Get Away Clean* (No Limit, 1991); *Mama's Bad Boy* (No Limit, 1992); *The Ghetto's Trying to Kill Me* (No Limit, 1994); *99 Ways to Die* (No Limit, 1995); *Ice Cream Man* (No Limit, 1996); Ghetto D (No Limit, 1997); *MP Da Last Don* (No Limit, 1998); *Only God Can Judge Me* (1999); *Ghetto Postage* (2000); *Game Face* (New No Limit/Universal, 2001); *Good Side: Bad Side* (New No Limit/Koch, 2004; double CD).

MC; MCING (Aka MC; MCing)

MC stands for Master of Ceremonies or Mic Controller. Traditionally, the MC is the person who controls and guides a program or an event. Within the context of Hip Hop, the MC originally began as someone who worked with the DJ to motivate the crowd by saying a few lines. The MC was sometimes called the master controller. The role of the MC expanded from saying a few phrases at the behest of the DJ to composing long form rhymes that are the focus of the event or party. The more modern usage of MC makes it fairly synonymous with the terms *rap artist* or *rapper*. The point of debate regarding calling someone an MC often revolves around the person's ability to perform before a live audience and to rhyme on the spot, contemporaneously, as opposed to being able to perform only previously written rhymes. Many purists believe that only the former should receive the MC designation.

MC BREED (Eric Breed)

MC Breed, from Flint, Michigan, is one of the first rap artists to come out the Midwest.

In 1991, MC Breed and da Flint Crew (DFC) released their debut album, MC Breed & DFC on the small independent label SDEG. The hit single "Ain't No Future in Yo' Frontin'," which sampled **Ice Cube**'s "Wicked," not only put Breed on the map for several years, it kept this album on the *Billboard* R & B charts for a year. This level of success was unprecedented for a rap artist from the Midwest. The success of the album is that it fused the sounds of the East Coast and West Coast rap styles.

In 1992, Breed, perhaps anxious to cash in on the success of the West Coast's style, followed up with the album *20 Below* (Ichiban Records), which ditched social consciousness and the East Coast aesthetic. It is no surprise that many fans on the East Coast and in the Midwest were not at all pleased. *20 Below* remains the least remembered of Breed's many albums.

In 1993, for his third album, *The New Breed* (Wrap Records), Breed teamed up with the D.O.C., who helped write and produce some of the songs. In 1994, Breed released his fourth album, *Funkafied* (Ichiban Records), which helped him to regain some ground, peaking at number 9 on the *Billboard* R & B chart. Unfortunately Breed's subsequent albums would never match the success of *Funkafied.* Several albums featuring **Too Short** (whom he met when he located to Atlanta, Georgia) did not do well, partly because Breed never signed with a major record company that would have the resources to market and promote them. As an **underground** artist, Breed continues to represent the Dirty South, releasing albums almost annually.

DISCOGRAPHY: *MC Breed and DFC* (SDEG, 1991); *20 Below* (Ichiban Records, 1992); *The New Breed* (Wrap Records, 1993; re-issued by Ichiban Records in 2002); *Funkafied* (Ichiban Records, 1994); *Big Baller* (Wrap Records, 1995); *To Da Beat Ch'all* (Ichiban Records, 1996); *Da Hood Tapes* (Ichiban Records, 1996); *Flatline* (Ichiban Records, 1997); *2 For the Show* (Roadrunner, 1999); *It's All Good* (Roadrunner, 1999); *Vol. 1 Present the Thugz* (Power, 2000); *Rare Breed* (R&D, 2000); *The Fharmacist* (Fharmacy, 2001); *Chopped and Screwed* (Ichiban Records/Ryko, 2002); *Mix Tape* (Ichiban Records/Ryko, 2004).

MC BREEZE (aka Joey B. Ellis) [Joseph Ellis]

MC Breeze is recognized as the first rap artist to have a record banned from radio. In 1985, the Philadelphia, Pennsylvania, native, used money that he had made delivering pizzas to produce and manufacture his debut EP *Discombobulatorbubalator.* The rap made derogatory references to Chinese restaurants cooking cats and dogs for meals sold in Black neighborhoods. The mayor of Philadelphia banned it because it was deemed insensitive to Chinese Americans and could negatively impact relations between Asian businesses and Black citizens. Before the song was taken off the radio, it was receiving over 500 requests a day on Philadelphia's Power 99 (WUSL-FM) radio station. While his single "It Ain't New York" was a hit (its title was used to promote the first ever Philly vs. New York rap **battle** at the Spectrum in 1986), it was *Discombobulatorbubalator* that put Breeze on the map.

At the 1987 New Music Seminar in New York, MC Breeze used the stuttering style that he created to defeat rap artist **Just-Ice**. Breeze later introduced his song "Superbad" to **MC Hammer**, who used it to open up his performances. In 1991, Breeze signed a deal with Hammer's Bust It Records, as an artist and producer. Since Atlantic Records was already promoting an artist named Breeze, he became known professionally as Joey B. Ellis. Breeze was the subject of immense local pride when he was tapped to write and perform three songs for the 1990 Sylvester Stallone film, *Rocky V*: "Go For It (Heart and Fire)," "Thought U Were The One For Me," and "All U Gotta Do Is Sing. Breeze is also the subject of the 2000 independent film *Philly Boy,* directed by Michael Dennis.
DISCOGRAPHY: *Discombobulatorbubalator* (Breeze Records, 1985).

MC EIHT [Aaron Tyler]

A veteran West Coast rap artist who retains a loyal following underneath the mainstream music radar, MC Eiht began his career as a teenager as a member of the group, Compton's Most Wanted (CMW). CMW received national attention for its 1990 album *It's a Compton Thang* (Capitol Records). Although CMW appeared to mine the same lyrical and musical influences as fellow Californians **N.W.A.**, they failed to ignite the same spark with record buyers.

CMW released two more albums, *Straight Checkn 'Em* (Sony Records, 1991) and *Music to Driveby* (Sony Records, 1992), before Eiht began his solo career. In 1993, Eiht with the help of CMW's, DJ Slip released his solo debut single, "Streiht Up Menace." The track was included on the *Menace II Society* soundtrack, a film that Eiht had appeared in. Eiht would thereafter sign a recording contract with Sony Records' Epic Street division. Again with production assistance from DJ Slip, Eiht recorded his 1994 solo debut album, *We Come Strapped* (Epic Street/Sony Records). Ironically the album is labeled "MC Eiht Featuring CMW," when in reality DJ Slip was the only other member of CMW on the album.

We Come Strapped topped *Billboard*'s R & B album chart and reached the Top Five of the Pop Album charts without spawning a strong lead single. The album also got headlines because of the controversy that ensued over his attack on racist police officers. Then-presidential candidate Bob Dole condemned the album. Epic Records felt compelled to issue an extra warning sticker on the CD, stating that Eiht's lyrics were not necessarily the opinions of the Sony Records. In 2000, vice presidential candidate Senator Joe Lieberman (D-CT) publicly condemned a host of rap and rock artists, including MC Eiht and **Tupac Shakur** in what he called the "Culture Wars." A September 2000 Federal Trade Commission report found that adult entertainment was being marketed to minors.

Eiht continued to release albums, some creatively better than his debut effort, but based on sales his career had peaked with his debut album. Eiht released his sophomore album, *Death Threatz* (Epic/Sony) in 1996 and *Last Man Standing* (Epic/Sony) in 1997. Both albums featured production by DJ Slip and were arguably better albums than Eiht's debut, but Epic Records nonetheless released the artist from his contract.

In 1998, Eiht's long-standing **beef** with **DJ Quik** went mainstream when Quik dissed Eiht on the single, "Dollaz & Sense," from his album *Safe & Sound* (Arista Records, 1998). Eiht went on to sign with **Mack 10**'s Hoo Bangin' label and in 1999 released the album, *Section 8*. Eiht would continue to release albums annually: *N' My Neighborhood* (Hoo Bangin'/Priority Records, 2000), *Tha8t'z Gangsta* (Half Ounce/Bayside, 2001), and *Underground Hero* (Hoo Bangin'/Priority Records, 2002). None of these successive albums has topped the charts, but MC Eight still retains a core of diehard fans. In 2000, Eiht reunited with CMW on the album *Represent* (Half-Ounce/Bayside).

MC Eiht left Hoo Bangin' records in 2001 and started his own label, Half Ounce Records. Of his departure from Hoo Bangin', Eiht publicly stated that he made the move because the label lacked direction and focus. MC Eiht has a role in the Rockstar Playstation II 2004 video game, "Grand Theft Auto: San Andreas" (the CMW song "Hood Took Me Under" is included on its soundtrack). East Coast rap artist Lloyd Banks, perhaps referencing MC Eiht as the leading spokesman for the streets, includes the line, "You don't have to go to L.A. to get your MC Eiht," on his debut album, *Hunger For More* (G-Unit/Interscope Records, 2004).

In July 2004, Eiht signed a distribution deal with Native Records to release the album *Veteran's Day* through Penalty Associated Labels/Ryko.

DISCOGRAPHY: *We Come Strapped* (Epic Street/Sony Records, 1994); *Death Threatz*; (Epic Street/Sony Records, 1996); *Last Man Standing* (Epic Street/Sony Records, 1997); *Section 8* (Hoo Bangin'/Priority Records, 1999): *N' My Neighborhood* (Hoo Bangin'/Priority Records, 2000); *Tha8t'z Gangsta* (Half Ounce/Bayside, 2001); *Underground Hero* (Hoo Bangin'/Priority Records, 2002); *Veteran's Day* (Penalty/Ryko/Native, 2004).

MC HAMMER [Stanley Kirk Burrell]

A rap artist known for his dance moves, harem pants, and pop appeal, MC Hammer has sold over 30 millions records, along the way winning

MC Hammer with James Brown. *Courtesy of Photofest.*

three Grammy awards, eight American Music Awards, and a People's Choice Award.

The Oakland, California, native got his first break when he got a job as a ball boy for the Oakland Athletic's baseball team. The young man entertained fans by dancing during game breaks and earned the nickname "Hammer" for his resemblance to all-time home run leader, "Hammerin'" Hank Aaron. Although he had aspirations to play professional baseball, he enlisted in the U.S. Navy for three years. Upon his return to Oakland, Hammer began performing at local clubs, even performing as a member of the religious rap group Holy Ghost Boys.

The financial help of baseball players Mike Davis and Dwayne Murphy allowed MC Hammer to form Bust It Records and release the solo single, "Ring 'Em'," a minor hit. In 1987, for the first time using the name MC Hammer, he recorded the album *Feel My Power* (Bust It Records). Hammer subsequently won over a Capitol Records executive with his live dance show. Hammer entered into a recording agreement that included a reported advance of $750,000, at that time unheard of for a rap artist. In 1988, Capitol Records re-issued his debut album under the title *Let's Get It Started* and it went on to sell triple-platinum. His 1990 second album, *Please Hammer, Don't Hurt 'Em* (Capitol Records), which includes the mega-single, "U Can't Touch This," would prove to be even more popular, selling 17 million units.

Following massive exposure due to Hammer's advertisement for **British Knights** footwear and Pepsi Cola, the album stayed at the top of the U.S. charts for a record-breaking twenty-one weeks. Hammer experienced utter failure, however, with the 1991 single, "Here Comes The Hammer" (Capitol Records), which stalled at number 54 in the U.S. music charts, despite its appearance on the *Rocky V* film soundtrack. During this period, Hammer's image was attached to the cartoon hero "Hammerman" and to a Mattel "Hammer" doll with an attached **boom box** radio.

In 1991, Hammer dropped the "MC" from his name and released the five-time platinum *Too Legit To Quit* (Capitol Records). The album liner notes discussed Hammer's wish that Black youth move closer to Christian values. Although the hit single "Addams Groove" from the *Addams Family* film (1991) soundtrack was heavily promoted, Hammer's career appeared to be on the decline. In 1992, The *San Francisco Examiner* newspaper reported that Hammer was nearly bankrupt after the poor attendance for his *Too Legit To Quit* tour. As a way to reignite his career, for his 1994 album, *The Funky Headhunter* (Capitol Records), Hammer adopted a more hardcore rap image; however, audiences did not accept the change. Although the album did sell platinum it was a poor showing in comparison to his earliest efforts.

In 1995, Hammer reverted to the MC prefix for the album *Inside Out* (Warner Bros. Records). Following the album's release, MC Hammer indicated that he was becoming a minister. Two years, later MC Hammer announced his decision to use his musical talents to praise God and emphasize traditional family values. In 2001, he released the album *Active Duty* on the independent label World Hit Records.

In 2003, Hammer's book *Enemies of the Father: A Message from the Heart on Being a Family Man* (New York: Atria) was published. Hammer also appeared in the WB television network reality series *The Surreal Life.* Hammer has also frequently appeared on the Trinity Broadcasting Network preaching the gospel.

DISCOGRAPHY: *Single*: "Ring 'Em" (Bust It Records). *Albums*: *Feel My Power* (Bust It Records, 1987), re-issued as *Let's Get It Started* (Capitol Records, 1988); *Please Hammer, Don't Hurt 'Em* (Capitol Records, 1990); *Too Legit To Quit* (Capitol Records, 1991); *The Funky Headhunter* (Warner Bros. Records, 1994); *Inside Out* (Warner Bros. Records, 1995); *Active Duty* (World Hit Records, 2001).

MC LYTE [Lana Michele Moorer]

MC Lyte is the first rap artist ever to perform at Carnegie Hall, the first solo female rap artist to ever receive a gold single, and also the first female MC considered to be on par with her male counterparts. Lyte's tomboy image was consistent with the 1980s B-girl style of the day: rather than revealing outfits, she favored large gold bamboo earrings, name plate belts, pressed jeans, **sheepskin coats**, and Puma or **Adidas** sneakers with fat laces.

Born in Queens, New York, and raised in Brooklyn, she began rhyming at age 12. Her first single, "I Cram to Understand U (Sam)," paved the way for her record deal with First Priority Records (which Lyte's stepfather, Nat Robinson, had founded). In 1988, she released the hit single, "I Got A Man," a duet with Positive K, and also her debut album, *Lyte as a Rock.*

MC Lyte. *Courtesy of Photofest.*

The single "10% Dis" sparked a running **beef** with rap artist **Antoinette**. The only live match-up between the rap artists took place at The World nightclub. Antoinette would hit back with the single "Light Outs," and Lyte responded with force on "Shut the Eff Up! (Hoe)," from her second album, *Eyes On This* (First Priority Records, 1989). Aside from the music, the *Eyes On This* album is important because the cover photograph directly appeals to the majority male rap audience by replacing the tomboy Lyte with a more femininely styled version. *Eyes on This* contained the hit singles "Cha, Cha, Cha," which reached number 1 on the rap music charts, and the antiviolence "Cappucino." In 1989 **KRS-ONE** invited Lyte to participate in the classic **Stop the Violence** "Self-Destruction" music video.

MC Lyte made history with her third album, *Act Like You Know* (First Priority Records, 1993). From this album came the thug–love anthem "Ruffneck," which earned her a Grammy nomination for Best Rap Single, making her the first solo female rap artist so honored. MC Lyte also made history with "Ruffneck" for becoming the first solo female rap artist to have a gold single.

In the mid-1990s Lyte moved to a major label, Elektra Records, and in 1996 released her fourth album, *Bad As I Wanna B*, which included the successful track "Cold Rock a Party," a duet with **Missy Elliott**. In 1996, she earned her second gold single for the Xscape track "Keep on Keepin' On," which appeared on the *Sunset Park* film soundtrack. In 1998, Lyte released the underrecognized *Seven & Seven* (Elektra Records). Lyte also turned up on the **remix** "Jammin'" from the album *Bob Marley: Chant Down Babylon* (Island Records, 1999), and on the film soundtrack for *Wild Wild West* (1999). She also made a guest appearance on **Common**'s album *Like Water for Chocolate* (MCA Records, 2000), and contributed a solo track and a duet with **Chuck D** for the *Dark Angel* soundtrack (Artemis, 2002).

As the environment for rap music changed, especially its expectations for female artists, Lyte moved from rapping to acting. Her television credits include *Moesha, In the House, Platinum,* New York Undercover, *The District,* Nickelodeon's *Cousin Skeeter,* and MTV's *DNC.* MC Lyte is currently starring in UPN's primetime hit sitcom *Half & Half.* In the 2004 season, she served as a celebrity judge on the CBS television program Star Search with Arsenio Hall. Lyte was also a familiar face on television with her recurring character Lana on the WB television network's long running comedy *For Your Love.*

With her distinctive husky voice, Lyte has also found success doing voice-overs for national commercials. Lyte has been the voice behind VH1 Hip Hop Honors, Wherehouse Music, Coca-Cola, McDonald's, and Nike advertisements. Lyte is also the voice of the popular Mattel Diva Stars "Chat Doll," Tia. Lastly, Lyte has her own weekend radio show on Sirius Satellite Radio.

After Lyte parted ways with Elektra Records, she signed with **Will Smith**'s company, Overbrook, but things were stalled when his distribution deal went south. Lyte subsequently joined iMUSIC. In 2003, Lyte made a musical comeback with the album, *Da Undaground Heat, Vol.* 1., hosted by Jamie Fox, released on her own label, SGI/CMM. The track "Ride Wit Me" from the album garnered the veteran rap artist her 2nd career Grammy nomination. The single also received a B.E.T. award nomination for Best Female Rap performance.

Lyte is also active with several social initiatives, including antiviolence campaigns, Rock the Vote, and AIDS charities.

DISCOGRAPHY: *Lyte as a Rock* (First Priority Records, 1988); *Eyes on This* (1989); *Act Like You Know* (First Priority Records, 1993); *Bad As I Wanna B* (Elektra, 1996); Seven & Seven (Elektra, 1998); *Da Undaground Heat, Vol. 1* (SGI/CMM, 2003).

MC SHAN [Shawn Moltke]

MC Shan is known for the **Marley Marl**–produced classic single, "The Bridge," which sparked the infamous lyrical **battle** with **Boogie Down Productions (BDP)**, led by **KRS-ONE**. BDP responded to "The Bridge" with "The Bridge is Over," attacking the Shan and the **Juice Crew All Stars**.

MC Shan was the cousin of producer Marley Marl, who would found **Cold Chillin'** Records, home of the Juice Crew All Stars. After recording several singles including "The Bridge," in 1987 he released his debut album *Down by Law* (Cold Chillin'/Warner Bros. Records) produced by Marley Marl. *Down By Law* showcases Shan, a clever and entertaining artist who aptly represents the typical New York City **B-boy** of the 1980s. He followed up in 1988 with another Marley Marl–produced album, *Born to Be Wild* (Cold Chillin'/Warner Bros.

Records); although tame by today's standards, in its time the album was considered rebellious.

On his 1990 album, *Play It Again, Shan* (Cold Chillin'/Warner Bros. Records), he attempted a more mature tone and enlisted the help of another producer. *Play It Again, Shan* is notable for the tracks "It Don't Mean a Thing," which was inspired by the Duke Ellington classic, and for "Death Was Quite a Surprise," which tells the story of a young man who, tired of working for minimum wage, becomes a drug dealer and gets killed.

Play It Again, Shan would be his last album and thereafter Shan worked largely as a producer, although he returned to the mic in 2000 on the track "Da Bridge 2001," from *QB Finest Nas & Ill Will Records Presents Queensbridge The Album* (Columbia Records, 2000). In the mid-1990s, MC Shan and KRS-ONE appeared in an advertisement for Sprite soft drinks.

DISCOGRAPHY: *Down By Law* (Cold Chillin'/Warner Bros. Records, 1987); *Born to Be Wild* (Cold Chillin'/Warner Bros. Records, 1987); *Play It Again, Shan* (Cold Chillin'/Warner Bros. Records, 1990).

MEDUSA [*unknown*]

Medusa is a Los Angeles–based rap artist who, because of her thought-provoking lyrics, trademark afro, and Afrocentric presence, has been called the "Angela Davis of Hip Hop."

A veteran of the **underground** Hip Hop scene, Medusa creates soulful, empowering music that is the antithesis of much of today's ego-driven rap music. Medusa considers herself a singer first, however, the former **locker** began MCing at the age of sixteen. In the early 1990s, she frequently performed at the Good Life café in Los Angeles, ground zero for the famed **Los Angeles Underground Movement** that incubated talent such as **Freestyle Fellowship** and **Jurassic 5**. Medusa subsequently formed her own 12-piece live band called, Feline Science.

She performs regularly at Hip Hop events as well as at other music events. Medusa is a respected MC who won the Rap Sheet MC World Championship in the 1990s. In 1997, Medusa released the EP *Do It the Way You Feel It* (Goodvibe Records). Since 1993, Medusa has hosted "Nappy @ Da Roots," a twice monthly event in Los Angeles that provides a venue for emerging rap artists and singers to perform. She performed on the track "Vocal Artillery" from Ozomatli's 2002 Latin Grammy Award-winning album, *Embrace the Chaos* (Interscope Records). The *Los Angeles Weekly* voted Medusa Best Hip-Hop Artist for in 2001 and 2002.

Medusa penned the single "My Momma Raised a G" for the 2001 HBO film *Stranger Inside,* as well as acting in the movie. She also appears in the 2003 documentary *Nobody Knows My Name,* Rachel Raimist's film about women artists in Hip Hop.

DISCOGRAPHY: *EP*: *Do It the Way You Feel It* (Goodvibe Records, 1997).

MELLE MEL. *See* Grandmaster Flash and the Furious Five

MERCEDES LADIES

The Mercedes Ladies, comprised of Baby D Sherri-Sher, RD Smiley, Zina-Zee, DJ LaSpank, and Eve-a-Def (with Sweet P and Sty-Sty as later members) are widely recognized as the first all-girl Hip Hop crew. With as many as four MCs and two DJs, the Mercedes Ladies were founded around 1976 and were the sister group to **Grand Wizzard Theodore** and the L Brothers. They were the opening act for such artists as **Kevvy Kev**, **Busy Bee**, **DJ Lovebug Starski**, Master Rob, **Afrika Bambaataa**, **Kool DJ Red Alert**, **Kool DJ Herc**, **The Furious Five**, The **Cold Crush Brothers**, and **Grand Mixer D.ST**. The Mercedes Ladies never had a record deal. After performing live shows for years, they appeared on the single, "Don's Groove" (Elektra Records, 1984) with male rap artist Donald D.
DISCOGRAPHY: "Don's Groove" (Elektra Records, 1984).

METHOD MAN (aka Ticallion Stallion, Johnny Blaze) [Clifford Smith]

The first and most successful solo rap artist from the **Wu-Tang Clan**, Method Man's distinctive, sandpaper-rough voice, and imaginative rhymes made him one of the most recognizable members of the Clan.

Born in Hempstead, Long Island, New York, Method Man divided his time between his father's home on Long Island and his mother's Staten Island, New York, residence. On Staten Island, he met future Wu-Tang members **RZA**, **Ol' Dirty Bastard**, and **GZA**, and in the early 1990s they formed the rap group, Wu-Tang Clan. Method Man's skills were showcased on the group's 1993 debut album, *Enter the Wu-Tang* (*36 Chamber*) (Loud Records), and even got his own track, "Method Man."

The Wu-Tang's unusual contract allowed members to pursue individual record contracts. In 1994, Method Man entered into a deal with Def Jam and became the first Wu-Tang member to release a solo project when *Tical* (Def Jam Recordings, 1995) hit the street. The highly anticipated album went platinum, helped by the singles "Bring the Pain" and "Release Yo' Delf." The single "All I Need" pounds with **B-boy** flavor and intensity, while the **remix** with **Mary J. Blige** is a smoothed-out version. The "All I Need (remix)" sold platinum and garnered Method Man a Grammy award, with accompanying major mainstream exposure.

Method Man released his sophomore album, *Tical 2000: Judgment Day* (Def Jam Recordings), in late 1998; it entered the charts at number

Method Man. *Courtesy of Photofest.*

2. The successful concept album, a many-layered affair with multiple skits and numerous guest appearances, demonstrated the range of Method Man's imagination.

In 1999, Method Man partnered up with **Redman** to form a duo act that performed with **Jay-Z** on his Hard Knock Life tour. The duo subsequently went into the studio and recorded the album *Blackout!* (Def Jam Recordings/Def Squad, 1999). The successful single from *Blackout!*, "How High," would inspire the 2001 comedy film *How High*, starring Method Man and Redman. After making guest appearances in Redman's Blues Brothers–inspired video "Whateva Man" and Erykah Badu's video for her single "Next Lifetime," Method Man leapt onto the big screen. He first appeared in the rap music documentary *The Show* (1995) and then took on acting roles in a succession of films: *The Great White Hype* (1996); *Copland* (1997); **Hype Williams**'s film *Belly* (1998), which featured **Nas** and **DMX**; *How High* (2001); *Undercover Brother* (2002); and *Soul Plane* (2004). In early 2001, Method Man also starred in the highly acclaimed HBO prison drama, *Oz*.

In 2004, Method Man released his third album, *Tical 0: The Prequel* (Def Jam Recordings). This proved to be his least successful effort to date. With only one RZA-produced track (it was rumored that RZA produced twenty tracks, but Def Jam released only one), the inclusion of producer **Sean "P. Diddy" Combs** and artists such as **Ludacris** and **Missy Elliott**, coupled with the lack of Wu-Tang artists, many fans and critics panned the album as too commercial. That same year, Method Man again joined with Redman for the Fox network television series, *Method and Red*, which has the rap duo moving into an upscale, predominantly White neighborhood. The short-lived series showed early signs of trouble that were confirmed when Method Man, an executive producer of the show, complained to the *Los Angeles Times* that the network would not let him keep the show "ghetto" enough. Method Man is also alleged to have had a physical altercation with one of the show's writers, who resigned.

DISCOGRAPHY: *Tical* (Def Jam Recordings, 1995); *Tical 2000: Judgment Day* (Def Jam Recordings, 1998); *Blackout*! [with Redman] (Def Jam Recordings/Def Squad, 1999); *Tical 0: The Prequel* (Def Jam Recordings, 2004).

MIAMI BASS (aka Booty bass)

Bass music emanates from two distinct sources: Detroit, Michigan's, electro music scene and Miami, Florida's, dance-derived music scene. Traditional bass music therefore covers a broad spectrum of sounds and speeds. Miami bass is known for its more frenetic tempo and its sexually oriented lyrics. Very often, Miami bass lyrics focus on women's rear ends, or "booties."

Modern Miami bass is often traced back to the 1985 single, "Bass Rock Express" (4-Sight Records) by MC A.D.E. (Adrian Hines). The song is based on Kraftwerk's "Trans Europe Express," previously used by **Afrika Bambaataa** in "Planet Rock." California transplants **2 Live Crew** helped to bring Miami bass to the attention of mainstream audiences. Their 1986 debut album, *2 Live Crew is What We Are* (Luke Skyywalker Records), featured songs such as "We Want Some P---y" and "Throw the D." They followed up in 1989 with the notorious album *Nasty As They Wanna Be* (Luke Skyywalker Records), which spawned the hit, "Me So Horny."

Other examples of Miami bass that have had national appeal include JT Money & Poison Clan's hit, "Shake Watcha Mama Gave Ya" (1992); 95 South's "Whoot, There It Is" (1993); "69 Boyz' "Tootsie Roll" (1994); and the Quad City DJs "C'mon N Ride It (The Train)" (1996).

MIA X [Mia Young]

The first female rap artist on **Master P**'s No Limit Records, Mia X was born in New Orleans, Louisiana, but her first music experience came in Queens, New York, as a member of the rap group, New York Incorporated. She performed with them for four years and then returned to Louisiana. Mia then recorded a few records that garnered her local attention.

Subsequently, Master P approached Mia to join his start-up label, No Limit Records. Mia joined with the stipulation that she would write her own lyrics and control her own image. She got her start on the multi-platinum **Tru** single, "I'm Bout It, Bout It," from the album *True* (No Limit Records/Priority Records, 1995). That same year, Mia released her debut album, *Good Girl Gone Bad* (No Limit/Priority Records, 1995). She followed it with the gold album, *Unlady Like* (No Limit/Priority Records, 1997), which included the radio-friendly track "Party Don't Stop," featuring Master P and **Foxy Brown**. In 1998, she released her third album, *Mama Drama* (No Limit/Priority Records).

DISCOGRAPHY: *Good Girl Gone Bad* (No Limit/Priority Records, 1995); *Unlady Like* (No Limit/Priority Records, 1997); *Mama* Drama (No Limit/Priority Records, 1998).

MISOGYNY AND HIP HOP

The subject of misogyny and Hip Hop is complex and sometimes contradictory. Although it is undeniable that misogyny and objectification of women exists within rap music and Hip Hop culture, it is noteworthy that perhaps the most influential female musical artist of this current era is **Missy Elliott**. Missy is a rap artist, songwriter, and producer; moreover, she has succeeded in a largely male entertainment industry, without disrobing or conforming to either musical or societal stereotypes about women or Black women in particular. Most significant, in relation to Missy and the development and mainstreaming of Hip Hop, Missy does not seem to have a female counterpart in the world of rock music.

Although rap lyrics and rap music videos are frequently criticized for misogynistic exploitation of women, this misogyny is rooted in American culture rather than in any musical genre in particular. The broader issue concerns the disparate treatment of the genders in American society. The hypermasculinity present in rap music specifically, and Hip Hop generally, is consistent with the male as conqueror and sexual adventurer. In fact, the misogyny in rap music is not necessarily distinct or more pronounced than that found in much of rock music. In the 1970s, and even more so in the 1980s, spandex-clad, heavy metal rock groups rode the charts and filled the arena with lyrics, videos, and album covers that portrayed women as sexual objects.

Race seems to play a factor, insofar as the bulk of critical attention has focused on rap music and its predominantly Black, male artists, rather than on rock music and its predominantly White, male artists. That being said, many rap music lyrics and their accompanying videos do promote and perpetuate negative images of women, and Black women particularly. Although all races of women are represented in rap music videos, Black women especially are depicted as sex objects. Many videos expressly foster this portrayal by including scantily clad women and/or focusing on the body parts of women. These media images usually accompany lyrics that negatively label women and declare that the only value of women is that of a short-term sexual partner.

In more extreme instances, rap artists glorify pimps and suggest that using women for financial gain is acceptable, as is physically assaulting women who disobey them. Certainly not every rap song is misogynistic, nor is every rap artist disdainful of women. However, mainstream rap music is rampant with sexualized images of women, coupled with derogative labels for them. This behavior not only disrespects and dishonors women, it also fosters an environment that dehumanizes women and thus implicitly justifies men's mistreatment of women.

Misogyny in rap music may also be symptomatic of Black men's experiences within a society that has devalued and dehumanized them. If Black men have been conditioned by society not to trust or love, even themselves, then it will be difficult for them to love and honor women, especially Black women. Misogyny in Hip Hop not only exposes societal influences on Black men, it also shows how Black women have been complicit in their own exploitation. Many women have simply detached themselves from the negative messages of rap music by saying that the rap artists are not referring to them; some go further and state that such labels are valid, given the conduct of some women. Furthermore, a large portion of consumers of misogynistic rap material are women, and hundreds of bikini-clad women show up for the music video shoots for the opportunity to be unpaid participants. Moreover, in clubs and backstage at concerts, there frequently are throngs of women of all races and ethnicities who pursue famous rap artists as well as neighborhood celebrities and express their willingness to exchange sexual favors for some type of compensation, or merely for the privilege being with that famous man.

There are indeed female rap artists and female rap music consumers who are attempting to fight against misogyny in Hip Hop, but it has proven a difficult task within a male-dominated entertainment industry, more interested in the financial bottom line than in social change and gender relations.

In May 2001, KBOO-FM, a Portland, Oregon radio station was fined $7,000 by the Federal Communications Commission (FCC) after it aired performance artist Sarah Jones's song, "My Revolution," which addressed the attitudes of male rap artists toward women. The FCC decided that the song contained "patently offensive" sexual references "designed to pander and shock." Ironically, what was deemed too explicit was her quoting **LL Cool J**. In published accounts, Jones is quoted as saying that "My Revolution,' originally a poem set to music by DJ Vadim, is "dedicated to all the women and men struggling to keep their self-respect in this climate of misogyny, money-worship, and mass production of hip hop's illegitimate child, 'hip-pop.'"

In 2004, in response to **Nelly**'s graphic video *Tip-Drill*, which depicts a scantily clad woman as a sexual appliance, women at Spelman College, a historical academic institution for Black women in Atlanta, Georgia, threatened to protest Nelly's appearance on their campus.

In January 2005 *Essence* magazine, the leading magazine for Black women, with circulation in excess of 1.6 million, launched a twelve-month initiative to combat the misogyny and sexism that is predominant in rap music and Hip Hop.

Rap music and Hip Hop culture, as experienced on the **underground,** often bears little resemblance to the music played on commercial radio stations and major music video outlets, it is nonetheless true that diverse, nonsexist material is not readily available and usually requires the consumer to actively search for it, while misogynist music is ubiquitous. Society at large continues to support an environment that condones sexism and misogyny, not only in rap music, but in other musical genres and in other entertainment vehicles such as film, television, and **video games**. Moreover, terms such as *pimpin'*, *wife-beater* (as in wife-beater T-shirt), and *bitch* have also entered the mainstream American language with little critical thought to the long-term effects on the gender relations of adults or on youth development.

MISSY "MISDEMEANOR" ELLIOTT [Melissa Arnette Elliott]

Missy Elliott is the first woman in Hip Hop to be recognized as a talented rap artist, songwriter, and producer.

Born in Portsmouth, Virginia, Missy's career began when Devante Swing of Jodeci signed her group, Sista, to his Wing Mob record label, a subsidiary of Elektra Records. Swing Mob's label deal fell through, as did Sista's debut album. Thereafter, Missy contacted her friend, producer **Timbaland**, who at the time was working on Aaliyah's hugely successful album, *One in a Million* (Atlantic Records, 1996). As a songwriter, Missy scored hits with the album's singles "One in a Million" and "If Your Girl Only Knew." Missy continued to work with a number of artists and made a breakthrough as an artist with her rap performance on Gina Thompson's single, "The Things You Do" (Mercury Records, 1996).

Despite her considerable talent, record companies did not believe that the zaftig Missy had the right image to be a female rap artist. Missy prevailed, however, and in 1996 she signed a production deal with Elektra Records. In 1997, Missy created her very own label, Gold Mind Inc., and released her platinum-selling debut album, *Supa Dupa Fly* (Elektra Records), which included the hit single, "The Rain." **Hype Williams**'s innovative music video for "The Rain" gave Missy even greater media exposure.

Aside from selling units, *Supa Dupa Fly* (Elektra Records) showcased Missy's versatility as an artist and as an industry trendsetter. Other standout singles from the album were "Sock It 2 Me," "Beep Me 911," "Hit 'Em Wit da Hee." Missy produced eight tracks for and also appeared on the soundtrack for the film *Why Do Fools Fall in Love* (Warner Bros. Records, 1998). In 1999, Missy released her follow-up album, the platinum-selling, *Da Real World* (Elektra Records), an even more ambitious album that featured two huge hits, "She's a Bitch" and "Hot Boyz," and an unexpected collaboration with **Eminem** on the track "Busa Rhyme." The album also includes performances by **Da Brat**, **Juvenile**, Beyoncé, and reggae artist Lady Saw.

Missy Elliott. *Courtesy of Photofest.*

In 2001, Missy released her third album, *Miss E . . . So Addictive* (Elektra), which featured mega hit singles, "Get Ur Freak On" and "One Minute Man." "Get Ur Freak On" helped Missy capture a Grammy award for Best Rap Solo Performance. Missy also produced and appeared in the MTV award-winning "Lady Marmalade" track, featuring **Lil' Kim**, Mya, Pink, and Christina Aguilera from the *Moulin Rouge* (2001) film soundtrack. Missy's Midas touch continued in late 2002 with the release of the double-platinum album, *Under Construction* (Elektra Records), which spawned the hit singles "Work It" and "Gossip Folks."

In 2003, Missy released her fifth album, *This is A Test* (Elektra) which while generally well-received, has some detractors who thought it was a rushed effort not worthy of Missy's talents.

In 2004, Missy would win her second Grammy Award, as Best Female Solo Performance for the single "Work It." In each of Missy's albums, she distinguished herself from other female rap artists by proving that she could deliver powerful and sexually charged lyrics with creativity and even humor. As a result, Missy has defied stereotypes about women rap artists without sacrificing her broad fan base.

In 2001, model Iman and Missy launched Misdemeanor Lipstick, which benefits Break the Cycle, an organization dedicated to helping young people break the chain of domestic abuse. In 2003, Missy became the organization's spokesperson.

Missy has parlayed her popularity into endorsements and in 2003 the Hip Hop icon appeared in Gap ads with Pop music icon Madonna. Missy also appeared in advertisements for Sprite. In addition to the two Grammy awards, Missy has won two B.E.T. awards, and five Lady Of Soul/Soul Train Awards. Twice within the past five years, *Rolling Stone* magazine has named her "Best Female Hip Hop Artist of the Year," and twice she has ranked as *Billboard*'s number 1 year-end female Hip Hop star. She was also awarded American Music Award for Favorite Rap/Hip-Hop Female in 2003.

In 2004, Missy joined with **Adidas** and unveiled her "Respect Me" clothing and footwear line. This is the first Adidas collaboration with a rap artist since **Run DMC** in the 1980s. In 2005, Missy launched her new UPN television reality series, *The Road to Stardom*, which spotlights thirteen aspiring rap artists and singers who travel on a dingy tour bus and compete for $100,000 and a recording contract. Missy serves as co-executive producer of the series and judges the contestants, along with R & B singer Teena Marie, producer Dallas Austin, and Mona Scott, President of Violator Management.

DISCOGRAPHY: *Supa Dupa Fly* (East/West Records, 1997); *Da Real World* (East/West Records, 1999); *Miss E ... So Addictive* (East/West Records, 2001); *Under Construction* (East/West Records, 2001); *This Is a Test* (Elektra Records, 2003).

MIXER

The core of the traditional DJ setup, the mixer provides a way to set the levels between different audio sources. Mixers vary, based on models and brands. In the simplest form, a mixer will have two channels, normally with each channel split into one phono input and one line input. The input type will be switchable, normally via a toggle switch. Each channel will have its own level control, in the form of a vertical channel fader, generally referred to as the "up" fader. This mechanism is essential in keeping the levels going to the **cross fader** consistent.

The cross fader, where the actual mixing occurs, is near the bottom of the mixer. The cross fader is a horizontal sliding lever, which allows the

DJ to affect a single record or to move easily back and forth between two turntables when working with multiple records. In Hip Hop, DJs usually use two turntables, with headphones connected to a mixer.

Kool DJ Herc and **Grandmaster Flash** were integral to the development of the modern mixer. Without it, Hip Hop DJing could not developed as it has. Before the invention of the cross fader, DJs had to use two hands to move sound between the two turntables, using the volume control. With the cross fader, the DJ needs only one hand and can use the free hand to perform techniques such as backspinning, cutting, scratching, mixing, blending, and punch-phrasing.

MIXTAPES

Beginning in the early 1970s in New York City with the advent of Hip Hop, audiocassettes that showcased DJ skills and captured DJ musical performances were sold on the street and in small, local record stores. Mixtapes progressed from mere recordings of music played at events to offerings that introduced new rap artists, commercially unreleased songs, and exclusive **remixes** of commercially released songs made by independent producers. Although mixtapes produced by major record companies are now available, the vast majority of mixtapes continue to be unauthorized, **underground** commodities made by independent record producers and are sold on the Internet, on the street by vendors, or by neighborhood record retailers.

Mixtapes remain crucial to rap music as a vehicle to scout talent and as a means to market to Hip Hop's urban base. In 1995, renowned record promoter Orpheous "Justo" Faison founded the annual Mixtape Awards in New York City to acknowledge the efforts of innovative Hip Hop, R & B, and reggae DJs and producers. Past Mixtape Award recipients include mixtape legends Ron G and Brucie B and **DJ Kay Slay**.

MOBB DEEP

As Mobb Deep, Havoc [Kejuan Muchita] and Prodigy [Albert Johnson] are widely recognized as exemplifying the best of East Coast hardcore rap music. While most hardcore rap music can be dismissed for its nihilism, materialism, and one-dimensional figures, Mobb Deep have risen above the crowd with their bleak stories about street life in New York City.

The two Queens, New York, natives met as teenagers while attending the High School of Graphic Arts in Manhattan. In 1993, the rap duo released their debut album, *Juvenile Hell,* on the 4th & Broadway label. *Juvenile Hell* did little to readily distinguish Mobb Deep from the pack of mediocre artists, either financially or creatively. It did, however, set the stage for Mobb Deep's unique sound. Not only did Mobb Deep produce their own beats, the duo also developed a street-wise, yet poetic approach to articulating the trials and tribulations of ghetto life.

Mobb Deep's unique sound brought them to the attention of the fledging Loud Records and in 1995 they signed a recording deal. Two years later, with the release of their sophomore album, *The Infamous* (Loud Records), Mobb Deep sent shock waves through the rap music **underground**. The album was definitely driven by the singles "Shook Ones, Pt. 2," as well as "Survival of the Fittest," and "Temperature's Rising." "Shook Ones, Pt. 2," would become an anthem for hardcore rap music fans. Mobb Deep's haunting lyrics were complemented by hard-hitting beats.

In 1996, Mobb Deep released their third album, *Hell on Earth* (Loud Records), which debuted at number 6 on the *Billboard* album chart. The album furthered the rap style that the duo had honed on *The Infamous,* with its evocative music and vivid rhymes about the grimy, underbelly of New York. Through their music video for the title single, "Hell On Earth (Front Lines)," and the photos in their CD booklet replete with guns and drugs, Havoc and Prodigy crafted a gangster image that had not firmly taken hold on the East Coast.

In June of that year, **Death Row Records** released the **Tupac Shakur** single "Hit 'Em Up," a brutal diatribe against a slew of East Coast figures, including **The Notorious B.I.G.**, **Bad Boy Entertainment**, and Mobb Deep.

The fourth album from Mobb Deep was highly anticipated to the point that, while *Murda Muzik* (Loud Records) was in its early stages of production, rough versions of nearly thirty songs were bootlegged on the streets and on the Internet. In the aftermath of the bootlegs and several delays, *Murda Muzik* was not released until early 1999. The album debuted at number 3 on *Billboard* album chart and quickly went platinum on the strength of the single "Quiet Storm," a track that represented the duo's dark, thugged-out style.

The **remix** version featuring **Lil' Kim** helped to give the single more radio play and thus wider exposure. In 2000, Prodigy released his solo album, *H.N.I.C.* (Relativity Records), which was well received by Mobb Deep fans. When *Infamy* (Loud Records) was released in 2001 with three tracks featuring R & B singers 112, Lil Mo, and Ronald Isley, it was met with mixed reactions. The radio-friendly track "Hey Luv," featuring 112, garnered the harshest criticism about Mobb Deep having gone commercial.

In 2002, Loud Records ceased to exist and in the aftermath Mobb Deep did a one-off deal with Land Speed Records and in 2003 released the double CD *Free Agents.* With forty-one tracks and guest appearances from numerous artists, including **Kool G Rap**, **50 Cent**, and **Ice-T**, it is a sloppy effort at best and thankfully is not a well-known or easily available recording. Despite the failure of *Free Agents,* Mobb Deep's body of work helped them to land a deal with Jive Records in 2003. In 2004, Mobb Deep released *Amerikaz Nightmare* (Jive Records), which included production help from **Lil Jon** and **Kanye West** and appearances by Nate Dogg and Twista. While the album was not exactly panned, the consensus seemed to be that even if it was better than quite a bit of rap music out that year, yet it did not compare with *The Infamous* or with *Hell on Earth.*

In October 2004, Mobb Deep released *Mix Tape Before 9/11* (Cleopatra Records).

DISCOGRAPHY: *Juvenile Hell* (4th & Broadway/Polygram, 1993); *The Infamous* (Loud Records, 1995); *Hell On Earth* (Loud Records, 1996); Murda Muzik (Loud Records, 1999); *Infamy* (Loud Records, 2001); *Free Agents* (Land Speed Records, 2003) *Amerikaz Nightmare* (Jive Records, 2004); *Mix Tape Before 9/11* (Cleopatra Records, 2004).

MONEY

Slang terms for money include benjamins, chedda, cheese, cream, dead presidents, dough, grip, loots, paper, and scrilla.

MONIE LOVE [Simone Johnson]

Recognized as the British rap artist who has had the most success with American rap music audiences in Hip Hop history, Monie Love is best known for her 1990 hit single, "Monie in the Middle" (Warner Bros. Records).

As a teenager, the rap artist was already a known entity in her native Great Britain. In 1989, she came to the United States and linked up with the **Native Tongues**, which included the **Jungle Brothers**, **De La Soul,** and **Queen Latifah**. Monie made her debut recording debut on Queen Latifah's classic single "Ladies First," from the album *All Hail The Queen*" (Tommy Boy Records, 1993). Monie also appeared on the De La Soul track "Buddy," from the album *3 Feet High and Rising* (Tommy Boy Records, 1989).

Known for her quick, lightning delivery, Monie Love released two solo albums, first *Down to Earth* (Warner Bros. Records, 1990), her debut album, which spawned the infectious singles "Monie in the Middle" and "It's a Shame (My Sister)," and then *In a Word or 2* (Warner Bros. Records, 1993). She contributed vocals to **Common**'s 2000 album, *Like Water for Chocolate*. Monie is currently an on-air personality for New York's Power 105.1 radio station (WWPR-FM).

DISCOGRAPHY: *Down to Earth* (Warner Bros. Records, 1990); *In a Word or 2* (Warner Bros. Records, 1993).

M.O.P.

As M.O.P., or Mash Out Posse, Lil Fame [Jamal Grinnage] and Billy Danze [Eric Murray] are recognized as one of the most lyrically confor-mational acts in rap music. Long before the hype around rock-rap bands such as **Limp Bizkit**, Korn, and Link, M.O.P. were using rock samples to create hardcore rap music.

The duo from the rough-and-tumble Brownsville section of Brooklyn, New York, hit the music scene in 1993. They are best known for their debut single, "How About Some Hardcore," as well as the singles "Ante Up" and "Cold As Ice." In 1992, Laze E. Laze put Lil Fame on a compilation album that he produced, called *The Hill That's Real* (4th and Broadway). Shortly thereafter Fame sent Laze a recording of a song of him rapping along side Billy Danze, produced by D.R. Period. The song was the duo's signature hit, the anthem "How About Some Hardcore."

The strength of that single, which was accompanied by an $8,000 video from a then-unknown director named **Hype Williams**, led to the release M.O.P.'s debut album, *To The Death* (Select Records, 1994). The album sold modestly, but caught the ear of **Gang Starr**'s DJ Premier. Premier created the first of the "Downtown Swinga" series of songs, which appeared on the M.O.P.'s sophomore album, *Firing Squad* (Relativity Records, 1996). Premier would also lend his considerable skills to future M.O.P. albums.

The group followed up with the album *First Family 4 Life* (Relativity Records, 1998) and with the EP *Handle Ur Bizness* (Relativity Records, 1998). Under financial strain, Relativity folded in 1999 and Loud Records acquired M.O.P.'s contract. In 2000, the group released their most successful album, *Warrioz* (Loud Records), which spawned two hits, "Cold as Ice" and the raucous "Ante Up." The "Ante Up Remix" featured **Busta Rhymes**, Teflon, and Remy Martin. M.O.P. was now primed to have their sales match their status as **underground** rap stars. Unfortunately, in 2002 while promoting *Warrioz* overseas, where both songs were chart hits, Loud Records closed its doors. In yet another record company shuffle, M.O.P. was now under the control of Loud's distributor, Columbia Records. The momentum of "Ante Up" and "Cold As Ice" soon fizzled and the duo wanted out of their contract. Negotiations with Columbia Records were at a standstill for about a year and a half.

Once released from Columbia, the duo joined forces with **Roc-A-Fella Records**. **Jay-Z** had made a guest appearance on the track "4 Alarm Blaze," from the album *First Family 4 Life* (Relativity Records, 1998), and Damon Dash had been interested in acquiring the group for some years. Once on Roc-A-Fella, M.O.P. quickly left the gate, first appearing on the single "Put It in the Air," featuring Jay-Z, which turned up on **mixtapes** for several months. The single "Wanna Be G's," produced by Billy Danze, was on the *Bad Boys II* film soundtrack and M.O.P. appeared on the Jay-Z track "U Don't Know" (**remix**) from his album, *The Blueprint 2: The Gift & The Curse*. M.O.P.'s first album to be released on Roc-A-Fella is *Ghetto Warfare*, is expected in 2005.

In the meantime, M.O.P. hooked up with New York–based rock band, Shiner Massive, to retool some M.O.P. classics for their self-titled album, *Mash Out Posse (M.O.P.)* (Fastlife Records).

DISCOGRAPHY: *Single*: "How About Some Hardcore." *EP: Handle Ur Bizness* (Relativity Records, 1998). *Albums*: *To the Death* (Select Records, 1994); *Firing Squad* (Relativity Records, 1996); *Family 4 Life* (Relativity Records, 1998); *Warrioz* (Loud Records, 2000); *Mash Out Posse (M.O.P.)* (Fastlife, 2004).

MOS DEF [Dante Terrell "Beze" Smith]

Originally a darling of the rap music **underground**, the multi-faceted Mos Def came aboveground as solo rap artist, actor, and member of the rap duo, **Black Star**.

Born in Brooklyn, New York, Mos Def pursued the arts at an early age, and showed promise as a versatile performer. Growing up in the 1980s, Mos was surrounding by the influences of Hip Hop. He began rhyming at age nine; however, he was also influenced by jazz and rock music. After high school, he began acting in a variety of television roles, and in 1994 appeared on the short-lived Bill Cosby series, *The Cosby Mysteries*. Mos became discontented with acting and turned to music.

With the encouragement of his younger brother, he formed the group Urban Thermo Dynamics (UTD), with his younger sister and DCQ. In 1994, UTD signed to Payday and released their first single, "My Kung Fu." They followed up with the classic single "Manifest Destiny." Although the two singles were the setup for their debut album, *Manifest Destiny*, Payday never released it. After the end of UTD, Mos would join up with members of the **Native Tongues** and in 1996 he appeared on the **De La Soul** track, "Big Brother Beat," from the album *Stake is High*

Mos Def in the 2004 film *The Woodsman*. *Courtesy of Photofest.*

(Tommy Boy Records) and Da Bush Babees' track "Love Song," from the album *Gravity* (Warner Bros. Records). These performances helped to launch Mos's music career.

In 1997, Mos released the single "Universal Magnetic" on his own Royalty Records. The popular single combined jazz-inspired beats and intelligent lyrics, instantly making Mos a star in the underground rap music scene. Soon thereafter Mos signed with the independent Rawkus Records and the label reissued "Universal Magnetic."

In 1997, Mos worked with **Talib Kweli**, for the first time producing the legendary "Fortified Live" collaboration, which appeared on the *Soundbombing Vol. I* compilation. In Talib Kweli, Mos found a kindred spirit, another socially conscious artist who understood the immense influence of Hip Hop. The two men officially joined forces to form **Black Star** (in honor of Marcus Garvey's, named for his Black Star Line). In 1998, they released their debut album, *Mos Def and Talib Kweli Are ... Blackstar* (Rawkus Records). Considered one of the most important albums of the year, it was a testament to Black love as well to social and political empowerment.

In 1999, Mos released his first solo album, *Black On Both Sides* (Rawkus Records). The gold-selling album represented Mos's journey both as an artist and as a Black man in America. Moreover, *Black on Both Sides* solidified his place among the rap music elite. People who have not really listened to the hit single from the album, "Ms. Fat Booty," a type of urban love song, might see it as sexist, rather than a stab at light-hearted humor. Mos, however, is dismissive of people who call his rap music "alternative" or even "conscious," seeing those labels as ways to distance him and his message from Black people and from his experience with Hip Hop, a diverse idiom. That same year, Mos Def reteamed with UTD member DCQ to form Medina Green. The underground hit single "Crosstown Beef" appears on Rawkus Records 1999 *Soundbombing Compilation II.*

Beginning in 1997, Mos Def appeared in his first film, *Where's Marlone.* Throughout the first few years of the 2000s, Mos would appear on numerous television programs and act in films such as Spike Lee's *Bamboozled* (2000), *Monster's Ball* (2001), *Brown Sugar* (2002), and *The Italian Job* (2003). He would also host the HBO series "**Russell Simmons** Presents Def Poetry." Preceding **Sean "P. Diddy" Combs** on the *Great White Way,* in 2002 Mos starred in the Tony Award-nominated, Pulitzer Prize-winning play, *TopDog/Underdog* by Suzan-Lori Parks. Mos received an Obie Award for his performance in the off-Broadway play *Fucking A,* also written by Parks.

In 2004, Mos Def received an Emmy nomination for Outstanding Lead Actor in a Miniseries or a Movie and then a 2005 Golden Globe Award nomination for his critically acclaimed role in the HBO film *Something the Lord Made.*

During this period, Mos Def formed a rock band, Black Jack Johnson, to create an authentic rap-rock hybrid album, where both rap and rock equally coexist on the tracks, as distinguished from rock bands who have adopted only the posturing of rap music. Moreover, Mos also wanted to use the project to instill the idea that rock, although co-opted by White artists such as Elvis Presley, is nonetheless part of the Black music tradition.

In 2004, Mos released, *The New Danger* (Geffen Records), five years after his solo album debut. Although the record received critical praise and debuted at number 5 on the *Billboard*'s Top 200 Album Chart, some fans were not enthusiastic about the blurring of genre lines. With some tracks by Black Jack Johnson, Mos explores rap, rock, jazz, soul, and blues. Other fans however loved the fact that, just as Saul Williams did on his underappreciated album *Amethyst Rock Star* (American Records, 2001), Mos expands the boundaries of rap music beyond percussion-influenced beats, tired ghetto tales, and rants about conspicuous consumption.

Mos received a 2005 Grammy Award nomination for Best Urban/Alternative Performance for the single, "Sex, Love and Money."

DISCOGRAPHY: *Singles*: "Universal Magnetic" (Royalty, 1997; re-issued by Rawkus Records in 1997). *Albums*: as Black Star, *Mos Def & Talib Kweli are ... Blackstar* (Rawkus Records, 1998); *Black On Both Sides* (Rawkus, 1999); *The New Danger* (Geffen, 2004).

MR. MAGIC'S RAP ATTACK

With his *Mr. Magic's Rap Attack* as the first regularly scheduled rap music radio program in the nation, the Connecticut native also became the first rap radio celebrity. He is credited with being the first to provide his listeners with gossip about rap artists. In 1979, the former rap artist debuted *Mr. Magic's Rap Attack* on a small New Jersey radio station, **WHBI** (WNWK), which aired on Saturday nights from 2 to 5 a.m. The show sold airtime for approximately $100 per hour and Mr. Magic, with an electronics store as his first sponsor, began *Magic's Disco Showcase*. The show's new name reflected the fact that the emerging genre was not yet called Hip Hop.

The radio program not only played music, but conducted interviews with rap artists and guests such as **Kurtis Blow** and **Melle Mel**, who began to rap on the show. Subsequently, the show changed it name to *Mr. Magic's Rap Attack*. Around 1981, *Mr. Magic's Rap Attack* moved to New York on the Black-owned radio station WBLS-FM with producer **Marley Marl** as the in-house DJ. *Mr. Magic's Rap Attack* would help to birth the **Juice Crew All Stars**. (Coincidentally Mr. Magic had attended Sarah J. Hale High School with **Big Daddy Kane**.)

The show competed with **DJ Red Alert** on KISS-FM (WRKS). *Mr. Magic's Rap Attack*'s tenure on WBLS-FM would end in 1989. Around

1995, Mr. Magic joined with Mister Cee (Big Daddy Kane's DJ) on New York's Hot 97 (WKYS-FM), where they played Old School classics every Sunday night. Mr. Magic, beginning in 1985, also released a series of compilations with performances culled from his radio show, which included many of rap music's luminaries. In 2002, Mr. Magic stepped into the video age, overseeing the soundtrack for the **video game** "Grand Theft Auto: Vice City, Vol. 5: Wildstyle." The compilation contains twenty-one tracks of Old School Hip Hop, including **Run DMC**, **Whodini**, and **Grandmaster Flash and the Furious Five**.

DISCOGRAPHY: *Mr. Magic's Rap Attack* (Profile Records, 1985); *Mr. Magic's Rap Attack, Vol. 2* (Profile Records, 1986); *Mr. Magic's Rap Attack, Vol. 3* (Profile Records, 1987); *Mr. Magic's Rap Attack, Vol. 4* (Profile Records, 1988); *Mr. Magic's Rap Attack, Vol. 5* (Profile Records, 1989).

Mystikal. *Courtesy of Photofest.*

MYSTIKAL [Michael Tyler]

Called the **James Brown** of rap because of his screaming, fast rhyming and sometimes less than crisp articulation, Mystikal became known as one of the top artists on **Master P**'s No Limit Records, and one of the first rap artists from New Orleans to get nationwide exposure.

After a stint in the U.S. army that included a tour in the first Gulf War, Mystikal returned to New Orleans and to the music career that he had begun as a teenager. In 1995, he released his debut album *Mystikal* in Big Boy Records. The album brought him to the attention of Jive Records, who signed him to a record deal. In 1996, Jive Records reissued the album as *The Mind of Mystikal*, with a few additional tracks. The album became a success on the **underground** and came close to selling gold.

With Steady Mobb'n's track "It's On," Mystikal made his first appearance on No Limit Records. Mystikal then made a guest appearance on the track "What 'Cha Think" from the *I'm Bout It* film soundtrack. Master P, impressed with Mystikal's flow signed him to No Limit Records. In 1997, Mystikal released his first No Limit album, the platinum-selling *Unpredictable*. In 1999, Mystikal released *Ghetto Fabulous*, another platinum-selling album.

During this period it was becoming clear that Mystikal's music had moved away from the No Limit message and his stature as an artist would require more than the Master P's inexpensive, assembly line treatment. Mystikal decided to leave No Limit and return to Jive Records. To capitalize on Mystikal's success in rapid fashion, Jive Records released *Let's Get Ready,* which debuted at number 1 on the *Billboard* album chart, driven by the monumental hit by radio-friendly singles "Shake Ya Ass" and "Danger." *Let's Get Ready* surpassed his prior album sales, and "Shake Ya Ass" became an MTV staple and provided Mystikal with crossover appeal.

In 2001, Mystikal's high-energy rap stylings came together for a fifth album, *Tarantula* (Jive Records). "Bouncin' Back (Bumpin' Me Against the Wall)" was one of 2002's hottest singles, although some critics called it nothing more than "Shake Ya Ass 2."

In 2002, Mystikal received two Grammy Award nominations, one for Best Male Rap Solo Performance and another for Best Rap Album. In July 2002, however, Mystikal's career came to a halt when he was charged with sexual battery. Police stated that Mystikal and two bodyguards forced his hairstylist to perform sex acts after he accused her of cashing $80,000 worth of his checks. Mystikal originally pleaded innocent; however, a videotape of the incident surfaced. In January 2005, he was found guilty in a Baton Rouge, Louisiana, court and sentenced to six years in prison.

DISCOGRAPHY: *Mystikal* (Big Boy Records, 1995), re-issued as *Mind Of Mystikal* (Jive Records, 1995); *Unpredictable* (No Limit Records, 1997); *Ghetto Fabulous* (No Limit Records, 1998); *Let's Get Ready* (Jive Records, 2000); *Tarantula* (Jive Records, 2001).

N

NAME BUCKLES (Name Belts)

Brass belt buckles worn on a wide, unadorned, black leather belt that spell out the name of the wearer and which came into fashion in the mid-1980s. Name belts resurfaced again around the year 2000.

NAMES

Performers within in the Hip Hop community have routinely renamed themselves, reflecting a common practice within African American culture. Artists adopt names that represent how they see themselves or how they wish to be seen. For example, artists Edward "Duke" Ellington and William "Count" Basie chose monikers that connoted royalty. Other artists, such as writer LeRoi Jones (Amiri Baraka) adopted African names, to reflect a rejection of names that originated in slavery. Hip Hop performers would continue the practice, choosing names that speak to their mastery of an aspect of Hip Hop, personal characteristics, or are just a play on real names. For instance, "Grandmaster," as used by DJs, is a term that represents the highest level of achievement, while "**Mos Def**" literally means the best, and **YoYo** is short for Yolanda.

NAS (aka Nas Escobar, aka Nasty Nas) [Nasir Bin Olu Dara Jones]

The self-proclaimed "King of New York," Nas is recognized as one of rap music's leading voices for his intelligent lyrics and superior storytelling skills, and he is considered by many to be the lyrical successor to the legendary Rakim (**Eric B & Rakim**).

Although Nas's career has had its peaks and valleys, his longevity and importance within rap music and Hip Hop may be due to his willingness to explore new aspects of himself as he matures, rather than sticking to pat formulas to get airplay or simply reworking the same ghetto tales on successive albums. In the ten years since his debut album, *Illmatic* (Columbia Records, 1994), Nas has moved from young hard head to cocksure Mafioso to a humbled elder dropping knowledge. With each album, Nas keeps listeners intrigued and interested in what he will do next.

Nas is the son of jazz musician Olu Dara. He dropped out of school in the eighth grade, and headed for the tough streets surrounding the **Queensbridge** housing projects, immortalized by producer **Marley Marl**

Nas. *Courtesy of Photofest.*

and his **Juice Crew All Stars** on the classic track, "The Bridge." Despite his lack of formal education, Nas nonetheless became highly literate and this characteristic filters into the fabric of his street-wise, yet incisive rhymes. Nas has been seen as a gifted rap artist from the time he appeared on the track "Live at the BBQ," from **Main Source**'s 1991 album *Breaking Atoms* (Wild Pitch Records). His cameo appearance instantly earned him the respect of East Coast rap music fans. Shortly thereafter, MC Serch (**3rd Bass**), the executive producer for the soundtrack for the film *Zebrahead* (1992), approached Nas about contributing a track. Nas submitted the track "Halftime," and the song so impressed Serch that he made it the soundtrack's lead single. Subsequently, Columbia Records signed Nas to a recording contract.

Producers **DJ Premier**, **Large Professor**, and **Pete Rock** worked with Nas to create his debut album, *Illmatic*. Upon release, *Illmatic* received unequivocal praise, spawning multiple hits, and was quickly hailed a rap music classic; however, *Illmatic* initially only sold gold (it went platinum in December 2001).

In 1996, Nas would follow with his sophomore album, *It Was Written* (Columbia Records), making production changes to attract a broader audience. The double-platinum album *It Was Written* was largely produced by Trackmasters and it distinguishes itself from *Illmatic* in that it contains tracks that seem specifically designed to gain radio play and have crossover appeal, notably "Street Dreams" and "If I Ruled the World (Imagine That)," which sample the Eurythmics and **Kurtis Blow**, respectively. *It Was Written* did garner Nas more widespread attention, but many Nas fans became concerned that he was moving away from his musical roots as he pursued more record buyers. This criticism would escalate with his next few albums.

In the aftermath of the killing of **The Notorious B.I.G.** in 1997, Nas, with only a handful of other artists, ruled the East Coast's rap elite. In 1998, Nas would make his acting debut in the **Hype Williams** film *Belly*, alongside fellow rap artist **DMX**, and he also contributed to the film's soundtrack. Nas would also lead the short-lived supergroup **The Firm**, comprised of rap artists, **Foxy Brown**, AZ, and Nature. The group released their eponymous debut in 1997 on Aftermath Records.

In 1999, Nas released two albums, the double-platinum *I Am* (Columbia Records) and the platinum *Nastradamus* (Columbia Records). On *Nastradamus,* Nas crafted an action-packed mafia tale, which played like an urban gangster film. In 2000, harking back to his Queensbridge roots, Nas assembled fellow Queensbridge rap artists for the compilation album *Nas and Ill Will Records Presents . . . Queensbridge: The Album* (Columbia Records, 2000).

After the release of the *Nastradamus* and *The Firm* albums, at a heightened pitch, detractors stated that Nas had abandoned thoughtful rap music for simplistic gangster stories as a means of gaining of cashing in on the popularity of **gangsta rap**. Ironically, as Nas gained more attention from the MTV audience, his reputation was flagging on the streets and among his core fan base.

In 2001, the trials of Nas's personal life and his music career came to a head when **Jay-Z** openly dissed Nas on the track "Takeover," the lead single on his popular *Blueprint* album (**Roc-A-Fella Records**, 2001). During this period, not only was Nas's mother suffering from cancer, but a soured romantic relationship became fodder for "Takeover." Jay-Z, whose multi-platinum albums have consistently appealed to traditional rap audiences and pop audiences, taunted Nas for not having had a "hot" album since *Illmatic.* Jay-Z had risen to the top of the East Coast rap scene, while Nas stepped back from the public eye to deal with his personal life and to reassess his career.

Nas came forward out of the shadows with a much-circulated **underground** freestyle rap over the beat to Eric B & Rakim's famous track, "Paid in Full." The 2001 album *Stillmatic* (Columbia Records), possibly Nas's best album since *Illmatic*, received tremendous praise from critics and fans alike. Nas blatantly attacks Jay-Z on the track "Ether," which features the chant "f*** Jay-Z." Perhaps Nas's most aggressive single ever, "Get Ur Self A . . . ," samples the theme song from the hit HBO television mafia series, *The Sopranos*.

With the release of these two tracks, Nas's star rose again on the streets and he regained fans who had lost interest in him. Moreover, the music video for his reflective and moving track, "One Mic," was played regularly on MTV and B.E.T. *Stillmatic* helped Nas to repair his professional reputation and reclaim his place among in the rap music pantheon.

Riding the wave of his renewed popularity, Nas made a number of guest appearances throughout 2002, among them on Brandy's "What About Us?," J-Lo's "I'm Gonna Be Alright," and **Ja Rule**'s "The Pledge." Columbia Records capitalized on Nas's comeback with the release of two albums comprised largely of archival material: *From Illmatic to Stillmatic (This is the Remix)* (2002) and *The Lost Tapes* (2002), the latter containing outtakes of Nas's tracks.

To thwart bootlegging of Nas's his next album, *God's Son,* Columbia Records quickly released it at the end of 2003. The platinum-selling *God's Son*, a more personally themed album, garnered acclaim for Nas, as well as sizable album sales, spawning the hits "Thugz Mansion (N.Y.)" and "Made You Look," a collaboration with **Tupac Shakur**, and the Top 40 hit "I Can," which features the voices of children and encourages them to reach their full potential. In 2004, Nas released the universally heralded album *Street's Disciple*, an ambitious album that goes beyond party-themed rap music by not only talking about women and the streets, but also about politics and Black culture. Aside from its musical value, the double CD *Street's Disciple* (Columbia Records), executive-produced by Nas, is important because, in several aspects, it is a family affair. The collection is dedicated to his mother, Ann Jones; it features his father Olu Dara on the tracks "Street's Disciple" and "Bridging the Gap" (he played the trumpet on Nas's debut album); and also includes his new wife, the singer Kelis, who appears on the tracks "American Way" and "Getting Married." Nas also pays homage to his rap family by including the track "U.B.R. (Unauthorized Biography of Rakim)" (which ends with a statement that he will profile **KRS-ONE** next go around) and by including Old School rap star **Doug E. Fresh** on the track "Virgo."

DISCOGRAPHY: *Illmatic* (Columbia Records, 1994); *It Was Written* (Columbia Records, 1996); *I am* (Columbia Records, 1999); *Nastradamus* (Columbia Records, 1999); *Stillmatic* (Columbia Records, 2001); *From Illmatic to Stillmatic (This is the Remix)* (Columbia Records, 2002); *The Lost Tapes* (Columbia Records, 2002); *God's Son* (Columbia Records, 2003); *Street's Disciple* (Columbia Records, 2004).

NATION OF ISLAM (aka The Nation)

The Nation of Islam is an Islamic denomination that has gained traction in Black communities throughout the United States. Male followers of the Nation of Islam are a familiar sight in urban areas. They are men traditionally dressed in dark suits with white shirts and red bow ties, often selling copies of the newspaper *The Final Call*, which currently claims a weekly circulation of half a million.

The Nation of Islam gained mainstream attention in 1964 when the world heavyweight boxing champion Cassius Clay joined the Nation of Islam and changed his name to Muhammad Ali. Malcolm Little ("Detroit Red") converted to Islam while in prison and became a minister within the Nation of Islam. The Nation of Islam was founded in 1930 in Detroit, Michigan, by Wallace D. Fard (later known as Master Fard Muhammad). Most of Fard's early followers were African American migrants from the South, who because of racial discrimination and economic conditions frequently resided in ghettos in the industrial cities of the North. Fard is believed to have at one time been an orthodox Muslim who came from Mecca. Fard's followers understood him to be an incarnation of Allah, who had come to liberate what he called the "Lost–Found Nation of Islam in the West." Fard promised Blacks that if they heeded his teachings and gained knowledge of themselves they would prevail over their White "slave masters" and become exalted people around the world.

There are Nation of Islam mosques in approximately 120 American cities. The Minister Louis Farrakhan became the leader of the Nation of Islam in 1975 after the death of the Minister Elijah Muhammad, whose followers had believed him to have been the most recent "messenger from Allah." The appeal of the Nation of Islam is not hard to fathom, in that it teaches Black people pride and self-respect, and not only provides a national identity, but more importantly hope and a sense of self-determination. Despite its social conservatism and dubious scholarship, the Nation of Islam attracts followers and sympathizers because of its commitment to social programs, particularly its outreach to prisoners, and because of its promotion of personal responsibility and morality.

Since the early days of Hip Hop and rap music, many artists have been attracted to or joined the Nation of Islam, subsequently including its teachings in their work. Minister Louis Farrakhan has been mentioned and his speeches sampled in many rap songs. He has also been a guest at Hip Hop conferences and called upon to mediate disputes between rap artists. Prominent rap artists who have been associated with the Nation of Islam as members or affiliates include **Ice Cube**, **Public Enemy**, Kam, Professor Griff, and **Paris**.

NATIVE TONGUE, THE (aka Native Tongues)

The Native Tongue was an informal group of artists united by the sense that rap music had grown stale with materialism and ghetto stylings. Beginning in 1988 with **A Tribe Called Quest**, **De la Soul**, and the **Jungle Brothers**, the Native Tongues movement did away with macho posturing in rap and instead embraced Afrohumanisn and social issues, with humor and creativity. Perhaps most novel was their inclusion of female rap artists **Queen Latifah** and **Monie Love**. By 1993, as asserted on the track "I am I Be" from *Bulhoone Mindstate* (Tommy Boy Records), the Native Tongues were fracturing. In 1996, on the album *Stake Is High* (Tommy Boy Records), De La Soul was indicating that the Native Tongues were back, but the declaration seems hollow in the absence of other original Native Tongues members. The final death knell for the Native Tongue movement was the demise of A Tribe Called Quest in 1998.

NAUGHTY BY NATURE

MCs Treach [Anthony Criss], Vinnie [Vincent Brown], and DJ Kay Gee [Keir Gist] make up Naughty By Nature, a rap trio known for creating popular, radio-friendly anthems while also maintaining street credibility.

In 1986, as students attending the same high school in East Orange, New Jersey, Treach, Vinnie, and Kay Gee formed a rap group, New Style. In 1988, The New Style would sign a recording contract with Bon Ami Records and in 1989 release the album, *Independent Leaders* (Bon Ami/MCA).

Naughty By Nature. *Courtesy of Photofest.*

New Style began performing at local talent shows and was discovered by fellow New Jersey native **Queen Latifah**, who ran Flavor Unit management. Queen Latifah would be instrumental in the group's securing a recording contract with Tommy Boy Records in 1990 under their new name, Naughty By Nature.

In 1991, the trio released their self-titled album on Tommy Boy Records. The platinum-selling album spawned the Top Ten hit, "O.P.P.," which stands for "Other People's Property (though there is also an X-rated alternative for the meaning of the third 'P'). The song had huge crossover appeal, yet the music did not alienate Naughty By Nature from **underground** audiences. In 1993, Naughty By Nature would build on their success with their album *19 Naughty III*, which included the track "Hip Hop Hooray," which became a ubiquitous chant. *19 Naughty III* hit the Top Five on the music charts and, like the previous album, went platinum.

Naughty By Nature's last album for Tommy Boy Records was the 1995 gold-selling *Poverty's Paradise.* A catchy single did not emerge from this album, but its value was acknowledged in 1996 with a Grammy for Best Rap Album and the single "Feel Me Flow" was nominated for Best Rap Performance By A Duo Or Group.

The group went on a hiatus and during this period Treach concentrated on an acting career that had begun in 1992 with his appearance in the film *Juice*, starring **Tupac Shakur**. Treach won acclaim for his recurring role on the HBO television prison drama *Oz.* In 1998, Treach would marry Pepa of the rap group **Salt 'N Pepa**; the couple would divorce two years later. Kay Gee continued to do production work for artists such Zhané, Aaliyah, and Krayzie Bone (of **Bone Thugs-N-Harmony**).

In 1998, Naughty By Nature and Tommy Boy Records were sued by Wesaline Music for breach of contract and related causes of action in connection to a 1988 songwriter's agreement that the group had entered into as New Style. In 1999 Naughty By Nature, now signed to Arista Records, released the gold-selling album *19 Naughty Nine: Nature's Fury.* The track "Jamboree," featuring Zhané, was a modest success. After the release of *19 Naughty Nine: Nature's Fury,* Kay Gee left the group amid internal friction; however, all members state publicly that he had chosen to focus on producing.

Continuing as a duo, Treach and Vinnie eventually entered into a recording deal with TVT Records, and in early 2002 they released the album *IIcons.* In recent years, Vinnie has become an advocate for young people and has worked directly with the mayor of his home city, East Orange, New Jersey, to take his message of social and political empowerment to high schools. Moreover, he has worked on various AIDS-related causes. Treach continues to act and appeared in the film *Empire* (2002) with John Leguizamo. He also cohosted the syndicated television show, *The Source All-Access.*

DISCOGRAPHY: *The New Styles—Independent Leaders* (Bon Ami/ MCA, 1989); *Naughty By Nature* (Tommy Boy Records, 1991); *19 Naughty III* (Tommy Boy Records, 1993); *Poverty's Paradise* (Tommy Boy Records, 1995); *19 Naughty Nine: Nature's Fury* (Arista Records, 1999); *IIcons* (TVT Records, 2002).

NELLY [Cornell Haynes Jr.]

Recognized for putting the Midwestern city of St. Louis, Missouri, on the rap music map, and so representing neither the East Coast or the Dirty South, Nelly's pop-infused style synthesizes his Southern-infected tone with colloquialisms culled from the Midwest's rap scene.

Nelly. *Courtesy of Photofest.*

Nelly remains a member of the St. Lunatics, a rap group he formed with some high school friends. In 1996, the group scored a regional hit with a self-produced single, "Gimmie What You Got." After failing to secure a recording contract as a group, the members of St. Lunatics decided that Nelly would be best able to obtain a deal as a solo artist and that the other members would then follow with their own solo albums. Nelly did gain the attention of Universal Records and was signed to a recording deal. When Nelly's debut album *Country Grammar* appeared in 2000, many considered Nelly a flash in the pan. Nelly, however, proved critics and many rap music fans wrong, gaining a cross section of fans with his catchy sing-along lyrics. The title single, "Country Grammar (Hot . . .)," became the summer anthem, and the album would sell nine times platinum.

In the summer of 2001, Nelly released his sophomore album, *Nellyville* (Universal Records) The album topped the *Billboard* album chart and the **Neptunes**-produced lead single, "Hot in Herre," stayed on top of the *Billboard* singles chart. Overall, Nelly held the number 1 spot on ten different *Billboard* charts for the week of *Nellyville's* release. In 2001, The St. Lunatics, with Nelly, released their debut album, *Free City* (Universal Records). After the release of *Nellyville*, Nelly founded several charities, including 4Sho4Kids foundation associated with bone marrow donation.

In 2002, Nelly and rap music legend, **KRS-ONE** engaged in a verbal **battle**. KRS-ONE recorded the track, "Clear Em Out," which appears on the CD *The Difference* (Official Jointz, 2002), a compilation album. The song was presumed to be a diss on Nelly, who offended many older rap artists and fans alike with his song, "Number One." The single dismisses the concept of "real Hip Hop" and touts record sales as the only important criterion in rap music. In response to "Clear Em Out," Nelly expressly took a direct swipe at KRS-ONE on rap artist Freeway's **remix** of "Rock The Mic," saying that the legend would do anything to have "one more hit" and claims the Blastmaster is the first rap artist in need of a pension plan. Shortly thereafter at a live performance called "Real Hip Hop," KRS-ONE responded back with a freestyled rhyme that slammed Nelly. New York radio personality, Wendy Williams played the two-minute sequence on her WBLS-FM show. Thereafter KRS-ONE recorded the track "The Real Hip Hop is Over Here" and called for a boycott of *Nellyville*.

Nelly again courted trouble in August 2003, when he launched his energy drink, Pimp Juice. Nelly's song, "Pimp Juice" from *Nellyville* was about attracting the opposite sex and this concept was critical to the promotion and marketing of the energy drink. Many African Americans in particular believe that the drink's name is offensive and seems to condone the pimping and exploitation of women. In 2004, Nelly became the center of further controversy when women at Spelman College, a historical Black women's academic institution in Atlanta, Georgia, threatened to protest his appearance on their campus in connection to a bone marrow drive sponsored by his charity 4Sho4Kids, over the "Tip-Drill" music video, which portrays a woman as a sexual appliance. The women's position was that Nelly's charitable work did not make up for his blatant disrespect for women.

In 2003, Nelly launched his Apple Bottom clothing company for women as an addition to his VOKAL clothing line, launched in 2001. Proceeds from Apple Bottom sales will go to Jes U 4 Jackie Foundation, dedicated to educating Black people about bone marrow and stem cell transplants. Nelly's older sister Jackie Donahue was diagnosed with lukemia, which is often treated with bone marrow transplants.

Nelly collaborated with **Sean "P. Diddy" Combs** in 2003 for the huge track "Shake Ya Tailfeather," which appeared on the *Bad Boys II* film soundtrack. That same year Nelly released the remix album, *Da Derrty Versions: The Reinvention*, on his Derrty Entertainment label. In 2003, Nelly won a Grammy award for Best Male Rap Solo Performance, for "Hot in Herre," and a second Grammy award for the Best Rap/Sung Collaboration, for "Dilemma," featuring Destiny Child's Kelly Rowland.

In July 2004, Nelly joined **Jay-Z** as the first rap artists to buy minority stakes in National Basketball Association teams. Nelly became a minority owner of the North Carolina Bobcats basketball team. In March of the prior year, Nelly had purchased part of Billy Ballew Motorsports, a NASCAR Craftsmen Truck team, for the rest of the season. The truck featured Nelly's Vokal clothing line label. In 2004, Nelly made history by releasing two new separate CDs simultaneously: *Suit* (Universal Records), a mellow love-rap collection, and *Sweat* (Universal Records), aimed at the clubs.

DISCOGRAPHY: *Country Grammar* (Universal Records, 2000); *Nellyville* (Universal Records, 2002); *Suit* (Universal Records, 2004); *Sweat* (Universal Records, 2004).

NEPTUNES (also commonly referred to as N.E.R.D.)

The Neptunes, the production duo of Pharrell Williams and Chad Hugo, has emerged as one of the most successful producers of the twenty-first century, applying their skills to both rap and pop music.

The Neptunes hail from Virginia Beach, Virginia, and met in high school. The duo began quietly producing party-themed rap tracks in the late 1990s and early 2000s, including **Ol' Dirty Bastard**'s "Got My Money" (1999) and **Mystikal**'s "Shake Ya Ass" (2000). In 2001, The Neptunes expanded into pop music, producing tracks for Britney Spears's "I'm a Slave 4 U" (2001), Usher's "U Don't Have to Call" (2001), and Justin Timberlake's "Rock Your Body"(2002) and 'N SYNC's "Girlfriend" (2002). At the same time, The Neptunes continued to man the production boards for some of rap music's biggest artists, including: **LL Cool J**

("Luv U Better," 2001), **Jay-Z** ("I Wanna Love U," 2001), **Busta Rhymes** ("Pass the Courvoisier," 2001), **Bow Wow** ("Take Ya Home," 2001), and **Nelly** ("Hot in Herre," 2003).

Pharrell is also known for singing falsetto hooks for rap superstars like Jay-Z ("Excuse Me Miss") and **Snoop Dogg** ("Beautiful"). Pharrell actually takes the vocal lead on the song "Frontin'," featuring Jay-Z. In 2001, Pharrell and Chad, working with longtime friend Shay, chose to expand their creativity by forming the rap-rock band, N.E.R.D. (which stands for No One Ever Really Dies). In 2001, N.E.R.D. released their critically acclaimed debut album, *In Search Of* (Virgin Records, 2001). In 2003, the Neptunes released their debut album, *Neptunes Present . . . Clones* (Star Trak Entertainment/Arista Records), which confirmed their wide appeal. The album topped *Billboard*'s album chart and sold 250,000 units during its first week.

Also in 2003, Pharrell as a fashion trendsetter entered into an agreement with Reebok International, Inc., for them to produce his "Billionaire Boys Club" apparel and "Ice Cream" footwear for men and women, billed as sexy, grown-up clothing. In 2004, Pharrell was asked to create a sunglasses range for French fashion house Louis Vuitton. The sunglasses were unveiled during Fashion Week in Paris, France. By year's end, however, Pharrell's relationship with Reebok had soured and Pharrell had filed a lawsuit for over $4.5 million against the company. Pharrell contended that Reebok did not produce garments up to Billionaire Boys Club standards and had failed to meet a shipping deadline. On January 18, 2005, the parties released a joint statement that their relationship had been amicably resolved. Details about the terms of the dissolution of the partnership were not publicly disclosed.

In 2004 N.E.R.D. released their second album, *Fly Or Die* (Virgin Records). In 2004, The Neptunes won a Producer of the Year, Non-Classical Grammy Award.

DISCOGRAPHY: Over 175 musical works. As the Neptunes: *Neptunes Present . . . Clones* (Star Trak Entertainment/Arista Records, 2003). As N.E.R.D.: *In Search Of* (2001); *Fly Or Die* (Virgin Records, 2004).

NEWCLEUS

The group Newcleus, comprised of Ben "Cozmo D" Cenac, Monique Angevin, Monique's brother Pete Angevin, Yvette "Lady E" Cook, and Bob "Chilly B" Crofton, is known for the electro single, "Jam on Revenge (The Wikki-Wikki Song)," which has appeared on hundreds of rap music **mixtapes** and was played by techno DJs.

In 1977, as teenagers in Brooklyn, New York, Ben "Cozmo D" Cenac and his cousins Monique Angevin and Pete Angevin formed the DJ collective Jam-on Productions, which played throughout the borough. By 1979, the core group consisted of Cenac, his future wife Yvette "Lady E"

Cook, Monique Angevin, and her future husband, Bob "Chilly B" Crafton. The name Newcleus stemmed from the family connections between the four members.

Newcleus recorded a demotape, including the track "Jam-On's Revenge," which took a favorite block party song and sped up the vocals to resemble the television cartoon characters "Alvin and The Chipmunks." Producer Joe Webb, impressed with "Jam-On's Revenge," signed the group to a recording contract. In 1983, "Jam-On's Revenge" (Mayhew Records) was released as Newcleus's first single. The song was a huge hit and became unofficially known as "The Wikki-Wikki Song," after the chorus. When it was rereleased later that year on Sunnyview Records, it had become "Jam on Revenge (The Wikki-Wikki Song)." In 1983, "Jam On Revenge" hit Top 40 on the R & B charts and was followed up by the successful singles "Jam on It," (Sunnyview Records, 1983), which made the Pop charts, and "Computer Age (Push the Button)" (Sunnyview, 1984).

Unfortunately, the group's two albums, *Jam on Revenge* (Sunnyview Records, 1984) and *Space is the Place* (Sunnyview, 1984), did poorly and the group soon faded into oblivion.

DISCOGRAPHY: *Singles*: "Jam-On's Revenge" (Mayhew Records, 1983), re-issued as "Jam On Revenge (The Wikki-Wikki Song)" (Sunnyview Records, 1984). *Albums*: *Jam on Revenge* (Sunnyview Records, 1984); *Space is the Place* (Sunnyview Records, 1985).

NEW JACK SWING

New Jack swing is used to describe the hybrid of contemporary soul music and rap music popularized by producer Teddy Riley in the late 1980s and early 1990s. *Village Voice* journalist Barry Michael Cooper, who wrote the screenplay for the 1991 film *New Jack City*, is credited with coining the phrase.

New Jack swing evolved in the late 1980s, when young R & B artists began incorporating rap music beats, samples, and other production techniques into their music. Some songs simply contained what had become known as rap rhythms; others incorporated actual raps, along with song choruses. New Jack swing produced a music that was edgier and more street-oriented than traditional R & B music. More importantly, New Jack swing blurred the dividing line between rap and R & B, not only musically, but also with regard to the artists themselves. New Jack Swing artists often adopted clothing styles and public personas that were similar to those of rap artists.

Some of the R & B artists that typified New Jack swing include Guy, Father MC, Keith Sweat, Bobby Brown, Blackstreet, Bell Biv Devoe, and Al B. Sure!. Some have also attributed New Jack swing as creating an environment that encouraged the media to create entertainment vehicles that reflected humor and styles of young African Americans, particularly television shows such as *The Arsenio Hall Show*, *A Different World*, *In Living Color*, *Martin*, ***New York Undercover***, and the *House Party* films.

NEW YORK CITY RAP TOUR

The first international Hip Hop tour, the New York City Rap Tour began in November 1982 in Paris, France, and featured **MCs**, **DJs**, **B-boy** dancers, and **graffiti** artists. The tour was conceived by a French music journalist, Bernard Zékri (New York correspondent for *Actuel* magazine) and was sponsored by the French radio station Europe1. **Fab 5 Freddy**, who himself had released the rap single "Change the Beat" (Celluloid, 1982), helped gather the array of participants, including **Afrika Bambaataa**, **Grandmixer D.ST** & The Infinity, Rammellzee, The Double Dutch Girls, **Rock Steady Crew**, and graffiti artists Phase 2, Dondi, and Futura 2000. The tour was promoted to the rock media in London and Paris, garnering nine dates in France and three dates in London.

"NEW YORK, NEW YORK"

The diss track "New York, New York" appeared on the 1995 album *Dogg Food* (Death Row Records) from West Coast group **Tha Dogg Pound** (**Kurupt** and Daz Dillinger) and featured **Snoop Dogg**. In the accompanying music video, Snoop Dogg is shown knocking over buildings in New York City. Once word got out about the music video's content, unknown gunmen fired at the film set. In 1996, **Capone-N-Noreaga**, **Mobb Deep**, and Tragedy responded on wax with the song "LA, LA." **Westside Connection** (**Mack 10**, **Ice Cube**, and WC) would also enter the fray, with their single "Bow Down" (Priority Records, 1996) from the album of the same name. The catalyst for "New York, New York" track may date back as early as 1991, when Tim Dog, an associate of the **Ultramagnetic MCs**, released the notorious anti-**N.W.A.** single, "F—k Compton," from his album *Penicillin on Wax* (Columbia Records). In 1994, he followed up with the single "Bitch Wid A Perm" (Talking Loud/Phonogram Records), dedicated to Snoop Dogg.

NEW YORK UNDERCOVER

The first television crime drama in history to pair a Black officer and a Latino officer together in lead roles. The Fox network television show *New York Undercover*, airing between 1994 and 1998, was also the first to have a music executive as a producer. **Andre Harrell**, president of Uptown Entertainment used the on-screen nightclub "Natalie's" to showcase a variety of musical talent, including **Mary J. Blige**, 112, Xscape, Johnny Gill, Chaka Khan, and Teena Marie.

Undercover detectives J. C. Williams and Eddie Torres, played by actors Malik Yoba and Michael DeLorenzo, respectively, were depicted as honest policemen working on the tough streets of New York City. They also realistically portrayed the times for young urban America by wearing current fashions and by using contemporary street terms. Even more, the show allowed the two officers to deal with issues associated with their personal lives: Officer Williams was a single father, doing his best to deal with his ex-wife and coparent his ten-year-old son, and Officer Torres grappled with his father's drug problem, which resulted in him contracting AIDS.

By the third season, Fox decided that a White detective should be cast alongside Williams and Torres so that the show would appeal to a wider audience. As a result, Tommy McNamara, played by Italian-American actor Jonathan LaPaglia, was added to the cast. (Ironically, White actress Patti D'Arbanville-Quinn, already cast as Lieutenant Virginia Cooper, was replaced by Thomas Mikal Ford, an African American actor.) The change did not improve the show, and McNamara was killed off by the end of the season, as was Torres, when DeLorenzo did not renew his contract. The show struggled for another year and then was cancelled.

NIGGA

A variant of the pejorative term *nigger* used to describe people of African descent. Over the years the term *nigga* has appeared frequently in rap lyrics. Some rap artists use the word as a political statement to discuss the status quo of Black people in the United States, but most have attempted to reinterpret the word as a term of endearment and/or kinship. Regardless of the usage, the term generally remains controversial and offensive to the majority of African Americans, particularly when used by people of other races.

Variant spellings abound, including *nigguh* or *niggah*, and a plural with either *-s* or *-z*.

NIGGA TWINS

Recognized as early **B-boy** pioneers and credited by some as being the first B-boy crew, very little has been has been written about the Nigga Twins (Keith and Kevin). Available accounts indicate that they were at their peak in the early to middle 1970s before many of the better-known B-boy crews were even established. Many of their routines were considered an innovative blend of moves culled from disparate sources such as singer **James Brown**, martial arts star Bruce Lee, and the legendary dancers, The Nicholas Brothers. The Nigga Twins are recognized as the first to take their moves to the floor with footwork, mixing in vertical moves such as the sling-shot. Additionally, the duo was known to wear trenchcoats and often sported cigars as part of their routines.

N.O.R.E./NOREAGA. *See* Capone-N-Noreaga

NOTORIOUS B.I.G., THE (aka B.I.G., aka Biggie Smalls, aka Big Poppa) [Christopher Wallace]

Considered by many to be one of the Hip Hop's best all-time rap artists, the late Notorious B.I.G. is widely recognized as a gifted lyricist whose distinctive mellow flows and superior freestyling abilities graced numerous rap music tracks and **underground** mixtapes.

B.I.G., born in Brooklyn, New York, started out as a Catholic school honors student who had aspirations of becoming a graphic artist. As a

The Notorious B.I.G. *Courtesy of Photofest.*

teenager and the only son of a struggling single mother, he became part of the drug trade in his tough Bedford–Stuyvesant neighborhood, dabbling with music on the side. Early on he performed with a local group called Old Gold Brothers, calling himself Biggie Smalls. For fun, B.I.G. **battled** rap artists in his neighborhood and even made some tapes.

One tape containing B.I.G.'s rhyming made its way to Mr. Cee, **Big Daddy Kane**'s former DJ, who submitted the tape to ***The Source*** magazine's "Unsigned Hype" column. They were impressed by B.I.G.'s skill, and he was asked to contribute to an "Unsigned Hype" compilation album. Although that album never materialized, the buzz around B.I.G. led to him securing a recording contract with Uptown Records, under the direction of **Sean "P. Diddy" Combs**, who at the time was the National Director of **A & R**.

In 1993, B.I.G. would make his recording debut on the **remix** for **Mary J. Blige**'s single, "Real Love" (Uptown Records). He also made a guest appearance on reggae artist Super Cat's single "Dolly My Baby." Once P. Diddy parted ways with Uptown Records, B.I.G. was also dismissed from the label and would go on to record for P. Diddy's new label, Bad Boy Entertainment.

B.I.G.'s first solo track was "Party And Bullshit" which appeared on the *Who's The Man* (1993) film soundtrack. In 1994, B.I.G.'s highly anticipated album, *Ready to Die* (Bad Boy Entertainment), hit the streets. This would be the only album that B.I.G. would release during his brief career. The album was an immediate success, based on singles such as such as "Juicy," "One More Chance," and "Big Poppa." The first single, "Juicy," was voted *Billboard*'s rap single of the year. "Juicy" tells the story of how B.I.G. went from street hustling to living the American dream by joining the ranks of the rap artists that he had read about and admired. The single went triple platinum by the end of that year and the *Ready to Die* album sold double platinum.

B.I.G. would go on to appear on Michael Jackson's album, *HIStory: Past, Present And Future, Book 1* (Sony Records, 1995). Not forgetting people from the old neighborhood, B.I.G. helped to launch the rap group **Junior M.A.F.I.A.**, which included **Lil' Kim,** who B.I.G. was romantically linked with. The group would release the CD *Conspiracy* in 1995 (Undeas/Big Beat).

In May 1995, B.I.G. was arrested in connection with the assault and robbery of a New Jersey promoter. A year later, he was again arrested for assault and possession of marijuana in New York City.

B.I.G., a former friend of **Tupac Shakur**, then became embroiled in the **East Coast–West Coast rivalry**. In the media, Tupac accused B.I.G. of being involved in a 1994 robbery where Tupac was shot several times. Tupac would also imply that he was having an affair with B.I.G.'s wife, singer Faith Evans, and publicly dissed B.I.G. along with several other

East Coast rap artists on the track, "Hit 'Em Up" (Death Row Records). When Tupac was murdered in September 1996, B.I.G.'s failure to attend a rap peace summit in Harlem was widely criticized and later fueled rumors about his involvement in the killing.

During this period, B.I.G. was in the studio, beginning work on a second album, prophetically titled *Life After Death* (Bad Boy Entertainment/Arista, 1997). Ironically, the twenty-four-year-old B.I.G. was gunned down in California, outside a Soul Train Awards after-party on March 9, 1997, and would never see the album's release.

Again, rumors swirled that B.I.G.'s murder was retaliation for the fatal shooting of Tupac. The posthumously released *Life After Death* debuted at number 1 on the *Billboard* album charts and broke first-week sales and sold over ten times platinum. Members of the Bad Boy Family, along with former wife, Faith Evans recorded the song, "I'll Be Missing You" to pay their respects to the late, great artist. The single, which samples The Police song, "Every Breath You Take," sold over 3 million copies.

In 1997, B.I.G.'s mother Violetta Wallace, a retired teacher, established the Christopher Wallace Memorial Foundation, an organization that provides books and school equipment to youth.

In 1999, B.I.G. Bad Boy Entertainment released the album *Born Again*, an uneven collection of formerly unreleased material, which nonetheless went on to top the charts.

DISCOGRAPHY: *Ready to Die* (Bad Boy Entertainment, 1994); *Life After Death* (Bad Boy Entertainment/Arista, 1997); *Born Again* (Bad Boy Entertainment, 1999); Also apppears on approximately sixty-nine musical tracks.

N.W.A.

N.W.A. was comprised of **Dr. Dre** [Andre Young], DJ Yella [Antoine Carraby], **Ice Cube** [O'Shea Jackson], **Eazy E** [Eric Wright], **Arabian Prince** [Mik Lezan], The D.O.C. [Terry Curry], and MC Ren [Lorenzo Patterson]. Perhaps the most notorious group in rap music history, N.W.A., which stands for Niggas with Attitude, popularized a hardcore rap music that seemed to celebrate the violence, **misogyny**, and nihilism associated with street life.

N.W.A. are important because they put Compton, California, on the Hip Hop map and catapulted the careers of rap entrepreneur Eazy E, rap artist and actor Ice Cube, and producer Dr. Dre. The group's bleak but powerful social commentary, including its attack on racist police officers, caused the F.B.I. to caution the group's record company. Initially, Dr. Dre, a member of the **World Class Wreckin' Cru**, and Ice Cube began writing songs for Eazy E's fledging Ruthless Records. When the company's artists, HBO, refused to record Ice Cube's song "Boyz N Tha Hood," Eazy E then formed the rap group, N.W.A., with Ice Cube and Dr. Dre to record it. N.W.A. would eventually consist of Eazy E, Ice Cube, Dr. Dre, fellow World Class Wreckin' Cru member, DJ Yella, the Arabian Prince, and Fila Fresh Crew member, The D.O.C. In 1988, MC Ren was added when Arabian Prince left the group.

In 1987, N.W.A. independently released their first album, *N.W.A. and the Posse* (Ruthless Records). The debut album contained sophomoric humor and party-themes that do not represent the sound that the group would develop on successive albums. *N.W.A. and the Posse* is best remembered for the tracks "Dopeman" and the original "Boyz N Tha Hood." The next year, N.W.A. added MC Ren and reshaped their sound, using some of the explosive sound innovations popularized by **Public Enemy**. N.W.A.'s new musical direction, coupled with unrepentantly violent lyrics, ushered in a new era of rap music.

In late 1988, N.W.A. released their second album, *Straight Outta Compton* (Ruthless Records), which became an underground hit without any radio play, media coverage, or appearances on music video programs. The album includes the title track "Straight Outta Compton," the pro–free speech "Express Yourself," and the infamous "Fuck tha Police," a track that resulted in the Federal Bureau of Investigations sending a warning letter to Ruthless Records and its distributor, Priority Records, suggesting that the group should rethink their lyrical content. In 1989, Priority Records re-issued N.W.A.'s debut album *N.W.A. and the Posse*.

Arabian Prince departed N.W.A. after the release of *Straight Outta Compton*. In 1989, amid fierce battles over the financial management of the group, Ice Cube left, and with him went much of the group's serious political and social commentary. The **beef** between Ice Cube and N.W.A. continued after his departure and led to Ice Cube's track "No Vaseline," from his 1991 *Death Certificate* (Priority Records) album, which directly attacks N.W.A.'s manager Jerry Heller and Eazy E. Many cultural critics contend that when businessman Eazy E took the front man position for N.W.A., the group became a parody of itself, exaggerating the violence and misogyny as a means to satisfy the fantasies of its primarily male, White, suburban audience.

In 1990, N.W.A. released an EP, *100 Miles and Runnin'* (Ruthless Records), and early the next year followed up with *Efil4zaggin* (Ruthless Records) ("Niggaz 4 Life" spelled backward). Despite the fact that N.W.A. was at the height of its popularity, issues related to the group's record deal and members' egos paved the way for Dr. Dre to leave the group in 1992. He would form **Death Row Records** with Marion "Suge" Knight. Rumors were widely circulated that Knight had threatened to kill N.W.A.'s manager Jerry Heller if he refused to let Dr. Dre out of his recording contract.

N.W.A. would disband in 1992. Over the next few years, Dr. Dre and Eazy E engaged in a highly publicized feud, with the two rap artists attacking each other in songs, including on Dr. Dre's album *The Chronic* (Death Row Records, 1992) and on Eazy E's EP, *It's on (Dr. Dre) 187um Killa* (Ruthless Records, 1993). MC Ren and DJ Yella both released solo albums, which were largely ignored, and Eazy E continued to record albums until his death from AIDS in March 1995. It was reported that he had mended fences with both Dr. Dre and Ice Cube before his death.

See also: Censorship

DISCOGRAPHY: *EP*: *100 Miles and Running* (Ruthless Records/Priority Records, 1990). *Albums*: *NWA and the Posse* (Ruthless Records, 1987); *Straight Outta Compton*, Ruthless Records/Priority Records, 1988); *Efil4zaggin* (Ruthless Records/Priority Records, 1991).

O

OL' DIRTY BASTARD (aka O.D.B., aka Dirt McGirt, aka Osirius, aka Big Baby Jesus) [Russell Tyrone Jones]

With his cousins **RZA** and **GZA/Genius**, Ol' Dirty Bastard is a founding member of the **Wu-Tang Clan**. The native of Brooklyn, New York, is best known for his eccentric personality and unorthodox delivery, which could alternately be slurred, growling, hyper, or nonsensical.

Most rap music listeners first heard the late O.D.B. on the track "Protect Ya Neck," the first single from Wu-Tang's debut album, *Enter the Wu-Tang (36 Chambers)* (Loud, 1993). His career actually began several years earlier, as a member of the rap group All in Together Now, with his cousins GZA/Genius and RZA.

In a skit included on the debut album, **Method Man** explains O.D.B.'s name saying, "there is no father to his style." His oddball antics outside the recording studio would made him a breakout star among the Wu-Tang members. In 1994, an MTV camera followed O.D.B. as he rode in his limousine to collect food stamps. O.D.B. charged the stage at the 1998 Grammy Awards to protest the Wu-Tang Clan's loss.

In 1994, O.D.B. appeared along with newcomer and fellow Brooklynite **Jay-Z** on **Big Daddy Kane**'s 1994 posse cut, "Show & Prove" (MCA Records). In 1995, O.D.B. released his entertaining solo debut, *Return of the 36 Chamber: The Dirty Version* (Elektra Records), which contained the hit single, "Shimmy Shimmy Ya." While the music of Wu-Tang Clan is often dark and enigmatic, in comparison O.D.B.'s was earthy and humorous.

In 1999, O.D.B. released his second album, *N***a Please* (Elektra Records), which included the **Neptunes**-produced hit, "Got Ya Money," featuring Kelis and O.D.B. singing a wobbling version of "Good Morning Heartache," a jazz standard closely associated with Billie Holiday. O.D.B.'s bouts with drug dependency were well known and included an arrest for the possession of crack cocaine, which landed him in prison for two years. After his release from jail, he signed a recording deal with Jay-Z's **Roc-A-Fella Records**, with plans to release an album in 2005.

In the interim, O.D.B. appeared on the track "When You Hear That" with **Beanie Sigel**, which appeared on the *State Property* (2001) film soundtrack and on **Kanye West**'s track, "Keep The Receipt," which was dropped from the *College Dropout* (Roc-A-Fella Records, 2004) album.

On Saturday, November 13, 2004, O.D.B. (who had complained of chest pains earlier in the day) collapsed and then died at Wu-Tang's Manhattan recording studio, 36 Records LLC. In December 2004, the New York City medical examiner concluded his death an accident, the result of a fatal interaction of cocaine and a prescription drug. O.D.B.'s mother and O.D.B.'s manager, Jarred Weisfield, created JC Records and in January 2005 the posthumous album *Osirius* (JC/Sure Shot), a collection of recordings made during the last six months of his life, was released.
DISCOGRAPHY: *Return of the 36 Chamber: The Dirty Version* (Elektra Records, 1995); *N***a Please* (Elektra Records, 1999); *Osirius* (JC/Sure Shot, 2005).

O'NEAL, SHAQUILLE (aka Enrico Gate, aka The Shaq)

A player for the Miami Heat National Basketball Association (NBA) team, Shaquille O'Neal has also recorded several rap music albums, sometimes using the rap name Enrico Gate. O'Neal made his first rap appearance on the Fu-Schnickens 1993 hit "What's Up Doc?" (Jive Records). He released his platinum-selling debut album *Shaq Diesel* (Jive Records) in 1993, following that up with the gold album, *Shaq-Fu: Da Return* (Jive Records) in 1994. His next two albums, *You Can't Stop the Reign* (Interscope Records, 1996) and *Respect* (A&M Records, 1998) were not commercially successful efforts.

In 2004, O'Neal appears on a DJ Slickmove mixtape, taking shots at Virginia-based rap artist Skillz, who attacked O'Neal's former teammate Kobe Bryant on his track "The Rap Up 2004."

Also in 2004, Shaquille O'Neal and Koch Records formed a partnership to launch the basketball star's new label, DEJA34 Records. Koch will provide marketing and distribution while Shaq will finance the label. **DJ Kay Slay** will head up the label's **A & R** department. DEJA34 Records' first release will be DJ Kay Slay's third album scheduled for an April 2005 release. Other NBA players who tried their hands at rap music include Shaq's former teammate and rival Kobe Bryant of the Los Angeles Lakers and Allen Iverson of the Philadelphia 76ers; however, neither of their records were released to the general public.
DISCOGRAPHY: *Shaq Diesel* (Jive Records, 1993); *Shaq-Fu: Da Return* (Jive Records, 1994); *You Can't Stop the Reign* (Interscope Records, 1996); *Respect* (A&M, 1998).

ONYX

Made up of Big DS [Marion Fletcher], Sticky Fingaz [Kirk Jones], Sonee Seeza (aka Suave Sonny Caesar), and Fredro Starr [Fredro Fragile Scruggs, Jr.], Onyx are best remembered for their aggressive, high-energy sound that brought a mosh pit feel to hardcore rap music.

In 1989, Onyx formed out of Queens, New York; consisting of Fredro Starr, Sonee Seeza (then known only as Suave), and Big DS. They released their first single under Profile Records, "Ah, and We Do It Like This," to not much success. After hearing a demo for the group, **Jam Master Jay** signed them to his JMJ label.

In 1993, Onyx released the twelve-inch single "Throw Ya Gunz" (JMJ Records), with the idea that they would thereafter record an EP. "Throw Ya Gunz," however, proved to be such a success that they were able to record a full-length album. In 1993, Onyx released their debut album, *Bacdafucup* (JMJ Records). The album, bolstered by their huge crossover hit single, "Slam," sold platinum. Onyx proved to be popular also with rock fans, and they collaborated with heavy metal band Biohazard for the *Judgment Night* film soundtrack (1993). Onyx was not able to recapture their original success on subsequent albums. By the second album, Big DS had left the group for undisclosed reasons. Onyx released *All We Got Iz Us* in 1995 and *Shut 'Em Down* in 1998, both without much fanfare.

In 2000, Sticky Fingaz released his first solo album, *Black Trash: The Autobiography of Kirk Jones* (Universal Records). Fredro would turn to acting, and has built an impressive resume without any formal training. Fredro has appeared in the 2000 Paramount/MTV film *Save the Last Dance* and for several seasons he appeared as Brandy's love interest on the WB's network television show *Moesha*. He has had roles on the television program *NYPD Blue*, in HBO's *Strapped* (1993), and in Spike Lee's *Clockers* (1995) and in the film *Light It Up* (1999). In 2001, Fredro released his solo debut album, *Firestarr* (Koch Records, 2001).

In 2002, after relatively lackluster solo efforts, the group made a comeback with *Bacdafucup, Pt. II* (Koch Records). In 2003, Fredro released his second solo album, *Don't Get Mad, Get Money* (D3 Entertainment/Riviera Records). Sticky Fingaz released his sophomore solo set, *Decade,* in April of that year. Onyx released the album, *Triggernometry* (D3 Entertainment/Riviera Records) in 2003.

Former Onyx member Big DS died of cancer in May 2003.

DISCOGRAPHY: *Singles*: "Ah, and We Do It Like This" (Profile Records, 1989); "Throw Ya Gunz" (JMJ Records). *Albums*: *Bacdafucup* (JMJ/Def Jam Recordings, 1993); *All We Got Iz Us* (JMJ/Def Jam Recordings, 1995); *Shut 'Em Down* (JMJ, 1998); *Bacdafucup Part II* (Koch Records, 2002); *Triggernometry* (D3 Entertainment/Riviera Records, 2003).

ORGANIZED KONFUSION

As Organized Konfusion, Prince Poetry [Larry Bakerfield] and Pharoahe Monch [Troy Donaldson Jamerson] are considered by many to be the best **underground** rap duo in Hip Hop history.

The rap artists from Queens, New York, may have called themselves Organized Konfusion because they were so adept at intelligently addressing a multitude of topical themes, sometimes humorously. Their unique sound and message were progressive for their time, and in retrospect may have even appeared futuristic. The complex lyrics and fast rhyming, however, did not lend themselves to commercial rap music listeners who desire catchy hooks and party-themes, and so the duo have often been underrated.

The high school friends worked with the late rap music producer Paul C., who was influential to them securing a recording deal with Hollywood Records. *Organized Konfusion*, their 1991 eponymous release, ranks among the best underground rap music albums of the 1990s. The standout tracks include "Who Stole My Last Piece of Chicken?" (a vivid reflection on Black family life) and "Fudge Pudge" (which details memories of family and friends). After three years of disillusioning experiences in the record industry, Organized Konfusion would follow up in 1994 with *Stress: The Extinction Agenda* (Hollywood Records). Their sophomore effort, while considered more cohesive than the first, is also less whimsical, showing the wear of their ties to the corporate music industry.

The duo would move to Priority Records and in 1997 released their third album, *The Equinox*, a concept album that traces the lives of two African American teenagers. After this release, the duo amicably called it quits. Pharoahe Monch went on to pursue a solo recording career. He signed a recording deal with independent label, Rawkus Entertainment, which allowed him as a solo artist to flex a more aggressive rap style. His guest appearances and his contribution to the 1999 *Rawkus Presents Soundbombing II* compilation heightened expectations about his debut solo album. His single "Simon Says" was released in 1999, a huge hit among rap music and club audiences, and set the stage for Pharoahe Monch's album, *Internal Affairs,* which hit the streets later that year.
DISCOGRAPHY: *Organized Konfusion* (Hollywood Records, 1991); *Stress: The Extinction Agenda* (Hollywood Records, 1994); *The Equinox* (Priority Records, 1997).

ORIGINAL FLAVOR

Original Flavor is best known as the crew that gave **Jay-Z** his start in rap music. Headed by Ski, an MC–producer, Original Flavor released its debut, *This Is How It Is* (Atlantic Records), in 1992. Although Ski worked with legendary DJ Clark Kent, the album was largely ignored. For the group's second album, novice producer Ski brought together more rap artists, including T-Strong, Chubby Chub, and a young Brooklynite named Jay-Z. Jay-Z had worked with fellow Brooklynite Big Jaz on the tracks "Hawaiian Sophie"(EMI Records, 1989) and "The Originators" (EMI Records, 1990), and the two were commonly referred to as Jaz and Jay-Z. The group's sophomore release, *Beyond Flavor* (Atlantic Records,

1994) also fizzled; however, the lead single "Can I Get Open" features Jay-Z's nascent style. Jay-Z's talents outshined the rest of the crew, and he pursued a solo career shortly thereafter.

Jay-Z, along with **Ol' Dirty Bastard**, appeared on **Big Daddy Kane**'s 1994 posse cut, "Show & Prove," from the album *Daddy's Home* (MCA Records), and he then released a number of singles, including "In My Lifetime." After Original Flavors disbanded, Jay-Z continued to work with Ski, making him a member of his Roc-A-Fella staff. Ski produced four tracks on Jay-Z's solo debut *Reasonable Doubt* in 1996 and two on *In My Lifetime, Volume One* (1997).

DISCOGRAPHY: *This Is How It Is* (Atlantic Records, 1992); *Beyond Flavor* (Atlantic Records, 1994).

OUTKAST

Big Boi [Antwan Patton] and Dre (aka Andre 3000) [Andre Benjamin], are known as Outkast. In the 1990s, Outkast was among the first rap groups, along with **Goodie Mob** and **Arrested Development**, to bring national attention to Atlanta, Georgia's, emerging rap music scene.

Rather than relying on aggressive lyrics, the duo (originally backed by Organized Noize's lush production) skillfully depict Southern life in a

Outkast. *Courtesy of Photofest.*

way that transcends regional divisions, striking a universal chord with listeners. Outkast's public persona also reflects the diversity of rap music: while Big Boi's image is that of a street-smart "playa," Andre 3000's outrageous outfits suggest a more bohemian bent. (In the September 2004 issue of *Esquire* magazine, Andre 3000 was named The World's Best Dressed Man.)

Dre and Big Boi attended the same East Point, Atlanta, high school and after competing against each other in rap **battles** the two self-proclaimed oddballs formed their first band, 2 Shades Deep. Dre would drop out of high school, but shortly before Big Boi was about to graduate the duo signed a record contract with LaFace Records.

Using the name Outkast, in 1993 the duo released their debut single, "Player's Ball," which rose to the number 1 spot on rap music charts and remained there for six weeks. The single went gold, spurring demand for a full-length album. In 1994, Outkast's debut album, *Southernplayalisticadillacmuzik* (LaFace Records), was certified platinum by the end of the year. In 1996, Outkast released their second album, *ATLiens* (LaFace Records), which went platinum with help from the gold-selling track "Elevators (Me & You)." In 1998, Outkast's third album *Aquemini* (LaFace Records) was released, selling over 2 million units.

On *Aquemini*, the duo produced much of the album themselves, sidelining longtime collaborators Goodie Mob and Organized Noize. Although the album did not produce any major singles, critics nonetheless praised it for taking rap music in a new, progressive direction. The album also spawned the single, "Rosa Parks," which became the basis of a lawsuit instituted in 1999 by civil rights icon Rosa Parks, who claimed that the group had defamed her and had unlawfully appropriated her name to promote their music. Outkast was eventually dismissed as a defendant, but a second suit was filed in 2003, demanding $5 billion from LaFace and its distributor Arista Records.

Prior to the release of Outkast's fourth album, *Stankonia* (LaFace Records), in 2000 Dre modified his name to Andre 3000. The album catapulted the rap duo into the superstar realm, with consistently strong reviews, especially for stellar singles such as "B.O.B." and "Ms. Jackson." Within months *Stankonia* had sold triple platinum, and "Ms. Jackson" became Outkast's first number 1 pop single.

Outkast's fifth album, *Speakerboxxx/The Love Below*, released in 2003, garnered the duo two 2004 Grammy awards, one for Best Album and another for Best Rap Album. Despite their statements to the contrary, the innovative double-disc album fueled rumors that there was a rift between the duo. The first CD, *Speakerboxxx*, is almost entirely the work of Big Boi; the second, *The Love Below,* is primarily Andre 3000. Debuting at number 1 on the U.S. music charts, the album produced two huge singles, Andre 3000's "Hey Ya" and Big Boi's "The Way You Move."

The two CDs of *Speakerboxxx/The Love Below* are, in effect, a retrospective of Black music history and incorporate facets of funk, psychedelic, soul, and rap. The album, like Outkast itself, is relevant in its willingness to expand the boundaries of rap music beyond tales of street life, simple hooks, and formulaic beats.

DISCOGRAPHY: *Singles*: "Player's Ball" (LaFace Records, 1993). *Albums: Southernplayalisticadillacmuzik* (LaFace Records, 1994); *ATLiens* (LaFace Records, 1996); *Aquemini* (LaFace Records, 1998); *Stankonia* (LaFace Records, 2000); *Speakerboxxx/The Love Below* (LaFace Records, 2003).

P

PANICCIOLI, ERNIE

Ernie Paniccioli is considered by many to be the premier Hip Hop photographer in the United States. Using a 35-millimeter camera, Paniccioli has photographed the development of Hip Hop since its inception. Paniccioli has been chronicling Hip Hop from 1973 and possibly has the most comprehensive collection of works by 1980s New York City graffiti artists in the world. Paniccioli's documentation of **graffiti** art spans from 1975 to 2001 and covers not only New York City, but also cities in northern New Jersey, including Newark, Jersey City, and Paterson. Along with aerosol art, Paniccioli photographed other components of Hip Hop, including **MCing**, **B-boying**, **DJing**, and fashion.

Paniccioli is distinguished from other art photographers because, where others concentrated primarily on subway art, he also photographed graffiti art in the urban communities where Hip Hop was emerging. In 1987, Paniccioli's commitment to Hip Hop earned him the position of chief photographer for the start-up magazine, *Word Up!*

Paniccioli has photographed across the span of Hip Hop's icons, including **Tupac Shakur**, **The Notorious B.I.G.**, **DMX**, **Jay-Z**, **Run DMC**, **Public Enemy**, **Wu-Tang Clan**, **Goodie Mob**, **Slick Rick**, **Nas**, **Dead Prez**, **Canibus**, **The Fugees**, **LL Cool J**, **Rakim**, Rob Base, **Redman**, **Naughty By Nature**, Michael Jordan, **Snoop Dogg**, **Master P**, **KRS-ONE**, **Afrika Bambaataa**, LEE, **DJ Kool Herc**, **Grandmaster Flash**, **Big Pun**, **Queen Latifah**, **Ice Cube**, **Lil' Kim**, Guru (**Gang Starr**), **Salt 'N Pepa**, **Crazy Legs**, **Big Daddy Kane**, **Roxanne Shante**, **Ice-T**, **Busta Rhymes**, **EPMD**, and **Method Man.** His work has been published in numerous publications including *The New York Times*, *Life Magazine*, *Time*, *Vibe*, *Rolling Stone*, ***The Source***, *Spin*, *Ebony*, and *Jet*. Paniccioli's photographs have been exhibited in The Brooklyn Museum of Art and The Rock and Roll Hall of Fame. In 2003, Paniccioli contributed forty-five never-before-seen photos to Kool Moe Dee's book on the fifty greatest MCs title *There's a God on the Mic* (New York: Thunder's Mouth Press). Paniccioli contended that **Kool Moe Dee** failed to pay him for the photographs and therefore he would not endorse or publicize the book. Paniccioli's own book, *Who Shot Ya?* (New York: Amistad/HarperCollins), published in 2002, covers twenty-seven years of his Hip Hop photography.

PARIS [Oscar Jackson, Jr.]

Often called the "Black Panther of Hip Hop," Paris is best known as one of rap music's most fiercely political artists. At a time when the majority of West Coast rap music was about gangbanging, cars, and the like, Paris's music was talking about Black consciousness. Paris used the ideology of figures such as Malcolm X, Minister Louis Farrakhan, and Huey Newton (of the Black Panthers) as the backdrop to create music that was a cross between the visceral rage of **Ice Cube** and the cerebral dialogue of **Public Enemy**.

The son of a medical doctor, Paris grew up in the Haight and Western Addition neighborhoods of San Francisco, California. After earning an undergraduate degree in economics from the University of California at Davis, he followed his interest in Hip Hop. On one occasion, Paris joined up with members of **Digital Underground** as they shot a music video, to gain some pointers about the process. At that time, a producer for Tommy Boy Records asked if he was a rap artist. Paris gave a tape to the producer, who, impressed with the music, offered Paris a recording deal.

In 1990, Paris released his acclaimed debut album, *The Devil Made Me Do It* (Tommy Boy Records), which received the most mainstream attention of his career because of the single "The Hate That Hate Made." The music video for the title single was banned from MTV. In 1992, Paris completed his second album, *Sleeping With the Enemy* (Tommy Boy Records), which included the anti–George Bush track "Bush Killa." Tommy Boy Records was owned by Time Warner, which as the distributor for **Ice-T**'s controversial track "**Cop Killer**" was still experiencing the aftermath of that maelstrom, and Tommy Boy Records refused to release *Sleeping With the Enemy.* Tommy Boy Records then, having decided that Paris's music was too inflammatory, opted to buy out his contract rather than release his music. Negotiations with Polygram and Def American also faltered, those labels likewise deeming Paris's music too incendiary.

With the settlement money from Tommy Boy Records, Paris formed Scarface Records and in 1993 finally released *Sleeping With The Enemy.* Although the album was hailed as a major political statement in some quarters of the rap music world, it failed to attract a broad audience. That same year, Paris signed a major artist and distribution deal with Priority Records for himself and Scarface Records and in 1994 released his third album, *Guerilla Funk.* The album went largely unnoticed.

In 1995, citing creative differences, Paris and Priority Records formally ended their business relationship. In 1997, Paris signed a one-off deal with now-defunct Whirling Records for his fourth album, *Unleashed*, released in 1998. On *Unleashed*, Paris largely set aside direct references to the **Nation of Islam** and the Black Panther Party, as a way of simplifying his message to appeal to mainstream rap fans whose tastes at the time ran toward groups such as **N.W.A.**, but the change in style did not help record sales.

In 1998, Paris retired from music and became a licensed stockbroker. Paris left the financial world after a few years, however, and in 2002 he scored and narrated *Aftermath: Unanswered Questions About 9/11*, a GNN (Guerrilla News Network) video documentary directed by Stephen Marshall that has played to packed houses in over twenty cities in Europe and North America, including San Francisco.

After a five-year hiatus, Paris returned with his fifth album, *Sonic Jihad* (Guerrilla Funk Recordings, 2003), which features appearances by Public Enemy and **Dead Prez**. The first single, "What Would You Do?" originally released via the Internet garnered media attention for implying that the Bush Administration was involved in the planning of the 9/11 attacks. Using the Internet as a means to get his message out, Paris emerged with his new label, Guerrilla Funk Recordings, and a Web site (http://www.guerrillafunk.com). The Web site does not just sell Paris's music and merchandise; it also provides Paris's thoughts on issues, a reading list, and links to articles related to politics and culture.

DISCOGRAPHY: *The Devil Made Me Do It* (Tommy Boy Records, 1990); *Sleeping with the Enemy* (Scarface, 1993); *Guerilla Funk* (Priority Records, 1994); *Unleashed* (Whirling Records, Rykodisc, 1998); *Sonic Jihad* (Guerilla Funk Recordings, 2003).

PARRISH, MANNY "MAN"

Manny "Man" Parrish is recognized as the first openly gay artist to impact Hip Hop. Parrish, a DJ and producer, is an important and influential figure in dance music history because he helped to lay the foundation for several subgenres, including electro, Hip Hop, freestyle, and techno. His nickname, "Man," first appeared in Andy Warhol's *Interview* magazine. Parrish's early live shows at Bronx Hip Hop clubs were spectacles of lights, glitter, and pyrotechnics that drew equally from the downtown aesthetic of Warhol's Factory and that of the **Cold Crush Brothers**.

In 1982, Parrish gained notoriety for the electro single, "Hip Hop Be Bop (Don't Stop)" (Sugarscoop Records). "Hip Hop Be Bop" is distinguished from other dance records not only because it lacked vocals, but also because it was popular with a diverse audience in New York City, including **B-boys** and downtown club kids. In 1983, Man Parrish, featuring Freeze Force Crew, released the single, "Boogie Down Bronx" (Sugarscoop Records), a single that remains an undisputed Hip Hop and electro classic. His debut album, *Man Parrish* (Importe, 1983), sold over 2 million copies worldwide. His second album, *DreamTime* (Strictly Rhythm), was released in 1997. Parrish continues to DJ in New York City and run several businesses related to adult entertainment.

DISCOGRAPHY: *Singles*: "Hip Hop Be Bop (Don't Stop)" (Sugarscoop Records, 1982); "Boogie Down Bronx" (Sugarscoop Records, 1983). *Albums*: *Man Parrish* (Importe, 1983); *DreamTime* (Strictly Rhythm, 1997).

P. DIDDY. *See* Combs, Sean "P. Diddy"

PETE ROCK [Peter Phillips]

Pete Rock is considered one of the best and most influential rap music producers in Hip Hop history. Although Pete Rock has extensive production credits, he is perhaps best known for his work with C. L. Smooth as Pete Rock and C. L. Smooth. Incorporating mellow beats and a heavy jazz influence into his work, Pete Rock has produced or done **remixes** for some of rap music's brightest stars, including **Public Enemy**, **Mos Def**, **Nas**, **Rakim**, **Kid 'N Play**, **Talib Kweli**, **Notorious B.I.G.**, **Run DMC**, Q-Tip (of **A Tribe Called Quest**), and **Mary J. Blige**.

A native of the Bronx, New York, the aspiring DJ Pete Rock had inherited a diverse collection of records from his father, who had been a DJ in Jamaica, West Indies. Pete Rock caught a major career break when his cousin, **Heavy D**, introduced him to legendary producer **Marley Marl**. During this period, Marley Marl had a radio show on New York's WBLS-FM and Pete Rock soon joined him, spinning records. After trying his hand at producing his own material, Pete Rock teamed up with long-time friend C. L. Smooth. In 1991, the duo of Pete Rock and C. L. Smooth, as they became known, released the EP *All Souled Out* (Elektra Records). Pete Rock and C. L. Smooth went on to create two of the most influential and timeless rap music albums, *Mecca & The Soul Brother* (Elektra Records, 1992) and *The Main Ingredient* (Elektra Records, 1994). *Mecca & the Soul Brother* was a groundbreaking effort and featured seminal hit singles ("Straighten It Out," "Ghettoes of the Mind") and their signature track, "They Reminisce Over You (T.R.O.Y.)," a tribute to Heavy D dancer Trouble TRoy who was killed in an accident while on tour. While melancholy-tinged "T.R.O.Y." was only a modest hit on the U.S. charts at the time, it remains a mainstay at funerals and family gatherings.

After the release of *Main Ingredient*, without any warning or public statement, the duo broke up. Four years later, Pete Rock came out with *Soul Survivor* (Relativity Records, 1998), which featured numerous guests, including Black Thought (**The Roots**), **Raekwon** (**Wu-Tang Clan**), and **Kool G Rap**. In 2001, he teamed up with BBE Records for their Beat Generation series, releasing the highly praised and largely instrumental album, *Petestrumentals*, which features an appearance by C. L. Smooth. In 2004, *Soul Survivor 2* (Rapster [Studio 7]) hit the streets. The album is more than just a sequel. Pete Rock acts as both MC and producer, and has assembled a stellar cast of rap artists, including Pharoahe Monch (**Organized Konfusion**), Slum Village and **Dead Prez**, **Talib Kweli**, **RZA**, **GZA/Genius**, and Canada's Kardinal Offishall.

In 2005, Pete Rock released *The Surviving Elements: From Soul Survivor II Sessions* (Rapster [Studio 7]), which provides outtakes and aural insights into Pete Rock's creative process.

DISCOGRAPHY: *EPs*: *Pete Rock and C.L. Smooth: All Souled Out* (Elektra Records, 1991); *The Main Ingredient* (Elektra, 1994). *Albums*: *Mecca & The Soul Brother* (Elektra Records, 1992). *Pete Rock: Soul Survivor* (Relativity Records, 1998); *Petestrumentals* (BBE Records, 2001); *Soul Survivor 2* (Rapster [Studio 7], 2004); *The Surviving Elements: From Soul Survivor II Sessions* (Rapster [Studio 7], 2005).

PHARCYDE

The Pharcyde, an influential West Coast rap quartet made up of Slim Kid Tre [Tre Hardson], Fat Lip [Derrick Stewart], Imani Wilcox, and Booty Brown [Romye Robinson], distinguished themselves from their peers with music that went beyond the hardcore guns, violence, and sex fare of the day. The group called itself the Pharcyde, stating that it is "a name that doesn't set any boundaries." The Pharcyde used humor and irony combined with multilayered production to create a previously uncharted listening experience.

Hailing from South Central Los Angeles, the Pharcyde was formed when Slim Kid Tre, Imani Wilcox, and Booty Brown, all dancers and choreographers, met in the late 1980s on the Los Angeles **underground** club circuit. As the group Two For Two, they appeared in several music videos and on the television program *In Living Color*. While attending "South Central Unit," an informal music business course run by high school teacher Reggie Andrews, the trio met the aspiring rap artist Fat Lip and producer J-Swift. The new quartet recorded a demo tape with J-Swift that ignited a bidding war among record companies. In 1990, they secured a recording deal with Delicious Vinyl. Their first single, the well-received "Soul Flower," was included on the compilation album *Heavy Rhyme Experience: Vol. 1*. In 1991, The Pharcyde released their eccentric gold debut album, *Bizarre Ride II*; the album's hit single, "Passing Me," garnered considerable radio and club play.

The Pharcyde would become the opening acts for rap groups such as **De La Soul** and **A Tribe Called Quest**, and in 1994 they performed on the second stage at Lollapalooza. That year, the group released its second album, *Labcabincalifornia* (Delicious Vinyl Records), a more subdued, but no less unique effort than the first. After touring for *Labcabincalifornia*, the Pharcyde and Fat Lip parted company. As a solo rap artist, Fat Lip released the single, "What's Up Fat Lip," which became an underground hit. Slim Kid Tre would also leave the group and record his solo album, *Liberation* (iMusic, 2002).

In 2000, a pared-down Pharcyde returned with an EP, *Testing the Waters* (Chapter 22), as well as a full album, *Plain Rap* (Edel America). In 2004, the Pharcyde released their fourth album, *Humboldt Beginnings* (Chapter One Entertainment).

DISCOGRAPHY: *EP*: *Testing the Waters* (Chapter 22, 2000). *Albums*: *Bizarre Ride II* (Delicious Vinyl, 1991); *Labcabincalifornia* (Delicious Vinyl Records, 1994); *Plain Rap* (Edel America, 2000); *Humboldt Beginnings* (Chapter One Entertainment, 2004).

PHAROAHE MONCH. *See* Organized Konfusion

PHILADELPHIA

Philadelphia, Pennsylvania, is recognized as the second home for the development of Hip Hop culture. Only two hours from New York City, for almost twenty years it has been a city where new talent has been scouted and then brought to the major record companies in New York.

In 1979, Philadelphian **Lady B** became one of the first female solo artists to release a rap single with "To The Beat Y'all" (TEC Records). That same year, the seventeen-year-old **Lady B** began playing rap records on WHAT-AM, furthering rap music's reach beyond New York City. Rap artists from Philadelphia include **Schoolly D**, **DJ Jazzy Jeff and The Fresh Prince**, **Bahamadia**, **The Roots**, **Eve**, and **Beanie Sigel**. Moreover, record companies also sent new artists to Philadelphia to record material and to hone their performance skills.

In 1984, Pop Art, Philadelphia's first rap music label released **Roxanne Shante**'s "Roxanne's Revenge" which set off the Roxanne Wars with **The Real Roxanne**. The next year **Salt 'N Pepa**, then known as Super Nature, recorded their first single, "Showstopper" as a response to **Slick Rick**'s single, "The Show" (Def Jam Recordings, 1985).

P.M. DAWN

P.M. Dawn is composed of Prince Be (aka The Nocturnal) [Attrell Cordes] and DJ Minute Mix (aka J.D. The Eternal) [Jarrett Cordes]. Although perhaps best known for their bohemian flair and Prince Be's physical altercation with **KRS-ONE**, P.M. Dawn nonetheless were innovative artists who enjoyed huge crossover appeal.

From Jersey City, New Jersey, the brothers were from a musical family that included a stepfather who was a member of the group, Kool and The Gang, as well as ten aunts and uncles who had been DJs or MCs in the early days of Hip Hop. The duo was also influenced by the death of their biological father from pneumonia and the drowning death of their two-year-old brother.

Heavily influenced by 1960s pop music and melodic Old School R & B, P.M. Dawn adopted the tag line, Daisy Age Soul. In 1989, they recorded several demos (including their first song, "Check The Logic") at a Long Island studio. Upon signing a recording deal with Gee Street Records, the duo took the name P.M. Dawn, representing "the transition from dark to light." P.M. Dawn's debut single, "Ode To A Forgetful Mind" (Gee Street Records), was released in 1991, as the B-side to the twelve-inch single "Paper Doll."

P.M. Dawn. *Courtesy of Photofest.*

Although the rap duo failed to gain permission to sample The Beatles' hit, "Let It Be," they had better luck with the new wave group Spandau Ballet, who allowed them to use their song "True" as the foundation for "Set Adrift On Memory Bliss." The single topped the American music charts and had major crossover success. In 1991, P.M. Dawn's debut album, *Of The Heart, Of The Soul And Of The Cross: The Utopian Experience*, was released to rave reviews. The album's critical acclaim also allowed P.M. Dawn to escape constant comparisons to **De La Soul**.

In 1992, while Prince Be took part in the live filming of a performance at New York's The Sound Factory, KRS-ONE and his associates charged the stage, forcing Prince Be off and in the process smashing a record on DJ Minute Mix's turntable. KRS-ONE reportedly was angry that in a *Detail* magazine article Prince Be had said, "KRS-ONE wants to be a teacher, but a teacher of what?" KRS-ONE later made a public apology to P.M. Dawn.

The duo's single "I'd Die Without You" would be included on the soundtrack to the Eddie Murphy film *Boomerang* (1992). That same year, Prince Be appeared in a Nike commercial.

In 1993, P.M. Dawn released their second album, *The Bliss Album . . . ? (Vibrations of Love And Anger And the Ponderance of Life and Existence)* (Gee Street). This album incorporated the work of three of the United Kingdom's biggest artists: the lead single, "Looking Through Patient Eyes," sampled George Michael's hit song "Father Figure;" former Culture Club frontman Boy George appeared on the track "More Than Likely"; and the track "Fly Me To The Moon" sampled U2's song "The Fly." Despite these hits and some glowing reviews, some critics nevertheless considered P.M. Dawn's *Bliss* less rewarding than their groundbreaking debut.

In the meantime, the artists changed their names, with Prince Be becoming The Nocturnal and Minute Mix taking the name J.D. The Eternal. P.M. Dawn also contributed to the AIDS benefit album *Red Hot + Dance*, as well as other charity events, including Earth Day and LIFEbeat's CounterAid. Although the quality of P.M. Dawn's work remained high, subsequent albums did not match the commercial potency of their earlier material. In 1995, P.M. Dawn returned with their third album, *Jesus Wept* (Gee Street Records), which received strong reviews but weak sales. In 1998, they followed up with *Dearest Christian, I'm So Very Sorry for Bringing You Here. Love, Dad* (Gee Street Records), which reflected The Nocturnal's experiences as a new father.

DISCOGRAPHY: *Single*: "Ode to a Forgetful Mind" (Gee Street Records, 1991); *Albums*: *Of The Heart, Of The Soul And Of The Cross: The Utopian Experience* (Gee Street Records, 1991); *The Bliss Album* (Gee Street Records, 1993); *Jesus Wept* (Gee Street Records, 1995); *Dearest Christian, I'm So Very Sorry for Bringing You Here. Love, Dad* (Gee Street Records/V2, 1998).

POOR RIGHTEOUS TEACHERS

Culture Freedom [unknown], Wise Intelligent [Timothy Taylor], and Father Shaheed [unknown] are recognized as among the leaders of Afrocentric, Islamic-influenced rap music. The Poor Righteous Teachers are members of the Nation of Gods and Earths, more commonly known as Five Percenters. The group's name comes directly from Five Percent Nation doctrine that says "Poor righteous teachers" are the five percent of humans who have full knowledge of themselves, their origins, and the way the world actually works. Ten percent of humans have some knowledge and conspire to hide it from the masses. The mission and responsibility of "poor righteous teachers" is to educate the eighty-five percent who are totally ignorant to the truth.

Intending to be an alternative voice to the hardcore rap that glorified the violence, drugs, and ill-gotten gains, Culture Freedom and Wise Intelligent formed the group Poor Righteous Teachers when they were teens in Trenton, New Jersey. DJ and producer Father Shaheed would later join the duo. The group in fact defended the right of hardcore rap artists to express their messages, but wanted to convey what they thought—that one "did not have to sin to be successful." The central theme of all of the Poor Righteous Teachers albums was the concept that the virtues of righteousness are personified in the struggle of poor people around the world.

Initially, the group put out a twelve-inch on New Jersey–based, independent label Northside Records. The record landed in the hands of **DJ Red Alert**, who began to play it at the start and end of his radio show. Poor Righteous Teachers then caught the attention of Profile Records, who subsequently signed them to a deal. In 1991, Poor Righteous Teachers released their debut album, *Holy Intellect* (Profile Records), which spawned the hit single, "Rock Dis Funky Joint." Both *Holy Intellect* and the following album, *Pure Poverty* (Profile Records, 1992), focused on their religious beliefs and philosophy. Sometimes criticized for sacrificing beats for the message, Poor Righteous Teachers's albums nonetheless sold respectable numbers.

Poor Righteous Teachers' 1993 album, *Black Business* (Profile Records), would be their most commercially successful effort. Wise Intelligent was praised for his ability to incorporate Caribbean-style toasting into his rhymes; however, critics faulted the album for its homophobic content. After a 1995 solo album by Wise Intelligent, *Killin' U for Fun*, Poor Righteous Teachers released the album *New World Order* (Profile, 1996). With guest appearances by **KRS-ONE**, the **Fugees**, and Brother J (**X-Clan**), it was considered by many to be Poor Righteous Teachers's best, but most slept-on, effort.

After Profile Records was bought out by Arista Records, Poor Righteous Teachers asked to be released from their contract. They then formed Exit 7a Records (7A is the Trenton exit on the New Jersey Turnpike) and continued to record. In 2000, they released the single "I Swear to God" (Exit 7a Records). During this same period, Poor Righteous Teachers contributed to the *Unbound Project, Vol. 1* (Ground Control, 2000), a compilation album dedicated to jailed journalist and activist, Mumia Abu-Jamal, and Wise Intelligent appeared on the maxi-single, *Hip-Hop For Respect* (Rawkus Entertainment, 2000) dedicated to Guinean immigrant Amadou Diallo, who was fatally shot by New York City undercover police when drawing out his wallet for identification. In 2002, they released the album, *Declaration of Independence* (Exit 7a Records). Wise Intelligent's second solo album, *The Talented Timothy Taylor*, is scheduled for release in 2005.

DISCOGRAPHY: *Single*: "I Swear to God" (Exit 7a Records, 2000). *Albums*: *Holy Intellect* (Profile Records, 1991); *Pure Poverty* (Profile Records, 1992); *Black Business* (Profile Records, 1993); *New World Order* (Profile Records, 1996); *Declaration of Independence* (Exit 7a Records, 2002).

POPPING

Popping is a style of dance created by the Los Angeles street dance crew Electric Boogaloo Lockers (aka Electronic Boogaloo Lockers). In 1976, The Electronic Boogaloo Lockers was formed in Fresno, California, by Sam "Boogaloo Sam" Soloman, Nate "Slide" Johnson, and Joe "Slim" Thomas. Originally, *popping* was the term used to describe specific dance moves comprised of sudden muscle contractions done with the triceps, forearms, neck, chest, and legs. These contractions emphasized the dancer's movement, causing a quick, jolting effect. Popping would later become the broad term used to describe various old and new dance forms.

After the Electric Boogaloo Lockers and the Campbellockers performed on television shows such as *Soul Train*, popping erroneously became known as the "Electric Boogie" and "Boogie," particularly among East Coast audiences. On the West Coast, dancers in Los Angeles also distorted the name, calling it "pop-locking" Although **B-boying**, Brooklyn uprocking, **locking**, and popping are all dances popularized by Black youth, each dance form is informed by the region of origin and is also inspired by different musical styles and possesses distinct dress codes and languages. The confluence of these distinct dances and their associated styles can in part be attributed to the mainstream media, who have passed along to the public their own misunderstandings of the various dance forms.

POSSE. *See* Crew

PRINCE PAUL [Paul Huston]

Founding member of **Stetsasonic**, Prince Paul has produced some of rap music's most important albums. Prince Paul has lent his skills to such rap artists as **Boogie Down Productions**, **Gravediggaz**, **MC Lyte**, **Big Daddy Kane**, and **Third Bass**. Paul's crowning achievement came when he produced **De La Soul**'s 1989 debut album, *3 Feet High and Rising* (Tommy Boy Records). Using a wide range of musical sources, Prince Paul was the first to expand the capabilities of **sampling,** successfully combining sounds not normally associated with rap music. He was also one of the first to use skits on albums, a technique that has since become commonplace among rap music producers.

In 1994, Prince Paul joined former Stetsasonic member Fruitkwan (aka Frukwan) and **RZA** as part of the conceptual rap supergroup **Gravediggaz**. The group made three albums. Prince Paul appears on the debut album, *6 Feet Deep* (1994), and on a skit track on the third album, *Nightmare in A Minor* (Empire Musicwerks, 2002). With *The Pick, the Sickle and The Shovel* (1997), the Gravediggaz developed a sound dubbed "horrorcore" for its ghoulish raps over hardcore beats.

In 1997, Prince Paul released his solo debut album, *Psychoanalysis: What Is It?* (initially released on Wordsound, an independent label, and Tommy Boy Records re-issued it that same year). The album evolved out of his 1995 one-man, off-Broadway show *A Prince Among Thieves.* Also in 1997, Chris Rock's comedy album *Roll With the New*, produced by Prince Paul, won a Grammy Award. In 1999, Prince Paul released the highly praised concept album, *A Prince Among Thieves* (Tommy Boy

Records). Reminiscent of ***Hustlers Convention***, this rap opera follows the story of two friends who become rivals. One young man is an aspiring rap artist and the other is a drug dealer who can rhyme; Black-on-Black violence is at the center of the story. The album includes appearances by numerous artists, including **De La Soul**, **Big Daddy Kane**, **Biz Markie**, and comedian Chris Rock.

In 1999, Prince Paul was integral to the forming of the Handsome Boy Modeling School project with Dan "The Automator" Nakamura, which resulted in the album *So ... How's Your Girl?* (Tommy Boy Records). His second solo album, 2003's *Politics of the Business* (Razor & Tie), a satire of the contemporary rap music, featured a star-studded lineup but failed to connect with audiences.

DISCOGRAPHY: Gravediggaz: *6 Feet Deep* (V2/BMG/Gee Street, 1997 re-issue); *Psychoanalysis: What Is It?* (Wordsound, 1997; Tommy Boy Records re-issue, 1997); *A Prince Among Thieves* (Tommy Boy Records, 1999); Handsome Boy Modeling School: *So ... How's Your Girl?* (Tommy Boy Records, 1999); *Politics of the Business* (Razor and Tie, 2003); *White People* (Elektra, 2004).

PRODUCERS

Producers are responsible for "making beats" or, rather, creating the underlying music for rap compositions. DJs are distinguished from producers in that DJs primarily rely on records and turntable techniques as the basis of their musical creations, but producers use not only recorded music but also other technologies to develop and manipulate music and sounds.

The concept of the producer most likely coincides with the advent of the drum machine, which gave DJs (and others) the ability to partially compose original scores. The ability of producers to create "new" music was further enhanced with the emergence of digital samplers, which allows a producer to digitally record and save small sound clips from an output device, such as a turntable. Digital samples replaced the need for live instrumentals, because a producer could sample horns, guitars, pianos, and upright basses to play along with their drum sequences to produce the sounds of a complete band.

The success of a rap music producer is most often dependent on his or her ability to select sounds and music (often spanning genres), and the appropriate studio equipment, with which to craft an original sounding track that seamlessly accompanies a rap's lyrics.

PUBLIC ENEMY (aka PE)

As Public Enemy, the foursome of **Chuck D** [Carlton Douglas Ridenhour], **Flava Flav** [William Jonathan Drayton, Jr.], Terminator X [Norman Lee

Public Enemy. *Courtesy of Photofest.*

Rogers], and Professor Griff [Richard Griffin] reinterpreted rap music and became one of the most influential and controversial rap groups of the 1980s. For many fans and critics, PE is the definitive rap group in Hip Hop history.

Although both rap and rock audiences embraced PE, the group were often in the midst of controversy because of lyrics that were considered radical, inflammatory, or anti-Semitic.

PE was founded in 1982 at Adelphi University on Long Island, where Chuck D, then a DJ at the student radio station WBAU, met Hank Shocklee. Shocklee had been assembling demo tapes, and Chuck D (then known as Chuckie D) rhymed over one song, "Public Enemy No. 1," Def Jam Recordings cofounder and producer Rick Rubin heard a tape of "Public Enemy No. 1" and immediately sought out Chuck D to sign with the start-up label. Initially reluctant, Chuck D conceptualized a group that would have a political message and extraordinary production. Chuck D recruited Shocklee as his main producer and DJ Terminator X and Professor Griff.

Following in the steps of the Black Panthers, **Nation of Islam** member Professor Griff became the group's Minister of Information; he also served as choreographer for the group's back-up dancers, the Security of the First World (aka S1W), who performed military-style moves, armed with fake Uzis. Flava Flav would round out the crew. With his large sunglasses and an oversized clock hanging from his neck, Flava Flav became the group's mascot, however he never obscured the music.

PE developed a brand of hardcore rap that was exponentially advanced, musically and politically. As PE's front man, Chuck D's powerful baritone voice articulated the social problems that affected African Americans. PE ushered in the era of pro-Black consciousness within Hip Hop, which was predicated on self-awareness, knowledge of history, and social activism. Arguably the most frequently sampled rap artists of all time, PE's production team, The **Bomb Squad**, created an innovative and unique sound that combined sounds such as police sirens, unknown samples, snippets from speeches, and pulsating beats. The music simultaneously energizes and calls the listener to attention, to listen to Chuck D's authoritative message or to trickster Flava Flav's off-center raps.

PE made its debut in 1987 with the album, *Yo! Bum Rush the Show* (Def Jam Recordings). While that album did garner attention from critics and rap music aficionados, PE's place in the Hip Hop canon was sealed with their sophomore album, *It Takes a Nation of Millions to Hold Us Back* (Def Jam Recordings, 1988). Under Hank Shocklee's guidance, The Bomb Squad created a dense, chaotic mix that relied as much on sounds and avant-garde noise as it did on Old School funk grooves. Chuck D's message had become sharper since the debut, and Flava Flav's rap was more outrageous and funny. Hailed as revolutionary, *It Takes a Nation of Millions to Hold Us Back* both raised the bar for political rap music and advanced the idea that rap music could be used for social change. In a famous statement, Chuck D said that rap was "the black CNN," meaning that, unlike most mainstream media, rap music was candidly detailing what was happening in Black communities across the country.

As PE gained more mainstream media attention, the group's lyrics and personal statement came under closer scrutiny. Many critics were unnerved with PE's praise of Nation of Islam leader Minister Louis Farrakhan on "Bring the Noise." Moreover, the track "Fight the Power," from Spike Lee's 1989 film, *Do the Right Thing*, also caused a furor for its attacks on American cultural icons Elvis Presley and John Wayne. These early controversies seem minor beside the one that erupted after Professor Griff's statement in an interview that Jews were responsible for "the majority of the wickedness that goes on across the globe." The subsequent maelstrom resulted first in Professor Griff's being fired from PE, then in his reinstatement, and then in the group's temporarily breaking up. Professor Griff recorded four solo projects during this time, rejoining PE in the late 1990s.

In 1990, Public Enemy released the single "Welcome to the Terrordome" from *Fear of a Black Planet* (Def Jam Recordings, 1990), which again raised the issue of anti-Semitism for the line "still they got me like Jesus." Despite the controversy, *Fear of a Black Planet* was enthusiastically received and spawned the hit singles "911 Is a Joke," "Brothers Gonna Work It Out," and "Can't Do Nuttin' for Ya Man."

On their 1991 album, *Apocalypse 91 ... The Enemy Strikes Black* (Def Jam Recordings), PE rerecorded "Bring the Noise" with thrash metal band Anthrax, thus creatively acknowledging their large White audience. The album also included the track "By The Time I Get to Arizona," which voices PE's anger over the state's refusal to make Martin Luther King, Jr.'s birthday a state holiday. Moreover, PE recruited activist **Sister Souljah**, who lends her vocals to the album. *Apocalypse 91* received overwhelmingly positive reviews; however, PE showed signs of wear when they toured the second leg of U2's Zoo TV tour. Furthermore, Flava Flav was making headlines for running afoul of the law.

In the fall of 1992, PE released the **remix** collection *Greatest Misses* (Def Jam Recordings), and for the first time their efforts were almost universally panned. In 1993, PE went on hiatus and in 1994 they returned with *Muse Sick-N-Hour Mess Age* (Def Jam Recordings), which received poor reviews prior to its release from leading music magazines *Rolling Stone* and ***The Source***. With bad reviews and no strong single to buoy it, *Muse Sick-N-Hour Mess Age* quickly fell off the radar.

In 1995, Chuck D retired PE from touring in an effort to retool the group. During this period, Chuck D departed Def Jam and started his own record label and publishing company. In 1996, he released his solo debut album, *The Autobiography of Mistachuck* (Polygram), announcing at the same time that he planned to record a new PE album the following year. In 1997, Chuck published an autobiography, *Fight the Power: Rap, Race, Reality* (New York: Delacorte Press, 1997), and also reassembled the original Bomb Squad and began work on three albums. In the spring of 1998, PE made a major comeback with their soundtrack to Spike Lee's film *He Got Game*. The soundtrack received the best reviews of any PE album since *Apocalypse '91 ... The Enemy Strikes Black*.

For the release of PE's seventh album in 1999, Chuck signed the group to the Internet record label Atomic Pop, who released their *There's a Poison Goin' On ...*. The label made MP3 files of the album available on the Internet. (One reason that PE had ended their twelve-year partnership with Def Jam Recordings was Def Jam's refusal to post the new PE single, "Swindler's Lust," on the Internet.) The physical album appeared in stores in July 1999.

After a three-year break from recording and a switch to the In the Paint label, PE released the album, *Revolverlution*, a mix of new tracks, remixes, and live cuts. In 2004, PE with Moby released the CD single, "Make Love, F*ck War" (Mute, 2004).

See also: Censorship

DISCOGRAPHY: *Yo! Bum Rush the Show* (Def Jam Recordings, 1987); *Nation of Millions to Hold Us Back* (Def Jam Recordings, 1988); *Fear of a Black Planet* (Def Jam Recordings, 1990); *Apocalypse 91 ... The Enemy Strikes Black* (Def Jam Recordings, 1991); *Greatest Misses* (Def Jam Recordings, 1992); *Muse Sick-N-Hour Mess Age* (Def Jam Recordings, 1994); *He Got Game* (Def Jam Recordings, 1988); *There's a Poison Goin' On ...* (Atomic Pop, 1999); *Revolverlution* (In the Paint, 2001).

Q

Q-BERT. *See* DJ Q-Bert

QUEEN LATIFAH [Dana Elaine Owens]

Queen Latifah became one of the first solo female rap artists to be commercially successful and to earn a gold album.

Born in East Orange, New Jersey, Queen Latifah is the daughter of a high school art teacher who once owned a jazz and poetry club in Newark, New Jersey, and her father was a policeman. As a young girl, she adopted the Arabic name Latifah, which means "delicate and sensitive." Queen Latifah began her music career while in high school, **beatboxing** for a girl group called Ladies Fresh. She would eventually hook up with producer **Mark The 45 King**, a fellow New Jersey resident, becoming a member of his informal Flavor Unit crew. Mark produced Queen Latifah's demo track, "Princess of the Posse," which helped her land a recording contract with Tommy Boy Records.

In 1988, at the age of eighteen, Queen Latifah released her debut single, "Wrath of My Madness," and in 1989 she released her debut album, *All Hail the Queen* (Tommy Boy Records). Donning African robes and a crown, Queen Latifah's image, coupled with intelligent lyrics and pro-woman stance, helped to garner her music industry attention and fans.

In 1991, Latifah released the underrated album *Nature of a Sista* (Tommy Boy Records). In 1993, however, *Black Reign* (Motown Records) was released to critical acclaim. This album made Latifah the first female solo rap artist with a gold album. The hit single "U.N.I.T.Y.," which discussed sexist attitudes and violence against women, earned Latifah a Grammy award for Best Solo Rap Performance.

Not long before the release of *Black Reign*, Latifah's beloved brother Lance, a policeman, had died in a motorcycle accident; she wears his motorcycle key around her neck to honor his memory. The track "Winki's Theme" is also dedicated to him.

Her last rap album, *Order in the Court* (Motown) was released in 1998.

Latifah made her first foray into acting in 1991 beginning with small parts on sitcoms such as *The Fresh Prince of Bel-Air, Hanging with Mr. Cooper*, and *Ellen.* Director Spike Lee gave Latifah her first major acting role in his 1991 classic, *Jungle Fever.* Latifah continued to act landing a small part in the 1992 film *Juice,* starring **Tupac Shakur**. In 1993 she played the role of a hospice nurse to Michael Keaton in the film *My Life*, and Hollywood took notice of her skills. Latifah landed a starring role as Kadijah James, owner of Flavor Magazine, a small magazine publication on the hit Fox network television sitcom *Living Single* which aired from 1993 to 1997.

Queen Latifah. *Courtesy of Photofest.*

Queen Latifah's acting abilities eclipsed her rap skills in the 1996 film *Set It Off*, which also starred Vivica A. Fox and Jada Pinkett-Smith. Latifah reportedly lost twenty-five pounds to take on the dramatic role of Cleo, a poverty-stricken lesbian trying to escape the 'hood by robbing banks. Subsequent acting roles paired Latifah with Hollywood heavyweights in the film *Living Out Loud* (1998) opposite Holly Hunter and Danny DeVito and in *The Bone Collector* (1999) with Denzel Washington.

In 2002, Latifah starred in the film *Chicago*, based on the Broadway show and received a Golden Globe award and an Oscar nomination. She was the Executive Producer and costar of the 2003 film *Bringing Down the House* with comedian Steve Martin.

In addition to her impressive skills on the mic and in front of the camera, Queen Latifah is also a savvy businesswoman. She is co-CEO of Flavor Unit, her own record label, talent management, and television and movie production company. In 1999, Latifah started her own syndicated television talk show, *The Queen Latifah Show*, which ran for two years. She also published her autobiography, *Ladies First: Revelations of a Strong Woman* (William Morrow & Co., 1999). In 2003, Latifah was named one of People magazine's "Most Beautiful People."

In 2004, Queen Latifah showcased her singing, rather than her rap skills, on *The Dana Owens Album* (Motown Records). The gold-selling album is a collection of jazz and pop standards. Latifah has appeared in commercials for Cover Girl, the Freedom Card Gold Master Card, Courtyard Inn at Marriott, and does voice-overs for Pizza Hut. She was also celebrity spokesperson for Lane Bryant clothing stores. Queen Latifah is scheduled to host the 2005 Grammy Awards.

DISCOGRAPHY: *All Hail The Queen* (Tommy Boy Records, 1989); *The Nature Of a Sista* (Tommy Boy Records, 1991); *Black Reign* (Motown Records, 1993); *Order in The Court* (Motown Records, 1998); *Non-rap: The Dana Owens Album* (Motown Records, 2004).

QUEENSBRIDGE

The New York City Queensbridge Housing Project was made famous in the lyrical **battle** between the **Juice Crew All Stars** and **Boogie Down Productions**. Queensbridge Houses, located in Long Island City, New York (in the borough of Queens), is the nation's largest public housing complex, with 3,100 apartments. Queensbridge is associated with such rap artists such as **Nas**, **Mobb Deep**, and producer **Marley Marl**.

Queensbridge was placed on the rap music map with the release of the 1986 single, "The Bridge," produced by Marley Marl, with **MC Shan** on the mic. "The Bridge" became Queensbridge's unofficial anthem. On the track, MC Shan would claim the start of Hip Hop in Queensbridge. In response, Boogie Down Productions released "The Bridge is Over," a classic response that has **KRS-ONE** verbally attacking Juice Crew members MC Shan, Marley, **Roxanne Shante,** and **Mr. Magic**. "The Bridge Is Over" not only declared that Bronx natives were the creators of Hip Hop, it also labeled Queens natives as people who were "faking it." Unfortunately Boogie Down Productions' "faking it" tag from the song became part of the Hip Hop lexicon, as did terms such as "Making Manhattan," "Crooklyn," and, later, "Shaolin" (Staten Island). For the next year, MC Shan and KRS-ONE would continue to trade barbs.

A 1996 album, *Battle For Rap Supremacy: KRS-ONE v. MC* Shan (Cold Chillin', 1996), captures the year-long feud. In 2000, "The Bridge 2001," a remake of the song by a collective of artists who called themselves QB's Finest, was featured on *Nas & Ill Will Records Presents Queensbridge the Album* (Columbia). Nas was the producer for this effort and he gathered many of Queensbridge's illustrious alumni, including Marley Marl, MC Shan, Mobb Deep, **Capone-N-Noreaga**, Cormega, Poet, Tragedy, Nature, and Big Noyd.

The original "The Bridge," released on Marley Marl's independent label **Cold Chillin'** had a limited release, and therefore the record's sales did not accurately represent the impact of the song on rap music fans and on the music industry. "The Bridge" became popular through word-of-mouth publicity. At least one music industry insider estimates that as many as 1 million bootleg copies of "The Bridge" were distributed.

R

RAEKWON (aka Raekwon "The Chef," aka Lex Diamonds) [Corey Woods]
A member of the **Wu-Tang Clan**, Raekwon is not as famous as fellow members **Method Man** and **RZA**, but his solo projects have deservedly received critical acclaim. People call Raekwon "the Chef," because he cooks up great musical recipes.

As a member of the Wu-Tang Clan, Raekwon contributed to the group's groundbreaking debut album, *Enter the Wu-Tang (36 Chambers)* (Loud Records, 1993), then in the following year he released his debut solo single, "Heaven and Hell" (Loud Records). In 1995, his debut solo album *Only Built 4 Cuban Linx* (Loud Records) reportedly went gold in three days. Although the album did not sell on a par with Method Man's *Tical* (Def Jam Recordings, 1994), nonetheless the Hip Hop **underground** hailed it a classic, citing Raekwon's vivid imagery and evocative Mafia tales (sometimes told by his alter ego, Lex Diamonds). His on-wax chemistry with partner in rhyme, fellow Wu-Tang member **Ghostface** also added even more hardcore texture to *Only Built 4 Cuban Linx*. The single "Verbal Intercourse" is notable because it features the first appearance of Nas Escobar, **Nas**'s alter ego.

Raekwon rejoined the Wu-Tang Clan for their second album, *Forever* (Loud Records, 1997). After changing record companies, Raekwon released his sophomore album, *Immobilarity* (Epic Records, 1999), to mixed reviews. Many fans loved the album and its new direction overall, but most listeners did not think it compared favorably to the first. Present on *Only Built 4 Cuban Linx*, RZA and Ghostface were absent on *Immobilarity*. As a result, some fans though that the production was lacking and needed RZA's skills while others missed Ghostface's verbal interplay with Raekwon.

In 2003, Raekwon released his third album, *Lex Diamond Story* (Universal Records), again to uneven reviews. It seems that fans were still expecting him to top *Cuban Linx*, which *Lex Diamond Story* did not. Moreover, the same complaints about lackluster production arose again. Ironically, Raekwon stated that RZA had done several tracks for the album, but one was rejected by Universal Records executives, RZA could not find the reel for another, and there were problems getting samples cleared for two others. Aside from the beats, some critics expressed the concern that Raekwon's Mafioso motif, so fresh in 1995, was perhaps a little stale nearly a decade later.

DISCOGRAPHY: *Single*: "Heaven and Hell" (Loud Records, 1994). *Albums: Only Built 4 Cuban Linx* (Loud Records, 1995); *Immobilarity* (Epic Records, 1999); *The Lex Diamond Story* (Universal Records, 2003).

RAH DIGGA [Rashia Fisher]

Rah Digga, the self-proclaimed "Harriet Thugman of Hip Hop," is best known as the female member of the **Flipmode Squad**, which is led by **Busta Rhymes**. Following in the footsteps of **MC Lyte**, Rah Digga has earned the respect of audiences and her male peers with rugged lyrics, a superior flow, and a take-no-prisoners attitude.

Far from having a troubled past, Rah Digga is the product of a two-parent home. She attended a private boarding school in Maryland and studied electrical engineering for one year at the New Jersey Institute of Technology before pursuing a music career. She is married to fellow rap artist Young Zee. The Newark, New Jersey, native began performing as a member of the rap group Twice the Flavor and was the only woman in the Da Outsidaz clique. Hanging with Da Outsidaz, she was able to complete a demo tape with help from Ski (from Rok-A-Blok). That demo ended up in the hands of Q-Tip (**A Tribe Called Quest**), who invited Rah Digga to perform at New York's **Lyricist Lounge**. When he saw Rah Digga (who was visibly pregnant at the time) perform live, he was struck by her hard-hitting lyrical skills and decided to bring her to Elektra Records.

Rah Digga did secure a recording deal with Elektra, but internal problems would cause Q-Tip to turn the project over to Busta Rhymes—who subsequently invited her to join the Flipmode Squad. As a part of the Flipmode Squad, she appeared on the Busta Rhymes album *When Disaster Strikes* (Elektra Records, 1997) and on the Flipmode Squad's *The Imperial Album* (Elektra Records, 1998). Without having to rhyme about hard times or about crimes she had not committed, Rah Digga's deep and rugged voice signals to listeners that she is no joke.

Aside from appearing with the Flipmode Squad, Rah Digga also appeared on the **Fugees** track "Cowboys," from their album *The Score* (Columbia Records, 1996), and she is paired with **Bahamadia** on the track "Be Ok" from the album *Lyricist Lounge, Vol. 1* (Rawkus Entertainment, 2002). Rah Digga released her long anticipated solo debut album, *Dirty Harriet* (J Records), in 2000 and it was praised by both commercial and **underground** audiences. According to Rah Digga, runaway slave Harriet Tubman inspired the album's title. Rah Digga stated that, like Harriet Tubman who led people to freedom, she is leading other female rap artists to realize that they can succeed using lyrical skills rather than their sexuality.

Refreshingly, *Dirty Harriet* has few guest appearances, only peppering the album with tracks such as "Do The Ladies," featuring **Eve** and

Sonja Blade. Rah Digga wanted her individual style to shine through, and not have it get lost in the midst of other voices. Even the Flipmode Squad's participation is limited to the track "Imperial," which features Busta Rhymes.

Four years after her debut album, Rah Digga was set to release her sophomore effort, *Everything Is a Story* (J Records), in February 2004, she said was influenced by the late **The Notorious B.I.G.** The first single, "Party & Bullsh*t," a reworking of The Notorious B.I.G. song, was well received by the public and got a significant amount of radio and video play. Unfortunately, there were persistent delays with the release of the album. In March 2004, following Busta Rhymes's lead, Rah Digga left J Records and *Everything Is a Story* remained unreleased.

DISCOGRAPHY: *Singles*: "Party & Bullsh*t" (J Records, 2003). *Albums*: *Dirty Harriet* (Elektra Records, 2000); *Everything is a Story* (J Records, unreleased).

RAKIM. *See* Eric B & Rakim

RAP

Rap is defined as the spoken element of Hip Hop and at its most elementary level rap is speaking to the beat of music. Although rap music is only one of the original four elements of Hip Hop (along with **DJing**, **B-boying**, and aerosol art or graffiti), it is the most commercial of the elements and over the years it has been seen as interchangeable with Hip Hop.

The original Hip Hop term for rapping was MCing. MC is an abbreviation for Master of Ceremonies or, alternatively, Mic Controller.

The origins of rap music are ancient, in the oral traditions of African countries. Those traditions spread to the African Diaspora and through slavery to the United States, South America, and into the Caribbean. In the United States, Black men were integral to the development of the oral poetry known as "toasts." A famous example is the "Signifying Monkey," whose main trickster character has direct links to African folklore. Toasts and later rapping were informed primarily by the experiences of low- income and transient men, who had been influenced by prison and street culture. The rhyming styles of early Black radio DJs such as **Jocko Henderson**, **Jack "The Rapper" Gibson**, and Daddy O would also contribute to the creation of rap music.

Within the context of 1960s African American culture, the term *rap* was a slang term for talking. For instance, Black activist, H. Rap Brown (later known as Jamil Abdullah Al-Amin) states in his 1969 autobiography *Die Nigger Die*, that he got his nickname because he was good at a competitive word game called the **Dozens**. During rounds of the Dozens, opponents hurl clever, but caustic, insults at each other (often focused on the opponent's mother). An offshoot of the Dozens was Signifying, whereby the opponent was the direct target of the wordplay. Signifying, unlike the Dozens, could be used to attack or praise. In either case, it was the response of the crowd or of fellow participants that determined which competitor was the best wordsmith.

Musically, in the 1970s, *rap* came to describe the spoken interludes in a record used by a myriad of R & B singers, including Barry White, Isaac Hayes, Marlena Shaw, Millie Jackson, and Bobby Womack. The immediate precursor to modern rap is most likely the music of artists such as The **Last Poets** and Gil Scott-Heron, who combined politically and socially relevant poetry with percussion-based music.

Caribbean immigrants to New York brought their toasts, which also influenced the development of rap music. "Toasting" is speaking in a syncopated manner to a beat. Many cite popular American radio DJ Jocko Henderson as being a causal link in the creation of toasting, since it was his style that was copied, either through radio transmissions that reached Jamaica (the show was broadcast in Florida for a time) or through the interactions between Jamaicans who visited the United States and heard Henderson's radio program with mainland artists such as U-Roy. In turn, Jamaican immigrant **DJ Kool Herc** imported the sound system (massive speakers and turntables) concept to the United States.

Initially, while manning the turntables he also "toasted" or rapped a bit, then turned over those duties to an MC, whose job was to keep the party-goers revved up. The MC's role then began to expand beyond crowd controlling to expressing his or her own thoughts, emotions, and interests in a rap or rhyme, as part of event's entertainment.

Lyrical **battles** between MCs followed in the traditions of the Dozens and of signifying, just as rapping has characteristics akin to American toasts. With the emergence of rap records such as "**King Tim III**" (Personality Rap) and "**Rapper's Delight**" (Sugar Hill Records) in 1979, the MC began to eclipse the DJ and took center stage. This was the easiest element of Hip Hop to commercialize and as such as become the genre's most recognized component.

RAPMANIA: ROOTS OF RAP. *See* Films

RAP-METAL

In the 1990s, rap-metal, a synthesizing of the most aggressive elements of hardcore rap and heavy metal, became a very popular subgenre of metal music. It was generally White musicians, whose leanings were in rock rather than in rap, who popularized the rap-metal subgenre.

Before the emergence of rap-metal as such, Hip Hop DJs such as **Afrika Bambaataa** used rock records as part of their musical creations, and several high-profile rap music artists had incorporated rock into their rap music production. In 1980, The Treacherous Three would use rock guitar riffs on their single "Body Rock" (Enjoy Records). In 1984, **Run DMC** released the single "Rock Box," which used aggressive guitar riffs. In 1986, Run DMC expanded their use of rock by collaborating with Aerosmith on a remake of the track "Walk This Way" (Def Jam Recordings). The **Beastie Boys** came from a punk rock background and therefore their 1986 album *Licensed to Ill* (Def Jam Recordings) represented an early rap-rock combination. The next year on their album *Lethal* (Select Records, 1987), the rap group **U.T.F.O.** teamed up with rock group Anthrax. Even **Sean "P. Diddy" Combs** produced two rock **remixes** of the 1998 single, "It's All About the Benjamins" (Bad Boy Entertainment).

Although bands such as Red Hot Chili Peppers and Faith No More played with the style, Anthrax is credited with its formation. The first acknowledged rap-metal single is Anthrax's 1987 EP, *I'm the Man* (Island Records), a comedic track that mixes a heavy guitar riff, the melody line from the popular Jewish song "Hava Nagila," with an actual full-length rap sequence. This prompts comparison to Blondie's 1980 single, "Rapture" (Chrysalis Records), which includes a snippet of rapping by Debbie Harry. In 1991, Anthrax would take the further step to remake **Public Enemy**'s "Bring the Noise" (Def Jam Recordings, 1988), featuring members of Public Enemy itself. Rap groups such as Public Enemy had large White followings and some metal bands therefore related rap music with the aggressive, street-wise attitude that they wanted to convey. "Bring The Noise" laid the foundation for this new musical pairing.

Most rap-metal bands were more interested in replicating the force of rap music than in mastering the complexities of its language and performance elements. More often than not, the result was shouting words linked together instead of words that flowed over the music with some discernable rhythm. With the exception of Rage Against the Machine's politically charged lyrics, most rap-metal bands during the mid- to-late 1990s combined ultra-aggressive and macho posturing either with juvenile humor or the reflective angst often found in alternative metal.

These rock-based compositions made use of traditional rap to varying degrees and with varying success. The much-hyped 1993 soundtrack for the film *Judgment Night* featured an array of celebrity rap artists and rock bands, but it failed to stem the decline of rap-metal collaborations as the 1990s progressed. Alternative metal bands such as Helmet, White Zombie, and Tool, known for a thick, booming sound instead of popular songs or memorable riffs based on a melodic sequence, would also influence rap-metal. While bands such as Korn used rap music beats in their music, recognizable rap-metal bands always had their front man rap to rock-infused music. Using this formula, **Limp Bizkit**, fronted by Fred Durst, became rap-metal's most popular band during the late 1990s.

"RAPPER'S DELIGHT"

Acknowledged as the first commercially successful "rap record" in Hip Hop history. It was also the first rap record subjected to radio censorship. In September 1979, Sugar Hill Records released the song recorded by the Sugar Hill Gang. A sexually-charged line that refers to a rival's "little worm" was deleted for airplay. Subsequently clean or edited rap songs that omitted profanity or controversial content were made to comply with radio decency standards. (See further in the Introduction.)

See also: Sugar Hill Gang

RAPPIN' 4-TAY (aka Four-Tay) [Anthony Forte]

Perhaps best known for his finger-wave-perm hairstyle, Rappin' 4-Tay detailed the rough side of urban living without glorifying the violence and crime. Moreover, he often provided advice about staying "legit" and changing negative behavior. With over ten years in the rap game, this West Coast artist gained the most attention for his appearance on **Tupac Shakur**'s single, "Only God Can Judge Me" from *All Eyez on Me* (Death Row Records, 1996).

A short time after finishing high school, Rappin' 4-Tay debuted on fellow Oakland, Californian **Too Short**'s single "Don't Fight the Feelin'," from his album *Life Is ... Too Short* (Jive Records, 1990). After the album's release, Rappin' 4-Tay would be convicted of selling marijuana and sentenced to ten months in prison. Upon his release from jail, he formed Rag Top Records with friends Franky J and Fly. In January 1991, Four-Tay, as he was originally known, released his debut album *Rappin' 4-Tay Is Back!!!.* With the release of his second album, *Don't Fight the Feelin'* (Capitol Records), Rappin' 4-Tay became a local favorite with his hardcore lyrics that did not romanticize the hood.

In April of 1995, 4-Tay stormed charts with a reworked version of the Spinners' 1972 hit, "I'll Be Around," featuring sampled vocals from the group. In 1996, Rappin' 4-Tay's album *Off Parole* (Capitol Records), which includes appearances by Too Short and **MC Breed,** was released while he was still in California's state prison, San Quentin, serving time for parole violations. The title expressed 4-Tay's goal, "to get off parole." In 1997, the album *4 Tha Hard Way* was released. Two years later, the album *Introduction to Mackin'* (Celeb Entertainment) featured a cameo by Max Julien, who starred in the 1970s **blaxploitation** film *The Mack.* After a four-year absence, 4-Tay released the album, *Gangsta Gumbo* (Liquid 8) in 2003.

DISCOGRAPHY: *Single*: "I'll Be Around" featuring the Spinners (Capitol Records, 1995). *Albums: Rappin' 4-Tay is Back* (Rag Top, 1991); *Don't Fight the Feelin'* (Capitol Records, 1994); *Off Parole* (Capitol Records, 1996); *4 Tha Hard Way* (Virgin, 1997); *Bigga Than Da Game*

(Rag Top, Ground Level, 1998); *Introduction to Mackin'* (Celeb. Entertainment, 1999); *Gangsta Gumbo* (Liquid 8, 2003).

RAY BENZINO [aka Ray Dogg] [Ray Scott]

An alumnus of **Almighty RSO** and Made Men, Ray Benzino is probably better known for his long-running feud with **Eminem** than for his rap artistry. Ray Benzino, a close associate of ***The Source*** magazine publisher, Dave Mays, incited verbal warfare with Eminem in the fall of 2002 on the song "Pull Your Skirt Up" (Surrender Records). The song accuses the multi-platinum rap artist of being allowed to play by a different set of rules because he is White. Benzino also contended that Eminem's rise was symbolic of the music industry's greed and indifference to Hip Hop's history and core fan base. In November 2003, to bolster his accusations against Eminem, Benzino and David Mays held a news conference and released Eminem tapes from 1993 that contained racial slurs against Black women.

In 2001, Benzino released his first solo effort, *The Benzino Project* (Surrender Records). In 2003, he released his second album, *Redemption* (Elektra Records).

DISCOGRAPHY: *Single*: "Pull Your Skirt Up" (Surrender Records, 2002); *Albums: The Benzino Project* (Surrender Records, 2001); *Redemption* (Elektra Records, 2003).

REAL ROXANNE, THE [Adelaida "Joanne" Martinez]

The Real Roxanne, best remembered as a player in the Roxanne Wars of the 1980s, must be acknowledged as the first successful Latina rap artist.

In 1984, the rap group **U.T.F.O.** recorded the song, "Roxanne, Roxanne," which criticizes a fictional "stuck-up" Roxanne. In the call-and-response pattern prevalent in music from the African Diaspora, over 100 response records were made, including **Juice Crew All Stars** member "Roxanne" Shante's debut single, produced by **Marley Marl**. Subsequently two female artists, **Roxanne Shante** and The Real Roxanne, both using the original U.T.F.O. track, would **battle** each other for prominence. Though many believe that The Real Roxanne's career began with U.T.F.O., she actually began rhyming in 1981, using the name Dimples Love. The teenager then joined the all-male Choices MCs and performed with the group in local clubs.

Martinez was not the first choice for The Real Roxanne role. Originally Elise Jacks, picked out of the crowd at the Funhouse Club, was slated to be The Real Roxanne. Things changed when Martinez, a self-described "light-skinned Puerto Rican chick with red hair," met Full Force member Paul Anthony at the diner where she worked as a waitress.

The Real Roxanne. *Courtesy of Photofest.*

Thereafter Martinez became involved with producer Hitman Howie Tee and became part of the Full Force family (which included U.T.F.O., Lisa Lisa, and Cult Jam) and so became The Real Roxanne. Howie Tee produced The Real Roxanne's musical response. It is generally agreed that Roxanne Shante was the better rap artist, particularly given the fact The Real Roxanne seemed to come to U.T.F.O.'s attention more for her good looks than because of her lyrical skills.

In 1988, Martinez released her debut album, *The Real Roxanne* (Select Records), and followed it up four years later with a sexually explicit sophomore album, *Go Down (But Don't Bite It)* (Select Records, 1992). Fellow rap artist **Chubb Rock**, rather than The Real Roxanne, is credited with writing the racy lyrics for the album.

DISCOGRAPHY: *Singles* (twelve inch): "Bang Zoom! Let's Go, Let's Go/Howies Teed Off" (Select Records, 1986); "Respect" (Select Records, 1988); "Roxanne's On A Roll" (Select Records, 1989). *Albums: The Real Roxanne* (Select Records, 1988); *Go Down (But Don't Bite It)* (Select Records, 1992).

REDMAN (aka Funk Doctor Spock) [Reggie Noble]

Redman, most often associated with **Method Man**, is a charismatic rap artist known for his blunt ability to deliver hilarious punch lines.

Legend has it that the Newark, New Jersey, native met **EPMD** at a New Jersey nightclub when the duo filled in for **MC Lyte**, who had cancelled a performance at the last minute. Subsequently, Redman hooked up with EPMD and was first was heard on their singles "Hardcore" and "Brothers on My Jock," from the album *Business as Usual* (Def Jam Recordings, 1991).

In 1992, Redman's debut album, *Whut? Thee Album* (RAL/Def Jam Recordings) hit the streets. The album combined reggae and funk influences, along with topical commentary. Redman's rap style is concise, yet fluid, and samples the tough, the silly, and the satirical. In 1994, he returned with his second album, *Dare Iz a Darkside* (Def Jam Recordings), a more hardcore album than his debut. Redman's third album, *Muddy Waters* (Def Jam Recordings), followed in 1996. In 2000, Redman released the album *Doc's Da Name* (Def Jam Recordings) and in 2001, *Malpractice* (Def Jam Recordings).

As part the Def Squad, he appeared on the crew's 1998 album, *El Niño* (Def Jam Recordings). In 1999, Redman would team up with Method Man and record the album *Blackout!* (Def Jam Recordings/Def Squad, 1999). The hit single from *Blackout!*, "How High," inspired the 2001 comedy film, *How High?* In 2004, the *Method and Red* program debuted on Fox television network, a short-lived show about the rap duo moving into an upscale, predominantly White neighborhood.

After a three-year hiatus, Redman released the slept-on *Ill At Will Mixtape, Vol. 1* (Gilla House, 2004). Clearly a move to expand beyond Def Jam's corporate grip, the album offers up unadulterated rap music. With plenty of freestyling, humor, and imaginative tracks such as "I See Dead People" (which contains samples of **Biggie Smalls**, **Big Pun**, **Big L**, and **Tupac Shakur**), the **mixtape** has received raves from **underground** and aboveground audiences.

DISCOGRAPHY: *Whut? Thee Album* (RAL/Def Jam Recordings, 1992); *Dare Iz a Darkside* (Def Jam Recordings, 1994) *Muddy Waters* (Def Jam Recordings, 1996); *Blackout!* [with Method Man] (Def Jam Recordings/Def Squad, 1999); *Doc's Da Name* (Def Jam Recordings, 2000); *Malpractice* (Def Jam Recordings, 2001); *Ill At Will Mixtape, Vol. 1* (Gilla House, 2004).

REGGAE AND RAP

The fusion of rap and reggae began when Jamaican immigrant **DJ Kool Herc** first set up his speakers and turntables in the Bronx. Herc was following in the footsteps of Jamaican DJs who set up their mobile "sound systems" in outdoor locations to entertain party-goers and to **battle** each other for supremacy within their communities.

The Hip Hop pantheon is rife with artists of Caribbean ancestry, including **Grandmaster Flash**, **Busta Rhymes**, **Heavy D**, **Slick Rick**, the **Fugees**, producer **Pete Rock,** and **Doug E. Fresh**, who, like Herc, brought these sensibilities to Hip Hop. The relationship between rap and reggae is more than simply the borrowing of bass lines and lyrical riffs. The concept of talking over records, called "toasting," had its origins in Jamaica with artists such as U-Roy, King Stitt, and Dennis Alcapone. Mobile sound systems that include massive speakers and turntables were also Jamaican innovations.

Dancehall reggae is probably closest to rap music in the United States, particularly since both have their roots in poor and working-class Black communities. Like its American cousin, critics contend that dancehall reggae tends to glorify criminal activity, is homophobic, and has the capacity to negatively influence the behavior of youths. Considered raunchier and earthier than traditional reggae, some believe that dancehall reggae has an overall lustier tone than rap music. While this assertion is debatable given the graphic nature of many rap lyrics, what is indisputable is that rap music and dancehall reggae are two art forms that are dependent on bass-laden beats and on lyricists who relay stories about life in the 'hood (or its Jamaican equivalent, the yard).

Dancehall reggae is not usually heard on mainstream commercial radio in the United States, but Jamaican artists such as Shabba Ranks, Cutty Ranks and Buju Banton, Beenie Man, Supercat, Shaggy, and Sean Paul nevertheless can attract and maintain audiences because of their collaborations with rap artists. The **Boogie Down Productions** song, "The Bridge is Over" (B-Boy Records, 1986), is widely recognized as the first record to fuse reggae with rap. DJ Scott La Rock's piano sequence on "The Bridge Is Over" is based on a Jamaican standard, Marcia Griffith's "Feel Like Jumping." Many other Hip Hop and reggae collaborations would follow, among them "Trash n' Ready," by Sound Dimensions (B-Boy Records, 1986); "Sexy," by Master of Ceremonies (1986); and "Na Touch da Just," by **Just-Ice** (Sleeping Bag Records, 1988). **Special Ed** includes two reggae-laced tracks on his album, *Youngest in Charge* (Profile Records, 1989); Asher D and Daddy Freddie released "Raggamuffin Hip Hop" (1989); **Poor Righteous Teachers**, rap over reggae-influenced beats on the album *Pure Poverty* (Profile Records, 1991); and **Run DMC** recorded the track "Roots, Rap, Reggae" with Yellowman, which appears on the *King of Rock* album (Def Jam Recordings, 1999). Jamaican producers Sly & Robbie collaborated with rap artists Willie D, **Young MC**, **Queen Latifah**, and Shah of Brooklyn on the 1989 album *Silent Assassins* (Island Records). The track "Shoot To Kill" (Weeded/Nervous, 1993), where Mad Lion rhymes over **KRS-ONE**'s "Black Cop," recently shot to number three on the *Billboard* chart. Queen Latifah's single "U.N.I.T.Y." (Motown Records, 1993) is yet another example of reggae-influenced rap music.

REMIX

A remix results when a producer takes the original multi-track recording and manipulates the separate tracks containing the original drums, bass, guitar, keyboards, and vocals, often inserting new performances, creating a new master recording.

With the emergence of digital samplers and drum loops or beats, remixes became popular as a way to make songs "danceable." Producers would accomplish this by speeding up the tempo or beats per minute (BPM). Then vocals are then cut up and stretched or compressed to fit the new melody line. Lastly, the bass and other instruments may be re-recorded, though snippets of the original tracks may be retained to reference the original composition.

RHYME AND REASON. *See* Films

RHYME SYNDICATE

The Rhyme Syndicate was a collective formed by **Ice-T** that included **Afrika Islam**, DJ Alladin, **Busy Bee**, Everlast (before **House of Pain**), MC Donald D, and Bronx Style Bob [Bob Khaleel]. Later, Ice-T would use the name for his record company.

RICHIE RICH

Richie Rich was the first artist from the Bay area signed to **Def Jam Recordings**. **Snoop Dogg** has stated that he was influenced by the underground legend to name his own supergroup **213**. Richie Rich is also distinct in that, despite his hardcore street content, he is equally comfortable using slang or standard English to convey his message. Richie Rich came onto the music scene in 1989 as a member of the group, 415, which was then the Oakland area code.

Of 415's group members, it was the distinctive, raspy voice and the hustler-infused lyrics of a young Richie Rich that made listeners take notice. The group's album *41Fivin* (Big League Records, 1990) was a Bay Area classic, independently selling 147,000 units. Catapulted by the success of his work with 415, Richie Rich released a solo album, *Don't Do It.*

Richie Rich was on the road to a promising music career when in 1990 he was convicted of drug solicitation and sent to prison. In the meantime, 415 entered into a recording agreement with Priority Records and replaced Richie Rich with another rap artist. After his release from prison, Richie Rich considered several record contract offers, but given the unscrupulous dealings that he had been exposed to, including a management contract that he could not break, Rich abandoned music and went back to the streets.

Richie Rich eventually bought his way out of his management contract and made appearances on several singles, most notably the **remix** for **The Luniz** track "5 On It" (Virgin Records, 1995) and on longtime friend **Tupac Shakur**'s track "Heavy in the Game," from *Me Against The World* (Interscope Records, 1995) and "Rather Be Yo Nigga" and "Ain't Hard 2 Find" from *All Eyez On Me* (Death Row Records, 1996). Rich's guest appearances were well received and subsequently he released his second album called *1/2 Thang* on his own record label, Oakland Hills 41510 (named after the former and current area codes).

Richie Rich's first release on Def Jam Recordings is the 1996 album *Seasoned Veteran*, which includes appearances by Tupac on "Niggas Done Changed," **E-40** on "It's On," and The Luniz on "Questions" and "Hard to Get" with Rick James that also appears on the *How to Be a Player* film soundtrack. Subsequent albums followed: *Game* (2000), *Nixon Pryor Roundtree* (Ten-Six Records, 2002), and *Richie Rich Presents Grabs, Snatches & Takes* (Ten-Six Records, 2004).

DISCOGRAPHY: *Don't Do It* (Big League, 1990); *1/2 Thang* (Shot Records, 1996); *Seasoned Veteran* (Def Jam Recordings, 1996); *Game* (Ten-Six Records, 2000); *Nixon Pryor Roundtree* (Ten-Six Records, 2002); *Richie Rich Presents Grabs, Snatches & Takes* (Ten-six, Records, 2004).

RICK RUBIN. *See* Def Jam Recordings

ROC-A-FELLA RECORDS

The Roc-A-Fella Records label was cofounded by rap artists **Shawn "Jay-Z" Carter**, Damon Dash, and Kareem "Biggs" Burke in New York City in 1995. The initial record company was created out of Damon Dash and Jay-Z's frustration in attempting to secure Jay-Z a record deal. The two began pressing up records, selling them out of the trunks of their cars, and requesting that DJs play their records on radio mix shows. Roc-A-Fella came to the attention of Priority Records and the two entities entered into a joint venture. In 1996, Roc-A-Fella released Jay-Z's debut album, *Reasonable Doubt.*

In 1997 Roc-A-Fella would enter into a partnership with **Def Jam Recordings**. The current artist roster includes Jay-Z, **Cam'ron**, **Kanye West**, **Beanie Sigel**, and Memphis Bleek. Aside from the record company, under the leadership of Damon Dash, Roc-A-Fella Enterprises, a $500-million company, houses several ventures, including a film division. In 1999, Roc-a-Wear was founded and as of 2004 had sales that total approximately $300 million a year, making it one of the most popular men's lines in the United States. In December 2002, Roc-A-Fella added liquor distribution to its portfolio, purchasing the U.S. distribution rights to Armadale vodka, a Scottish liquor. Under the Roc-A-Fella Enterprises umbrella are also Tiret luxury watches and *America*, an urban luxury fashion magazine. Dash also brought the Pro-Keds name to use on a new line of athletic shoes and is slated to introduce Roc Digital, a line of MP3 players.

In November 2004, Roc-A-Fella Records released the film *Fade to Black*, which chronicles Jay-Z's Madison Square Garden performance in November 2003. The film includes appearances by artists and record executives such as **Missy Elliott**, **Foxy Brown**, **Mary J. Blige**, **Slick Rick**, Rick Rubin, and **P. Diddy**.

In December 2004, Roc-A-Fella Records was bought by Island Def Jam for a reported $10 million. Def Jam already owned a 50 percent stake in the company and purchased the remaining 50 percent. (In 1997, Def Jam Recordings had paid $1.5 million for its stake.) Several years later, the Roc-A-Fella co-CEOs renegotiated their contract for approximately $20 million. In December 2004, Jay-Z was appointed president of Def Jam Recordings. Dash will reportedly continue in various other ventures, including his movie production house, Dash Films, and Rocawear Clothing. Dash is also reportedly in talks related to launching another music company.

ROCK STEADY CREW

Rock Steady Crew is perhaps the best known of the original **B-boy** crews. Membership has included Ken Swift [Kenny Gabbert], Mr. Freeze, Eazy Mike, Mr. Wiggles [Steve Clemente], Lil' Crazy Legs, Pop Master Fabel [Jorge Pabon], Frosty Freeze [Wayne Frost], Jimmy D, JoJo; **Crazy Legs** [Richie Colón], Johnny Jay, Rip Ski, Lenny Len, and deceased members Kuriaki, Buck 4, and Kippy D.

The group dates back to 1977, when Jimmy Dee, JoJo, and JoJo's brother Eazy Mike formed Rock Steady Crew in the Bronx, New York. JoJo is also often credited with inventing the backspin, a B-boy move. People interested in joining Rock Steady Crew had to subject themselves to a **battle** with current members. In 1979, Jimmy D added Manhattan residents Richard "Crazy Legs" Colón and Lenny Len, who began spreading the Rock Steady Crew name into Manhattan. Mr. Freeze was one of the first White B-boys. Frosty Freeze was a veteran B-boy (a member of the Rock City Crew), who at the time was without a crew. Still interested in B-boying, he gave his support to younger Rock Steady Crew members if they needed him in a battle.

The Rock Steady Crew's big break came in 1981 when photographer Henry Chalfant (who co-directed the 1983 documentary **Style Wars**), gave them the chance to perform at the Lincoln Center Outdoors Program. The event turned into a battle with the Dynamic Rockers. The show, and therefore also B-boying, received international media attention. In 1982, Rock Steady Crew became members of **Afrika Bambaataa**'s **Zulu Nation**. Rock Steady Crew designated ninety-eighth and Amsterdam Avenues in New York City as Rock Steady Park, and this became a meeting place for all Rock Steady Crew members.

Shortly after, Crazy Legs was appointed president of the Rock Steady Crew, with Frosty Freeze and Ken Swift (who was part of a crew called The Young City Boys and was brought in as an Rock Steady Crew member after battling Crazy Legs) as co-vice presidents. The profile of Rock Steady Crew was raised even more when members Mr. Freeze, Ken Swift, Crazy Legs, and Frosty Freeze appeared in the 1983 box office smash *Flashdance*. Their dance sequences lead to a nationwide craze that the media called break dancing. Other pioneering B-boy crews include The Furious Rockers, Dynamic Rockers, and New York City Breakers.

In 1991, Rock Steady Crew began to have an annual gathering to celebrate their founding. The New York City event includes numerous performances and offerings and has become a get-together for domestic and international B-boys and B-girls, as well as other people who identify with Hip Hop.

RODRIGUEZ, IVAN "DOC" (aka DJ Doc)

Ivan "Doc" Rodriguez is acknowledged as the first Latino producer–engineer–DJ to have a creative role in the production of early rap music records, some of which have become classics within the Hip Hop canon. Under the name DJ Doc, Rodriguez began his career as **KRS-ONE**'s first DJ and progressed to becoming a sound engineer or record producer for such rap artists as **EPMD**, KRS-ONE, **Biz Markie**, **Eric B & Rakim**, **MC Lyte**, **LL Cool J**, **Redman**, Ed OG, **The Fugees**, and **Das EFX**.

ROOTS, THE

Comprised of Black Thought [Tariq Trotter], ?uestlove [Ahmir Khalib Thompson], Hub [Leon Hubbard], and Malik B [Malik Abdul Basit] and following in the footsteps of **Stetsasonic**, The Roots are known for performing live rap music, with traditional instruments, instead of relying on samples and drum machines. The Roots have developed a distinctly jazzy sound supported by intelligent lyrics that span an array of subjects from romance to politics.

The Roots remain a rap music paradox, in that they are consistently praised for their albums and live shows and yet have failed to achieve huge sales. Many fans and critics, it seems, have adopted the notion that traditional instrumentation and a jazz sound are not consistent with authentic rap music. The Roots have therefore relied on extensive touring, rather than on record sales, to sustain their musical mission for the past fifteen years.

The origins of The Roots began in 1987 in Philadelphia, Pennsylvania, when rap artist Black Thought and drummer ?uestlove (pronounced *Quest Love*) became friends at the Philadelphia High School for the Creative and Performing Arts. The cash-poor duo did not have money to purchase basic DJ equipment: two turntables, a microphone, plus a **mixer** and plenty of records. They compensated for their lack of a DJ setup by re-creating classic rap music tracks with Black Thought rhyming over ?uestlove's drum kit. The duo eventually earned money by playing at school and on sidewalks, then at local talent shows. Through their performances,

The Roots. *Courtesy of Photofest.*

the pair met up with bassist Hub and rap artist Malik B. The Roots came together as a group in 1989 and generated buzz by playing the clubs on Philadelphia's and New York's **underground** rap music circuits.

While representing the United States in a rap music concert in Germany, The Roots recorded their debut album, *Organix*, to be sold at their shows. *Organix* was officially released in the United States in 1993 on Remedy Recordings. As ascendant underground stars, The Roots were solicited by several record companies and in 1993 signed with Geffen Records. In 1995, The Roots' second album, *Do You Want More?!!!??!* (Geffen Records) was released. Bucking convention, this album contains only original music and forgoes samples or any previously recorded material. Standout singles include the title track, and also "Mellow My Man," and "Proceed." The album was largely ignored by rap music fans, however, instead gaining traction among alternative rock audiences. In 1995, the Roots' popularity in alternative music circles got them invited to perform on the second stage at Lollapalooza; they also performed at the Montreux International Jazz Festival in Switzerland.

The Roots released their second album *Illadelph Halflife* (Geffen Records) in 1996; this spawned the popular single "Clones/Sections." The album made a small concession to conventional rap music by using samples of material that they had previously produced and recorded. The Roots released their first platinum-selling album, *Things Fall Apart* (MCA Records), in 1999; this album stands as their biggest critical and commercial success. The title references Chinua Achebe's classic 1958 novel of the same name. On the album, The Roots display an encyclopedic knowledge of African American music as well as the capacity to forge a new musical vision. Their live album, *The Roots Come Alive* (MCA Records) was also released in 1999.

In 2000, the single "You Got Me," featuring Erykah Badu from *Things Fall Apart*, earned the group a Grammy award for Best Performance for a Duo or Group. Fellow Philadelphian, singer Jill Scott, wrote the verses that Badu sang. In 2002, the long-awaited *Phrenology* (MCA Records), the Roots' most experimental album to date, was released to mixed reviews. Some applauded the group's willingness to expand their musical horizons; others accused them of going commercial.

In January 2004, The Roots launched Okayplayer Records, in partnership with Decon, a multimedia design and entertainment company. The label's name comes from group's popular Web site, Okayplayer.com. Okayplayer.com was founded in 1999 by ?uestlove as the online community that houses artists such as The Roots, Jill Scott, D'Angelo, **Talib Kweli**, and **Dilated Peoples**.

The Tipping Point (Geffen Records), released in 2004 appears to be The Roots bid to get their anti-bling message to a wider audience. As they continue to meld together musical genres, throughout *The Tipping Point* The Roots discuss political issues such as the war in Iraq and apathy while celebrating the victories of common folks who work hard on demanding, low-paying jobs, ever struggling to stay afloat.

DISCOGRAPHY: *Organix* (Remedy Recordings, 1993); *Do You Want More?!!!??!* (Geffen Records, 1995); *Illadelph Halflife* (Geffen Records, 1996); *Things Fall Apart* (MCA Records, 1999); *The Roots Come Alive* (MCA Records, 1999); *Phrenology* (MCA Records, 2002); *The Tipping Point* (Geffen Records, 2004).

ROXANNE SHANTE [Lolita Shante Gooden]

Roxanne Shante is best known for the single "Roxanne's Revenge" (Pop Art, 1984), which in the 1980s set off the Roxanne Wars with **The Real Roxanne**.

The rap artist from the famous **Queensbridge** housing projects has stated in interviews that **Marley Marl** offered to pay her for her rhyming with a pair of $35 Sergio Valente designer jeans (Marley Marl worked at the factory). The fourteen-year-old agreed, and the collaboration resulted in the classic 1984 single, "Roxanne's Revenge." Allegedly, Marley Marl was mad at U.T.F.O. for missing a performance and it appears that he used Roxanne Shante to retaliate on wax. The inexpensive music video for the single depicted Roxanne Shante stepping out of a limousine wearing a white fur. Roxanne Shante's street tough delivery juxtaposed with ghetto-fabulous style paved the way for later female rap artists such as **Lil' Kim** and **Foxy Brown**. Roxanne Shante did not write her rhymes, but most often composed them while listening to a beat. Moreover, as with The Real Roxanne, and other female artists, many of the lyrics and insults that were written were done so by men.

Aside from her **battle** with The Real Roxanne, Roxanne Shante was attacked by numerous other artists, including **KRS-ONE**, who provided a scathing insult on "The Bridge is Over" (B-Boy Records, 1987). She had several more hit twelve-inch records, with "Def Fresh Crew" with **Biz Markie** (Pop Art Records, 1986), "Have a Nice Day" (Cold Chillin' Records, 1987), and also "Go on Girl" from the *Colors* film soundtrack (Warner Bros. Records, 1988) (both written by **Big Daddy Kane**), and she made an appearance on Rick James's "Loosey's Rap" (Reprise Records, 1988).

In 1990, Roxanne Shante released her debut album, *Big Mama* (Cold Chillin' Records), and in 2000 she appeared on the track "We Live This," from the album *Nas and Ill Will Records Presents: Queensbridge The Album* (Columbia Records). In October, 2004, Roxanne Shante filed a lawsuit against Janet Jackson, alleging that Jackson had used a sample of her voice on the song "Like You Don't Love Me" on her album *Damita Jo* and failed to pay her. According to Roxanne Shante, Jackon's song samples the phrase "so fresh" from the song "Def Fresh Crew." Roxanne Shante has owned the masters to her own recordings for over nine years. She is currently a psychologist working in New York City.

DISCOGRAPHY: *Singles* (twelve-inch): "Roxanne's Revenge" (Pop Art, 1984); "Bite This" (Pop Art Record, 1985; "Runaway" (Pop Art Records, 1985); "Queen of Rox (Shante Rox On)" (Pop Art Records, 1985); "Def Fresh Crew" [with Biz Markie] (Pop Art Records, 1986); "Pay Back" (Pop Arts Records, 1987); "Have a Nice Day" (Cold Chillin' Records, 1987); "Go on Girl" (Warner Bros. Records, 1988); "Live On Stage" (Cold Chillin' Records, 1989). *Album*: *Big Mama* (Cold Chillin' Records, 1990).

RUFF RYDERS

Ruff Ryder is a management company and record label founded by New York siblings Joaquin, Darren, and Chivon Dean. In 2001, the company reportedly generated over $35 million in revenue. The collective of artists and producers associated with Ruff Ryders includes **DMX**, **Eve**, the **LOX**, Drag-on, and producer Swiss Beats. In 1999, the Ruff Ryder crew released the album *Ryde or Die Compilation Vol. 1* (Ruff Ryders/Interscope Records). Subsequent Ruff Ryder albums were *Ryde or Die Vol. 2* (Ruff Ryders/ Interscope Records, 2000) and *Ryde or Die: In the "R" We Trust* (Ruff Ryders/Interscope Records, 2001).

RUN DMC

Run [Joseph Simmons], DMC [Darryl McDaniels], and **Jam Master Jay** [Jason Mizell] make up Run DMC, arguably the most important rap group in Hip Hop history. Moreover, Run DMC is considered by many to be a stylistic bridge between rap music's early pioneers, such as **Grandmaster Flash and the Furious Five** and **Cold Crush Brothers**, and more current artists. For two generations of rap fans, Run DMC epitomized the face and sound of 1980s rap music.

The Run DMC story does not begin in the ghettos of New York City, but rather in the middle-class neighborhood of Hollis, Queens. Joseph Simmons is the younger brother of **Def Jam** cofounder **Russell Simmons** and artist Daniel Simmons Jr. The three brothers were born to Daniel Simmons, an educator, and his wife Evelyn. Joseph, nicknamed "Run" for "running at the mouth," became the DJ for **Kurtis Blow**, one of Russell Simmons's first management clients. At local rap events where he performed in the early 1980s, Simmons became known as "DJ Run Love, the Son of Kurtis Blow."

Run shared tapes of his performances with childhood friend Darryl McDaniels, the son of an engineer and a nurse. Eventually, McDaniels was coerced into joining Run on stage at a local event, but a music career was not immediately in their futures. The two continued their friendship as they prepared to enter college in New York City. Run was slated to attend La Guardia Community College (to study mortuary science) and McDaniels was admitted to St. John's University. Encouraged by his older brother to form a rap duo, Simmons and McDaniels teamed up and enlisted their mutual friend, DJ Jam Master Jay (Jason Mizell). The group, now known as Run D.M.C., sent their demo tape around and were subsequently signed to Profile Records, an independent label.

In 1983, the three released their first single, "It's Like That." The twelve-inch was a huge success among New York area **B-boys** and then caught on rapidly across the country. The B-side, "Sucker MC's," was innovative for its time, with stripped-down beats and a sophisticated rhyme style. The tone and message of "Sucker MCs" have caused some to consider it the first hardcore rap. Run DMC released two more singles, "Hard Times" (Profile Records, 1983) and the "Rock Box" (Profile Records, 1984). With its use of guitar riffs, the video for "Rock Box" earned Run DMC airplay on MTV, a rare feat for a rap group at a time when even the "King of Pop" Michael Jackson was complaining that he was not getting play on the cable video channel.

Run DMC. *Courtesy of Photofest.*

In 1984, Run DMC's self-titled debut album became the first rap album to go gold. During this time, Russell Simmons formed Rush Management and a record label, Def Jam, with producer and New York University student, Rick Rubin. Now clients of Rush Management, Run DMC performed alongside groups such as **U.T.F.O.**, **Newcleus**, and **Whodini** in several of the **Fresh Fests**, the first nationwide rap tour. Dressed in black jeans, unlaced **Adidas** sneakers, and fedoras, Run DMC departed from the glitzy outfits previously worn by rap performers and in doing so created a new Hip Hop aesthetic. With their modern look, rap-rock singles (such as "Rock Box" and "King of Rock"), and with MTV airplay, Run DMC quickly became the first rap group to have a broad appeal among White youth.

The group's second album, 1985's *King of Rock* (Def Jam Recordings), which would eventually go platinum) featured several hits, including the title track, "You Talk Too Much," and "Can You Rock It Like This," which includes lyrics ghostwritten by **LL Cool J**, then sixteen. In early 1986, Run DMC starred in the film ***Krush Groove***, loosely based on Russell Simmons's music career, costarring the **Fat Boys,** Kurtis Blow, LL Cool J, and (then unknowns) the **Beastie Boys**. The film's release was marred by violence at movie theaters across the country. Despite the resulting bad publicity for themselves and for rap music, Run DMC they released the album *Raising Hell* later that year. Landing at number 3 on the *Billboard* charts, it sold over 3 million copies on the strength of singles such as "My Adidas" and "Walk This Way," featuring Aerosmith. This was the biggest-selling album in rap music history.

"Walk This Way," became the first rap song to become a Top 10 single in American history and also resurrected Aerosmith's flagging career. The subsequent *Raising Hell* tour made Run DMC into pop stars; however, violent outbreaks at the venues would also make them a lightning rod for attacks on rap music. On August 17, 1986, fighting broke out between Los Angeles Crips and Bloods gang members attending the Long Beach Arena date of Run DMC's *Raising Hell* tour. Police, summoned by promoters at 7:35 p.m., when first the melee erupted, did not arrive until 11 p.m. Forty-two people were injured in what was, up to then, rap music's most notoriously violent event. The Long Beach arena already had established a sixteen-year history of violence at concerts. In 1970, for instance, forty-six people were arrested at a Jethro Tull show; and in 1972, thirty-one were arrested on drug charges at a Led Zeppelin performance.)

The Long Beach Arena concert made national headlines, and the media blamed Run DMC and rap music for the violence. Undeterred, Run DMC continued both to tour and to release music. By the time Run DMC's fourth album, *Tougher Than Leather* (Def Jam Recordings, 1988), was released, it was evident that the rap music landscape had changed. In the wake of groups such as **Public Enemy** and **N.W.A.**, not only had rap lyrics become more confrontational, Run DMC's rock music elements and chants seemed passé, given that rap music was now more syncopated and sample-driven. Although the single "Run's House" was an attempt to be current, *Tougher Than Leather* failed to connect with music buyers, unlike the previous Run DMC albums. Although the album eventually sold platinum (1 million units), Def Jam Recordings had initially shipped out 1.23 million copies to stores, therefore, the sales were disappointing news for the group.

Run DMC's second movie, the action drama *Tougher Than Leather*, flopped in theaters. In 1990, Run DMC released *Back from Hell* (Def Jam

Recordings), which became their first album not to go platinum. Creatively it is also considered by some to be their worst effort. The album lacks the rock influence, and includes a fair amount of profanity, perhaps an attempt to compete with current rap trends.

After the release of *Back from Hell*, personal and financial problems would plague Run DMC. Simmons was falsely accusing of raping a Cleveland, Ohio, woman, and Daniels succumbed to alcoholism. Daniels and Simmons thereafter turned to religion, with Run taking the additional step of becoming an ordained minister. On their 1993 comeback album *Down With the King* (Def Jam Recordings), they touted their religious conversion. The title single, produced by **Pete Rock**, became the group's biggest-selling single to date. Aside from Pete Rock, the album featured guest appearances and production assistance from artists as diverse as Public Enemy, **EPMD**, **Naughty By Nature**, **A Tribe Called Quest**, Neneh Cherry, and **KRS-ONE**.

In the aftermath of *Down With the King*, Run DMC lowered their profile. At the beginning of the 1990s Jam Master Jay set up JMJ Records, most notably the record company for rap group **Onyx**. Jam Master Jay continued to produce and was credited with discovering rap artist **50 Cent**. Run DMC continued to tour worldwide. In 2000, Reverend Run published the book *It's Like That: A Spiritual Memoir* (St. Martin's Press). After a long hiatus, which included rumors of DMC's departure and delays at Def Jam, Run DMC released the album *Crown Royal*, named after the whiskey, in 2001. The album did little to boost their declining record sales. In support of the album, Run DMC joined Aerosmith and Kid Rock for a blockbuster performance on MTV Awards. In 2001, following Run's lead, DMC published *King of Rock: Respect, Responsibility, and My Life with Run-DMC* (Thomas Dunne Books). In October 2002, weeks after Run DMC had completed a tour with Aerosmith, Jam Master Jay was murdered in his Queens recording studio. Soon thereafter the two remaining members announced that Run DMC had retired.

Run DMC pioneered several firsts for rap artists: first gold album (*Run DMC*, 1984); first platinum album (*King Of Rock*, 1985); first multi-platinum album (*Raising Hell*, 1986); first to reach the Top 10 on *Billboard's* Hot 100 ("Walk This Way," 1986); the first to appear on MTV, first on *American Bandstand*, and first on *Saturday Night Live*; and the first to become a household name across the nation.

DISCOGRAPHY: *Singles*: "It's Like That" w/Sucker MCs (Profile Records, 1983); "Hard Times" (Profile Records, 1983); "Rock Box" (Profile Records, 1984). *Albums: Run DMC* (Def Jam Recordings, 1984); *King Of Rock* (Def Jam Recordings, 1985); *Raising Hell* (Def Jam Recordings, 1986); *Tougher Than Leather* (Def Jam Recordings, 1988); *Back from Hell Down* (Def Jam Recordings, 1990); *With the King* (Def Jam Recordings, 1993); *Crown Royal* (Def Jam Recordings, 2001).

RZA (aka the Abbott, aka Prince Rakeem, aka the Rzarector, aka Bobby Digital, aka Bobby Steels) [Robert Diggs]

Known primarily as the main producer for Wu-Tang Clan, RZA's musical career began in the 1990s as a member of the rap group All in Together Now, with his cousins and future Wu-Tang members **GZA/Genius** and **Ol' Dirty Bastard**. After All in Together dissolved, RZA entered into a recording deal with Tommy Boy Records under the name Prince Rakeem, and released the 1991 EP *Ooh We Love You Rakeem*, a poorly executed project that was little more than the average braggadocio accompanied by the giggles of girls. It suffices to say that EP was not successful, and that afterwards RZA made music in his own unique way.

RZA produced the Wu-Tang Clan's landmark debut album, *Enter the Wu-Tang (36 Chambers)* (Loud Records, 1993), which is considered one of the most influential works of that time. RZA would also man the boards for **Method Man**'s debut solo album, *Tical* (Def Jam Recordings, 1994), and **Raekwon**'s first solo album, *Only Built 4 Cuban Linx* (Loud Records, 1995). At the end of 1995, RZA worked with GZA on his album *Liquid Swords* (Geffen Records, 1995). During this period, RZA also joined the supergroup the **Gravediggaz**, using the name Rzarector, and supervised the production of their 1994 debut album *6 Feet Deep* (V2/BMG, 1997 re-issue). RZA has also done production for Wu-Tang affiliates Shyheim, Cappadonna, and Killah Priest as well as Tricky, **Cypress Hill**, and **Shaquille O'Neal**. He has also created **remixes** for R & B group SWV and dancehall reggae performer Super Cat.

In 1998, RZA released his solo album debut, *RZA As Bobby Digital: In Stereo* (V2/BMG). On this funny and smart album, RZA adopts the alter ego Bobby Digital, a lover man–pimp. The following year, RZA composed the excellent score for Jim Jarmusch's 1999 film *Ghost Dog: The Way Of The Samurai*, starring Forrest Whitaker. In 1999, *The RZA Hits* (Sony), was released, a collection of his work on Wu-Tang albums and on members' solo projects. RZA released two additional solo albums, *Digital Bullet* (Koch Records, 2001) and *Birth of a Prince* (Sanctuary Records, 2003).

DISCOGRAPHY: *EPs: Ooh We Love You Raheem* (Tommy Boy Records, 1991). *Albums: RZA As Bobby Digital: In Stereo.*(V2/BMG, 1998); *The RZA Hits* (Sony Records, 1999); *Digital Bullet* (Koch Records, 2001); *Birth of a Prince* (Sanctuary Records, 2003).

S

SALT 'N PEPA

Comprised of Salt [Cheryl Renee James], Pepa [Sandra Jacqueline Theresa Denton], and Spinderella [Deidre "Dee Dee" Roper], Salt 'N Pepa is the most successful female rap group to date and the first since **The Mercedes Ladies** to also have a female DJ. They were also one of the first rap artists to cross over into the pop mainstream, laying the groundwork for the music's widespread acceptance in the early 1990s.

Cheryl James, a Brooklyn native, and Sandra Denton, a transplant from Kingston, Jamaica, met while studying nursing at Queensborough Community College in the mid-1980s. Cheryl James's rap style supposedly first appeared in a church play, with the nine-year-old playing a rhyming witch. Denton and James worked as telephone sales representatives for the retail store Sears, alongside fellow undiscovered talents **Kid 'N Play** and comedian Martin Lawrence. At Sears, the girls would also meet aspiring record producer–writer, Herbie "Luv Bug" Azor. Luv Bug was studying record production at the Center of Media Arts, and asked Cheryl and Sandy to record for him as a class project.

The resulting song was a response to **Doug E. Fresh** and **Slick Rick**'s extremely popular 1985 song, "The Show" (Def Jam Recordings). The relationship of the trio would remain complicated by the long-term romantic relationship between Luv Bug and Salt. In 1985, the duo, then known as Super Nature, recorded "The Showstopper (Is Stupid Fresh)" (Pop Art Records). The success of their single led them enter into a recording agreement with Next Plateau Records, an independent label. At this point the duo was now named Salt 'N Pepa after a line in "The Showstopper." Luv Bug reportedly wrote the lyrics (an assertion disputed by Salt 'N Pepa) and produced the tracks for Salt 'N Pepa's 1986 debut album, *Hot, Cool and Vicious* (Next Plateau Records). Three singles from the album were moderate hits: "My Mike Sounds Nice," "Tramp," and "Chick on the Side."

In 1987, Cameron Paul, a DJ at a San Francisco radio station, **remixed** "Push It," the B-side of "Tramp" (a reworking of the 1967 Otis Redding–Carla Thomas song) and it became a local hit. "Push It" was released nationally and climbed to number 19 on the pop charts. "Push It" then also became one of the first rap records to be nominated for a Grammy award.

Aside from supervising Salt 'N Pepa's music, Luv Bug, just as **Sean "P. Diddy" Combs** would later do with **Mary J. Blige**, was also instrumental in crafting Salt 'N Pepa's image and sound. Luv Bug's notion was to present Salt 'N Pepa as "around the way" girls, having fun. In a departure from the past, Salt 'N Pepa intentionally did not diss fellow female rap artists. Luv Bug's Idolmaker management company, aside from Salt 'N Pepa also boasted as clients Kid 'N Play, **Dana Dane**, and **Kwamé**. Reportedly, Luv Bug owns 50 percent of Salt 'N Pepa's copyrighted material and thus receives a portion of all royalties that the group receives.

In 1987, Brooklyn, New York, native, Deidre "Dee Dee" Roper auditioned to become the duo's DJ, replacing the original Spinderella, Pamela LaToya Greene. Roper had learned to DJ from a boyfriend while attending Franklin K. Lane High School in Brooklyn, New York. Salt 'N Pepa's 1988 follow-up album, *A Salt With a Deadly Pepa* (Next Plateau Records), spawned the Top Ten R & B hit "Shake Your Thang," which was recorded with the **go-go** band E.U. In 1990, the album *A Blitz of Salt-N-Pepa Hits: The Hits Remixes* (Polygram Records) was released. Prior to releasing their fourth album, the duo ended their business relationship with Luv Bug (Salt's personal relationship with him had ended several years earlier) and signed with London/Polygram.

Salt 'N Pepa's *Blacks' Magic* (FFRR/London/Polygram, 1990) received strong reviews and support from rap music fans. One criticism that had been leveled at Salt 'N Pepa was that they were too pop-oriented and too concerned with crossover success. The track "Expression" spent eight weeks at the top of the rap charts and went gold before it even cracked the pop charts, where it would later peak at twenty-six. The single "Let's Talk About Sex" became their biggest pop hit to date. In 1992, the song later was later rerecorded and released as "Let's Talk About AIDS," a safe-sex rap.

In 1993, the group released the multi-platinum album, *Very Necessary*. The album was bouncy and sexy without being either exploitative or too soft for traditional rap audiences. *Very Necessary* included the gold-selling single "Shoop," which reached number 4 on the pop charts, and "Whatta Man," a duet with the female R & B group En Vogue, which reached number 3 on both the pop and R & B charts in 1994. The single "None of Your Business," although not as popular as the other two singles, nonetheless won the Grammy for Best Rap Performance by a Duo or Group in 1995. After problems with their record company, which eventually filed for bankruptcy, in 1997 Salt 'N Pepa released their fifth album, *Brand New* (London/Polygram); this included an array of guest appearances from performers such as **Queen Latifah**, Sheryl Crow, Kirk Franklin, and the Sounds of Blackness, The album covered a range of musical styles and proved that Salt 'N Pepa were still on top of their game.

In 1999 Pepa would marry **Naughty By Nature** member Treach (the duo would divorce in 2001; the union produced a daughter). Salt, now a born-again Christian, performed on the Kirk Franklin 1997 gospel hit, "Stomp," from the album, *God's Property From Kirk Franklin's Nu Nation* (Gospocentric, 1997).

In the intervening years, Salt 'N Pepa formed Jireh Records and embarked on solo business ventures: Spinderella opened the "She Thing" salon and day spa in Queens, New York, and Pepa opened the clothing store "Hollyhood" in Atlanta, Georgia. The group recorded four new tracks for the *Best of Salt 'N Pepa* (FFRR) album released in the United Kingdom in 2000. Salt was scheduled to release her solo debut album, *Salt of the Earth*, on her GavFam record label in 2001, but the promotional CD for the track "Pardon Me" was the only public release.

DISCOGRAPHY: *Singles*: "Showstopper" (Pop Art Records, 1986). *Albums: Hot, Cool and Vicious* (Next Plateau, 1986); *A Salt With a Deadly Pepa* (Next Plateau, 1988); *Blacks' Magic* (FFRR/London/Polygram, 1990); *A Blitz of Salt-n-Pepa Hits: The Hits Remixes* (Polygram, 1990); *Very Necessary* (London/Polygram, 1993); *Brand New* (London, Polygram, 1997).

SAMPLING

In sampling, a music producer takes an excerpt of one sound recording and reuses it as an element in the creation of a new recording.

The sample is generally made with a piece of equipment called a sampler, or using a specialized computer program. Early on, loops (i.e., the continuous play of a sampled sequence) were made with actual loops of magnetic tape using a reel-to-reel audiotape machine.

One of the first recognized samples is Chic's song "**Good Times**," which appears on the Sugar Hill Gang's 1979 "**Rapper's Delight**" (Sugar Hill Records). Not chic songwriters originally credited for their work, Bernard Edwards and Nile Rodgers would sue over copyright infringement. Other defendants in "sampling lawsuits" include **De La Soul**, **Biz Markie**, and most recently **LL Cool J**, who was sued in 2001 by four member of the **Furious Five** who claimed that he used an unauthorized sample of their 1979 song, "Superrappin'" for his 1997 song "4,3,2,1" (Def Jam Recordings).

SCARFACE (aka Mr. Scarface, aka Face) [Brad Jordan]

Scarface broke away from the **Geto Boys** in 1991 and quickly distinguished himself as one of the most important rap artists to hail from the South. Known for his vivid story telling, Scarface defined hardcore South rap music through his numerous albums of the 1990s.

During this period, major rap artists including **Ice Cube**, **Dr. Dre**, **Tupac Shakur**, and **Master P** collaborated with Scarface, to benefit from his loyal Southern fan base. Critics contend that Scarface did not cross over into the mainstream partly because of his allegiance to producer Mike Dean, which led to albums having a predictable sound. Others assert that Scarface's lyrics were too caustic for radio and that his albums contained too much filler material. Scarface, however, remained close to the streets and, although the popularity of other rap artists chasing mass appeal has waned, his influence has never diminished.

Brad Jordan, was born in San Antonio, Texas, and was raised in Houston. He began his rap career in the mid-1980s as a solo artist known as Akshen, working for the start-up record company, Rap-A-Lot. In 1988, Rap-A-Lot chief James Smith was attempting to launch a group called the Ghetto Boys and asked Akshen to join. In 1990, the group released their debut album, *Grip It On That Other Level* (Rap-A-Lot Records), which shocked many with its graphic depictions of violence. The track "Scarface" introduced Akshen's alter ego, and he would be known by that name thereafter.

The renamed Geto Boys benefited from the controversy surrounding their music and in 1991 released their successful second album, *We Can't Be Stopped* (Rap-A-Lot Records). That same year Scarface released his debut, *Mr. Scarface Is Back* (Rap-A-Lot Records, 1991), which suddenly showed who was the most talented member of the Geto Boys. Two years later, Scarface released his solo follow-up, *The World Is Yours* (Rap-A-Lot Records, 1993). By this time, his reputation clearly overshadowed that of the Geto Boys. Tensions between group members ensued, and although members at times left and at times came back, the Geto Boys failed to regain the success of *We Can't Be Stopped*.

In the interim, Scarface continued to release solid solo albums. *The Diary* (Rap-A-Lot Records, 1994), a platinum-selling album, is considered a Hip Hop classic. *Untouchable* (Rap-A-Lot Records, 1997), with performances by Dr. Dre, Ice Cube, and **Too Short**, and the double-disc *My Homies* (1998) are best remembered for numerous guest appearances. In 2000, Scarface received kudos from the national rap community for his gold album, *Last of a Dying Breed* (Rap-A-Lot Records), considered to be his best album in years.

The following year, **Def Jam Recordings** tapped Scarface to run its newly formed Def Jam South division, although Scarface had one more album to complete under his contract with Rap-A-Lot. As the CEO of Def Jam South, Scarface made his first signing **Ludacris**, who has become a multi-platinum-selling artist. In 2002, Scarface released his own album, *The Fix*, already considered another Hip Hop classic. *The Fix* includes the track "Guess Who's Back," a collaboration with **Jay-Z** that is produced by **Kanye West**. The album also spawned the popular single, "My Block." Additionally, *The Fix* sparked new interest in Scarface's earlier works, prompting his former label, Rap-A-Lot, in 2003 to release the rap artist's first greatest hits collection, *Balls and My Word*, previously recorded material packaged as a new album. The title is taken from the film *Scarface*, in which gangster Tony Montana (played by Al Pacino) states: "All I have in this world is my balls and my word, and I don't break 'em for no one." In 2004, squashing rumors that he was going to **Death Row Records**, Scarface re-signed to Rap-A-Lot, which had recently secured a distribution deal with Warner Bros. Records.

An upcoming Scarface album, *My Homies Vol. 2,* is scheduled to be released in 2005. In January 2005, the Geto Boys made a triumphant return with their reunion album *Foundation* (Rap-A-Lot/WEA).

DISCOGRAPHY: *Mr. Scarface Is Back* (Rap-A-Lot Records, 1991); *The World Is Yours* (Rap-A-Lot Records, 1993); *The Diary* (Rap-A-Lot Records, 1994); *Untouchable* (Rap-A-Lot Records, 1997); *My Homies* [double disc] (Rap-A-Lot Records, 1998); *The Fix* (Def Jam Recordings, 2002); *Balls and My Word* (Rap-A-Lot Records, 2003).

SCHOOLLY D [Jesse B. Weaver Jr.]

With his DJ, Code Money [Lance Allen], the Philadelphia, Pennsylvania, rap artist Schoolly D is credited with being among the first to use graphic depictions of gang violence, street crime, and sex as the basis for his rhymes.

Schoolly D began his career in 1984, with the independent release of the singles "Maniac" and "Gangsta Boogie." The following year he would release his self-titled debut album on his independent label, Schoolly D Records. The album is best remembered for the Schoolly D the track "PSK—What Does It Mean?" The PSK is an acronym for Park Side Killers, a Philadelphia gang with which Schoolly D claimed an affiliation. The other notable track is "Gucci Time," which appears as the B-side of the twelve-inch single release of "PSK—What Does It Mean."

There was public outrage in Philadelphia over Schoolly D's next two albums, *Saturday Night! The Album* (Schoolly D Records) in 1986 and *Smoke Some Kill* (Jive Records) in 1988, both of them explicit and horrific ghetto narratives on inner-city strife, and some city officials publicly supported the removal of the albums from record stores. The controversy, however, made Schoolly D a hot property, despite his less than stellar rap skills. He signed with Jive Records, who reissued *Saturday Night! The Album* in 1987. Aside from the explicit nature of the music, *Smoke Some Kill* would receive attention for the track "Signifying Rapper," which references the famous African American toast, Signifying Monkey.

Schoolly D's 1989 album *Am I Black Enough For You?* (Jive Records) was his first attempt to incorporate some social commentary into his repertoire. He would release his fifth album, *How a Blackman Feels*, in 1991 (Capitol Records). In between, he gained national attention for his contribution on the soundtrack for the 1990 film, *King of New York*.

Schoolly D would not release another album until 1994, with *Welcome to America*, released on Philadelphia's Ruffouse Records. The comeback album omitted **sampling** in favor of the label's live band. The 1995 *Reservoir Dogs* saw Schoolly D revert to his original sound and depart Ruffhouse for his own label, PSK Records, releasing *A Gangster's Story* (PSK, Records, 1996) and *Funk N' P**sy* (PSK Records, 2000). His career was temporarily revived in 1997 after the Chemical Brothers sampled him on their 1997 *Dig Your Own Hole* album.

DISCOGRAPHY: *Schoolly D* (Schoolly D Records, 1985); *Saturday Day Night! The Album* (Schoolly D Records, 1986; re-issued by Jive Records in 1987); *Smoke Some Kill* (Jive Records, 1988); *Am I Black Enough For You?* (Jive Records, 1989); *How a Black Man Feels* (Capitol Records, 1991); *Welcome to America* (Ruffhouse Records, 1994); *Reservoir Dogs* (PSK Records, 1995); *A Gangster's Story* (PSK Records, 1996); *Funk N' Pu**y* (PSK Records, 2000).

SCOTT LA ROCK [Scott Sterling]. *See* Boogie Down Productions; KRS-ONE

SCRATCH. *See* Films

SCRATCHING

Scratching is a DJ or turntablist technique developed by **Grand Wizzard Theodore** and honed by **Grandmaster Flash**. At its simplest, a scratching is done by moving a vinyl record back and forth with your hand while it is playing on a turntable; the result is a distinctive sound that has become universally associated with rap music. If done properly, the record is not damaged because the needle remains in the grooves and does not move horizontally across the record's surface.

SEQUENCE

The group called Sequence, comprised of Cheryl "The Pearl" Cook, Gwendolyn "MC Blondie" Chisolm, and Angela "Angie B" Brown, is recognized as the first all-girl rap group to release a record.

The high school cheerleaders from Columbia, South Carolina, were able to parlay their cheers into raps and secured a recording deal with Sugar Hill Records. Their 1979 classic single "Funk You Up," was the second record released by the label. They also teamed up with **Spoonie Gee** on the single "Monster Jam" (Sugar Hill Records, 1980) and the Sugar Hill Gang on "Rappers Reprise" (Jam-Jam). Additional singles were "Funky Sound (Tear the Roof Off)" (Sugar Hill Records, 1981), a remake of the 1976 Parliament's hit "Tear the Roof Off the Sucker" and "I Don't Need Your Love (Part One)" (Sugar Hill Records, 1982). The glitzy disco-influenced group incorporated singing with their rhymes. Angie B went on to become the R & B singer Angie Stone.

SHA ROCK [Sharon Jackson, née Green]

Sha Rock is the most celebrated Old School female rap artist and was the "+1" with the **Funky 4 + 1**. She inspired a whole generation of female rap artists and later formed **US Girls** with Debbie Dee and Cosmic Force member Lisa Lee.

SHEEPSKIN COATS

A type of winter coat that was staple outerwear for B-girls and **B-boys** in the New York metropolitan area in the 1980s, sheepskin, similar to shearling, has leather skin on the outside and wool fur on the inside. The popular sheepskin coats were similarly styled, three-quarter length, and came in various colors: brown, beige, blue, black, and white.

SHOW, THE. *See* Films

SHOWBIZ AND A.G.

Showbiz [Rodney LeMay] and A.G. (aka Andre the Giant) [Andre Barnes] were instrumental in the forming the famous **Diggin' in the Crates** crew (D.I.T.C.). The duo represented the next generation of Bronx-bred Hip Hop.

The cost of making unadulterated rap music is that it sometimes remains underneath the mainstream radar. Andre The Giant and producer Showbiz hail from the Bronx, New York, and got their start on **Lord Finesse**'s album *Funky Technician* (Wild Pitch Records). Lord Finesse asked Showbiz to work on the track "Keep it Flowing," which A.G. also performed on. From these recording sessions the duo Showbiz and A.G. was born.

The duo created a buzz on the street by selling their tapes out of the trunks of their cars. Revenue from street sales helped them refine their 1991 debut single "Soul Clap," b/w "Party Groove." "Soul Clap" was a blend of Old School beats under a classic call-and-response refrain. In March 1992, Showbiz and A.G. released a self-titled EP. Showbiz and A.G. signed with Payday/FFRR and in 1992 they released the full-length album *Runaway Slave*. The album contained tracks from the EP album and also included Showbiz kicking some lyrics along with A.G.

Runaway Slave also marked the official birth of the D.I.T.C., which originally included rap artist–producer **Diamond D** (his classic debut solo album *Stunts, Blunts, and Hip Hop* was released the same week in 1992), **Fat Joe**, Lord Finesse, **Big L**, and Deshaun; later on, **DJ Premier** and O.C. would be added. The album introduced the tracks "Bounce ta this" with Dres from **Black Sheep**, "Fat Pockets," "Silence of the Lambs," and the posse cut "Represent."

In 1995, the duo released their sophomore album, *Goodfellas* (Payday/FFRR). The promotional version was released under the name Show featuring A.G. and was titled *Goodfellas ... The Medicine*; it was well received by fans, and had a similar feel to their debut effort. The official version of the album, however, would be a different affair. The new version, however, had been redone to Showbiz and A.G.'s (now Show & A.G.) satisfaction. On *Goodfellas*, the duo's sound was less jazzy and more somber; moreover, Showbiz did not rap and only contributed on production. Underrated when it was released, *Goodfellas* nonetheless contains classics tracks such as the DJ Premier–produced "Next Level" and "Got Tha Flava," featuring new crew, the Ghetto Dwellaz and **Method Man**. The album also floundered because Showbiz was accused of being involved with the murder of their manager. He was jailed, but later released when he was cleared of the charges.

In 1998, Showbiz & A.G. independently released the vinyl-only EP *Full Scale* (D.I.T.C. Records). The track "Drop it Heavy" features **Big Punisher** and **KRS-ONE**. Showbiz has also done production work for Big Punisher and KRS-ONE. Show & A.G. appeared on the D.I.T.C. albums *Worldwide* (Tommy Boy Records, 2000) and *The Official Version* (D.I.T.C. Records, 2000) A.G. released his solo album *The Dirty Version,* along with a twelve-inch single, "The Rude Awakening," to promote the album. A.G. appeared on the **Big L** twelve-inch single "Holdin' It Down." Showbiz has also been producing and **remixing** on the Big L and D.I.T.C. albums.

DISCOGRAPHY: *Singles*: "Soul Clap," b/w "Party Groove" (1991). *EPs*: *Showbiz and AG* (Polygram, 1992); *Full Scale* (1998). *Albums*: *Runaway Slave* (Payday/FFRR, 1992); *Goodfellas* (Payday/FFRR, 1995).

SIMMONS, RUSSELL

Usually attired in sneakers, jeans, and a baseball cap, Russell Simmons is best known for his Def Jam entertainment empire. Simmons, whose official title is founder and chairman of Rush Communications, is recognized as an adept businessman who used rap music as a base to Hip Hop the terrain of Hip Hop into other entertainment vehicles and more recently politics.

The first element of Rush Communications was its management company, which he and partner Rick Rubin established in 1979. After

Russell and Kimora Lee Simmons. *Courtesy of Photofest.*

landing a production deal at CBS that made **Kurtis Blow** the first rap artist released on a major label, the duo established **Def Jam Recordings** in 1984. Def Jam remained the predominant rap music label for nearly twenty years, with an artist roster that included leading artists such as **Run DMC** (member Joseph Simmons is Russell's younger brother), the **Beastie Boys**, **Public Enemy**, **LL Cool J**, and **Slick Rick**.

Def Jam subsequently branched off into Def Pictures, RSTV, Phat fashion, Rush Media (an **advertising** concern), and *OneWorld* magazine, though Rush Media and *OneWorld* have since been eliminated from the company's business portfolio. Most recently, Simmons entered theater with the *Def Poetry Jam*, which had a stint on Broadway.

Simmons, the son of a college professor and a preschool teacher, hails from the middle-class community of Hollis in Queens, New York. Simmons got the nickname Rush as a youngster because he was always "rushing" around.

Back in the day Simmons tried his hand at rhyming. His first effort as a solo vocalist was the 1985 twelve-inch single "Def Jam," b/w "Cold

Chillin' In The Spot." Simmons also was featured on the LL Cool J song "That's a Lie," from his 1985 album *Radio* (Def Jam Recordings).

Simmons, however, began his career while still a student at City College in Manhattan. In the middle 1970s, Simmons and a friend, Curtis Walker, calling themselves "The Force," gave parties in Harlem at Small's Paradise and the now defunct Charles Gallery. Walker would become Hip Hop's first superstar, rap artist Kurtis Blow. As the Hip Hop expanded uptown, so too did competitors. The Force began promoting parties in Queens, New York, touting Blow as the best rap artist in Queens—a dubious label, given the dearth of rap artists in the borough.

Although **Sean "P. Diddy" Combs** is credited with inventing street promotion, years before him Simmons would produce and distribute 15,000 flyers and thousands of stickers to promote his parties, often netting more than one thousand people. The Force eventually moved their parties to the Hotel Diplomat on West 43rd Street, near Times Square in Manhattan. This central location allowed Black kids from all of the five boroughs to come to events, as well as any White kids in the area who by chance might have wandered into the rap events.

Simmons was one of the first entrepreneurs to appreciate the value of rap music and Hip Hop culture. Not seeking to change the culture or attitudes about it, he influenced Hip Hop by how he marketed it. Simmons realized that hardcore, rebellious street culture was most appealing to White youth. With that knowledge he developed the mindset that he would market Black culture to anyone who was willing to buy it. Unlike other rap artists and Black executives who are primarily concerned with Black people validating a particular rap track or album, Simmons in comparison has been quoted as saying that "I don't feel that a record has to be number one in Harlem to be number one in America" [Kierna May, "When Russell Talks..." ***The Source*** magazine, February, 1993].

Simmons's idea that Hip Hop should be marketed to everyone has been controversial. Many believe that he and executives like him promote negative racial stereotypes of Black youth to satisfy the appetites of White rap music consumers. Minister Conrad Muhammad, known as the "Hip Hop Minister," engaged in a public dispute with Simmons in 2001. Muhammad (who is now a Christian minister known by his birth name, Conrad Tillard) accused Simmons of condoning violence by refusing to curtail the frequent use of terms such as "nigga" and "bitch" in rap lyrics. Conrad, founder of A Movement for CHHANGE (Conscious Hip Hop Activism Necessary for Global Empowerment), was quoted as saying, "Whites have accepted Russell Simmons as the guru of urban Black youth culture. He has sold them a bill of goods—that we are a penny-chasing, champagne drinking, gold-teeth-wearing, modern day Sambos, pimps, and playas" [Peter Noel. "The Minster vs. the Mogul." *Village Voice*, April 25, 2001; available at http://www.villagevoice.com/

issues/0117/noel.shtml]. Simmons dismissed Muhammad's statements as an obsessive desire to censor rap artists.

Also in 2001, in response to a *Village Voice* article about Simmons, New York activist Rosa Clemente circulated on the Internet an open letter to Simmons titled, "You Are Not Hip Hop" (available at http://www.daveyd.com/youarenothiphop.html). The letter charges Simmons with exploiting Hip Hop for the financial gain of a few elites and ignoring the concerns of fans and activists about the content and direction of Hip Hop. Although Simmons is often referred to in the media as the Godfather of Hip Hop, among Hip Hop purists that title is usually reserved for Hip Hop pioneers **Afrika Bambaataa** or **DJ Kool Herc**.

Simmons in 2001 established the Hip Hop Summit Action Network which states its mission as being "dedicated to harnessing the cultural relevance of music to serve as a catalyst for education advocacy and other societal concerns fundamental to the well-being of at-risk youth throughout the United States" (http://www.hiphopsummitactionnetwork.org/). The group has held numerous regional summits laden with rap artists, as well as voter education drives. With a board of directors heavily populated with record industry executives, however, and with its focus seemingly on rap artists, critics question how relevant are the group's activities to improving the lives of average young people.

Simmons tangentially entered the political arena in 1999 when he hosted a $1,000-a-plate fundraiser for New York Senate candidate Hillary Clinton at his home. He also endorsed New York City mayoral candidate Mark Green in 2000 and former Housing and Urban Development chief, Andrew Cuomo for Governor in 2001. Simmons then used his clout to lobby for the abolishment of draconian Rockefeller drug laws, which imposed mandatory minimum sentences for drug offenses, even for first-time and low-level offenders. Many in New York State applauded Simmons's efforts, which brought more media attention to the thirty-year-old law, but some activists believed that Simmons had derailed years of work. In private meetings with Governor Pataki (that longtime activists were neither informed of nor invited to), Simmons agreed to the proposed changes to the law, which many called only cosmetic modifications.

Like Hip Hop culture itself, Simmons is complex and multifaceted. The married father of two children, a practitioner of yoga, he remains an important, yet controversial, figure within Hip Hop.

See also: Def Jam, Kurtis Blow, Run DMC

SIR MIX-A-LOT [Anthony Ray]

Sir Mix-A-Lot is best known for his hit comical pimp persona and for one particular single.

The humorous and crude "Baby Got Back" pays tribute to women with large butts. The 1992 single sparked controversy on grounds of both race and gender. Was the song just sexist objectification, or did it indeed celebrate Black women (whose physiques are not usually recognized under European beauty standards) and the Black men who admire them? "Baby Got Back" spent five weeks atop the pop charts and sold over 2 million copies. *Billboard* magazine ranked the song as the second biggest single of the year, behind only Boyz II Men's phenomenal hit song, "End of the Road."

Well before the "Baby Got Back" single, Sir Mix-A-Lot had already released a platinum album. In 1983, the Seattle, Washington native cofounded the Nastymix record label in 1983 with his DJ, Nasty Nes, who also hosted Seattle's first rap radio show. In 1987, he released his first single "Posse on Broadway," referring to a street in Seattle, not New York. The song was a local hit and then, with some airplay on MTV, became Sir Mix-A-Lot's first national single in 1988. On the strength of "Posse on Broadway," in 1988 Sir Mix-A-Lot released his first album, *Swass* (Nastymix), which included the novelty track "Square Dance Rap," as well as the rock-rap track "Iron Man," a cover of the Black Sabbath song.

In 1989, Mix-A-Lot released his second album, *Seminar* (Nastymix), spawning three singles: "Beepers," "My Hooptie," and "I Got Game." Although none were crossover hits, the album again sold platinum. Sir Mix-A-Lot split with Nastymix over financial disputes and thereafter signed with **Rick Rubin**'s Def American. In 1992, he released his first Def American album, *Daddy Mack*. The lead single, "One Time's Got No Case," a critique of racial profiling, hit a brick, but the follow-up single was "Baby Got Back." It, and the accompanying music video, became a pop sensation.

Sir Mix-A-Lot followed with the 1994 album *Chief Boot Knocka* (Def American), which included the "Baby Got Back" clone "Put 'Em on the Glass," but he failed to reach the same level of success again. In 1996, Def American released the album *Return of the Bumpasaurus*, but in the midst of personnel problems and lack of promotional push, Sir Mix-A-Lot ended his relationship with Def American and spent several years out of the studio. During this period, Mix-A-Lot briefly hooked up with The Presidents of the United States of America and in 1998 began to perform under the group name Subset. He also partnered with Mudhoney on the track "Freak Momma" for the *Judgment Day* (1999) film soundtrack. In 2003, Sir Mix-A-Lot released his sixth album, *Daddy's Home* (Artist Direct).

DISCOGRAPHY: *Swass* (Nastymix, 1988); *Seminar* (Nastymix, 1989); *Daddy Mack* (Def American, 1992); *Chief Boot Knocka* (Def American, 1994); *Return of the Bumpasaurus* (Def American, 1996); *Daddy's Home* (Artist Direct, 2003).

SISTER SOULJAH [Lisa Williamson]

A community activist, rap artist, and author, Sister Souljah received national attention after being excoriated by then-presidential candidate Bill Clinton for an allegedly racist comment she made in the aftermath of the 1992 Los Angeles riots. Born into poverty and raised on welfare, Sister Souljah decided early on not only to improve her own lot in life, but also that of other Black people.

An excellent student, the Bronx, New York, native also became a voracious reader, trying to fill the educational gap left by a school curriculum that included little about Black history. While in high school, Williamson interned in the House of Representatives, and among the many other honors won during her teen years were The American Legion's Constitutional Oratory Contest, a scholarship to attend Cornell University's Advanced Placement Summer Program, and study abroad at the University of Salamanca in Spain. Souljah went on to graduate from Rutgers's University with a double major in American History and African Studies. In the 1980s as a college student, she was well known on campus as an activist and writer for the school paper, and continued her travels abroad. During those college years, she met the Reverend Benjamin Chavis (now Minister Benjamin Muhammad), head of the United Church of Christ Commission for Racial Justice, who offered her a job. Under his supervision for the next three years Souljah developed, organized, and secured funding for a number of programs such as the African Youth Survival Camp, a six-week academic and cultural sleep-away camp for 200 children of homeless families, located in Enfield, North Carolina.

As a means to get her political message out to a wide audience, she joined forces with **Public Enemy** and provided background vocals for their album, *Apocalypse 91 ... The Enemy Strikes Black* (Def Jam Recordings, 1991). Souljah released a single, "Final Solution," in 1991 (Epic Records), and her debut album, *360 Degrees of Power*, in 1992 (Epic Records).

About her album, Souljah has been quoted saying, "As Sister Souljah, I reserve the right to fight against White racism. I have not ordered anyone to kill anyone. My album creates pressure on White America—a lot of pressure, and pressure is what America needs, deserves, and inherited. No justice, no peace!" Throughout the 1990s, Sister Souljah continued her commitment to fighting social injustice and her strong opinions placed her in the center of national controversy in 1992. That year, Presidential candidate Bill Clinton admonished Souljah at a Rainbow Coalition event for comments she made on her in an interview with the *Washington Post*, while promoting her album.

Souljah reemerged in 1995, with the publication of her first book, *No Disrespect* (New York: Crown Books), a candid and passionate memoir that critiqued the relationship between Black men and Black women in today's America. She is also the executive director of Daddy's House, a nonprofit organization for youth started by Bad Boy Records CEO **Sean "P. Diddy" Combs**. The program provides educational and mentorship opportunities to over 600 young people, ages six to sixteen, from the low-income neighborhoods of New York, New Jersey, and Philadelphia, Pennsylvania. She was also one of the founders of the 1999 Million Woman March in Philadelphia.

In 1999 Souljah published her first novel, *The Coldest Winter Ever* (New York: Atria), a cautionary tale highlighting the toll that drugs and violence take on one young woman from Brooklyn, New York. Souljah subsequently wrote a screenplay for the novel, but plans for an HBO film version of the *The Coldest Winter* (to be executive produced by Souljah and actress Jada Pinkett Smith) have been canceled. The film rights will again be available for purchase in January 2006. Sister Souljah continues her work as an activist, lecturer, and writer. She is currently working on the sequel to *The Coldest Winter*. She has been married for over a decade and has one child.

SKEE-LO [unknown]

Skee-Lo is best remembered for profanity-free, good-time stories and his self-deprecating humor. Skee was born in Poughkeepsie, New York, (approximately ninety miles from the city) and moved to Riverside, California, at age nine. When he began recording in the 1990s, Skee-Lo's G-rated content was an anomaly, given the prevalence of hardcore rap music laden with profanity, violence, drugs, and sex. Skee-Lo was not only a novelty, but was actually considered a good lyricist.

His first single, "I Wish," released in 1995, was a self-deprecating rhyme. The accompanying music video parodied the Tom Hanks film *Forrest Gump*, and became a huge hit on radio and MTV. His debut album, also called *I Wish* (Scotti Bros., 1995), was released shortly thereafter. In 2000, Skee-Lo released his long-awaited follow-up, *I Can't Stop* (Maddtrax).

DISCOGRAPHY: *I Wish* (Scotti Bros, 1995); *I Can't Stop* (Maddtrax, 2000).

SLICK RICK (aka MC Ricky D) [Ricky Walters]

Slick Rick, best known as one of rap music's greatest storytellers, is a modern rap music genius. His debut album *The Great Adventures of Slick Rick* (Def Jam Recordings) would influence a generation of rap artists with rhymes that painted lyrical pictures rather than just stringing words together.

A Hip Hop icon, Slick Rick was easily recognizable with his massive gold chains and eye patch. The London-born rap artist was blinded by broken glass as an infant and took to wearing an eyepatch from an early age. In the late 1970s, Slick Rick and his family immigrated to the Bronx, New York, where he attended La Guardia High School of Music & Art. It was at La Guardia that he met **Dana Dane**. Rick and Dana formed the Kangol Crew, and began performing in rap **battles** around New York.

Slick Rick. *Courtesy of Photofest.*

In 1984, Rick met **Doug E. Fresh**, at a battle in the Bronx and began performing with his Get Fresh Crew, which also included Chill Will and Barry Bee. As part of the Get Fresh Crew, MC Ricky D (as he was then known) gave an unforgettable performance on the 1985 twelve-inch single "The Show," b/w "La Di Da Di" released by Reality Records. Rick personified a new type of rap artist: suave, debonair, but also possessing humor and insight. "The Show," exploded and hit number 4 on the R & B charts.

One year later, MC Ricky D became a solo artist and thereafter signed to **Def Jam Recordings**. In 1988, he released the single, "Treat Her Like A Prostitute," considered by many to be **misogynistic** in tone. The song became an **underground** hit, but mainstream radio was reluctant to play it. In 1989, Rick released his debut album, the platinum-selling *The Great Adventures of Slick Rick*. Classic tracks such as "Children's Story," "Mona Lisa," and "Hey Young World" displayed Slick Rick's remarkable talent for narratives.

In 1990, Slick Rick was incarcerated for attempted murder in the shooting of his cousin. In the aftermath of the shooting, Slick Rick had led police on a high-speed chase. Slick Rick claimed that he had shot his cousin because the cousin had harassed Slick Rick's mother. **Russell Simmons** bailed Slick Rick out of jail, and during a three-week period he recorded twenty-one songs for his sophomore album, *The Ruler's Back* (Def Jam Recordings). The album flopped, although the track "I Shouldn't Have Done It" did make the charts in 1991. Slick Rick released his third album, *Behind Bars* (Def Jam Recordings, 1994). The underrated album reteamed Slick Rick with Doug E. Fresh on the track "Sittin' In My Car." He was released on a work program in 1996.

In 1999 Slick Rick released his successful comeback album, *Art of Storytelling* (Def Jam Recordings), which solidified his reputation as a lyricist. The album included guest performances by top-flight rap artists **Outkast** and **Snoop Dogg**, but did even more to emphasize his talents as a solo artist. In 2001, singer Macy Gray asked Slick Rick to perform on her version of his song "Hey Young World," which appears on her for album *The It*. The original song appeared on Slick Rick's debut album.

Slick Rick's prison stint would almost get the rap artist deported to the United Kingdom, although he had not lived there since he was a child. In the summer of 2002, while he was performing in Florida, the Immigration and Nationalization Service (INS) arrested Slick Rick. The government agency had been trying to deport Slick Rick since 1991. The Board of Immigration Appeals now ruled in favor of INS. Slick Rick, who had come to the United States at age eleven, never officially became a citizen (although his wife, children, and parents are all United States citizens). According to U.S. immigration law, any noncitizen who serves more than five years in prison for a felony conviction is automatically to be deported, and Slick Rick had served five years and twelve days when released from prison in 1996 for attempted murder. Russell Simmons and Dr. Benjamin Muhammad of the Hip-Hop Summit Action Network called on President George W. Bush to issue an executive order overturning the deportation ruling. Simmons and Chavis also worked with Congressman John Conyers (D-MI) to call for a fair hearing on the case. On October 31, 2003, a U.S. District Court judge reinstated the legendary MC's U.S. residency and ruled that he not be deported to England, where he was born. Rick was released from jail in early November.

While he was fighting deportation, Slick Rick was the victim of identity theft. Twenty-eight-year-old Steven Glenn of Raleigh, North Carolina, had Rick's mail rerouted to North Carolina sometime in 2002. Glenn forged Slick Rick's name on royalty checks and attempted to withdraw the funds after depositing them into an account. He also registered a car, received hospital care, and sent out express mail packages under the name Ricky Walters.

DISCOGRAPHY: *The Great Adventures of Slick Rick* (Def Jam Recordings, 1989); *The Ruler's Back* (Def Jam Recordings, 1991); *Behind Bars* (Def Jam Recordings, 1994); *Art of Storytelling* (Def Jam Recordings, 1999).

SMITH, WILL

Will Smith began his musical career as the rap artist for the 1980s duo **DJ Jazzy Jeff and the Fresh Prince**. In 1990, he became the star of the NBC sitcom, *Fresh Prince of Bel Air*, which catapulted him to numerous big screen film. Will Smith has since become a box office hit, starring in numerous films, including *Bad Boys* (1995), *Independence Day* (1996), *Men In Black* (1997), *Enemy of the State* (1998), *Ali* (2001), *I, Robot* (2004), the animated film *Shark Tale* (2004), and the comedy *Hitch* (2005).

Four years after the DJ Jazzy Jeff and the Fresh Prince album *Code Red* (Jive Records, 1993), Will Smith released his solo debut album, *Big Willie*

Style (Columbia Records). Rap fans either like Will Smith's pop-flavored raps or they do not; few folks stay in the middle. Will Smith as a solo artist basically expands on the feel-good, PG-rated material that DJ Jazzy Jeff and the Fresh Prince became famous with. The multiplatinum *Big Willie Style* is Smith's best-selling solo effort to date. The album spawned several hit singles including the bouncy "Getting Jiggy Wit It," "Men in Black" (from the film soundtrack), and "Just the Two of Us" (an ode to fathers). Cameo's Larry Blackmon joins Will on the track "Candy," and TLC's Left Eye makes an appearance on the track "Big Willie Style."

In 1999, Will's follow-up album *Willennium* (Columbia Records) liberally uses The Clash's song "Rock the Casbah," to create the track "Will2K." *Willennium* mixes Old Schools with new, with performances by **Lil' Kim**, **Eve**, **Slick Rick**, and **Biz Markie**. DJ Jazzy Jeff makes a brief appearance on the track "Pump Me Up." Will's third album, the overlooked *Born to Reign* (Columbia Records), was released in 2002 to generally good reviews. Standout tracks include "Block Party," How Da Beat Goes" (which samples **Newcleus**'s 1984 hit "Jam On It"), and "Nod Ya Head" (the **remix**). Will's fourth album, *Lost and Found* (Interscope Records), is scheduled for release in 2005.

DISCOGRAPHY: *Big Willie Style* (Columbia, 1997); *Willennium* (Columbia, 1999); *Born to Reign* (Columbia, 2002); *Lost and Found* (Interscope Records, [2005]).

SNIPES. See Films

SNOOP DOGG (aka Snoop, aka Snoop Doggy Dogg) [Calvin Broadus]

Snoop Dogg is the poster child for the transitional character of rap celebrities. In the 1990s, Snoop epitomized hardcore rap music and the sullen gangster attitudes and criminal lifestyle often associated with it. Today, however, Snoop is a frequent guest on mainstream television programs, has appeared in films and commercials, and even had his own comedy show on MTV.

Nicknamed Snoop by his mother as a joke about how he looked, Snoop Dogg was raised in Long Beach, California, where he had numerous run-ins with the law. Shortly after he graduated from high school, he was incarcerated for three years for cocaine possession. Once released, Snoop began recording tapes with his friend **Warren G**, who was **Dr. Dre**'s stepbrother. After hearing Snoop's rhymes, Dr. Dre was impressed enough to begin collaborating with him.

Snoop came to the public's attention on the title song from soundtrack for the 1992 film *Deep Cover* (Death Row Records, 1992), the music produced by Dr. Dre on **Death Row Records**. Snoop then performed on the

Dre's album *The Chronic* (Death Row Records, 1993). Snoop's distinctive slow drawl on Dre's singles "Nuthin' but a 'G' Thang" and "Dre Day" set the stage for Snoop's much-anticipated debut album, *Doggystyle*.

While he was recording his album that summer, however, Snoop was arrested in connection with the drive-by shooting death of Phillip Woldermarian. According to the charges, Snoop drove the car as his bodyguard, McKinley Lee, shot the victim. Snoop claimed that the shooting was in self-defense, alleging that the victim was stalking Snoop. In true rap fashion, after performing at the MTV Music Awards in September 1993, Snoop turned himself in to authorities. The arrest perhaps further legitimized his street credentials; and his debut album *Doggystyle* became the first debut rap album to enter the charts at number 1. It stayed on the top of the charts in 1994, helped enormously by the hit singles "What's My Name?" and "Gin & Juice." Controversies based on assertions that Snoop's lyrics were exceedingly violent and sexist also increased demand for the album.

In 1994, when Snoop Dogg was on tour in the United Kingdom, a Tory minister pleaded for the government to expel Snoop from the country. Snoop capitalized on the impending trial by shooting a short film based on the track "Murder Was the Case" from *Doggystyle*. Snoop also released an accompanying soundtrack, which debuted at number 1 in 1994. During this period, *Doggystyle* had sold quadruple platinum. Snoop's popularity surge was not permanent, however, since he had to fight charges throughout 1994 and 1995.

In February 1996, when he was finally cleared of all charges, Snoop began working on his second album (produced without Dr. Dre, who had left Death Row Records). By the time his second album, *The Doggfather,* was released in November 1996, the public's appetite for hardcore rap music was dying out and *The Doggfather* sold only half as well as its predecessor. Death Row Records was also in disarray, after the death of **Tupac Shakur** and the indictment of Suge Knight on racketeering charges, all which may also have caused the album to receive less than stellar promotion and marketing.

Snoop, perhaps sensing the changing rap music landscape, began to distance himself from his gangster image and eventually from Death Row Records. In 1997, he performed in the Lollapalooza tour and collaborated with rock artists Beck and Marilyn Manson. Snoop also signed to No Limit Records and in 1998 released the solo *Da Game Is to Be Sold Not to Be Told*. In 1999, *No Limit Top Dogg* appeared, *Dead Man Walkin'* appeared in 2000, with *Tha Last Meal* following in December of that year.

Although the almost annual releases were of inconsistent quality, Snoop was forging a bigger career as a rap personality, acting in several big-budget movies, including *Baby Boy* (2001), *Training Day* (2001), *The Wash* (2001), *Malibu's Most Wanted* (2003), *Starsky and Hutch* (2004), and *Soul Plane* (2004). In late in 2002, Snoop released his first album for Capitol Records, *Paid tha Cost to Be da Bo$$*. Between June and August in 2003, he starred in his own MTV comedy show *Doggy Fizzle Televizzle*.

Snoop released his next album, *R&G (Rhythm & Gangsta): The Masterpiece* (Geffen Records) in 2004. The album contains the **Neptunes**-produced hit "Drop It Like It's Hot." That year Snoop also scored big with the single "Beautiful" (featuring Pharell Williams) from the *Soul Plane* film soundtrack.

In 2004, he filed for divorce from his wife, Shanté, citing irreconcilable differences. He is seeking joint custody of their children, Corde, Cordell, and Cori.

DISCOGRAPHY: *Doggystyle* (Death Row Records, 1993); *The Doggfather* (Death Row Records, 1996); *Da Game Is to Be Sold Not to Be Told* (No Limit, 1998); *No Limit Top Dogg* (No Limit, 1999); *Dead Man Walkin'* (No Limit, 2000); *Tha Last Meal* (No Limit, 2000); *Paid tha Cost to Be da Bo$$* (Capitol Records, 2002); *R&G (Rhythm & Gangsta): The Masterpiece* (Geffen Records, 2004).

SOURCE, THE

The Source magazine, the leading rap publication in the country, got its start at Harvard University when sophomores David Mays (a college radio DJ) and Jon Schecter (an erstwhile rap artist) decided to capitalize on the growing interest in rap music by producing the one-page "The Source: Boston's First and Only Rap Music Newsletter" in the summer of 1988. Initially distributed free of charge, Mays sold advertising space to local record stores.

In the fall of 1989, Mays and Schecter decided to make "The Source" a business, publishing the newsletter from their dorm room, and doing all of the work from the writing to the administrative tasks. The newsletter was now sold for about $1.00 per copy. In 1989, two African Americans joined "The Source"—Harvard law student James Bernard on the editorial team and undergraduate Ed Young, who oversaw business affairs. When Mays and Schecter graduated in 1990, they moved their offices to New York City.

In 1994, Jon Schecter, James Bernard, and other editors defected from the publication after an article written by David Mays about the Boston rap group The **Almighty RSO** was published in the magazine without the editors' knowledge. Members of the Almighty RSO were alleged to be personal friends of Mays. David Mays and Ed Young would retain control of the magazine. In 1997, several editors who left *The Source*, including Reginald Dennis and James Bernard, founded the magazine *XXL*, a competing Hip Hop magazine, only to resign after a dispute with Harris Publishing over editorial and financial control of the publication.

SOURCE, THE: 1999 HIP HOP MUSIC AWARDS. *See* Films

SPECIAL ED [Ed Archer]

Special Ed is best known for his 1989 Hip Hop classic, the single "I've Got it Made," from his debut album, *Youngest In Charge* (Profile Records).

Born in Brooklyn, New York, Special Ed began his music career at age 16. Before signing with Profile Records, Special Ed had earned a reputation, first in his Flatbush neighborhood and later all around New York City, for his superior freestyling ability.

His debut album, *Youngest In Charge*, produced by Howie "Hitman" Tee, showcased Special Ed's lyrical quickness and the music video for "I've Got it Made" was shot at Brooklyn landmarks such as Prospect Park, the Brooklyn Museum of Art and the Brooklyn Public Library at Grand Army Plaza. The album also spawned the hits "I'm the Magnificent" and "Taxin'."

In 1990, Special Ed released his follow-up album, *Legal* (Profile Records), which contained the tracks "On a Mission" and "C'mon Let's Move It." *Legal* combined Special Ed's witty rhymes with Caribbean inflections, for a memorable album. Special Ed tried his hand at acting, making guest appearances on *The Cosby Show* and in the 1992 film *Juice*, which starred **Tupac Shakur**. In 1994, Special Ed appeared on the single "Crooklyn Dodgers," released from the Spike Lee film *Crooklyn*, featuring Buckshot (**Black Moon**) and **Master Ace** and produced by Q-Tip (of **A Tribe Called Quest**).

After the release of his third album, *Revelations* (Profile Records, 1995), Ed focused on producing. He lent his talents to Tupac's 1993 album *Strictly 4 My N.I.G.G.A.Z.* (Interscope Records), producing and performing on the track "Guess Who's Back." Special Ed works the boards on **Junior M.A.F.I.A.**'s first and only album, *Conspiracy* (Undeas Entertainment, 1995). In 2002, Special Ed was featured on the track "Don't Make a Wrong Move" from **Snoop Dogg**'s Doggystyle All-Stars compilation *Welcome to the House Vol. 1.* (MCA Records) In 2005, Special Ed reteamed with Howie Tee to produce his fourth album, *Still Got It Made*, released on his independent label, Semi Records.

DISCOGRAPHY: *Youngest In Charge* (Profile, 1989); *Legal* (Profile Records, 1990); *Revelations* (Profile Records, 1995); *Still Got It Made* (Semi, 2005).

SPOONIE GEE [Gabriel Jackson]

Originator of the Old School Hip Hop rap phrase "One for the trouble, two for the time," Spoonie Gee influenced a generation of rap artists and is considered by many to be the first great rap storyteller.

When Spoonie Gee was signed to **Enjoy Records**, which was owned by his uncle, R & B producer Bobby Robinson, he became one of rap music's earliest recorded artists. The Harlem, New York, native began his rap career in 1977, inspired by seeing **DJ Hollywood**. In 1979, Peter Brown, owner of the independent label Sound of New York, came to Robinson's record shop in search of a rap artist. Spoonie Gee stepped up and, a few days later, the sixteen-year-old Spoonie released his debut single, "Spooning Rap" The correct title for the single was Spoonie Rap, but a typo caused the song to be known as "Spoonin' Rap."

Spoonie (it was originally spelled "Spoony") got his nickname as a child, for always preferring to eat with a spoon. In 1980, Spoonie Gee released the mature-themed single "Love Rap" (Enjoy Records), which used only a drum and conga as the musical accompaniment. Similar in vibe to the intimate talking segments found in soul music, it helped to establish Spoonie Gee's reputation as a "love rapper."

Originally it was Spoonie Gee and not **Kool Moe Dee** who was the front man for legendary **Treacherous Three**, and under the group name "Spoonie Gee and The Treacherous Three" they released the twelve-inch single "New Rap Language," with "Love Rap" on the B-side. Robinson sold Enjoy Records artists' contracts to Sugar Hill Records, leading to Spoonie Gee's collaboration with the all-female group **Sequence** in 1980 on a classic twelve-inch single, "Monster Jam." In 1981, he released the single "Spoonie is Back" (Sugar Hill), dedicated to his mother, who had died in 1977.

Spoonie Gee acted as ghostwriter for the 1982 **Grandmaster Flash and the Furious Five** song, "Message II (Survival)," to meet his contract obligations with Sugar Hill Records and get off the label. Spoonie then moved to Tuff City Records, where he went recorded several twelve-inch singles: "The Big Beat" (1983), produced by **Davy DMX**; "Get Off My Tip" (1984); and "Street Girl" (1985). In 1987, Spoonie Gee released his first and only U.S. album, *The Godfather of Rap*, which benefited from production help from **Marley Marl** and Teddy Riley. Standout tracks were the "The Godfather" and "Take It Off." He released other singles: "All Shook Up" (Tuff City, 1987) and "You Ain't Just a Fool (You's an Old fool)" (Tuff City, 1988).

In the early 1990s **LL Cool J** and the **Beastie Boys** kept Spoonie Gee's name current by included it in lyrics for their respective tracks, "The Booming System" (Def Jam Recordings, 1990) and "So Whatcha Want" (Def American/Capitol Records, 1992). Despite Spoonie Gee's musical legacy, he has largely faded from the public's view, primarily because the private artist rarely grants interviews to U.S.-based publications.

DISCOGRAPHY: *Singles*: "Spoonin' Rap" (Sound of New York, 1979); "The New Rap Language" b/w "Love Rap" (Enjoy Records, 1980) "Monster Jam" w/Sequence (Sugar Hill Records, 1980); "Spoonie is Back" (Sugar Hill Records, 1981); "The Big Beat" (Tuff City Records, 1983);

"Get Off My Tip" (Tuff City Records, 1984); "Street Girl "(Tuff City Records, 1985); "All Shook Up" (Tuff City Records, 1987); "You Ain't Just a Fool (You's an Old fool)" (Tuff City Records, 1988). *Album*: *The Godfather of Rap* (Tuff City Records, 1987).

STETSASONIC

Before there was **The Roots**, there was Stetsasonic, the original "Hip Hop band," who created rap with live instruments and jazz samples. Comprised of "**Prince Paul**" Huston, Leonard "Wise" Roman, Marvin "DBC" Nemley, Glenn "Daddy O" Bolton, Martin "Delite" Wright, and Anthony "Frukwan" Hamilton, Stetsasonic helped usher in a new wave of Black consciousness that would be popularized in later groups such as **De La Soul** and the **Jungle Brothers**. For example, proceeds from the twelve-inch single "A.F.R.I.C.A.," b/w "Free South Africa" (1987) were donated to the Africa Fund for humanitarian relief projects.

Hailing from Brooklyn, New York, Daddy O and Delite founded the group in 1981, originally calling themselves the Stetson Brothers (after the hat). The duo began performing in New York clubs, and along the way the other members joined. Stetsasonic's debut album *On Fire* (Tommy Boy Records), was released in 1986, but it was the follow-up, *In Full Gear* (Tommy Boy Records, 1988), that brought the group critical acclaim, buoyed by the single, "Sally."

According to Hip Hop lore, the outstanding Stetsasonic track "Talking All That Jazz" (1988) is a direct response to Grammy Award winner James Mtume's public criticism of rap music's use of samples. Mtume also questioned whether rap was even a legitimate musical form. In the album liner notes, Stetsasonic calls Hip Hop "the most progressive form of music since jazz." In true B-boy **battle** style, along with a jazzy, percussion heavy melody line, "Talkin' All That Jazz" contains samples from several soul and jazz samples tracks, including Mtume's "Juicy Fruit" (1983), Banbarra's "Shack Up" (1976), Sly and the Family Stone's "You Can Make It if You Try" (1969), and Donald Byrd's "(Fallin' Like) Dominoes" (1976). To step the retort up even more, Stetsasonic worked in lyrical references to one or two of the tracks they sample.

In 1991, the group released *Blood, Sweat & No Tears* (Tommy Boy Records), which would be their last album. Although not generally ranked with *In Full Gear* as a classic Hip Hop album, many nevertheless consider *Blood, Sweat & No Tears* to be Stetsasonic's best and most diverse album. Reportedly, Daddy-O indicated that Stetsasonic had run out of ideas and therefore the Hip Hop band parted ways.

Before the group's formal breakup, Prince Paul had already produced De La Soul's 1989 debut album. **Prince Paul** and Frukwan would become members of the group the **Gravediggaz**. In 1993, Daddy-O released his debut solo album, *You Can Be a Daddy, But Not Daddy-O* (Island

Records). Daddy-O has also written and produced jingles and radio or television commercials for products such as Casio Electronics, Alka Seltzer, and Pepsi.

DISCOGRAPHY: *On Fire* (Tommy Boy Records, 1986); *In Full Gear* (Tommy Boy Records, 1988); *Blood, Sweat & No Tears* (Tommy Boy Records, 1991).

STOP THE VIOLENCE MOVEMENT–"SELF DESTRUCTION"

In 1988 at a **Public Enemy** and **Boogie Down Productions** concert, a young fan was killed in a fight. Inspired by the track "Stop the Violence" track from **KRS-ONE**'s album *By Any Means Necessary*, executives at Jive Records asked KRS-ONE to put together a collective of artists to record the single "Self Destruction," to bring attention to violence among young African Americans as part of a Stop The Violence Movement.

The collection of rap artists included KRS-ONE (Boogie Down Productions), Ms. Melodie (Boogie Down Productions) **Heavy D**, Daddy-O (**Stetsasonic**), **MC Lyte**, **Just-Ice**, **LL Cool J**, and **Kool Moe Dee**. The twelve-inch single "Self Destruction" sold over 500,000 units and raised approximately $600,000, which was donated to the National Urban League in 1989. Nelson George authored an accompanying book, *Stop the Violence: Overcoming Self-Destruction* (New York: Pantheon **Books**, 1990).

STRICTLY HIP HOP MAGAZINE

Founded in Philadelphia, Pennsylvania, in 1988 by **Lady B** and Mike Elliott (who would later join ***The Source*** magazine), *Strictly Hip Hop* was the first national magazine dedicated exclusively to rap music and Hip Hop.

STYLE WARS. *See* Films; Graffiti

SUGAR HILL GANG

A group assembled by Sylvia Robinson of Sugar Hill Records, the Sugar Hill Gang released the single "**Rapper's Delight**" in 1979, which would become the first commercially successful rap record.

As a group prefabricated by its recording company, the Sugar Hill Gang started the controversy about what and who constitutes real Hip Hop, particularly because numerous talent groups who had honed their skills in New York venues were not given the opportunity to record their work. Notably, **Grandmaster Caz** of the legendary **Cold Crush Brothers** is reported to be the author of much of "Rapper's Delight," but his work was used by his acquaintance Big Bank Hank without credit and without his knowledge or permission.

Although the Sugar Hill Gang never received the critical acclaim given to label mates **Grandmaster Flash and the Furious Five**, they continued to release records. In 1980, they released the album *Sugar Hill Gang* (Sugar Hill Records), which was followed by *8th Wonder* in 1982. Re-issue house Rhino Records would release a new Sugar Hill album, *Jump on It*, a children's album in 1999. There also have been numerous Sugar Hill albums and remixes released over the years abroad.

DISCOGRAPHY: *Single*: "Rapper's Delight" (Sugar Hill Records, 1979). *Albums*: *The Sugar Hill Gang* (Sugar Hill Records, 1979); *8th Wonder* (Sugar Hill Records, 1982); *Jump On It* (Rhino Records, 1999).

SWEET T [Tanya Winley]

Sweet T is recognized as the first female solo rap recording artist, for the single "Vicious Rap," released in November 1979. The song was recorded on Paul Winley Records, owned by Paula's father.

T

TAG; TAGGING. *See* Graffiti

TALIB KWELI. *See* Black Star

TECHNICS 1200

Technics was the legendary brand and model of turntables favored by early Hip Hop DJs; these were often used with a Gemini 626 **mixer**.

TEMPLE OF HIP HOP, THE

The motto of The Temple of Hip Hop is "Rap is something that you do, Hip Hop is something you live." Founded by **KRS-ONE** in 1998, the organization that that it is "a Hiphop preservation society that seeks to define and teach the accumulated wisdom of Hiphop to Hiphoppas."

In January 2005, KRS-ONE announced plans to develop a learning institution, The Temple of Hip Hop, located in Los Angeles, California, which would include a library and archive and would teach the principles of Hip Hop and as well as offering training and developing Hip Hop's first "cultural specialists," "Teachas," and "certified Hiphop instructors," some of whom would be the actual architects and pioneers of "Hiphop Kulture" itself. "It's time to do this. I think the physical establishment of such a Hiphop institution is long over-due." Registered members include **Fat Joe**, Kid Capri, **Busta Rhymes**, **Redman**, **Lauryn Hill**.

TERROR SQUAD

Terror Squad is the rap crew founded by Latino rap artists **Fat Joe**, and the late **Big Pun** in 1996. The two Latino superstars anchored the Terror Squad, which would later add fellow Bronx rap artists Cuban Link (who later left the crew), Armageddon, Prospect, and Triple Seis and singer Tony Sunshine, as well as Remy Ma.

The group debuted on the 1998 Fat Joe album, *Don Cartagena* (Relativity Records). In 1999, the Terror Squad released their self-titled debut album on Atlantic Records. Five years later, they released a second album, *True Story* (Universal Records). By this time, Fat Joe had added female **battle** rap champion Remy Ma to the Terror Squad. Remy Ma had been discovered by Big Pun and signed to Loud Records. The album's lead single, "Lean Back," became a quick hit.

DISCOGRAPHY: *Terror Squad* (Atlantic Records, 1999); *True Story* (Universal Records, 2004).

THA ALKAHOLIKS (aka Tha Liks)

The West Coast rap trio of J-Ro [James Robinson], Tash [Rico Smith], and DJ E-Swift [Eric Brooks], founded in the early 1990s, came on the Hip Hop scene by working with **King Tee** on his 1993 single, "I Got It Bad Y'All," from *Tha Triflin' Album* (Capitol Records).

Cincinnati natives, DJ E-Swift and Tash had worked together in the rap group Disturbers of the Peace (D.O.P.) and the two relocated to Los Angeles and met J-Ro, who had worked in Total Control with rap artist Suavee D and **King Tee**. Although J-Ro had opened for artists such as **The Real Roxanne** and **Dana Dane**, he was ready to move on. After working with King Tee the three joined together and named themselves Tha Alkaholiks.

Thereafter they toured with **KRS-ONE**, **Ice Cube**, and **Too Short**. They subsequently secured a record contract with Loud Records in 1993 and released the single, "Likwit/Only When I'm Drunk." The trio released their debut album *21 & Over* (Loud Records) in 1993. On their second album, *Coast II Coast* (Loud Records, 1995), the trio worked with East Coast heavyweight Q-Tip (**A Tribe Called Quest**) while maintaining their West Coast party vibe. Tha Alkaholiks moved to Relativity Records and in 1999 they released their third album, *Likwidation*. In 2001, as Tha Liks they released the album *X.O. Experience* (Sony Records). In 1999, Tash released his solo debut, *Rap Life*, which gained critical acclaim and commercial success.

DISCOGRAPHY: *Single*: "Likwit/Only When I'm Drunk" (Loud, 1993). *Albums*: *21 & Over* (Loud/RCA, 1993); *Coast II Coast* (Loud/RCA, 1995); *Likwidation* (Relativity Records, 1999); *X.O. Experience* (Sony, 2001).

THA DOGG POUND

The duo, Tha Dogg Pound, comprised of rap artists Daz Dillinger and **Kurupt**, each gained exposure as solo artists on **Death Row Records**, and each was a minor player in the success of **Dr. Dre**'s 1992 album, *The Chronic* (Death Row Records). Their contributions were more evident a year later, on **Snoop Dogg**'s album *Doggystyle* (Death Row Records). Riding on their new-found success, the duo were labeled Snoop's protégés and given the name Tha Dogg Pound.

Tha Dogg Pound subsequently released their debut album, *Dogg Food* (Death Row Records). The album spawned two minor hits, "Let's Play

House" and the diss track "**New York, New York**," but was not considered a major success. Daz Dillinger and Kurupt then went back to their solo careers, which proved to be lackluster in both instances.
DISCOGRAPHY: *Dogg Food* (Death Row Records, 1995).

3RD BASS (aka Third Bass)

3rd Bass, comprised of Pete Nice [Peter J. Nash], MC Serch [Michael Berrin], and DJ Richie Rich [Richard Lawson], are best known for their singles "Pop Goes the Weasel," "The Gas face," and "Step Into the A.M." This largely underrated White rap group gained early legitimacy with Black rap fans. 3rd Bass were embraced by core rap music fans because, rather than relying on the novelty of being White rap artists, they had rhyme skills and demonstrated a respect for Hip Hop, and its history. Even so, multi-platinum-selling **Vanilla Ice**, eclipsed 3rd Bass, because his simple, pop-influenced rhymes appealed to a wider music audience. (Vanilla Ice would later be exposed as having lied about his rough background as a means of selling more records.)

Brooklyn native, MC Serch began rhyming as a youth and honed his skills at the High School of Music and Art. In the mid-1980s, he began performing with groups such as Gangster 5 and SZ Connection. He then recorded his first solo single "Melissa" (Warlock Records) in 1986 and followed that up with the single "Hey Boy" (Idlers Records, 1987). Prime Minister Pete Nice, hailing from Queens, New York, took an interest in rap music while in junior high school. Fast-forward to 1985, and he would win a basketball scholarship to Columbia University and begin hosting his own rap music radio show with DJ Clark Kent on the campus station WKCR-FM. In 1988, the show was cancelled and he began focusing his attention on rap music. At this time he began working with DJ **Richie Rich**. Through Sam Sever and Dante Ross, Serch was introduced to Pete Nice and they did a few songs under the group name Three the Hard Way, including an early "Wordz of Wizdom."

Once signed to **Def Jam Recordings**, they renamed themselves 3rd Bass and in 1989 they released their debut album, *Cactus Album* (Def Jam Recordings), which includes their "Wordz of Wizdom" track. In 1990, *The Cactus Collection: 3rd Bass Remixes* (Def Jam Recordings) was released. In 1991, they followed with *Derelicts of Dialect* (Def Jam Recordings), which contained the track "Pop Goes the Weasel," their biggest chart single. The track, a viciously funny attack on Vanilla Ice, is accompanied by an equally humorous video, which includes a fake Vanilla Ice. The song was also a means for 3rd Bass to distance themselves from Vanilla Ice and the entire White rap artist phenomenon. In 1992, the 3rd Bass disbanded after recording the song "Gladiator" for the film soundtrack of the same name. That year MC Serch released a solo album titled, *Return of the Product* (Def Jam Recordings). While recording his album, MC Serch also executive-produced the 1992 *Zebrahead* film soundtrack, which introduced the world to **Nas**. Nas also appeared on MC Serch's solo album on the track "Back to the Grill." MC Serch was the executive producer on Nas's classic debut album *Illmatic* (Columbia, 1994), which was met with rave reviews. Under the name Pete Nice & Daddy Rich, the two released the album *Dust to Dust* (Def Jam Recordings, 1993). In October 1998, 3rd Bass briefly reunited to play a party for Andy Hilfiger, brother of fashion designer Tommy Hilfiger.

Despite rumors that a new album was being discussed, no album ever materialized. In late 2002, MC Serch could be heard on Detroit, Michigan, radio station WJLB-FM. After his Hoppoh Records label (founded with DJ Bobbito Garcia) folded, Pete Nice left the music industry and opened a baseball memorabilia store in Cooperstown, New York. He was also the curator for the Chadwick Collection, a traveling exhibit of nineteenth-century baseball memorabilia. In 2003, as Peter J. Nash, he published the book *Baseball Legends of Brooklyn's Green-Wood Cemetery (Images of Baseball)* (New York: Arcadia Publishing).

DISCOGRAPHY: *The Cactus Album* (Def Jam Recordings, 1989); *The Cactus Album Revisited* (Def Jam Recordings, 1990); *Derelicts of Dialect* (Def Jam Recordings, 1991).

THROUGH THE YEARS OF HIP HOP. *See* Films

THROW-UP. *See* Graffiti

TIMBALAND [Tim Mosely]

The hit-making producer Timbaland helped to reshape rap music in the 1990s with his distinctive signature sound. The Timbaland sound does not rely on samples, and frequently includes stuttering bass-heavy bounce beats offset resounding high-end synthetic stabs, all of this often studded with his trademark quiet murmuring beneath the track.

The Norfolk, Virginia, native initially worked with a close group of associates that included **Missy Elliott** singers Aaliyah and Ginuwine. As Timbaland branched out, he would produce successful tracks for A-list artists including **Jay-Z** ("Big Pimpin'"), **Snoop Dogg** ("What's My Name, Pt 2"), **Nas** ("You Won't See Me Tonight"), and Justin Timberlake and **Ludacris** ("Rollout (My Business)"). He also worked occasionally with lesser-known rap artists, such as Petey Pablo ("Raise Up"), Pastor Troy ("Are We Cuttin'"), and Tweet ("Oops (Oh My)").

Beginning in the late 1980s, Timbaland worked on and off with rap artist Magoo, a fellow Virginian. Under the name Timbaland & Magoo, the duo released three albums: The double-platinum-selling *Welcome to our World* (Blackground Records, 1997), followed by *Indecent Proposal* (Virgin Records, 2001) and *Under Construction Pt. 2* (Universal Records, 2003). In 1998, Timbaland released his solo album, *Tim's Bio: From the Motion Picture "Life from Da Bassment"* (Blackground Records, 1998), which included appearances by Jay-Z, Aaliyah, and Ginuwine.

Timbaland's first big breaks as a solo entity came as a result of his work on the Jodeci albums *Diary Of A Mad Band* (MCA Records, 1993) and *The Show, The After-Party, The Hotel* (MCA Records, 1995). On *The Show, The After-Party, The Hotel*, Timbaland co-wrote the track "Bring On Da Funk." In 1996, Timbaland's work on Aaliyah's successful sophomore album, *One In A Million* (Virgin Records, 1996), would put him firmly on the Hip Hop map. In 2001, Timbaland established his own label, Beat Club, and on his roster was White rap artist **Bubba Sparxxx**, whose debut single, "Ugly," on the album *Dark Days, Bright Nights* (Interscope Records, 2001) celebrated country rap.

DISCOGRAPHY: *Albums* [Timbaland & Magoo]: *Welcome to our World* (Blackground Records, 1997); *Indecent Proposal* (Virgin Records, 2001); *Under Construction Pt. 2* (Universal Records, 2003). *Albums* [solo]: *Tim's Bio: From the Motion Picture "Life from Da Bassment"* (Blackground Records, 1998).

T LA ROCK [Clarence Keaton]

T La Rock is best known for recording the 1984 classic single, "It's Yours." The record helped to propel the fledging **Def Jam Recordings** label, being the first record to bear the Def Jam logo. The single was not actually released by Def Jam, but by Arthur Baker's Partytime/Streetwise Records.

T La Rock is the older brother of **Treacherous Three**'s Special K and, according to Hip Hop lore, "It's Yours" was written by both of the brothers, but Special K convinced T La Rock to record it. T la Rock went on to the albums *Lyrical King* (Fresh Records, 1987) and *On a Warpath* (Sleeping Bag Records, 1989).

DISCOGRAPHY: *Single*: "It's Yours" (Partytime/Streetwise, 1984). *Albums*: *Lyrical King* (Fresh Records, 1987); *On a Warpath* (Sleeping Bag Records, 1989).

TONE LŌC (aka Tony Loco) [Anthony Terrell Smith]

The Los Angeles rap artist Tone Lōc is best known for his raspy voice, which graces his hit singles "Wild Thing" (Delicious Vinyl Records, 1990) and "Funk Cold Medina" (Delicious Vinyl Records, 1990), both co-written by **Young MC**. The former gang member got his name Tone Lōc when his people called him Antonio Loco (Spanish for Crazy Anthony).

Tone's debut album, *Loc-ed After Dark* (Delicious Vinyl Records, 1989), became the only second rap album ever to top the pop charts; the **Beastie Boys** debut album *Licensed to Ill* (Def Jam Recordings, 1986) was the first. In 1991, he released his second album *Cool Hand Loc* (Delicious Vinyl).

In 1990, Tone Lōc began acting; he would appear on television shows such as *Roc*, *Martin*, *Living Single*, and *Thieves*. He did voice-over work for the animated features *FernGully: The Last Rainforest* (1992), *Bébé's Kids* (1992), and *Titan A.E.* (2000). Tone Lōc also appeared in the films *Car 54, Where Are You?* (1994), *Ace Ventura: Pet Detective* (1994), *Heat* (1995), and *Freedom Strike* (1998). Most recently, he was a panelist on the talent show *Superstar USA* (2004).

DISCOGRAPHY: *Loc-ed After Dark* (Delicious Vinyl Records, 1989); *Cool Hand Loc* (Delicious Vinyl, 1991).

TOO SHORT (aka Short Dog, aka Too $hort) [Todd Shaw]

Best known for songs extolling the pimp lifestyle, street violence, and his own sexual prowess (with an occasionally socially conscious track), Too Short preceded most hardcore **gangsta rap** and therefore became the West Coast's first major solo rap star. His high-pitched voice, coupled with the infectious bass-heavy, mid-tempo funk known throughout the Bay area as "Dope Fiend" beats, creates Too Short's unique sound. Frequent collaborator, producer **Ant Banks** also often contributes to Short's musical trademark.

Too Short, the son of two college-educated accountants, was born in South Central Los Angeles. Too Short moved to East Oakland while he was a youth, his father having decided that South Central was becoming too dangerous.

Like his peers, Too Short was heavily influenced by the **blaxploitation** film, *The Mack* (1973). By the eleventh grade, he had decided that he wanted to be a rap artist. In the early 1980s, Short and his high school friend Freddie B (Benz) were making homemade, thirty-minute rap tapes with titles such as "F**king a Basehead Bitch" that they sold for $5 each at local weed spots.

Short got his big break in 1984 when he was asked to open for rap group U.T.F.O. Still in his teens, Too Short began his professional recording career as an artist on the independent label 75 Girls Records and Tapes. In 1983, he released his first album, *Don't Stop Rappin'*, followed by the albums, *Raw, Uncut and X-Rated* (1984) and *Players* (1985). Although his albums sold well locally, he failed to see any royalties or further money from the releases. Subsequently, in 1986, Too Short and partner Randy Austin formed the Dangerous Music label and released the album *Born To Mack*. The fledging independent company sold 50,000 units of the album, primarily by driving around Oakland and selling tapes from the trunk of the car. As a production company, Dangerous Music was instrumental in advancing the careers of Ant Banks, Spice 1, and Pooh-Man.

On the strength of the buzz that *Born to Mack* had generated, Jive Records signed Too Short to a recording deal. Jive then reissued *Born to Mack* in 1988 and, with virtually no airplay, the album went gold. Too Short's second album, *Life Is ... Too $hort* (Dangerous Music/Jive Records, 1988) sold platinum. as did his next three albums. Too Short's record sales success at last translated into airplay. The track "The Ghetto" from *Short Dog's In The House* (Dangerous Music/Jive Records, 1990) went to number 12 on the R & B charts. Too Short continued to have a string of hit albums: *Shorty the Pimp* (Jive Records, 1992) and *Get in Where You Fit In* (Jive Records, 1993), both of which went platinum.

By the time he released the album *Cocktails* (Jive Records, 1995), Short found himself competing with a slew of sound-alike West Coast artists, and *Cocktails* was not as successful as its predecessors. Short rebounded in late 1996 with *Getting It (Album Number 10)*, his fifth platinum album. After the release of *Getting It*, Too Short announced that he was establishing his own Short Records and retiring from performing. Only three years later, however, Too Short was back in the recording studio; he released the album *Can't Stay Away* (Short Records/Jive Records), which debuted in the Top Ten and went gold. Subsequent albums are: *You Nasty* (Short Records/Jive Records, 2000); *Chase the Cat* (Short Records/Jive Records, 2001); *What's My Favorite Word?* (Jive Records, 2002); *It's About Time* (75 Girls Records, 2003); and *Married to the Game* (Jive Records, 2003).

Over the years Too Short has graced the mic with many of rap's elite, including **Ice Cube**, **Jay-Z**, **The Notorious B.I.G.**, **Lil' Kim**, **Scarface**, and **Dr. Dre**. In 2003, the documentary *Life I$*, produced by former Tony! Toni! Tone! member D'wayne Wiggins, was released on his Grass Roots Entertainment. *Life I$* explores Too Short's life as well as the reasons why he left California for Atlanta in 1994.

As Short states in his song, "These are the Tales," he has the dubious distinction of coining the phrase "Bee-yatch" in rap music. Also relevant is the fact that Short was putting out sex-filled rhymes even before the likes of **Luke Campbell** and **2 Live Crew**. In recent years, Short, like Luke, has entered into the adult entertainment industry.

Too Short is also an astute businessman. As Todd Shaw, he has stated that Too Short is a "marketing vehicle," as well as being a character that he has created. Although there are aspects of Too Short in Shaw, he's clear that Too Short's rhymes contain a great deal of exaggeration and hyperbole, because that is what sells records.

DISCOGRAPHY: *Twelve-inch singles*: Girl (Cocaine)/Shortrapp (75 Girls Records and Tapes, 1985); Playboy Short/Don't Stop Rappin' (75 Girls Records and Tapes, 1985); Whip It/Girl (Cocaine) Rap (75 Girls Records and Tapes, 1985). *Albums*: *Don't Stop Rappin'* (75 Girls Records and Tapes, 1983); *Players* (75 Girls Records and Tapes, 1984); *Raw, Uncut and X-Rate* (75 Girls Records and Tapes, 1985); *Born To Mack* (Dangerous Music, 1987, re-issued, Jive Records, 1989) *Life Is . . . Too $hort* (Jive Records, 1989); *Short Dog's In The House* (Jive Records, 1990); *Shorty the Pimp* (Jive Records, 1992); *Get in Where You Fit In* (Jive Records, 1993); *Cocktails* (Jive Records, 1995); *Getting It (Album Number 10)* (Jive Records, 1996); *Can't Stay Away* (Short Records/Jive Records, 1999); *You Nasty* (Short Records/Jive Records 2000); *Chase the Cat* (Short Records/Jive Records, 2001); *What's My Favorite Word?* (Short Records/Jive Records, 2002); *It's About Time* (75 Girls Records, 2003); *Married to the Game* (Short Records/Jive Records, 2003).

TOUGHER THAN LEATHER. *See* Films

TREACHEROUS THREE

One of the most important of the Old School rap groups, the Treacherous Three briefly included rap artist **Spoonie Gee** [Gabriel Jackson], as well as the legendary rap artist **Kool Moe Dee** [Mohandas Dewese] and the rest of the crew: L.A. Sunshine [Lamar Hill], Special K, Kevin Keaton, DJ Easy Lee [Theodore Moyé], and at times DJ Dano B and Reggie Reg.

The Treacherous Three was founded in the late 1970s, when Harlem, New York, resident Kool Moe Dee joined fellow Norman Thomas High School students Special K and DJ Easy Lee. L.A. Sunshine went to Brandeis High School, also located in Manhattan. The friends began to perform around New York City. Rap artist Spoonie Gee introduced his friends to his uncle Bobby Robinson, who owned **Enjoy Records**, and Spoonie Gee initially recorded with The Treacheous Three.

In 1980, the group released their first twelve-inch single, "The New Rap Language" (Enjoy Records), which raised the bar for rhyming with its complex fast rap style. The B-side of "The New Rap Language" was the Spoonie Gee's classic single "Love Rap," and Spoonie Gee continued to record as a solo artist.

Also in 1980, the Treacherous Three became the first rap group to use rock guitars, on the song "Body Rock" (Enjoy Records). In 1981, the group also released the hit single "Feel the Heat Beat" (Enjoy Records), based on the Taana Gardner club song "Heart Beat" (West End, 1981), and "At the Party" released in 1983 by Enjoy Records. The group moved to Sugar Hill Records and in 1982 recorded the party jams "Whip It" and "Yes We Can-Can." One of their live performances with **Funky Four + 1** appeared on a long-playing twelve-inch titled *Live Convention '81* (Disco Wax Records). In 1984, the trio also made a cameo appearance in the Hip Hop film *Beat Street,* in which they performed the hilarious rhyme

"Santa's Rap" (Atlantic Records), featuring newcomer **Doug E. Fresh**. The song is also known as "X-mas Rap."

Kool Moe Dee and Special K were cohosts on the short-lived television Hip Hop show "**Graffiti Rock**" in 1984, which included a mini-**battle** between **Run DMC** and Kool Moe Dee and Special K.

In 1985, the Treacherous Three recorded "Gotta Rock" (Sugar Hill Records), but for the B-side "Turn It Up" only Kool Moe Dee showed up at the recording studio, so it is actually (despite the Treacherous Three labeling) his first solo recording. Kool Moe Dee graduated from State University of New York at Old Westbury and then officially embarked on a successful solo career in 1986.

In 1987, Special K did a twelve-inch for Republic Records called "Special K Is Good" and DJ Easy Lee did some producing. In 1994, the trio released a reunion album, *Old School Flava* (Wrap Records), which was produced by DJ Easy Lee and included Grandmaster Flash as one of the engineers.

DISCOGRAPHY: "The New Rap Language" (Enjoy Records, 1980) backed with "Love Rap" [Spoonie Gee]; "Body Rock" (Enjoy Records, 1980); "Feel the Heat Beat" (Enjoy Records, 1981); "Put The Boogie In Your Body" (Enjoy Records, 1981); "Whip It" (Sugar Hill Records, 1982); "Yes We Can-Can" (Sugar Hill Records, 1982); "Action" (Sugar Hill Records, 1983); "At the Party" (Enjoy Records, 1983); "Turning You On" backed with "U.F.O." (Sugar Hill Records, 1983); "Santa's Rap" (Atlantic Records, 1984); "Gotta Rock" backed with "Turn It Up" (Sugar Hill Records, 1985).

TR-808

A Roland model drum machine that became the standard for rap music, the TR-808 (introduced in late 1980) was originally intended for studio musicians creating demos. The TR-808 is known for its deep kick drum, snappy snares, and strange cowbell sound. The TR-808 has separate outputs, so DJs can isolate the various sound elements and customize the resulting final sound creation. The TR-808 was used on some early R & B and rap music tracks tunes, including, Marvin Gaye's "Sexual Healing" and **Afrika Bambaataa**'s "Planet Rock." House music was born after Chicago DJs would play the 808 over, between, and under other tracks. This allowed DJs to mix tracks together, creating long dance tracks.

TRIBE CALLED QUEST, A

A Tribe Called Quest (or ATCQ for short) is comprised of Q-Tip (aka Kamaal) [Jonathan Davis], Phife Dog [Malik Taylor], Ali Shaheed Muhammad, and sometime member Jairobi White. ATCQ remains one of the most critically acclaimed rap groups in Hip Hop history. Like other members of the **Native Tongue** movement, **De La Soul** and the **Jungle Brothers**, ATCQ favored jazz-infused tracks rather than recycled R & B and soul samples and an Afrocentric aesthetic. Moreover, the music of ATCQ more often than not successfully combined smart lyrics, head-nodding beats and straight-up fun.

The group formed in 1988. Q-Tip and Phife had grown up together in Queens. Q-Tip met DJ Ali Shaheed Muhammad, a native of Brooklyn, New York, while at high school. The trio was christened by Afrika Baby Bambaataa (The Jungle Brothers), who attended the same high school as Q-Tip and Phife, and thereafter they began performing.

In August 1989, ATCQ's debut single, "Description of a Fool" was released on a small independent label. By that time, Q-Tip had already recorded guest appearances on the De La Soul track from their debut album *3 Feet High and Rising* (Tommy Boy Records, 1989).

Signed to Jive Records in 1989, ATCQ released their debut album, *People's Instinctive Travels And The Paths Of Rhythm* (Jive Records, 1990), which included the classic hits "Anita Applebaum" and "Can I Kick It?" The "Can I Kick It?" track sampled rocker Lou Reed's classic single, "Walk on the Wild Side."

Their second album, *The Low End Theory* (Jive Records, 1991), may be their best. It showcases the group's musical versatility, featuring the jazz musician Ron Carter on the track "Rap Promoter," along with **Leaders of the New School** on "Scenario" and **Diamond D** (**D.I.T.C.**), Sadat X (**Brand Nubian**), and Lord Jamal (Brand Nubian) on the track "(Show-Business)." Aside from "Scenario," the other famous tracks from this album are the controversial "The Infamous Date Rape" and "Check the Rhime."

In 1993, ATCQ released the album *Midnight Marauders* (Jive Records), thought to be an album that moved ATCQ closer to the center of the rap music spectrum and perhaps away from the group's more experimental roots. The album cover and accompanying insert booklet present the faces of over fifty artists who represent the diversity of rap music including De La Soul, the Jungle Brothers, the **Beastie Boys**, **Ice-T**, and **Heavy D**. Although the album is perhaps best known for the single, "Award Tour," it also spawned other popular singles, including "Electric Relaxation" and "Sucka N***a," and had a harder sound than the first two albums.

The following year, the span of ATCQ's musical influence was evident through their performance at the alternative rock gathering Lollapalooza. In 1996, the group returned with their fourth album *Beats, Rhymes and Life* (Jive Records), which debuted at number 1 on the *Billboard* album chart. The standout single from this album is "Stressed Out," which may have described the state of the group at the time. The album contained less bawdy humor and language than before. Some attribute the change in tone to Q-Tip's conversion to the Islam during this period; others simply cite the maturation of the group members.

Two years later, ATCQ released the album *The Love Movement* (Jive Records, 1998), which most believe to be the least energized of the group's works. It was not surprising, then, that while on tour to support the album the group announced their intention to stop recording as a group, with members pursuing solo projects.

The following year, Q-Tip would release the album, *Amplified* (Arista Records), which contained the hit singles "Vibrant Thing" and "Stop and Breath." Some longtime ATCQ fans were confused with the stylistic departure that Q-Tip took on the album, from the bare-chested photo on the album cover to the booty-shaking and gloss-influenced music videos. In 2001, He followed up with the album *Kamaal The Abstract* (Arista), combining his Muslim name with the his rap handle he used as a member of ATCQ; the album was never officially released.

In 2000, Phife released his solo album, *Ventilation: Da LP* (Groove Attack Productions), but despite production help from **Pete Rock**, Hi-Tek, and Jay Dee the album made little noise in the United States.

Ali Shaheed Muhammad cofounded the short-lived supergroup Lucy Pearl, with Raphael Saadiq and ex–En Vogue member Dawn Robinson. In 2004, he released his debut solo album, *Sheedullah & Stereotypes* (Penalty [Ryko]).

In 2003, the group announced that they would be releasing a new album in 2004. As a prelude, the trio of Phife, Q-Tip, and Ali Shaheed Muhammad teamed to record the song "(ICU) Doin' It," which will be a track on the upcoming Violator Records compilation *V3: The Good, the Bad and the Ugly.* It appears that the release date for the compilation has been pushed back to sometime in 2005. In December 2004, the reunited ATCQ blazed the stage at club Mansion in Miami, Florida, performing several songs from their five-album collection.

DISCOGRAPHY: *People's Instinctive Travels and the Paths of Rhythm* (Jive Records, 1990); *The Low End Theory* (Jive Records, 1991); *Midnight Marauders* (Jive Records, 1993); *Beats, Rhymes and Life* (Jive Records, 1996); *The Love Movement* (Jive Records, 1998).

TRICK DADDY (aka Trick Daddy Dollars) [Maurice Young]

Best known as one of the thuggish artists in rap music, Trick Daddy gained national attention with his 2001 hit "I'm a Thug." Although **Tupac Shakur** may have popularized the term "thug life," Trick Daddy, the menacing-looking, gold-toothed, tattooed rap artist has actively promoted himself as thug life incarnate.

The Miami, Florida native, originally known as Trick Daddy Dollars, started making waves in 1996 as one of the lead rap artists on the **Luke Campbell** track "Scarred" (Luke Records). The song was a considerable hit on the booty bass circuit and Trick Daddy Dollars received a great deal of attention. The fledging Slip-N-Slide Records signed the artist and in 1997 Trick Daddy Dollars released his largely autobiographical debut album, *Based on a True Story,* which includes J.T. Money on vocals. Although the independent album sold well regionally, it did not make much noise outside of the Miami area.

In 1998, things changed substantially with the release of the album *www.Thug.com* (Slip-N-Slide Records). Trick Daddy dropped the "Dollars" from his name and scored himself a breakout hit with "Nann Nigga," that had him trading rhymes with a then-unknown female rap artist, **Trina**. The single spread rapidly through the South and then on into the Midwest and Southwest. The independent label Slip-N-Slide signed a distribution deal with Atlantic Records, and in 2000 Trick Daddy released *Book of Thugs: Chapter AK Verse 47* (Slip-N-Slide/Atlantic), his first album under the partnership. Along with other tracks on *Book of Thugs*, the club track "Shut Up," which also featured Trina, expanded Trick Daddy's reputation nationally.

In 2001, Trick Daddy released his next album, *Thugs Are Us* (Slip-N-Slide/Atlantic Records), which included the boom-banging club track, "I'm a Thug." The extremely popular song garnered Trick Daddy immediate radio play on mainstream and urban radio stations. To date, "I'm a Thug" is Trick Daddy's biggest hit. In 2002, Trick Daddy released his fifth album in six years, *Thug Holiday* (Slip-N-Slide/Atlantic), and in 2004 *Thug Matrimony: Married to the Streets* (Slip-N-Slide/Atlantic) hit the streets.

DISCOGRAPHY: *Based on a True Story* (Slip-N- Slide, 1997); *www.Thug.com* (Slip-N-Slide, 1998); *Book of Thugs: Chapter AK Verse 47* (Slip-N-Slide/Atlantic, 2000); *Thugs Are Us* (Slip-N-Slide/Atlantic Records, 2001); *Thug Holiday* (Slip-N-Slide/Atlantic, 2002); *Thug Matrimony: Married to the Streets* (Slip-N-Slide/Atlantic Records, 2004).

TRINA [Katrina Laverne]

Much like **Lil' Kim** and **Foxy Brown**, Trina is a female rap artist who is not afraid to flaunt her curves or love of sex and money.

The Miami, Florida-based artist established her career by making guest appearances on **Trick Daddy**'s albums. Her hardcore style on Trick Daddy's hit "Nann Nigga," made noise in the rap world. Trick Daddy's record label, Slip-N-Slide, liked Trina's style and continued to pair her up with him. Her presence is particularly strong on Trick Daddy's album, *Thugs Are Us* (Slip-N-Slide, 2001). Fans soon wanted more of Trina's in-your-face lyrics, and Slip-N-Slide Records signed Trina to a recording deal. In 2000, she released her debut gold album *Da Baddest B***h* (Slip-N-Slide) filled with profanity and sexually direct lyrics such as the track "69 Ways." The album, however, also includes the inspirational track "Mama."

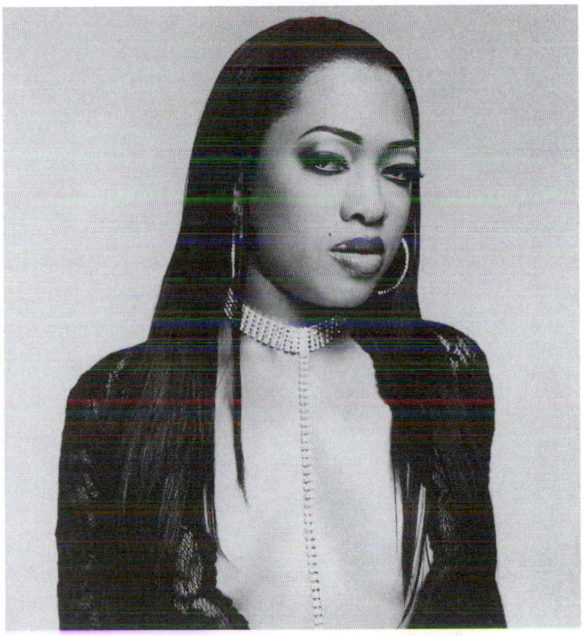

Trina. *Courtesy of Photofest.*

Trina lent her talents to the **remix** for **Missy Elliott**'s hit "One Minute Man" (Elektra Records, 2001). Trina went on to join the Jingle Baller tour with top-selling rap artists such as **Nelly** and Lil' Kim. Moreover her track from the soundtrack for the 2002 film *All About the Benjamins* helped attract more fans. Trina penned most of the lyrics on her first album, and took even more control of the creative process on her second. In 2002, Trina released her second album, *Diamond Princess* (Slip-N-Slide Records), which was created in just four months. Her sophomore set also spawned hits such as "No Panties," featuring Tweet and "B R Right" with **Ludacris**, and "Told Y'all."

In 2003, like many rap artists before her, 2003 Trina launched an apparel line, in this case called Diamond Princess Wear. Trina loves performing live, which keeps her on the road. Her charity work involves children afflicted with meningitis.

DISCOGRAPHY: *Da Baddest B***h* (Slip-N-Slide Records, 2000); *Diamond Princess* (Slip-N-Slide Records, 2002).

TRU

Master P [Percy Miller] and his younger brothers, Silkk the Shocker, and C-Murder, formed the trio Tru.

In 1993, Tru released the debut album, *Who's Da Killer*, on the independent label Me & Mine Records. The following year, they released the album, *Understanding the Criminal Mind* on No Limit Records. In 1995, Tru released the album *True,* which was released under No Limit's new pressing and distribution deal with Priority Records. The album is best known for popularizing the phrase from their track of the same name. *Tru 2 Da Game* (No Limit Records) was released in 1997 followed by *Da Crime Family* (No Limit Records) in 1999. In 2004, a reconstituted Tru released the album *The Truth* (Koch Records), which is really a No Limit Presents effort. C-Murder is currently incarcerated on murder charges. Newcomers Halleluyah and Afficial are heavily featured while Silkk and Master P's son **Lil' Romeo** make limited appearances.

DISCOGRAPHY: *Who's Da Killer* (Me & Mine Records, 1993); *Understanding the Criminal Mind* (No Limit Records, 1994); *True* (No Limit Records, 1995); *Tru 2 Da Game* (No Limit Records, 1997); *Da Crime Family* (No Limit Records, 1999); *The Truth* (Koch Records, 2004).

TUCKER, C. DOLORES

The veteran civil rights activist and head of the National Political Congress of Black Women, is best known as an outspoken critic of **gangsta rap** music, maintaining that the lyrics and imagery of hardcore rap music poison the minds of African American children. In 1994, Tucker became famous for launching an anti-rap campaign with former U.S. Secretary of Education and drug czar, William Bennett. In 1995 the duo pressured Time-Warner to dump its 50 percent share in Interscope Records, distributor of **Death Row Records**. In 1996, Tucker filed a $10-million lawsuit in federal court against the estate of **Tupac Shakur**, contending that lyrics on from the tracks "*Wonda Why They Call U Bytch*" and "*How Do U Want It,*" from Tupac's 1996 *All Eyez On Me* (Death Row Records), defamed her and negatively impacted her relationship with her husband.

TUPAC SHAKUR (aka 2Pac, aka Makaveli, aka MC New York) [Lesane Parish Crooks]

Tupac Shakur is one of the most important figures in rap music and Hip Hop history. Tupac's legacy springs from how his life reflected the contradictions and complexities of the genre and of the lives of those people who identify with it. Although Tupac is most often associated with Los Angeles, California, the rap artist was actually born in Brooklyn, New York. Tupac's embrace of thug life was emblematic of his hardcore persona; however, he also wrote poetry and as a youth acted in the theater.

Tupac Shakur had the words "thug life" tattooed across his midriff—but he defined the term as "The Hate U Give Lil' Infants F*cks Everybody." Through his parentage, Tupac directly links the Hip Hop generation with the Black Power generation. Like many of his generation, Tupac embodied a fragmented understanding of the Black Power ideology, often made cloudy in the face of contemporary financial and emotional pressures. Tupac's music catalog is thus a combination of thought-provoking and even socially aware content and vulgar, nihilistic, and banal rhymes.

Tupac Shakur had a chaotic family life and it was the pain of his own experiences that he channeled into lyrics. On April 2, 1969, Afeni Shakur (Alice Faye Williams) was arrested with twenty other New York–based Black Panthers for allegedly conspiring to kill police officers and bomb department stores, a railroad, and the Bronx Botanical Gardens. While out on bail, Afeni, became pregnant with Tupac, by one of two

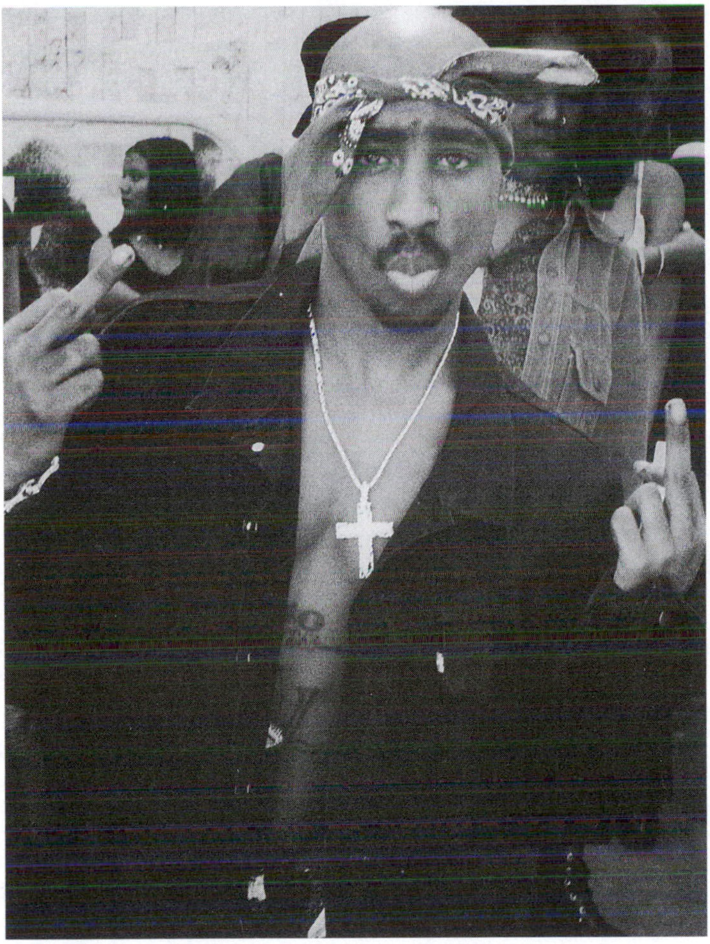

Tupac Shakur. *Courtesy of Photofest.*

men she was involved with at the time. In 1971, her bail was revoked and she was held in the Women's House of Detention in Greenwich Village, incarcerated for withholding information that could have led to the arrest of leading members of the Black Panther Party.

Afeni, a high school dropout in her early twenties who was facing life in prison demanded to act as her own attorney. After cross-examining detective Ralph White for twenty minutes, Afeni had single-handedly destroyed the prosecution's case. She was released after authorities found no evidence for her conviction. After her acquittal, Afeni worked as a paralegal and tenant organizer for over ten years at Bronx Legal Service. Afeni renamed her son *Tupac Amaru*, which is Quechua (Inca descendent) for "shining serpent," and Shakur, which is Arabic for "thankful to God."

Afeni would establish a family with Mutulu Shakur, who became Tupac's stepfather and confidante for the rest of his life. That family unit was shattered when Mutulu was accused of planning and executing the

1981 Brinks robbery, where two New York policemen and a Brinks guard were killed. Maintaining his innocence, Mutulu went underground for several years but was arrested in 1986. He was convicted and sentenced to sixty years in prison, though he continues to steadfastly deny his involvement with the holdup.

From the mid-1970s through the early 1980s, Tupac's family shuttled between Harlem and the Bronx. In 1983, a boyfriend of Afeni's introduced her to crack cocaine, after which the family eventually went on welfare, often staying in homeless shelters.

During the years in New York City, Tupac became interested in acting and writing poetry. In 1983, Afeni enrolled the 12-year-old Tupac in the 127th Street Ensemble, a Harlem theater group, where he debuted in the role of Travis in Lorraine Hansberry's play, "A Raisin the Sun." (That play would also be the vehicle for **Sean "P. Diddy" Combs**, who made his 2004 theater debut in the starring role of Walter Lee.)

In 1985 Afeni would seek greener pastures for her family in Baltimore, Maryland, where Tupac attended the Baltimore School for the Performing Arts. At the school Tupac met actress Jada Pinkett (**Will Smith**'s wife), who became a lifelong friend. As MC New York, Tupac wrote his first rhyme, about gun control, after a close friend was fatally shot. In 1988, Afeni pulled Tupac out of the Baltimore School for the Performing Arts, moving the family to Marin City, California, known as "The Jungle."

Tupac has been quoted as saying that leaving school profoundly affected him. Moreover, with his mother in the throes of drug addiction, Tupac was the man of the house and began to take on the accompanying financial responsibilities, using street figures as his role models. He moved out of the house and begin to sell drugs. During this period he dropped the name MC New York and began calling himself Tupac.

Tupac began his career performing locally in a group called "Strictly Dope," which led him to audition for Shock G, of the rap group **Digital Underground**. In 1990, Tupac was brought on as a roadie–dancer–rap artist. In 1991, Tupac made his recording debut on Digital Underground's *This Is an EP Release*, appearing on several songs: "Same Song," "DFLO Shuffle," and "Wassup Wit Tha Luv."

In November 1991, the twenty-year-old Tupac released his first solo album, *2pacalypse Now* (Interscope Records). Shortly thereafter, Tupac filed a $10 million lawsuit against the Oakland, California police for alleged brutality following an arrest for jaywalking. *2pacalypse Now* included the popular track, "Brenda's Got a Baby." Tupac is said to have written the song after reading a newspaper story about a twelve-year-old girl who became impregnated by her cousin. The young girl threw her newborn baby down an incinerator.

The *2pacalypse Now* album sold decently and brought Tupac some industry attention, but it is perhaps most notable for bringing the first of Tupac's many brushes with the law as a rap artist. In April 1992, nineteen-year-old Ronald Ray Howard shot a Texas trooper and his attorney claimed that the album *2pacalypse Now,* which was in Howard's tape deck, incited him to kill. The youth, an alleged crack dealer, was sentenced to death by lethal injection.

Then Vice President Dan Quayle targeted Tupac's music, saying that "*2pacalypse Now* has no place in our society." Tupac's music was again implicated in a murder when in 1995 two Milwaukee teens murdered a police officer and then cited the track "Souljah's Story" from *2pacalypse Now* as their inspiration.

In 1992, Tupac received rave reviews for his performance as Bishop in his film debut, *Juice.* The famous quote "I am crazy, and I don't give a f--k," was taken from this film. In August 1992, Tupac had an altercation with old acquaintances at a Marin City outdoor festival. As a result, a six-year-old bystander was fatally shot in the head. Tupac's half brother, Maurice Harding, was arrested, but then released for lack of evidence. The dead child's parents sued Tupac, who in 1996 agreed to an out-of-court settlement.

In 1993, Tupac released his second album, "Strictly 4 my NIGGAZ" which includes guest appearances by **Ice Cube**, **Ice-T**, and Digital Underground. The album eventually went platinum and included the hits "I Get Around" and "Keep Ya Head Up." The same year Tupac was sentenced for ten days in jail after threatening a local rap artist with a baseball bat during a concert. Tupac also fought with a limousine driver after the driver accused him of using drugs in the car. Tupac was arrested for that incident, but the charges later dropped.

When Tupac starred in the 1993 John Singleton movie, *Poetic Justice*, Janet Jackson demanded that Tupac take an HIV test before she consented to doing the kissing scenes with him.

Tupac was arrested again in 1993, this time for allegedly shooting two armed, off-duty police officers who were harassing an African American motorist. It was determined that the police officers had a gun that had been stolen from the evidence locker and all charges against Tupac were eventually dropped. In November 1993, a nineteen-year-old woman whom Tupac had met four days earlier at Nell's nightclub alleged that she was sodomized and sexually abused by the rap artist and three of his friends. Witnesses had stated that the accuser, Ayanna Jackson, had performed a sex act on the rap artist in the corner of the club. (See further in Bruck, Connie, "The Takedown of Tupac," *The New Yorker Magazine*, July 7, 1997.) That accusation resulted in John Singleton being forced by Columbia Pictures to drop Tupac from the cast of his upcoming movie, *Higher Learning.*

Still more legal troubles were on the way, with a fifteen-day jail term in 1994 for assault and battery in an incident involving director Allen Hughes after Hughes and his brother, Albert, had dropped Tupac from their film, *Menace II Society.* That same year Tupac gave a stellar performance as

Birdie, a troubled drug dealer, in *Above the Rim*. The film soundtrack, which sold 2 million copies, featured the song "Pour out a Little Liquor," recorded by Tupac's group Thug Life, which includes his stepbrother Mopreme.

In November 1994, while on trial for sex and weapons charges, Tupac was shot five times and robbed of $40,000 worth of jewelry in the lobby of a Times Square recording studio. Indicating concerns for his own safety, Tupac checked himself out of the hospital less than three hours after surgery. While in the hospital, Tupac met his biological father Billy Garland, whom he had thought dead. In December 1994, a bandaged and wheelchair-bound Tupac went to court and was acquitted of sodomy and weapons charges stemming from 1993 charges, but was found guilty of sexual abuse. At the sentencing in February 1995, Tupac was given a prison term of up to four and a half years in a maximum-security facility.

Two months into his prison term, Tupac released his third album, *Me Against the World* (Interscope Records). The double-platinum album debuted at number 1 on *Billboard*'s pop chart and featured the single "Dear Mama." Tupac became the first (and so far only) performer to have an album reach number 1 while in prison.

In an interview that was published in April 1995, Tupac told *Vibe* magazine journalist Kevin Powell that he had renounced the "thug life" and stated his new commitment to positivity. In that interview, Tupac also accused members of the **Bad Boy Entertainment** family (Sean "P. Diddy" Combs, **The Notorious B.I.G.**, and **Andre Harrell**) as instigators of the attack on him the previous November. To date, that case remains unsolved. In the August 1995 issue of *Vibe* magazine, the three men denied any involvement with this shooting.

While in jail, Tupac wed Keisha Morris, a woman whom he had been dating for six months. In October 1995, after serving eight months in prison, Death Row Records CEO Marion "Suge" Knight posted $1.4 million bond to release Tupac. Knight had previously pursued Tupac, but Tupac had shown no interest in leaving Interscope Records for Death Row Records. Now Tupac immediately flew to Los Angeles, signed with Death Row Records, and began recording *All Eyez on Me* (Death Row Records), which would eventually sell quintuple platinum. Moreover, shortly after his release from prison, Tupac's marriage was annulled.

Three days after he finished making *All Eyez on Me*, Tupac began work on *Makaveli: The Don Killuminati*, but he would not live to see the album's release. On November 30, 1995, exactly one year after Tupac's shooting in New York, Randy "Stretch" Walker, whom Tupac had accused as being part of the ambush, was murdered execution style in Queens.

In February 1996, *All Eyez on Me* was released; rap music's first official double CD, it reached number 1 on the charts. In the February issue of *Vibe* magazine, Tupac suggested an intimate relationship between himself and Faith Evans, the wife of his former friend and Bad Boy Entertainment star, The Notorious B.I.G. On March 29, 1996, a gun was drawn in a confrontation of Death Row Records and Bad Boy Entertainment employees after the Soul Train awards in Los Angeles. In May 1996, Tupac and fellow Death Row label mate, **Snoop Dogg** released the track "2 Of Amerikaz Most Wanted." The accompanying music video depicts caricatures of The Notorious B.I.G. and P. Diddy being punished for setting up Tupac's shooting. The next month, Tupac released the track "Hit 'Em Up" (Death Row Records, 1996), a brutal diss against East Coast artists, including The Notorious B.I.G, **Lil' Kim**, and **Mobb Deep**.

On September 4, 1996, Tupac, accompanied by security guards and his fiancée Kidada Jones (Quincy Jones's daughter) returned to New York City for the MTV Music Awards. When members of Bad Boy Entertainment and Death Row camps met, the ensuing scuffle required the New York City police department to break it up. According to reports, including those in Ronin Ro's book, *Have Gun Will Travel*, it also appears that during this period Tupac may have been reconsidering his association with Death Row Records: he left his Death Row-leased home and fired Death Row attorney David Kenner as his personal representative.

On September 7, 1996, Tupac and Suge Knight attended the Mike Tyson–Bruce Seldon fight at the MGM Grand Hotel in Las Vegas, Nevada. After leaving the hotel, Tupac and his entourage were on their way to a charity concert at Death Row Records' Club 662. Tupac was riding in the car with Knight when another car pulled up to the right of them. The men got out of the car and unloaded their guns into the car containing Tupac and Knight. Although Knight was slightly injured, Tupac sustained serious wounds. Tupac's right lung was removed in emergency surgery and after six days in a medical coma he died on September 13, 1996.

When Tupac's estate was reviewed, he had only $100,000, having signed away a fortune in an onerous contract issued by Death Row Records. News reports stated that although Tupac had sold over $60 million in records, he owed Death Row Records $4.9 million. Tupac's mother, his sole heir, waged a battle with Death Row Records to receive a fairer share of Tupac's earnings. She also founded Amaru Records and released new and previously released Tupac records.

Rumors that Tupac is still alive abound and are driven by the musical material that continues to be released years after his death. In 1999, *The Rose That Grew from Concrete* (New York: Simon and Schuster), a collection of Tupac's poems was published. Tupac was a prolific writer who loved being in the recording studio, which explains the huge backlog of songs available for periodic release. Similarly, the interest in Tupac remains fueled by the numerous documentaries and books that have been written about him.

FILMOGRAPHY: *Juice* (1992); *Poetic Justice* (1993); *Above the Rim* (1994); *Bullet* (1996); *Gang Related* (1997); *Gridlock'd* (1997).

DISCOGRAPHY: *Albums: 2Pacalypse Now* (Interscope Records, 1991); *Strictly 4 My N.I.G.G.A.Z.* (Interscope Records, 1993); *Me Against the World* (Interscope Records, 1995); *All Eyez On Me* (Death Row Records, 1996). *Posthumous Albums: Makaveli—The Don Killuminati: The 7 Day Theory* (Death Row Records, 1996); *R U Still Down?* (Amaru Records, 1997); *Greatest Hits* (Amaru/Death Row/Interscope Records, 1998); *Still I Rise* [with Outlawz] (Interscope Records, 1999); *The Lost Tapes: Circa 1989* (Lightyear Records, 2000); *The Rose That Grew From Concrete* (Interscope Records 2000); *Until the End of Time* (Amaru Records, 2001); *Better Dayz* (Interscope Records, 2002).

2 LIVE CREW

Many rap artists have courted controversy, and 2 Live Crew reside somewhere at the top of the heap, known for sexually graphic raps and for the furor that ensued over their 1989 album, *As Nasty As They Wanna Be*. It seems as if one needs a scorecard to keep track of the various 2 Live Crew members, which include Fresh Kid Ice [Chris Wong Won], Mr. Mixx [David Hobbs], Brother Marquis [Mark Ross], **Luther "Luke" Campbell**, Verb [Larry Dobson], and Amazing V.

The 2 Live Crew literally became the poster children for lewd rap lyrics in the late 1980s and early 1990s. When *As Nasty As They Wanna Be* was ruled obscene by a Florida court and effectively banned, First Amendment advocates were caught in the unenviable position of having to defend 2 Live Crew's constitutional right to release sophomoric, vulgar, and often **misogynistic** lyrical content. 2 Live Crew is also credited with popularizing booty bass music outside of Miami, Florida.

Although 2 Live Crew is associated with Miami, the group actually got their start in California. In 1984, Fresh Kid Ice, Mr. Mixx, and Amazing V, then living in California, recorded the first 2 Live Crew single, "Revelation" (Fresh Beat Records). The single sold well in California, Texas, and Florida, and the crew decided to move to Miami, Florida. The next year, the group released their second single, "What I Like" (Fresh Beat Records). By this time, the Amazing V had left and Fresh Kid Ice took over the lead rhyming duties. Once in Miami, new addition Brother Marquis led the group.

2 Live Crew hooked up with Miami entrepreneur–promoter **Luther "Luke" Campbell** (aka Luke Skyywalker), who not only offered them a record contract with his Skyywalker Records, but also acted as their manager. Luke would eventually begin to accompany the trio on stage and so became a member of the group.

In 1986, the 2 Live Crew, now including Luke, released their first album *The 2 Live Crew Is What We Are* (Skyywalker Records), which includes the raunchy tracks "We Want Some Pu**y" and "Throw the Di*k." The street buzz on the album was strong, and it eventually sold gold.

Even at this early stage, 2 Live Crew songs were already being targeted as obscene. In 1987, a Florida record store clerk was acquitted of felony charges after selling *The 2 Live Crew Is What We Are* to a fourteen-year-old girl. The incident spurred Campbell to be the first to record both "clean" (with most profanity and graphic violent or sexual references deleted) and "dirty" versions of 2 Live Crew albums, so that younger fans could buy less explicit albums. Their second album, *Move Somethin'* (Skyywalker Records), released in 1988, was the first album recorded in two versions. This second album became an even bigger hit. One reason for the success was the track "One and One," an X-rated interpretation of the Kinks' song, "All Day and All of the Night."

2 Live Crew was again the subject of an obscenity charge in 1988, when an Alabama record store was fined for selling a copy of *Move Somethin'* to an undercover cop; the conviction was later overturned on appeal.

In 1989, 2 Live Crew released their infamous third album, *As Nasty as They Wanna Be* (Skyywalker Records). With virtually no radio airplay, the album reached the Top 40 charts and sold over 2 million units, primarily on the strength of the track "Me So Horny."

By this time, 2 Live Crew had attracted the attention of an ultraconservative watchdog group, the American Family Association (AFA), who did not believe that parental advisory warning stickers were enough of a deterrent. The AFA was determined to get the album off the store shelves. AFA supporter Jack Thompson, a lawyer, convinced then-Florida governor Bob Martinez to decide whether *As Nasty as They Wanna Be* violated Florida obscenity laws. According to the state prosecutor, local rather than state action was recommended.

In early 1990, Broward County sheriff Nick Navarro obtained a copy of the album and then County Circuit Court Judge Mel Grossman ruled that there was probable cause to ascertain that the album was legally obscene. In the aftermath of the judge's decision, Navarro warned record stores around the county that *Nasty as You Wanna Be* was legally obscene and that selling it would make them subject them to prosecution. In turn, the 2 Live Crew filed a lawsuit against Navarro asserting that his actions were unconstitutional. In June, a Florida District judge ruled that *As Nasty as They Wanna Be* was legally obscene, making it against the law to sell it.

Two days after the ruling, record retailer Charles Freeman was arrested for selling the album to an undercover cop. During this period two members of the 2 Live Crew were arrested at an adult-only nightclub for a performance deemed obscene performance; the charges were later dropped. Similarly, the charges against Charles Fuller were overturned on appeal.

The travails of 2 Live Crew brought them to the attention of George Lucas, creator of *Star Wars* films, who sued Luther Campbell for copyright infringement for calling his record company Skyywalker Records. In September 1990, Campbell settled the lawsuit for a reported $300,000 and changed the record company's name to "Luke Records." Riding high on the publicity, Campbell signed a distribution deal with Atlantic Records.

In 1990, 2 Live Crew secured the rights to Bruce Springsteen's song, "Born in the U.S.A." The group, under the name Luke Featuring 2 Live Crew, released the album *Banned in the U.S.A.* (Luke Records), with a title track using the Springsteen material. The album sold briskly, and the lead single became the group's second Top 40 hit.

After this, all of the members of the 2 Live Crew begin to pursue solo careers. Luke released the album *I Got Shit on My Mind* (Luke Records, 1992) and Fresh Kid Ice released the album *The Chinaman* (Chinaman Records, 1992). Kid Fresh Ice and Mr. Mixx, calling themselves Rock on Crew, released the album *Deal With This* (Dance Factory Records, 1992), which was pre–Skyywalker Records 2 Live Crew music.

The popularity of 2 Live Crew appeared to be waning by 1991. The group released the first full-length live rap album ever, *Live in Concert* (Luke Records, 1991). The follow-up was *Sports Weekend (As Nasty as They Wanna Be Pt II)* (Luke Records, 1990) and both albums sold poorly. *Sports Weekend* would also be the group's last album together.

In 1991, MC Shy D successfully sued Luke Records for $1.6 million in royalties. In 1992, the Court of Appeals in Atlanta, Georgia overturned a Florida district court ruling that *As Nasty as They Wanna* Be was legally obscene. The Supreme Court upheld the Appeals court decision. In 1994, 2 Live Crew was again victorious as advocates for the First Amendment. The late Roy Orbison's music publisher sued 2 Live Crew alleging that their use of the song "Oh Pretty Woman" on the album *As Clean as They Wanna Be* was plagiarism and damaged the value of the original. The Supreme Court ruled that the 2 Live Crew's reinterpretation was a parody, which is a protected use under the Constitution. In 1993, Luke released his second solo album *In the Nude* (Luke Records).

In 1994, Luke Campbell and The Fresh Kid Ice partnered with rap artist Verb to form short-lived The New 2 Live Crew and released the album *Back at Your Ass for the Nine-4* (Luke Records). That same year, Luke also released his third solo album, *Freak for Life* (Luke Records, 1994).

In June 1995, Luke Campbell filed for bankruptcy and he and the remaining 2 Live Crew ended up on Lil Joe Records, a label founded by his ex-business partner, Joe Weinberger. Also in 1995, Fresh Kid Ice and Mr. Mixx released the album *The Original 2 Live Crew* on independent Blue Dolphin Entertainment. The album is essentially a re-issue of the 1992 Rock on Crew album, *Deal With This* (Dance Factory Records), with five additional songs. In 1996, Fresh Kid Ice, Brother Marquis, and

Mr. Mixx reconstituted 2 Live Crew to release the album *Shake a Lil Something* (Lil Joe Records). This the first 2 Live Crew album not released on Luke Records, and it should also be noted that Luke did not perform with the group on the album.

In 1997, Luke released his fourth solo album *Uncle Luke* (Luke Records) followed by *Changin' the Game* (Luke Records) in 1997. The next year, another incarnation of the 2 Live Crew appeared, this time Mr. Mixx and Fresh Kid Ice, two original members, released *The Real One* (Lil Joe Records), which includes a performance by **Ice-T**. In 2001, Luke released the album *Luke: Something Nasty* (Luke Records, 2001). 2 Live Crew released the albums *Private Personal Parts* (Lil Joe Records) in 2000 and *Stop Playin'* (Biggest Hits Records) in 2004.

See also: Censorship

DISCOGRAPHY: *Singles*: "Revelation" (Fresh Beat Records, 1984); "What I Like" (Fresh Beat Records, 1985); *Selected albums: The 2 Live Crew Is What We Are* (Skyywalker Records, 1986); *Move Somethin'* (Skyywalker Records, 1988); *As Nasty as They Wanna Be* (Skyywalker Records, 1989); *Luke Featuring 2 Live Crew: Banned in the U.S.A.* (Luke Records, 1990); *Live in Concert* (Luke Records, 1990); *Sports Weekend (As Nasty as They Wanna Be Pt II)* (1991); *Rock on Crew: Deal With This* (Dance Factory Records, 1992); *The New 2 Live Crew: Back At Your Ass For The Nine-4* (Luke Records, 1994); *The Original 2 Live Crew* (Blue Dolphin Entertainment, 1995); *Shake A Lil Something* (Lil Joe Records, 1996); *The Real One* (Lil Joe Records, 1998); *Private Personal Parts* (Lil Joe Records, 2000); *Stop Playin'* (Biggest Hits Records, 2004).

213

The supergroup 213 is composed of **Snoop Dogg**, Nate Dogg, and **Warren G**. In 2004, their first album was released. *The Hard Way* (TVT Records) takes a trip back a decade to revisit that G-Funk sound that was popular in the 1990s. *The Hard Way* is a familiar ode to the wine, women, and weed. The album includes a remake of Rick James's classic single "Mary Jane;" James died shortly before the album's release. Some fans were disappointed because the album did not include the song "Dollar Bill," which was originally heard on **mixtapes**.

U

ULTRAMAGNETIC MCs

Kool Keith [Keith Thornton], TR Love [Trevor Randolph], DJ Moe Love, and Ced Gee [Cedric Miller] are the Ultramagnetic MCs (UMC), best remembered for their classic 1988 album, *Critical Beatdown* (Next Plateau Records). This legendary rap group's claim to fame rests on their creation of futuristic rhyme style.

Three years before their debut album, UMCs released their first single, "I'm Gonna Give You Love" (Sutra/DNA, 1985), under the name "Bronx Vice," with **Kool DJ Red Alert**. This rare record, filled with its strange sexual tone, is a prelude to what front man Kool Keith would lay down in subsequent offerings. In 1986, the UMCs would release "Ego Trippin'," their first commercially released twelve-inch single, on Next Plateau Records. The single is important, because it is the first to highlight the group's complex and otherworldly approach to rap music. The twelve-inch also featured Ced Gee's then-innovative production work. Ced Gee, one of rap music's most underrated producers, not only helped to create a good deal of UMCs best material, he also was integral to the production of **Boogie Down Productions'** album *Criminal Minded* (B-Boy Records, 1987).

The UMCs would release three additional twelve-inch records, "Mentally Mad" (Next Plateau, 1987), "Watch Me Now" (Next Plateau, 1988), and "Ease Back" (Next Plateau, 1988). In 1988, after releasing five twelve-inch recordings, the UMCs released their groundbreaking debut album, *Critical Beatdown* (Next Plateau Records).

The UMCs moved to the larger Mercury records, to be positioned to take fuller advantage of the growing rap music market. Their first Mercury release was the 1991 twelve-inch "Make it Happen". Four years after the release of their 1988 debut album, the UMCs released their second album, *Funk Your Head Up* (Mercury Records, 1992). The follow-up album received a lukewarm response, in part because the rap music landscape had changed significantly since 1988; fan tastes had changed and they had moved on to other artists. *Funk Your Head Up* failed to sell also because, musically, it was simply not as strong of an album as *Critical Beatdown*. After the release of *Funk Your Head Up*, the UMCs would release the twelve-inch "Poppa Large" (Mercury Records, 1992) before severing ties to Mercury Records.

In 1993, they released their third album, *The Four Horsemen,* on Wild Pitch Records. *The Four Horsemen* helped the UMCs regain their reputation for being cutting edge and in the process it gave listeners information about the long-forgotten Negro Baseball League, something other rap artists were not discussing at all. After the album release, the UMCs released two twelve-inch records, "Two Brothers With Checks (San Francisco, Harvey)" (Wild Pitch 1993) and "Raise It Up" (Wild Pitch, 1993). Despite its critical appeal, *The Four Horsemen* sold poorly and the UMCs faded into obscurity.

Kool Keith was the only member to establish a successful solo career, using the aliases Dr. Octogon, Big Willie Smith, Sinister6000, Mr. Gerbik, Mr. Clean, 'Ultra' (with Tim Dog), and Reverend Tom. Ced Gee divided the group over his decision to sell unreleased UMCs material to Tuff City Records, without other members' permission. Because copyright laws prevented Tuff City from using the UMCs name, the three albums and two twelve-inch recordings were released under the group name Ultra.

DISCOGRAPHY: *Singles*: "I'm Gonna Give You Love" [as Bronx Vice] (Sutra Records/DNA, 1985); "Ego Trippin'" (Next Plateau Records, 1986); "Mentally Mad" (Next Plateau Records, 1987); "Watch Me Now" (Next Plateau Records, 1988); "Ease Back" (Next Plateau Records, 1988); "Make It Happen" (Mercury Records, 1991); "Poppa Large" (Mercury Records, 1992); "Two Brothers With Checks (San Francisco, Harvey)" (Wild Pitch Records, 1993); "Raise It Up" (Wild Pitch Records, 1993). *Albums*: *Critical Beatdown* (Next Plateau Records, 1988); *Funk Your Head Up* (Mercury Records, 1992); *The Four Horsemen* (Wild Pitch Records, 1993).

UNCLE JAMM'S ARMY

Uncle Jamm's Army was a collective of DJs in the 1980s who played an important role in pioneering Los Angeles, California's independent rap scene. The DJ collective was started by former dancer, Robert Clayton, who appropriated the name "Uncle Jamm's Army" from the George Clinton fan club. The DJs associated with Uncle Jamm's army often wore army fatigues and created identifiable characters, essentially roles that they played onstage at performances.

Uncle Jamm's Army, which played Culver City going east to Pomona, often produced events large enough to be accommodated in Los Angeles's 16,000-seat sports arena. The DJ collective was instrumental in promoting electro, which was the first step in the development of West Coast Hip Hop. The extended crew of producers, DJs, and vocalists included **Ice-T**, **Egyptian Lover**, the **Unknown DJ**, and Chris "The Glove" Taylor.

On the Freak Beat label, Uncle Jamm's Army released a string of popular and influential electro cuts during 1984–1986, including "What's

Your Sign," "Dial-a-Freak," and "Yes, Yes, Yes." Other influential West Coast groups during this period include: **Disco Daddy and Captain Rap**, **World Class Wreckin' Cru**, and L.A. Dream Team.

UNDERGROUND

Underground is a term to describe rap music that is not associated with a major record company, or that reflects the more diverse and often socially aware rap music and Hip Hop culture developing around the United States but not usually promoted by commercial entertainment outlets, including radio and music video programs.

"UNITY PART I (THE THIRD COMING)." *See* Afrika Bambaataa; Brown, James

UNITY SUMMIT

The first Hip Hop Summit was convened as the **Unity Summit** by **KRS-ONE** and **Afrika Bambaataa** and was held at the Latin Quarters nightclub in Manhattan in 1987. Other major Hip Hop summits to follow include the National African America Leadership (Philadelphia, Pennsylvania, 1997) in a response to the **East Coast–West Coast** conflict, the National Action Network (New York City, 2000), and Russell Simmons's Hip Hop Summit Action Network (New York City, 2002).

UNKNOWN DJ, THE [Andre Manuel]

In the 1980s, The Unknown DJ pioneered the electro music popularized by West Coast artists such as **Egyptian Lover** and the **World Class Wreckin' Cru**, which would serve as the foundation for the development of Hip Hop in that region of the country.

The Unknown DJ, a member of the **Uncle Jamm's Army**, recorded only a few twelve-inch singles: primarily for the independent, West Coast labels Techno Hop and Techno Kut. Although the records were not commercially successful, they nonetheless influenced the techno bass music that emerged in the 1990s. He would move from electro music and produce **Ice-T**'s hardcore rap single, "Six 'N the Mornin'," from the *Rhyme Pays* album (Sire Records). Several years later The Unknown DJ experienced success as the producer for the group Compton's Most Wanted, led by **MC Eiht**.

DISCOGRAPHY: "Rhythm Rock Rap" (Saturn, 1984); "Beatronic" (1984); "808 Beats" (Techno Hop, 1984); "Let's Jam" (Techno Hop, 1985); "Basstronic" (Techno Kut, 1988); "Breakdown" (Techno Kut, 1988); "X-Men" (Techno Kut, 1988); "Revenge of the X-Men" (Techno Kut, 1988).

US GIRLS

US Girls **Sha Rock**, Lisa Lee, and Debbie Dee became first female rap artists to appear in a major motion picture when they performed in the film *Beat Street* (1984).

U.T.F.O.

U.T.F.O., comprised of Doctor Ice, the Kangol Kid, the Educated Rapper, and Mix-Master Ice, are best remembered for their 1985 single, "Roxanne, Roxanne" (Select Records), a witty song about an attractive young woman who rebuffs the men's advances.

Formed in 1983, U.T.F.O. stands for UnTouchable Force Organization. Initially dancers, they began their careers on tour with **Whodini**. The group signed with Select Records in 1984, and that year released their debut twelve-inch single, "Beats and Rhymes." The group at first referred to themselves as "the Village People of Rap," because each member adopted a specific image: Doctor Ice was the "Hip-Hop Physician"; The Educated Rapper was a college student in a suit and tie; Mix Master Ice was a ninja, because he would "cut things up" on the turntables; and Kangol Kid got his name because of his ever-present **Kangol** hat.

The group's 1985 follow-up single, "Roxanne, Roxanne," would be a huge hit for the group. Moreover, "Roxanne, Roxanne" sparked hundreds of response songs, including the most infamous dialogue between fourteen-year-old **Roxanne Shante** (produced by **Marley Marl**) and Latina siren, **The Real Roxanne** (a U.T.F.O. creation produced by Hitman Howie T and **Jam Master Jay**).

In 1985, U.T.F.O. released their self-titled debut album. The album U.T.F.O. included their own "Roxanne, Roxanne" and its sequel, "Calling Her a Crab (Roxanne Part 2)," which failed to match the original's success. Subsequently the group went on the thirty-city New York **Fresh Fest** tour with the likes of rap artists such as **Run DMC**, **Kurtis Blow**, the **Fat Boys**, and **Newcleus**. The group would continue to release albums almost annually, although they never recaptured the success of "Roxanne, Roxanne."

DISCOGRAPHY: *Singles*: "Beats and Rhymes" (Select Records, 1984); "Roxanne, Roxanne" (Select Records, 1984). *Albums*: *U.T.F.O.* (Select Records, 1985); *Skeezer Pleezer* (Select Records, 1986); *Lethal* (Select Records, 1987); *Doin' It!* (Select Records, 1989); *Bag It & Bone It* (Jive Records, 1990).

V

VANILLA ICE [Robert Van Winkle]

The White rap artist Vanilla Ice rose to international attention with the single "Ice Ice Baby." Prior to that, the **Beastie Boys** had been the only commercially successful White rap artists.

Vanilla's Ice's star rapidly fell when his tough, street background was exposed as a lie. With his **high top fade** and Hammer-esque dance steps, many music critics who reviewed his debut album, *To the Extreme* (Capitol Records, 1990), thought that Vanilla Ice had no future in rap music. To gain street credibility, the Miami, Florida native publicly announced that he had been a gang member who had been stabbed five times in street brawls. While debates about Vanilla Ice's authenticity were being argued within the music industry and among rap music fans, the crossover appeal of "Ice, Ice Baby," helped the album go quadruple-platinum in just one month.

Trying to exploit a waning popularity, Vanilla Ice starred in the film, *Cool as Ice.* Unfortunately, by the time it was released in the fall of 1990, his popularity had dramatically fallen off and the movie bombed, as did the soundtrack, *Cool As Ice O.S.T.* (Capitol Records, 1991). The same year, Vanilla Ice's live album, *Extremely Live* was also released (Capitol Records, 1991). After lying low for several years, Vanilla Ice returned in 1994 and released the album *Mind Blowin'* (Ultrax Records), which had a harder sound, reminiscent of **Cypress Hill**; even so, the album was considered a commercial and critical failure.

Vanilla Ice. *Courtesy of Photofest.*

Four years later, Vanilla Ice abandoned rap for metal rock on the album *Hard To Swallow* (Universal Records, 1998). Using the name V-Ice, he continued down the rock path again in 2001 with the album, *Bi-Polar* (Liquid 8 Records). In 2003, coming full circle, he came back to rap, releasing the album, *Hot Sex* (Liquid 8 Records), which appears to be Vanilla Ice's take on the Dirty South.

DISCOGRAPHY: *To the Extreme* (Capitol Records, 1990) *Cool As Ice O.S.T.* (Capitol Records, 1991); *Extremely Live* (Capitol Records, 1991); *Mind Blowin'* (Ultrax Records, 1994); *Hard To Swallow* (Universal, 1998); *Bi-Polar* (Liquid 8, 2001); *Hot Sex* (Liquid 8, 2003).

VAN SILK [Ralph Blandshaw]

Van Silk is recognized as one of Hip Hop' earliest promoters. The South Bronx native credits Kool DJ AJ for teaching him about the business of music promotion. Aside from promoting, Van Silk's long career in Hip Hop led him to work alongside many of the leading figures on both coasts. He is also recognized for discovering Full Force and **Doug E. Fresh**.

In 1988, Van Silk provided narrations between tracks for the compilation album, *Posse All Star Classic* (Posse Records, 1988), which includes appearances by **DJ Hollywood**, radio DJ **Mr. Magic**, and Jimmy Spicer. In 1991, he joined Grandmaster **Melle Mel** on the twelve-inch single, "What's the Matter With Your World" (Rickster, Penthouse4, 1989). He was integrally involved in the production of the compilation album *Raiders of the Lost Art* (Scotti Bros., 1994), which includes **Afrika Bambaataa**, **Busy Bee**, **Kurtis Blow**, **Whodini**, **Grandmaster Flash and the Furious Five**, and **Kool Moe Dee**.

In 1991, he created the pay-per-view program ***Rapmania***, which celebrated fifteen years of Hip Hop. He would also use the same format for the "*Sisters in the Name of Rap"* in 1992. (Both are available as video releases.)

VIDEO GAMES AND HIP HOP

Video games have become an important marketing tool for both new and established artist of all musical genres. As with film scores, video game soundtracks complement the visual content and thus enhance the gaming experience. Overall, music in video game soundtracks allows its players to hear familiar classics, discover new artists, or see established artists stretching their creativity.

Perhaps one of the earliest instances of rap artists being involved with video games is "**Kris Kross**: Make My Video" (Digital Pictures, Sega CD, 1992). Other collaborations followed, such as "RapJam Vol. 1" (Motown Games, Super Nintendo, 1995) and "**Wu-Tang Clan** Shaolin Style" (Activison PSOne, 1999). In 2002, **Mr. Magic** supervised the soundtrack for "Grand Theft Auto: Vice City, Vol. 5: Wildstyle, and Old School Compilation." In 2003, **Def Jam Recordings** entered into an agreement with Electronic Arts that led to the video games "Def Jam Vendetta" (2003) and "Def Jam: Fight For New York" (2004). These video games not only feature the music of rap artists, but also their likenesses. **Snoop Dogg** covers The Doors song "Riders of the Storm" for the video game soundtrack "Need for Speed Underground 2" from Electronic Arts. **Ice-T** has also agreed to provide the voice of the main character for Fox Interactive's forthcoming science-fiction adventure game, "Sanity: Aiken's Artifact."

According to Nielsen Interactive Entertainment, the number of men aged eighteen to thirty-four who play video games increased 26 percent per year over the past five years.

VIDEO MUSIC BOX

Recognized as the first rap music video show, the *Video Music Box* program was founded by Ralph McDaniels and Lionel "Kid Vid" Martin in April 1984 on WNYC-TV, Channel 31, in New York City. The program aired daily from 3:30 to 4:30 p.m. The popularity of the show waned with the creation of ***Yo! MTV Raps***, but it remained a staple for New York teenagers without cable access. WNYC-TV was sold in 1996.

W

WARREN G [Warren Griffin III]

Warren G is best known for his 1994 single "Regulate." The album *Regulate ... G Funk Era* (Def Jam Recordings) followed thereafter.

Warren G grew up in Long Beach, California, listening to his parents' extensive collection of jazz, soul, and funk records. He was also frequented the local V.I.P. record store. As a teenager, he and his friends Nate Dogg and **Snoop Dogg** formed a rap group called **213**, after their area code. After each member spent time in jail, however, they were inclined to get jobs and to do music only in their spare time.

When Snoop recorded his demo "Super Duper Snooper," at the V.I.P. record store, Warren G played the demo for his half brother, **Dr. Dre**, at a party. Dre invited all three to his recording studio and wound up collaborating with Snoop.

Warren decided to develop his talents away from the spotlight of Dr. Dre, honing his musical skills while producing such artists as **MC Breed** and **Tupac Shakur**. Warren got a career break when he collaborated with Mista Grimm on "Indo Smoke," from the *Poetic Justice* film soundtrack (Sony Records, 1993). Warren signed to **Def Jam Recordings**, and released his debut album *Regulate ... G Funk Era* (1994). The lead single "Regulate," featuring Nate Dogg, appeared on the *Above the Rim* film soundtrack

Warren G. *Courtesy of Photofest.*

(Death Row Records, 1994). The *Regulate ... G Funk Era* album eventually went triple platinum.

After a three-year hiatus, Warren G released his second album, *Take A Look Over Your Shoulder* (Def Jam Recordings), which received mixed reviews and lackluster sales. In 1999, Warren G released his third album, *I Want It All* (Restless Records), and in 2001 his fourth album, *Return of the Regulator* (Universal Records).

DISCOGRAPHY: *Regulate ... G Funk Era* (Def Jam Recordings, 1994); *Take A Look Over Your Shoulder* (Def Jam Recordings, 1997); *I Want It All* (Restless Records, 1999); *Return of the Regulator* (Universal Records, 2001).

WATTS PROPHETS

The Watts Prophets, comprised of Father Amde Hamilton, Otis O'Solomon, and Richard Anthony Dedeaux, are best known as The West Coast counterparts to East Coast artists **The Last Poets** and Gil Scot-Heron. The group performed spoken word over percussion rhythms and improvisational jazz, credited as a forerunner of rap music. The Watts Prophets formed out of the Watts Writers Workshop, a cultural laboratory for Black ideology developed in the aftermath of the 1965 Watts riots. Rap artists such as **Digable Planets**, **Coolio**, and **Ice Cube** have sampled the Watts Prophets.

The group's professional career began when they entered the Inner City Culture Talent Show and won second place. The group then embarked on a sixteen-week engagement at the legendary Maverick's Flat, where people such as Richard Pryor, Earth Wind & Fire, and George Clinton performed. In the 1970s, they recorded two legendary albums: *Black Voices: On The Streets of Watts* (1969) and *Rappin' Black In A White World* (1973). The group was branded as militants for songs such as "There's a Difference Between a Black Man and a Nigger" and "I'll Stop Calling You Nigger When You Start Acting Like a Black Man," songs that even put off some African Americans.

They made a guest appearance on Quincy Jones's *Mellow Madness* (A&M, 1975) and Stevie Wonder's *Songs In The Key of Life* (Motown Records, 1976). Despite their word-of-mouth acclaim, The Watts Prophets still remained much less well known than The Last Poets. In 1997, Full Frequency/PGD released the album *When The 90's Came*, a compilation of poems that The Watts Prophets had written in the 1960s and some more recent raps, laid over dance and jazz rhythms. **DJ Quik** and US3 lent production help to the album, which puts the fight for civil rights in a historical context.

DISCOGRAPHY: *Black Voices: On The Streets of Watts* (1969; re-issued by Full Frequency/Pgd in 1997); *Rappin' Black In A White World* (1973; re-issued by Full Frequency/Pgd in 1997); *When The 90's Came* (Frequency/Pgd, 1997).

WEST, CORNEL

A renowned academic, lecturer, activist, and public intellectual, Cornel West released a CD, *The Journey, Sketches of My People* (Artemis Records), in 2001. The ten-track concept album contains spoken work over Hip Hop, jazz, and R & B rhythms. West's monologues range from heroes of the Civil Rights Movement to 1970s soul.

Sketches is the debut project of 4 Black Men Who Mean Business, a production team and independent label that West put together with his older brother Clifton, songwriter and producer Mike Daily, and Derrick "D.O.A." Allen. West was quoted in an Africana.com article as stating that his motivation for recording the CD "was really to try and communicate more directly, especially with the younger generation, to ensure that the struggle for freedom remains alive in them."

West released his second double CD, *Street Knowledge*, in 2004. At the time of *Sketches* release, West held a position as the Alphonse Fletcher, Jr., Professor at Harvard University, teaching philosophy of religion and Afro-American Studies. He left Harvard in 2002 after the university's president, Lawrence H. Summers, questioned West's most recent scholarship, as well his political activism and the wisdom of releasing a rap music CD. West is now teaching at Princeton University as the Class of 1943 University Professor of Religion. (He had earlier taught at Princeton from 1988 to 1994, directing the Program in African American Studies.)
DISCOGRAPHY: *"The Journey, Sketches of My People"* (Artemis Records, 2001); *Street Knowledge* (Roc Diamond Records, 2004).

WEST, KANYE OMARI

Kanye West was the first secular rap artist to be nominated for gospel's prestigious Stellar Award. The producer-turned-artist opened a long simmering debate as to whether a rap artist can rap about the profane on one song and the sacred on another. (Themes of religion and spirituality are in fact often tackled by mainstream rap artists, from **Run DMC** to **Tupac Shakur** to **Nas**.)

In 2004, the Stellar Award committee nominated Kanye West's debut album, *College Dropout* (Roc-A-Fella Records, 2004), for best rap/Hip Hop album. The single "Jesus Walks" has become popular in nightclubs and on the music charts. The single also has three versions of a music video, which aired on MTV and Black Entertainment Television's (B.E.T.) rap and gospel programs. The openly religious track "2 Words" features the Boys Choir of Harlem. After nearly 100 letters and e-mails to the Stellar Committee, and threats of a boycott of the awards ceremony, West's nomination was rescinded and 4,000 new ballots omitting Kanye West's name were sent to voting members.

In the same year, Kanye West, who has produced songs for such rap music heavyweights as **Jay-Z**, **Ludacris**, and **Talib Kweli** reaped a larger

prize by winning ten Grammy nominations, as an artist for his debut *College Dropout* and as a producer and songwriter for the R & B album, *The Diary of Alicia Keys* (J Records, 2004). Kanye West's nominations include Album of the Year. Only Michael Jackson (1983) and Kenneth "Babyface" Edmonds (1996), who each received twelve Grammy nominations, have surpassed Kanye West's ten nominations. *College Dropout* garnered the Grammy nominations because it is an album that mixes humor, superior beats, social commentary, and spirituality with stand out tracks that include "Through the Wire" and "All Falls Down." Like Hip Hop, the album is contradictory, complex, and explosive.
DISCOGRAPHY: *College Dropout* (Roc-A-Fella Records, 2004).

WESTSIDE CONNECTION

The rap music trio Westside Connection is comprised of **Ice Cube**, **Mack 10**, and WC (WC & The Madd Circle).

In 1995, the group members joined forces on Mack 10's eponymous debut album on the single "Westside Slaughterhouse" (Priority Records). The following year, the trio released their first album, *Westside Connection* (Priority Records), which was successful on the strength of the East Coast–diss track, "Bow Down." In 2003, seven years after the first album, the trio followed up with the album *Terrorist Threats* (Priority Records). They used basically the same style and vibe as with the first album, but the formula did not prove to be a winner the second time around.
DISCOGRAPHY: *Westside Connection* (Priority Records, 1996); *Terrorist Threats* (Priority Records, 2003).

WHATZ BEEF: A HIP HOP DOCUMENTARY ON BEEFS IN 2002.

See Films

WHBI-FM

WHBI-FM (later WNWK), a radio station located in Newark, New Jersey, served the New York metropolitan area and was home to several rap programs, including ***Mr. Magic's Rap Attack***, *World's Famous Supreme Team*, *Sweet G*, the ***Awesome Two***, and **Afrika Islam**'s *Zulu Beats*.

WHODINI

The group Whodini, comprised of Jalil Hutchins and John "Ecstasy" Fletcher, (and DJ Drew "Grandmaster Dee" Carter, added in 1986), are best known for the singles "Friends," "Freaks Come Out At Night," and "One Love." They were also the first rap artists to have a promotional video, and the first to perform with their own dancers. Whodini was

Whodini. *Courtesy of Photofest.*

also among the first rap groups to incorporate R & B singing into their rhymes.

Formed in 1982, the Brooklyn, New York–based rap group released their debut single, "Magic's Wand," a tribute to the pioneering Hip Hop DJ **Mr. Magic**, who gave them a start. The song was also the first rap single on the Jive Records label. Jive was a subsidiary of the UK-based company, Zomba Publishing. UK keyboardist Thomas Dolby, best known for "She Blinded Me With Science," received production credit for the single. "Magic's Wand" was also the first single in Hip Hop history to have an accompanying music video.

The group would follow up with the singles "Rap Machine" (Jive Records) and "The Haunted House Of Rock" (Jive Records) in 1983, and that year they would also release their self-titled album, which included already released singles as well as new material.

Whodini gained national fame for their 1984 hit, the twelve-inch single "Friends," with the B-side "Five Minutes Of Funk." Also in 1984, they released their sophomore album, *Escape* (Jive Records), which included the old tracks "Friends" and "Five Minutes of Funk," as well as new hit singles "Freaks Come Out At Night" and "Big Mouth." Grandmaster Dee made his first appearance on this album, before formally joining the group.

Whodini was widely renowned for their innovative stage performances, where they originated the concept of back-up dancers for rap artists. With dancers Doctor Ice and Kangol Kid, who would gain their own fame with the rap group **U.T.F.O.**, Whodini went on world tours in 1983 and 1984. In 1985, they would be part of the second leg of the Swatch Watch–sponsored New York City **Fresh Fest** tour, which also included **Run DMC**, **Kurtis Blow**, the **Fat Boys**, and **Newcleus**.

In 1986, the Whodini officially added DJ Grandmaster Dee, known for being able to scratch records with nearly every part of his body. In the autumn of 1986, they released "Growing Up," an anti-drug video financed by the New York State Division Of Substance Abuse. Whodini released the album *Back In Black* (Jive Records) in 1986, followed by *Open Sesame* (Jive Records) in 1987.

The group toured again in 1987, with **LL Cool J**, but their music career was sidelined, not only by marriage and children, but also management and record label problems. The trio regrouped and in 1991 released the album *Bag-A-Trix* on MCA Records. Unfortunately, the record company and Whodini did not click and *Bag-A-Trix* was not commercially successful. In 1993, Whodini again came together, for Terminator X's compilation album *The Godfathers Of Threatt*, which included **DJ Kool Herc** and **Cold Crush Brothers**. In 1996, five years after their last album, Whodini (now on **Jermaine Dupri**'s label, So So Def) returned with their sixth album, apted titled *Six*. The album spawned the modest hit, "Keep Running Back to You."

DISCOGRAPHY: *Whodini* (Jive Records, 1983); *Escape* (Jive Records, 1984); *Back In Black* (Jive Records, 1986); *Open Sesame* (Jive Records, 1987); *Bag-A-Trix* (MCA Records, 1991); *Six* (Columbia Records, 1996).

WILD STYLE. *See* Films; Graffiti

WILLIAMS, HAROLD "HYPE"

The music video director Hype Williams changed the aesthetic of rap music videos, largely by moving away from (inexpensive) gritty street backdrops and creating extravagant, highly stylized productions that celebrated living large. The video music director has worked with every major rap artist in the business.

Hype Williams, born in Hollis, Queens, New York, aspired to be an artist. Influenced by the works of Jean-Michel Basquiat and Keith Haring, Williams took to creating **graffiti** art in the streets of New York City. "Hype" was Williams's tag. In the late 1980s Williams studied film at Adelphi University on Long Island. Williams got his first job at Classic Concept Production, a pioneering rap music video company run by Ralph McDaniels and Lionel C. Martin (who created the television music video program ***Video Music Box***), reportedly sweeping the floor on music video sets.

In 1993, he established, his own production company, Big Dog Films, and the following year he made his first major video for **Wu-Tang Clan**'s single "Can It All Be So Simple" (Loud Records). Once the video aired, Williams was deluged with offers and he took on as many projects as possible, throughout the rest of the decade.

In 1998, Williams made his big screen directorial debut with the film *Belly*, which starred rap artists **DMX**, **Nas**, and **Method Man**. Williams also began directing commercials for major brands, such as **FUBU**, The Gap, and Nike.

WILLIAMS, PHARRELL. *See* The Neptunes

WORD UP! MAGAZINE

As a Black music fan magazine, *Word Up!* preceded rap music publications such as ***The Source***, *Vibe*, *XXL*, *Blaze*, and *Rappages*. Since the early 1980s, the New Jersey–based publication has covered rap and R & B music. *Word Up!* magazine routinely includes artist posters, interviews, special celebrity tributes, and entertainment news. The magazine is immortalized in **The Notorious B.I.G.**'s 1994 track "Juicy," in the line, "It was all a dream; I used to read *Word Up!* magazine. . . ."

"Word Up" is a 1980s slang phrase that can (loosely put) convey or confirm—or question—the truth or validity of a statement: "Word Up!" or just "Word."

WORLD CLASS WRECKIN' CRU

Made up of Lonzo [Alonzo Williams], **Dr. Dre** [Andre Young], Cli-N-Tel [Marquette Hawkins], DJ Yella [Antoine Carraby], Shakespeare [Barry Severe], Mona Lisa Young, Michel'le [Michelle Toussaint], and Arabian Prince [Mik Lezan], the West Coast electro-rap group known as World Class Wreckin' Cru launched the careers of future **N.W.A.** members Dr. Dre and DJ Yella.

The focal point for the creation of the World Class Wreckin' Cru was the Eve After Dark nightclub. The group had existed for several years as mobile DJs until 1983 when club owner Alonzo Williams decided to transition to recorded music. Around 1984 Dr. Dre joined the World Class Wrecking Cru.

In 1984, the group released its debut single, "Surgery," on Williams's Kru-Cut record label, followed by the single "Juice." Both singles were popular on the West Coast. In 1985, the group released their first album, World Class (Kru-Cut), and released their second in 1986, *Rapped in Romance* (Epic Records).

In 1987, **Ice Cube** is credited as a co-writer on tracks of twelve-inch single "House Calls," with B-side "Cabbage Patch" (Macola Records Co.). Just before the group broke up in 1988 over financial disputes, they scored a national hit with the slow jam "Turn Off The Lights," featuring Michel'le (Kru-Cut Records). Michel'le went on to marry Dr. Dre and released one album on Ruthless Records.

To capitalize on their new-found success, Lonzo formed a new World Class Wreckin' Cru for the 1988 album *The Lights Are Off In The Fast Lane* (Techno Cut Records).

DISCOGRAPHY: *Singles*: "Surgery" (Kru-Cut Records, 1984); "Juice" (Kru-Cut Records, 1984) "House Calls" with B-side "Cabbage Patch" (Macola Records Co., 1987); "Turn Off The Lights" [featuring Michel'le] (Kru-Cut Records, 1987). *Albums*: *World Class* (Kru-Cut, 1985); *Rapped in Romance* (Epic Records, 1986); *The Lights Are Off In The Fast Lane* (Techno Cut Records, 1988).

WORLD'S FAMOUS SUPREME TEAM

Malcolm McLaren (on vocals), Justice, and Divine (rap vocals) make up a group whose full name of the group is Malcolm McLaren & The World's Famous Supreme Team (TWSFT).

Old School–heads automatically associate the words "we're on a world tour" with the TWSFT single, "World Famous" (Island Records, 1983). United Kingdom performance artist Malcolm McLaren, best known for his management of the punk rock group the Sex Pistols, is credited with bringing this rap collective to the attention of U.S. audiences. The core Hip Hop element of TWFST had already gained fame in the 1980s for their own nightly show on New Jersey–based radio station **WHBI-FM**, which aired in the New York metropolitan area. WHBI-FM was also home to pioneering radio shows such as **Afrika Islam**'s *Zulu Beats*, ***Mr. Magic's Rap Attack***, and ***Awesome Two***.

On the McLaren-produced single, "Buffalo Gals" (Charisma, 1983), TWFST rapped over T-Ski Valley's "Catch The Beat" (Groove Records, 1982), and the song became a Top Ten hit in the United Kingdom. The "Buffalo Gals" would become popular not only in dance clubs in the United States, but also among Hip Hop audiences. On the B-side of the twelve-inch "Double Dutch" (Charisma, 1982), TWFST performs on the tracks "She's Looking Like a Hobo" and "D'ya Like Scratchin."

Duck Rock (Charisma, 1983), a mélange of African, Caribbean, and American folk music, contains the singles "Buffalo Gals" and "World Famous." It is notable that Malcolm McLaren is listed as the artist, although he does not contribute any vocals or production. In 1984, TWFST released the twelve-inch single, "Hey DJ" (Charisma). In February 1984, the cassette maxi-single *D'Ya Like Scratchin'* (Island Records, 1983), which contained TWFST hits, "She's Looking Like A Hobo," "Buffalo Gals," and "World Famous" became McLaren's first American album chart entry. In 1986, TWFST released their first official album,

Rappin (Charisma). In 1990, Atlantic Records released the album *World's Famous Supreme Team Show,* a McLaren creation that mixes rap with classical references to Shakespeare and opera and which featured Mona Lisa Young, formerly of the **World Class Wreckin' Cru**. In 1992, under the name McLaren Presenting the World Supreme Team Show they would follow up with *Round The Outside! Round The Outside!* (Virgin, 1992), Once again, McLaren has fun recycling bits of pop culture, Hip Hop, opera, and literature.

In 1998, as part of its United Hip-Hop Nation Series, Priority Records released the album *Buffalo Gals Back to the Old Skool,* which has artists such as **De La Soul**, **KRS-ONE**, and **Rakim** paying tribute to a true New York phenomenon, the World's Famous Supreme Team.

DISCOGRAPHY: *Singles*: "Double Dutch" (Charisma, 1982), b/w "She's Looking Like a Hobo" and "D'ya Like Scratchin"; Buffalo Gals" (Charisma, 1983); "Hey DJ" (Charisma, 1984); Maxi-single "D'Ya Like Scratchin'" (Island, 1983). *Albums*: *Duck Rock* (Charisma, 1983), listed under Malcolm McLaren; *Rappin* (Charisma, 1986); *World's Famous Supreme Team Show* (Atlantic Records, 1990); *Round The Outside! Round The Outside!* (Virgin Records, 1992).

WRITER'S BENCH

The last active writer's bench was located at 149th and Grand Concourse in the Bronx, New York. In the history of aerosol art (**graffiti** art), meeting places for writers were known as *writer's corners* or *writer's benches*, with the majority of them located in the subway system.

The writer's bench at the subway station at 149th Street Grand Concourse, where the number 2 and number 5 IRT trains converge, was active from the 1970s until the decline of subway aerosol art in the late 1980s. At the bench located at the back of the "Uptown" platform, writers from all over the city congregated, watched trains, inspected the artwork, made plans, settled arguments, and signed black books. Because these lines traveled between Brooklyn and the Bronx, through Manhattan, artists were competitive in seeing that their work got on the trains on these highly visible lines, and as a result the number 2 and number 5 train lines featured some of the most artistic works in the city.

WU-TANG CLAN

The Wu-Tang Clan is comprised of **RZA** [Robert Diggs], **GZA** (Genius/GZA) [Gary Grice], **Ol' Dirty Bastard** [Russell Jones], **Method Man** [Clifford Smith], **Raekwon** the Chef [Corey Woods], **Ghostface Killah** [Dennis Coles], U-God [Lamont Hawkins], Inspectah Deck [Jason Hunter], and Masta Killa [Elgin Turner]. The groundbreaking rap group from

Wu-Tang Clan. *Courtesy of Photofest.*

Staten Island, New York, revolutionized the rap music industry on three fronts: musically, their hardcore style helped to revitalize East Coast Hip Hop in the early 1990s; culturally, they created a group mythology based on **martial arts** principles and ideology peppered with tenets of the **Nation of Islam**, which is articulated by their language Wu-speak; and, as businessmen, rather than stepping into the music industry as one entity, they had the innovative idea of signing one contract as a group but with other members signing separate contracts as individual artists and releasing spin-off projects.

The origins of the Wu-Tang Clan are based in the earlier rap group All In Together Now, formed by RZA, the Genius/GZA, and Ol' Dirty Bastard. When the group fizzled, RZA and GZA embarked on solo careers, without much success. RZA, then known as Prince Rakeem, signed to Tommy Boy Records and released the embarrassing single "Ooh, We Love You Rakeem" in 1991 and the equally poor follow-up single, "My Deadly Venom." GZA released the single "Come Do Me" (Cold Chillin' Records) and the full-length album *Words From the Genius* (Cold Chillin' Records).

RZA's experiences with the music industry caused him to come back and prevail on his own terms. RZA reteamed with GZA and Ol' Dirty Bastard and formed the crew that within a year would become the Wu-Tang Clan, once they were joined by Method Man, Ghostface Killah, Raekwon, U-God, Inspectah Deck, and Masta Killa (who rarely rhymes).

The first Wu-Tang Clan single, "Protect Ya Neck," was released independently by the Wu-Tang Clan. The record became an **underground** hit and shortly major record labels came offering recording contracts. In November 1993, the Wu-Tang Clan released the seminal album *Enter the Wu-Tang (36 Chambers).* The group's name is taken from a powerful, mythical kung fu sword wielded by an invincible collective of warriors—fitting enough, given that the Wu-Tang Clan is a loose collective of nine lyricists.

The Wu-Tang Clan as a group signed with Loud Records, with the contract provision that each member be able to sign a separate agreement with the record label of his choosing. GZA joined Geffen Records, Method Man went with **Def Jam Recordings**, Ol' Dirty Bastard signed with Elektra Records and Raekwon remained with Loud Records. *Enter the Wu-Tang (36 Chambers)* received critical acclaimed and proved to be commercially successful. The breakthrough single, "C.R.E.A.M." (which stands for Cash Rules Everything Around Me), released in early 1994, helped Wu-Tang to develop a loyal following.

The members of the Wu-Tang thereafter did their solo projects. RZA would join the horrorcore rap group the **Gravediggaz**, working alongside **Prince Paul** and Fruitkwan (ex-**Stetsasonic**) as well overseeing the production of all Wu-Tang Clan music and later launching up his own Razor Sharp record label. In 1994, Raekwon released his first single, "Heaven and Hell," produced by RZA and featuring Ghostface Killah; this single appeared on the 1994 *Fresh* film soundtrack. In November 1994, Method Man became the first Wu-Tang member to become a major solo star, releasing his debut album, *Tical* (Def Jam Recordings). The RZA-produced album spawned several hits, including Method Man's duet with **Mary J. Blige**, "I'll Be There for You (You're All I Need to Get By)."

In March 1995, Ol' Dirty Bastard followed Method Man's breakthrough success with his debut, *Return to the 36 Chambers* (Elektra Records), which reached gold with the hit singles "Brooklyn Zoo" and "Shimmy Shimmy Ya."

Inspectah Deck's first solo track appeared on the 1995 *Tales From the Hood,* a film soundtrack. That same year, Raekwon and GZA released albums that were highly praised by both critics and rap music fans: Raekwon's *Only Built 4 Cuban Linx* (Loud Records), which featured Ghostface Killah on numerous tracks, and GZA's *Liquid Swords* (Geffen Records). In February 1996, Ghostface Killah's first solo track, "Winter Warz," appeared on the *Don't Be a Menace to South Central While You're Drinking Your Juice in the Hood* film soundtrack and in October he released his solo debut album, the 1970s soul-flavored *Ironman*, on RZA's label Razor Sharp Records, an Epic Records subsidiary.

In June 1997, The Wu-Tang Clan reconvened and released their second album, the double-CD *Wu-Tang Forever* (Loud Records). Hugely anticipated, the album entered the charts at number 1 and sold over 600,000 copies in its first week, spawning the hit single "Triumph."

In addition to the official Wu-Tang Clan members, a slew of associates began to produce music. In 1997, Killarmy released their debut album, *Silent Weapons for Quiet Wars* (Priority Records). In March of the same year, Cappadonna released his solo debut, *The Pillage* (Columbia Records), and Killah Priest released his made his debut solo album *Heavy Mental* (Geffen Records). Killah Priest was not an official member of the Wu-Tang Clan, but he was a frequent guest on tracks and was a member of another Wu protégé group, called the Sunz of Man. Killah Priest's album, filled with spiritual imagery, received high praise from critics and helped to distinguish him from the other Wu-Tang Clan satellites. In July, the group Sunz of Man released its debut album, *The Last Shall Be First* (Red Ant Entertainment).

In November 1998, RZA released his own solo debut, the soundtrack-styled *RZA as Bobby Digital in Stereo* (V2). In 1999, the next round of solo projects from official Wu-Tang Clan members were released: Method Man's album *Tical 2000: Judgment Day* (Def Jam Recordings); Genius/GZA's *Beneath the Surface* (Geffen Records); Ol' Dirty Bastard's *Nigga Please* (Elektra Records) (released while the rap artist was in drug rehab); and Method Man's album with Redman, *Blackout*! (Def Jam Recordings).

In 2000, Ghostface Killah released his well-received sophomore album, *Supreme Clientele* (Razor Sharp/Epic). Raekwon also returned with his second album, *Immobilarity* (Loud Records). That year, first albums would come from Wu members Inspectah Deck, who released the album *Uncontrolled Substance* (Relativity Records), and U-God, who released his album *Golden Arms Redemption* (Priority Records).

Although individual Wu members have had scrapes with the law, in early 1999 the entire Wu-Tang Clan was accused of heading a gun-running operation between Staten Island, New York, and Steubenville, Ohio; however, the unsubstantiated charges were never proven. Even among the most ardent of Wu-Tang fans, there is agreement that the group has not been flawless: the large output of Wu-related music has been inconsistent, and there has been overexposure as a result of their myriad of endeavors, including a clothing line, a **video game**, a comic book, and more.

In 2000, RZA produced the soundtrack for the indie film *Ghost Dog: The Way of the Samurai*, starring Forrest Whitaker, and without much fanfare the Wu-Tang Clan released their third album, *The W* (Loud Records), in November of that year. Ol' Dirty Bastard appeared on only one album track and Cappadonna was photographed as an official member of a member of the group (however, the Wu's contract with Loud Records reportedly had not changed to include him). Subsequent Wu-Tang Clan albums were *Wu Tang Iron Flag* (Loud Records, 2001), *Disciples Of The 36 Chambers: Chapter 1* (Wu/Sanctuary 2004).

After several run-ins with the law as well as battles with drugs, Ol' Dirty Bastard had been incarcerated in April 2001 on drug possession charges. In November 2004, Ol' Dirty Bastard, now released from prison and signed to **Roc-A-Fella Records**, collapsed at a New York recording studio and subsequently died. In January 2005, his mother released the posthumous album *Osirius* (JC/Sure Shot). In 2004, *The Wu-Tang Manual: Enter the 36 Chambers, Volume One* (New York: Riverhead) was published. In this comprehensive concordance, RZA lays out their complex philosophy and history of this powerful musical dynasty.

DISCOGRAPHY: *Enter The Wu-Tang (36 Chambers)* (Loud Records, 1993); *Wu-Tang Forever* (Loud Records, 1997); *The W* (Loud Records, 2000); *Iron Flag* (Loud Records, 2001); *Disciples Of The 36 Chambers: Chapter 1* (Wu/Sanctuary, 2004).

X

X-CLAN

Members of X-Clan are Paradise, Brother J, and Prof X [Lumumba Carson]. This was the best known of the Afrocentric rap groups of the 1980s. The name X-Clan is a reference to the fact that African Americans have no way of knowing which family or clan in Africa that they are descended from.

Prof X's father was Sonny Carson, a controversial activist who as a young man had been a gang member and in 1974 was convicted of kidnapping. Sonny Carson's life was the subject of a movie, *The Education of Sonny Carson*, based on his autobiography. In later years, Carson became a fierce advocate for African Americans in Brooklyn, New York. He was a founding board member of the oldest community development corporation (CDC) in America, the Bedford-Stuyvesant Restoration Corporation. He was also one of the founders of Medgar Evers College (City University of New York).

X-Clan was easily recognizable because they adorned themselves with nose rings, ankhs, carved wooden canes, and ornate leather crowns. They evoked the ancient mysticism of Egypt and promoted knowledge of ancient Africa.

X-Clan was the center of a Black youth organization called, "Black Watch," which included Queen Mother Rage, Isis, and YZ. This collective also participated in marches and protests, including the 1989 protest over the unprovoked killing of Black youth Yusef Hawkins by a White mob in the Bensonhurst section of Brooklyn. Their debut album, *To the East Blackwards* (4th & Broadway) was released in 1989.

DISCOGRAPHY: *To the East Blackwards* (4th & Broadway, 1989).

X-ECUTIONERS (aka X-Men)

Past and current members of the X-Ecutioners include Rob Swift [RobAguilar], Dr. Butcher [Andrew Venerable], Grandmaster Spin [Chris Forte], Sinister [Joe Wright], Sean C [Sean Matthews], Roc Raida [Anthony Williams], Johnny Cash [John Rolle], Diamond J, DJ Boogie Blind, and DJ Precision. Considered the nation's premier turntablist crew, the X-Ecutioners were known for many years as *The X-Men*, until copyright issues forced them to change their name to the X-Ecutioners.

The X-Men were formed in New York in 1989, during a period when Clark Kent's Superman DJ Crew dominated all DJ competitions. The original members of the X-Ecutioners (Steve D, Johnny Cash, Sean C, and Roc Raida) joined together to defeat the Superman DJ Crew. Although the anticipated **battle** did not occur, the X-Men stayed together and began entering professional competition. They elevated the art of DJing to new heights with dexterity and showmanship.

Along with West Coast crews Invisibl Skratch Piklz and the Beat Junkies, the X-Ecutioners were integral to the development of turntablism, whereby turntables are treated and manipulated as musical instruments, rather than just as equipment to transmit recorded sounds. The X-Ecutioners have become became perennial winners in international competitions and are considered pioneers in the art of beat juggling. Rob Swift is quoted as explaining beat juggling as "manipulating a kick, snare, and high hat off a record and reorganizing the sounds to create a totally different composition, the same way one would do with a **sampling** machine."

The X-Ecutioners signed to Asphodel Records in1997, and that same year they released their debut album *X-pressions* to wide praise. After a five-year hiatus from the studio and a move to Sony Records, the X-Ecutioners released their sophomore album, *Built from Scratch*, in 2002. Rap artists **M.O.P.**, **Kool G Rap**, **Large Professor**, and Pharoahe Monch (**Organized Konfusion**) join the turnablists on the album.

In September 2004, after thirteen years as an X-Ecutioner, DJ Rob Swift left the group on amicable terms to work on solo music projects. Rob Swift has released his first solo album, *Ablist*, in 1999 (Asphodel Records).

The X-Ecutioners' latest album, *Revolutions*, was released in 2004 (Sony Records).

DISCOGRAPHY: *X-pressions* (Asphodel Records, 1997); *Built from Scratch* (Sony, 2002); *Revolutions* (Sony Records, 2004).

XZIBIT [Alvin Nathaniel Joiner]

Best known for his powerful and rugged delivery, as well as for his hardcore, but intelligent lyrics, the respected West Coast rap artist Xzibit remains an undervalued commodity. Ironically, Xzibit has perhaps received the most attention, not as an lyricist, but as host of the popular MTV series, *Pimp My Ride*.

After the death of his mother, the Detroit, Michigan, native moved to New Mexico with his father; he experienced a troubled childhood. At seventeen, he moved to California to pursue a recording career. A producer's introduction led Xzibit to **Tha Alkaholiks** (later known as Tha Liks), which then led him to perform on the **King Tee** track "Freestyle Ghetto" from his album *King Tee: IV Life* (MCA Records, 1995). Subsequently he appeared on Tha Liks' tracks "Hit and Run"

Xzibit. *Courtesy of Photofest.*

and "Flashback," from their album *Coast II Coast* (Priority Records, 1995). After working with King Tee and Tha Alkaholiks, he became part of their **Likwit Crew**.

Xzibit's talents came to the attention of Steve Rifkind, head of Loud Records who offered him a recording deal. In 1996, Xzibit released his debut album *At the Speed of Life* (Loud Records/RCA), which became an **underground** hit. The album includes the singles "Paparazzi," an observation about the rap game, and "Foundation," produced by DJ Muggs (**Cypress Hill**), a song from Xzibit to his son about the struggles of growing up, and "Carry The Weight," which details Xzibit's turbulent life story.

Xzibit's second album, *40 Dayz & 40 Nightz* (Loud/RCA) was released in 1998 and also earned praise. The underground success of his first two albums gained Xzibit a reputation for being a rising new talent. He got major career breaks when he appeared on **Snoop Dogg**'s album, *No Limit Top Dogg* (No Limit/Priority Records, 1999) (on the track

"Bi**h, Please"), and **Dr. Dre**'s album, *Dre's 2001* (Aftermath/Interscope Records, 1999) (on the track "L.A. Niggaz").

In 1999 Xzibit made approximately thirty guest appearances on various rap music tracks. Xzibit would go on to join the "Up in Smoke tour," which featured Dr. Dre, Snoop Dogg, **Eminem**, and **Ice Cube**, among others. In 2000, Xzibit released his first platinum-selling album, *Restless* (Loud Records), which was executive-produced by Dr. Dre. *Restless* would be Xzibit's best-selling effort to date.

Next, Xzibit would crossover into acting, appearing in the comedy film *The Wash* (2001) with Snoop Dogg and Dr. Dre. He also has a small role in Eminem's film, *8 Mile* (2002). Xzibit's fourth album, the gold-selling *Man vs Machine* (Columbia Records), was released in 2002. During this period Xzibit increased his visibility as part of Eminem's successful "Anger Management" tour. Xzibit, however, continued to balance his commercial success with his underground roots by maintaining links to West Coast mainstays such as Tha Liks and Ras Kass.

In 2004, Xzibit gained mainstream fame as the host of the MTV series, *Pimp My Ride*, which also features Los Angeles car shop, West Coast Customs. In each episode, young Southern Californians have their old clunker cars transformed into top-notch vehicles. The fifth Xzibit album, *Weapons of Mass Destruction* (Sony Records), was released in late 2004.

DISCOGRAPHY: *At the Speed of Life* (Loud Records, 1996); *40 Dayz & 40 Nightz* (Loud Records, 1998); *Restless* (Loud Records, 2000); *Man Vs Machine* (Columbia Records, 2002); *Weapons of Mass Destruction* (Sony Records, 2004).

Y

YO! MTV RAPS

Prior to creation of their rap music video program, *Yo! MTV Raps*, MTV had been criticized for ignoring music videos made by African American artists. The pilot debuted in August 1988, with Hip Hop impresario **Fab 5 Freddy** as the host. By September, *Yo! MTV Raps* was established as a weekly show and by January 1989 it was a daily program, with radio personalities Ed Lover and Doctor Dre as hosts.

Not only did *Yo! MTV Raps* air rap music videos, the program also included live rap music performances and interviews with artists. *Yo! MTV Raps* was instrumental in promoting rap music to White audiences, as well as to others who lived outside of the urban centers of the United States.

YOUNG MC [Marvin Young]

Best known for the hit single "Bust A Move" (Delicious Vinyl Records, 1989), Young MC was born in England and raised in a middle-class home in Queens, New York. Young's music career began in California, however, when he was an economics student at University of Southern California and met Michael Ross and Matt Dike, cofounders of the start-up record label Delicious Vinyl.

In 1988, under the name Young MC, he released the single "I Let 'Em Know" (Delicious Vinyl Records). Young co-wrote the hit singles "Wild Thing" and "Funky Cold Medina" on **Tone Lōc**'s debut album, *Loc-ed After Dark* (Delicious Vinyl Records, 1989). That same year he released his own debut album, *Stone Cold Rhymin'* (Delicious Vinyl Records). The album spawned the single "Bust a Move," a light-hearted rhyme about the ups and downs of romance. The affable track won a Grammy Award for Best Rap Performance and helped the album go platinum.

In the aftermath of this success, Young MC engaged in a bitter split from Delicious Vinyl Records, asserting that the label had tampered with his album without permission and had placed unwarranted restrictions on his work. The label countersued, citing breach of contract. The parties eventually settled out of court. After signing with Capitol Records, Young MC released his second album, *Brainstorm*, in 1991. The album, which focused less on humor and more on messages related to personal responsibility, was not well received. In the new, more hardcore rap

Young MC. *Courtesy of Photofest.*

music environment, his third album, *What is the Flavor?* (Capitol Records, 1993), also flopped. Young MC continued to release albums on independent labels, with little impact: *Return of the 1 Hit Wonder* (Overall Records, 1997), *Ain't Going Out Like That* (Young Man Moving, 2000), and *Engage the Enzyme* (Stimulus Records, 2002).

DISCOGRAPHY: *Single*: "I Let 'Em Know," (Delicious Vinyl Records) *Albums*: *Stone Cold Rhymin'* (Delicious Vinyl Records, 1980); *Brainstorm* (Capitol Records, 1991); *What is Flavor?* (Capitol Records, 1993) *Return of the 1 Hit Wonder* (Overall Records, 1997); *Ain't Going Out Like That* (Young Man Moving, 2000); *Engage the Enzyme* (Stimulus Records, 2002).

YO YO [Yolanda Whitaker]

A protégé of rap artist **Ice Cube**, Yo Yo began rapping in high school. She got a break when Ice Cube discovered her in a Los Angeles shopping mall. He asked her to appear on the track "It's a Man's World," off his debut album, *AmeriKKKa's Most Wanted* (Priority Records, 1990). Yo Yo signed with EastWest Records for the release of her debut album, *Make Way for the Motherlode*, in 1991. Ice Cube, Sir Jinx, and **Del Tha Funkee Homosapien** acted as producers on the album.

Yo Yo was initially promoted as a feminist rap artist because of her strong messages to women. On tracks such as "Girl Don't Be a Fool," she urged women to respect themselves, to demand respect from men, and to practice sexual restraint. In 1991, she teamed up with Ice Cube on the single "You Can't Play With My Yo Yo" (EastWest). She also cofounded the IBWC (Intelligent Black Women's Coalition) to spread her pro-woman message.

Follow-up albums include *Black Pearl* (East/West, 1992), *You Better Ask Somebody* (East/West, 1993), *Total Control* (East/West, 1996), and *Ebony* (East/West, 1998). On the album, *You Better Ask Somebody*, produced by Ice Cube, Yo Yo talks less about feminism and more about street life and women doing unto men before the men do unto them. She would again pair up with Ice Cube on the track "The Bonnie and Clyde Theme."

Yo Yo's acting credits include 1991's ***Boyz n the Hood*** (1991), *Who's the Man* (1993), *Sister Act II* (1993), and *Panther* (1995). She also wrote an advice column in *Vibe* magazine for several years.

DISCOGRAPHY: *Make Way for the Motherlode* (East/West, 1991); *Black Pearl* (East/West, 1992); *You Better Ask Somebody* (East/West, 1993); *Total Control* (East/West, 1996); *Ebony* (East/West, 1998).

Z

ZULU NATION (aka Universal Zulu Nation)

Founded by **Afrika Bambaataa** on November 12, 1973, in the Bronx, New York, the Zulu Nation is the organization that fostered the development of the elements of Hip Hop and currently acts to preserve its integrity. Zulu Nation would produce the first **B-boy** crew, the Zulu Kings, and a member, **Afrika Islam**, would produce the first radio Hip Hop mix show, *Zulu Beats*. Zulu parties or "throwdowns" initially showcased Bambaataa's superior **DJing** skills, but later expanded to include B-boy contests, **MC battles**, and **graffiti** murals.

As specified in their manifesto, this international Hip Hop movement advocates principles such as peace, unity, knowledge, wisdom, understanding, justice, equality, love, and respect. Its mission is to improve and uplift the lives of people and communities, using music and its many incarnations to spread its message. Many rap artists, Hip Hop celebrities, and Hip Hop fans are members.

Chapters of the Universal Zulu Nation are located in New York; Philadelphia; Chicago; Washington, DC; Miami; Virginia Beach; Los Angeles; Detroit; New Haven; Hartford; New Jersey; Texas; Belgium; Norway; London; Paris; Canada; Germany; Japan; Switzerland; Africa; as well as other cities, countries, and continents around the world.

Appendix I

Selected Rap Discography

The albums selected for this discography represent a broad scope of rap music styles and eras. Although this list is not definitive, it includes albums that are widely considered the best of the genre. For each album, the listing is for the earliest known release, however, there may be other versions of the album in existence. A resurgence of interest in an artist may result in a subsequent rerelease of an original album by the original record company or by the artist. Additionally, a producer or the recording artist may decide to release an updated or alternative version of the original album through a major record company or through an independent record label.

A Tribe Called Quest, *People's Instinctive Travels and the Paths of Rhythm* (Jive Records, 1990).

A Tribe Called Quest, *The Low End Theory* (Jive Records, 1991).

A Tribe Called Quest, *Midnight Marauders* (Jive Records, 1993).

Beastie Boys, *Licensed to Ill* (Def Jam Recordings, 1986).

Beastie Boys, *Paul's Boutique* (Capitol Records, 1989).

Big Daddy Kane, *Long Live the Kane* (Cold Chillin'/Warner Bros. Records, 1988).

Big Daddy Kane, *It's A Big Daddy Thing* (Cold Chillin'/Warner Bros. Records, 1989).

Big L, *Lifestylez Ov Da Poor and Dangerous* (Sony, 1995).

Biz Markie, *Goin' Off* (Cold Chillin', 1988).

Black Sheep, *A Wolf In Sheep's Clothing* (Mercury/Universal, 1991).

Boogie Down Productions, *Criminal Minded* (B-Boy Records, 1987).

Boogie Down Productions, *By Any Mean Necessary* (Jive Records/Novus, 1988).

Bone Thugs-N-Harmony, *Creeping on Ah Come Up* (Ruthless Records, 1994).

Bone Thugs-N-Harmony, *E. 1999 Eternal* (Ruthless Records, 1995).

Brand Nubian, *One for All* (Elektra, 1990).

Company Flow, *Funcrusher Plus* (Rawkus, 1997).

The Coup, *Genocide and Juice* (Wild Pitch Records, 1994).

Cypress Hill, *Cypress Hill* (Ruffhouse/Columbia Records, 1991).

De La Soul, *3 Feet High and Rising* (Tommy Boy Records, 1989).

De La Soul, *De La Soul is Dead* (Tommy Boy Records, 1991).

The D.O.C., *No One Can Do It Better* (Ruthless Records/Atlantic, 1989).

Dr. Dre, *The Chronic* (Death Row Records, 1992).

Dr. Dre, *2001* (Aftermath Entertainment/Interscope Records, 1999).

DMX, *It's Dark and Hell Is Hot* (Def Jam Recordings, 1998).

Eminem, *The Slim Shady LP* (Interscope Records, 1999).

EPMD, *Strictly Business* (Priority Records, 1988).

EPMD, *Unfinished Business* (Priority Records, 1989).

Eric B & Rakim, *Paid in Full* (4th & Broadway, 1987).

Eric B & Rakim, *Follow the Leader* (Uni Records, 1988).

Eric B & Rakim, *Let the Rhythm Hit' Em* (MCA Records, 1990).

50 Cent, *Get Rich Or Die Tryin'* (Aftermath Entertainment/Interscope Records, 2003).

Freestyle Fellowship, *To Whom It May Concern* (Sun Records, 1991).

DJ Jazzy Jeff and The Fresh Prince, *He's the DJ and I'm The Rapper* (Jive Records, 1988).

The Fugees, *The Score* (Ruffhouse/Columbia Records, 1996).

Gang Starr, *Step in the Arena* (Chrysalis, 1990).

Gang Starr, *Daily Operation* (Chrysalis, 1992).

Geto Boys, *Grip It! On That Other Level* (Rap-A-Lot Records, 1995).

Ghostface Killah, *Ironman* (Razor Sharp/Epic, 1996).

Ice Cube, *Amerikkka's Most Wanted* (Priority Records, 1990).

Ice Cube, *Death Certificate* (Street Knowledge/Priority Records, 1991).

Jay-Z, *Reasonable Doubt* (Roc-A-Fella Records, 1996).

Jay-Z, *The Blueprint* (Roc-A-Fella Records, 2001).

Jay-Z, *Black Album* (Roc-A-Fella Records, 2003).

Jungle Brothers, *Straight Out the Jungle* (Idler, 1988).

Juvenile, *400 Degreez* (Uptown/Universal/Cash Money Records, 1998).

Kanye West, *The College Dropout* (Roc-A-Fella Records, 2004).

Kool G. Rap & DJ Polo, *Road to the Riches* (Cold Chillin'/Warner, 1989).

Kool G. Rap & DJ Polo, *Wanted: Dead or Alive* (Cold Chillin'/Warner, 1990).

Kool Moe Dee, *Kool Moe Dee* (Jive Records, 1986).

Kool Moe Dee, *How Ya Like Me Now* (Jive Records, 1987).

Lauryn Hill, *The Miseducation of Lauryn Hill* (Sony/Columbia Records, 1998).

LL Cool J, *Radio* (Def Jam Recordings, 1985).

LL Cool J, *Mama Said Knock You Out* (Def Jam Recordings, 1990).

Lord Finesse & DJ Mike Smooth, *Funky Technician* (Wild Pitch Records, 1990).

Ludacris, *Word of Mouf* (Def Jam South, 2001).

Main Source, *Breaking Atoms* (Wild Pitch Records, 1990).

Makaveli, *The Don Killuminati (The 7 Day Theory)* (Death Row Records, 1996).

MC Lyte, *Lyte as a Rock* (First Priority, 1988).

Master Ace, *Take A Look Around* (Cold Chillin'/Warner Bros. Records, 1990).

Masta Ace Incorporated, *Slaughtahouse* (Delicious Vinyl, 1993).

Mobb Deep, *The Infamous* (Loud Records/RCA, 1995).

Mobb Deep, *Hell on Earth* (Loud Records/RCA, 1996).

Mos Def and Talib Kweli, *Mos Def and Talib Kweli are Black Star* (Rawkus, 1998).

Mos Def, *Black On Both Sides* (Rawkus, 1999).

Nas, *Illmatic* (Columbia Records, 1994).

Nas, *Stillmatic* (Columbia Records, 2001).

N.W.A., *Straight Outta Compton* (Ruthless Records/Priority Records, 1988).

The Notorious B.I.G., *Ready To Die* (Arista, 1994).

The Notorious B.I.G., *Life After Death* (Bad Boy Entertainment/Arista, 1997).

Organized Konfusion, *Organized Konfusion* (Hollywood Basic, 1991).

Outkast, *Southernplayalisticadillacmuzik* (LaFace Records/Arista, 1994).

Outkast, *Stankonia* (LaFace Records/Arista, 2000).

Outkast, *Speakerboxxx* (LaFace Records/Arista, 2003).

Pete Rock & C. L. Smooth, *Mecca and the Soul Brother* (Elektra, 1992).

Prince Paul, *A Prince Among Thieves* (Tommy Boy Records, 1999).

Public Enemy, *It Takes a Nation of Millions to Hold Us Back* (Def Jam Recordings, 1988).

Public Enemy, *Fear of a Black Planet* (Def Jam Recordings, 1990).

Queen Latifah, *All Hail The Queen* (Tommy Boy Records, 1989).

Raekwon, *Only Built 4 Cuban Linx* (Loud Records, 1995).

Rah Digga, *Dirty Harriet* (Elektra Records/Flip Mode, 2000).

Run DMC, *Run DMC* (Profile Records/Arista, 1984).

Run DMC, *King of Rock* (Profile Records/Arista, 1985).

Run DMC, *Raising Hell* (Profile Records/Arista, 1986).

Salt 'N Pepa, *Hot, Cool & Vicious* (Next Plateau, 1986).

Salt 'N Pepa, *Very Necessary* (Next Plateau/London/Polygram, 1993).

Scarface, *The Diary* (Rap-A-Lot Records, 1994).

Scarface, *The Fix* (Def Jam South, 2002).

Slick Rick, *The Great Adventures of Slick Rick* (Def Jam Recordings, 1988).

Snoop Doggy Dogg, *Doggystyle* (Death Row Records, 1993).

Stetsasonic, *In Full Gear* (Tommy Boy Records, 1988).

3rd Bass, *The Cactus Album* (Def Jam Recordings, 1989).

Talib Kweli & Hi-Tek, Reflection Eternal (Priority Records/Rawkus, 2000).

Too Short, *Life is ... Too Short* (Dangerous Music/RCA, 1988).

2 Live Crew, *As Nasty As They Wanna Be* (Luke Skyywalker Records/ Atlantic, 1989).

2Pac, *All Eyez on Me* (Death Row/Interscope Records, 1995/1996).

2Pac, *Me Against the World* (Death Row/Interscope Records, 1995).

Ultramagnetic MCs, *Critical Beatdown* (Next Plateau, 1985).

Whodini, *Whodini* (Jive Records/Arista, 1983).

Wu-Tang Clan, *Enter the Wu-Tang* (36 Chambers) (Loud Records, 1993).

Wyclef Jean, *The Carnival* (Sony/Columbia Records, 1997).

X-Clan, *To the East, Blackwards* (4th & Broadway, 1990).

Appendix 2

Statements to Preserve and Appreciate Hip Hop Culture

HIP HOP DECLARATION OF PEACE: UNVEILED BY KRS-ONE'S THE TEMPLE OF HIP HOP AT THE UNITED NATIONS ON MAY 16, 2002

INTRODUCTION

This Hiphop (*sic*) Declaration of Peace guides Hiphop Kulture (*sic*) toward freedom from violence, and establishes advice and protection for the existence and development of our Hiphop community. Through the "overstandings" of this Hiphop Declaration of Peace, we establish a foundation of health, love, awareness, wealth, peace and prosperity for ourselves, our children and their children's children, forever.

For the purpose of establishing a respectable international framework by which Hiphop Kulture may achieve and contribute to a lasting peace in the world we, the founders, pioneers, inventors, artists, photographers, authors, teachas, and other kultural contributors of Hiphop Kulture, ordain and decree, the manifestation of this Hiphop Declaration of Peace.

That Hiphop Kulture may come to know, and act upon, its true intention, meaning and purpose we, the B-Boys, B-Girls, Emcees, DeeJays, Writers, Beatboxers, and other legitimate contributors to Hiphop Kulture have united on this day May 16, 2002 at the United Nations headquarters in New York to document, establish, fulfill, and promote the vision of Hiphop as an International kulture for peace and prosperity.

For the clarification of Hiphop's meaning and purpose, or when the intention of Hiphop is questioned, or when disputes between parties arise, Hiphoppas shall have access to the advice of this document, the "Hiphop Declaration of Peace," as guidance, advice and protection.

FIRST OVERSTANDING

Hiphop is the name of our collective consciousness. It is commonly expressed through Breakin, Emceein, Graf, Deejayin, Beatboxin, Street

Fashion, Street Language, Street Knowledge and Street Entrepreneurialism or Street Trade. Wherever and whenever the elements, and expressions of Hiphop Kulture manifest, this Hiphop Declaration of Peace shall advise its use and interpretation.

SECOND OVERSTANDING

Hiphop Kulture respects the dignity and sanctity of life, without discrimination or prejudice. We shall consider our duty to protect the development of life, over and before our individual free choice to destroy it or seek to alter its natural development.

THIRD OVERSTANDING

Hiphop Kulture respects the laws and agreements of its kulture, its country, its institutions, and those it does business with. Hiphop does not irresponsibly break laws.

FOURTH OVERSTANDING

Hiphop Kulture encourages womanhood, manhood, sisterhood, brotherhood and family. We are also conscious not to bring any disrespect to the dignity and reputation of our ancestors.

FIFTH OVERSTANDING

The right to define and educate ourselves shall be encouraged, developed, preserved, protected and promoted as a means toward peace and prosperity.

SIXTH OVERSTANDING

Hiphop honors no relationship, person, event, act, or otherwise, wherein the preservation and further development of Hiphop's kulture, principles and elements are not considered nor respected. Hiphop Kulture does not participate in activities that clearly destroy its ability to productively exist.

SEVENTH OVERSTANDING

The elements of Hiphop Kulture may be traded for money, honor, power, respect, food and other resources. However, Hiphop's Kulture is never for sale—nor can it be bought. It is the priceless principle of our self-empowerment.

EIGHTH OVERSTANDING

Companies, corporations, non and not-for-profit organizations, as well as individuals and groups that are clearly benefiting from the use, interpretation and/or exploitation of Hiphop, and the expressions and terminologies of Hiphop; shall be encouraged to commission and/or employ a certified Hiphop specialist to answer sensitive kultural questions, and guide businesses, cities and countries through the principles and proper presentations of Hiphop Kulture to the world.

NINTH OVERSTANDING

Every third week in May, Hiphoppas shall be encouraged to remember its ancestors and appreciate the elements, principles and history of Hiphop.

TENTH OVERSTANDING

Hiphop is the name of our collective consciousness. As a conscious way of life we recognize our influence on society, especially on children, and we shall forever keep the rights and welfare of both in mind.

ELEVENTH OVERSTANDING

Within the collective Hiphop consciousness there are no competing races, tribes, countries, religions, occupations, kultures, nor languages. All are one in consciousness. Hiphop Kulture is one multi-skilled, multi-cultural, multi-racial people.

TWELFTH OVERSTANDING

Hiphop Kulture does not intentionally participate in any form of hate, deceit, or theft at any time. At no time shall Hiphop engage in any violent war within itself.

THIRTEENTH OVERSTANDING

Hiphop Kulture rejects the immature impulse for unwarranted acts of violence, and always seeks diplomatic, non-violent strategies first in the settlement of all disputes. Revolution is preserved as a final solution, when all other means of diplomatic negotiation has failed repeatedly.

FOURTEENTH OVERSTANDING

Hiphoppas respect nature wherever we are; on this planet as well as on others.

FIFTEENTH OVERSTANDING

Hiphop holds sacred our duty to contribute to our survival and salvation as a human race on planet Earth. Native American kulture teaches us to respect Mother Earth as our mother.

SIXTEENTH OVERSTANDING

No one should be a self-proclaimed Hiphop pioneer or "legend" unless they can prove with facts and/or witnesses to their credibility and contributions to Hiphop Kulture.

SEVENTEENTH OVERSTANDING

Hiphop is shown the highest respect when Hiphoppas respect each other. Hiphop Kulture is preserved, nurtured and developed when Hiphoppas preserve, nurture and develop one another.

EIGHTEENTH OVERSTANDING

For the purpose of promoting, interpreting and defending the principles of the Hiphop Declaration of Peace; Hiphop Kulture shall maintain a healthy, caring, fully aware, and wealthy central Hiphop committee. Such committee shall be made up of seven dedicated Hiphoppas invested with the power to promote, interpret and defend the principles of the Hiphop Declaration of Peace.

THE NEW YORK STATE SENATE'S PROCLAMATION RECOGNIZING NOVEMBER AS HIP HOP HISTORY MONTH AS ADOPTED ON DECEMBER 12, 2002

Whereas, it is the sense of this legislative body that those who enhance the well-being and vitality of their community and have shown a long and sustained commitment to excellence certainly have earned our recognition and applause; now, therefore, be it resolved that this legislative body pause in its deliberations to honor the rich traditions of hiphop culture. The month of November is now recognized by the State of New York as Hiphop Culture History Month.

THE RESOLUTION WAS INTRODUCED IN OCTOBER 2002 BY NEW YORK STATE SENATOR PEDRO ESPADA, JR.

BRONX BOROUGH PRESIDENT FERNANDO FERRER AT CITY HALL PROCLAIMS HIP HOP APPRECIATION WEEK, ON MAY 14, 2001

Whereas: Hiphop culture, which originated in the Bronx, is a lifestyle for countless people around the world which unites and establishes a common identity; it was developed with the purpose of ensuring health, love, awareness, and wealth for ourselves, our children and our children's children forever.... Now, therefore, I, Fernando Ferrer, do hereby proclaim every third week in May herein Hiphop Appreciation Week.

Selected Bibliography

BOOKS

Adler, Bill. *Rap: The Lyrics of a Generation of Black Rockers*. Photographs by Janette Beckman. New York: St. Martin's Press, 1991.

Chuck D, with Yusuf Jah. *Fight The Power: Rap, Race, and Reality*. Foreword by Spike Lee. New York: Delacorte Press, 1997.

Fernando, S. H., Jr. *The New Beats: Exploring the Music, Culture, and Attitudes of Hip-Hop*. New York: Anchor/Doubleday, 1994.

George, Nelson. *Hip Hop America*. New York: Viking, 1998 [Penguin editions: 1999, 2005].

———. *Buppies, B-Boys, Baps, and Bohos: Notes on Post-Soul Black Culture*. New York: HarperCollins, 1992 [paperback: Cambridge, MA: Da Capo Press, 2001].

Ice-T, as told to Heidi Siegmund. *The Ice Opinion: Who Gives a Fu*k?* New York: St. Martin's Press, 1994.

KRS-ONE. *The Science of Rap*. 2nd ed. New Jersey: L. Parker, 1996.

Jackson, Bruce. *Get Your Ass in the Water and Swim Like Me: African-American Narrative Poetry from the Oral Tradition*. New York: Routledge, 2004 [first published in 1974 by Harvard University Press].

Lewis, Miles Marshall. *Scars of the Soul Are Why Kids Wear Bandages When They Don't Have Bruises*. New York: Akashic Books, 2004.

Light, Alan, ed. *The* Vibe *History of Hip Hop*. New York: Three Rivers Press, 1999.

Nelson, Havelock, and Michael A. Gonzales. *Bring the Noise: A Guide to Rap Music and Hip-Hop Culture*. New York: Harmony Books, 1991.

Paniccioli, Ernie, photographer, and Kevin Powell, ed. *Who Shot Ya? Three Decades of Hiphop Photography*. New York: Amistad, 2002.

Queen Latifah with Karen Hunter. *Ladies First: Revelations of a Strong Woman*. New York: William Morrow, 1999.

Ro, Ronin. *Have Gun Will Travel: The Spectacular Rise and Violent Fall of Death Row Records*. New York: Doubleday, 1998.

Shakur, Tupac. *The Rose That Grew From Concrete*. Preface by Afeni Shakur. Foreword by Nikki Giovanni. Introduction by Leila Steinburg. New York: Pocket Books, 1999.

Simmons, Russell, with Nelson George. *Life and Def: Sex, Drugs, Money + God*. New York: Crown, 2001.

Spady, James G., Stefan Dupres, and Charles G. Lee. *Twisted Tales: In the Hip Hop Streets of Philly*. Philadelphia: UMUM/LOH, 1995.

Toop, David. *The Rap Attack: African Jive to New York Hip Hop*. 1st ed. London: Pluto Press; Boston, MA: South End Press, 1984.

———. *Rap Attack 2: African Rap to Global Hip Hop*. Rev. ed. London: Serpent's Tail, 1991.

Vibe Magazine, the editors of. *Hip Hop Divas*. New York: Three Rivers Press, 2001.

Wang, Oliver, ed. *Classic Material: The Hip-Hop Album Guide*. Foreword by Dante Ross. Toronto: ECW Press, 2003.

ARTICLES

Bradsher, Keith. "Suit on Song, Rosa Parks, is Rejected." *New York Times*, November 19, 1999, A28.

Coates, Ta-Nehisi. "Dropping the Bomb: An Oral History of Go-Go." *Washington City Paper*, January 14–20, 2000.

Copage, Eric V. "Brazilian Martial Art for the Mind and Body." *New York Times*, March 9, 1999.

Dunning, Thad. "Circle of Liberation: New York's First Female Capoeira Mestranda. *Village Voice*, February 1998.

Hedges, Chris. "His Beat Goes on, as a Hip-Hop Empire." *New York Times*, February 20, 2001 [Available at: http://www.nytimes.com].

Leland, John, with Lola Ogunnaike and Laura Holson. "Feuding for Profit: Rap's War of Words; In Rap Industry, Rivalries as Marketing Tool." *New York Times*, November 2, 2002 [Available at: http://www.nytimes.com].

———. "Requiem for a Gangsta." *Newsweek*, March 24, 1997, p.74.

Mayo, Kierna, "When Russell Talks...." *The Source*, February 1993, p. 50.

Noel, Peter. "Hip Hop War: The Minister vs. The Mogul." *Village Voice*, May 1, 2001, p. 60.

Quinones, Eric R., "Hip-Hop Music Seen As a Lifestyle." Associated Press, July 1, 1998.

Richardson, Lynda. "A Diva of the Spoken Word Who Irritates the F.C.C." Public Lives. *New York Times*, July 21, 2001 [Abstract available at: http://query.nytimes.com/gst/abstract.html?res=F40713FA3D5F0C718DDDAE0894D9404482].

Roberts, Johnnie L. "Music, Money, Murder." *Newsweek*, March 24, 1997, p. 76.

Samuels, David. "The Vanished Writing on the Subway Wall." [Music] *New York Times*, May 11, 2003, p. 11.

Sanneh, Kelefa, "Sticker Shock: The FTC Markets Censorship as Consumer Protection." *Village Voice*, May 2–8, 2001 [Available at: http://www.villagevoice.com/news/0118,sanneh,24347,1.html].

———. "Rap With Its 'Props' Under Glass. Why Not?" Music. *New York Times*, November, 12, 2000, Arts & Leisure, p. 36 [Available at: http://www.nytimes.com].

———. "Rappers Who Definitely Know How to Rock." *New York Times*, December 3, 2000, Arts and Leisure, p. 30 [Available at: http://www.nytimes.com].

Siegal, Nina, "Billboard Sets Off Angry Chorus." [Neighborhood report: Harlem] *New York Times*, May 22, 1999 [Available at: http://www.nytimes.com].

———. "For Some, Hip-Hop show is Not Hip Enough." *New York Times*, September 27, 2000, p. E1 [Available at: http://www.nytimes.com].

Stewart, David O. "Rock Around the Docket," *ABA Journal*, May 1994.

Wartofsky, Alona. "Rap vs. the Press." *Newsday*, January 11, 1999, B3 [Available at: http://www.newsday.com].

Various authors. "Rap, Inc." [four-part series] *New York Daily News*, April 1, 1997–April 4, 1997.

INTERNET RESOURCES

http://www.allhiphop.com. "AllHipHop.com: The World's Most Dangerous Site!" Copyright: Infinity, AllHipHop.com, Inc.

http://www.b-boys.com. " Representin' all aspects of Hip Hop culture and music—B-Boys.com." Copyright: B-Boys.com.

http://www.daveyd.com. "Davey D's Hip Hop Corner: The World from a Hip Hop perspective." Produced by: Davey D in association with eLine Productions.

http://www.discogs.com. "Discogs: a user-built database of music information.: Copyright: Discogs.

http://ericnuzum.com/banned/incidents/90s.html. Censorship incidents, 1990s. Copyright: Eric Nuzum.

http://www.hiphoparchive.org. "The Hiphop Archive: Respect – Build – Represent." Copyright: The Hiphop Archive.

http://www.icebergradio.com. Streaming audio from about 250 stations; some premium services. Copyright: IcebergMedia.com Inc.

http://www.jahsonic.com. "A Vocabulary of Culture: Part online encyclopedia, part music criticism, part blog." Curated, compiled and edited by Jan Geerinck.

http://www.mtv.com. Multifaceted Internet presence of the MTV; some premium services. Copyright: MTV Networks.

http://www.ohhla.com. "The Original Hip-Hop Lyrics Archive." Copyright OHHLA.com.

http://www.okayplayer.com. "An online community made up of like-minded recording artists (who keep their official Internet homes here) and visitors to the site." Copyright: Okayplayer.com.

http://www.oldschoolhiphop.com. "This Site Focuses Solely On Preserving The Four Elements of Hip Hop Prior to 1986." Copyright: Oldschoolhiphop.com.

http://www.rap.about.com. "Your Guide to Rap/Hip Hop." By Ifè Oshun. Optional newsletter. Copyright: About, Inc., part of the New York Times Co., and Ifè Oshun.

http://www.rockonthenet.com. "Your music resource and more." Includes chart standings, music awards, birthday almanac, and music-specific search tools. Copyright: Rock On The Net.

http://www.rollingstone.com. The magazine. Copyright: Rolling Stone.

http://www.sing365.com. A lyrics database. Copyright: Sing365.com

http://www.sohh.com. An online Hip Hop community, with news, blogs, and other features, Copyright: 4Control Media, Inc.

http://www.tvtome.com.

http://www.villagevoice.com. The New York City–based newspaper. Copyright: The Village Voice.

Index

About the Author

YVONNE BYNOE is an author and lecturer whose work combines the relevant issues of politics, culture, and economics within the context of American popular culture. She is the author of the book *Stand and Deliver: Political Activism, Leadership and Hip Hop Culture* (2004). Bynoe's writings have appeared in such publications as *The Georgetown Journal of International Affairs* and the *National Urban League's 2001 State of Black America.* Bynoe currently provides political and social commentary to the National Public Radio program *News and Notes with Ed Gordon.*